Veb Data Management

Springer
New York
Berlin
Heidelberg
Hong Kong
London
Milan
Paris
Tokyo

Sourav S. Bhowmick   Sanjay K. Madria
Wee Keong Ng

Web Data Management

A Warehouse Approach

With 106 Illustrations

 Springer

Sourav S. Bhowmick
  and Wee Keong Ng
School of Computer Engineering
Nanyang Technological University
50 Nanyang Avenue
Blk N4 2A-32
Nanyang, 639798
Singapore
assourav@ntu.edu.sg
awkng@ntu.edu.sg

Sanjay K. Madria
University of Missouri
Department of Computer Science
1870 Miner Circle Drive
310 Computer Science Building
Rolla, MO 65409
USA
madrias@umr.edu

Library of Congress Cataloging-in-Publication Data
Bhowmick, Sourav S.
    Web data management : a warehouse approach / Sourav S. Bhowmick, Sanjay K.
Madria, Wee Keong Ng.
        p. cm. — (Springer professional computing)
    Includes bibliographical references and index.

    1. Web databases.   2. Database management.   3. Data warehousing.   I. Madria, Sanjay
Kumar.   II. Ng, Wee Keong.   III. Title.   IV. Series.
    QA76.9.W43B46   2003
    005.75′8—dc21   2003050523

ISBN 978-1-4419-1806-2   Printed on acid-free paper.

9 8 7 6 5 4 3 2 1   SPIN 10901038

Typesetting: Pages created by the author using a Springer TeX macro package.

www.springer-ny.com

Springer-Verlag   New York Berlin Heidelberg
A member of BertelsmannSpringer Science+Business Media GmbH

SOURAV:
Dedicated to my parents,
Himanshu Kumar Saha Bhowmick, and
Gouri Saha Bhowmick, and
to my wife Rachelle
for her infinite love, patience, and support.

SANJAY:
To my parents Dr. M. L. Madria and Geeta Madria
for their encouragement, and
to my wife Ninu and
sons Priyank and Pranal
for their love and support.

WEE KEONG:
To my parents and family.

Preface

Overview

The existence of different autonomous Web sites containing related information has given rise to the problem of integrating these sources effectively to provide a comprehensive integrated source of relevant information. The advent of e-commerce and the increasing trend of availability of commercial data on the Web has generated the need to analyze and manipulate these data to support corporate decision making. Decision support systems now must be able to harness and analyze Web data to provide organizations with a competitive edge. In a recent report on the future of database research known as the Asilomar Report, it has been predicted that in a few years from now, the majority of human information will be available on the Web. The Web is evolving at an alarming rate and is becoming increasingly chaotic without any consistent organization. To address these problems, traditional information retrieval techniques have been applied to document collection on the Internet, and a panoply of search engines and tools have been proposed and implemented. Such techniques are sometimes time consuming, and laborious, and the results obtained may be unsatisfactory. Thus there is a need to develop efficient tools for analyzing and managing Web data. In this book, we address the problem of efficient management of Web information from the database perspective. We build a data warehouse called WHOWEDA (**Ware**h**ouse Of We**b **Da**ta) for managing and manipulating Web data. This problem is more challenging compared to its relational counterpart due to the irregular unstructured nature of Web data. This has led to rethinking and reusing existing techniques in a new way to address the current challenges in Web data management.

A web warehouse acts as an information server that supports information gathering and can provide value-added services such as personalization, summarization, transcoding, and knowledge discovery. A web warehouse can also be a shared information repository. By building a shared web warehouse (in a company), we aim to maximize the sharing of information, knowledge, and experience among users who share common interests. Users may access the warehouse data from appliances such as PDAs and cell phones. Because these devices do not have the same rendering capabilities as desktop computers, it is necessary for Web contents to be adapted, or transcoded, for proper presentation on a variety of client devices. Second, for very large documents, such as high-quality pictures, or video files, it is reasonable and efficient to deliver a small segment to clients before sending the complete version. A web warehouse supports automated resource discovery by integrating technologies for the search engine, filtering, and clustering.

The Web allows the information (both contents and structural modification) to change or disappear at any time and in any way. How many times have we noticed that bookmarked pages have suddenly disappeared or changed? Unless we store and archive these evolving pages, we will continue to lose some valuable knowledge over time. These rapid and often unpredictable changes or disappearances of information create the new problems of detecting, representing, and querying these changes. This is a challenging problem because the information sources in the Web are autonomous and typical database approaches to detect changes based on triggering mechanisms are not usable. Moreover, these information sources typically do not keep track of historical information in a format accessible to the outside user. When the versions of data are available, we can explore how a certain topic or community evolved over time. Web-related research and mining will benefit if the history of data can be warehoused. This will help in developing a change notification service that will notify users whenever there are changes of interest. The web warehouse can support many subscription services such as allowing changes to be detected, queried, and reported based on a user's query subscription.

Managing data in a web warehouse requires (1) design of a suitable data model for representing Web data in a repository, (2) development of suitable algebraic operators for retrieving data from the Web and manipulating the data stored in a warehouse, (3) tools for Web data visualization, and (4) design of change management and knowledge discovery tools. To address the first issue, we propose a data model called WHOM (WareHouse Object Model) to represent HTML and XML documents in the warehouse. To address the second issue, we define a set of web algebraic operators to manipulate Web data. These operators build new web tables by extracting relevant data from the Web, and generating new web tables from existing ones. To address the next issue, we introduce a set of data visualization operators to add flexibility in viewing query results coupled from the Web. Finally, we propose algorithms to perform change management and knowledge discovery in the web warehouse.

Organization and Features

We begin by introducing the characteristics of Web data in Chapter 1. We motivate the need for new warehousing techniques by describing the limitations of Web data and how conventional data warehousing techniques are ill-equipped to manage heterogeneous autonomous Web data. Within this context, we describe how a web warehouse differs from those studied in traditional data warehousing literature. We present an overview of our framework for modeling and manipulating Web data in the web warehouse. We present the conceptual architecture of the web warehouse, and identify its key modules and the subproblems they address. We define the scope of this book by identifying the portion of the architecture and their subproblems that is addressed here. Then we briefly describe the key research issues raised by the need for storing and managing data in the web warehouse. Finally, we highlight the contributions of the book.

In Chapter 2, we discuss prior work in the Web data management area. We focus on high-level similarities and differences between prior work and our work, deferring detailed comparisons to later chapters that present our techniques in detail. We focus on three classes of systems based on the task they perform related to information management on the Web: modeling and querying the Web, information extraction and integration and, Web site construction and restructuring. Furthermore, we discuss recent research in XML data modeling, query languages, and data warehousing systems for Web data. The knowledgeable reader may omit this chapter, and perhaps refer back to comparisons while reading later chapters of the book.

In Chapter 3, we describe the issues that we have considered in modeling warehouse data. We provide a brief overview of WHOM, the data model for the web warehouse. We present a simple and general model for representing metadata, structure, and content of Web documents and hyperlinks as trees called node and link metadata trees, and node and link data trees. Within this context, we identify HTML elements and attributes considered useful in the context of the web warehouse for generating tree representations of content and structure of HTML documents.

Chapter 4 describes a flexible scheme to impose constraints on metadata, content and structure of HTML and XML data. An important feature of our scheme is that it allows us to impose constraints on a specific portion of Web documents or hyperlinks, on attributes associated with HTML or XML elements, and on the hierarchical structure of Web documents, instead of simple keyword-based constraints similar to the search engines. It also presents a mechanism to associate two sets of documents or hyperlinks using comparison predicates based on their metadata, content, or structural properties.

In Chapter 5, we present a mechanism to represent constraints imposed on the hyperlinked connection in a set of Web documents (called *connectivity*) in WHOM). An important feature of our approach is that it can represent interdocument relationships based on partial knowledge of the user about the hyperlinked structure. We discuss the syntax and semantics of a connectivity element. In this context, we motivate the syntax and semantics of connectivities by identifying various real examples.

In Chapter 6, we present a mechanism for querying the Web. The complete syntax is unveiled and some examples are given to demonstrate the expressive power of the query mechanism. Some of the important features of our query mechanism are the ability to query metadata, content, internal and external (hyperlink) structure of Web documents based on partial knowledge, ability to express constraints on tag attributes and tagless segments of data, the ability to express conjunctive as well as disjunctive query conditions compactly, the ability to control execution of a web query and preservation of the topological structure of hyperlinked documents in the query results. We also discuss various properties, validity conditions, and limitations of the query mechanism.

In Chapter 7, we present a novel method for describing schema of a set of relevant Web data. An important feature of our schema is that it represents a collection of Web documents relevant to a user, instead of representing any set of Web documents. We also describe the syntax, semantics, and properties of a web schema and introduce the notion of web tables. Again, an important advantage of our web schema is that it provides the flexibility to represent irregular, heterogeneous structured data. We present the mechanism for generating a web schema in the context of a web warehouse.

In Chapter 8, we focus on how web tables are generated and are further manipulated in the web warehouse by a set of web algebraic operators. The web algebra provides a formal foundation for data representation and manipulation for the web warehouse. Each web operator accepts one or two web tables as input and produces a web table as output. A set of simple web schemas and web tuples are produced each time a web operator is applied. The global web coupling operator extracts web tuples from the Web. In particular, portions of the World Wide Web (WWW) are extracted when it is applied to the WWW. The web union, web cartesian product, and the web join are binary operators on web tables. Web select extracts a subset of web tuples from a web table. Web project removes some of the nodes from the web tuples in a web table. The web distinct operator removes duplicate web tuples from a web bag.

A user may wish to view web tuples in a different framework. In Chapter 9, we introduce a set of data visualization operators such as web nest, web unnest, web coalesce, web pack, web unpack, and web sort to add flexibility in viewing query results coupled from the Web. The web nest and web coalesce operators are similar in nature. Both of these operators concatenate a set of web tuples over identical nodes and produce a set of directed graphs as output. The web pack and web sort operations produce a web table as output. The web pack operator enables us to group web tuples based on the domain name or host name of the instances of a specified node type identifier or the keyword set in these nodes. A web sort, on the other hand, sorts web tuples based on the total number of nodes or total number of local, global or interior links in each tuple. Web unnest, web expand and web unpack perform the inverse functions of web nest, web coalesce and web pack respectively.

In Chapter 10, our focus is on detecting and representing changes given old and new versions of a set of interlinked Web documents, retrieved in response to a user's query. We present a mechanism to detect relevant changes using web algebraic operators such as web join and outer web join. Web join is used to detect identical documents residing in two web tables, whereas outer web join, a derivative of web join, is used to identify dangling web tuples. We discuss how to represent these changes using delta web tables. We have designed and discussed formal algorithms for the generation of delta web tables.

In Chapter 11, we introduce the concept of the web bag in the context of the web warehouse. Informally, a web bag is a web table that allows multiple occurrences of identical web tuples. We have used the web bag to discover useful knowledge from a web table such as visible documents (or Web sites), luminous documents, and luminous paths. In this chapter, we formally discuss the semantics and properties of web bags. We provide formal algorithms for various types of knowledge discovery in a web warehouse using the web bag and illustrate them with examples.

In Chapter 12, we conclude by summarizing the contributions of this book and discussion on promising directions for future work in this area. Readers can benefit by exploring the research directions given in this chapter.

Audiences

This book furnishes a detailed presentation of relevant concepts, models, and methods in a clear, simple style, providing an authoritative and comprehensive survey and resource for web database management systems developers and enterprise Web site developers. The book also outlines many research directions and possible extensions to the ideas presented, which makes this book very helpful for students doing research in this area.

The book has very strong emphasis and theoretical perspective on designing the web data model, schema development, web algebraic operators, web data visualization, change management, and knowledge discovery. The solid theoretical foundation will provide a good platform for building the web query language and other tools for the manipulation of warehoused data. The implementation of the discussed algorithms will be good exercises for undergraduate and graduate students to learn more about these operators from a system perspective. Similarly, the development of tools for application developers will serve as the foundation for building the web warehouse.

Prerequisites

This book assumes that readers have some introductory knowledge of relational database systems and HTML or XML as well as some knowledge of HTML or XML syntax and semantics for understanding of the initial chapters. A database course at the undergraduate or graduate level or familiarity with the concepts of relational schema, data model, and algebraic operators is a sufficient prerequisite for digesting the concept described in the later chapters. For professionals, working knowledge of relational database systems and HTML programming is sufficient to grasp the ideas presented throughout this book. Some exposure to the internals of search engines will help in comparing some of the methodology described in the context of the web warehouse. A good knowledge of C++/Java programming language at a beginner's level is sufficient to code the algorithm described herein. For readers interested in learning the area of Web data management, the book provides many examples throughout the chapters, which highlight and explain the intrinsic details.

Acknowledgments

It is a great pleasure for us to acknowledge the assistance and contributions of a large number of individuals to this effort. First, we would like to thank our publisher Springer-Verlag for their support. In particular, we would like to acknowledge the efforts, help, and patience of Wayne Wheeler, Wayne Yuhasz, Frank Ganz, and Timothy Taylor, our primary contacts for this edition.

The work reported in this book grew out of the Web Warehousing Project (WHOWEDA) at the Nanyang Technological University, Singapore. In this project, we explored various aspects of the web warehousing problem. Building a warehouse that accommodates data from the WWW has required us to rethink nearly every aspect of conventional data warehouses. Consequently, quite a few doctoral and master's dissertations have resulted from this project. Specifically, the chapters in this book are larger extensions in terms of scope and details of some of the papers published in journals and conferences and some initial chapters of Sourav's thesis work. Consequently, Dr. Wee Keong Ng, who was also Sourav's advisor, deserves the first thank you. Not only did he introduce Sourav to interesting topics in the database field, he was also always willing to discuss ideas, no matter how strange they were. In addition to Dr. Wee Keong Ng, the WHOWEDA project would have not been successful without the contributions made by Dr. Lim Ee-Peng who advised on many technical issues related to the WHOWEDA project.

In addition, we would also like to express our gratitude to all the group members, past and present, in the WHOWEDA project team. In particular, Feng Qiong, Cao Yinyan, Luah Aik Kee, Pallavi Priyadarshini, Ang Kho Kiong, and Huang Chee Thong made substantial contributions to the implementation of some of the components of WHOWEDA.

Quite a few people have helped us with the initial vetting of the text for this book. It is our pleasure to acknowledge them all here. We would like to thank Samuel Mulder for carefully proofreading the complete book in a short span of time and suggesting the changes which have been incorporated. We would also like to acknowledge Erwin Leonardi and Zhao Qiankun (graduate students in NTU) for refining some of the contents of this book.

Sourav S. Bhowmick would like to acknowledge his parents who gave him incredible support throughout the years. Thanks to Diya, his cute and precocious two year old niece, who has already taught him a lot; nothing matters more than drinking lots of milk, smiling a lot, and sleeping whenever you want to. A special thanks goes to his wife Rachelle, for her constant love, support, and encouragement. A special thanks goes to Rod Learmonth who was Sourav's mentor and a great motivator during his days in Griffith University. He was the major force behind the development of Sourav's aspiration to pursue a doctoral degree.

Sanjay would also like to mention his source of encouragement: his parents and the constant love and affection of his wife Ninu and sons Priyank and Pranal for giving him time out to work on the book at various stages, specially making a visit to Singapore in December 2002. He would also like to thank his friends and students who also helped him in many ways in completing the book.

Finally, we would like to thank the School of Computer Engineering of Nanyang Technological University, Singapore for the generous resources and financial support provided for the WHOWEDA project. We would also like to thank the Computer Science Department at the University of Missouri-Rolla for allowing the use of their resources to help complete the book.

DR. SOURAV S. BHOWMICK, DR. SANJAY MADRIA, DR. WEE KEONG NG
Nanyang Technological University, Singapore
University of Missouri-Rolla, USA
April 5th, 2003

Contents

1

Introduction

The growth of the Internet has dramatically changed the way in which information is managed and accessed. We are now moving from a world in which information management was in the hands of a few devotees to the widespread diffused information consumption of the World Wide Web (WWW). The World Wide Web is a distributed global information resource residing on the Internet. It contains a large amount of data relevant to essentially all domains of human activity: art, education, travel, science, politics, business, etc. What makes the Web so exciting is its potential to transcend geography to bring information on myriad topics directly to the desktop. Yet without any consistent organization, the Web is growing increasingly chaotic. Moreover, it is evolving at an alarming rate. In a recent report on the future of database research known as the Asilomar Report [12], it has been predicted that in ten years, the majority of human information will be available on the Web. To address these problems, traditional information retrieval techniques have been applied to document collection on the Internet, and a panoply of search engines and tools have been proposed and implemented. Such techniques are sometimes time consuming, and laborious, and the results obtained may be unsatisfactory. In [165], Zaine demonstrates some of the inefficiency and inadequacy of the information retrieval technology applied on the Internet. In this book, we present techniques to improve Web information management. Specifically, we discuss techniques for storing and manipulating Web data in a warehousing environment.

We begin motivating the need for new warehousing techniques by describing the limitations of Web data and how conventional data warehousing techniques are ill-equipped to manage heterogeneous, autonomous Web data. Within this context, we describe how a web warehouse differs from those studied in traditional data warehousing literature. In Section 1.2, we present an overview of our framework for modeling and manipulating Web data in a *web warehouse*. We present the conceptual architecture of the *web warehouse*, and identify its key modules and the subproblems they address. In Section 1.3, we briefly describe the key research issues raised by the need for storing and managing data in the *web warehouse*. In Section 1.4, we summarize the contributions of this book.

1.1 Motivation

In this section, we discuss the motivation behind the building of a web warehouse. We begin by identifying the problems associated with Web data. In Sections 1.1.2 and 1.1.3, we describe the existing technologies currently available and their limitations in alleviating the problems related to Web data. Specifically, we address the limitations of search engines and conventional data warehousing techniques in addressing these problems. Finally, we introduce the notion of a web warehouse in Section 1.1.4 to resolve these limitations.

1.1.1 Problems with Web Data

In this subsection, we identify the main problems associated with Web data, namely, lack of credibility, productivity, and historical data, and the inability to transform data into information. Note that these problems are analogous to the problems with naturally evolving architectures as described in [94] which were behind the germination of traditional data warehousing techniques. However, the implications of these problems are multiplied to a greater degree due to the autonomous, *semistructured* [40] nature of the Web.

Lack of Credibility of Data

The lack of credibility problem is illustrated with the following example. Let there be two Web sites A and B that provide information related to hotels in Hong Kong (there can be hundreds of them). These Web sites are operated by independent, often competing, organizations, and vary widely in their design and content. Moreover, assume that these Web sites are not controlled by the hotels in Hong Kong. Suppose we are interested in finding the cheapest three-star hotel in the Kowloon area of Hong Kong from the Web. Site A shows that the "Imperial Hotel" is the cheapest three-star hotel with rent 400 HK Dollars per room per night. However, Site B shows that the "Park Hotel" is the cheapest (390 HK Dollars per room per night) and the rent of "Imperial Hotel" is higher than " Park Hotel". When users receive such conflicting information they do not know what to do. This is an example of the crisis in credibility of the data in the Web. Such crises are widespread on the Web and the major reasons for this are: (1) no time basis of data, (2) autonomous nature of the Web sites, (3) selection of Web sites or information sources, and (4) no common source of data. We elaborate on these reasons one by one.

The lack of time basis is illustrated as follows. In the above example, let the last modification date of Sites A and B be February 15th and January 15th respectively. Suppose the rent of Park Hotel is increased to 430 HK Dollars per room per night on February 7th. Site A has incorporated this change in its Web site but Site B has failed to do so. Hence Site B does not provide current accommodation rates of hotels in Hong Kong.

The second reason for the crisis of credibility of Web data is the autonomous nature of related Web sites. There may exist significant content and structural differences between these Web sites. These sites are often mutually incompatible and inconsistent. This is primarily because the content and structure of Web sites are determined by the respective owner(s) of the sites. Hence Site A may only include information about hotels in Hong Kong thatr= it considers to be good accommodations. It may not include all hotels in Hong Kong. Therefore, 'Imperial Hotel' is considered to be the cheapest hotel by Site A simply because it does not consider 'Park Hotel' to be a good three-star hotel and does not record it in the Web site.

The third reason is the problem posed by the selection of information sources or Web sites. In the above example, the user has considered the Web sites A and B. However, these Web sites may not be the "authorities" pertaining to hotel-related information in Hong Kong. There may exist some other site(s) that provides more comprehensive data related to hotels in Hong Kong. Yet the user may not be aware of the existence of such Web sites.

The last contributing factor to the lack of credibility is that often there is no common source of data for these related Web sites. Different web sites belong to different autonomous and independent organizations with no synchronization or sharing of data whatsoever. These sites may cooperate to only a limited extent, and do not expose sensitive or critical information to each other. Such autonomy is most often motivated by business and legal reasons. The aftermath of this situation is that the content of different related Web sites may widely vary. Given these reasons, it is not surprising that there is a crisis of data credibility brewing in the Web.

Lack of Productivity

Credibility is not the only major problem with Web data. The productivity (or lack thereof) that is achieved while searching for relevant information in the Web is abysmal. For example, suppose a user wishes to find a list of locations in Singapore where the rent of a two-bedroom flat is less than 1500 Singapore Dollars per month that also has a movie theater and a Thai restaurant. Suppose there are three independent autonomous Web sites that contain such information. The first Web site contains information about apartment rental in Singapore. The second and third Web sites contain information about movies and restaurants in Singapore, respectively. In order to retrieve such information the user has to do the following three tasks: locate the relevant Web sites, obtain relevant data from these sites, and combine these related data to accomplish the above.

The first task is to locate relevant Web sites for answering the queries. To do this, many Web sites and their content must be analyzed. Furthermore, there are several complicating factors. Such information is rarely provided by a single Web site and is scattered in different Web sites in a piecemeal fashion. Moreover, not all such Web sites are useful to the user. For instance, not all Web sites related to restaurants in Singapore provide information about Thai restaurants. Also there may exist Web sites containing information about apartments that do not provide exact details of the type of apartment a user wishes to rent. Hence the process of having to go through different Web sites and analyze their content to find relevant information is an extremely tedious one.

The next tasks involve obtaining the desired information by combining relevant data from various Web sites, that is, to get information about the location of two-bedroom apartments with specified rent, and the location of those Thai restaurants and movie theaters that match the location of the apartment. However, comparing different data in multiple Web sites to filter out the desired result can be a very tiresome and frustrating process.

Lack of Historical Data

Web data are mercurial in nature. That is, Web data can change at any time. A majority of Web documents reflect the most recently modified data at any given instance of time. Although some Web sites such as newspaper and weather forecast sites allow users to access news of previous days or weeks, most of the Web sites do not have any archiving facility. However, the time period of historical data is not necessarily enough. For instance, most of the newspaper Web sites generally do not archive news reports that are more than six months old. Observe that once data in the Web change there is no way to retrieve the previous snapshot of data.

Such lack of historical data gives rise to severe limitations in exploiting time-based information on the Web. For instance, suppose a business organization (say Company A) wishes to determine how the price and features of "Product X" have changed over time in Company B. Assume that Company B is a competitor of Company A. To gather such information from the Web, Company A must be able to access historical data of "Product X" for the specified period of time to analyze the rate of change of the price along with the product features. Unfortunately, such information is typically impossible to retrieve from the Web.

Observe that the importance of previous snapshots of Web data is not only essential for analyzing Web data over a period of time, but also for addressing the problem of broken links ("Document not found" Error). This common problem arises when a document pointed to by a link does not exist anymore. In such a situation the most recent snapshot of the document may be presented to the user.

From Data to Information

As if productivity, credibility and lack of historical data were not problems enough, there is another major fault with Web data is the inability to go from data to information. At first glance, the notion of going from data to information seems to be an ethereal concept with little substance. But such is not the case at all. Consider the following request, typical of an e-commerce environment; "Which online shop sells a palmtop at the lowest price?" The first thing a user encounters in the Web is that many online shops sell palmtops. Trying to draw the necessary information (lowest price in this case) from the data in these online shops is a very tedious process. These Web sites were never constructed with comparison shopping in mind. In fact, most of the online shops do not support comparison shopping because it may be detrimental to their business activities.

The following example concerns the health care environment. Suppose a user wishes to know the following; "What are the new drugs for AIDS that have been made available commercially during the last six months?" Observe that there are many Web sites on health care providing information about AIDS. To answer this query, one not only needs access to data about drugs for AIDS but also different snapshots of the list of drugs over a period of six months to infer all new drugs that have been added to the Web site(s). Hence data in the Web simply are inadequate for the task of supporting such informational needs.

To resolve the above limitations so that Web data can be transformed into useful information, it is necessary to develop effective tools to perform such operations. Currently, there are two types of tools to gather information from different sources: search engines enable us to retrieve relevant documents from the Web; and conventional data warehousing systems can be used to glean information from different sources. In subsequent sections, we motivate the necessity of a web warehouse by describing how contemporary search engines and data warehouses are ill-equipped to satisfy the needs of individual Web users and business organizations with a web presence.

1.1.2 Limitations of Search Engines

Currently, information on the Web may be discovered primarily by two mechanisms: browsers and search engines. Existing search engines such as Yahoo and Google service millions of queries a day. Yet it has become clear that they are less than ideal for retrieving an ever-growing body of information on the Web. This mechanism offers limited capabilities for retrieving the information of interest, still burying the user under a heap of irrelevant information. We have identified the following shortcomings of existing search engines in the context of addressing the problems associated with Web data. Note that these shortcomings are not meant to be exhaustive. Our intention is to highlight only those shortcomings that act as an impediment for a search engine to satisfy the informational needs of individual Web users and business organizations on the Web.

Inability to Check Credibility of Information

The Web still lacks standards that would facilitate automated indexing. Documents on the Web are not structured so that programs can reliably extract the routine information that a human indexer might find through cursory inspection: author, date of last modification, length of text, and subject matter (this information is known as metadata). As a result, search engines have so far made little progress in exploiting the metadata of Web documents. For instance, a Web crawler might turn up the desired article authored by Bill Gates. But it might also find thousands of other articles in which such a common name is mentioned in the text or in a bibliographic reference.

Such a limitation has a significant effect on the credibility problem. Search engines fail to determine whether the last modification time of a Web site is more recent compared to another site. It may also fail to determine those Web sites containing comprehensive information about a particular topic. Reconsidering the example of credibility in the previous section, a search engine is thus incapable of comparing timestamps of Sites A and B or determining if these sites provide comprehensive listings of hotel information in Hong Kong.

Inability to Improve Productivity

It may seem that search engines could be used to alleviate some of the problems in locating relevant Web sites. However, the precision of results from search engines is low as there is an almost unavoidable existence of irrelevant data in the results. Considerably more comprehensive search engines such as Excite (`www.excite.com`) and Alta Vista (`www.altavista.com`) will return a long list of documents littered with unwanted irrelevant material. A more discriminating search will almost certainly exclude many useful pages. One way to help users describe what they want more precisely is to let them use logical operators such as AND, OR, and NOT to specify which words must (or must not) be presented in retrieved pages. But many users find such Boolean notation intimidating, confusing, or simply unhelpful. When thousands of documents match a query, giving more weight to those containing more search terms or uncommon keywords (which tend to be more important) still does not guarantee that the most relevant pages will appear near the top of the list. Moreover, publishers sometimes abuse this method of ranking query results to attract attention by repeating within a document a word that is known to be queried often.

Even if we are fortunate enough to find a list of relevant sites using search engines (sites related to apartment rental, restaurants, and movie theaters in Singapore), it does not provide an efficient solution to the productivity problem. To find information about the location of apartments where there also exist a Thai restaurant and a movie theater from the results of one or more search engines requires considerable manual effort. Currently, integrating relevant data from different Web sites can be done using the following methods

1. Retrieve a set of Web sites containing the information and then navigate through each of these sites to retrieve relevant data.
2. Use the search facilities, if any, provided by the respective Web sites to identify potentially relevant data and then compare the data manually to compute the desired location of the apartment.
3. Use the search facilities in the Web sites to get a list of potentially relevant data and then write a program to compare the data to retrieve information about the desired location of the apartment.

The first two methods involve manual intervention and generate considerable cognitive overhead for finding answers to the query. Hence these two methods do not significantly improve the productivity of users. The last method, although more efficient than the previous two methods, is not a feasible solution as a user has to write different programs every time he or she is looking for different information. To produce the answer to the query, the exercise of locating desired Web sites must be done properly.

Inability to Exploit Historical Data

Queries in search engines are evaluated on index data rather than the up-to-date data. In most search engines, once the page is visited, it is marked read and never visited again (unless explicitly asked). But, because of its mercurial nature, information in each document is everchanging along with the Web. Thus, soon after an update, the index data could become out of date or encounter "404 Error" (error for "document not found" in the Web). Moreover, the search engines do not store historical data. Hence any computation that requires access to previous snapshots of Web data cannot be performed using search engines.

Due to these limitations, the search engines are not satisfactory tools for converting data to information. Next we explore the capabilities (or limitations) of traditional data warehousing systems in managing Web data.

1.1.3 Limitations of Traditional Data Warehouse

Data warehouses can be viewed as an evolution of management information systems [49]. They are integrated repositories that store information which may originate from multiple, possibly heterogeneous, operational or legacy data sources. There has been considerable interest in this topic within the database industry over the last several years. Most leading vendors claim to provide at least some "data warehousing tools" and several small companies are devoted exclusively to data warehousing products. Data warehousing technologies have been successfully deployed in many industries: manufacturing (for order shipment and customer support), retail (for user profiling and inventory management), financial services (for claim analysis and fraud detection), transportation (for fleet management), telecommunications (for call analysis and fraud detection), utilities (for power usage analysis), and health care (for outcomes analysis) [49]. The importance of data warehousing in the commercial segment appears to be due to a need for enterprises to gather all of their information into a single place for in-depth analysis, and the desire to decouple such analysis from online transaction processing systems. Fundamentally, data warehouses are used to study past behavior and possibly to predict the future. It may seem that the usage of traditional data warehousing techniques for Web data could alleviate the problem of harnessing useful information from the Web. However, using traditional data warehousing techniques to analyze irregular, autonomous, and semistructured Web data has severe limitations. The next section discusses those limitations.

Translation of Web Data

In a traditional data warehousing system, each information source is connected to a wrapper [90, 104, 156] which is responsible for translating information from the native format of the source into the format and data model used by the warehousing system. For instance, if the information source consists of a set of flat files but the warehouse model is relational, then the wrapper must support an interface that presents the data from the information source as if they were relational. Note that most commercial data warehousing systems assume that both the information sources and the warehouse are relational, so translation is not an issue. However, such a technique becomes very tedious for translating Web data to a conventional data warehouse. This is because different wrapper components are needed for each Web site, since the functionality of the wrapper is dependent on the content and structure of the Web site. Hence for each relevant Web site, one has to generate a wrapper component. Consequently, this requires knowledge of the content and structure of the Web site. Moreover, as the content and structure of the site change, the wrapper component has to be modified. We believe that this is an extremely tedious and undesirable approach for retrieving relevant data from the Web. Therefore a different technique is required to populate a data warehouse for Web data without exploiting the capabilities of wrappers. Thus it is necessary to use different warehouse data modeling techniques that nullify the necessity of converting Web data formats. That is, the data model of the warehouse for Web data should support representation of Web data in their native format. It is not required to convert to another format such as into relational format.

Rigidity of the Data Model of the Conventional Data Warehouse

Even if we are fortunate enough to find Web sites whose structure and content are relatively stable so that constructing wrappers for retrieving data from these Web sites in the warehouse data model format is a feasible option, it is desirable to model the data in the warehouse appropriately for supporting data analysis.

To facilitate complex analysis and visualization, the data in a traditional data warehouse are typically modeled *multidimensionally*. In a multidimensional data model [89], there is a set of numeric measures that are the objects of analysis. Examples of such measures are sales, budget, etc. Each of these numeric measures depends on a set of dimensions that provide the content for the measure. Thus the multidimensional data views a measure as a value in the multidimensional space of that dimension. Each dimension is described by a set of attributes. The attributes of a dimension may be related via a hierarchy of relationships. A multidimensional model is implemented directly by MOLAP (Multidimensional Online Analytical Processing) servers. However, this multidimensional model is ill-equipped to model semistructured, irregular Web data. For instance, it is very difficult to identify a set of numeric measures for the Web data (HTML or XML pages) that are the object of analysis. Moreover, identifying a set of attributes for Web data to describe dimensions in a multidimensional model is equally difficult. This is because related data in different Web sites differ in content and structure. Furthermore, as the sites are autonomous there may not exist any common attribute among these data. Consequently, we believe that a multidimensional model is not an efficient mechanism to model Web data in a conventional data warehouse.

A traditional data warehouse may also be implemented on Relational OLAP (ROLAP) servers. These servers assume that data are stored in relational databases. In this case, the multidimensional model and its operations are mapped into relations and SQL queries. Most data warehouses use a star or snowflake schema [49] to represent multidimensional data models on ROLAP servers. Such a technique is suitable for relatively simple data types having rigid structure. Most of the traditional data warehousing paradigms first create a star or snowflake schema to describe the structure of the warehouse data and then populate the warehouse according to this structure. However, the data that are received from a Web site may appear to have some structure but may widely vary [149]. The fact that one page uses H2 tags for headings does not necessarily carry across to other pages, perhaps even from the same site. Moreover, the type of information described in pages across different Web sites may be related but may have different formats and content. Also, insertion of new data on these Web sites may cause a schema to be inconsistent or incomplete to describe such data. Thus we believe that the current rigidity of conventional warehouse schemas and the warehouse data model in general becomes an impediment to address in the issues of representing irregular inconsistent data from the Web.

Rigidity of Operations in a Conventional Data Warehouse

Adding to the problem of modeling Web data in a traditional warehousing environment, the operations defined in the multidimensional data model are ill-equipped to perform similar actions on Web data. Typical OLAP operations include roll-up (increasing the level of aggregation), drill-down along one or more dimension hierarchies (decreasing the level of aggregation or increasing detail), slice-and-dice (selection and projection), and pivot (reorienting the multidimensional view of data) [89]. Note that the distinctive feature of a multidimensional model is its stress on aggregation of measures by one or more dimensions as one of the key operations. Such aggregation makes sense for data such as sales, time, budget, etc. However, the varied nature and complexity of Web data containing text, audio, video, and executable programs makes the notion of aggregation and the set of operations described above extremely difficult to perform. Hence there is a need to redefine operations that are applicable on a data warehouse containing Web data.

Change Monitoring

Detection and management of changes in the base data are performed by *monitors* and *integrators* in traditional data warehousing environments [156]. Monitors detect changes to an information source that are of interest to the warehouse and propagate the changes to the integrators. The function of the integrators is to receive change notifications from the monitors for the information sources and reflect these sources in the data warehouse. Also, a different set of monitors is required to detect changes in the information sources. Moreover, a different integrator is needed for each data warehouse since different sets of views over different base data may be stored.

When we consider Web data, the change detection and management techniques used in traditional database systems cannot be used due to the uncooperative nature of Web sites. In conventional databases, detecting changes to data is made easier by the availability of facilities such as transaction logs, triggers, etc. However, in the Web such facilities are often absent. Even in cases where these facilities are available, they may not be accessible by an outside user. Therefore we often need to detect changes by comparing two or more snapshots of the Web data. Here the unstructured nature of the Web adds to the problem. Thus, finding changes in Web data is much more challenging than in structured relational data. Consequently, conventional monitors are not an efficient solution to reflect the changes in Web sites. Moreover, as modified data are added to the warehouse, the warehouse schema used to represent the data may become incomplete or inconsistent. Thus the warehouse for Web data must contain schema management facilities that can adapt gracefully to the dynamic nature of Web data. The maintenance of views in the warehouse containing Web data becomes a much more challenging and complex problem.

1.1.4 Warehousing the Web

Based on the above discussion, it is evident that there is a necessity to develop novel techniques for managing Web data such that they will be able to support individual users as well as business organizations in decision making. Consequently, developing such techniques necessitates a significant rethinking of traditional data warehousing techniques. We believe that a special data warehouse design for Web data (a *web warehouse*) [116, 13, 140] is necessary to address the needs of Web users to support decision making. In this context, we briefly introduce the notion of a web warehousing system. In the next section, we discuss the architecture of a web warehouse.

Similar to a data warehouse, a web warehouse is a repository of integrated data from the Web, available for querying and analysis. Data from different relevant Web sites are extracted and translated into a common data model (*Warehouse Object Model* (WHOM) in our case), and integrated with existing data at the warehouse. At the warehouse, queries can be answered and data analysis can be performed quickly and efficiently. Moreover, the data in the web warehouse provide a means to alleviate the limitations of Web data discussed in Section 1.1.1. Furthermore, similar to a conventional data warehouse, accessing data at a web warehouse does not incur costs that may be associated with accessing data from the Web. The web warehouse may also provide access to data when they are not available directly from the Web (Document not found error).

Availability, speed of access, and data quality tend to be the major issues for data warehouses in general, and web warehouses in particular. The last issue is a particularly hard problem. Web data quality is vital to properly managing a web warehouse environment. The quality of data will limit the ability of the end users to make informed decisions. Data quality problems usually occur in one of two places: when data are retrieved and loaded into the web warehouse, or when the Web sources themselves contain incomplete or inaccurate data. Due to the autonomous nature of the sources, the latter is the most difficult to change. In this case, there is nothing in the way of tools and techniques to improve the quality of data. Hence improving the data quality of the Web sources is not supported in our web warehouse. However, we provide a set of techniques for improving the quality of data in the web warehouse when data are retrieved and loaded into the web warehouse. We discuss this briefly by specifying the techniques we adopt to address the following indicators of data quality

- *Data are not irrelevant:* Retrieving relevant data from the Web using a *global web coupling* operation may also couple irrelevant information. The existence of irrelevant information increases the size of the web warehouse. This adversely affects the storage and query processing cost of coupled Web information and also affects the query computing cost. We address this problem by eliminating the irrelevant data from the warehouse using the *web project* operation. We discuss this in Chapter 8.

- *Data are timely:* The Web offers access to large amounts of heterogeneous information and allows this information to change at any time and in any way. These changes take two general forms. The first is existence: Web pages and Web sites exhibit varied longevity patterns. The second is structure and content modification: Web pages replace their antecedents, usually leaving no trace of the previous document. Hence one significant issue regarding data quality is that copying data may introduce inconsistencies with the Web sites. That is, the warehouse data may become obsolete. Moreover, these information sources typically do not keep track of historical information in a format accessible to the outside user. Consequently, historical data are not directly available to the web warehouse from the information sources. To mitigate this problem, we repeatedly scan the Web for results based on some given criteria using the *polling global web coupling* technique. The *polling frequency* is used in a *coupling query predicate* of a web query to enforce a global web coupling operation to be executed periodically. We discuss this in Chapters 6 and 8. Note that the web warehousing approach may not be appropriate when absolutely current data are required.

- *There are no duplicate documents:* Due to the large number of replicated documents in the Web, the data retrieval process may harness identical Web documents in the web warehouse. Note that these duplicate documents may have different URLs. This makes it harder to identify such replicated documents autonomously and remove them from the web warehouse. One expensive way is to compare the content of a pair of documents. In this book, we do not discuss how to mitigate this problem.

One drawback of the warehousing approach is that the warehouse administrator needs to identify relevant Web sites (*source discovery*) from which the warehouse is to be populated. Source discovery usually begins with a keyword search on one of the search engines or a query to one of the web directory services. The works in [46, 127, 69] address the resource discovery problem and describe the design of *topic-specific PIW crawlers*. In our study, we assume that a potential source has already been discovered. In any case, the importance of a web warehouse for analyzing Web data to provide useful information that helps users in decision making is undeniable. Next we introduce our web warehousing system called WHOWEDA (**W**are**H**ouse **O**f **WE**b **DA**ta).

1.2 Architecture and Functionalities

Figure 1.1 illustrates the basic architecture of our web warehousing system. It consists of a set of modules such as the *coupling engine*, *web manipulator*, *web delta manager*, and *web miner*. The functionalities of the warehousing modules are briefly described as follows

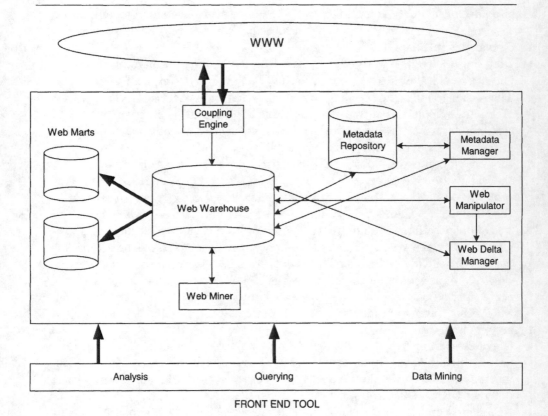

Fig. 1.1. Architecture of WHOWEDA.

Coupling Engine

The coupling engine is responsible for extracting relevant data from multiple Web sites and storing them in the web warehouse in the form of *web tables*. In essence, it translates information from the native format of the sources into the format and data model used by the warehouse. These sources are Web sites containing image, video, or text data. The coupling engine is also responsible for generating *schemas* of the data stored in web tables.

Web Manipulator

The web manipulator is responsible for manipulating newly generated web tables (from the coupling engine) using a set of web algebraic operators to generate additional useful information. It returns the result in the form of a web table.

Web Delta Manager

The web delta manager is responsible for generating *web deltas* and storing them in the form of *delta web tables*. By web delta we mean relevant changes in Web information in the context of a web warehouse. The web delta manager issues polling queries over information sources in the Web (via the coupling engine) and the result of each query is stored by the warehouse as the current snapshot for that query. The current and previous snapshots are sent to the web delta manager which identifies changes and stores them in the warehouse in the form of *delta web tables*.

A web delta manager also assists in generating a "trigger" for a certain user's query. Such a trigger will automatically notify the user if there has been an occurrence of user-specified changes. Users interact with the web delta manager through the front end tools, creating triggers, issuing polling queries, and receiving results.

Web Miner

The web miner is responsible for performing mining operations in the warehouse. It uses the capabilities of the web manipulator as well as a set of data mining operators to perform its task. Specifically, it is involved in generating summarization of data in the web warehouse and providing tools for generating useful knowledge that aids in decision making. A preliminary list of research issues on Web mining in the context of WHOWEDA is given in [21].

Metadata Manager

Finally, the metadata manager is a repository for storing and managing metadata, as well as tools for monitoring and administering the warehousing system. The metadata manager manages the definitions of the web schemas in the warehouse, predefined queries, web marts location and content, user profiles, user authorization and access control policies, currency of data in the warehouse, usage statistics, and so on.

In addition to the main web warehouse, there may be several topic-specific warehouses called *web marts*. The notion of a web mart is similar to that of data marts in a traditional data warehousing system. Data in the warehouse and web marts are stored and managed by one or more warehouse servers, which present different views of the data to a variety of front-end tools: query tools, analysis tools, and web mining tools.

Similar to the conventional data warehouse [49], a web warehouse may be distributed for load balancing, scalability, and higher availability. In such a distributed architecture, the metadata repository is usually replicated with each fragment of the warehouse, and the entire warehouse is administered centrally. An alternative architecture, implemented for expediency when it may be too expensive to construct a single logically integrated web warehouse, is a federation of warehouses or web marts, each with its own repository and decentralized administration.

1.2.1 Scope of This Book

In this book, we focus our discussion in detail on the coupling engine and web manipulator modules as shown in the architecture in Figure 1.1. The remaining modules for data mining in the web warehouse, change management, and metadata managements are briefly discussed. We do not discuss issues related to distributed architecture of web warehouses, or federations of web warehouses or web marts. In other words, this book explores the underlying data model for representing and storing relevant data from the Web, the mechanism for populating the warehouse and the generation of *web schemas* to describe the warehouse data and various web algebraic operators associated with the web warehouse. In essence, these goals are to be achieved:

- The design of a suitable data model for representing Web data;
- Designing a mechanism for populating a web warehouse with relevant data from the Web;
- Designing a Web algebra for manipulating the data to derive additional useful information; and
- Developing applications of the web warehouse.

Although the WWW is a dynamic collection of distributed and diverse resources that change from time to time, we assume throughout this book that whenever we refer to the WWW, we are referring to a particular snapshot of it in time. This snapshot is taken to be a *typical* instance of the WWW at any point in time. Furthermore, we restrict our discussion based on the following assumptions

- Modeling of Web data is based on the HTML specification (version 3.2) as described in [147] and the XML specification (version 1.1) as described in [37].
- This work does not include modeling and manipulation of images, video, or other multimedia objects in the Web.
- Web sites containing nonexecutable textual content that are accessible through HTTP, FTP, and Gopher are considered in this book. These are sites containing HTML or XML documents, or plain texts. Pages that contain forms that invoke CGI scripts are not within the scope of this work.

1.3 Research Issues

We now summarize the research issues raised by the modeling and manipulation of data in a web warehouse. We present only a brief description of the issues here, with details deferred to later chapters.

Web Data Coupling Mechanism

Data in the Web are typically *semistructured* [40], meaning they have structure, but the structure may be irregular and incomplete, and may not conform to a fixed schema. This semistructured nature of data introduces serious challenges in retrieving relevant information from the Web to populate a web warehouse. We address this issue in detail in Chapters 6 and 8.

Representation of Web Data

It is essential for us to be able to model Web documents in an efficient way that will support metadata, content, and structure-based querying and analysis of these documents. Note that a Web document has content and some structure and also a set of metadata associated with it. However, there is no explicit demarcation between these sets of attributes. Thus, materializing only the copy of a Web document is not efficient for querying and analysis of Web data as we need to extract the content, structural, and metadata attributes every time we query the document. In order to facilitate efficient querying and analysis over the content, structure, and metadata associated with Web documents we need to extract these attributes from the documents. In Chapter 3, we show how HTML and XML documents are modeled in the web warehouse.

Mechanism for Imposing Constraints

In a web warehouse, we are not interested in any arbitrary collection of Web documents and hyperlinks, but documents and links that satisfy certain *constraints* pertaining to the metadata, content, and structural information. In order to exploit interdocument relationships, i.e., the hyperlink structures of documents in the Web, we also need to define a way to impose constraints on the interlinked structure of relevant Web documents. In Chapters 4 and 5, we describe how we address the problem of imposing constraints on Web data.

Schemas of Warehouse Data

The reliance of traditional work on a fixed schema causes serious difficulties when working with Web data. Designing a relational or object schema for Web data is extremely difficult. Intuitively, the reason for the difficulties in modeling Web data using a schema is the following: every schema relies on a set of assumptions. For example, relational database schema design is guided by the presence and absence of functional dependencies. Web data by their very nature lack the consistency, stability, and structure implied by these assumptions. In Chapter 7, we present a novel method of generating schema for a set of related Web documents.

Manipulation of Warehouse Data

In this book, we are not only interested in how to populate the web warehouse with relevant information, but also how to manipulate the warehouse data to extract additional useful information. In order to achieve this, we need to have a set of algebraic operators to perform selection, reduction, and composition of warehouse data. We address the panoply of web operators in detail in Chapter 8 of this book.

Visualization of Warehouse Data

It is necessary to give users the flexibility to view documents in different perspectives that are more meaningful in the web warehouse. We discuss a set of data visualization operators in detail in Chapter 9 of this book.

1.4 Contributions of the Book

The major contributions of this book are summarized as follows

- We described a data model called the Warehouse Object Model (WHOM), which is used to describe data in our web warehouse and to manipulate these data.
- We present a technique to represent Web data in the web warehouse in the form of *node* and *link objects*.
- We present a flexible scheme to impose constraints on metadata, content, and structure of HTML and XML data. An important feature of our scheme is that it allows us to impose constraints on a specific portion of Web documents or hyperlinks, on attributes associated with HTML or XML elements, and on the hierarchical structure of Web documents, instead of simple keyword-based constraints used in search engines.
- We describe a mechanism to represent constraints imposed on the hyperlinked connection within a set of Web documents. An important feature of our approach is that it can represent interdocument relationships based on *partial* knowledge of the user about the hyperlinked structure.
- We discussed a novel method for describing and generating schema(s) for a set of relevant Web data. An important feature of our schema is that it represents a collection of Web documents that are relevant to a user, instead of representing any set of Web documents.
- We present a query mechanism to harness relevant data from the Web. An important feature of the query mechanism is that it can exploit *partial* knowledge of the user to retrieve relevant data.
- We present a set of *web algebraic operators* to manipulate hyperlinked Web data in WHOWEDA.
- We present a set of *data visualization operators* for visualizing web data.
- We present two applications of the web warehouse, namely, Web data change management and knowledge discovery.

A Survey of Web Data Management Systems

The popularity of the Web has made it a prime vehicle for disseminating information. The relevance of database concepts to the problems of managing and querying this information has led to a significant body of recent research addressing these problems. Even though the underlying challenge is how to manage large volumes of data, the novel context of the Web forces us to significantly extend traditional techniques [79]. In this chapter we review some of these Web data management systems. Most of these systems do not have a corresponding algebra. We focus on several classes of systems that are classified based on the tasks they perform related to information management on the Web: (1) modeling and querying the Web, (2) information extraction and integration, and (3) Web site construction and restructuring [79]. Furthermore, we discuss recent research in XML data modeling and query languages and data warehousing systems for Web data.

For each system, we provide the following as appropriate: a short summary of the system along with the data model and algebra, if any, a rough idea of the expressive power of the query language or algebra, implementation status (where applicable and known), and examples of algebraic or web queries (similar queries are used as often as possible throughout to facilitate comparison). As the discussion moves to Web data integration systems, the examples are largely omitted due to space constraints.

Note that we do not discuss the relative power of the underlying data models or other theoretical language issues. Many of these issues are covered in [79]. The purpose of this survey is to convey some idea of the general nature of web query systems in the hope of gaining some insight into why certain operations exist and of identifying common themes among these systems. We do not compare the similarity and differences of the features of these systems with those of WHOWEDA in this chapter. Such discussion is deferred, whenever appropriate, to subsequent chapters.

It is inevitable that some web information management systems have been either omitted or described only briefly. This is by no means a dismissal of any kind, but reflects the fact that including them in this particular survey would have added little to its value and greatly to its length. Section 2.1 reviews the existing query systems for the Web. Section 2.2 discusses various data integration systems for integrating data from multiple Web sources. In Section 2.3 we discuss various web data restructuring systems. The next section covers semistructured data [40] management systems. Note that the Web is an instance of semistructured data. Next we review various data models and query languages for XML data in Section 2.5. The last section summarizes this survey and draws some conclusions.

2.1 Web Query Systems

Given the high rate of growth of the volume of data available on the WWW, locating information of interest in such an anarchic setting becomes a more difficult process every day. Thus there is the recognition of the immediate need for effective and efficient tools for information consumers, who must be able to easily locate disparate information in the Web, ranging from unstructured documents and pictures to structured, record-oriented data. When doing this, one cannot just ask for the information he is interested in; instead one has to search for it. If the information happens to be found, it may be scattered everywhere, in a piecemeal fashion. An appealing alternative is querying the data in the Web. This has led to an increasing research effort in developing efficient query mechanisms for the Web. The most popular form of query system is the panoply of available Web search engines. We elaborate on the features and limitations of these search engines.

2.1.1 Search Engines

In search engines (such as Google, and Alta Vista), a user submits keywords to a database of Web pages, and get back a different display of documents from each search engine. Results from submitting very comparable searches can differ widely, but also contain some of the same documents. Some of the features of popular search engines are shown in Table 2.1 [159]. Note that the feature "Other sources" means that the search service may search Internet sources other than Web pages: most commonly the message archives of Usenet newsgroups. Many also link to services providing email address directories and may have a directory of Internet resources arranged by subject. "Implied OR, AND" indicates search keywords will be automatically OR'd together to look for pages with any of the words or AND'd to look for pages containing all of them. The feature "+ and -" means that the terms that must be present can be prefixed with '+' (require). Those not required can be indicated with '-' (reject). "AND, OR, NOT" specifies that terms can be linked with AND to show all words must be present. With OR the search can look for synonyms and NOT to exclude words. Some services have options such as "any words" or "all these words" which have the same purpose. Next the feature "fields" indicates that in some search engines it may be possible to search, for example, just the document title or the URL. "Truncation" allows the system to search for a number of words beginning with the same stem, eg., "medic★" would find medical and medicine. "Adjacency" specifies that words must be next to each other, as in a phrase or person's name. Finally, the feature "proximity" ensures that search words are near each other, say, in the same sentence.

Features	Alta Vista	Excite	Google	Hotbot	Infoseek	Lycos
Other sources	Usenet sounds pictures	Usenet news email address	None	Usenet sounds pictures	Usenet news email addresses	Sounds pictures
Implied OR, AND	Implied OR	Implied OR	AND	Implied AND	Implied OR	Implied AND
+ or -	Yes	Yes	Yes	Yes	Yes	Yes
AND, OR, NOT	In Advanced Search	Yes	No	Yes	No	Yes
Fields	title, URL, text, etc.	No	No	title, domain, etc	title, URL, etc.	URL, title, text, etc.
Truncation	Uses *	No	No	Uses *	No	No
Adjacency (phrase)	Uses " "	Uses " "	Uses " "	Uses " " or from menu	Uses " "	Uses " " from menu
Proximity	Uses NEAR	No	No	No	No	Uses NEAR or from menu

Table 2.1. Features of popular search engines.

The search engines offer limited capabilities for retrieving the information of interest, still burying the user under a heap of irrelevant information. We have identified the following shortcomings of the existing search engines:

- **Lack of support for metadata queries:** The current Web lacks standards that would facilitate automated indexing using metadata information such as author, last date of modification, anchor keywords associated with hyperlinks and URLs, length of the text, summary of documents, etc.

- **Lack of support for querying interlinked documents:** Search engines have so far made little progress in exploiting the topological nature of documents in the Web. Not only do most search engines fail to support queries utilizing link information, they also fail to return link information as part of a query's result. Most of the search engines always return a set of disconnected documents as their search results. They do not allow users to input constraints on the hyperlink structure of a set of documents. We believe that searches related to the hypertext structure of sites are very important. Such searches are difficult to pose using the query mechanism offered by search engines. In these mechanisms users pose queries by defining conditions that a Web page must satisfy in order to be in the solution set. It is extremely difficult to define complex conditions about relationships between pages.

- **Lack of support for structural queries:** Search engines do not exploit the structure of Web documents. One cannot express conditions based on the hierarchical nature of the tag elements in a query. For instance, consider the query to retrieve documents that include the list of features of a digital camera in the form of a table in the Web page. A search engine may return thousands of documents containing a wide variety of information related to digital cameras most of which are not necessarily structured in the form of a table.

- **Search engines recognize text only:** The search is limited to string matching. Numeric comparisons, as in conventional databases, cannot be done. For example, the following query cannot be expressed: *Find 3-bedroom houses for sale in Clementi whose price is less than $500,000;* Moreover, most search engines recognize text only. The intense interest in the Web, though, has come about because of the medium's ability to display images, whether graphics or video clips. Some research has moved toward finding colors or patterns within images, but no program can deduce the underlying meaning and cultural significance of an image (for example, that a group of men dining represents the Last Supper).

- **Existence of duplicate documents:** Due to such large numbers of replicated documents in the Web, there is the almost unavoidable existence of identical Web documents in the query results of the search engines. These identical documents may be scattered in a piecemeal fashion in the query result returned by the search engines. The only way to find these duplicate documents is by manually browsing each Web document and comparing them to each other.

- **Limitation in querying dynamic Web pages:** Present-day search engines retrieve content only from a portion of the Web, called the *publicly indexable Web* (PIW) [108]. This refers to the set of web pages reachable exclusively by following hypertext links, ignoring search forms and pages requiring authorization or registration. However, recent studies [109, 96] observed that a significant fraction of Web content lies outside the PIW. A great portion of the Web is hidden behind search forms (lots of databases are available only through HTML forms). This portion of the Web was called the *hidden Web* in [80] and the *deep Web* in [96]. Pages in the hidden Web are dynamically generated in response to queries submitted via the search forms. These dynamically generated pages, unlike static files, cannot be analyzed and indexed by Web crawlers. Thus search results ignore such dynamic Web documents.

- **Lack of support for querying XML data:** Currently, none of the search engines support querying XML documents. They also do not provide the facility to specify query conditions in the form of *path expressions*. This condition plays an important role for querying XML data.

2.1.2 Metasearch Engines

In a metasearch engine, Dogpile (www.dogpile.com), Inference Find (www.infind.com) and MetaCrawler (www.metacrawler.com), a query is submitted in the form of keywords in its search box, and is transmitted simultaneously to several individual search engines and their databases. The search then returns results from various search engines combined together. For instance, MetaCrawler submits a query simultaneously to the following search services: about.com, Alta Vista, Excite, Infoseek, Looksmart, Lycos, Thunderstone, Web Crawler, and Yahoo. It consolidates the results in one large list, ranked by a score derived from the rankings of each of the search engines listing each site. It normalizes the confidence scores used by each of the services, sums the scores, and ranks them 1 to 1000.

Although this sounds too good to believe, it may not always be a useful engine for answering a query. Of course, metasearch engines are useful when a user is looking for a unique term or phrase contained in the database of several search engines. However, the following are the shortcomings of metasearch engines.

- Metasearch engines only spend a short time in each database and often retrieve only a small portion of any of the results in any of the databases queried.
- Since metasearch engines retrieve results from different search engines, the limitations of these search engines as discussed above also appear in the results of metasearch engines.
- If the query contains more than one or two keywords or very complex logic, then most of that will be lost while searching the relevant databases. It will only make sense to the few search engines that support such logic (see Table 2.1).

The above limitations of search and meta-search engines have triggered considerable research activity to build efficient web query systems for querying HTML and XML data [79]. If the Web is viewed as a large graph-like database, it is natural to pose queries that go beyond the basic information retrieval paradigm supported by today's search engines and take structure into account, both the internal structure of Web pages and the external structure of links that interconnect them. In this chapter, we discuss the web query languages proposed so far: W3QS [101], WebSQL [132], WebLog [106], RAW [77], and NetQL [119]. These systems view the WWW as a huge database that can be queried using a declarative language. We now briefly describe each of these query systems.

2.1.3 W3QS

W3QS (WWW Query System) [101, 102] at Technion (Israel Institute of Technology) is a project to develop a flexible, declarative, and SQL-like Web query language, W3QL. This language supports effective and flexible query processing addressing the structure and content of WWW nodes and their various kinds of data. Some of the notable features of W3QL [101] are the use of external programs for specifying content conditions on files rather than building conditions into the language syntax, and providing a mechanism for handling forms encountered during navigation. In [102], Konopnicki and Shmueli describe additional features in W3QL such as modeling internal document structure, hierarchical web modeling that captures the notion of the Web site explicitly, and replacing the external program method of specifying conditions with a general extensible method based on the MIME standard. In summary, some of the main features of W3QL are as follows.

- It enables both content queries (queries about the content of the WWW accessible information) and structural queries (queries about the hypertext organization of the WWW accessible data) [9, 63, 134].
- It allows easy interfacing to user-written programs and standard UNIX utilities.
- It takes advantage of existing WWW indexes and search services.
- It provides a view update specification facility.

W3QS is an operational prototype system that executes W3QL queries. Some of the main features of this system are:

- It is accessible via any WWW browser;
- It provides an application program interface (API) that can be used by programs running anywhere in the Internet;
- It supports queries on the Web structure by specifying a starting page, a search domain, and the depth of links;
- It provides utilities for file content analysis and is capable of filling out online forms automatically; and
- It simplifies the building of WWW search programs by providing a library of Perl classes.

We now briefly discuss the expressiveness of W3QL with some examples. The data model of W3QL is based on a labeled multigraph. The topology of the W3QL multigraph is specified in the text of the query by a set of path specifications. A path is specified by a comma-separated list of distinct node names and distinct edge names. For example, n_1, ℓ_1, n_2, ℓ_2, n_3 specifies a three-node path from node n_1 to node n_2 via an edge called ℓ_1 and from node n_2 to node n_3 via an edge called ℓ_2. In order to pose queries without knowing exactly how the hypertext is organized, W3QL allows specification of *unbounded* length paths. We illustrate this with an example. Suppose we are interested in all the Web pages containing the keyword "product" in the title accessible from the Web page at www.druginfonet.com/maninfo.htm (Figure 2.1). The query may be expressed as follows.

```
1 Select
2 From            n₁, ℓ₁, (n₂, ℓ₂), ℓ₃, n₃;
3 Where
4 n₁ in           {http://www.druginfonet.com/maninfo.htm };
5 ℓ₁ in           {/www.druginfonet.com/};
6 n₃: PERLCOND    '(n₃.title.content = /product/i)';
7 Using ISEARCHd -d 5 -1 1000;
```

The from clause in the above query expresses the hypertext path to be searched from the Web page at www.druginfonet.com/maninfo.htm(see Figure 2.1). Here n_1, n_2, and n_3 are node variables and ℓ_1, ℓ_2, and ℓ_3 are link variables. (n_2, ℓ_2) is an unbounded length path of pages accessible from n_1. Line 6 specifies that the content of the title of the pages must contain "product". The expression PERLCOND is an external program for content analysis. It can analyze some file formats (HTML, Latex, Postscript) and can evaluate content conditions stated in a PERL-like fashion. The ISEARCHd in line 7 takes two arguments: -d, the maximum length of the unbounded length path and -1, the maximum number of HTTP requests allowed during the search. ISEARCHd traverses the WWW from the starting points and searches for solutions for the other W3QL nodes in the path. The default format for a query result is an HTML table. The table contains the URLs of the WWW nodes and WWW links' strings that satisfy the query, organized in rows. The URLs in the column that correspond to W3QL nodes are hyperlinks to the WWW nodes that are in the solution. If the result table is displayed in a WWW browser, clicking on the node URL generates a request to display the node content.

W3QS is capable of learning how to fill out forms and of doing so automatically. Consider the form in Figure 2.4. It can be used to ask for details of products for

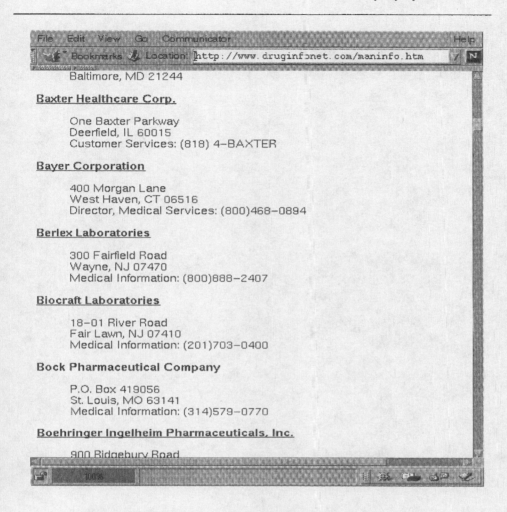

Fig. 2.1. Web page at www.druginfonet.com/maninfo.htm.

treatment of different diseases or a list of products in a particular category. The following query uses this form.

```
1 Select                      n₂:
2 From                        n₁, ℓ₁, n₂
3 Where
4 n₁ in                       {http://www.bms.com/products/index.html };
5 Fill n₁ as in               Product;
6 Run learnform n₁ cs76:0 if n₁ unknown in Product;
7 Using                       ISEARCHd;
```

In the from-clause in line 2, the node n_1 contains the form and the node n_2 is the "answer" to the filled form. In W3QL, forms and their answers are considered linked by hypertext links. The Product file is a *Dictionary of Forms* (DOF)

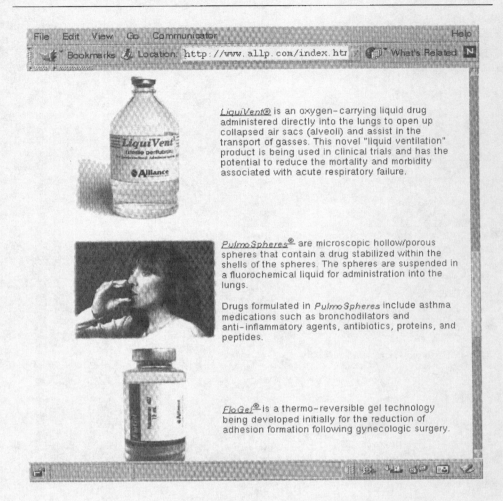

Fig. 2.2. Web page of Drug Infonet Web Site.

which is a database of known forms. Line 5 in the query specifies that the form must be filled out as described in the DOF file Product. If this is the first time this form is encountered, and therefore cannot be found in the DOF file Product, then the condition in line 6 specifies a recovery statement: learnform n_1 cs76:0. Here, learnform is an external program designed to take appropriate actions if an unknown form is encountered during a search. The learnform program receives two arguments: the node containing the form that needs to be learned, and the user's X-Terminal name. The learnform program opens a window on the user's X-terminal and activates a browser in that window. The browser, in turn, displays a request to the user to fill out the form (Figure 2.4). The filled-out form is then saved in the specified DOF file. The next time the query is run, the form will be filled out automatically, using the information in the DOF file Product. The in-

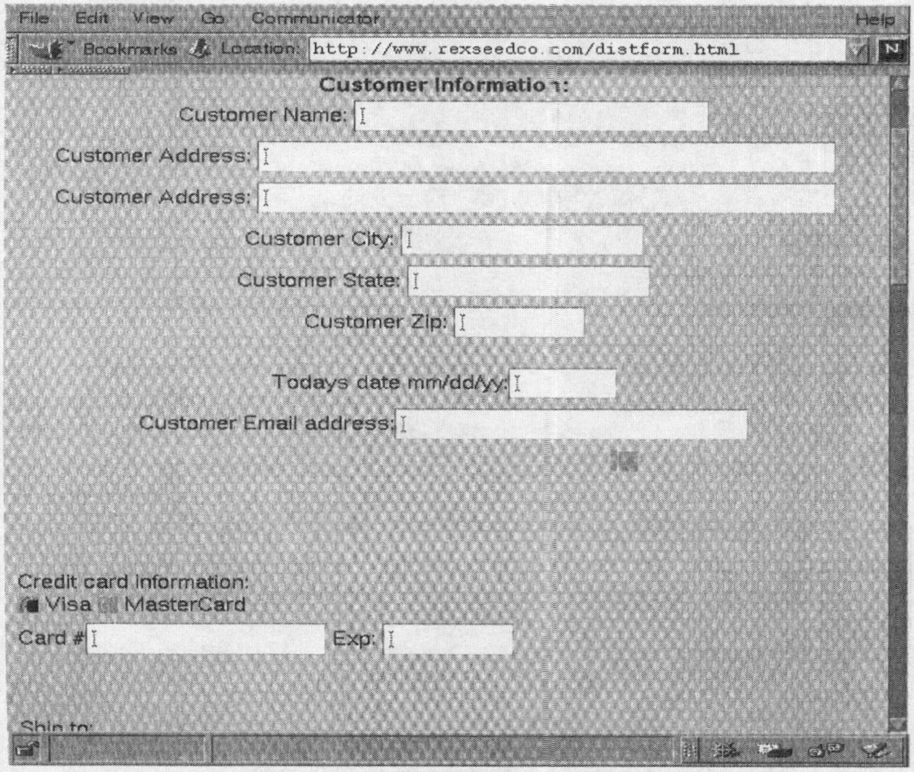

Fig. 2.3. A hypertext-free form.

formation in the DOF file may be used to fill out the form in different ways, for example, to find different types of hair color products one may write: Fill n_1 as in Product With product type = "Hair color products". The effect is that the value "hair color products" overwrites the value of the field product type that was saved in the DOF. The result of the form learning query is a table. Clicking on the link in the n_2 column of the table shows the result of the form filling. Similarly, to find different products for the treatment of cancer one may write: Fill n_1 as in Product With condition = "Cancer". Note that the form filling learning mechanism can be used to access information supplied by indexers. Essentially, one can turn indexers into traditional relational database indices; i.e., use the pointers returned by the indexers as starting point for more precise search.

Finally, W3QS allows us to reevaluate a query periodically to identify new changes in the Web pages or to track broken links. For example, the following query is executed weekly to identify any broken links in the home page of www.druginfonet.com (Figure 2.1).

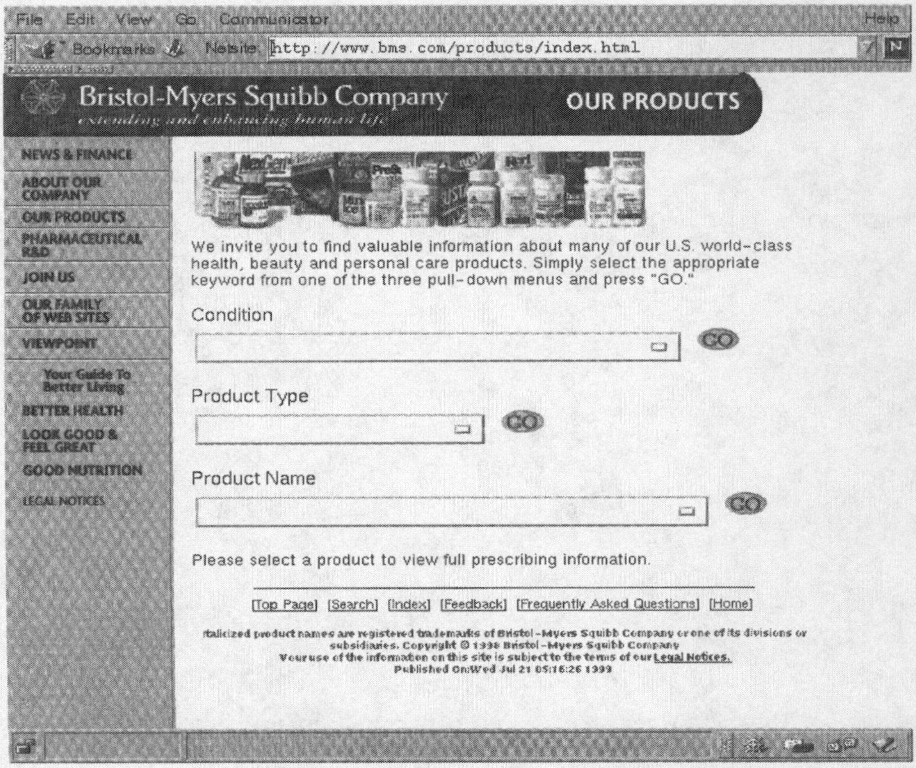

Fig. 2.4. A non-hypertext-free form.

```
1 Select
2 From          n₁, ℓ₁, (n₂, ℓ₂), ℓ₃, n₃;
3 Where
4 n₁ in         {http://www.druginfonet.com/maninfo.htm };
5 ℓ₁ in         {/www.druginfonet.com/};
6 n₃: PERLCOND  '(n₃.title.content = /404 Not Found/i)';
7 Using ISEARCHd -d 2;
8 Evaluated     every week
```

Note that if n_3 has an erroneous address, the request will return a default node whose title is "404 Not Found". This will qualify ℓ_3 as a broken link. To find where this broken link resides, one can examine the table of results, and look for the last n_2 entry in the (n_2, ℓ_2) column.

Also note that in W3QL queries are always made to the WWW. Past query results are not manipulated for the evaluation of future queries. There is no formal algebra for manipulating tables generated by W3QL queries. This limits the manipulation of Web data to derive additional information from the past queries.

2.1.4 WebSQL

WebSQL [131] is a project at the University of Toronto to develop a Web query facilitation language. WebSQL expresses any content query, that is, a query that refers only to the content of documents using an SQL-like notation. WebSQL is also capable of querying the hypertext structure of the Web. A prototype of Web-SQL has been implemented. It makes hypertext links first-class citizens in the data model. In particular, the WebSQL system concentrates on HTML documents and on hypertext links originated from them. To realize content and structural queries, it proposes to model the Web as a relational database composed of two virtual relations:

$$\text{Document}[\text{url.title}, \text{text}, \text{type}, \text{length}, \text{modif}]$$
$$\text{Anchor}[\text{base}, \text{label}, \text{href}]$$

where the url is a key and all other attributes can be null. In the relation Anchor, base is the URL of the HTML document containing the link, href is the referred document, and label is the link description. The Document relation has one tuple for each document in the Web and the Anchor relation has one tuple for each anchor in each document in the Web. This relational abstraction of the Web allows us to use a query language similar to SQL to pose the queries.

Note that if Document and Anchor were actual relations, we could simply use SQL to write queries on them. But as these relations are completely virtual and there is no way to enumerate them, we cannot operate on them directly [79, 131]. The WebSQL semantics depend instead on materializing portions of them by specifying the documents of interest in the FROM clause of a query. The basic way of materializing a portion of the Web is by navigating from known URLs. Path regular expressions are used to describe such navigation. We now illustrate WebSQL with some examples.

Suppose we wish to find the URL and title of documents containing the keyword "cancer". Such a query is expressed as follows using WebSQL.

```
select    d.url, d.title
from      Document d
such that
d         mentions "cancer";
```

The result of this WebSQL query is constructed by sending the string pattern "cancer" to an index server. Note that the FROM clause instantiates a document variable d. The variable d is bound in turn to each document that contains the keyword "cancer". The next example illustrates queries that refer to the links present in documents.

Suppose we wish to find all links to "lung cancer" from documents about "cancer". This query is expressed as follows.

```
select y.label, y.href
from    Document x
        such that x mentions "cancer"
        Anchor y such that base = x
where   y.label contains "lung cancer";
```

Finally, WebSQL allows us to query the topology of the Web by making a distinction between types of hyperlinks. A hypertext link in an HTML document is said to be *interior* if the destination document coincides with the anchor document; *local* if the destination and the anchor documents are different but located on the same server, and *global* if the destination and the anchor documents are located on different servers. Next, WebSQL assigns an arrowlike symbol to each of the three link types to express path regular expressions in a compact intuitive way. Therefore $\mapsto$ denotes an interior link, $\rightarrow$ a local link, and $\Rightarrow$ a global link. Also $=$ denotes an empty path. Path regular expressions are built from these symbols using concatenation, alternation, and repetition. We illustrate this with the following example.

Starting from the Web page at `www.druginfonet.com/maninfo.htm`, suppose we wish to find all documents whose title contains the keyword "product" and that are linked through paths of two or three containing a global link followed by local links. This is expressed by the following WebSQL query.

```
select d.url, d.title
from    Document d
        such that "http://www.druginfonet.com/maninfo.htm" ⇒→|⇒→→ d
where   d.title contains "product";
```

Note that WebSQL uses two different keywords, `mentions` and `contains`, to do string matching in the `from` and `where` clauses, respectively. `Mentions` is used with the first argument free and the second bound; that is, given a string, it returns the set of all documents that contain that string. `Contains` is used with both arguments bound; that is, it checks whether a given document contains a given string. Note that, unlike W3QL, WebSQL does not support form processing. Furthermore, similar to W3QS, WebSQL does not have any algebra to manipulate the data retrieved from the Web.

2.1.5 WebLog

Inspired by concepts in declarative logic, Lakshmanan, Sadri, and Subramanian at Concordia University designed WebLog [106] as a declarative language for Web queries based on SchemaLog [105, 107]. No implementation of WebLog has yet been reported. Some of the highlights of WebLog are:

- providing a declarative interface for querying as well as restructuring (the language is logic-based);
- accommodating partial knowledge the user may have on the information being queried;
- providing ways for seamlessly integrating libraries of document analysis and string processing algorithms, thus putting their combined power to work for querying and restructuring the Web (the language has facilities for specifying foreign functions in the form of built-in predicates); and
- recognizing the dynamic nature of Web information.

We first highlight the conceptual model of WebLog for HTML information. The model for WebLog is based on the notion that each Web document consists of a heterogeneous mix of information about the topic mentioned in the title of the document. In practice, a typical Web document would consist of groups of related information that are spatially close together in the page. Information within each such group would be homogeneous. For instance, information enclosed within the tag <HR> in a document could form a group of related information. Each such group is called a *rel-infon*. A page is a set of rel-infons. The notion of what constitutes a rel-infon is highly subjective and the choice is left to the user. A rel-infon has several *attributes*. The attributes come from a set consisting of strings "occurs", "hlink", and various tags in the HTML documents. The attributes of a rel-infon map to string values, except for the "hlink" attribute that is mapped to an hlink-id. That is, the attribute "occurs" is mapped to the set of strings occuring in a rel-infon and the tag attributes, if defined, are mapped to the tokens they adorn in the rel-infon. Note that the tag attribute `title` is considered special and is mapped to the same string (the title of the document) in all rel-infons in the document. Also each rel-infon has a unique id.

We now informally present the semantics of WebLog with some examples. Through these examples we illustrate the power of WebLog to navigate hyperlinks, search titles as well as the document for keywords, recognize patterns appearing in documents, and perform restructuring.

One of the features of WebLog is that it treats hyperlinks as first-class citizens. This provides a facility for navigating across HTML documents using the WebLog program. Hyperlinks can also be queried and used for restructuring. The following examples illustrate these ideas. Suppose we are interested in collecting all hyperlinks refering to HTML documents that appear at www.druginfonet.com/maninfo.htm[1]. We would also like this collection to contain the title of the document to which the link refers. The following WebLog program expresses this need.

```
ans.html[title→'all links', hlink⇒L, occurs⇒T]  ←— drugurl[hlink⇒L],
href(L, U),
U[title→T]
```

Variable L in the first subgoal ranges over all hyperlinks in *drugurl*. The built-in predicate `href` is used to navigate over the citations in the page at *drugurl*. This predicate captures the relationship between an hlink-id and the destination anchor in its corresponding hyperlink. The rule generates a new HTML document `ans.html` that is a collection of all links in *drugurl*, annotated with the title of the destination document. Note that the result illustrates a primitive instance of restructuring using WebLog. It is also possible to express sophisticated restructuring capabilities using WebLog. Also this example illustrates just one level of traversal. Navigation of a more general kind is illustrated in the next example.

Suppose we would like to find all documents in the Web site of Abbott Laboratories, located at www.abottrenalcare.com, that have information related to "products". We know that these documents can be reached by navigating links originating in the Web page at www.abottrenalcare.com and that their URLs will have the prefix http://www.abottrenalcare.com The following WebLog program expresses this query.

---

[1] In order to avoid repeating the URL of the Web page, we refer to it as *drugurl*.

```
abbott_pages(http://www.abottrenalcare.com/)
abott_pages(U)←—abbot_pages(V), V[hlink⇒L], href(L, U),
substring(U, http://www.abottrenalcare.com/)
interesting_urls(U)←—abott_pages(U), U[occurs⇒I], synonym(I,'product')
```

Rules 1 and 2 help identify the documents belonging to www.abottrenalcare.com. The recursive rule (Rule 2) essentially captures the properties known to the user. Navigation is done via recursion. Rule 3 searches for occurrences of keywords related to "product" (captured using the predicate synonym) in the server of Abbott Laboratories and returns the relevant URLs in the relation interesting_urls.

2.1.6 NetQL

NetQL [119] is a project at the University of Regina, Canada to develop a query language over the World Wide Web. NetQL follows the approach of structure-based queries; however, it attempts to overcome the problems unsolved by WebSQL, W3QS, and WebLog. First, a novel approach to mine information from Web pages is presented so that queries which involve information or structures inside pages can be issued. Second, various methods are provided to control the complexity of query processing. We elaborate on these two features of NetQL. A preliminary version of NetQL has been implemented.

NetQL currently supports *keyword-based mining* and *string* or *structure pattern-based mining*. Keyword-based mining is used to extract values associated with *keywords*, e.g., Email, Publication, or Research interests. When a keyword is given, the system first looks for the keyword in pages. If it is located, a set of heuristic rules are applied to mine the corresponding value automatically. For example, if the word is in a label of a hyperlink, then the value is the content of the page pointed to by the link.

A string pattern contains a set of *constant words* or *variables* and is delimited by a pair of brackets. When it is given, the system first locates strings from pages to match the *constant words* in patterns. If successful, the *noun phrase* or *number* corresponding to variables is assigned to the variables. For example, a pattern [Dr. Name] can be matched against a string starting with "Dr." and then the first *noun phrase* after "Dr." is assigned to variable *Name* :. For string "Dr. Ng is ...", then "Ng" is assigned to *Name* :. In addition, wildcards can be used in string patterns.

Structure pattern-based mining means that a *structure pattern* is given to match a textual line or a row of tables (defined by tags <TABLE> and </TABLE>) in Web pages. NetQL treats each textual line or a row of tables as a set of fields. For example, structure pattern $\{X, \text{"Cancer"}, \star, Z < 30\}$ is matched against a textual line or a row of a table, in which the second field is a string "Cancer" and the last field is a number less than 30. The processing of a structure pattern is used to find the values of all fields in a textual line or row and then match them against the pattern. For textual lines, *fields* are separated by delimiters, which are defined as two or more spaces, <tab>, or a HTML tag. The value of a string field is the textual string between two delimiters and the value of a number field is the first number between two delimiters. Note that structure-based patterns cannot handle all structural information such as complex tables.

We now illustrate the query language NetQL with some examples. The syntax of NetQL is similar to a SQL Select statement but the data consist of Web documents instead of relational databases. Suppose we wish to find the name and email address of all doctors at Johns Hopkins Medical School who are expert in "human genetics". This query can be posed as follows using NetQL.

```
select  Name:, E − mail
from    http://www.jhu.edu/www/academics/faculty.html →*
contain human genetics
match   [Dr. Name:];
```

In the above query, $Name$: and $E − mail$ are variables used to indicate the object of our search. $E − mail$ is a keyword variable whose value is mined directly from Web pages specified in the from clause (all pages containing keyword " human genetics" at the Johns Hopkins Medical School site). In contrast, $Name$: is a variable occurring in patterns Dr. $Name$:. The query first finds the pages containing the keywords "human genetics" at the above site and then locates the constant string "Dr." in the returned pages and assigns the first noun phrase after it to variable $Name$:.

The next example illustrates structural pattern mining. Suppose we wish to find the brand names and generic names of the drugs manufactured by "Pfizer" that are listed in the top 200 drugs at www.rxlist.com. The following NetQL query can be used to extract such information from the Web page at www.rxlist.com/top200.htm.

```
select X, Y
from   http://www.rxlist.com/top200.htm
match  {X, -, "Pfizer", Y};
```

This query matches structure pattern {X, -, "Pfizer", Y} against the contents of the page whose URL is www.rxlist.com/top200.htm. It matches the table in the Web page consisting of four fields with the third field containing the keyword "Pfizer".

NetQL provides methods to control the complexity of query processing. This is controlled in NetQL in two levels. Users are given various choices to control run-time. The following methods are provided for users to control the run-time of a web query. This helps users avoid waiting for a long time for the query results.

1. Restrict the search to local data. The search only follows the links inside a web server.
2. Restrict the search to a specified limited depth of links.
3. Restrict the search to a certain number of returned results. If the specified number of results is exceeded, the search stops.
4. Restrict the search to a specified amount of time. When the time reaches its limit, the search stops and returns the results found thus far.

For example, consider the previous query related to the Johns Hopkins Medical School. This query can be restricted to 20 results by using the following clause in the query: restricted RESULTS < 20. The restricted clause is used to control the complexity of query processing.

Second, an optimizing technique based on semantic similarity is developed to guide the search in the most promising direction so that the expected results are obtained as soon as possible. Note that queries restricted by time and the number of results will be benefited directly. NetQL uses semantic information on hyperlink labels for heuristic searching. The semantic similarity between the current set of links and the goal can help an optimizer to decide which is preferred for the next step. For example, when we need to locate the pages containing "lung cancer", it is better to navigate links whose label contains "cancer" or "pulmonary diseases", etc. The key point for this method is the computation of semantic distances between words or noun phrases that has been widely studied in the fields of Natural Language Processing (NLP) and Information Retrieval (IR) [95, 103, 150]. NetQL follows the approach of word-word similarities based on WordNet [74] presented in [95, 150].

2.1.7 FLORID

FLORID (**F-LO**gic **R**easoning **I**n **D**atabases) [93, 122] is a prototype implementation of the deductive and object-oriented formalism F-logic [97]. FLORID has been extended to provide declarative semantics for querying the Web. The proposed extension allows extraction and restructuring of data from the Web and a seamless integration of local data. To use FLORID as a web query engine, a Web document is modeled by the following two classes:

```
url::string[get⇒ webdoc].
webdoc::string[url ⇒ url; author ⇒ string;
                        modif ⇒ string;
type ⇒ string;         hrefs@(string) ⇒> url;
                        error ⇒> string].
```

The first declaration introduces a class `url`; a subclass of `string` with the only method `get`. The notation `get ⇒ webdoc` means that `get` is a single-valued method that returns an object of type `webdoc`. The method `get` is system-defined; the effect of invoking `u.get` for a URL `u` in the head of a deductive rule is to retrieve from the Web the document with that URL and cache it in the local FLORID database as a `webdoc` object with object identifier `u.get`.

The class `webdoc` with methods `self`, `author`, `modif`, `type`, `hrefs`, and `error` models the basic information common to all Web documents. The notation `href@(string) ⇒> url` means that the multivalued method `hrefs`takes a string as argument and returns a set of objects of type `url`. That is, if d is a `webdoc`, then d.`hrefs@(Label)` returns all URLs of documents pointed to by links labeled `Label` in the document d.

Computation in FLORID is expressed by sets of deductive rules. For example, the program below extracts from the Web the set of all documents reachable directly or indirectly from the URL `www.druginfonet.com/maninfo.htm` by links whose labels contain the string "products".

Fig. 2.5. List of diseases at www.pedianet.com.

```
("www.druginfonet.com/maninfo.htm":url).get.
(Y:url).get                              ←
                                         (X:url).get[hrefs@(L)⇒>{Y}],
                                         substr("products", L).
```

Let us consider another example to illustrate extraction and querying of Web data. Consider the Web site at www.pedianet.com (Figure 2.5) which provides information about various diseases. The source page at www.pedianet.com/news/illness/disease/disease.htm contains links to the individual disease pages. Let these links be used to populate the class disease with instances D and the URLs U of D.

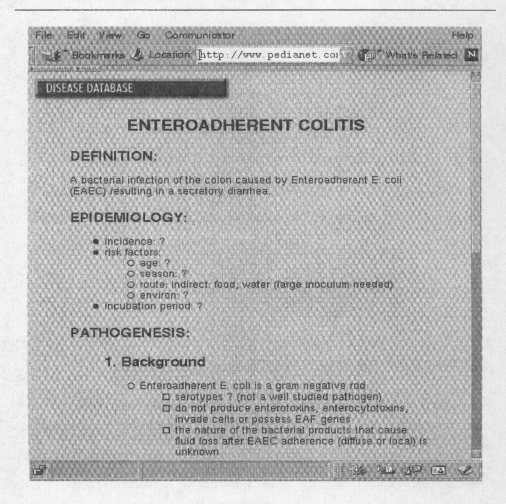

Fig. 2.6. Web page of a disease.

```
U.get ← D:disease[url→U].

        ("http://www.pedianet.com/news/illness/
        disease/disease.htm":url)
        .get [hrefs@(L) ⇒> {U}],
        match(L, "(..+)", D).
```

The labels L at www.pedianet.com/news/illness/disease/disease.htm are
the names of the diseases. Here the built-in predicate match is used to find all strings
in the input string (or Web document) that contain more than one character. This
is to ignore the links on the alphabets in this page.

Finally, data from the disease pages (Figure 2.5) can be extracted and stored in
the F-Logic database. For example, among others, the following can be extracted.

```
D[definition → X] ←              match(D:disease.url.get,
"Definition: *\n\(.*\)", X),
D[clinical → X] ←                match(D:disease.url.get,
"Clinical Features: *\n\(.*\)", X),
```

The above declarations extract the definition and clinical features of each disease from the disease pages. Once the data have been extracted, they can be queried, restructured ,and integrated with data from other sources, using the features of F-logic and FLORID.

2.1.8 RAW

Fiebig, Weiss, and Moerkotte extended relational algebra to the World Wide Web by augmenting the algebra with new domains (data types) [77, 154], and functions that apply to the domains. The extended model is known as RAW (Relational Algebra for the Web). Only two low level operators on relations, *scan* and *index-scan*, have been proposed to expand the URL address attribute in a relation and to rank results returned by web search engine(s), respectively. RAW provides a minor improvement on the existing relational model to accommodate and manipulate web data.

2.2 Web Information Integration Systems

Ideally, we would like programs that answer a user's query based on information obtained from many different online sources. Such a program is called an *information-integration system*, because to answer queries it must integrate the information from the various sources into a single coherent whole. This program primarily performs two tasks. The first task is to actually extract a structured representation of the data (e.g., a set of tuples) from the HTML pages. This task is performed by a set of *wrapper* programs [143], whose creation and maintenance raises several challenges. A wrapper is a piece of software that interprets a request (expressed in SQL or some other structured language) against a Web source and returns a structured reply (such as a set of tuples). The other task is to respond to queries that require the integration of data and is addressed by a *mediator*. Information mediators [82, 113, 136, 158], such as the SIMS system [5], provide an intermediate layer between information sources and users. Queries to a mediator are in a uniform language, independent of such factors as the distribution of information over sources, the source query languages, and the location of sources. The mediator determines which data sources to use, how to obtain the desired information, how and where to temporarily store and manipulate data, and how to efficiently retrieve information from the sources. As an example, consider the domain of movies. The Internet Movie Database (www.imdb.com) contains comprehensive data about movies, their casts, genres, and directors. Reviews of movies can be found in multiple other Web sources, and several Web sources provide schedules of movie showings. By combining data from these sources we can answer queries such as: *Give me a movie, playing time, and a review of movies starring Matt Damon, playing tonight in Singapore.* Hence, in addition to the obvious benefit of reducing the number of sites a user must visit, integrating this information has several important and nonobvious advantages. First, often more queries can be answered using the integrated information than using any single source. A second and more important advantage of integration is that making it possible to combine information sources also makes it possible to decompose information so as to represent it in a clean, modular way [61].

Several systems have been built with the goal of answering queries using a multitude of Web sources [61, 100, 113, 114, 136, 160]. Many of the problems encountered in building these systems are similar to those addressed in building heterogeneous database systems. Web data integration systems have, in addition, to deal with (1) a large and evolving number of Web sources, (2) few metadata about the characteristics of the source, and (3) a large degree of source autonomy [79]. We briefly describe some of these Web data integration systems.

2.2.1 Information Manifold

The Information Manifold Project at the University of Washington [78, 113, 114, 112, 115] aimed to develop a system that would flexibly integrate many data sources with closely related content and that would answer queries efficiently by accessing only the sources relevant to the query. The approach in designing the Information Manifold is based on the observation that the data integration problem lies at the intersection of database systems and artificial intelligence. Hence the solution combines and extends techniques from both fields, for example, a representation language and a language for describing data sources that was simple from the knowledge representation perspective, but that had the necessary added flexibility concerning previous techniques developed in the database community.

The Information Manifold is most importantly a mechanism for describing data sources. This mechanism lets users describe complex constraints on a data source's contents, thereby letting them distinguish between sources with closely related data. Also this mechanism enables users to add or delete data sources from the system without changing the descriptions of other sources. Informally, the contents of a data source are described by a query over the mediated schema. For example, we might describe a data source as containing American movies that are all comedies and were produced after 1985.

The Information Manifold employed an expressive language Carin [115], for formulating queries and for representing background knowledge about the relations in the mediated schema. Carin combined the expressive power of the Datalog database-query language and Description Logics, which are knowledge representation languages designed especially to model complex hierarchies that frequently arise in data integration applications.

The query-answering algorithms used in the Information Manifold guarantee that only relevant sets of data sources are accessed when answering a query, even in the presence of sources described by complex constraints. They also developed a method for representing local-source completeness and an algorithm for exploiting

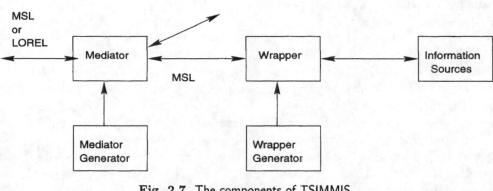

Fig. 2.7. The components of TSIMMIS.

such information in query answering [113]. One of the novel features in this system is that they pioneered the use of probabilistic reasoning for data integration (representing another example of the combined AI and DB approach to the data integration problem) [78]. When numerous data sources are relevant to a given query, a data-integration system needs to order the access to the data sources. Such an ordering is dependent on the overlap between the sources and the query and on the coverage of the sources. In [78], Florescu, Koller, and Levy developed a probabilistic formalism for specifying and deducing such information and algorithms for ordering the access to data sources given such information.

Finally, the Information Manifold developed several novel algorithms for adapting to differing source capabilities. When possible to reduce the amount of processing done locally, the system would fully exploit the query-processing capabilities of its data sources [114].

2.2.2 TSIMMIS

TSIMMIS (The Stanford-IBM Manager of Multiple Information Sources) [136] is a system for integrating information. It offers a data model and a common query language that are designed to support a combination of information from many different sources. It also offers tools for automatically generating the components that are needed to build systems for integrating information. We briefly describe the architecture of TSIMMIS.

The TSIMMIS approach is to integrate different information sources that deal with the same real-world entities to create a mediator, which is a facility capable of answering queries about these entities. The mediator uses the raw sources (suitably interfaced by a wrapper), and/or other mediators to answer the queries. The principle components of TSIMMIS are as follows (Figure 2.7).

OEM Model. A "lightweight" object model called OEM (Object Exchange Model) serves to convey information among components. It is "lightweight" because it does not require strong typing of its objects and is flexible in other ways. Data represented in the OEM are *self describing*, in the sense that they can be parsed without reference to an external schema. A second feature of the OEM is flexibility in data organization, both in the structures that can be described and in the tolerance of alternative forms for "similar" objects, differences in terminology, and differences in the kinds of information obtainable from "similar" sources. The OEM can be visualized as object-oriented in the sense that the fundamental OEM concept is an object. OEM objects have several components: (1) an *object id* which is an identifier of the object. However, unlike object-oriented database systems, OEM object ids may be local to a query and they also need not be persistent; (2) *label* to specify what the object represents. However, there is no schema. Objects with a given label are not required to have a particular set of subobjects. Labels carry all the information there is about objects which is why the OEM is called self describing; (3) *type* of the object's value, either a set or atomic type such as a string; and (4) *value*, either an atomic value or a set of objects. Note that objects are not organized into classes. A query will address all objects whose structure matches the conditions of the query.

Mediators. The next component of TSIMMIS is a mediator. The mediator-generator *MedMaker* provides a high-level language, *Mediator Specification Language (MSL)*, that allows the declarative specification of mediators. MSL is an object-oriented, logical query language targeted to the OEM data model. It contains features that facilitate the integration of heterogeneous systems. MSL borrows many concepts from logic-oriented languages such as Datalog, HiLog [54], and F-Logic [97]. A complete specification of MSL, including formal syntax and semantics is found in [144]. Given a set of sources with wrappers that export OEM objects, the mediators integrate and refine the information. It provides integrated OEM "views" of the underlying information. At run-time, when the mediator receives a request for information, MedMaker's *Mediator Specification Interpreter (MSI)* collects and integrates the necessary information from the sources, according to the specification. These sources can be either wrappers of raw information sources or other mediators.

Wrappers. Recall that wrappers provide access to heterogeneous information sources by converting application queries into source-specific queries or commands. Wrappers are specified with the *Wrapper Specification Language (WSL)* that is an extension to MSL to allow for the description of source contents and querying capabilities. Thus a TSIMMIS wrapper takes a query and decides first whether its underlying source can answer the query, i.e., whether the query is directly supported. If so, it converts the answer into the appropriate OEM objects and returns this result. If the query is not directly supported, the wrapper determines whether the query can be answered by applying local filtering to a directly supported query. The wrapper then again converts the answer received from the source into the appropriate OEM object, applies the filter, and returns the result. The architecture of a wrapper implementation toolkit for generating wrappers is described in [143].

Common Query Language. A common query language links the components of TSIMMIS. TSIMMIS uses MSL as both the query language and the specification language for mediators and as the query language for wrappers. It uses LOREL (**L**ightweight **O**bject **RE**pository **L**anguage), an OQL-based query language for the OEM model, as the end-user query language. A complete specification of LOREL, including formal syntax and semantics is found in [1]. We illustrate LOREL in the context of query languages for semistructured data and XML data in Sections 2.4 and 2.5.

2.2.3 Ariadne

The Ariadne project's [100] goal is to make it simple for users to create their own specialized web-based mediators. The prime focus was to develop the technology for rapidly constructing mediators to extract, query, and integrate data from Web sources. The system includes tools for constructing wrappers that make it possible to query Web sources as if they were databases and the mediator technology required to dynamically and efficiently answer queries using these sources. A simple example illustrates how Ariadne can be used to provide access to Web-based sources. There are numerous sites that provide reviews on restaurants, but none are comprehensive, and also, checking each site can be time consuming. In addition, information from other Web sources can be useful in selecting a restaurant. For example, the LA County Health Department publishes the health ratings of all restaurants in the county, and many sources provide maps showing the location of restaurants. Using Ariadne, one can integrate these sources to create an application where people could search these sources to create a map showing the restaurants that meet their requirements.

For building wrappers, the project developed the Stalker inductive-learning system [137], which learns a set of extraction rules for pulling information from a page. The user trains the system by marking up example pages to show the system what information it should extract from each page. Stalker can learn rules from a relatively small number of examples by exploiting the notion that there are typically landmarks on a page that help users visually locate information.

Another important feature of Ariadne is that it uses planning algorithms to determine how to integrate information efficiently and effectively across sources. Ariadne breaks down query processing into a preprocessing phase and a query planning phase. In the first phase, the system determines the possible ways of combining the available sources to answer a query. Because sources might be overlapping (an attribute may be available from several sources) or replicated, the system must determine an appropriate combination of sources that can answer the query. The Ariadne source-selection algorithm preprocesses the domain model so that the system can efficiently and dynamically select sources based on the classes and attributes mentioned in the query. In the second phase, Ariadne generates a plan using a method called Planning-by-Rewriting [4, 3]. This approach takes an initial, suboptimal plan and attempts to improve it by applying rewriting rules. With query planning, producing an initial suboptimal plan is straightforward, the difficult part is finding an efficient plan. The rewriting process iteratively improves the initial query plan using local search processes that can change both the sources used to answer a query and the order of the operation on the data. The system also features a mechanism that determines when to prefetch data depending on how often the target sources are updated and how fast the databases are.

2.2.4 WHIRL

William Cohen describes an interesting variation on the theme, focusing on "informal" information integration. The idea is that, as in related fields that deal with uncertain and incomplete information, an information-integration system should be allowed to take chances and make mistakes. His WHIRL [61] (Word-based Heterogeneous Information Representation Language) system uses information retrieval algorithms to find approximate matches between different databases, and as a consequence knits together data from diverse sources.

Of the many mechanisms required by an integration system, Cohen has chosen to concentrate on general methods for integrating information without object identity knowledge. His approach in dealing with uncertain object identities relies on the observation that information sources tend to use textually similar names for the same real-world entity. This is particularly true when sources are presenting information to people of similar background in similar contexts. To exploit this, the WHIRL query language allows users to formulate SQL-like queries about the similarity of names. The query language has a "soft" semantics; the answer to such a query is not the set of all tuples that satisfy the query, but a list of tuples, each of which is considered a plausible answer to the query and each of which is associated with a numeric score indicating its perceived plausibility. WHIRL supports "similarity joins", a "soft" version of a equijoin which allows textual descriptions to be used as keys. The basic idea in similarity joins is that tuples are paired, not when keys for the entities involved are identical, but when textual descriptions of the entities involved are sufficiently similar [61]. It computes the similarity of two names using the cosine distance in a vector space model, a metric widely used in statistical information retrieval.

In typical use, WHIRL returns only the K highest-scoring answers, where K is a parameter set by the user. From the user's perspective, interacting with the system is thus much like interacting with a search engine: the user requests the first K answers, examines them, and then requests more if necessary.

WHIRL data are not semistructured, but instead are stored in simple relations. The problem of query planning is simplified by collecting all data with spiders online. WHIRL maps individual information sources into a global schema using manually constructed views. Access knowledge is represented in hand-coded extraction programs.

2.3 Web Data Restructuring

In order to express web restructuring, the query language must be capable not only of manipulating the structure of documents, but also of providing a mechanism for generating arbitrarily linked sets of documents. This facility is present in Web site restructuring systems such as ARANEUS [7, 128, 129] and STRUDEL [75]. These systems exploit knowledge of a Web site's structure for defining alternative views over its content. In this chapter, we briefly describe these systems. Furthermore, we describe the WebOQL system [6], proposed recently by Arocena and Mendelzon,

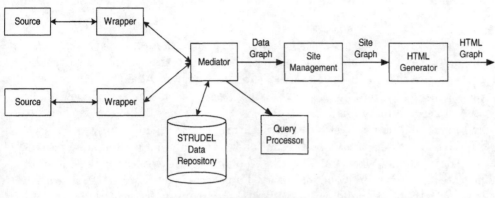

Fig. 2.8. STRUDEL architecture.

which synthesizes ideas from query languages for the Web, for semistructured data and for Web site restructuring.

2.3.1 STRUDEL

The web-site management system STRUDEL [75], was developed at AT&T, and applies familiar concepts from database management systems to the process of building Web sites. The main motivation for developing STRUDEL was the observation that with current technology, creating and managing large sites is tedious, because a site designer must simultaneously perform at least these tasks:

1. choosing what information will be available at the site,
2. organizing that information in individual pages or in graphs of linked pages, and
3. specifying the visual presentation of pages in HTML.

Furthermore, since there is no separation between the physical organization of the information underlying a Web site and the logical view we have on it, restructuring a site is an unwieldy task.

The key idea in the STRUDEL system is the separation of the logical view of information available at a Web site, the structure of that information in linked pages, and the graphical presentation of pages in HTML. STRUDEL follows two steps for building a Web site. The Web-site manager defines independently the data that will be available at the site. The information may be stored in multiple sources (e.g., existing Web sites and various types of external databases) and STRUDEL integrates the information when building the Web site. Second, the web-site manager decides how to structure and present those data. Intuitively, the structure of the Web site is defined as a view over the underlying data. STRUDEL allows users to manipulate the underlying data independently of where they are stored or how they are presented and to customize the Web site by creating different views of the underlying data. STRUDEL provides a single graph model in which all data sources are uniformly modeled and provides a query language for both data integration and view definition. Using STRUDEL to build and manage Web sites provides several benefits.

- The separation between the logical view of the information underlying a Web site and its storage presents several advantages. First, the Web site builder need not be concerned with issues such as updating and maintaining coherence of the HTML files containing the underlying data. Second, the logical view of the underlying information is more appropriate for the task of building a Web site and manipulation tasks such as restructuring, querying, and analysis.
- STRUDEL provides a mechanism that allows the automatic integration of multiple data sources when building the Web site. The system is not required to migrate all the data into one repository. Furthermore, since the data integration is a separate step in building the Web site, the resulting integrated view can be reused for creating different versions of the Web site.
- The declarative nature of STRUDEL's view-definition language, the language that is used for specifying Web sites, makes it easy to restructure the site and specialize it for different classes of users.
- Defining Web sites as queries makes it possible to enforce constraints on sites.
- By defining Web pages as queries, a user can concisely specify sets of similar pages and the corresponding links between them instead of designing each page individually.
- Because STRUDEL uses a graph data model, existing Web sites can be incorporated directly in the STRUDEL system.

STRUDEL Architecture

In every level of the STRUDEL system data are viewed uniformly as a graph. At the bottom-most level, data are stored in STRUDEL's *data graph* repository or in external sources. External sources may have a variety of formats and are translated into the graph data model using a wrapper (Figure 2.8). STRUDEL's graph model is similar to that of OEM [145]; graphs contain objects, or named nodes, connected by edges labeled with attribute names. STRUDEL also provides *collections*, which are named sets of objects and supports several atomic types that commonly appear in Web pages such as URLs, Postscript, text, image, and HTML files.

The *data graph* describes the logical structure of all the information available on a site, and may be obtained by integrating information from various sources using a mediator. The STRUDEL approach to data integration is similar in spirit to those developed in systems such as TSIMMIS [136] and Information Manifold [113] in the sense that STRUDEL defines a virtual loose schema and a mapping between the contents of the data sources and the virtual schema.

Given the data graph, a site builder can define one or more *site graphs*; each site graph represents the logical structure of the information displayed at that site (i.e., a node for every Web page and attributes describing the information in the page and links between pages). Finally, the *HTML generator* constructs a browsable HTML graph from a graph site. The HTML generator creates a Web page for every node in the site graph, using the values of the attributes of the node.

StruQL

In STRUDEL, querying and/or transforming graphs take place at two levels: at the integration level, where data from different external sources are integrated into the data graph, and at the site graph definition level, where site graphs are constructed from a data graph. It uses the same query and transformation language, StruQL (**Site TR**ansformation **U**nd **Q**uery Language), at each of these levels. Note that even though StruQL was developed in the context of a specific web application, it is a general-purpose query language for semistructured data (discussed previously), based on the data model of labeled graphs.

An expression in STRUDEL's manipulation language has two parts: a query expression, which selects a subgraph of an existing graph, and a graph creation expression, which creates new nodes and links. A StruQL query is a set of possibly nested blocks, each of the form:

$$[\texttt{where} C_1, \ldots, C_k]$$
$$[\texttt{create} N_1, \ldots, N_n]$$
$$\texttt{link} L_1, \ldots, L_p]$$
$$\texttt{collect} G_1, \ldots, G_q]$$

The **where** clause can include either membership conditions or conditions on pairs of nodes expressed using regular path expressions The **where** clause produces all bindings of node and arc variables to values in the input graph, and the remaining clauses use Skolem functions [73] to construct a new graph from these bindings.

We illustrate StruQL with a query defining a Web site, starting with a Bibtex bibliography file related to AIDS research, modeled as a labeled graph. The Web site consists of three kinds of pages: an **AIDS-Paper** page for each bibliography entry; a **YearPage** for each year, pointing to all AIDS-related papers published in that year; and a **RootPage** pointing to all the **Year** pages.

```
create RootPage()
where  Publications(x),    x→l→v
create AIDS-Paper(x)
link   AIDS-Paper(x)→l→ v
{
       where            l = "year"
       create           YearPage(v)
       link

                        YearPage(v)→"Year" → v
                        YearPage(v)→"Paper" → AIDS-Paper(x),
                        RootPage()→"Year Page" → YearPage(v)

}
```

In the **where** clause, the notation Publications(x) means that x belongs to the collection Publications, and the atom $x \to \hat{l} \to v$ denotes that there is a link in the graph from x to v and the label on the arc is l. The same notation is used in the link clause to specify the newly created edges in the resulting graph. After creating the Root page, the first **create** generates a page for each publication (denoted by the Skolem function, **AIDS-Paper**). The second **create**, nested within the outer

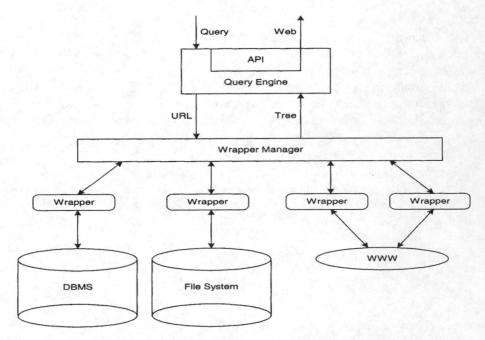

Fig. 2.9. The architecture of WebOQL system.

query, generates a Year page for each year, and links it to the Root page and to the AIDS-Paper pages of the publications published in that year.

2.3.2 WebOQL

The WebOQL system [6] (Figure 2.9), developed at the University of Toronto, supports a general class of data restructuring operations in the context of the Web. WebOQL synthesizes ideas from the query languages for the Web, for semistructured data and for Web site restructuring. It provides a framework for approaching many Web data management tasks from a unified perspective. The WebOQL data model supports the necessary abstractions, such as records, ordered trees, hyperlinks, and *webs*. Furthermore, it provides a query language to navigate, query, and restructure graphs of trees. Both the data model and the query language are capable of accommodating lack of knowledge of the structure of the data to be queried and potential irregularities, or even lack of explicit structure in these data, which are common issues in the context of the Web. The three main types of applications of WebOQL are document restructuring, Web data warehousing, and generation of HTML from databases and other sources.

The main data structure provided by WebOQL is the *hypertree*. Hypertrees are ordered arc-labeled trees with two types of arcs, internal and external. Internal arcs are used to represent structured objects and external arcs are used to represent references (hyperlinks) among objects. Arcs are labeled with *records*. This tree can be built from an HTML file, using a generic HTML wrapper. Sets of related hypertrees are collected into *webs*. In WebOQL, a web can be used to model a small set of related pages (for example, a manual), a larger set (for example, all the pages in a corporate intranet), or even the whole WWW. Both hypertrees and webs can be manipulated using WebOQL and created as the result of a query.

WebOQL is a functional SQL-like language. For example, suppose disease-related information at `www.pedianet.com` is stored as hypertrees. Let *diseaseBase* denote such a database. Suppose we wish to extract from it the title and URL of the pages whose title contains "Chronic".

```
select [y.Title, y'.Url]
from   x in diseaseBase, y in x'
where  y.*[Title - "Chronic"]
```

In this query, x iterates over the simple trees of *diseaseBase* and, given a value for x, y iterates over the simple trees of x'. The primed variable x' denotes the result of applying to tree x the Prime operator, which returns the first subtree of its argument. The same operator is used to extract from tree y its first subtree in $y'.Url$. The square brackets denote the Hang operator, which builds an arc labeled with a record formed with the arguments. Finally, the tilde represents the string pattern-matching predicate: its left argument is a string and its right argument is a pattern.

The query above maps a hypertree into another hypertree; more generally, a query is a function that maps a web into another. For example, the following query creates a new page for each disease (using the disease name as the URL). Each page contains the information related to a particular disease.

```
select x' as x.disease
from   x in diseaseBase
```

In general, the select clause has the form "select q_1 as s_1, q_2 as s_2, ... , q_m as S_m", where the q_is are queries and each of the s_is is either a string query or the keyword schema. The "as" clauses create the URL's s_1, s_2, ... , s_m, which are assigned to the new pages resulting from each query q_i.

2.3.3 ARANEUS

Atzeni, Mecca, and Merialdo proposed the ARANEUS system [7] for managing and restructuring data coming from the World Wide Web. They presented a specific data model, called the ARANEUS Data Model (ADM), inspired by the structures typically present in Web sites. The model allows us to describe the scheme of a Web hypertext, in the spirit of databases. The ADM is a page-oriented model, in the sense that the main construct of the model is that of a page scheme, used to describe the structure of a set of homogeneous pages in a site; the main intuition behind the model is that an HTML page can be seen as an object with an identifier, the URL, and several attributes, one for each relevant piece of information in the page. The scheme of a Web site can be seen as a collection of page schemes, connected using links. The attributes in a page can be either *simple*, such as text, images, binary data, or links to other pages, or *complex*, such as lists of items, possibly nested. In essence, web pages are instances of page schemes. Consider the page at `www.informatik.uni-trier.de/~ley/db/indices/a-tree/index.html`, which is the search page for author names at the Web site of the DB & LP Bibliography Server. The page returned by searching for a particular author has a similar structure in the site. The page has a monovalued attribute, the name of the author; it also has a multivalued attribute consisting of the list of works; each item in the list can in turn be described as a tuple having attributes such as the title, the authors, and so on.

The ADM also provides the *heterogeneous union* and the *form* type specifically needed to model the organization of Web pages. The form type is used to model HTML forms and is essentially considered as a virtual list of tuples; each tuple has as many attributes as the fill-in fields of the form along with a link to the resulting page. This structured view of the site abstracts some of the properties of the pages, reflecting the user's perspective, and provides a high-level description to be used as a basis of successive manipulations. Consider the search page of authors' names again. The search form has a rather involved behavior: when a string is specified, the database of author names is searched; if a single name matching the query string is found, the author's page is returned; on the other hand, if the query string matches several names, a different page containing the list of all matching names along with links to the corresponding pages is returned. Heterogeneous union is used to model this behavior. In this case, the form returns a link to a type which is the union of two different page-schemes; one for authors' pages and the other for name-index pages.

Essentially, pages are grouped into *page-schemes*, which recall the notion of objects of homogeneous structure. It is possible to see an instance of a page-schema as a set of nested tuples, one for each page of the corresponding type. A Web site is a collection of page-schemes connected by links.

Based on the ADM, Atzeni, Mecca, and Merialdo propose two languages to define views over the Web. First, the ULIXES language is used to build relational views over the Web. In ULIXES, the knowledge about the structure based on the ADM description of the site highly facilitates the process of extracting data. When an external site is to be queried, an ADM description of the site has to be derived by analyzing its content. Then the site needs to be wrapped in order to extract data from pages and see them as instances of page-schemes. Wrappers are written using text-management tools called EDITOR [128] and MINERVA. They allow searches and restructuring of semistructured documents. ULIXES allows us to express and evaluate queries over a Web site. It is implemented as a *navigational algebra* [129] over nested structures. The notion of *navigational expressions* is used as a means to express a set of navigations, i.e., paths through pages in a site along which selections/projections and joins can be performed to select data of interest and return a set of tuples. In this way, data can be extracted from a site and stored in the database; these database abstractions over sites can be further processed for reorganization, integration, or application development.

Second, the PENELOPE language [8] is used to present the resulting database as a derived hypertext, that is, a hypertextual view over the original data sources that can be explored using a Web browser. PENELOPE uses the ADM to describe the structure of the resulting hypertext, and allows us to define new page schemes to present data under the form of derived pages, which are correlated using a suitable URL invention mechanism. These views are declaratively defined using the PENELOPE Definition Language (PDL) and maintained using the PENELOPE Manipulation Language (PML). When a new site is to be generated, its ADM scheme is first designed. Then the ADM structure is mapped to the database using PDL, which provides a `Define-page` command to describe the structure of a page-scheme in terms of database tables. Then the actual site is generated using PML. PML provides two instructions: `Generate` and `Remove`, which can refer to (a) the whole site, (b) all instances of a page-scheme, or (c) pages that satisfy a condition in a `Where` clause.

The view definition process in the ARANEUS system can be summarized as follows.

- Web sites of interest are identified and relevant data are described using the ADM.
- The ULIXES view language is used to define a set of database views over the sites of interest; these views can be analyzed, manipulated, and integrated.
- Finally, the resulting table-based data are restructured using PENELOPE to generate a derived hypertext to be browsed by the user, possibly involving existing portions of the Web.

2.4 Semistructured Data

The main obstacles to exploiting the internal structure of Web documents are the lack of a schema or type and the potential irregularities that can appear for that reason. The problem of querying data whose structure is unknown or irregular has been addressed, although not in the context of the Web, by the query languages for semistructured data Lorel [1] and UnQL [41]. By semistructured, we mean that although the data may have some structure, the structure is not as rigid, regular, or complete as the structure required by traditional database management systems [40]. Furthermore, even if the data are fairly well structured, the structure may evolve rapidly. In this chapter, we briefly describe Lorel and UnQL systems.

Note that these languages were not developed specifically for the Web, and do not distinguish, for example, between graph edges that represent the connection between a document and one of its parts and edges that represent a hyperlink from one Web document to another. Their data models while elegant, are not very rich, lacking such basic comforts as ordered collections [79].

2.4.1 Lore

Lore (**L**ightweight **O**bject **RE**pository) is a project at Stanford to provide a convenient and efficient storage, querying, and updating mechanism for semistructured data [1]. In Lore, data are self-describing, so they do not need to adhere to a schema fixed in advance. All data in a Lore database follow the Object Exchange Model

(OEM) [145], originally designed for Stanford's TSIMMIS project [136], as discussed earlier in Section 2.2.2. The OEM is a "lightweight" self-describing object model that supports the concepts of object identity and nesting, and not much else. Under the OEM, each object is either atomic (such as integer, string, or image) or complex. A complex object consists of a collection of labeled subobjects. Thus an OEM object can be thought of as a rooted graph, with objects as nodes and labeled edges representing object-subobject relationships. The root of the graph also has a label associated with it. Queries are formed based on *path expressions*, which are sequences of labels traversable from the root. Lore supports storage of arbitrary atomic data within an OEM object, including integers, reals, strings, images, audio, video, HTML text, and Java applets. Atomic objects have type tags to aid in query processing and user interface displays. Note that these type tags are not used to enforce any type-checking; Lore never returns type errors. Note that Lore itself also is "lightweight", in the sense that it is a repository and a query engine but not a full-feature database management system. Currently, Lore does not provide transaction management, concurrency control, or recovery.

Lorel is the query language of the Lore system for querying semistructured data effectively. The language is a compatible extension to OQL [45], with numerous features to enhance queries over semistructured databases: partially specified path expressions, wild cards, automatic type coercion in comparisons, and a special semantics for disjunction. Unlike OQL, Lorel does not enforce strong typing, thus allowing similar objects to be compared and retrieved despite minor differences in their structure. Finally, Lorel allows querying and schema browsing when the object structure is unknown or only partially known. Lorel queries bind variables to objects in the **from** clause, navigate using path expressions, test conditions in the **where** clause, and return objects in the **select** clause. In summary, the highlights of Lorel are as follows.

- Queries return meaningful results even when some data are absent.
- Queries operate uniformly over single- and set-valued attributes.
- Queries operate uniformly over data having different types.
- Queries can return heterogeneous sets, i.e., where objects in the query result have different types and structures.
- Meaningful queries are possible even when the object structure is not fully known.
- The query language syntax is similar in spirit to SQL.

We illustrate some of the important features of Lorel with the following examples. Consider the OEM data in Figure 2.10. Here &113, &114 are object ids. Suppose we wish to find the name of drug manufacturing companies whose area code is greater than 200. This query is expressed as follows in Lorel.

```
select X.name
       from   manufacturers.company X
       where  X.phone.area > 200
```

This query will return a name if its area code is "300" (a string) or 300 (an integer). Note that Lorel simply ignores companies missing any of the phone or

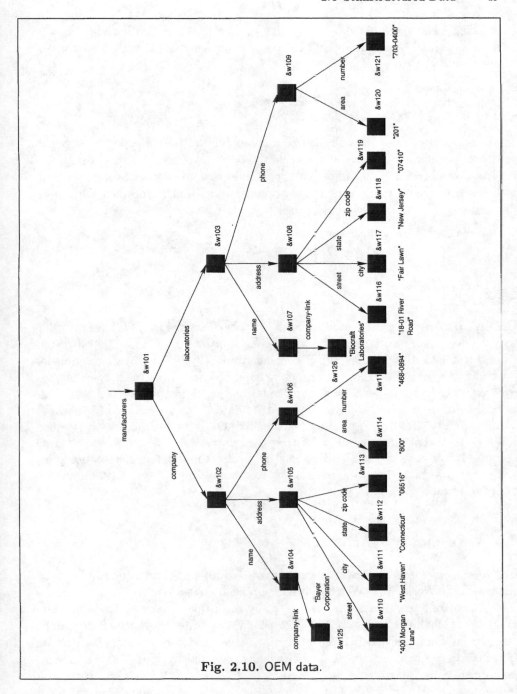

Fig. 2.10. OEM data.

area code attributes, unlike OQL, which generates an error if the query is applied to data missing any attribute. Also if X has several phone attributes, then X will be selected as long as at least one of them has a area code greater than 200. Finally, to query data with partially unknown structure, Lorel introduces generalized path expressions. These are extended OQL-like path expressions with wild-cards and arbitrary regular expressions, for example, to find companies with area code of phone equal to 200.

```
select X.name
    from   manufacturers.company X
    where  X(.phone)?.area = 200 )})
```

The above query obtains the name of companies with area code 200 either in the phone number or directly as a field of the company.

Note that Lorel does not require a from clause, and has a rule stating that common paths in the query correspond to the same object (unless specified otherwise). For instance, the first query above can be rewritten as:

```
select manufacturers.company.name
    from                        manufacturers.company.phone.area > 200
```

2.4.2 UnQL

UnQL, a language closely related to Lorel, was also designed at AT&T for querying semistructured data. UnQL is based on a model consisting of rooted labeled graphs similar to OEM. UnQL's semantics is specified formally by UnCAL, a calculus for unstructured data. UnQL queries are expressed in UnCAL as recursive functions over graphs. UnQL allows a user to query both a graph's structure (e.g., the relationships between linked HTML files) and its data (e.g., the values of hyperlinks and text in HTML files). A primary feature of UnQL is a powerful construct called *traverse* that allows restructuring of trees to arbitrary depth. Such restructuring operations are not expressible in Lorel. UnQL also supports regular path expressions that match the values of edge labels and node contents and that bind edge, node, and graph values to variables.

2.5 XML Query Languages

The recent emergence of XML as a new standard for data representation and exchange on the World Wide Web has drawn significant attention [37]. Simultaneously, a large body of research has been motivated by the attempt to extend database manipulation techniques to data on the Web [79]. Most of these research efforts; which range from the definition of Web query languages and related optimizations, to systems for Web-site development and management and to integration techniques (as discussed in the preceding sections); started before XML was introduced, and therefore have striven for a long time to handle the highly heterogeneous nature of HTML pages. In the meanwhile, Web data sources have evolved from small home-made collections of HTML pages into complex platforms for distributed data access and application development, and XML promises to impose itself as a more appropriate format for this new breed of Web sites [130]. XML brings data on the Web closer to databases, since, unlike HTML, it is based on a clean distinction between

```
⟨ manufacturers ⟩
   ⟨ company id = c12356, year = 1993⟩
      ⟨ name ⟩
         ⟨ company-link HREF ="www.bayer.com/bayer/index.xml"
         TITLE = "Bayer Home page" ⟩
            Bayer Corporation
         ⟨ /company-link ⟩
      ⟨ /name ⟩
      ⟨ address ⟩
         ⟨ street ⟩ 400 Morgan Lane ⟨ /street ⟩
         ⟨ city ⟩ West Haven ⟨ /city ⟩
         ⟨ state ⟩ Connecticut ⟨ /state ⟩
         ⟨ zip code ⟩ 06516 ⟨ /zip code ⟩
      ⟨ /address ⟩
      ⟨ phone ⟩
         ⟨ area code ⟩ 800 ⟨ /area code ⟩
         ⟨ number ⟩ 468-0894 ⟨ /number ⟩
      ⟨ /phone ⟩
   ⟨ /company ⟩
   ⟨ laboratories id = I00089, year = 1989⟩
      ⟨ name ⟩
         ⟨ company-link HREF ="www.tevapharmusa.com/biocraft.xml"
         TITLE = "Biocraft Home page" ⟩
            Biocraft Laboratories
         ⟨ /company-link ⟩
      ⟨ /name ⟩
      ⟨ address ⟩
         ⟨ street ⟩ 18-01 River Road ⟨ /street ⟩
         ⟨ city ⟩ Fair Lawn ⟨ /city ⟩
         ⟨ state ⟩ New Jersey ⟨ /state ⟩
         ⟨ zip code ⟩ 07410 ⟨ /zip code ⟩
      ⟨ /address ⟩
      ⟨ phone ⟩
         ⟨ area code ⟩ 201 ⟨ /area code ⟩
         ⟨ number ⟩ 703-0400 ⟨ /number ⟩
      ⟨ /phone ⟩
   ⟨ /laboratories ⟩
⟨ /manufacturers ⟩
```

Fig. 2.11. An example of XML data at www.xml-man.com/maninfo.xml.

the way the logical structure (the DTD) of the data and the chosen presentation (the stylesheet) are specified. Also researchers have casually observed a striking similarity between semistructured data models and XML. While similarities abound, some key differences dictate changes to any existing data model, query language, or DBMS for semistructured data in order to fully support XML. By virtue of this, most of the early research proposals for data management on the Web and semistructured data in general are now being reconsidered in this new perspective.

```
⟨ !DOCTYPE manufacturers [
  ⟨ !ELEMENT manufacturers (company|laboratories)* ⟩
  ⟨ !ELEMENT company (name, address, phone?) ⟩
  ⟨ !ELEMENT name (company-link) ⟩
  ⟨ !ELEMENT address (street, city, state, zip code) ⟩
  ⟨ !ELEMENT street (# PCDATA) ⟩
  ⟨ !ELEMENT city (# PCDATA) ⟩
  ⟨ !ELEMENT zip code (# PCDATA) ⟩
  ⟨ !ELEMENT phone (area code, number) ⟩
  ⟨ !ELEMENT area code (# PCDATA) ⟩
  ⟨ !ELEMENT number (# PCDATA) ⟩
  ⟨ !ATTLIST company-link
        ROLE CDATA#IMPLIED
        XML-LINK CDATA #FIXED "SIMPLE"
        HREF CDATA #REQUIRED
        TITLE CDATA #IMPLIED
        SHOW (EMBED|REPLACE|NEW) "EMBED"
        ACTUATE (AUTO|USER) "USER" ⟩
  ⟨ !ATTLIST company year CDATA # REQUIRED ⟩
] ⟩
```

Fig. 2.12. DTD of XML data in Figure 2.11.

Recently, a few XML query languages have been proposed by the database community: XML-QL [67], Lorel [84], and YAT$_L$ [58, 59]. In this section, we discuss two of these existing XML query languages, i.e, Lorel and XML-QL. For each of these languages we describe the underlying data model and illustrate some of the features of the query language. A comprehensive examination of the features of these query languages is available in [76]. One word of caution is needed here: although very popular, XML is still a new proposal, and there are very few (if any) real XML-based applications on the Web. It is therefore quite difficult to reason about the data management problems that will come with XML, since we still haven't experienced them.

2.5.1 Lorel

In Lore's new XML-based data model [84], an XML element is a pair $\langle eid, value\rangle$ where eid is a unique element identifier and $value$ is either an atomic text string or a complex value containing the four components:

- A string-valued *tag* corresponding to the XML tag for that element;
- An ordered list of attribute-name/atomic-value pairs, where each attribute name is a string and each atomic value has an atomic value drawn from integer, real, string, etc., or ID, IDREF, or IDREFS. The list of attribute-name/attribute-value pairs in the data element is derived directly from the document element's attribute list;
- An ordered list of *crosslink subelements* of the form $\langle label, eid\rangle$ where *label* is a string. Crosslink subelements are introduced via an attribute of type IDREF or IDREFS; and

- An ordered list of *normal subelements* of the form $\langle label, eid \rangle$ where *label* is a string. Normal subelements are introduced via lexical nesting within an XML document. The subelements of the document element appear, in order, as the normal subelements of the data element. The label for each data subelement is the tag of that document subelement, or text data if the document subelement is atomic.

Once one or more XML documents are mapped into the data model, they can be visualized as a directed, labeled, ordered graph. The nodes in the graph represent the data elements and the edges represent the element-subelement relationship. Each node representing a complex data element contains a tag and an ordered list of attribute-name/attribute-value pairs; atomic data element nodes contain string values. There are two different types of edges in the graph: normal subelement edges, labeled with the tag of the destination subelement; and crosslink edges, labeled with the attribute name that introduced the crosslink. For example, consider the XML document in Figure 2.11. The graph representation of this document in this data model is shown in Figure 2.13.

Next we discuss the modifications made to the Lorel query language [1] to accommodate the differences between the new XML data model and the OEM, and to exploit XML features not present in the OEM. First, for XML, the notion of path expressions in Lorel is extended to navigate both attributes and subelements, and the notion of *path expression qualifiers* is introduced to distinguish between the two when desired. When no qualifier is given, both attributes and subelements are matched. Secondly, to facilitate different types of comparison, Lorel treats each XML component as atomic value either through default behavior or via explicit transformation functions that can transform an element into a string. Next, Lorel is extended to handle a *range qualifier*. The expression [range] can optionally be applied to any path expression component or variable. The *range* is a list of single numbers and/or ranges, e.g., [2-4, 7]. When such a range qualifier is applied to a label in a path expression, Lorel limits matched values to those within the range. For example, if x.drug[1-3] is a path expression in a Lorel query, then it considers the first two drug subelements of every manufacturer. When a range is applied to a variable, it limits the entire set of variable bindings to the specified range. Lorel also extends its query language to incorporate an order-by clause so that the result of a query is an ordered list of eids identifiers selected by the query.

Finally, using queries to restructure XML data may be more common than it was in the OEM, so Lorel has introduced two new query language constructs to transform data and return structured query results. The first construct, the **with** clause, is added to the standard **select-from-where** query form and was introduced originally in Lorel's view specification language. When a **with** clause is present in a query, the query result replicates all data selected by the **select** clause, along with all data reachable via any of a set of path expressions in the **with** clause. The second construct is the usage of *Skolem functions* [73]; for more expressive data restructuring than was provided in Lorel previously. In Lorel, a Skolem function accepts an (optional) list of variables as arguments and produces one unique element for every binding of elements and/or attributes to the argument(s). When a new set

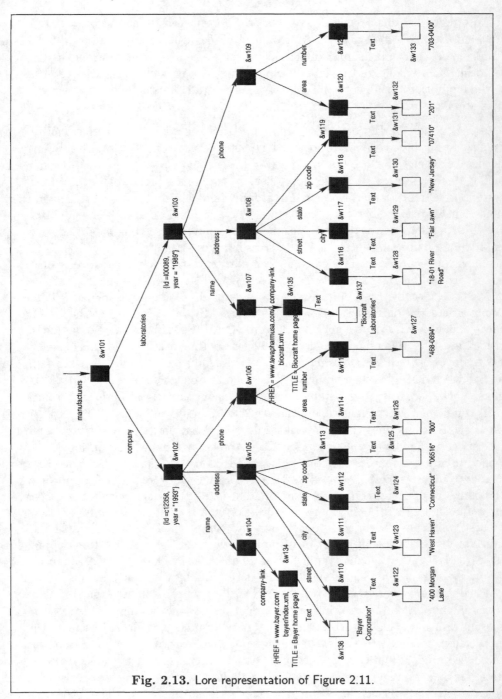

Fig. 2.13. Lore representation of Figure 2.11.

of bindings for the arguments is passed into a Skolem function, then a new database element is created and returned.

We now illustrate some of the features of Lorel in querying XML data with examples. We use the XML data in Figure 2.11 as our running example. We assume that queries specify a fixed data source (via one or more URLs) and return a well-formed XML tree. Also note that all the query languages discussed in this section consist of three parts: a *pattern* clause, which matches nested elements in the input documents and binds variables; a *filter* clause, which tests the bound variables; and a *constructor* clause which specifies the result in terms of the bound variables [76]. Typically, in a Lorel query, the constructor appears in the `select` clause, patterns appear in the `from` clause, and both patterns and filters appear in the `where clause`.

Example 2.1. Our first example selects all companies that were established after 1991.

```
select xml(manufacturers: {
     (select              xml(company: {@year:y, name:n} )
     from                 manufacturers.company c, c.name, c.year y
     where                y > 1991)})
```

In the above query, `manufacturers` is used as the entry point for the data in the XML document. The `from` clause binds variables to the element ids of elements denoted by the given pattern, and the `where` clause selects those elements that satisfy the given filters. The `select` clause constructs a new XML `company` element with a year attribute and its name.   ∎

Example 2.2. Sometimes the result of a query needs to have a structure different from the original XML document. The next query illustrates restructuring by grouping each state with the companies in that state. This requires joining elements on their `state` value; the example query treats two states as equal when they have the same value.

```
select xml(results: {
select xml(result:{ state: s,
     (select              xml(name: n} )
     from                 manufacturers.company c, c.name n
     where                c.address.state = a)})
     from                 manufacturers.company.name.address.state a})
```

Note that Lorel uses a nested query to join `state` elements on their character data.   ∎

Now we show how to combine information collected from different portions of documents, which is necessary to merge information from multiple documents. For the next query, assume that we have a second data source at `www.drugs.com/druginfo.xml` that contains details of drugs manufactured by different companies, with the DTD in Figure 2.14.

Example 2.3. Suppose we wish to identify the state and name of the company where each drug is manufactured. For the corresponding Lorel query, we use the entry point `drugs-man` to access the data in the second XML document.

```
⟨ !DOCTYPE drugs-man [
⟨ !ELEMENT drugs-man (manufacturer-name)* ⟩
⟨ !ELEMENT manufacturer-name(company-name, drugs)* ⟩
⟨ !ELEMENT drugs (name, side-effects, usage, disease-list, price) ⟩
⟨ !ELEMENT company-name (# PCDATA) ⟩
⟨ !ELEMENT name (# PCDATA) ⟩
⟨ !ELEMENT side-effects (# PCDATA) ⟩
⟨ !ELEMENT usage (# PCDATA) ⟩
⟨ !ELEMENT disease-list (# PCDATA) ⟩
⟨ !ELEMENT price (# PCDATA) ⟩
] ⟩
```

Fig. 2.14. DTD of www.drugs.com/druginfo.xml.

```
select xml(drugs-state: {
select xml(drugs-state:{ state:s,
      name-man:nm}
      from                        manufacturers.company c,
                                  c.name nm, c.address.state s,
                                  drugs-man d,
                                  d.manufacturer-name.company-name nd,
                                  d.manufacturer-name.company-name nd,
      where                       nm = nd)})
```

Note that Lorel uses an explicit equality predicate on the manufacturer's name to perform the join operation.   ∎

Example 2.4. Some queries may be conveniently specified by constraining the path through the tree via the use of a regular-path expression. For instance, suppose we wish to retrieve all the names of companies containing the string "lab", regardless of the nesting level at which they occur.

```
select xml(results: {
      (select       xml(name:n)
      from          manufacturers(.company)* c, c.name n
      where         c like "*lab*")})
```

The path expression component `manufacturers(.company)* s` binds the variable s to all elements reachable by following a manufacturers element and a sequence of company elements.   ∎

2.5.2 XML-QL

XML-QL is a query language for XML proposed by Deutsch et al [67]. This query language is based on the notion that an XML document is a database and a DTD is the schema of the database. XML-QL is a declarative, "relational complete" query language that can extract data from existing XML documents and construct new XML documents. To better understand XML-QL it is necessary to describe its data models. We describe both *unordered* and *ordered* data models as proposed in [67].

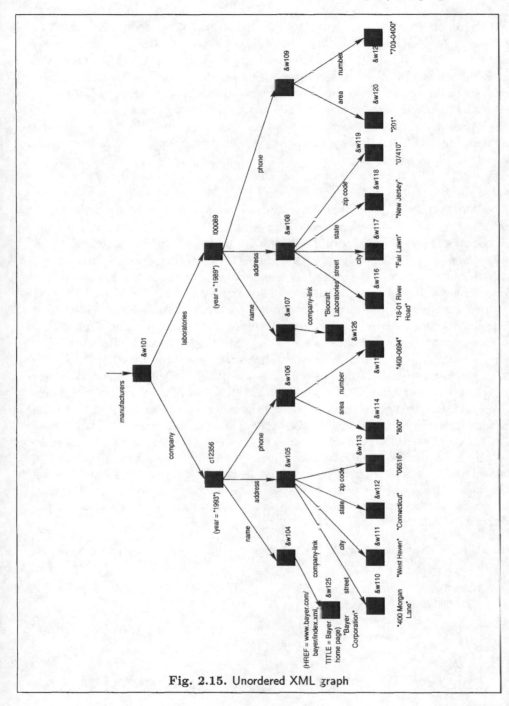

Fig. 2.15. Unordered XML graph

XML-QL's unordered data model is expressed as an unordered *XML Graph* which consists of a graph in which each node is represented by a unique string called the *object identifier* (OID) and edges are labeled with element tags. Note that the object id is the ID attribute associated with the corresponding element or is a generated OID, if no ID attribute exists. The nodes of the graph are labeled with sets of attribute-value pairs to model tag attributes and their values. The leaves of the graph are labeled with one string value. Note that the graph has a distinguished node called the *root*. This model allows several edges between the same two nodes, but with the following restriction. A node cannot have two outgoing edges with the same labels and the same values. Here value means the string value in the case of a leaf node, or the OID in the case of a nonleaf node. As in Lorel, an IDREF attribute is represented by an edge from the referring element to the referenced element; the edge is labeled by the attribute name. For example, the data in Figure 2.11 would be represented by the XML graph in Figure 2.15.

An ordered XML graph is an XML graph in which there is a total order on all nodes in the graph. For graphs constructed from XML documents a natural order for nodes is their document order. Given a total order on nodes, a local order is enforced on the outgoing edges of each node. Also in an ordered model, many edges with the same source, same edge label, and same destination value are possible. For example, the data in Figure 2.11 would be represented by the ordered graph in Figure 2.16. Nodes are labeled by their index (parenthesized integers) in the total node order and edge labels are labeled with their local order (bracketed integers).

Finally, another important feature of the data model of XML-QL is that only leaf nodes in the XML graph may contain values, and they may have only one value. As a consequence, the XML fragment: <disease>Down <type> Syndrome </type></disease> cannot be represented directly as an XML graph. In such cases, XML-QL introduces extra edges to enforce the invariant of one value per leaf. The data above would be transformed into: <disease><CDATA>Down<CDATA><disease> <CDATA><type><CDATA>Syndrome </CDATA></type></disease>.

We now illustrate some of the features of XML-QL with examples. We use the same examples as we used for Lorel in the previous section and show how we can express these queries using XML-QL. Also note that in an XML-QL query, patterns and filters appear in the where clause, and the constructor appears in the construct clause.

Example 2.5. Consider Example 2.1. This query can be expressed using XML-QL as follows.

```
CONSTRUCT <manufacturers> {
    WHERE
        <manufacturers>
            <company year = $y>
                <name>$n </name>
            </company>
        </manufacturers> IN "www.xml-man.com/maninfo.xml"
    $y > 1991
    CONSTRUCT <company year = $y><name>$n</name></company>
} </manufacturers>
```

In the above query the result of the inner WHERE clause is a relation that maps variables to tuples of values that satisfy the clause. In this case, the result contains

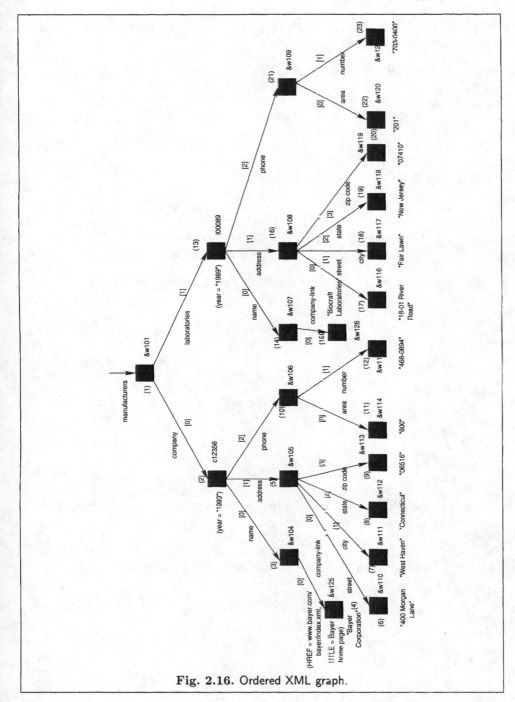

Fig. 2.16. Ordered XML graph.

all pairs of year and name values bound to (**$y, $t**) that satisfy the clause. The result of the complete query is one **<manufacturers>** element, constructed by the outer `CONSTRUCT` clause. It contains one `<company>` element for each company that satisfies the `WHERE` clause of the inner query. ∎

Example 2.6. Consider the Example 2.2. This query can be expressed using XML-QL as follows.

```
CONSTRUCT <results> {
   WHERE
      <manufacturers>
         <company >
            <address>
               <state> $s </state>
            </address>
         </company>
      </manufacturers> IN "www.xml-man.com/maninfo.xml"
   CONSTRUCT
   <result>
      <company><address><state> $s </state></address></company>
      {
         WHERE
            <manufacturers>
               <company>
                  <name> $n </name>
                  <address><state>$s</state></address>
               </manufacturers>
            </manufacturers> IN "www.xml-man.com/maninfo.xml"
         CONSTRUCT <name> $n </name>
      }
   </result>
} </results>
```

In this XML-QL query, the occurrence of `$s` in the outer `WHERE` clause causes them to be bound, while their occurrence in the inner `WHERE` clause tests for equality. One `result` element is constructed for each state and contains one or more name elements, which are constructed by the nested query. ∎

Example 2.7. Next consider Example 2.3 in the preceding section. The XML-QL version of this query is shown below.

```
CONSTRUCT <man-state> {
   WHERE
      <manufacturers>
         <company >
            <name> $n </name>
            <address>
               <state> $s </state>
            </address>
         </company>
      </manufacturers> IN "www.xml-man.com/maninfo.xml"
      <drugs-man>
         <manufacturers-name>
            <company-name> $n </company-name>
            <drugs> <name> $d </name></drugs>
         </manufacturers-name>
      </drugs-man> IN "www.drugs.com/druginfo.xml"
   CONSTRUCT
      <man-state>
         <name> $n </name>
         <state> $s </state>
         <drugs> $d </drugs>
      </man-state>
   }
</man-state>
```

Note that the use of the same variable $n for both names causes a join between the two data sources. ∎

Example 2.8. Finally, consider the last example in the previous section illustrating regular path expressions. This query can also be expressed using XML-QL as follows.

```
CONSTRUCT <results> {
   WHERE
      <manufacturers.(company)*>
         <name>$n </name>
      </> IN "www.xml-man.com/maninfo.xml"
   $n LIKE '*lab*'
   CONSTRUCT <name>$n</name>
} </results>
```

Here `manufacturers.(company)*` is a regular-path expression, and matches a manufacturers element followed by a sequence of zero or more nested company elements. Regular path expressions are combined with the alternation, concatenation, and Kleene-star operators. ∎

2.6 Summary

We conclude the survey by summarizing the salient features of the query systems described above. In the preceding sections we have seen many different ways of defining a Web querying and manipulation mechanism. The most important common theme here, clearly, is the inadequacy of the relational model and its algebra. Specifically, these query systems imply that the relational model falls short in the areas of modeling Web data and manipulating them effectively.

W3QL, WebLog, WebSQL, NetQL, FLORID, and WebOQL are all intended for information gathering from the World Wide Web. These are based on the metaphor of the Web as a huge database. It is assumed that partial knowledge on structure is available to the users. A query starts from one or more entry points and performs an exhaustive search to match user-defined paths. While WebLog, FLORID, and WebOQL aim at restructuring Web documents using Datalog-like rules or graph tree representations, WebSQL and W3QL are languages for relevant documents retrieved by several search engines in parallel. The results of a WebSQL query are flattened immediately to linear tuples. Moreover, it is built on top of already existing search engines that suffer from many limitations. In W3QL users may specify content and structure queries on the WWW and maintain the results of queries as database views of the WWW. In W3QL, queries are always made to the WWW. However, the results are not manipulated further. NetQL follows the approach of structure-based queries. The main contributions of NetQL are that it provides an approach to extracting information from irregular textual Web pages and that it supports various methods to control the complexity of queries. A Web document structuring language like WebOQL or WebLog is capable of retrieving information from a subset of the web defined in the queries and also extracting interesting and useful information from within a given set of Web pages.

The Information Manifold, TSIMMIS, Ariadne, and WHIRL systems highlight the recent research activities for integrating information from various Web sources. These systems allow a user to query a database (possibly a virtual one) that combines information from several Web sites. In particular, Information Manifold uses probabilistic reasoning for deducing the order of access to data sources. It also has algorithms for adapting to differing source capabilities. The novel feature in TSIMMIS is the usage of the OEM data model to represent objects of varying structure. Furthermore, TSIMMIS offers tools for automatically generating the components such as wrappers and mediators that are needed to build systems for information integration. The distinguishing features of Ariadne are its use of wrapper algorithms to extract structured information from semistructured data sources and its use of planning algorithms to determine how to integrate information efficiently and effectively across sources. WHIRL, on the other hand, takes a different approach, focusing on "informal" information integration. It combines properties of logic-based and text-based representation systems. WHIRL is basically a subset of Datalog and uses information retrieval algorithms to find approximate matches between different databases. Observe that all these data integration systems are used to retrieve relevant data. They do not further manipulate the data.

Other proposals, namely, Lorel [1] and UnQL [41], aim at querying heterogeneous and semistructured information. These languages adopt a lightweight data model to represent data based on labeled graphs and concentrate on the development of powerful query languages for these structures.

The query languages for XML, i.e., XML-QL and Lorel, provide powerful tools to query and manipulate XML data. The data models of these query languages are extensions of data models for semistructured data (labeled graphs). Some of the major features of these languages are: first, they provide constructs to impose nesting and order upon relations. These may retain the structure of the original document or may allow its complete restructuring. These constructs include nested queries, grouping related data items together via Skolem functions or explicit grouping operators, indexing, and sorting. They also use a join operator to combine data from different portions of documents, corresponding to the join operation on relations. However, this join is based only on equality of values and has limited power in combining different types of information in the Web. Also these languages use tag variables and path expressions to support querying without precise knowledge of the document structure and access to arbitrarily nested data.

3

Node and Link Objects

3.1 Introduction

The World Wide Web contains an enormous collection of documents connected by hyperlinks. Thus in a data warehouse designed for Web information it is imperative to represent and store these relevant hyperlinked documents effectively for further querying and manipulation. In this chapter, we describe a model for representing the metadata, structure, and textual content of Web documents and their hyperlinks.

3.1.1 Motivation

The primary objective of our web warehousing project is to design and implement a repository of integrated information from the Web to support analytical processing of the data and decision making. To realize this objective, it is imperative to model Web documents in an efficient way that will support metadata, content, and structure-based querying and analysis of these documents. Recall that a Web document has content and some structure and also a set of metadata associated with it. However, there is no explicit demarcation between these attributes. Thus materializing only a copy of a Web document is not efficient for querying and analysis of Web data as we need to extract the content, structural attributes, and metadata attributes every time we query the document. In order to facilitate efficient querying and analysis over the content, structure, and metadata of Web documents, we need to extract these attributes from the documents. We elaborate on this with an example.

Consider the Web site at www.ninds.nih.gov containing information related to neurological diseases. Suppose we wish to identify those pages containing information about diseases where one of the symptoms is "spasticity". In order to retrieve such information, it is necessary to have knowledge about the metadata and content of the pages in the Web. For instance, for the above example, the host name of the URLs of the relevant web pages must be www.ninds.nih.gov. Moreover, the Web pages must contain information about symptoms of neurological diseases. Figure 3.1 is an example of a Web page satisfying these conditions. Note that the URL of this page is part of the metadata of the page and is not embedded in it as

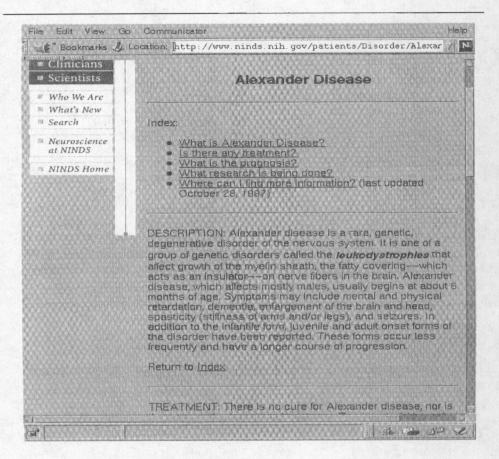

Fig. 3.1. Web page of Alexander disease at www.ninds.nih.gov.

textual content. Moreover, the textual content has an implicit structure defined by the tags in this page. The source code of the page is shown in Figure 3.2.

Next, Web data and XML data in particular may contain attributes associated with a tag. It is imperative that our data model be able to query and manipulate not only the content and structure (defined by the tags) of the Web page but also the attribute values associated with the tags. For example, consider the XML data in Figure 2.11. The element company has an attribute id with a value of c12356. Note that id is an identifier and has relevance only to a central database someplace. It should not be a part of the visible content of the XML data, but it may prove useful to a database, allowing it to connect to the original source and collect more information. Thus modeling attributes associated with a tag in our data model provides us the opportunity to enhance the querying and analysis capabilities.

Finally, the hyperlink structure of the Web is one of the major reasons for the explosive popularity. In order to exploit this hyperlinked structure, it is imperative to include the hyperlink information in the logical data model of our web warehouse.

```
<hr>

<p><a name="whatis">DESCRIPTION</a>: Alexander disease is a rare, genetic, degenerative
disorder of the nervous system. It is one of a group of genetic disorders called the <b><i>leukodystrophies</i></b>
that affect growth of the myelin sheath, the fatty covering--which acts as an
insulator--on nerve fibers in the brain. Alexander disease, which affects mostly males,
usually begins at about 6 months of age. Symptoms may include mental and physical
retardation, dementia, enlargement of the brain and head, spasticity (stiffness of arms
and/or legs), and seizures. In addition to the infantile form, juvenile and adult onset
forms of the disorder have been reported. These forms occur less frequently and have a
longer course of progression.</p>

<p>Return to <a href="alexander.htm#index">Index</a></p>

<hr>

<p><a name="treatment">TREATMENT</a>: There is no cure for Alexander disease, nor is there
a standard course of treatment. Treatment of Alexander disease is symptomatic and
supportive.</p>

<hr>

<p><a name="prognosis">PROGNOSIS</a>: The prognosis for individuals with Alexander disease
is generally poor. Most children with the infantile form do not survive past the age of 6.
In the juvenile form death usually occurs within 10 years after the onset of symptoms.</p>

<hr>

<p><a name="research">RESEARCH</a>: The NINDS supports research on genetic disorders
including leukodystrophies such as Alexander disease. The goals of this research are to
find ways to prevent, treat, and, ultimately, cure these disorders.</p>

<p>Return to <a href="alexander.htm#index">Index</a></p>

<hr>
```

Fig. 3.2. Source code.

Note that the current search engines available on the Web allow us to query only the textual content of documents. They return a set of URLs of Web documents satisfying a given query. However, they fail to return a set of interlinked documents that may be relevant to a query. Sometimes we may be interested in several documents connected by hyperlinks in lieu of a set of disconnected Web documents. We elaborate on this with an example.

Consider the Web page at www.druginfonet.com/maninfo.htm (Figure 2.1) containing information about various drug manufacturing companies in the United States. Specifically, this page contains contact information for different drug manufacturers in different states and provides links to their Web sites. Suppose we wish to find information about the products manufactured by companies in New Jersey and Connecticut. Figures 3.3 and 2.4 are screen shots of pages containing lists of products manufactured by two such companies: Bayer Corporation and Bristol-Myers Squibb Company. Note that pages containing such information can be reached from www.druginfonet.com/maninfo.htm by following the links of the respective manufacturers. However, these pages do not indicate whether these two companies are in New Jersey or Connecticut. This can be determined from the Web page at www.druginfonet.com/maninfo.htm as the state code in the addresses of the manufacturers reveals the state in which the company is physically located. For instance, the state codes CT and NJ indicate that Bayer

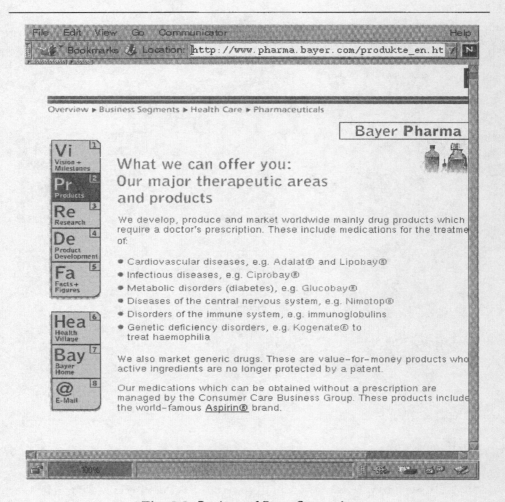

Fig. 3.3. Products of Bayer Corporation.

Corporation and **Bristol-Myers Squibb Company** are physically located in Connecticut and New Jersey, respectively. Thus the interconnectivity of the Web page at www.druginfonet.com/maninfo.htm and Web sites of different drug manufacturers must be preserved to correlate the products of companies located in different states.

Based on the above discussion, it is evident that in order to exploit querying and manipulation of Web data, it is imperative to model the metadata, content, and structure (interdocument as well as intradocument) associated with Web documents. In the subsequent sections, we discuss our approach for modeling Web data.

3.1.2 Our Approach - An Overview of WareHouse Object Model (WHOM)

We introduce the *Node* and *Link types* to represent metadata, structure, and content of Web documents and hyperlinks [20]. A *Node type* consists of a *name*, a set of *node metadata attributes*, and a set of *node structural attributes*. To facilitate metadata queries on Web documents in our web warehouse, we introduce the data type *node metadata attribute*. Node metadata attributes are used to capture the meta-data information associated with Web documents (excluding hyperlinks) such as URL, date of last modification, and size. Each attribute may either be atomic or *complex*. A complex metadata attribute contains another level of metadata attribute components. The *node structural attribute* is used to model the content and structure of Web documents. It consists of the attributes *name*, *attribute list*, *content*, *identifier*, and *location attribute*, which we elaborate on subsequent sections.

A *Link type* consists of a *name*, a set of *link metadata attributes*, a set of *link structural attributes*, and a *reference identifier*. Similar to the node metadata attributes, the metadata information associated with hyperlinks (such as link_type, source URL, and target URL) is represented using the *link metadata attribute* type. The *link structural attribute* consists of three components: *name*, *attribute_list*, and *content*. We elaborate on this later.

3.2 Representing Metadata of Web Documents and Hyperlinks

In this section, we discuss the modeling of metadata information associated with Web documents and hyperlinks. Specifically, we elaborate on the *node metadata attribute* and *link metadata attribute* components in Node type and Link type, respectively. We begin by identifying the metadata associated with HTML and XML documents.

3.2.1 Metadata Associated with HTML and XML Documents

Currently, an HTML or XML document may have the following metadata. Note that some of these metadata may be *hierarchical*. That is, they may be further decomposed into metadata having finer granularity.

- At the highest level of abstraction, every Web document is identified by its URL. The URL can be decomposed into host-name, domain name, protocol, path, file name, and geographical location.
- Web servers provide some additional information such as the format, size (in bytes), and the date of the last modification of the document. Note that the metadata date can be further decomposed to month, month-date, year, day, and time.

Similarly, a hyperlink in a Web document has the metadata:

- Source URL or the URL of the Web document containing the link;

- **Target** URL or URL of the referred document;
- *Type* of hyperlink or **link type**. Note that in order to study the topology of the Web, we sometimes want to make a distinction between links that point within the same document, to another document stored at the same site, or to a document on a remote server. This is expressed by the values of the link type object: **interior**[1], **local**, or **global**, respectively [131].

Note that like the URL of a Web document, the **source url** and **target url** may be further decomposed into metadata having finer granularity.

3.2.2 Node Metadata Attributes

The data type *node metadata attribute* is used to capture the metadata information associated with Web documents (excluding hyperlinks). Again each attribute may either be atomic or *complex*, the latter consisting of another level of metadata attribute components. For instance, the node metadata attribute URL can further be decomposed into **server**, **port**, **protocol**, **path**, and **file name**. For simplicity, we assume all attributes to be character strings. Figures 3.4(a), (b), and (c) depict the atomic and complex metadata attributes associated with a Web document.

An instance of a node metadata attribute can be represented by a tree called a *node metadata tree* where the internal vertices of the tree are metadata attribute names and the leaf vertices are values of metadata attributes. For example, the URL **http://www.ninds.nih.gov/ patients/Disorder/Alexander/ Alexander.htm** and date **Thursday, 15th July, 1999, 04:50:53** can be represented as trees as shown in Figure 3.5.

3.2.3 Link Metadata Attributes

Similarly, the metadata information associated with hyperlinks (such as **link_type**, **source URL**, and **target URL**) can be represented using the *link metadata attributes* data type. Each attribute may be atomic or complex. Analogous to the node metadata attributes, an instance of a link metadata attribute can be represented by a tree called the *link metadata tree* where the internal vertices of the tree are metadata attribute names of hyperlinks and the leaf vertices of the tree are values of metadata attributes.

3.3 Representing Structure and Content of Web Documents

In the preceding section, we described how to represent metadata associated with Web documents and hyperlinks. We now discuss the representation of content and

---

[1] In HTML, links can point to specific named fragments within the destination document; the fragment name is incorporated into the URL. For example, **http://www.cais.ntu.edu.sg:8000/intro.html#staff** refers to the fragment named **staff** within the document with URL **http://www.cais.ntu.edu.sg:8000/intro.html**. We ignore this detail in the rest of the chapter.

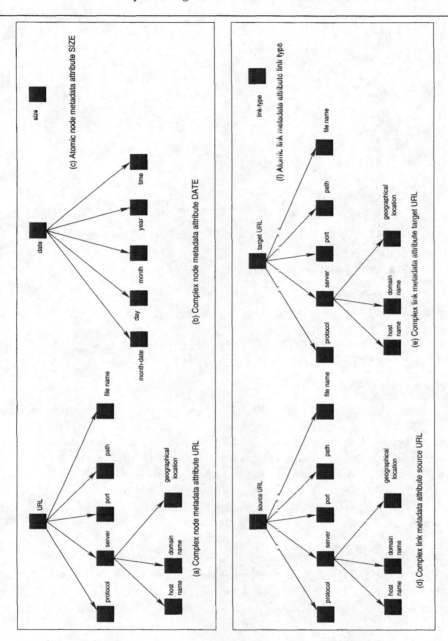

Fig. 3.4. A set of node and link metadata attributes.

structure of Web documents. To achieve this objective, we present the *node structural attributes* associated with a `Node type`.

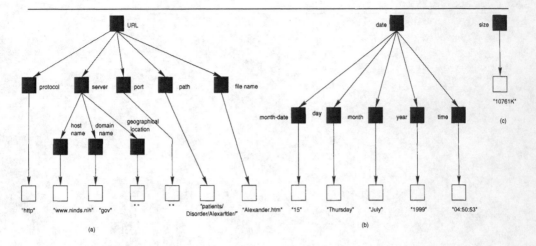

Fig. 3.5. An instance of some of the node metadata attributes.

3.3.1 Issues for Modeling Structure and Content

We first discuss some issues that we have considered for modeling the content and structure of Web documents.

Tags and Tagless Data

An HTML or XML document consists of text, which defines the content of the document, and tags, which define the structure and appearance (for HTML only) of the document. The tags and content are collectively referred to as HTML or XML elements. In XML, the tags are used only for specifying the structure of the document but not for the appearance of the document. We ignore tags (called *noisy tags*) that are used for formatting purposes in HTML and consider all XML tags in WHOM. The node structural attribute must be able to represent these tags and tagless segments of data.

Modeling Hierarchical Structure

The content of an HTML or XML element may be *hierarchical* in nature. That is, the content of an HTML or XML element may consist of another level of HTML or XML elements. Node structural attributes must be able to model this hierarchical structure of Web documents.

Attribute Value Pairs Associated with Tags

A tag in a Web document may also contain a set of attribute value pairs for passing along extra information about the element to an automated processor. For example, consider the XML data in Figure 2.11. The tag <company id = c12356> is an example of a start tag where the name of the tag is company and the attribute id may have relevance to some database somewhere. Thus modeling attributes associated with a tag in our data model provide us the opportunity to enhance the querying and analysis capabilities of WHOM.

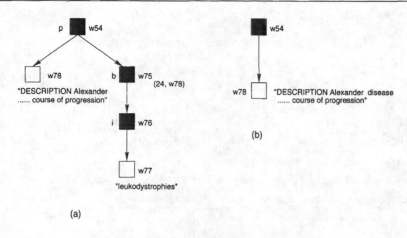

Fig. 3.6. A portion of a NDT.

"Order" of Text

Because HTML and XML documents represent textual documents, it is necessary to preserve the order of the textual components of the documents while representing the structure and content of Web documents.

Locality Information of a Portion of Tagless Data

It is necessary to maintain the *locality information* of portions of tagless data with respect to an actual document. Once a Web document is mapped to instances of *node structural attributes*, the relative locality information of some portions of text may be lost. We elaborate this with some examples. Consider the Web page in Figure 3.1. The source code of this page is shown in the screen shot (Figure 3.2). The word "leukodystrophies" is embedded in a paragraph that describes the "Alexander disease". From the structural perspective, observe that this keyword is emphasized by the tags <b> and <i> in the Web document. Disregarding the details of structural representation of Web documents using *node data tree* for the moment, a portion of the structure of the Web page involving this keyword is depicted in Figure 3.6(a). Observe that the leaf vertices (identified by the vertices having identifiers $w77$ and $w78$ in Figure 3.6(a)) represent the tagless data of this paragraph. However, they do not express the position of the word "leukodystrophies" in the segment "Alexander disease ... genetic disorder ... course of progression". This locality information may serve an important purpose: Suppose we wish to identify all documents in which the keywords "genetic disorder" and "leukodystrophies" are not separated by more than four words (the intention is to identify genetic disorders of type "leukodystrophies". Alexander disease is one such disorder). Without the locality information of "leukodystrophies", i.e., location of vertex $w77$ in the paragraph represented by the vertex $w78$, it is not possible to evaluate the condition correctly from the structural representation of the document in Figure 3.1. "leukodystrophies" is located after

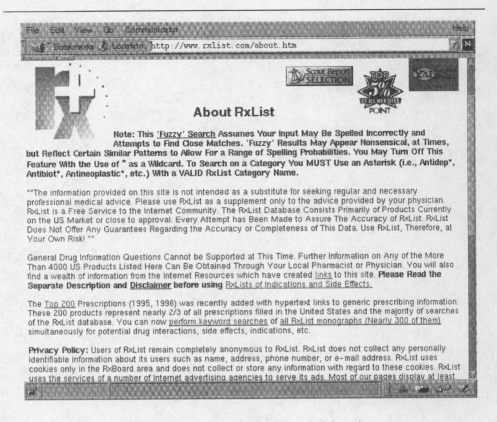

Fig. 3.7. Web page at www.rxlist.com/about.htm.

the 24th word in the paragraph identified by the vertex $w78$. In WHOM, we should be able to represent such locality information of a tagless segment of data.

One may decide to ignore the tags `<b>` and `<i>` while extracting structural information from HTML documents so that the specified paragraph can be represented simply as shown in Figure 3.6(b). However, in HTML documents the tags `<b>`, `<i>`, and so on are often used to emphasize certain information in the documents that is considered to be relatively more important for retrieval than the rest of the text [64]. For instance, the emphasis on the keyword "leukodystrophies" is due to the fact that the disease "Alexander Disease" falls under the category of the genetic disorder called "leukodystrophies".

In the next section, we discuss the components of a node structural attribute and show how the above issues are modeled in WHOM.

3.3.2 Node Structural Attributes

A node structural attribute consists of the following.

```
<html>
<head>
    <title>About RxList - The Internet Drug Index
</title>
    <meta name="GENERATOR" content="Mozilla/2.01Gold (Win32)">
</head>
<body text="#000000" bgcolor="#FFFFFF" link="#0000EE" vlink="#551A8B" alink="#FF0000">

<CENTER><TABLE><TR><TD WIDTH=468><nolayer><iframe src="http://ad.doubleclick.net/adi/www

<center><p><a href="http://www.rxlist.com">
<img src="rx.gif" alt="Click to search RxList" vspace=2 border=0
height=125 width=125 align=left>
</a><a href="http://www.zdnet.com/yil/url/9901/9901e.html"><img src="yil.gif"
alt="Best of The Best '98" vspace=2 align=right border=0></a>  
<a href="http://point.lycos.com/reviews/Medications_30M1.html">
<img src="topf.gif" alt="Lycos top" vspace=2 border=0 height=72 width=72
align=right>
</a>     
<a href="http://scout7.cs.wisc.edu/page/00000013.html">
<img src="scoutsel.gif" alt="Scout Report" border=0 height=29 width=100
align=right>
</a>     
</center><pre>

</pre><center>
<h1>About RxList</H1></center>
<h4>Note: This <a href="http://www.calweb.com/~Frank">"Fuzzy"
Search</a> Assumes
Your Input May Be Spelled Incorrectly and Attempts to Find Close Matches.
"Fuzzy" Results May Appear Nonsensical, at Times, but Reflect Certain Similar
Patterns to Allow For a Range of Spelling Probabilities. You May Turn Off
This Feature With the Use of <font SIZE=+1>*</font> as a Wildcard.
To Search on a Category You MUST Use an Asterisk (i.e., Antidep*,
Antibiot*, Antineoplastic*, etc.) With a VALID RxList Category Name. </h4>

<p>**The information provided on this site is not intended as a substitute
for seeking regular and necessary professional medical advice. Please use RxList as a
only to the advice provided by your physician. RxList is a Free Service to the Interne
Consists Primarily of Products Currently on the US Market or close to approval.
Every Attempt Has Been Made to Assure The Accuracy of RxList. RxList Does
Not Offer Any Guarantees Regarding the Accuracy or Completeness of This
Data. Use RxList, Therefore, at Your Own Risk! ** </p>
```

Fig. 3.8. Source code of the Web page in Figure 3.7.

- **Name**: the name is a finite set (possibly empty) of character data corresponding to the name of an HTML or XML start-tag. The name attribute of node structural attributes includes all tag names associated with Web documents except those used to represent hyperlinks. For HTML documents, the name attribute can have any value that is a name of any valid HTML tag except the *noisy tags* (Appendix E).

- **Attribute_list**: A finite set (possibly empty) of attributes associated with the tag. The attributes are always strings. Recall that it is necessary to consider attributes associated with a tag to exploit *analysis* of extra Web information.

- **Content**: The content between a start- and end-tag. It is a finite and possibly empty set of character data and/or it may contain data of node structural attributes type. This attribute models the textual content of Web documents and its hierarchical structure.

- **Identifier**: A nonempty string that uniquely identifies an object of the node structural attributes type.

- **Location_attribute**: This attribute is used to specify the location of a portion of tagless data as discussed in the previous section. It is represented by a pair

(location_identifier, position) where location identifier is of type
identifier and position is a string denoting the position of a portion of
tagless data (the number of words counted from the head of the content of
identifier).

A Web document can be represented as a set of instances of the node structural
attributes called *node structural objects* which is either a start-tag (called a *tag
object*) or a data content (called a *data object*) in a Web document. These objects
satisfy some *dependency constraints* and collectively they can be visualized as a
rooted directed tree called a *node data tree* (NDT). Intuitively, the vertices in NDTs
are node structural objects and the edges between the vertices are the dependency
constraints between two node structural objects. Figure 3.9 shows an example of a
node data tree of the HTML document in Figure 3.7 (the source code for which is
shown in Figure 3.8) and Figure 3.10 is an example of a NDT of the XML data in
Figure 2.11. From these examples of NDTs, we can identify the following features.

Rooted Directed Tree

An interior vertex of a node data tree represents a tagged element containing a tag
name, a list of attribute name/value pairs, and a unique identifier. The leaf vertices
contain string values and represent the textual data in the Web document. They
may also represent tagged elements. The edges represent the element/subelements
relationship. Furthermore, each vertex in the node data tree has a unique identifier.

The interior vertex of the tree is labeled by the start tag name. A leaf vertex
is labeled by the tagless data content if it represents textual data or by the start
tag name if it represents an HTML or XML element. For instance, the labels of
the interior vertices of the NDT in Figure 3.9 are p, title, head, and so on which
are HTML tags. The label of the root vertex for a tree generated from an HTML
document is fixed and is equal to html. This is because the root element of all
HTML documents is <html>. For NDTs generated from XML documents, the label
of the root vertex is not fixed and is defined by the user.

Loss of Structural Information

Recall that while modeling HTML documents, we ignore some tags and tag attributes (called *noisy tags* and *attributes*) as these tags and attributes are used
to impose conditions on the appearance and format of HTML documents or their
executable contents. Complete lists of these noisy tags and noisy tag attributes are
given in Tables E.7 and E.8 (Appendix E), respectively. Thus the NDT generated
from an HTML document may suffer some loss of structural information. Note that
the selection of noisy tags is application dependent. The user may modify the list
of noisy tags by adding or deleting one or more tags from the list.

No Loss of Content Data

The textual contents of Web documents are represented by leaf vertices in a node
data tree. Some of these leaf vertices may represent a tag element. For example,
the exterior vertices in Figure 3.9 with identifiers $w15$, $w16$, $w17$, and so on are

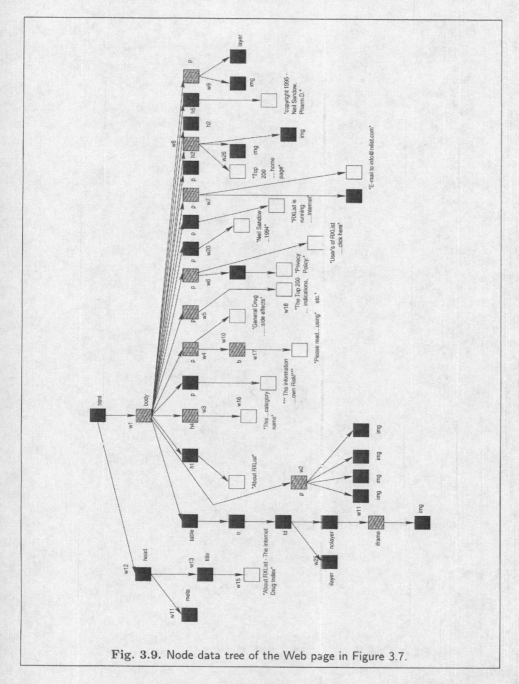

Fig. 3.9. Node data tree of the Web page in Figure 3.7.

tagless data. On the other hand, the vertices with identifiers $w11$, $w25$, $w26$ are tagged elements labeled as meta, iframe, and img, respectively. We do not ignore any textual content of Web documents while generating the NDT. Hence there is no loss of textual data during this transformation.

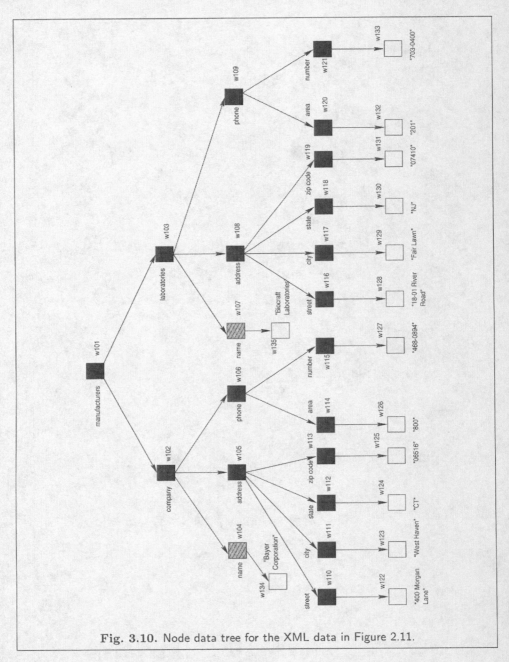

Fig. 3.10. Node data tree for the XML data in Figure 2.11.

Exclusion of Anchor Tags

A NDT does not represent hyperlinks embedded in a Web page. In WHOM, we model hyperlinks separately from a Web document. As we show later, a hyperlink is represented by a *link data tree* (LDT). Thus a NDT that is generated from an

HTML document does not contain any vertex whose label is A. Similarly, a NDT for XML data does not contain any vertex where one of the attributes is xml:link.

3.3.3 Location Attributes

Sometimes a portion of a document may be represented by more than one data object. A location attribute indicates the relative position of a tag object with respect to its predecessor tag object. Observe that not all node structural objects have a location attribute value in a NDT. Specifically, the location attributes of the data objects in a NDT are empty and only some of the tag objects (called *locator vertices*) contain a location attribute value. In this section, we determine how to identify these location vertices. Within this context, we first illustrate a few examples for representing location attributes in NDTs based on the Web pages in Figures 3.1 and 3.7. We then identify the common features of these representations and show that the locator vertices of a NDT can be represented by a set of subtrees called *location subtrees*.

We set the stage for our discussion by depicting the following examples. Consider the third paragraph, i.e., "General Drug, ...", at www.rxlist.com/about.htm (Figure 3.7). The source code of this section is shown in Figure 3.11(a). The portion of the NDT representing this paragraph is shown in Figure 3.11(b). Observe that the content of the paragraph is not being expressed by a single-node structural object or data object. Specifically, two data objects $w30$ and $w17$ are used to represent the content. This is because of the existence of text formatting tags b in the paragraph. The location attribute of the tag object labeled b ($w10$) is ($w30, 51$). It indicates that the content enclosed by the b tag is located after the 51st word in the data object $w30$. Consider now the section related to the index in the Web page at www.ninds.nih.gov/patients/Disorder/Alexander/Alexander.htm (Figure 3.1). The source code of this portion of the document is shown in Figure 3.12(a). The portion of the NDT representing this section is shown in Figure 3.12(b). Similar to the previous example, observe that rather than representing the content of the paragraph with a single data object in the NDT, a set of data objects is used due to the existence of the ul element in the paragraph. The location attribute of the tag object $w111$ (labeled as ul) is ($w110, 1$) indicating that the element ul is located after the first word in the data object $w110$. Based on these examples, we can infer the following.

- The tag objects, called *locator vertices*, which have a nonempty location attribute are located in a set of specific subtrees of the NDT. These objects are children of the root of the subtrees. For instance, the tag objects $w75$, $w10$, and $w111$ of the subtrees in Figures 3.6(a), 3.11(b), and 3.12(b), respectively, are locator vertices. These objects are children of the roots $w54$, $w4$, and $w109$ respectively. Observe that one of the children of the root of the subtree is always a data object; i.e., the vertices $w78$, $w30$, and $w110$ are data objects. These data objects are called *reference vertices*. Each subtree is called a *location subtree*.
- Let the reference vertex of a location subtree, with identifier i, contain w number of words. Then the location attribute of each locator vertex is equal to (i, w_k),

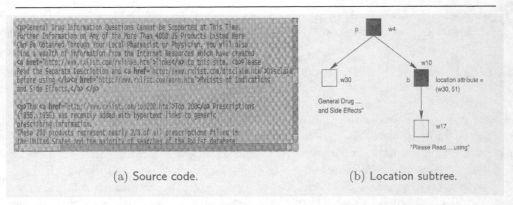

(a) Source code.   (b) Location subtree.

Fig. 3.11. Example of location subtree.

where $0 \leq w_k \leq w$. For instance, consider the location subtree in Figure 3.11(b). The number of words in the reference vertex $w30$ is 57. Hence the location attribute of the locator vertex $w10$ is $(w30, 51)$. Similarly, the number of words in the reference vertex $w110$ is 1 in Figure 3.12(b). Hence the location attribute of locator vertex $w111$ is $(w110, 1)$.

- There must exist at least one locator vertex that has one or more child vertices. For instance, the locator vertices $w75$, $w10$ and $w111$ in Figures 3.6(a), 3.11(b), and 3.12(b), respectively, have at least one child vertex.
- There must be one at least one data object that can be reached from each locator vertex which is not a leaf node in the subtree. For instance, the data object $w77$ in Figure 3.6(a) can be reached from the locator vertex $w75$. Similarly, the data objects $w117$, $w118$, $w119$, $w120$, and $w121$ can be reached from the locator vertex $w111$ in Figure 3.12(b). Observe that none of these locator vertices is the leaf nodes of the location subtrees.
- If one of the child vertices of a locator vertex is a data object, then the remaining children of the locator vertex must be tag objects with no children.

3.4 Representing Structure and Content of Hyperlinks

Hyperlinks are perhaps most important for relating parts of data that are not near each other in terms of prose flow. In the Web environment, the authors inclination to create many small pages, rather than single monolithic documents, makes this even more important. Authors' are motivated to create small pages to keep retrieval latencies low [155]. A hyperlink, as the term is used here, is an explicit relationship between two or more data objects or portions of data objects. In WHOM, we define a hyperlink by the data type **Link type**. Recall that a **Link type** consists of three components: a set of link metadata attributes, a set of link structural attributes and a reference identifier. We discussed link metadata attributes in Section 3.2.3. In this section, we elaborate on the *link structural attributes*, and *reference identifiers*. Intuitively, link structural attributes are used to express the structure and content

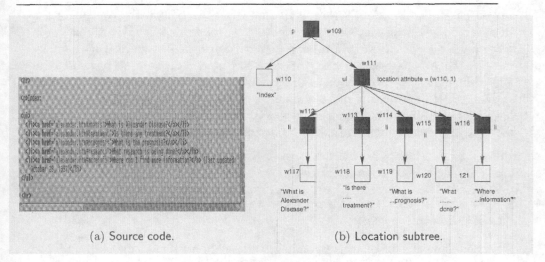

| (a) Source code. | (b) Location subtree. |

Fig. 3.12. Example of location subtree.

of hyperlinks and the reference identifier is used to specify the location of hyperlinks in Web documents.

3.4.1 Issues for Modeling Hyperlinks

We have identified the following issues that are to be considered for modeling hyperlinks in WHOM.

Modeling Tags and Tag Attributes

Hyperlinks in Web documents are specified by tags and tag attributes. Tags may in turn contain other tags. For instance, the <a> tag and the attributes **href** or **name** are used to specify hyperlinks in HTML documents. The <a> tag may contain subelements such as <b>, <i>, and so on. Similarly, extended XML links contain another level of hyperlinks. Thus we should be able to model the hierarchical structure of hyperlinks.

Modeling Tagless Data or Anchors

Typically, when authors add a hyperlink to a document D, they include in the anchor tag a description of D in addition to its URL. These descriptions can be important for retrieval since they include the perception of the authors about the contents of D. Hence it is imperative to represent the textual content between the hyperlink tags.

Location of Hyperlinks

A Web page may have one or more hyperlinks located in different parts of the Web page. Sometimes, two links may have an identical anchor but different locations in a Web page. The location of these hyperlinks is important in the context of the web warehouse as we may need to impose constraints in a query to follow only those links that are located in a particular portion of a Web page. For example, consider the Web page at `www.druginfonet.com/maninfo.htm`. This page provides a hyperlinked list of a collection of drug manufacturers in the United States. The anchor text related to drug manufacturers is contained inside the element `strong`. In order to specify a query that follows only these links, one may need to specify the location of these hyperlinks, i.e., inside the `strong` element.

3.4.2 Link Structural Attributes

Similar to `node structural attributes`, the `link structural attribute` consists of three components.

- `Name`: The name of the corresponding start-tag of an HTML or XML link. For XML, there is no specific link tag; an XML link is specified with an XML element. The `xml:link` attribute is used to specify a link. Thus, given an XML document, the instances of `link structural attributes` are those elements where one of the attributes is `xml:link`.
- `Attribute_list`: Similar to the `attribute list` of node structural attributes, it is a finite (possibly empty) set of attributes associated with the tag. The attributes are always strings.
- `Content`: The `content` between the start- and end-tags. It is a finite (possibly empty) set of character data or it may contain data of `link structural attributes` type.

Observe that unlike the `identifier` attribute in node structural attributes there is no attribute that uniquely identifies a link structural attribute. We envisage that it is not important for these to be a unique identifier in the context of link structural attributes as there is no need to correlate the link structural attributes with the node structural attributes based on a common identifier.

3.4.3 Reference Identifier

We now discuss the attribute `reference identifier` associated with a `Link type`. Recall that the link metadata attribute `source URL` enables us to correlate hyperlinks with Web documents in which these links are embedded. Furthermore, we are interested in the location of a hyperlink in a particular document. As the attribute `source URL` does not represent such information, we use a `reference identifier` to incorporate such location details of hyperlinks.

Consider the hyperlink "all RxList monographs ..." in the Web page in Figure 3.7. The NDT of the Web page is shown in Figure 3.9. Observe that the hyperlink is located in the tag object having identifier $w5$ in the NDT. Thus the reference identifier of this hyperlink is $w5$.

As in Web documents, the structure and content of each hyperlink can be represented by a set of instances of link structural attributes. Note that once an HTML

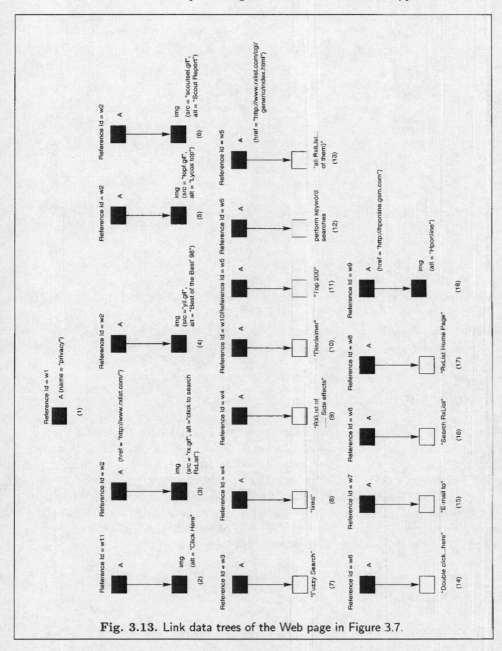

Fig. 3.13. Link data trees of the Web page in Figure 3.7.

or XML link is mapped into an instance of the link structural attribute called the *link structural object*, the object and the *dependency constraints* on the object can be visualized as a rooted directed tree. This tree is called the *link data tree* or LDT, in short. Intuitively, the vertices in LDT are link structural objects and the edges between the vertices are the dependency constraints between two link structural

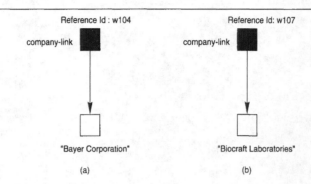

Fig. 3.14. Link data tree for XML data in Figure 2.11.

objects. Figure 3.13 shows a set of link data trees of the hyperlinks contained in the Web page of Figure 3.7. Each tree in the figure represents a hyperlink. Note that the reference identifier in each tree is not a component of a link data tree and is used only for clarity. Figure 3.14 is the LDT for the XML link in the XML data in Figure 2.11. Observe that unlike node data trees, the vertices in a link data tree do not have any unique identifier associated with them.

3.5 Node and Link Objects

We now formally discuss *node* and *link* objects. A node object (*node* for brevity) is an instance of the **Node type** and has two components: a set of node metadata trees and a node data tree. It represents the metadata, content, and structure of an HTML or XML document excluding the hyperlinks embedded in it.

A link object (*link* for brevity), on the other hand, is an instance of the **Link type** and consists of three components: a set of link metadata trees, a link data tree, and a reference identifier. Similar to the node object, it represents the metadata, content, and structure of hyperlinks embedded in a Web document.

3.6 Node and Link Structure Trees

In the preceding sections, we have seen how to generate NDTs and LDTs from Web documents and hyperlinks. We now discuss the generation of *node structure trees* (NST) and *link structure trees* (LST) from NDTs and LDTs, respectively. Intuitively, NSTs and LSTs are tree representations of the structure of a Web document and a hyperlink, respectively excluding the textual data contents. That is, NSTs and LSTs only contain tag objects and no data objects. These trees are generated from NDTs and LDTs, respectively, by eliminating the tree nodes representing data objects from these trees and the corresponding edges to these nodes. For instance, the NST of the NDT in Figure 3.9 is shown in Figure 3.16. Observe that the vertices representing the data objects (i.e., $w15$, $w16$, $w17$, $w18$, and so

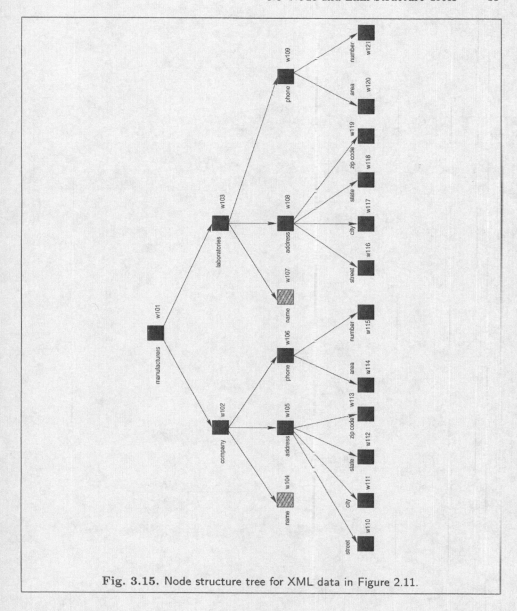

Fig. 3.15. Node structure tree for XML data in Figure 2.11.

on) are deleted from the NST. Similarly, Figure 3.15 depicts the NST generated from the NDT of the XML data in Figure 3.10. As a NST does not contain any data objects, the location_attributes of the tag objects are removed from the vertices. To summarize, the transformation of a NDT to a NST consists of the two steps:

- deletion of data objects from the NDT; and
- removal of the location_attribute from the tag objects in the NDT.

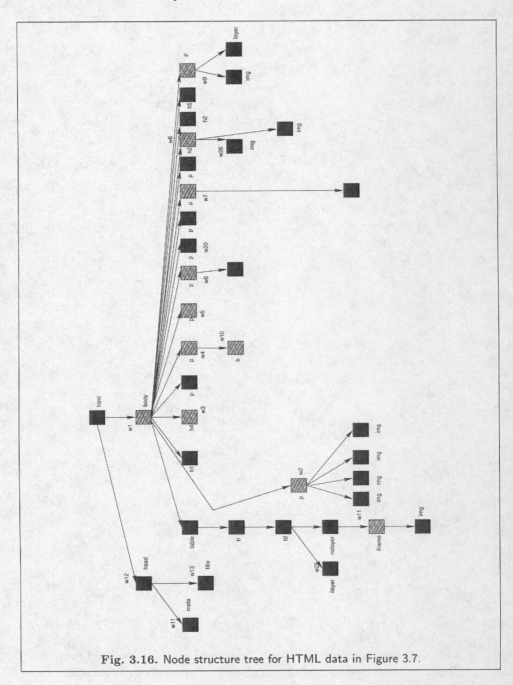

Fig. 3.16. Node structure tree for HTML data in Figure 3.7.

A *link structure tree* (LST) represents the structure of an HTML or XML link excluding the anchor text. Similar to the NST, a LST is generated from a LDT by removing the leaf vertices of the LDT that represents the data object. For example,

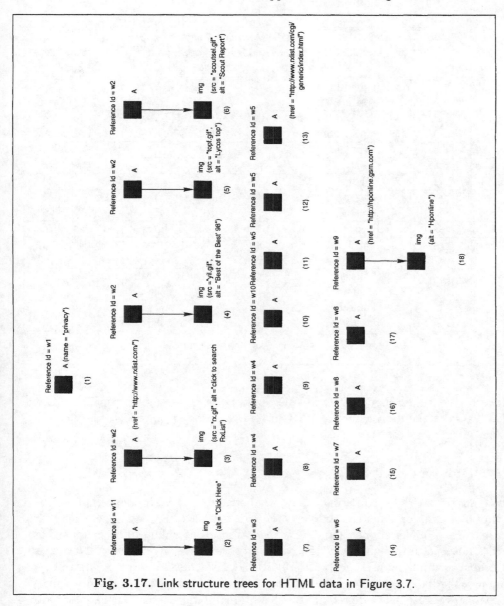

Fig. 3.17. Link structure trees for HTML data in Figure 3.7.

the set of LSTs generated from the LDTs of the hyperlinks (Figure 3.13) in the Web page in Figure 3.7 are shown in Figure 3.17. Observe that the data objects in the LDTs are removed while transforming to corresponding LSTs.

3.7 Recent Approaches in Modeling Web Data

In this section, we compare our modeling technique with some of the related research discussed in Chapter 2. We focus on high-level similarities and differences

System	Model HTML	Model XML	Data Model	Internal structure modeling	Metadata modeling	Content modeling	Hyper-link	Order	tag attri-bute	Mixed tag
WHOM	Yes	Yes	Labeled tree	Yes	Yes	Yes	Yes	Yes	Yes	Yes
W3QS	Yes	No	Labeled multigraph	Yes	Yes	Yes	Yes	No	No	No
WebSQL	Yes	No	Relational	No	Yes	Yes	Yes	No	No	No
WebLog	Yes	No	Relational	No	Yes	Yes	Yes	No	No	No
FLORID	Yes	No	F-Logic	Yes	Yes	Yes	Yes	No	No	No
ARANEUS	Yes	No	Page scheme	Yes	Yes	Yes	Yes	No	No	No
WebOQL	Yes	No	Hypertrees	Yes	No	Yes	Yes	Yes	No	No
STRUDEL	Yes	No	Labeled graph	Yes	No	Yes	Yes	Yes	No	No
Lore	No	Yes	Labeled graph	Yes	No	Yes	XML-link	Yes	Yes	No
XML-QL	No	Yes	Labeled graph	Yes	No	Yes	XML-link	Yes	Yes	Yes

Table 3.1. Comparison of web data models.

between recent data modeling techniques and our work. A summary of the differences between the data model of WHOM and the existing approaches is given in Table 3.1.

3.7.1 Semistructured Data Modeling

The main obstacles to exploiting the internal structure of Web documents are the lack of a schema or type and the potential irregularities that can appear for that reason. The problem of querying data whose structure is unknown or irregular has been addressed, although not in the context of the Web, by the query languages for semistructured data, Lorel [1] and UnQL [41]. By semistructured, we mean that although the data may have some structure, the structure is not as rigid, regular, or complete as the structure required by traditional database management systems [40]. Furthermore, even if the data are fairly well structured, the structure may evolve rapidly.

Comparison with WHOM

In WHOM, we model specifically Web data. Unlike the OEM, the documents and hyperlinks are represented separately as trees. We also ignore *noisy* elements in Web documents while transforming them to tree form. Moreover, we model the metadata associated with Web data. Note that the languages discussed earlier were not developed specifically for the Web, and do not distinguish, for example, between graph edges that represent the connection between a document and one of its parts and edges that represent a hyperlink from one Web document to another. Their data models, while elegant, are not very rich, lacking such basics as ordered collections [79].

3.7.2 Web Data Modeling

If the Web is viewed as a large, graphlike database, it is natural to pose queries that go beyond the basic information retrieval paradigm supported by today's search engines and take structure into account, both the internal structure of Web pages and the external structure of links that interconnect them. In this section, we discuss the data models of some of the web query languages proposed thus far: W3QS [101], WebSQL [132], WebLog [106], and so on.

Comparison with WHOM

In WHOM, we represent not only HTML but also XML data. We also separate the representation of documents and hyperlinks in WHOM. Furthermore, we separately model the metadata associated with Web documents and hyperlinks in a tree form. Such metadata modeling is not expressed in the above systems. The data models of W3QS, WebSQL, Florid, WebLog, and ARANEUS do not support modeling of tree-structured data. Furthermore, they do not address the problem of modeling mixed tags (we model it using location attributes), tag attributes, and a hierarchy of tag elements.

3.7.3 XML Data Modeling

Recently, few XML query languages have been proposed by the database community: XML-QL [67], Lorel [84], and YAT$_L$ [58, 59]. In this section, we discuss the data models of two of these existing XML query languages, i.e., Lorel and XML-QL.

Comparison with WHOM

In WHOM, we do not represent attributes of type IDREF or IDREFS as edges but as a simple string. Hence the representation of a document is always a tree in WHOM. Moreover, we model the hyperlinks and the XML documents separately using node and link data trees, respectively. Furthermore, we represent mixed tags using location attributes instead of introducing extra edges in XML-QL to enforce the notion of one value per leaf to represent mixed tag elements. Note that the XML data model of Lorel does not address the problem of modeling mixed tags. Also, unlike XML-QL, we do not express the order of a node data tree using explicit indices. Finally, we model hyperlinks and documents separately and represent metadata of XML documents explicitly in our data model.

Note that like all models in the literature, the label of nodes in a tree or graph can be used both to represent data such as strings, and to represent metadata attributes or structural attributes. While it might seem natural to represent metadata or structural attributes as edge labels and textual data as node labels, for convenience usually one of the two kinds of labels is used. For our work, node labels seem to have an advantage. It is easy to convert edge labels to node labels; create a node to represent the edge and move the label to it. Thus our model applies to edge-labeled trees as well.

XPath

The World Wide Web Consortium has recommended Xpath (www.w3c.org) as a language for operating on the logical structure of XML document. It models XML as a tree of nodes at a level higher than the DOM (document object model) but does not describe the abstract logical structure.

3.7.4 Open Hypermedia System

Open hypermedia [44, 87, 88, 65] is an approach to relationship management and information organization. Relations are stored and managed separately from the information they relate. This approach allows content and relationships to evolve independently, enables links to read-only content, and allows multiple sets of links to be maintained over the same set of information. Open hypermedia provides hypermedia services to all integrated applications. The underlying motivation is that eventually hypermedia services, such as link navigation, should be available from all of the applications in a user's computing environment and not arbitrarily restricted to a special hypermedia browser.

Open hypermedia systems (OHS) provide advanced hypermedia data models to enable the modeling of complex relationships and to provide sophisticated hyper-media services, such as guided tours, anchor and link attributes, filtering, etc., over these relationships. Open hypermedia environments emphasis the separate nature of links and data, where the semantics of the data is controlled by the viewers and the semantics of the links is controlled by link services. A link is more than a user navigation issue: it is a fundamental mechanism for document construction. From a document-oriented perspective, an open hypermedia system is a system that does not have a single, fixed hypermedia document model.

An OHS is able to process an extensible set of document types (each having a different markup scheme), to recognize the (possibly complex) hyperlink structures that are encoded into the documents, and to present the documents in an appropriate way to the user. From this perspective, the Web currently does not qualify as an OHS, because browsers cannot be easily extended with new document types: there are only very limited facilities to tell the browser how to recognize links encoded differently from HTML links, or to define how new document types should be presented to the user. In contrast, open hypermedia document models focus on the facilities supporting structural, domain-dependent markup, facilities to use common link structures across different document sets, and generic ways of defining how to present the encoded information, usually in the form of stylesheets. From an architecture- or protocol-oriented perspective, an open hypermedia system needs to be able to offer generic hypermedia services to different applications. From this perspective, the Web does not qualify as an OHS, because it requires other applications to adopt HTML as the main document format, which would require (at least) a major rewrite for most applications. In contrast, an OHS can be seen as a middleware component offering link services and/or storage facilities to a wide variety of applications, each with its own data models and document formats. Open hypermedia system models focus on the design of the OHS architecture, the interfaces and (link)protocols that are defined by the various components in the OHS environment and the main component technology used (e.g., CORBA, DCOM, etc.).

The Distributed Link Service (DLS) implements an open hypermedia system above the infrastructure of the World Wide Web [92]. This provides a powerful framework to aid navigation and authoring and solves some of the issues of distributed information management. WWW-related work has been investigated to augment it with the functionality of the open hypermedia style link facilities such as those found in the Microcosm system [43]. Recently, in [120], a conceptual model has been used to model HTML documents and a query language developed. However, it models HTML documents at a higher level in comparison to ours.

Comparison with WHOM

In DLS [44] and Open hypermedia environments, links can be inserted over existing WWW links, whereas in WHOM we only keep original links inserted by authors of the web pages. We make a distinction between the creators of web pages and readers of those web pages by disallowing web pages to be modified unless the owners of the web pages change them. This is very important in WHOM as queries are like graph queries and they depend on the original link structure. Another important distinction is that WHOM is a data model to store web pages (together with links) to facilitate query of those web pages and not an external link providing facility. The semantics of the data contained in the documents is generally ignored in an open hypermedia environment that is concerned only with links. In the WWW [141], the link semantics are defined as a part of the data semantics, and understood and implemented (fairly) uniformly by each browser. There exist some similarities with WHOM such as the fact that links and data are considered different entities in both approaches. Our objective is to query resources based on content and original links rather than link creation. We treat the Web as a huge database rather than just as a hypertext structure and resources are located based on their content. We believe that bringing hyperlink facility (such as in [43]) once the results are retrieved by the query will definitely make the model richer and able to provide more meaningful data to users.

3.8 Summary

We conclude this chapter by summarizing the salient features of the node and link objects described above. In this chapter, we have shown that Web documents and hyperlinks are represented as node and link objects in WHOM. These objects are first-class objects in WHOM. The most important theme, here, clearly is the logical separation of the hyperlinks from the Web documents and the representation of metadata, structure, and content of HTML and XML data as a treelike structure. Specifically, the metadata of Web documents and hyperlinks are represented as a set of node and link metadata trees, respectively. The content and structure of Web documents and hyperlinks are represented by a node and link data tree. The correlation between nodes and their links is maintained by the metadata source and target URL and the reference identifier of the link object.

Predicates on Node and Link Objects

Recall that the node and link objects represent the metadata, content, and structure of arbitrary Web documents and hyperlinks between Web documents, respectively. However, in a web warehouse, we are not interested in any arbitrary collection of Web documents and hyperlinks, but documents and hyperlinks that satisfy *certain constraints*. There are essentially two ways one may find documents on the Web that satisfy these *constraints*; navigation starting from known documents or querying search engines. In practice, navigation is done by following only certain links, based on their properties related to the constraints. On the other hand, the search engines return a set of URLs of documents that satisfy the specified constraints. For example, consider the Web sites of different universities around the world. Suppose a user wishes to find documents containing a list of publications in a particular research area, say "data warehousing" from all the universities. Note that "data warehousing" can be found not only in the publication of computer science department pages, but also in many other pages; for instance, it is presumably used as an anchor in every page that contains a link to a page dealing with data warehousing. It also appears in "non-university" pages, i.e., pages belonging to commercial organizations that build data warehousing products.

A user may find these pages by navigating through known documents or by using web search engines. For instance, she may start from a Web page containing a list of all major universities in the world (i.e., `http://www.mit.edu:8001/people/cdemello/univ.html`) and start navigating via each link pertaining to a university in the page. Note that in this case the user follows only certain links that are related to publications in data warehousing: "computer science department", "database research", "publications", etc. The user may also issue a keyword-based query "data warehousing + publications" to a search engine to retrieve a set of documents containing these keywords. Thus it is evident that in order to get relevant documents from the Web it is necessary to impose certain conditions to restrict the retrieval of those documents that satisfy these constraints. In WHOM, these constraints are imposed using *predicates* and *connectivities*. In this chapter, we introduce the notion of *predicates*. In the next chapter, we discuss *connectivities*.

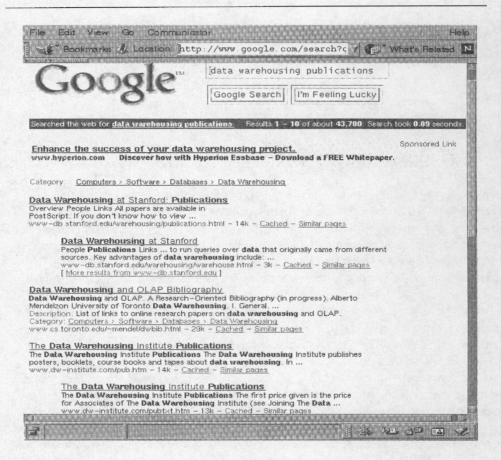

Fig. 4.1. A page retrieved by Google.

4.1 Introduction

A *predicate* is a logical expression that can be evaluated to true or false, with respect to some documents or hyperlinks. Predicates are the main mechanisms of expressing what portions of Web data a query or retrieval task should or should not match. The notion of predicates is similar to that of keyword-based constraints in search engines. However, the expressiveness of predicates in WHOM is more powerful than the keyword-based constraints used in conventional search engines. For instance, a keyword-based searching method is incapable of locating accurately a desired list of publications on data warehousing for a number of reasons.

- Data warehousing-related information may appear in university Web sites (.edu sites) as well as commercial sites (.com sites) and it is not possible in a conventional search engine to differentiate between these two instances. For instance, Figure 4.1 shows a screen shot of the results of the query "data warehousing

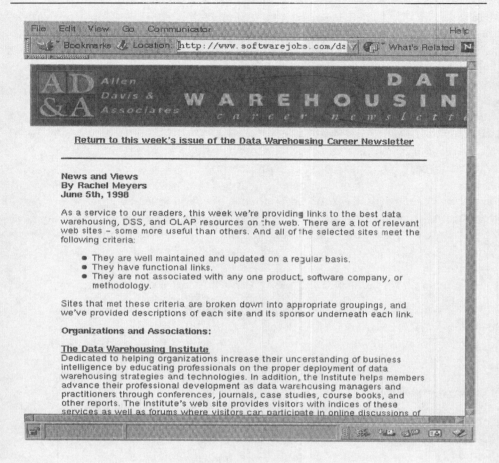

Fig. 4.2. Results returned by Google.

publications" using the Google search engine. Observe that the last two results in Figure 4.1 retrieve documents from commercial sites.

- Many search engines rank documents based on the number of times the words "data warehouse" and "publication" occur on the Web page. Advanced search engines such as Google use Pagerank [38] crawl and index the Web more efficiently and produce higher-quality results than existing systems. The score of a page with respect to a query is obtained by combining the position, font, and capitalization information stored in *hitlists* with the Pagerank measure. However, it may still retrieve pages containing these keywords but not contain a list of publications. For example, Figure 4.2 displays a Web page retrieved by the Google search engine with respect to the above query. Note that although this page contains the keywords "data warehousing" and "publication", it does not contain a list of publications.

In WHOM, as we show later, predicates can exploit not only simple keyword-based matching but also metadata associated with Web documents and hyperlinks, and the hierarchy of data content in Web pages. Predicates provide a greater flexibility in imposing constraints on Web data and a way to overcome the limitations in keyword-based retrieval techniques. We call such predicates *comparison-free predicates*.

Moreover, a predicate in WHOM can also impose conditions on associated metadata, content, or structure-related properties of a set of Web documents or hyperlinks to the corresponding properties of another set of documents or hyperlinks. In conventional search engines, constraints are basically a set of keywords that are to be matched against a set of documents. It does not support the retrieval of Web documents that satisfy a certain correlation with other documents. These types of predicates are called *comparison predicates*. A slight drawback of predicates in WHOM is that it may be difficult for a novice to formulate them. However, in many cases this drawback is not a significant problem and is outweighed by its advantages.

In summary, the main contributions of this chapter are the following.

- We present a flexible scheme to impose constraints on metadata, content, and structure of HTML and XML data. An important feature of our scheme is that it allows us to impose constraints on a specific portion of Web documents or hyperlinks, on attributes associated with HTML or XML elements, and on the hierarchical structure of Web documents, instead of simple keyword-based constraints similar to the search engines.
- We present a mechanism to associate two sets of documents or hyperlinks using comparison predicates based on their metadata, content, or structural properties.
- We describe the syntax and semantics of comparison and comparison-free predicates for imposing constraints on Web data.

The remainder of the chapter is organized as follows. Section 4.1.1 identifies a set of features that are to be associated with a predicate in the context of Web data. We provide a brief overview of the two types of predicates, i.e., *comparison-free* and *comparison* predicates, in Section 4.1.2. In Section 4.2, we introduce the components associated with a comparison-free predicate, i.e., *attribute path expression*, *predicate qualifier*, *predicate operator*, and *value* of a predicate, which are aimed at addressing the various features associated with a comparison-free predicate. Next we describe the *comparison predicates*. Within this context, we present the *components* of comparison predicates. Finally, the last section summarizes the notion of predicates.

4.1.1 Features of Predicate

We believe a predicate should have the following features.

- Satisfiability of predicate: For any predicate, there may be zero or more documents and hyperlinks in a given set of documents or hyperlinks satisfying it. For any given document or hyperlink, there will be a large (perhaps infinite) set of predicates that may be satisfied by it. Thus there is a many-to-many mapping between predicates in WHOM and the set of Web documents and hyperlinks.

- **Conditions on metadata, content, and structure:** Recall that a node or link provides information not only on textual content but also a metadata and structure associated with Web documents or hyperlinks. Thus predicates must be able to impose conditions on all of these components.

- **Assumption of zero or partial knowledge:** It is unrealistic to assume that a user has complete knowledge about the content and structure of Web pages in a Web site as one may not necessarily know anything about the architecture of a given site or how the desired information is represented in the source. Thus predicates should be able to support constraint specifications based on zero or partial knowledge about the structure or content of Web data.

- **Constraints on tag attributes:** A user must be able to impose constraints on the attributes associated with tags as well as tagless segments of data. The textual content in HTML or XML as described by the tagless data segment is viewable by users. However, not all useful information is enclosed by tags. Some information is found in the attribute/value pairs associated with tags. Thus a predicate must be able to impose constraints on tag attributes in order to exploit this extra information.

- **Demarcation among metadata, structure, and content:** Since metadata, structure and textual content are found in every Web document and hyperlink, predicates should be able to distinguish the application of it with respect to these components. As we show later, there may not exist a distinct demarcation among these components.

- **Associating Web data based on similar properties:** Predicates must be able to impose constraints on the *association* between two sets of Web documents or hyperlinks based on certain *conditions* related to metadata, content, or structural properties of the Web data. For instance, we may wish to associate those hyperlinks whose label is contained in the title of some Web documents.

4.1.2 Overview of Predicates

In WHOM, we define two types of predicates: *comparison-free* and *comparison* predicates. Comparison-free predicates are *value-driven* predicates where a string value or a regular expression over string values must be specified. It extends the notion of conventional keyword-based search techniques on the Web. Comparison-free predicates are used to impose constraints on the metadata, content, and structure of Web documents or hyperlinks. Each predicate is imposed on a single *node* or *link type identifier*. For instance, suppose we wish to retrieve documents whose title contains the keyword *Cancer*. A conventional search engine will not only retrieve documents whose title contains this keyword, but also many documents in which *cancer* occurs only in the text. In WHOM, we can specify the particular location of the keyword to be matched using a comparison-free predicate. Disregarding the syntax for the moment, the following predicate will satisfy only those documents whose title contains the keyword *cancer*.

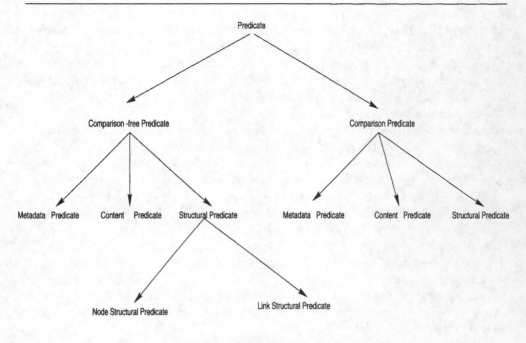

Fig. 4.3. Taxonomy of predicates.

$$p(x) \equiv \texttt{CONTENT::}x\texttt{[html.head.title] NON-ATTR\_CONT}$$
$$\texttt{":BEGIN\_WORD: + } \textit{Cancer} \texttt{ + :END\_WORD:"}$$

Comparison-free predicates can also be used to impose constraints on the metadata and structure of Web documents or hyperlinks. For instance, the following predicate satisfies only those documents located on servers in Singapore or Australia:

$$p(x) \equiv \texttt{METADATA::}x\texttt{[url.server.geo\_location] EQUALS } \textit{"sg/au"}$$

The next predicate can be used to retrieve only those documents that contain a table.

$$p(z) \equiv \texttt{STRUCTURE::}z \texttt{ SATISFIES } \textit{"table"}$$

Note that as of this writing the above two types of retrieval are not supported by conventional search engines. Also observe that comparison-free predicates are value-driven. That is, a string value or a regular expression over string values is to be specified in order to match it against the metadata, content, or structure of Web data. A comparison-free predicate cannot be evaluated without such values.

Comparison predicates are *value-free* predicates. They are used to correlate the metadata, content, and structural properties of a set of documents or hyperlinks with the corresponding properties of another set of documents or hyperlinks. Hence such predicates, unlike comparison-free predicates, are not value-driven. For instance, suppose we wish to identify that set of documents, denoted by x, whose title is contained in the anchor text of a set of hyperlinks represented by link type identifier y. Disregarding the syntactic details of the comparison predicate for the moment, the above constraint can be expressed as follows.

$$p(x, y) \equiv \texttt{CONTENT::} x \texttt{[head.title] IS\_CONTAIN } y \texttt{[A]}$$

Observe that in this case the user does not specify any value for the title or the anchor text. He or she only correlates the title of the documents with the anchor text of the hyperlinks. Hence such predicates, unlike comparison-free predicates, are not value-driven. Moreover, it provides a mechanism to impose constraints on a pair of node or link type identifiers, instead of on a single node or link type identifier as in comparison-free predicates.

Comparison and comparison-free predicates are further classified into *metadata*, *content*, and *structural* predicates depending on whether the constraints are imposed on the metadata, content, or structure of Web documents or hyperlinks, respectively. The complete taxonomy of predicates in WHOM is shown in Figure 4.3.

Observe that the choice of the terms comparison-free and comparison predicates may not follow the traditional mechanism of defining a predicate. First, they evoke echoes of the terms "equality" and "equality-free" that arise in logic and model theory, where the prime concern with the presence of the equality operator tends to be decision complexity. The issue here is certainly different. Second is the significance of treating these as substantially distinct notions Broadly speaking, comparison predicates take two object parameters, while comparison-free predicates effectively take a single parameter. Equivalently we could treat the second parameter as a constant. In spite of these similarities, we treat them distinctly for the following reasons.

- First, we wish to distinguish between the type of predicates that are currently supported by conventional search engines and those that are not. Observe that comparison-free predicates stem from the conventional keyword-based search techniques in the Web. It extends the notion of keyword-based search by providing the mechanism of imposing constraints not only on the content, but also on the metadata and structure of Web documents. On the other hand, comparison predicates are value-free predicates and are not currently supported by the conventional search engines.
- Second, the primary motivation for introducing the notion of predicates is to use them for formulating meaningful web queries. However, as we show in Chapter 6, we cannot impose constraints on the *source vertex* of a *web query* by using comparison predicates only. There must be at least one nontrivial comparison-free predicate imposed on the source vertex. This is due to the *computability* of a *web query*. Hence, unlike comparison-free predicates, comparison predicates have restricted application in a web query.

In the subsequent sections, we discuss comparison and comparison-free predicates in detail. We begin with the comparison-free predicate.

Predicate Qualifier	Attribute Path	Operator	Value	Examples
METADATA	Exist	EQUALS	RE on ASCII characters	$p(x) \equiv$ METADATA::x[url] EQUALS "$www[./]hotmail[./]com/$", $p(x)$ $\equiv$ METADATA::x[url.filename] "EQUALS .+[.]MATCH(xml + :END_STR:)"
CONTENT	Exist	ATTR_CONT, ATTR_ENCL, NON-ATTR_ENCL, NON-ATTR_CONT, CONT	RE on ASCII characters, Attr/value pairs, proximity values	$p(x) \equiv$ CONTENT::x[body(.b)?] NON-ATTR_CONT ":BEGIN_WORD: + $treatment$ + :END_WORD:", $p(z) \equiv$ CONTENT:: z[name(.last name)?] NON-ATTR_ENCL "Smith", $p(z) \equiv$ CONTENT::z[customer] ATTR_ENCL "[':START_STR: + $customer\ id$ + :END_STR:']"
STRUCTURE	Optional	SATISFIES, EXISTS_IN*	collection of tag names, attribute path expression	$p(z) \equiv$ STRUCTURE::z SATISFIES "document (name)", $p(f) \equiv$ STRUCTURE::f EXISTS_IN "orders.item"

* Applicable to link objects only

Table 4.1. Synopsis of comparison-free predicates.

4.2 Components of Comparison-Free Predicates

In this section, we formally introduce the notion of a comparison-free predicate. A synopsis of the different types of comparison-free predicates is shown in Table 4.1. A *comparison-free predicate* is defined over a *node* or *link type identifier* and is used to impose *conditions* on the metadata, content, or structure of instances of the type identifier. Hereafter, for brevity, unless otherwise stated, when we use the term "predicate", we mean a comparison-free predicate.

A comparison-free predicate consists of the following components: *predicate qualifier*, *attribute path expression*, *predicate_operator*, and *value*. The following is a form of a comparison-free predicate p on x,

$$p(x) \equiv \text{predicate\_qualifier}::x\{[\text{attribute\_path\_exp}]\}$$
$$\text{predicate\_operator } "V"$$

where x, the argument of p, is called a *node* or *link type identifier* depending on the application of constraints on Web documents or hyperlinks, respectively. A node or link type identifier represents a set of node or link objects, respectively. That is, given a predicate $p(x)$, all node or link objects that conform to $p(x)$ are represented by the type identifier x. The component predicate_qualifier determines the *scope* of the predicate. It can have any one of the values: "METADATA", "CONTENT", or "STRUCTURE". It indicates whether the predicate is to be used to impose constraints on the metadata, textual content, or structure of instances of x.

The component `attribute_path_exp` is essentially a sequence of tags which may include wild cards and regular expression operators. It is used to specify constraints on specific position(s) of a Web document and hyperlink. It may also be used to impose structural constraints on Web data. The component `predicate_operator` represents operators for testing string regular expression matching. V is called the *value* of the predicate and is a regular expression over the ASCII character set when the `predicate_qualifier` is either METADATA or CONTENT. Specifically, when the qualifier is CONTENT, V may also be a regular expression over a set of attribute name/value pairs. When the qualifier is STRUCTURE, V may be an attribute path expression or a collection of tag element names. The curly brackets are used to indicate 0 or 1 occurrence of the components. Disregarding details of the components for the moment, some examples of comparison-free predicates are:

$$p(x) \equiv \texttt{CONTENT::}x\texttt{[company] ATTR\_CONT "}\textit{(id, c12356)}\texttt{"}$$
$$p(x) \equiv \texttt{STRUCTURE::}x \texttt{ SATISFIES "}\textit{manufacturers(company+)}\texttt{"}$$
$$p(x) \equiv \texttt{METADATA::}x\texttt{[url.server.domain name] EQUALS "}\textit{edu}\texttt{"}$$
$$p(e) \equiv \texttt{CONTENT::}e\texttt{[A] NON-ATTR\_CONT}$$
$$\texttt{":BEGIN\_STR: + }\textit{health information}\texttt{ + :END\_STR:"}$$

The first predicate imposes a constraint on the attribute/value list associated with documents containing the element `company`. Instances of x must contain an element `company` where one of the attributes "id" has value equal to *c12356* (Figure 2.11 is an instance of x). The next predicate specifies that the instances of x have a tagged element `manufacturers` that immediately contains one or more `company` elements (Figure 2.11). The third expression is a predicate on the metadata of a node type identifier x that indicates that all instances of x must belong to the domain "edu". Finally, the last predicate is imposed on a link type identifier e. It specifies that the anchors of instances of e contain the string "health information". In the following sections, we elaborate on the various components of a predicate.

Note that throughout this book, we denote the argument, attribute path expression, predicate qualifier, predicate operator and value of a comparison-free predicate p as $arg(p)$, $attr\_path(p)$, $qual(p)$, $op(p)$, and $val(p)$, respectively. Also two predicates p_1 and p_2 are *identical* if $attr\_path(p_1) = attr\_path(p_2)$, $qual(p_1) = qual(p_2)$, $op(p_1) = op(p_2)$, and $val(p_1) = val(p_2)$.

4.2.1 Attribute Path Expressions

When querying Web data, especially when the exact content or structure of the Web page or hyperlink is not known, it is convenient to use a form of "navigational" querying based on path expressions. The idea is to specify paths in the tree representation of metadata and structural attributes in order to impose constraints on the content, structure, and metadata of node and link objects. In this section, we discuss *simple attribute path expressions* and *regular attribute path expressions* which are used to impose constraints on the content, structure, and metadata of node and link objects. The function of attribute path expressions depends on the *domain* of application of the predicates. When imposing constraints on metadata, the attribute path expression is used to specify the value of a particular metadata attribute. In *content predicates* the attribute path expression is used to specify the location of a particular portion of the document. For predicates imposed on the structure of Web documents or hyperlinks, the attribute path expression specifies the location of an HTML or XML element which is the root of the subtree that is to be matched against the structure of Web data.

We begin our discussion by introducing the notion of *containment* of metadata and structural attributes. We use this to define simple and regular attribute path expressions. Next we discuss the syntax and semantics of an attribute path and illustrate them with examples. Then we classify an attribute path expression into one of three types, *metadata*, *content*, or *structure*, based on its domain of application.

Attribute Containment

Recall from the previous chapter that tagged elements are the building blocks of HTML or XML documents. Each tagged element has a sequence of zero or more attribute/value pairs and a sequence of zero or more subelements. These subelements may themselves be tagged elements or they may be "tagless" segments of text data.

Given metadata or an HTML or XML element o and its content c, we say that o *immediately contains* c, denoted by $o \leftarrow c$, and that o is called the *container* of c. Note that c is contained in o with no intermediate containers between o and c; i.e., $o \leftarrow c$ holds but $o \leftarrow o_1 \leftarrow o_2 \leftarrow \cdots \leftarrow c$ do not hold. Note that o_1, o_2, and so on are the submetadata attributes or subelements of o. We label o_i with the meta-attribute name or the start tag name. For example, in Figure 2.11, the `company` element is the container of `name`, `address`, `street`, `city`, and `phone`. However, `street` and `city` are immediately contained in `address` but not in `company`; i.e., `company` $\leftarrow$ `address` $\leftarrow$ `street` and `company` $\leftarrow$ `address` $\leftarrow$ `city`.

Simple Attribute Path Expressions

As the metadata and structural attribute of a Web document or hyperlink are representable in the form of a tree, an attribute path expression captures the notion of a path in the tree. A simple attribute path expression $A = o_1.o_2.o_3 \ldots o_n$ is a sequence of containment $o_1 \leftarrow o_2 \leftarrow o_3 \leftarrow \cdots \leftarrow o_{n-1} \leftarrow o_n$, where $n > 0$ and o_i is *simple* $\forall\, 0 < i \leq n$. n is called the *path length* of the attribute path expression. $o_1, o_2, \ldots, o_n$ are called *labels* or *elements* of attribute path expression A. A label is basically a string and is considered simple if it does not contain any regular expression defined over it. The labels o_1 and o_n are called *start* or *root* and *terminal* or *end* labels, respectively. For instance, `URL.server.domain name` is a simple attribute path containing metadata attributes and `company.address.street` is a simple attribute path expression containing node structural attributes. The length of each of these simple attribute path expressions is three. The labels `URL` and `company` are the start labels and `domain name` and `street` are the terminal labels.

Regular Attribute Path Expressions

Note that simple attribute path expressions enable a user to specify constraints on specific elements of Web documents provided he knows the exact structure and relative ordering of tag elements in which the concerned element is enclosed. However in reality it may not be always possible for a user to know the exact hierarchical structure of a set of documents ahead of time. In order to specify constraints on specific segments of a collection of documents based on zero or partial knowledge we extend the notion of simple attribute path expressions to a more powerful syntax for attribute path expression, called *regular attribute path expressions*. Regular attribute path expressions allow both regular expressions including wild cards to be used in paths, thus providing more flexibility in imposing constraints on the metadata, content, and structure of Web data.

A regular attribute path expression allows the labels to be followed by one or more *complex attribute components*, rather than just a sequence of labels as in simple attribute paths. The syntax of a complex attribute component is given by:

1. If o is a label, then $.o$ is a complex attribute component; and
2. If o_1 and o_2 are complex attribute components, then the following are also complex attribute components: o_1o_2, $o_1|o_2$, $(o_1)?$, $(o_1)+$, $(o_1)^*$, $(o_1)\{m, n\}$.

In Case 2, the symbol $|$ is used for disjunction, ? means 0 or 1 occurrences, + means 1 or more, * means 0 or more, and m and n are positive integers indicating at least m occurrences and at most n occurences.

In this definition, we use "." as a separator between element and subelement and not to match any character. Instead, we use "%" as the wild card to match 0 or more characters in an element name. In standard regular expressions, the matching of 0 or more characters is achieved by the expression ".*". However, we do not use this symbol here for two reasons. First, the period "." will create confusion if it is used as the element subelement separator. Second, having too many "*" may not be comprehensible as attribute path expressions can become lengthy collections of metacharacters, making them difficult to read and understand. For example, the attribute path expression document(.customer)*(..*)+(.phone)* is not very easy to read. Moreover, "..*" in this path is confusing as one period is used as an element subelement separator and another is used in the standard regular expression sense. Thus we replace .* with the symbol "%" to simplify its usage and to make it compact.

Classification of Attribute Path Expression

In this section, we classify an attribute path expression based on its domain of application. For the time being, consider that a *predicate qualifier* is used to define the domain of a comparison-free predicate. That is, if the value of the predicate qualifier is METADATA, then it is used to impose constraints on the metadata of Web documents or hyperlinks. Similarly, if the value is CONTENT or STRUCTURE, then it is used to impose conditions on the textual content or structure of Web data. We elaborate on predicate qualifiers in the next section. Based on different values of a predicate qualifier, the attribute path expressions are classified as the following. Note that each of these attribute path expressions can be simple or regular.

Metadata Attribute Path Expression

Metadata attribute path expressions are associated with predicates defined on the metadata of Web data. Let $A_m = o_{m_1}.o_{m_2}\ldots o_{m_n}$ be an attribute path expression in the predicate $p(x)$. Then A_m is a metadata attribute path expression if the predicate qualifier of $p(x)$ is equal to METADATA. For instance, the attribute path expression url.server.domain name in the predicate $p(x) \equiv$ METADATA::x[url.server.domainname] EQUALS "*edu*" is a metadata attribute path expression. Note that in this case, we only consider simple attribute path expressions and exclude regular attribute path expressions. The justification for this is that the attribute path expressions related to metadata are much simpler than those for structure and content of Web documents and hyperlinks. The length of any metadata attribute path expression is always less than four and the value of the labels in these attribute paths are metadata attributes and are known ahead of time for any Web document or hyperlink. Hence there is no pragmatic need to specify regular attribute path expressions in a metadata comparison-free predicate.

Content Attribute Path Expression

Content attribute path expressions are associated with predicates defined on the textual content or tag attributes of Web data. Let $A_c = o_{c_1}.o_{c_2}\ldots o_{c_n}$ be an attribute path expression in the predicate $p(x)$. Then A_c is a content attribute path expression if the predicate qualifier of $p(x)$ is equal to CONTENT. For instance, the attribute path html(.%)+.p in the predicate $p(x) \equiv$ CONTENT::x[html(.%)+.p] NON-ATTR_CONT "*cancer* " is a content attribute path expression.

Structural Attribute Path Expression

Finally, the structural attribute paths are associated with predicates defined on the structure of Web data. Let $A_s = o_{s_1}.o_{s_2}\ldots o_{s_n}$ be an attribute path expression in the predicate $p(x)$. Then A_s is a structural attribute path expression if the predicate qualifier of $p(x)$ is equal to STRUCTURE. For instance, the attribute path expression manufacturers(.%)+.location in the predicate $p(x) \equiv$ STRUCTURE::x[manufacturers(.%)+.location] SATISFIES "*city, country, zip code*" is a structural attribute path expression.

Note that for the structural attribute path expression the start label and terminal label must be simple. That is, they must not contain regular expressions. Hence manufacturers(.%)+.location is a valid structural attribute path expression, whereas the path manufacturers(.%)+ is not. We justify the reasons behind this later in this chapter.

4.2.2 Predicate Qualifier

When imposing constraints on Web data, we have seen that it is convenient to use an attribute path expression to impose conditions on the structure and textual and metadata content as well as on the attributes associated with tagged elements in HTML or XML documents. However, using only attribute path expressions to define comparison-free predicates may create the following types of ambiguities.

- In the case of an HTML document, the set of metadata attributes and the set of tag names are disjoint. Hence, given an attribute path, it is clear whether it refers to a metadata attribute or to a tag name. For example, `url.server.domain name` and `table.tr.td` automatically suggest paths containing metadata attributes and tag elements, respectively. However, in XML data, this distinction is blurred due to user-defined tags. Given an attribute path expression, say `date.year.month`, the labels `date`, `year`, and `month` may be metadata attributes or they may be tag names defined by the user.
- The value of a predicate may contain a string that is to be matched against the textual content of the Web document or it may contain an attribute path expression or tag element that imposes constraint over the structure of the Web document. Without a qualifier, it is not possible to distinguish whether the predicate is meant for the metadata, content, or structure of a Web document.

In order to resolve these ambiguities, we introduce the notion of a *predicate qualifier* as a component of a comparison-free predicate. A predicate qualifier may have any one of the following values, METADATA, CONTENT, and STRUCTURE, and the usage of a particular qualifier in a predicate is self-explanatory. That is, a predicate is either a metadata predicate of the form:

$$p(x) \equiv \texttt{METADATA}::x\,[\texttt{metadata\_attribute\_path\_exp}] \ \texttt{op} \ "V"$$

where V is a regular expression over the ASCII character set, or a content predicate of the form:

$$p(x) \equiv \texttt{CONTENT}::x\,[\texttt{content\_attribute\_path\_exp}] \ \texttt{op} \ "V"$$

It may also be a predicate on the structure of Web documents or hyperlinks. A *node structural predicate* imposes constraint(s) on the structure of Web documents and is of the form:

$$p(x) \equiv \texttt{STRUCTURE}::x\{[\texttt{structural\_attribute\_path\_exp}]\} \ \texttt{op} \ "V"$$

where x is a node type identifier, op is "SATISFIES", and V is a *collection* of tag element names or regular expressions over the tag element names. A *link structural predicate* is expressed in the form:

$$p(e) \equiv [\texttt{STRUCTURE}::e\{[\texttt{structural\_attribute\_path\_exp}]\} \ \texttt{op} \ "V"]$$

where e is a link type identifier, op $\in$ {"EXISTS_IN","SATISFIES"} and V can be an attribute path expression or a collection of tag element names.

4.2.3 Value of a Comparison-Free Predicate

The *value* of a comparison-free predicate depends on the predicate qualifier and *predicate operator*. As mentioned earlier, the value is a regular expression over the ASCII character set when the predicate qualifier is either METADATA or CONTENT. When the predicate qualifier is STRUCTURE, the value can be an attribute path expression or a *collection* of tag elements.

Observe that tags, tagless segments of data, and attributes associated with tags and metadata in Web documents are essentially collections of strings. Thus the metadata, content, and structure of Web documents and hyperlinks are expressed as a meaningful collection of strings. However, it is not always simple to *correctly* impose conditions on these strings. Defining a predicate value for finding documents containing the keyword *genetic disorder* is fairly simple. However, expressing predicates to locate documents containing information about job opportunities may not be simple. Due to the lack of central authority on the Web, some pages may use *job opportunities* while others may use *career opportunities* or *employment opportunities*. To enhance the ability to impose constraints on documents we allow the specification of predicate values using regular expressions. Appendix B depicts different types of regular expression operators supported in the predicate values.

Values for Content Comparison-Free Predicates

The value of a content predicate is either a string that will be matched with segments of data between tags or a set of attribute/value pairs that will be matched with the attribute/name value pairs of the specified element. We illustrate with examples of some of the possible values for content predicates that express tagless segments of data, tag attribute names, and their corresponding values.

Tagless Data

Let $p(x) \equiv$ CONTENT::x[attribute_path_exp] op "V" be a content predicate. Then the value of the predicate V for tagless segments of data can have any one of the following syntax.

1. V is a regular expression over the ASCII character set as discussed in the previous section. The following are examples of different values of content predicates.

    ```
    ":BEGIN_WORD: + treatment + :END_WORD:"
    ":START_STR: + brain tumou?r + :END_STR:"
    ":START_STR: + Zellw[ea]ger Disease + :END_STR:"
    ":START_STR: + (no cure)|(no treatment) + :END_STR:"
    "(:START_STR: + genetic disorder + :END_STR:)+"
    "(:BEGIN_WORD: + treatment + :END_WORD:){4, }"
    ```

    The first expression matches the word *treatment*; it does not match words where *treatment* is embedded as part of the word. The second expression matches the occurrence of keywords *brain tumor* or *brain tumour*. The next expression matches the occurrence of *Zellweger Disease* or *Zellwager Disease*. Here, we use :START_STR: and :END_STR: instead of :BEGIN_WORD: and :END_WORD:, respectively, as the string *Zellweger Disease* consists of two words. The fourth expression indicates that the keyword *genetic disorder* must occur one or more times. Finally, the last expression indicates that the keyword *treatment* must occur at least four times.

The next two values are used to match those strings that satisfy certain constraints.

```
":BEGIN_WORD: + MATCH(AE4).* + :END_WORD:"
":BEGIN_WORD: + UNMATCH(AE4).* + :END_WORD:"
```

The first value matches those documents that contain a word which begins with *AE4* followed by one or more characters. The next value identifies those words that do not contain the string *AE4*.

2. The predicate value can also be of the form $NEAR(v_1,v_2,m,n)$ where v_1 and v_2 are simple strings or regular expressions over the ASCII character set and m and n are integers. Such values are called *proximity values*. We now elaborate on the motivation of proximity values and their syntax. Due to the lack of central authority we observe the following cases in the Web. First, the same entities having web presence may be represented by different sets of keywords in different Web pages across different Web sites. For instance, the department of computer science for various universities may be listed as *Department of Computer Science*, *Computer Science Department*, or *Department of Computing Science* in different Web pages. Thus trying to express a unique and accurate set of keywords for searching for a certain expression may be difficult. Second, sometimes the accurate meaning and context of a keyword is determined by the appearance of other keywords in the proximity of the specified keyword. For example, in Figure 3.1 the occurrence of *dementia* in the neighborhood of the keyword *symptoms* may indicate that *dementia* is a symptom of the particular disease, i.e., *Alexander Disease*. Note that *dementia* occurring in various locations in different Web pages may be used in completely different contexts.

In order to express the above cases in a predicate we use *proximity values*. In $NEAR(v_1,v_2,m,n)$ v_1 and v_2 are keywords and m and n denote the minimum and maximum number of words separating v_1 and v_2. Note that n is mandatory in this expression. However, m is optional. For example, we may express constraints on the department of computer science that occur in different Web pages as follows.

```
"NEAR('Department', 'MATCH(Compu).* + :END_STR: + :BEGIN_WORD:
+ Science + :END_WORD:', 0, 3)"
```

The above expression matches those documents in which there are at most 3 words between the words *Department* and *Compu.* Science*. Observe that this expression matches the string *Department of Computer Science*, *Computer Science Department* and *Department of Computing Science*.

Similarly, the keyword *dementia* can be correlated with *symptoms* using the following proximity value in a predicate: "NEAR('*symptoms*', 'dementia', 1, 10)". This value matches those documents in which the minimum and maximum number of words separating the keywords *symptoms* and *dementia* are 1 and 10, respectively.

Attribute/Value Pairs

V can be used to express attribute/value pairs associated with elements. Formally, $V = \{(\alpha_{a_1}, \alpha_{v_1}), (\alpha_{a_2}, \alpha_{v_2}), \ldots, (\alpha_{a_n}, \alpha_{v_n})\}$ where α_{a_i} and α_{v_i} are regular expressions over attribute names and their corresponding values, respectively. Some examples of V are given below.

```
"[:BEGIN_WORD: + clerk + :END_WORD:, :BEGIN_WORD: + Smith +
:END_WORD:]"
"[:BEGIN_WORD: + clerk + :END_WORD:, :BEGIN_WORD: + Smith +
:END_WORD:],
[type + :END_STR:, :BEGIN_WORD: + (phone)|(web) + :END_WORD:]"
"[id + :END_STR:, MATCH(AE4).* + :END_STR:]"
"[:BEGIN_WORD: + complete + :END_WORD:, UNMATCH(yes).* + :END_STR:]"
"[:BEGIN_STR: + (clerk)?(staff) + :END_STR:, :BEGIN_WORD: +
Smith + :END_WORD:]"
"[id + :END_STR:, .*]"
```

The first expression indicates that the value of the tag attribute *clerk* is equal to *Smith*. The second expression specifies that the attribute *clerk* has the value *Smith* and the attribute *type* has the value *phone* or *web*. The next expression matches those documents where the tag attribute *id* has a value beginning with the string *AE4*. The fourth expression specifies that the value of the attribute *complete* must not start with the string *yes*. The next expression says that the attribute labeled *clerk* or *staff* has the value *Smith*. Finally, the last expression says that the attribute *id* can have any value.

Values for Metadata Comparison-Free Predicates

Metadata predicates are used to impose constraints on the metadata attributes of Web documents and hyperlinks. The value of a metadata predicate is a regular expression over the ASCII character set that is to be matched with the value of the specified metadata attribute. Note that the metadata attribute is specified using an attribute path expression. We illustrate the values of metadata predicates with some examples below.

```
"http://www[.]ntu[.]edu[.]sg/"
"(edu)|(com)"
"19.*"
```

Observe that in the first expression which specifies the value of a URL, the "." character needs to be treated specially because it is a metacharacter. Thus we use [ ] to express "." as a literal character.

Values for Structural Comparison-Free Predicates

Structural predicates impose constraints on the hierarchical structure of Web documents and hyperlinks and on the location of hyperlinks in the Web documents. There are two possible forms of values for structural predicates. V can be an attribute path expression when the predicate is imposed on link objects. For example, ul.li is a value of a link structural predicate. In addition , the value can be a collection of tag names or regular expressions over tag names. Let us illustrate the predicate values with some examples:

```
"{table}"
"{item ( itemno, itemdes, quantity)}"
"{purchase ( date, account?, item+)}"
"{customer ( name, date, order+)}, {name (first name, second name)}"
"{purchase (date, account, item/product)}"
```

The first expression specifies only one element, table. The next expression says that the element item has the subelements itemno, itemdes, and quantity. The third expression illustrates the use of regular expressions in element names. The element purchase contains an element date, followed by an optional element account, and one or more elements of type item. The next value indicates that the element customer contains the subelements name, date, and one or more order. Furthermore, the element name contains the subelements first name and last name. The last expression specifies that the element purchase contain a date element, an account element, and an item or product element.

Observe that the first expression (attribute path expression) imposes only structural constraints on a path of hierarchical structure of documents or hyperlinks. The subsequent values of V impose constraints on the tree structure of Web documents and hyperlinks.

4.2.4 Predicate Operators

We have introduced attribute path expressions, predicate qualifiers, and predicate values as components of a comparison-free predicate. We now discuss the final component, the *predicate operator*. We discuss different predicate operators for each type of predicate and illustrate them with examples. A synopsis of the set of predicate operators is given in Table 4.2.

The set of predicate operators depends on the type of comparison-free predicate, i.e., content, metadata, and structure. We first discuss the set of operators for content predicates and then proceed to discuss operators for metadata and structural predicates.

Predicate Operators for Content Predicates

Recall that attribute path expressions enable us to impose constraints on specific metadata and structural attributes without being fully aware of the complete structure of the Web documents. As HTML and XML elements may contain zero or more

Qualifier	Operator	Explanation	Examples
METADATA	EQUALS	Test equality for metadata attribute values	`METADATA::x[date.year] EQUALS "1999"`
CONTENT	ATTR_ENCL	Test if the specified attr/value pairs are the only attributes in the element	`CONTENT::z[customer] ATTR_ENCL "[customer id, 100025]"` `CONTENT::z[customer] ATTR_ENCL "[customer id, .*]"`
CONTENT	ATTR_CONT	Test if specified attr/value pair(s) are contained in the element	`CONTENT::z[purchase] ATTR_CONT [id, E-208765]`
CONTENT	NON-ATTR_ENCL	Test if specified value is enclosed as tagless data in the element	`CONTENT::z[item.itemdes] NON-ATTR_ENCL 3 1/2 Floppy Disk`
CONTENT	NON-ATTR_CONT	Test if specified value is contained in tagless data in the element	`CONTENT::z[item.itemdes] NON-ATTR_CONT ":START_WORD: + disk + :END_WORD:"`
CONTENT	CONT	Test if specified value is contained in tagless data or in the attr/value pairs in the element	`CONTENT::e[A] CONT ":START_WORD: + patients + :END_WORD:"`
STRUCTURE	SATISFIES	Test if the instances satisfy the specified structure	`STRUCTURE::z[item] SATISFIES "itemno, itemdes, quantity"`
STRUCTURE	EXISTS_IN	Test if the hyperlinks exist in the specified structure of the source document	`STRUCTURE::z EXISTS_IN "ul.li"`

Table 4.2. Synopsis of predicate operators.

sequences of attribute/value pairs and/or tagged subelements, an attribute path expression cannot distinguish between the attribute/value pair(s) associated with tagged elements and the textual content between tagged elements. For instance, the value *(id, c12356)* in a content predicate may appear as textual content between some tags or as an attribute/value pair. Moreover, the value V in a content predicate may be a *complete* or *partial* data segment, or a list of attribute/value pairs. For example, the keyword *Bayer* may occur as `<company>` *Bayer* `</company>` in some documents or as a portion of the text in the tagged element in others, i.e., `<company>` *Bayer Corporation* `</company>`.

We resolve these ambiguities by introducing five types of *predicate operators*; NON-ATTR_CONT, NON-ATTR_ENCL, ATTR_CONT, ATTR_ENCL, and CONT. Operators beginning with ATTR and NON-ATTR are used to distinguish between an attribute/value pair associated with an HTML or XML element and the textual content between a pair of tagged elements. Thus operators NON-ATTR_CONT and NON-ATTR_ENCL indicate constraints imposed on the textual content of documents or hyperlinks only, whereas operators ATTR_CONT and ATTR_ENCL indicate constraints imposed on attributes associated with tags only. The suffixes CONT and ENCL in these operators are used to further distinguish between partial and complete data segments in an element or in the attribute set associated with an element. Some examples of these

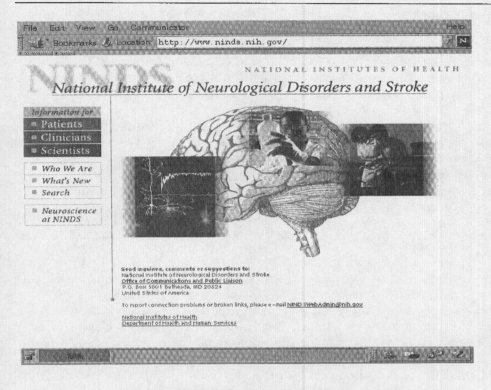

Fig. 4.4. Web page at www.ninds.nih.gov.

operators in the context of content predicates are:

```
NON-ATTR_CONT ":BEGIN_WORD: + treatment + :END_WORD:"
NON-ATTR_ENCL "Bayer"
ATTR_ENCL "[':START_STR: + id + :END_STR:',
':START_STR: + c12356 + :END_STR:']"
ATTR_CONT "[(':BEGIN_WORD: + id + :END_WORD:', .*)]"
```

The first expression indicates that the textual content of the document or hyperlink contains the keyword *treatment*. The second expression specifies that the segment of data enclosed between a specified element is equal to *Bayer*. Observe that as the predicate operator NON-ATTR_ENCL is used, it indicates that *Bayer* is the only tagless segment of data in the specified element. Moreover, as these two expressions contain predicate operators beginning with the prefix NON-ATTR, the values indicate textual content in Web documents or hyperlinks. The next expression indicates that the only attribute associated with the specified element is *id* and that its value is *c12356*. Finally, the last expression states that one of the attributes associated with the specified element is *id*. Note that *id* may have any arbitrary value. In the last two expressions, as the predicate operators contain the suffix ATTR, the values refer to attribute/value pairs.

We now describe the final operator CONT. It is used to impose constraints on the attribute/value pairs or the tagless segment of data but not both. It may seem that the operator CONT is superfluous in this context as the objective of CONT may be achieved by the operators ATTR_CONT and NON-ATTR_CONT. However, there exists *some disambiguity* that has motivated us to incorporate a separate operator in lieu of composite usage of ATTR_CONT and NON-ATTR_CONT. We explain this with an example. Suppose we wish to impose constraints on those hyperlinks (denoted by e) which have the string *patients* as anchor text or in the attribute/value pairs of the tags associated with the hyperlinks. Note that it may not be possible for a user to know the exact position of occurrence of the string *patients* ahead of time. An example of such a hyperlink is the graphic link "Patients" in the Web page at www.ninds.nih.gov as depicted in Figure 4.4. Intuitively, this condition on the hyperlinks can be imposed by the following predicates.

$p_1(e) \equiv$ CONTENT::e[A(.%)*] ATTR_CONT "MATCH(*patients*).*+:END_STR:"
$p_2(e) \equiv$ CONTENT::e[A(.%)*] NON-ATTR_CONT "MATCH(*patients*).*+:END_STR:"

The predicate $p_1(e)$ imposes a condition on the attribute/value pairs on the element A or on the subelements that are contained in A. It specifies that the attribute/value pair of the element A or a subelement of A must contain the string *patients*. The second predicate specifies that the anchor text of A must contain the string *patients*. Observe that the implication of these two predicates when combined is *conjunctive*. That is, a hyperlink satisfies the link type identifier e if its attribute/value pairs contain *patients* and also the anchor text between the A tag contains the keyword *patients*. However, we are typically interested in hyperlinks that satisfy one of the above constraints but not necessarily both. For example, reconsider the graphic link "Patients" in Figure 4.4. The source code of this hyperlink is given below.

```
<a
href= "patients/default.htm" onmouseout= "MM_swapImgRestore()"
onmouseover= "MM_swapImage('document.patients','document.patients',
'images/pat2.gif', 'document.mainrule', 'document.mainrule',
'images/patrule.gif', 'document.mainpop', 'document.mainpop',
'images/patpop.gif', '#927743526150')"><img src="images/pat1.gif"
name="patients" alt="Patients" border="0" width="108" height="22">
</a>
```

Observe that the element A contains an IMG element. It does not contain any textual data. The word *patients* appears as an attribute/value pair in IMG; i.e., it appears as the value of the attributes alt and name in the element IMG. Thus this hyperlink satisfies only the first predicate but not the second one. Hence it is not an instance of e. Clearly, this is not desirable in this context. In order to resolve this limitation, we introduce the operator CONT. An example of a comparison-free predicate containing this operator is $p(e) \equiv$ CONTENT::e[A(.%)*] CONT ":BEGIN_STR:+MATCH(*patients*).*+:END_STR:". This predicate specifies that the instances of e must contain the string *patients* in the anchor text or as a value of one of the tag attributes. Observe that in this case the conditions on tagless data and the value of tag attributes is disjunctive. One of them must be satisfied but not necessarily both. Hence the hyperlink "Patients" in Figure 4.4 is an instance of e. Later in Chapter 6, we show that in a query we only allow a set of predicates that are in conjunction.

One may think that similar to CONT, the operator ENCL may be used to impose constraints on the complete segment of tagless data or on the complete list of attribute/value pairs associated with elements. To elaborate further, let v be a data segment. Then, ENCL may be used to impose constraints on HTML or XML elements of the type: $\langle o_n \rangle v \langle /o_n \rangle$ or $\langle o_n \ v \rangle \cdots \langle /o_n \rangle$. Typically the predicate containing ENCL will be of the form $p(e) \equiv$ CONTENT::e[attribute_path_exp] ENCL "v". However, we do not include ENCL as one of the predicate operators as the syntax for imposing constraints on a complete list of attribute/value pairs is different from the data segment enclosed in a tag. Thus the predicate value v cannot exist as tagless data as well as attribute/value pairs. For instance, consider the following expressions.

```
ENCL "Bayer"
ENCL "[':START_STR: + id + :END_STR:',
      ':START_STR: + c12356 + :END_STR:']"
```

In the first expression, *Bayer* may appear as tagless data, but it cannot appear as an attribute/value pair. Note that it may be a value of a tag attribute or a tag attribute itself but it syntactically does not represent an attribute/value pair. Similarly, in the second expression *(id, c12356)* may be an attribute/value pair associated with an element but it is unlikely to be tagless data enclosed inside an element. Hence we do not envisage any practical usage of ENCL.

Predicate Operators for Metadata Comparison-Free Predicates

Note that unlike content predicates, metadata predicates do not have a set of attribute/value pairs associated with them. Each metadata attribute and its corresponding value is a string. Thus we do not use ATTR and NON-ATTR in the predicate operator of metadata predicates. There is only one predicate operator, EQUALS, to express metadata predicates. We now give a few examples.

```
EQUALS "edu"
EQUALS ".+[.]MATCH(xml + :END_STR:)"
EQUALS "sg|au"
```

The first expression states that one of the specified metadata attributes is equal to *edu*. The next expression says that the specified attribute matches those strings that end with *.xml*. The last expression specifies that the metadata attribute may have either of the values: *sg* or *au*.

Predicate Operators for Structure Comparison-Free Predicates

Structural predicates are used to impose constraints on the hierarchical structure of Web documents or hyperlinks and the location of the hyperlinks in the source Web documents. In order to distinguish between these two types, we define two operators SATISFIES and EXISTS_IN. Operator SATISFIES specifies constraints on the hierarchical structure of Web documents or hyperlinks and the operator EXISTS_IN imposes constraints on the location of link objects. We elaborate on these operators with the following examples:

```
SATISFIES "company(name, address, phone)"
EXISTS_IN "ul.li"
```

The first expression says that the company element contains the subelements name, address, and phone. The next expression specifies that the specified link objects are contained in a list.

4.3 Comparison Predicates

In the preceding sections, we have seen how to impose constraints on the metadata, content, and structure of a set of Web documents or hyperlinks using comparison-free predicates. Recall that a comparison-free predicate on node or link objects consists of four components: predicate qualifier, attribute path expression, predicate operator, and predicate value. One must specify each of these components correctly in order to impose meaningful constraints on the Web documents and hyperlinks. Typically, any predicate on node or link objects is based on a user's complete or partial knowledge of the predicate value.

Although it may seem that this type of value-driven predicate is sufficient to impose constraints on all Web documents and hyperlinks, this may not be the case in a web warehouse where data are not only retrieved from the Web but also manipulated locally. Sometimes it may be necessary to impose constraints without specifying the predicate value in order to evaluate *certain* queries. There are some major reasons for these types of *value-free* predicates. First, it may not be possible to specify a predicate value simply because there may not exist a fixed set of values or constraints that can be imposed on node or link objects. For instance, the user may not be aware of the value, if any, ahead of time. One may wish to retrieve documents whose title is also contained in one of the header tags. Observe that the title of the document may have any arbitrary value and that it is not realistic to assume that a user is aware of the value ahead of time. Second, it may be necessary to impose constraints on the *association* between two node and link type identifiers based on certain *conditions*. In a web warehouse, one may wish to identify those instances of a link x whose anchor text is contained in the anchor text of instances of a link y. This type of constraint cannot be specified by comparison-free predicates because there does not exist a fixed predicate value to correlate these hyperlinks, and the predicates discussed until now only impose constraints on a single node or link type identifier; it fails to define association between two node or link type identifiers.

In order to enhance the flexibility of predicates, we introduce the notion of *comparison predicates*. A comparison predicate imposes constraints on node or link objects when the predicate value is not known.

4.3.1 Components of a Comparison Predicate

A comparison predicate consists of the components: predicate qualifier, attribute path expression(s) or *data path(s)*, and *comparison_operator* for imposing constraints over node and/or link objects represented by two type identifiers. Let p be a comparison predicate, and x and y be node or link type identifiers. Then the following is a comparison predicate on x and y,

$$p(x,y) \equiv \texttt{predicate\_qualifier}::x\{[\texttt{path}]\} \ \texttt{comparison\_operator} \ y\{[\texttt{path}]\}$$

where the `predicate_qualifier` is identical to that of comparison-free predicates. The component `path` can be an attribute path expression or *data path*. The `comparison_operator` is used to specify the *types* of comparisons between the node or link type identifiers x and y. Note that the comparison of constraints on node and link type identifiers can be of the types: *containment*, *equality*, and *equality-containment*. The curly brackets are used to specify 0 or 1 occurrence. That is, the components, attribute path expression(s) and data path(s) may not occur always in a comparison predicate. For brevity, unless otherwise stated, a predicate refers to a comparison predicate. We now elaborate on the *data path* and *comparison operator* components of the comparison predicates. As we have discussed attribute path expressions and predicate qualifiers before in Sections 4.2.1 and 4.2.2, we do not elaborate on them further.

Similar to comparison-free predicates, we denote the arguments, predicate qualifier, data path(s), and value of a comparison predicate $p(x,y)$ as $arg(p)$, $qual(p)$, $path(p,x)$, $path(p,y)$, and $op(p)$, respectively. Two comparison-free predicates $p_1(x,y)$ and $p_2(a,b)$ are *identical* if $qual(p_1) = qual(p_2)$, $path(p_1,x) = path(p_2,a)$, $path(p_2,y) = path(p_2,b)$, and $op(p_1) = op(p_2)$.

Data Path

In Section 4.2.1, we introduced the notion of an attribute path expression. A *data path* is a special type of attribute path expression whose terminal label represents an atomic HTML or XML element. To elaborate further, let $A_d = o_{d_1}.o_{d_2}. \ldots .o_{d_n}$ be an attribute path expression where $o_{d_1} \leftarrow o_{d_2} \leftarrow \cdots \leftarrow o_{d_n}$. Then A_d is a data path if the element with label o_{d_n} in the Web documents or hyperlinks contains only a tagless segment of data; i.e., the element o_{d_n} is an atomic element and does not immediately contain any subelements. For instance, `html.head.title` is an example of a data path as `html` ← `head` ← `title` and the element with label `title` in HTML documents only contain a tagless segment of data. All data paths are attribute path expressions but the converse is not always true.

Similar to attribute path expressions, data paths can be *simple* or *regular*. A simple data path is identical to a simple attribute path expression and does not contain any regular expressions. Regular data paths are similar to regular attribute path expressions with one important difference: the terminal label cannot be a regular expression.

Comparison Operators

A comparison operator defines the *type* of comparison between the metadata, content, or structure of a Web document or hyperlink with that of another document or hyperlink. There are three types of correlation in the context of comparison predicates: *containment*, *equality*, and *equality-containment*. Containment correlation specifies that *some* properties related to metadata, content, or structure of instances of x are contained in the metadata, content, or structural properties of instances of y. Equality correlation specifies that certain properties of an instance of x are identical to those of an instance of y. Lastly, the equality-containment correlation is a *disjunctive* combination of the containment and equality association. It specifies that certain properties of an instance of x are contained in or are equal to some properties of an instance of y. We define the following operators: IS_CONTAIN, IS_EQUAL, and IS_CONT_EQUAL to specify these three types of correlations.

Given two node or link type identifiers x and y the comparison operator IS_CONTAIN is used to specify constraints on the containment of some properties of instances of x with respect to their metadata, content, and structure in y. For instance, let x represent a set of hyperlinks where the label of these links represents a drug name and y represent a set of Web documents containing information about different drugs. Then a comparison predicate with the IS_CONTAIN operator may be used to specify conditions on those instances of x whose label is contained in the title of the instances of y. That is, if a_1 is the label of x_1 (an instance of x) and t_1 is the title of y_1 (an instance of y) then the operator IS_CONTAIN is used to evaluate whether a_1 is contained in t_1; i.e., $a_1 \subset t_1$. The following comparison predicates depict the usage of the IS_CONTAIN comparison operator.

$$p(x,y) \equiv \text{METADATA}::x[\text{url.server}] \; \text{IS\_CONTAIN} \; y[\text{url}]$$
$$p(e,y) \equiv \text{CONTENT}::e[\text{A}] \; \text{IS\_CONTAIN} \; y[\text{html.head.title}]$$
$$p(x,y) \equiv \text{STRUCTURE}::x \; \text{IS\_CONTAIN} \; y$$

The first predicate is a constraint on the metadata of instances of x and y and specifies that the server name in the URL of an instance of x must be contained in the URL of an instance of y. The predicate $p(e,y)$ specifies that the anchor text of an instance of e must be contained in the title of an instance of y. The IS_CONTAIN operator in the last predicate specifies that the structure of an instance of x must be contained in the structure of an instance of y.

We now discuss the IS_EQUAL operator. Given two node or link type identifiers x and y, the IS_EQUAL operator is used to impose constraints on the equality of metadata, content, or structural properties of x with the corresponding properties in y. For instance, let x represent a set of hyperlinks where the label of each link represents a particular issue related to diseases (i.e., treatment, side effects, description, and so on). Let y represent a node type identifier where each instance of y contains a detailed description of a particular disease. Then an equality comparison operator, i.e., IS_EQUAL, may be used to identify those pairs of instances of x and y satisfying some equality conditions. For instance, it may be used to identify those instances of x and y where the label of x_1 (an instance of x) is equal to tagless data enclosed in a header tag in y_1 (an instance of y). That is, if a_1 is the label of

x_1 and h_1 is a header in y_1 then the IS_EQUAL operator can be used to evaluate if $a_1 = h_1$. Some examples of comparison predicates containing the IS_EQUAL operator are shown below.

$$p(x, y) \equiv \texttt{METADATA::}x\texttt{[url] IS\_EQUAL } y\texttt{[url]}$$
$$p(e, y) \equiv \texttt{CONTENT::}e\texttt{[A] IS\_EQUAL } y\texttt{[html(.\%)+.h\%]}$$
$$p(x, y) \equiv \texttt{STRUCTURE::}x \texttt{ IS\_EQUAL } y$$

The first predicate specifies that the URLs of instances of x must be identical to the URLs of instances of y. In the next example, the equality comparison operator is used to specify that the labels of instances of e must be equal to the data enclosed in a header tag in the instances of y. Finally, the last predicate is a comparison predicate on structural properties and the equality comparison operator is used to specify that the structure of an instance of x must be equal to the structure of an instance of y.

Lastly, we elaborate on the IS_CONT_EQUAL operator used to express an equality-containment correlation. From the nomenclature it is clear that this operator is used to express the containment and equality association between the properties of x and y. Note that the containment and equality correlation are in disjunctive form in IS_CONT_EQUAL. That is, a predicate containing this operator is evaluated true if containment or equality correlation between the node or link type identifiers, say x and y in the predicates, holds. It is not necessary for both of the correlations to be satisfied by instances of x and y. For example, the equality-containment operator can be used to identify those sets of hyperlinks whose label is equal to or is contained in the title of the documents pointed to by these hyperlinks. Similarly, IS_CONT_EQUAL may be used to identify those Web documents whose URL is equal to or contained in the URL of another document. Some examples of comparison predicates containing IS_CONT_EQUAL operator are shown below.

$$p(x, y) \equiv \texttt{METADATA::}x\texttt{[url] IS\_CONT\_EQUAL } y\texttt{[url]}$$
$$p(e, y) \equiv \texttt{CONTENT::}e\texttt{[A] IS\_CONT\_EQUAL } y\texttt{[html.head.title]}$$
$$p(x, y) \equiv \texttt{STRUCTURE::}x \texttt{ IS\_CONT\_EQUAL } y$$

The equality-containment operator in the first predicate specifies that the URL of an instance of x must be either equal to or contained in the URL of an instance of y. The next example says that the label of instances of e must be equal to or contained in the title of the documents represented by y. The last predicate containing an equality-containment operator is used to specify that the structure of an instance of x is either identical to the structure of an instance of y or contained in the structure of an instance of y.

4.3.2 Types of Comparison Predicates

In this section, we discuss different types of comparison predicates that are supported in WHOM. They are the *metadata, content,* and *structural* predicates based on the correlation constraints specified on the metadata, content, and structure of Web documents or hyperlinks, respectively. A synopsis of the different types of comparison predicates is shown in Table 4.3.

Predicate qualifier	Attribute path	Operator	Syntax
METADATA	Exist	IS_EQUAL, IS_CONTAIN, IS_CONT _EQUAL	$P(x,y) \equiv$ METADATA::$x[A_x]$ comp_op $y[A_y]$
CONTENT	Exist	IS_EQUAL, IS_CONTAIN, IS_CONT _EQUAL	$P(x,y) \equiv$ CONTENT::$x[A_x]$ comp_op $y[A_y]$
STRUCTURE	Optional	IS_EQUAL, IS_CONTAIN, IS_CONT _EQUAL	$P(x,y) \equiv$ STRUCTURE::$x\{[A_x]\}$ comp_op $y\{[A_y]\}$

Table 4.3. Synopsis of comparison predicates.

Metadata Comparison Predicates

A metadata comparison predicate specifies comparison conditions on the metadata of Web documents or hyperlinks. Let x and y be either node or link type identifiers. Then metadata comparison predicates on x and y are used to correlate some metadata properties of instances of x with those of instances of y. The syntax of a metadata comparison predicate is as follows.

$p(x,y) \equiv$ METADATA::x[metadata attribute path expression] comp_operator
$\qquad y$[metadata attribute path expression]

where comp_operator $\in \{$'IS_EQUAL', 'IS_CONTAIN', 'IS_CONT_EQUAL'$\}$ and $x \neq y$. For reasons similar to those in metadata comparison-free predicates, attribute path expressions in metadata comparison predicates are simple and do not contain regular path expressions.

Let us illustrate metadata comparison predicates. We begin with predicates containing a containment comparison operator as shown below.

$\qquad p_1(x,y) \equiv$ METADATA::x[url] IS_CONTAIN y[url]
$\qquad p_2(x,y) \equiv$ METADATA::x[url.server.name] IS_CONTAIN y[url]
$\qquad p_3(x,y) \equiv$ METADATA::x[url.filename] IS_CONTAIN y[url]

The first predicate specifies that the URL of an instance of x must be contained in the URL of an instance of y. For example, the document with URLs http://www.ntu.edu.sg/sas/ (an instance of x) and http://www.ntu.edu.sg/sas/research/ (an instance of y) satisfies this predicate. Predicate $p_2(x,y)$ says that an instance of x, i.e., x_1, and an instance of y, say y_1, satisfy this predicate if the name of the server of the URL of x_1 is contained in the URL of y_1. For instance, the documents with the above-mentioned URLs also satisfy $p_2(x,y)$ as the server name www.ntu is contained in http://www.ntu.edu.sg/sas/research/. The predicate $p_3(x,y)$ states that the file name in the URL of an instance of

x must be contained in the URL of an instance of y. For instance, the URLs
http://www.ntu.edu.sg/jobs.html and http://www.nus.edu.sg/jobs.html
represent documents that satisfy $p_3(x, y)$.

Note that not all metadata attribute path expressions in this context generate a
meaningful metadata comparison predicate. For instance, the following predicates
do not have any significance in the context of the web warehouse as they are never
satisfied when evaluated. That is, $p_{a,b}(x, y) =$ false for any arbitrary documents
or hyperlinks a and b.

$p_4(x, y) \equiv$ METADATA::x[url.filename] IS_CONTAIN y[url.filename]
$p_5(x, y) \equiv$ METADATA::x[url.server.domain name] IS_CONTAIN
    y[url.server.domain name]
$p_6(x, y) \equiv$ METADATA::x[size] IS_CONTAIN y[size]
$p_7(x, y) \equiv$ METADATA::x[date.month] IS_CONTAIN y[date.month]
$p_8(e, f) \equiv$ METADATA::e[link_type] IS_CONTAIN f[link_type]

Observe that $p_4(x, y)$ is never satisfied as the filename of a URL is suffixed by .html,
.htm, or .xml and hence cannot be contained in another file name. Similarly, the
domain name of a URL cannot be contained inside the domain name of another
URL and hence the predicate $p_5(x, y)$ is never satisfied. Based on similar reasons
the predicates $p_6(x, y)$, $p_7(x, y)$, and $p_8(e, f)$ are always evaluated false.

We now illustrate with examples of metadata predicates containing an equality
comparison operator. Consider the following predicates.

$p_9(x, y) \equiv$ METADATA::x[url] IS_EQUAL y[url]
$p_{10}(x, y) \equiv$ METADATA::x[url.server] IS_EQUAL y[url.server]
$p_{11}(x, y) \equiv$ METADATA::x[size] IS_EQUAL y[size]
$p_{12}(e, f) \equiv$ METADATA::e[link_type] IS_EQUAL f[link_type]

The first predicate specifies that the URL of an instance of x must be identical to
the URL of an instance of y. The predicate $p_{10}(x, y)$ indicates that the server of
an instance of x and y must be same. The next predicate says that the size of a
document representing x must be same as the size of a document representing y.
The last predicate $p_{12}(e, f)$ is defined on link objects and states that the link type
of an instance of e and f must be identical.

Observe that in metadata equality predicates the simple metadata attribute
path expressions associated with the two node or link type identifiers must be
identical in order to identify instances of node or link type identifiers that satisfy
the imposed constraints. If the metadata attribute path expressions are not identical
then the predicate will never be satisfied. For instance, the following predicates are
never satisfied for any Web document or hyperlink.

$p_{13}(x, y) \equiv$ METADATA::x[url] IS_EQUAL y[url.server]
$p_{14}(x, y) \equiv$ METADATA::x[size] IS_EQUAL y[url.filename]
$p_{15}(x, y) \equiv$ METADATA::x[url.server.name] IS_EQUAL y[url.server]
$p_{16}(e, f) \equiv$ METADATA::e[link_type] IS_EQUAL f[source_URL]

Lastly, we discuss metadata predicates containing the equality-containment
comparison operator. Note that unlike predicates containing equality and containment comparison operators, the application of an equality-containment comparison

operator in a metadata predicate is *limited*. That is, its usage is only meaningful for metadata predicates with *specific* metadata attribute paths. In fact, the following predicate is the only example for which the predicate may be evaluated true or false.

$$p_{14}(x, y) \equiv \texttt{METADATA::} x \texttt{[url]} \texttt{ IS\_CONT\_EQUAL } y \texttt{[url]}$$

This predicate specifies that the URL of an instance of x is either equal to the URL of an instance of y or it is contained in the URL of an instance of y. In all other cases, there is no need to use an equality-containment operator for imposing constraints on metadata. There are two major reasons for this.

- Metadata attribute path expressions containing the labels `date`, `size`, `link_type`, `file name`, and so on can only be evaluated meaningfully using the equality comparison operator. That is, the values of these metadata attributes for a document or hyperlink can never be contained in the corresponding attribute value for another document or hyperlink. Hence they can only be meaningfully evaluated using the `IS_EQUAL` operator.
- Attributes such as `server`, `name`, `domain name`, and so on can only be contained in the attributes `URL`, `source URL`, or `target URL`. The value of these attributes can never be equal to a URL. Hence they can only be evaluated meaningfully by the `IS_CONTAIN` operator.

Content Comparison Predicates

A content comparison predicate specifies comparison conditions on the textual content of Web documents or hyperlinks. Let x and y be either node or link type identifiers. Then content comparison predicates on x and y are used to correlate some textual content of instances of x with that of instances of y. The syntax of a content comparison predicate is as follows.

$$p(x, y) \equiv \texttt{CONTENT::} x \texttt{[data path]} \texttt{ comp\_operator}$$
$$y \texttt{[content attribute path expression]}$$

where `comp_operator` $\in \{$ '`IS_EQUAL`', '`IS_CONTAIN`', '`IS_CONT_EQUAL`'$\}$.

Observe that a data path instead of a content attribute path expression is associated with x as we want to restrict the containment of data specified in x to character data only. If we associate content attribute path expressions with x, then the data specified in x may not always be tagless segments of data in the instances of x. Some of the instances of x may contain tagged elements in the location specified by the content attribute path expression. In this case, the evaluation of the predicate involves not only content but also the hierarchical structure of Web documents or hyperlinks. However, our intention is to separate the structural constraints from the constraints on textual content.

We now illustrate content comparison predicates with some examples. We begin with content predicates containing the containment comparison operator. Consider the following predicates.

$$p_1(x,y) \equiv \texttt{CONTENT::} x\texttt{[body.p] IS\_CONTAIN } y\texttt{[html(.\%)+]}$$
$$p_2(x,y) \equiv \texttt{CONTENT::} x\texttt{[html(.\%)+.p] IS\_CONTAIN } y\texttt{[html(.\%)+]}$$
$$p_3(x,y) \equiv \texttt{CONTAIN::} x\texttt{[customer.name.first name] IS\_CONTAIN}$$
$$y\texttt{[employer(.\%)+.name]}$$
$$p_4(x,x) \equiv \texttt{CONTENT::} x\texttt{[head.title] IS\_CONTAIN } x\texttt{[html(.\%)+.h\%]}$$
$$p_5(e,f) \equiv \texttt{CONTENT::} e\texttt{[A] IS\_CONTAIN } f\texttt{[A]}$$

The first two predicates specify that the tagless data enclosed in a paragraph inside the body of a HTML document which is an instance of x must contain an instance of y. The predicate $p_3(x,y)$ imposes a constraint on XML documents. It specifies that instances of x must contain an element customer and a subelement name. The element name must contain an atomic element first name. Data enclosed in first name must contain the element name in the instances of y. The predicate $p_4(x,x)$ is an example of a comparison predicate on a single node type identifier x. It specifies that the title of the HTML documents representing instances of x must also be contained in a header in the documents. Finally, the last predicate is imposed over link objects and indicates that the label of an instance of e must be contained in the label of an instance of f.

Next we illustrate content comparison predicates containing equality or equality-containment comparison operators. Consider the following predicates.

$$p_6(x,y) \equiv \texttt{CONTENT::} x\texttt{[cancer-drugs(.\%)+.state] IS\_EQUAL}$$
$$y\texttt{[manufacturer.company(.\%)+.state]}$$
$$p_7(x,e) \equiv \texttt{CONTENT::} x\texttt{[html.head.title] IS\_EQUAL } e\texttt{[A]}$$
$$p_8(x,y) \equiv \texttt{CONTAIN::} x\texttt{[customer.name] IS\_CONT\_EQUAL}$$
$$y\texttt{[employer(.\%)+.name]}$$
$$p_9(e,f) \equiv \texttt{CONTENT::} e\texttt{[A] IS\_CONT\_EQUAL } f\texttt{[A]}$$

The first two content comparison predicates in the above example contain an equality comparison operator. The first predicate is on XML data. It specifies that the tagless data enclosed in element state, which is an instance of x and reached by the path matching cancer-drugs(.%)+.state, must be equal to some character data enclosed in the element state in an instance of y. The predicate $p_7(x,e)$ specifies that the title of an instance of x is identical to the label of a hyperlink represented by e. The next two predicates contain equality-containment comparison operators. The predicate $p_8(x,y)$ indicates that the tagless data inside the name element of an instance of x are either contained inside or are equal to the character data in the name element of an instance of y. Finally, the last predicate is imposed on link objects and indicates that the label of an instance of e must be either contained in or equal to the label of an instance of f.

Structural Comparison Predicates

Structural comparison predicates are used to specify comparison conditions on the hierarchical structure of Web documents or hyperlinks. Let x_1 and y_1 be instances of node type identifiers x and y, respectively. Then the structural comparison predicate on x and y specifies that the instances of x and y are *structurally related* based on some given condition.

```
⟨ cancer-drugs ⟩
   ⟨ name ⟩ ⟨ Beta Carotene ⟨/name ⟩
   ⟨ company ⟩
      ⟨ name ⟩ Bayer Corporation ⟨ /name ⟩
      ⟨ address ⟩
         ⟨ street ⟩ 400 Morgan Lane ⟨ /street ⟩
         ⟨ city ⟩ West Haven ⟨ /city ⟩
         ⟨ state ⟩ CT ⟨ /state ⟩
         ⟨ zip code ⟩ 06516 ⟨ /zip code ⟩
      ⟨ /address ⟩
      ⟨ phone ⟩
         ⟨ area code ⟩ 800 ⟨ /area code ⟩
         ⟨ number ⟩ 468-0894 ⟨ /number ⟩
      ⟨ /phone ⟩
   ⟨ /company ⟩
   ⟨ side effects ⟩
      Liver and skin problem. People who smoke appeared to be at increased risk
   ⟨ /side effects ⟩
⟨ /cancer-drugs ⟩
```

Fig. 4.5. An example of XML data containing cancer drug information.

The syntax of a structural comparison predicate is as follows.

$$p(x,y) \equiv \texttt{STRUCTURE::} x\{[A_x]\} \ \texttt{comp\_operator} \ y\{[A_y]\}$$

where $\texttt{comp\_operator} \in \{\texttt{`IS\_EQUAL'}, \texttt{`IS\_CONTAIN'}, \texttt{`IS\_CONT\_EQUAL'}\}$.
We can classify structural comparison predicates into the following types.

- **Type 1**: The syntax of this type of structural predicate is as follows.

$$p(x,y) \equiv \texttt{STRUCTURE::} x[\texttt{structural attribute path expression}]$$
$$\texttt{comp\_operator} \ y[\texttt{structural attribute path expression}]$$

Let $T_s(x_1)$ and $T_s(y_1)$ be the NSTs or LSTs of x_1 (an instance of x) and y_1 (an instance of y), respectively. Type 1 of structural predicates specifies that a subtree of $T_s(x_1)$, whose root is reachable by the corresponding structural attribute path expression, is contained in (in the case where the comparison operator is IS_CONTAIN) or equal to (when the comparison operator is IS_EQUAL) a subtree of $T_s(y_1)$, whose root is *specified* by the structural attribute path expression associated with y. We now elaborate on how the root of the subtrees is specified in the predicate. Let $A_x = o_{x_1}.o_{x_2}\ldots o_{x_n}$ and $A_y = o_{y_1}.o_{y_2}\ldots o_{y_k}$ be the structural attribute path expressions associated with x and y, respectively. Observe that A_x and A_y are used to specify the location of the roots of the subtrees of the NSTs or LSTs of instances of x and y, respectively. Specifically, the terminal labels of A_x and A_y, i.e., o_{x_n} and o_{y_k}, respectively, represent the labels of the roots of the subtrees in the NSTs or LSTs. The structural attribute path expressions A_x and A_y specify the path in NSTs or LSTs that must be matched to reach the root nodes of the subtrees.

- **Type 2**: The syntax of this type of structural predicate is as follows:

    $p(x, y) \equiv$ STRUCTURE::x[structural attribute path expression]
    comp_operator y

    Let $T_s(x_1)$ and $T_s(y_1)$ be the NSTs or LSTs of x_1 (an instance of x) and y_1 (an instance of y), respectively. The above type of structural predicate specifies that a subtree of $T_s(x_1)$ whose root is reachable by the attribute path expression is contained in or equal to $T_s(y_1)$.

- **Type 3**: The syntax of this type of structural predicate is as follows.

    $p(x, y) \equiv$ STRUCTURE::x comp_operator
    y[structural attribute path expression]

    Type 3 of structural predicates is the inverse of Type 2 and specifies that $T_s(x_1)$ is contained in or equal to a subtree of $T_s(y_1)$ whose root is reachable by the attribute path expression associated with y.

- **Type 4**: Finally, the last case does not contain any structural attribute path expressions. The syntax of this type of structural predicate is as follows.

    $p(x, y) \equiv$ STRUCTURE::x comp_operator y

    That is, $T_s(x_1)$ is contained in or equal to $T_s(y_1)$.

Note that there is an important difference between structural predicates containing IS_CONTAIN and IS_EQUAL comparison operators. The terminal labels of structural attribute path expressions A_x and A_y for predicates containing the IS_CONTAIN comparison operator may not be identical, whereas, for predicates containing the IS_EQUAL comparison operator, the terminal labels must be identical. For example, the following predicates are valid.

$p_1(x, y) \equiv$ STRUCTURE::x[manufacturers.company]
    IS_CONTAIN y[cancer-drugs]
$p_2(x, y) \equiv$ STRUCTURE::x[manufacturers.company] IS_EQUAL
    y[cancer-drugs.company]

Observe that the terminal labels for attribute path expressions in $p_1(x, y)$, i.e., company and cancer-drugs, are not identical. However, the terminal labels in $p_2(x, y)$ containing the IS_EQUAL operator are the same.

For each category of structural comparison predicates we depict different examples based on different types of comparison operators. We begin with Case 1.

Case 1: Consider the following structural comparison predicates.

$p_1(x, y) \equiv$ STRUCTURE::x[manufacturer.company] IS_CONTAIN
    y[cancer-drugs]
$p_2(x, y) \equiv$ STRUCTURE::x[html(.%)+.table] IS_CONTAIN y[html.body.p]
$p_3(x, y) \equiv$ STRUCTURE::x[manufacturer.company] IS_EQUAL
    y[cancer-drugs.company]
$p_4(x, y) \equiv$ STRUCTURE::x[manufacturer.company] IS_CONT_EQUAL
    y[cancer-drugs]

Assuming that the x and y are node type identifiers, the first predicate specifies the following.

- The NST of an instance of x and y must contain the paths `manufacturer.company` and `cancer-drugs` respectively.
- The subtree with root labeled `company` in the NST of an instance of x must be contained in the subtree with root `cancer-drugs` in the NST of an instance of y.

For instance, consider the XML-data in Figures 2.11 and 4.5. The NSTs of the data are shown in Figures 3.15 and 4.6(a), respectively. Observe that these figures contain the paths `manufacturer.company` and `cancer-drugs`, respectively. Hence Figures 2.11 and 4.5 are instances of x and y, respectively. Moreover, the subtree with root labeled `company` having identifier $w102$ in Figure 3.15 is contained in Figure 4.6(a) (the subtree with root $a1000$). Hence these two instances of XML data satisfy the predicate $p_1(x, y)$.

Case 2: We now illustrate Case 2 type structural predicates. Consider the following predicates.

$$p_5(x, y) \equiv \texttt{STRUCTURE::}x\,\texttt{[manufacturer.company] IS\_CONTAIN } y$$
$$p_6(x, y) \equiv \texttt{STRUCTURE::}x\,\texttt{[html(.\%)+.table] IS\_CONTAIN } y$$
$$p_7(x, y) \equiv \texttt{STRUCTURE::}x\,\texttt{[manufacturer.company] IS\_EQUAL } y$$
$$p_8(x, y) \equiv \texttt{STRUCTURE::}x\,\texttt{[manufacturer.company] IS\_CONT\_EQUAL } y$$

The first predicate says that an instance of x must contain a path `manufacturer.company`. Moreover, the subtree rooted at the node labeled `company` in the instance of x must be contained in the NST of an instance of y. For example, consider the NST in Figure 3.15 of the Web data in Figure 2.11. It contains a path `manufacturer.company` and hence it is an instance of x. Let Figure 4.6(a) be an instance of y. Observe that the subtree rooted at `company` in Figure 3.15 is the same as the subtree rooted at the tree node `company` ($a1000$) in Figure 4.6(a). Hence these two documents satisfy $p_5(x, y)$. The next predicate $p_6(x, y)$ specifies that the subtree rooted on the node labeled `table` in an instance of x must be contained in the NST of an instance of y. The predicate $p_7(x, y)$ is similar to $p_5(x, y)$ except that the comparison operator is `IS_EQUAL`. For example, let Figure 4.6(b) be the NST of an instance of y. Then the instances of x and y with NSTs in Figure 3.15 and 4.6(b) satisfy the predicate $p_7(x, y)$. The last predicate is used to illustrate the usage of the `IS_CONT_EQUAL` operator and specifies that the subtree rooted at node `company` is contained in or equal to the NST of an instance of y.

Case 3: Case 3 is the inverse of Case 2. Some examples of Case 3 are shown below.

$$p_9(x, y) \equiv \texttt{STRUCTURE::}x\ \texttt{IS\_CONTAIN } y\,\texttt{[cancer-drugs]}$$
$$p_{10}(x, y) \equiv \texttt{STRUCTURE::}x\ \texttt{IS\_EQUAL } y\,\texttt{[cancer-drugs.company]}$$
$$p_{11}(x, y) \equiv \texttt{STRUCTURE::}x\ \texttt{IS\_CONT\_EQUAL } y\,\texttt{[cancer-drugs]}$$

The predicate $p_9(x, y)$ specifies that the NST of an instance of x is contained as a subtree or portion of the subtree rooted at the node labeled `cancer-drugs` in the NST of an instance of y. Similarly, the predicates $p_{10}(x, y)$ and $p_{11}(x, y)$ are examples of equality or containment of the NST of an instance of x in the specified subtree of the NST of an instance of y.

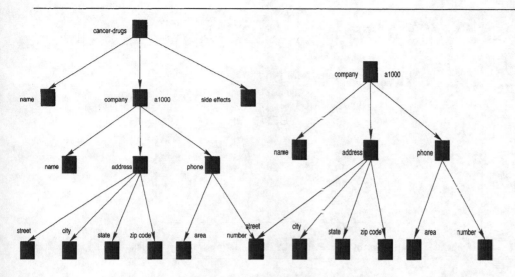

(a) NST for XML-data in Figure 4.5.   (b) NST for XML-data in Figure 4.7.

Fig. 4.6. NSTs of XML data.

Case 4: In Case 4 there is no structural attribute path expression in the structural comparison predicates. Hence there can be only three possible forms of Case 4 type structural comparison predicates as shown below.

$$p_{12}(x,y) \equiv \texttt{STRUCTURE}::x \text{ IS\_CONTAIN } y$$
$$p_{13}(x,y) \equiv \texttt{STRUCTURE}::x \text{ IS\_EQUAL } y$$
$$p_{14}(x,y) \equiv \texttt{STRUCTURE}::x \text{ IS\_CONT\_EQUAL } y$$

Predicate $p_{12}(x,y)$ states that the NST of an instance of x must be contained in the NST of an instance of y. Figures 4.6(b) and 4.6(a) are examples of NSTs of an instance of x and y, respectively, satisfying $p_{12}(x,y)$. Predicate $p_{13}(x,y)$ specifies that the NST of an instance of x must be equal to the NST of an instance of y. Finally, the last predicate indicates that the NST of an instance of x must be contained in or equal to the NST of an instance of y.

4.4 Summary

In this chapter, we have discussed the notion of predicates on node and link objects. A predicate is a mechanism for expressing those portions of Web data a query or other retrieval task should or should not match. We have presented two types of predicates: comparison-free and comparison predicates. Each of these predicates is further classified into metadata, content, or structural predicates based on the constraints imposed on the metadata, content, or structure of the Web data, respectively. Note that predicates only impose conditions on the metadata, structure, and content of Web documents and hyperlinks, and they do not impose constraints

⟨ company ⟩
    ⟨ name ⟩ Bayer Corporation ⟨ /name ⟩
    ⟨ address ⟩
        ⟨ street ⟩ 400 Morgan Lane ⟨ /street ⟩
        ⟨ city ⟩ West Haven ⟨ /city ⟩
        ⟨ state ⟩ CT ⟨ /state ⟩
        ⟨ zip code ⟩ 06516 ⟨ /zip code ⟩
    ⟨ /address ⟩
    ⟨ phone ⟩
        ⟨ area code ⟩ 800 ⟨ /area code ⟩
        ⟨ number ⟩ 468-0894 ⟨ /number ⟩
    ⟨ /phone ⟩
⟨ /company ⟩

Fig. 4.7. An example of XML data containing company information.

on interdocument relationships. In the next chapter, we introduce the notion of *connectivities* to express the hyperlinked connection between the node and link objects.

Imposing Constraints on Hyperlink Structures

In Chapter 4, we have seen how to impose constraints on a set of Web documents or hyperlinks using predicates. In this chapter, we introduce the notion of *connectivities* to express the hyperlinked connection between the node and link objects.

5.1 Introduction

Given a node or link type identifier x, a predicate $p(x)$ enables us to identify a set of documents or hyperlinks that conform to $p(x)$. That is, all documents or hyperlinks for which $p(x)$ is evaluated to be true belong to the node or link type identifier x. Hence a predicate in WHOM enables us to *categorize* a set of documents or hyperlinks into different types based on their metadata, content, or structural properties. To elaborate further, suppose the following set of predicates is defined to impose constraints on a set of documents and hyperlinks denoted as D and H, respectively.

$$p_1(x) \equiv \texttt{METADATA::x[url] EQUALS}$$
$$\texttt{"}http{:}//rex[.]nci[.]nih[.]gov{/}SQUAREFIELD3[.]html\texttt{"}$$
$$p_2(z) \equiv \texttt{CONTENT::z[html.head.title] NON-ATTR\_CONT}$$
$$\texttt{":BEGIN\_WORD: + } tumour \texttt{ + :END\_WORD:"}$$
$$p_3(e) \equiv \texttt{CONTENT::e[A] NON-ATTR\_ENCL "} Treatment\ Statements \texttt{"}$$

The above predicates categorize some of the documents in D into two types, x and z. Type x represents a document whose URL is equal to $http{:}//rex.nci.nih.gov/$ $SQUAREFIELD3.html$. Also, there can be only one node object or Web document that satisfies $p_1(x)$. Type z represents a set of documents where the title of each document contains the keyword *tumour*. Note that these two categories do not necessarily classify all documents in D. Similarly, some of the hyperlinks in H are represented as type e. The anchor text of these hyperlinks is *treatment statement*. Note that similar to the documents in D, the labels of some of the hyperlinks embedded in documents in D may not be equal to *treatment statement*.

It may seem that predicates are sufficient to retrieve and manipulate relevant information from the Web. This belief stems from the increasing popularity of search engines for locating information on the Web. A user's query is formulated by specifying a set of keywords analogous to values in a comparison-free predicate. For a user, predicates are a more comprehensive, expressive, and flexible mechanism than keyword-based search techniques on the Web.

Although predicates are useful for expressing query conditions, they are not a sufficient mechanism for expressing all *types* of conditions in the context of the Web. Predicates can only impose conditions on the metadata, structure, and content of Web documents and hyperlinks. They do not impose constraints on how these documents are connected to one another. We elaborate on this with an example. Consider again the above predicates. Note that these predicates are sufficient to categorize the set of documents and hyperlinks to different types based on the metadata, content, or structural properties of these documents or hyperlinks. Suppose we wish to identify those documents of type z that are directly or indirectly linked from the document of type x. In particular, one of the hyperlinks between an instance of x and z must be of type e. That is, we wish to determine those documents whose title contains the keyword *tumour* and are linked from the Web page at *http://rex.nci.nih.gov/SQUAREFIELD3.html* via a hyperlink labeled **treatment statement**. Note that some of the documents of type z may not be reached from the document of type x. There may also exist instances of z that may be reached from the instance of x without following any hyperlink labeled *treatment statement*. For instance, since the title of the Web page at http://www.ncl.ac.uk/ nchwww/guides/guide2w.htm is *Wilms' Tumour Resources*, it is an instance of z. However, this page cannot be reached from http://rex.nci.nih.gov/SQUAREFIELD3.html by following the hyperlinks embedded in this page. Hence the predicates are not sufficient to impose conditions on the hyperlinked structure of a set of Web documents.

In order to exploit interdocument relationships, i.e., the hyperlink structures of Web documents, we need to define a way to specify the interlinked structure of relevant Web documents. This is achieved by *connectivities*. This limitation of predicates is not visible in a traditional search engine-based query because search engines do not exploit interdocument connectivity. They only return a set of disconnected documents satisfying the query conditions. With the tremendous growth of the number of available relevant documents in a specified area in different Web sites, it is imperative to be able to exploit these interlinked structures of relevant Web data.

Traditionally, in the field of graph theory, the term connectivity of a connected graph refers to the minimum number of vertices whose removal disconnects the graph or reduces the graph to a single vertex [11]. However, in this book, we do not use the notion of connectivities in this context. Informally, a *connectivity* is a way to impose conditions on the interlinked structure of relevant Web documents in order to exploit interdocument relationships. Connectivity is a mechanism to specify conditions that documents of type z can be reached from documents of type x via a set of hyperlinks represented by one or more link type identifiers.

The remainder of this chapter is organized as follows. Section 5.1.1 presents a brief overview of the notion of connectivities. Section 5.1.2 addresses the inherent difficulties associated with modeling connectivities. Based on these difficulties,

Section 5.1.3 identifies the features that are required in connectivities. We identify various components, i.e., *source and target node type identifiers* and *link path expressions*, of a connectivity in Section 5.2. We introduce two types of connectivities, *simple* and *complex*, and illustrate them with examples in Section 5.3. In Section 5.4, we show how different types of *complex* connectivities are transformed into a set of *simple* connectivities. Section 5.5 presents the *conformity conditions* of a connectivity. Finally, the last section summarizes this chapter.

5.1.1 Overview

In this section, we provide a brief overview of a connectivity or connectivity element. A connectivity is a predicate on the interdocument relationship of one or two classes of Web documents. To define a connectivity element, one first categorizes the set of documents and hyperlinks into different types by using a set of predicates. Then connectivities are defined by using the type identifiers of these documents and hyperlinks. Intuitively, a connectivity consists of three components: a *source identifier*, a *target identifier*, and a *link path expression*. We illustrate these components informally now. The detailed treatment follows in Sections 5.2.1 and 5.2.2.

A connectivity k is an expression of the form: $x \equiv s\langle\rho\rangle t$, where s is the *source node type identifier* (*source identifier*, in short), t is the *target node type identifier* (*target identifier* in short) and ρ is called a *link path expression*, which is essentially a sequence of link type identifiers that may include regular expressions, e.g., e, efg, $ef\{1,3\}$. The angle brackets around ρ are used for delimitation purposes only. Note that the connectivity $s\langle\rho\rangle t$ specifies how the instances of s are connected to the instances of t. The interlinked structure between an instance of s and t identifiers is specified by the link path expression. Throughout this book, we denote the source and target identifiers of a connectivity k as $lnode(k)$ and $rnode(k)$, respectively. The set of link type identifiers in ρ is denoted as $link(k)$.

A connectivity element is categorized into two types: *simple* and *complex*. A *simple* connectivity contains only a *simple* link path expression. By a simple link path expression we mean that there are no regular expressions defined over it. Hence a simple connectivity contains only one link type identifier in the link path expression. For instance, $x\langle e\rangle y$ is a simple connectivity. On the other hand, in a complex connectivity, the link path expression may contain regular expressions. For instance, $x\langle efgh\rangle y$, $x\langle(ef?)|(g-)\rangle y$, $x\langle e-\{1,5\}\rangle y$ are examples of complex connectivities.

5.1.2 Difficulties in Modeling Connectivities

The modeling of interdocument relationships causes serious difficulties when working with heterogeneous, autonomous Web documents. The reasons are as follows.

Necessity of Node Type Identifiers

The definition of a connectivity requires node type identifiers. Recall that a predicate requires the instances of a node or link type identifier to satisfy the specified constraints. However, in reality it may not be possible for a user to specify the properties associated with the metadata, content, and structure of a set of nodes or links ahead of time without inspecting each instance. There may exist common constraints of which the user may not be aware. Thus it may not be possible to bind a node or link type identifier with one or more predicates. Consequently, due to the lack of existence of node type identifiers, it is not possible to define a connectivity to express the hyperlink structure of these documents. For instance, consider the Web page at the Web site `http://www.ninds.nih.gov/` containing a list of neurological diseases. Each disease is the anchor of a link that connects to a Web page containing details about the disease. Observe that the anchors of the disease do not share any common keyword. Furthermore, the diseases are organized in the Web page as a list of items. The structure of these links is shown in Figure 5.1. Suppose a user wishes to bind all these links related to diseases using a link type identifier, say d. However, it may not be possible to enforce a meaningful predicate on d simply because the user may not be aware of any common properties to bind these links ahead of time. To elaborate further, it may not be possible for a user to know the organizational structure of these links to various diseases ahead of time without viewing the Web page. Note that a predicate of the form given below may be used to bind these hyperlinks.

$$p(d) \equiv \texttt{STRUCTURE::}d \ \texttt{EXISTS\_IN} \ \texttt{"}ul.li\texttt{"}$$

But the user must be familiar with the structure of the page in order to impose such a predicate.

Consequently, due to the lack of existence of node type identifiers, it is not possible to define a connectivity to express the hyperlinked structure of these documents. Therefore identification of a set of node type identifiers by defining predicates over them is an important factor in specifying a set of connectivities.

Prior Knowledge of Interdocument Structure

Even if we are able to identify node or link predicates, one must also possess partial or complete knowledge about the hyperlink structure in order to specify a connectivity. For example, suppose we classify some of the relevant documents and hyperlinks into x, z, and e based on a set of predicates. To specify the interdocument structure between the documents of type x and z, one must know how documents of type x are connected to documents of type z. Note that the connectivities between x and z can be expressed as any of the expressions: $x\langle e \rangle z$, $x\langle - \rangle z$, $x\langle -\{0,5\} \rangle z$, $x\langle -e \rangle z$, $x\langle e(-)\{1,5\} \rangle z$, and so on. The selection of one of these expressions depends on the user's perception of the interdocument structure between x and z.

Lack of Homogeneous Interlinked Structure

It may not be possible to impose a meaningful constraint that is satisfied by all node or link objects simply because there may not exist such a constraint. This may happen because the content and interlinked structure of Web documents in different Web sites are different. Thus it may not be possible to enforce a rigid interlinked structure of node and link objects. For instance, consider the Web page at the Web

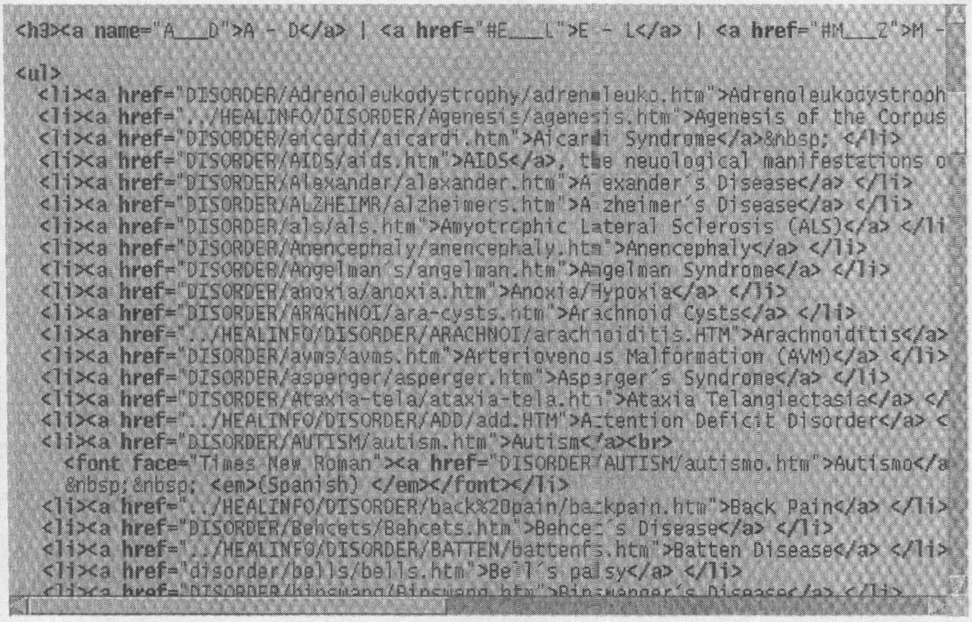

```
<h3><a name="A___D">A - D</a> | <a href="#E___L">E - L</a> | <a href="#M___Z">M -

<ul>
  <li><a href="DISORDER/Adrenoleukodystrophy/adrenoleuko.htm">Adrenoleukodystroph
  <li><a href="../HEALINFO/DISORDER/Agenesis/agenesis.htm">Agenesis of the Corpus
  <li><a href="DISORDER/aicardi/aicardi.htm">Aicardi Syndrome</a>  </li>
  <li><a href="DISORDER/AIDS/aids.htm">AIDS</a>, the neuological manifestations o
  <li><a href="DISORDER/Alexander/alexander.htm">Alexander's Disease</a> </li>
  <li><a href="DISORDER/ALZHEIMR/alzheimers.htm">Alzheimer's Disease</a> </li>
  <li><a href="DISORDER/als/als.htm">Amyotrophic Lateral Sclerosis (ALS)</a> </li
  <li><a href="DISORDER/Anencephaly/anencephaly.htm">Anencephaly</a> </li>
  <li><a href="DISORDER/Angelman's/angelman.htm">Angelman Syndrome</a> </li>
  <li><a href="DISORDER/anoxia/anoxia.htm">Anoxia/Hypoxia</a> </li>
  <li><a href="DISORDER/ARACHNOI/ara-cysts.htm">Arachnoid Cysts</a> </li>
  <li><a href="../HEALINFO/DISORDER/ARACHNOI/arachnoiditis.HTM">Arachnoiditis</a>
  <li><a href="DISORDER/avms/avms.htm">Arteriovenous Malformation (AVM)</a> </li>
  <li><a href="DISORDER/asperger/asperger.htm">Asperger's Syndrome</a> </li>
  <li><a href="DISORDER/Ataxia-tela/ataxia-tela.htm">Ataxia Telangiectasia</a> </
  <li><a href="../HEALINFO/DISORDER/ADD/add.HTM">Attention Deficit Disorder</a> <
  <li><a href="DISORDER/AUTISM/autism.htm">Autism</a><br>
    <font face="Times New Roman"><a href="DISORDER/AUTISM/autismo.htm">Autismo</a
       <em>(Spanish) </em></font></li>
  <li><a href="../HEALINFO/DISORDER/back%20pain/backpain.htm">Back Pain</a> </li>
  <li><a href="DISORDER/Behcets/Behcets.htm">Behcet's Disease</a> </li>
  <li><a href="../HEALINFO/DISORDER/BATTEN/battenfs.htm">Batten Disease</a> </li>
  <li><a href="disorder/bells/bells.htm">Bell's palsy</a> </li>
```

Fig. 5.1. Structure of the Web page containing disease-related links.

site **www.lycos.com** containing a list of AIDS-related Web sites. Each link is an anchor of a link that connects to a Web site containing details about AIDS. For instance, the link **AIDS-HIV-GIS** points to the Web site at **www.aegis.com** which is one of the largest HIV-AIDS databases in the world. Note that the architecture of these AIDS-related Web sites are different from each other. In fact, there does not exist a common architectures of these heterogeneous Web sites. A partial view of the structure of these Web sites is shown in Figure 5.2.

Suppose we have downloaded a set of interlinked documents related to information about the treatment of AIDS (Figure 5.2). Observe that the interdocument structure of each Web site is different from the other. Suppose a user wishes to specify the interlinked structure of these nodes and links related to diseases using a set of connectivities. However, in reality, this may not be possible due to the heterogeneous structure of different Web sites. That is, there may not exist some meaningful common properties to bind all the nodes and links. For example, the links labeled "Medical" in Figure 5.2 cannot be bound to a single link type identifier as it does not appear in all instances. Hence, as the number of different Web sites grows, the likelihood of any specific interdocument structure specified by connectivities being valid for all sites may drop sharply.

Lack of Necessity for Knowledge of Hyperlink Properties

There may not be a need to specify constraints on link objects because they may not be relevant to the user. For example, consider the Web page at

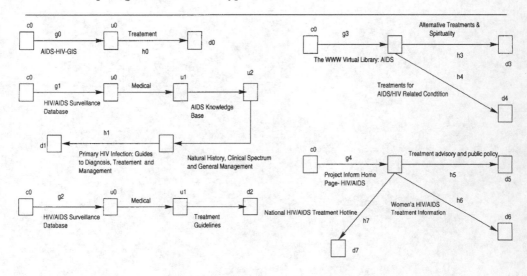

Fig. 5.2. Partial structure of AIDS-related Web sites.

http://www.druginfonet.com/maninfo.htm which connects a user to several pharmaceutical manufacturers. Suppose a user wishes to find information about all "products" that are sold by different manufacturers. There are two node type identifiers x and y with the following predicates that are relevant to the user.

$p(x) \equiv$ METADATA::x[url] EQUALS
    "$http://www[.]druginfonet[.]com/maninfo[.]htm$"
$p(y) \equiv$ CONTENT::y[body.(%)*] NON-ATTR_CONT ":BEGIN_WORD: + $products?$
    + :END_WORD:"

Note that the links between the instances of x and y are irrelevant to the user and hence there is no necessity to capture common properties using predicates.

5.1.3 Features of Connectivities

Based on the above difficulties, we now identify a set of features that must be supported by a connectivity element.

Interconnectivity Based on Node and Link Type Identifiers

Given a set of documents and hyperlinks, we specify the interdocument connectivity of the node and link objects in terms of their node and link type identifiers. It must not be expressed at the instance level because a set of documents may share the same connectivity structure and expressing connectivity for each of these documents is cumbersome and repetitive. Hence each connectivity must express the hyperlinked structure of a group of documents.

Connectivities Between Nonadjacent Node Objects

A connectivity must be able to express hyperlinked structure between nonadjacent node objects. As we have seen in the preceding section, it is not always possible to identify the properties of all the node and link objects by defining predicates over them. We illustrate this with an example. Suppose we have a set of documents and hyperlinks denoted by D and H, respectively. Let some of the documents in D be instances of node type identifiers x and y. Similarly, suppose some the hyperlinks in H are instances of link type identifiers e, f, and g. Suppose each instance of x is connected to an instance of y by following the sequence of links of type e, f, and g, respectively. In this case, an instance of x is not adjacent to an instance of y. In fact, following a link of type e from an instance of x leads to a node object whose property is not specified by any predicate.

Heterogeneous Hyperlink Structure

Recall from the previous section that the hyperlinked structure between documents can be heterogeneous in nature. A connectivity must be able to express such irregular heterogeneous structures. For example, the instances of node types x and y may be connected through hyperlinks of type e and f. Or they may be connected directly via links of type g. It may also be possible that some instances of x and y are connected by one or more links of type e. A connectivity must be able to express such irregular structures clearly and compactly.

Connectivity Based on Partial Knowledge

A user should be able to impose constraints on interdocument connectivity based on *zero* or partial knowledge of the hyperlink structure of the documents. For instance, if x and y are node type identifiers of two sets of documents, then a connectivity must be able to express the hyperlinked structure between instances of x and y based on zero knowledge of how these documents are connected. By zero knowledge, we mean no knowledge about the hyperlinked structure between instances of x and y; it does not indicate the lack of knowledge of the properties of node objects represented by source or target node identifiers.

A connectivity should also be able to express connectivities based on partial knowledge. It is not always necessary to know the exact interlinked structure between sets of documents in order to specify a connectivity. For instance, a user may be aware that the instances of x are connected to instances of y via the hyperlinks represented by link type identifiers e or f. However, he or she may not be sure of the exact type of the hyperlink between an instance of x and y.

5.2 Components of Connectivities

In this section, we discuss the components of a connectivity and show how the above features are incorporated.

5.2.1 Source and Target Identifiers

The source and target identifiers of a connectivity represent the initial and terminal sets of interconnected node objects, respectively. Source or target node type identifiers can be classified into *bound* and *free* identifiers. Node instances of a *bound* type identifier share some *common properties* in terms of their metadata, content, or structure. Some of these properties are expressed explicitly using predicates. A *free* type identifier does not have any predicate defined over it; i.e., there are no conditions in terms of metadata, content, or structure imposed by the user on the node instances of the free type identifier. In WHOM, we denote a free node type identifier using the special symbol "#". When there is a need to further differentiate free identifiers, we use $\#_1$, $\#_2$, and so on. Note that instances of free type identifiers represent arbitrary nodes.

5.2.2 Link Path Expressions

A link path expression specifies how a set of documents is connected to another set of documents. We begin by defining *simple* and *complex link components* that are used for defining link path expressions. We then classify link path expressions into *simple* and *regular*.

A *simple link component* is a link type identifier that represents a set of hyperlink instances. As with source and target node type identifiers, it can be bound or free. We use the symbol "-" to denote a free link component. A *complex link component* contains regular expressions defined over simple link components. Let ℓ_1 and ℓ_2 be two simple link components. Then

1. $\ell_1?$, $\ell_1|\ell_2$, $\ell_1\ell_2$ and $\ell_1\{m,n\}$ are complex link components, where $m \geq 0$, $n > 1$, and $m < n$. The existence of m is optional;
2. If c_1 and c_2 are simple or complex link components, then c_1c_2, $c_1?$, $c_1|c_2$, and $c_1\{m,n\}$ are complex link components; and
3. Nothing else is a complex link component.

Examples of complex link components are efg, $e?$, $e|f$, $e\{1,4\}$.

Observe that we have ignored the quantifiers $+$ and $\star$ in complex link components for the followings. First, an expression of the form $(\ell)^+$ or $(\ell)^\star$ matches any number of links of type ℓ. As there is no upper bound, this may result in an intractable traversal of the Web. In the worst case, constraints of this form may trigger a traversal of the whole Web. The immediate aftermath of this situation is infinite query execution time and degradation of system performance. Second, connectivities containing $+$ and $\star$ quantifiers in link path expressions may retrieve a large number of irrelevant Web documents. Proliferation of such irrelevant Web data has direct implications on the storage cost and further processing of Web queries in the warehouse. To avoid these limitations, we use the quantifier $\{m,n\}$ to specify the lower and upper bounds.

With the above two types of link components, link path expression is *simple* if the path expression contains only a simple link component. Otherwise, it is a *regular* link path expression.

5.3 Types of Connectivities

In the preceding section, we discussed the components of a connectivity. In this section, we discuss the connectivity element. We define two types of connectivities and illustrate them with examples.

5.3.1 Simple Connectivities

A connectivity $k \equiv x\langle\rho\rangle y$ is simple if ρ is a simple link path expression. Examples of simple connectivities are: $k_1 \equiv x\langle e\rangle y$, $k_2 \equiv \#_1\langle f\rangle \#_2$ and $k_3 \equiv \#_1\langle - \rangle \#_2$. The first connectivity k_1 specifies that instances of x must be connected to instances of y via links of type e. The connectivity k_2 states that starting from an instance of $\#_1$, follow a link of type f to reach an instance of $\#_2$. The last connectivity k_3 illustrates the usage of free node and link type identifiers. It says that from an instance of $\#_1$, follow an arbitrary link instance to reach an arbitrary node object.

5.3.2 Complex Connectivities

A connectivity $k \equiv x\langle\rho\rangle y$ is complex if ρ is a regular link path expression. The following are examples of complex connectivities.

$$k_1 \equiv x\langle efgh\rangle y \qquad\qquad k_2 \equiv x\langle (ef)|(gh)\rangle y$$
$$k_3 \equiv x\langle ef?\rangle y \qquad\qquad k_4 \equiv x\langle ef\{2,4\}\rangle y$$
$$k_5 \equiv x\langle e\text{-}\{1,5\}\rangle z$$

The first expression specifies that starting from a node of type x, one may reach a node of type y by following the link instances of type e, f, g and h. The next connectivity specifies that an instance of x and an instance of y must be connected by any of the set of link instances:

- from an instance of x there must exist a hyperlink of type e that connects to a Web page containing a link of type f and that links to an instance of y;
- from an instance of x there must exist a link of type g that connects to a page containing a link of type h that points to an instance of y.

The third connectivity specifies that from an instance of x, there must be a link of type e followed by an optional link of type f that connects to an instance of y. That is, an instance of x may be directly connected to an instance of y through an instance of e or it may be connected to an instance of y via instances of e and f, respectively. The connectivity k_4 specifies that from an instance of x, there must be a link of type e followed by at least two and at most four links of type f that connect to an instance of y. Hence a set of documents and links of type x, y, e, and f must satisfy any one of the connectivities: $x\langle eff\rangle y$, $x\langle efff\rangle y$, or $x\langle effff\rangle y$. Note that the number of occurrences of f type hyperlinks is specified by the *quantifier* "$\{2,4\}$". The last connectivity k_5 expresses the usage of free link type identifiers in a connectivity. It specifies that from an instance of x, there must exist a link of type e followed by at most five arbitrary links that connect to a document of type y. In this case, the properties of the links following e are not defined by any predicate. Observe that the term *quantifier* has a well-established usage in logic theory. However, in this book, we do not use the term in this context. It is used to describe a constraint interval. Note that such constraint intervals on regular expressions are also defined as quantifiers in [81].

5.4 Transformation of Complex Connectivities

In this section, we discuss how a complex connectivity can be reduced to a *set* of simple connectivities. We show how these simple connectivities can be represented in Disjunctive Normal Form (DNF). Note that in this book a *set* of connectivities or a *connectivity set* extends the traditional notion of set. It is not only an unordered collection of distinct simple or complex connectivities but also these connectivities are in conjunction or disjunction to one another.

The justification of transforming a complex connectivity into a set of simple connectivities is twofold: reduction of complex connectivities is useful for *coupling query* evaluations (we discuss this in Chapter 6). In addition, transformation of a complex connectivity to a set of simple connectivities is necessary for generating schemas of a web table. We discuss this in detail in Chapter 7. We proceed by elaborating on the transformation of several basic cases of complex connectivities as shown below.

- **Case 1:** Connectivity containing a link path expression of the form $\ell_1\ell_2\cdots\ell_n$. That is, the link path expression does not contain any other type of regular expression operators.
- **Case 2:** Connectivity containing "|" and "?" regular expression operators in the link path expression.
- **Case 3:** Connectivity containing the "{m , n}" operator in the link path expression.
- **Case 4:** Connectivity containing "|", '?', and "{m , n}" operators in the link path expression. Observe that it is the combination of the above cases.

We first discuss the transformation of these four cases informally. In Section 5.4.5, we provide the formal procedure for the transformation of the four cases.

5.4.1 Transformation of Case 1

Connectivities belonging to Case 1 are the simplest form of complex connectivities. We illustrate the graphical representation of this type of connectivities with some examples first and then discuss its transformation. Consider the following complex connectivities: $k_1 \equiv x\langle e\text{-}g\rangle y$ and $k_2 \equiv x\langle efgh\rangle\#$. The tree views of these connectivities are shown in Figure 5.3. Observe that for a Case 1 connectivity the number of edges in the tree is equal to the number of link type identifiers in the link path expression.

This type of connectivity can be reduced to a set of simple connectivities adjacent to each other, i.e., $x\langle\rho\rangle y \equiv x\langle\ell_1\rangle\#_1 \wedge \#_1\langle\ell_2\rangle\#_2 \wedge \cdots \wedge \#_{n-1}\langle\ell_n\rangle y$. Observe that

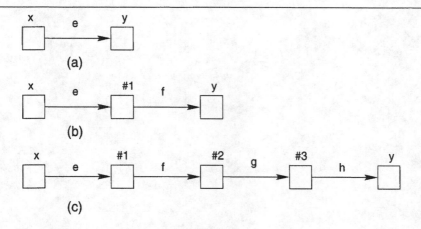

Fig. 5.3. Pictorial representation of Case 1.

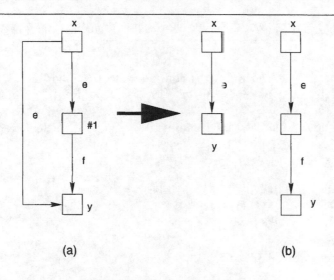

Fig. 5.4. Connectivity $x\langle ef?\rangle y$.

the identifier # represents any arbitrary collection of node objects. For instance, the connectivity $k \equiv x\langle e\text{-}g\rangle y$ can be transformed to the following set of simple connectivities in conjunction to one another, $x\langle e\rangle \#_1 \wedge \#_1\langle\text{-}\rangle \#_2 \wedge \#_2\langle g\rangle y$.

5.4.2 Transformation of Case 2

Consider the connectivity $k_1 \equiv x\langle e|f\rangle y$. It specifies a link of type e or f from a node of type x to a document of type y. Hence the connectivity can be represented as $C_1 \vee C_2$, where $C_1 \equiv x\langle e\rangle y$ and $C_2 \equiv x\langle f\rangle y$. Either of the two simple connectivities must be satisfied in order to conform to the connectivity k_1. Similarly, the connectivity $k_2 \equiv x\langle ef?\rangle y$ can be represented as $x\langle e\rangle y \vee (x\langle e\rangle \#_1 \wedge \#_1\langle f\rangle y)$ (Figure 5.4). The

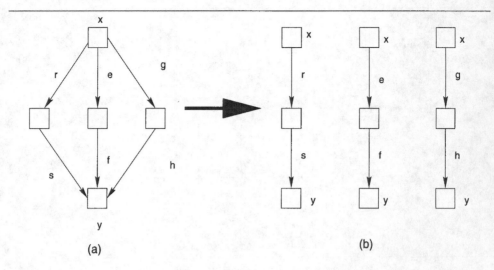

Fig. 5.5. Connectivity $x\langle(ef)|(rs)|(gh)\rangle y$.

connectivity $k_3 \equiv x\langle(ef)|(gh)|(rs)\rangle y$ is equivalent to the following set of simple connectivities in disjunction: $(x\langle e\rangle\#_1\wedge\#_1\langle f\rangle y) \vee (x\langle r\rangle\#_2\wedge\#_2\langle s\rangle y) \vee (x\langle g\rangle\#_3\wedge\#_3\langle h\rangle y)$ (Figure 5.5).

We now consider connectivities containing "|" and "?" metacharacters. The connectivity $k_4 \equiv x\langle e(fg?)|hr\rangle y$ can be expressed as sets of simple connectivities in DNF, i.e., $k_4 \equiv C_1 \vee C_2 \vee C_3$ where

$$C_1 \equiv x\langle e\rangle\#_1 \wedge \#_1\langle f\rangle\#_2 \wedge \#_2\langle g\rangle\#_3 \wedge \#_3\langle h\rangle\#_4 \wedge \#_4\langle r\rangle y$$
$$C_2 \equiv x\langle e\rangle\#_1 \wedge \#_1\langle f\rangle\#_4 \wedge \langle r\rangle y$$
$$C_3 \equiv x\langle e\rangle\#_3 \wedge \#_3\langle h\rangle\#_4 \wedge \#_4\langle r\rangle y$$

5.4.3 Transformation of Case 3

Next we discuss the transformation of Case 3 connectivities into sets of simple connectivities in DNF. Consider the connectivity $k_1 \equiv x\langle e\text{-}\{1,4\}\rangle y$. It specifies that there exists a link of type e from a node of type x followed by at most four arbitrary links to a document of type y. Hence k_1 can be represented as $k_1 \equiv C_1 \vee C_2 \vee C_3 \vee C_4$ where $C_1 \equiv x\langle e\text{-}\rangle y$, $C_2 \equiv x\langle e\text{--}\rangle y$, $C_3 \equiv x\langle e\text{---}\rangle y$, and $C_4 \equiv x\langle e\text{----}\rangle y$. Each connectivity element in the above expressions is a Case 1 type. Thus they can be further reduced to a set of simple connectivities in conjunction to each other. Observe that a set of interlinked documents must satisfy any one of the above connectivities in order to conform to the connectivity k_1. Also notice that each connectivity represents a path with start vertex x and end vertex y in the digraph of k_1 in Figure 5.6(a). The set of paths corresponding to C_1, C_2, C_3, and C_4 are shown in Figure 5.6(b).

5.4.4 Transformation of Case 4

We now illustrate a transformation of the the complex connectivities of Case 4. The transformation of such a connectivity to a set of simple connectivities involves the following two steps.

- Given a connectivity of Case 4, it is first transformed to a set of connectivities (in DNF) of Case 2.
- Then each of these connectivities is reduced to a set of simple connectivities as described in Section 5.4.2.

For example, consider the connectivity $k_1 \equiv x \langle e(f|g)\{1,3\}\rangle y$. It is first transformed to a set of connectivities of Case 2 in disjunction, i.e., $k_1 \equiv C_1 \vee C_2 \vee C_3$, where $C_1 \equiv x \langle ef|g\rangle y$, $C_2 \equiv x \langle ef|gf|g\rangle y$, and $C_3 \equiv x \langle ef|ef|gf|g\rangle y$.

Next each of these connectivities can be reduced to a set of simple connectivities in DNF. We have already described the reduction procedure in Section 5.4.2.

5.4.5 Steps for Transformation

In the preceding sections we have seen informally how a complex connectivity is transformed into a set of simple connectivities in DNF. In this section, we provide the steps for such transformation. That is, given a complex connectivity we show the steps that must be followed to transform it into a set of simple connectivities in DNF.

Let $C \equiv x \langle \rho \rangle y$ be a complex connectivity where ρ is a regular expression over a set of link type identifiers containing the operators "|", "?" or "$\{m,n\}$". This expression may contain any number of nestings. The steps for the transformation are as follows.

1. Note that ρ serves as a name for sets of strings (finite sequences of link type identifiers). Therefore generate the set of strings $E = \{\rho_1, \rho_2, \cdots, \rho_n\}$ from ρ. This set denotes the strings involving the link type identifiers in C that match the expression ρ. Hence $\rho_i = \ell_{i1}\ell_{i2}\cdots\ell_{ir}$ where $r > 0$ and is less than or equal to the maximum length of a string in E.
2. Arrange the strings in E in a descending order based on the length of each string. That is, $E = \{\rho_1, \rho_2, \cdots, \rho_n\}$ where $|\rho_1| \geq |\rho_2| \geq \cdots \geq |\rho_n|$.
3. Each string in E represents a sequence of link type identifiers between x and y. Generate $C \equiv C_1 \vee C_2 \cdots \vee C_n$, where $C_i \equiv x \langle \rho_i \rangle y \ \forall \ 0 < i \leq n$. Observe that as ρ_i is a finite sequence of link type identifiers, C_i is a simple connectivity or a complex connectivity of Case 1 type. Furthermore, let $|C|$ be the length of a connectivity. Then $|C_1| \geq |C_2| \geq \cdots \geq |C_n|$.
4. Each complex connectivity C_i (for $i \in [1,n]$) is of Case 1 and is reduced to a set of simple connectivities in CNF as discussed in Section 5.4.1. That is, $C_i \equiv x \langle \ell_{i1} \rangle \#_1 \wedge \#_1 \langle \ell_{i2} \rangle \#_2 \wedge \cdots \wedge \#_{(r-1)} \langle \ell_{ir} \rangle y$. Observe that this is an *ordered* reduction where the connectivities are reduced in descending order of their length. The selection of a free node type identifier in this context is based on the following rules.

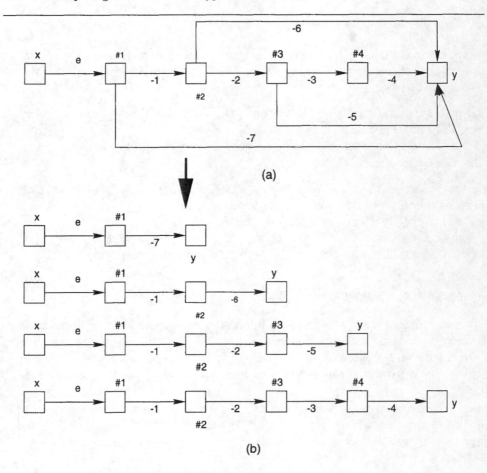

Fig. 5.6. Pictorial representation of $x\langle e(-)\{1, 4\}\rangle y$.

- Suppose C_i is being reduced, and k_i is a connectivity in C_i. If there exists a connectivity k_j in C_j (already reduced) such that $rnode(k_j) \neq y$, $lnode(k_j) = lnode(k_i)$, $link(k_j) = link(k_i)$, then $rnode(k_i) = rnode(k_j)$.
- If $link(k_i) \neq link(k_j)$, then a distinct free node type identifier is generated for $rnode(k_i)$.
- If $lnode(k_i) \neq lnode(k_j)$ and $link(k_i) = link(k_j)$, then the node type identifier $rnode(k_i)$ is chosen from C_j based on the position of the identifier in C_i.

Hence the following property holds.

Proposition 5.1. *Let k be a complex connectivity. Then $k \equiv C_1 \vee C_2 \vee \cdots \vee C_n$, where $C_i \equiv k_{i_1} \wedge k_{i_2} \wedge \cdots \wedge k_{i_r}$, $\forall\ 0 < i \leq n$ and k_{i_j} is a simple connectivity $\forall$ $0 < j \leq r$. C_i is called the* **conjunctive connectivity set**. ∎

5.4.6 Graphical Visualization of a Connectivity

Based on the above discussion, it is evident that a connectivity $k \equiv x\langle \rho \rangle y$ can be visualized as an acyclic digraph $G(k)$ where the edges of the graph correspond to the link type identifiers in the connectivity. $G(k)$ has a single source vertex x (vertex with zero in-degree) and a single leaf vertex y (vertex with zero out-degree). Also some of the edges may be in disjunction with other edges. If k is simple, then $G(k)$ does not have any interior vertices and represents a path of length one. On the other hand, if k is complex, then $G(k)$ contains a set of internal vertices each of which is labeled by a free node type identifier. Moreover, k is equivalent to a set of simple connectivities in DNF; i.e., $k \equiv C_1 \vee C_2 \vee \cdots \vee C_n$ where each C_i represents a path between the root and leaf vertex of $G(k)$.

Definition 5.2. *Let $k \equiv x\langle \rho \rangle y$ be a connectivity. Then, k can be represented by an* **acyclic digraph** *$G(k) = (V_k, E_k)$, where*

- *$V_k = V_{k_r} \cup V_{k_i} \cup V_{k_\ell}$ is a finite set of labeled vertices where $V_{k_r} = \{v_r\}$ is the root vertex of $G(k)$ and $id(v_r) = x$, $V_{k_\ell} = \{v_\ell\}$ is the leaf vertex of $G(k)$ and $id(v_\ell) = y$, and $v_i \in V_{k_i}$ is a set (possibly empty) of interior vertices such that $label(v_i) = \#_j$ where $j > 0$. Moreover, $V_{k_r} \cap V_{k_i} \cap V_{k_\ell} = \emptyset$.*
- *E_k is a set of labeled edges. If $e_k \in E_k$, then $e = (a, \alpha, b)$ where $a \in V_k$, $b \in V_k$, and $\alpha \in \{\ell_1, \ell_2, \ldots, \ell_n\}$, where $\ell_i \; \forall \; 0 < i \leq n$ is the link type identifier in ρ.*
- *Let $k \equiv C_1 \vee C_2 \vee \cdots \vee C_n$. Then C_i is a path between the root and a leaf vertex in $G(k) \; \forall \; 0 < i \leq n$.* ∎

5.5 Conformity Conditions

In this section, we discuss *conformity conditions* to a connectivity. Given a set of documents D, we identify the conditions these documents and hyperlinks must satisfy such that D conforms to a connectivity k. We begin with conformity conditions for simple connectivities and then discuss complex connectivities.

5.5.1 Simple Connectivities

Let $k \equiv x\langle \ell \rangle y$ be a simple connectivity, and d_1 and d_2 be two documents. Then d_1 and d_2 satisfy k if they satisfy the following conditions. First, these two documents must satisfy the predicates defined on x and y (if any). Second, there must exist a hyperlink in d_1 that satisfies the predicates (if any) defined on ℓ and links to the document d_2. We represent this with the symbol $D_s \dashv k$, where $D_s = \{d_1, d_2\}$. We now elaborate this formally.

We first define a function *existLink* which we subsequently use to define the conformity conditions for a simple connectivity k. Let ℓ be a link type identifier. If ℓ is bound, then given a predicate set on ℓ, i.e., P_ℓ and a document d, the function *existLink* determines whether there exists any hyperlink in d that satisfies the predicates in P_ℓ. If there is, then it returns a set of hyperlinks that satisfy the predicates P_ℓ. If ℓ is a free link type identifier, then the function *existLink* returns all the hyperlinks in d. Formally,

$$existLink(P_\ell, d) = \begin{cases} H_b & \text{if } P_\ell(h_i) = \text{true where } h_i \in H_b \ \forall \ 0 < i \leq |H_b| \\ \emptyset & \text{otherwise and } \ell \text{ is bound} \\ H_f & \text{if } \ell \text{ is free} \end{cases}$$

Let $k \equiv x\langle \ell \rangle y$ be a simple connectivity and $D = \{d_s, d_t\}$ be a set of Web documents. Then the documents in D conform to k, denoted by $D \dashv k$, if the following conditions are true.

1. If x is a bound node type identifier, then $P_{d_s}(x) = \text{true}$;
2. If y is a bound node type identifier, then $P_{d_t}(y) = \text{true}$;
3. If $H = existLink(P_\ell, d_s)$ and $H \neq \emptyset$, then $\exists \ h \in H$ such that $h \Rightarrow d_t$. The symbol $\Rightarrow$ indicates the hyperlink h points to the document d_t,

5.5.2 Complex Connectivities

We now discuss the conformity conditions of complex connectivities. Note that the conformity conditions of a complex connectivity k can be defined in terms of conformity conditions of simple connectivities discussed above. This is because based on Proposition 5.1, a complex connectivity k can be represented as a set of simple connectivities in DNF. Therefore a set of documents will satisfy k if it conforms to any one of the conjunctive connectivity sets. For example, a set of documents D satisfies the connectivity $k \equiv x\langle (ef)|(rs)|(gh) \rangle y$ in Figure 5.5(a) if it satisfies any one of the simple connectivities $C_1 \equiv x\langle e \rangle \#_1 \wedge \#_1 \langle f \rangle y$ or $C_2 \equiv x\langle r \rangle \#_2 \wedge \#_2 \langle s \rangle y$ or $C_3 \equiv x\langle g \rangle \#_3 \wedge \#_3 \langle h \rangle y$ (depicted in Figure 5.5(b)). Hence the following condition holds.

Definition 5.3. [Conformity Condition of Complex Connectivity] *Let* $k \equiv C_1 \vee C_2 \vee \cdots \vee C_n$ *be a complex connectivity where* $C_i \equiv k_{i_1} \wedge k_{i_2} \wedge \cdots \wedge k_{i_r}$, $\forall$ $0 < i \leq n$. *Let* D *be a set of documents. Then* $D \dashv k$ *if* $D_j \dashv k_{i_j} \ \forall \ 0 < j \leq r$, *where* $0 < i \leq n$, $D = D_1 \cup D_2 \cup \cdots \cup D_r$, *and* $|D_j| = 2$. ∎

5.6 Summary

In this chapter, we discussed the notion of connectivity. A connectivity is a predicate on the interdocument relationship of a set of Web documents. To define a connectivity element, one has to first categorize the set of documents and hyperlinks into different types using predicates. Then the connectivities are defined by using the type identifiers of these documents and hyperlinks. A connectivity consists of three components: a source identifier, a target identifier, and a link path expression. A connectivity element is categorized into two types: simple and complex. A simple connectivity contains only simple link path expressions. A complex connectivity contains regular link path expressions. We describe how to transform a complex connectivity into a set of simple connectivities in DNF.

In the next chapter, we discuss how the notion of predicates and connectivities can be used to formulate a meaningful query for retrieving relevant Web documents from Web sites.

6

Query Mechanism for the Web

In order to populate a web warehouse one has to retrieve relevant data from the Web. In WHOWEDA, we harness relevant Web data by querying the Web. In this chapter, we discuss how to specify a web query to garner a set of relevant Web data. In Chapter 8, we discuss the execution of a web query which we call the *global web coupling* operation.

We express a web query in the form of a *coupling query* [16, 14, 32, 33]. We begin by discussing some of the major features associated with a web query mechanism. Then we explain how we incorporate these features into the coupling query by describing the components of a coupling query in Section 6.2. Within this context, we formally define coupling queries and introduce two types of coupling queries, i.e., *canonical* and *noncanonical*. Next, in Section 6.3, we discuss how to formulate canonical and noncanonical queries. In Section 6.4, we show how to convert a *noncanonical* coupling query to a *valid canonical* one. Next, in Section 6.5, we discuss how to formulate canonical and noncanonical queries in text form and pictorially. These two forms of queries are called *coupling text* and *coupling graph*, respectively. In Section 6.6, we discuss the results generated after the execution of a *valid* canonical coupling query. We explore issues related to the *computability* of coupling queries in Section 6.7. Section 6.8 compares our approach with recent approaches for querying the Web. Finally, we conclude by summarizing the chapter.

6.1 Introduction

In this section, we begin by discussing the motivation behind coupling queries. Then we provide an overview of our approach. In the subsequent sections, we discuss our approach in detail.

6.1.1 Motivation

Currently, the majority of Web data is in HTML format. However, in the near future more and more XML documents will coexist with HTML documents. Consequently, querying the Web implies querying a large collection of interlinked HTML and XML documents. As a result a large body of research has been motivated by the attempt to extend database manipulation techniques to data on the Web [79, 58, 59, 67, 84] and several web query mechanisms such as W3QS [101], WebSQL [132], WebLog [106], RAW [77], NetQL [119], WebOQL [6], ULIXES in the ARANEUS system [8], XML-QL [67], Lorel [84], and YAT$_L$ [59] have been proposed thus far. Given the existence of so many query systems for Web and semistructured data, it is natural to question the necessity of yet another query mechanism for gleaning relevant data from the Web. We justify our intention by outlining the following features of a web query system that we consider significant in the context of WHOWEDA. Note that to the best of our knowledge no single query system has all these desirable features. Some of the query systems may possess some of these features but not all.

Constraints on Specific Portions of Documents or Hyperlinks

If the Web is viewed as a large graphlike database, it is natural to pose queries that go beyond the basic information retrieval paradigm supported by today's search engines and take structure into account, both the internal structure of Web pages and the external structure of links that interconnect them. Thus a coupling query should be able to provide the capabilities to exploit the internal and external structure of both HTML and XML documents. The web query languages proposed so far: W3QS [101], WebSQL [132], WebLog [106], RAW [77], FLORID [122], NetQL [119], WebOQL [6], ULIXES in the ARANEUS system [8], XML-QL [67], Lorel [84], and YAT$_L$ [59] view the WWW as a huge database that can be queried using a declarative language. Exploitation of internal structure is restrictive in W3QS, FLORID, NetQL, RAW, and ULIXES. Although WebOQL, XML-QL, Lorel [84], and YAT$_L$ are rich in expressing constraints on the structure of documents in a web query, XML-QL, YAT$_L$, and Lorel are used specifically for XML data only. Query languages for semistructured data such as Lorel [1], UnQL [42], and StruQL [75] were not specifically developed for the Web, and do not distinguish between graph edges that represent the connection between a document and one of its parts and edges that represent a hyperlink from one Web document to another. Thus a coupling query should be able to provide the capabilities to exploit the internal and external structure of both HTML and XML documents. These constraints are expressed as a set of predicates and connectivities in the coupling query.

Queries Based on Partial or Zero Knowledge

It is unrealistic to assume the user has complete knowledge about the content and structure of Web pages in Web sites. The user knows what she is looking for, but she may not have a clear idea of how to express her needs. This is primarily because one may not necessarily know anything about the architecture of a given site, anything about the structure used to represent the data, or how the desired information is represented in the source. Thus a web query language must allow a user to express some incomplete requests based on partial knowledge. WebSQL, WebLog, and W3QS can express partial knowledge with respect to hyperlink structure only. Expressiveness of these languages is limited in the context of expressing partial knowledge with respect to content, metadata, and structure of Web documents. ULIXES of the ARANEUS system [8] is only capable of expressing queries with simple path expressions without recursion. This limits the expressive power of ULIXES. Next, ULIXES is based on page-schemes used to model the structure of a Web site. Hence, in order to use ULIXES, one has to be familiar with the Web site structure to generate the scheme of the site. This limits the usage of ULIXES as a user may not always be aware of the Web site structure. WebOQL [6], however, is capable of accommodating lack of knowledge of the structure of the data to be queried and potential irregularities, or even lack of explicit structure in these data. Query languages for semistructured data [1, 42] and XML data [59, 67, 84] use regular expressions to facilitate querying based on partial knowledge. As shown, we address queries based on partial knowledge using predicates and connectivities containing regular expressions.

Conditions on Tags and Tag Attributes

A user must be able to impose constraints on the attributes associated with tags as well as tagless segments of data. The textual content in HTML or XML as described by the tagless data segment is viewable by users. However, not all useful information is enclosed by tags. Some information is found in the attribute/value pairs associated with tags. Thus a web query mechanism must be able to impose constraints on tag attributes in order to exploit this extra information. Query mechanisms such as XML-QL [67], Lorel [84], and YAT$_L$ [59] allow the user to impose conditions on tags and tag attributes. However, as mentioned earlier, these languages are specifically designed for XML data. HTML query systems such as WebSQL [132], WebLog [106], W3QS [102], NetQL [119], WebOQL [6], FLORID [122], and ARANEUS [8] are not capable of imposing constraints on tag attributes. As shown later, our query mechanism enables us to impose constraints on both tags and tag attributes using the notion of predicate operators.

Control Query Execution

In contrast to conventional database systems, there should be a mechanism to impose *conditions* on the execution of a web query. The primary motivation is to address *some* of the limitations of the Web. Because the Web is large and the content and structure of relevant information may not be completely determined ahead of time, a web query based on partial knowledge can take a considerable amount of time. Thus a user may ask a query with a condition set on the time allowed to answer the query. This condition may also be expressed by a condition on the number of query results returned, number of documents, and so on. However, only NetQL [119] provides the mechanism for controlling query execution. In WHOWEDA, these conditions are imposed on a coupling query by *coupling query predicates*.

Express Disjunctive Query Conditions

Due to the irregular and semistructured nature of Web data, it is important for a web query language to express disjunctive constraints on the hyperlinked structure compactly. Informally, such disjunctive queries may be decomposed into a set of conjunctive queries that are in disjunction to each other. A set of documents satisfies such a disjunctive query if it satisfies any one of the conjunctive query conditions. Consequently, one may argue the justification of disjunctive queries as such queries can be represented by conjunctive query sets which are relatively easier to formulate. However, we believe that it is necessary for a web query mechanism to express disjunctive conditions for the following reasons.

- First, disjunctive queries allow us to overcome the limitations of the irregular structure of interlinked Web documents and pose meaningful queries over it.
- Second, sometimes query evaluation is relatively less expensive if a query is formulated and evaluated using disjunctive constraints rather than repeated evaluation of each query in the equivalent conjunctive query set.
- Third, expressing all possible sets of conjunctive queries accurately for a disjunctive condition incurs significant cognitive overhead which may result in an erroneous query.
- Finally, a disjunctive query can be expressed compactly using regular expressions. Expressing all possible sets of conjunctive queries can be quite cumbersome and frustrating.

Although the importance of imposing disjunctive constraints on interdocument structure is undeniable, most of the web query systems support very limited [59, 67, 79, 84, 102, 132, 106, 77, 119, 6, 8] forms of disjunctive constraints, if any, on the interdocument structure of the Web. NetQL, WebSQL, W3QS, WebLog, and FLORID do not address the issue of such constraints on interlinked documents extensively. A limited form of disjunctive condition that involves the variability of the depth of traversal of a query can be expressed by these languages. In addition, these systems do not support querying of XML data. Query systems for semistructured data and XML query languages such as XML-QL, Lorel, and YAT$_L$ also support a limited form of disjunctive constraints on the interlinked structure of Web documents. Query languages for semistructured data such as Lorel [1] and UnQL [42] were not specifically developed for the Web, and do not distinguish between graph edges that represent the connection between a document and one of its parts and edges that represent a hyperlink from one Web document to another. On the other hand, XML-QL, YAT$_L$, and Lorel are designed specifically for XML.

Formulating Web Queries

Intuitively, a web query represents a graphlike structure with constraints on some of its vertices and edges that are matched against the Web. Conventionally, graphs can be represented in text form as well as pictorially. Consequently, a web query may take both textual and pictorial forms. Textual formulation of a web query enables us to express any complex web query accurately. As a result, most of the contemporary Web query mechanisms as well as query languages for semistructured data focus on text-based query languages. However, text-based queries have some disadvantages. To express such queries, a user must be completely familiar with the syntax of the query language, and must be able to express his needs accurately in a syntactically correct form. Otherwise, a text-based query may be error prone and may contain superfluous query conditions. Also due to the nature of Web data, specifying such queries in text form requires considerable effort. For instance, query languages such as XML-QL, Lorel, YAT$_L$, WebOQL, and FLORID, although powerful languages, are definitely not easy to formulate in textual form Although it is possible to apply syntactic sugar to these languages, issues involved with such efforts are not discussed in [67, 84, 59, 6, 122]. W3QS [102] allows us to use query templates to minimize the complexity associated with the formulation of web queries. Note that research on visual querying has been done in traditional database research [72, 166]. To a greater or lesser extent, all these research efforts focused on devising novel visual querying schemes to replace data retrieval aspects of SQL. Specifically, forms have been popular building blocks for visual querying mechanisms. For instance, Embley [72] proposed the NFQL as a communication language between humans and database systems. It uses forms in a strictly nonprocedural manner to represent queries. As shown in Section 6.5, we allow a user to formulate a coupling query both in text form and pictorially.

Preservation of Topological Structure

Results of a web query are directed connected graphs that can be further manipulated in a web warehouse. Hence it is necessary to preserve the hyperlinked structure of the query results of a coupling query to facilitate subsequent query formulation and evaluation. However, due to flattening of query results, the topological structure of these results is lost in WebSQL [132], W3QL [101, 102], WebLog [106], FLORID [122], NetQL [119], and ULIXES [8]. On the other hand, XML-QL [67], YAT$_L$ [59], UnQL [42], and Lorel [1, 84] allow us to preserve the topological structure in query results and provide the flexibility to restructure these results. However, these languages are designed specifically for XML or semistructured data and do not scale up well with HTML documents.

Based on the above issues, rather than using an existing query system, we have developed a separate query mechanism for populating the web warehouse. In the next section, we illustrate with an example how to specify a coupling query step-by-step. In subsequent sections, we discuss in detail various issues related to coupling queries.

6.1.2 Our Approach

We now provide a brief overview of a *coupling query*. Informally, a coupling query consists of five components: sets of node and link type identifiers, a set of connectivities, a set of predicates, and a set of *coupling query predicates*. It is evaluated by a global web coupling operation and a set of documents satisfying this query is garnered from the Web and stored in a web table in the form of *web tuples*. Each web tuple satisfies the coupling query. We now illustrate with an example how to specify a query in WHOWEDA step-by-step. In subsequent sections, we discuss in detail various issues related to coupling queries.

Consider the NCI Web site at `rex.nci.nih.gov`. Suppose a user wishes to retrieve information related to treatment of different types of cancer. This site pro-

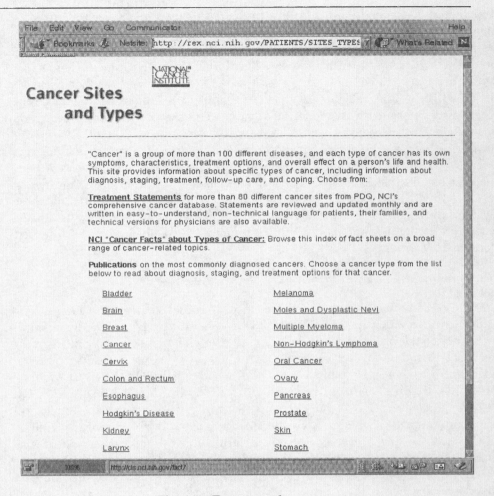

Fig. 6.1. Treatment of cancer.

vides information about specific cancer types, including information about diagnosis, staging, treatment, follow-up care, and coping. Specifically, links in the Web page at rex.nci.nih.gov/PATIENTS/SITES_TYPES.html provide links to information related to different types of cancer. The link "treatment statement" points to a page containing a list of links to cancer-related diseases (Figure 6.2). Each of these links points to a page containing information on diagnosis, treatments, and so on of a particular disease. There are also hyperlinks labeled "bladder", "brain", and so on in the Web page at rex.nci.nih.gov/PATIENTS/SITES_TYPES.html (Figure 6.1) which directly connect to a page containing details of these diseases. Observe that some of the links such as "AIDS-related lymphoma", "Anal Cancer", "Endometrical Cancer", and so on in Figure 6.2 are not available in the Web page at http://rex.nci.nih.gov/PATIENTS/SITES_TYPES.html. Similarly, links related to "Non-Hodgkin's Lymphoma", "Hodgkin's Disease", and "Stomach" in

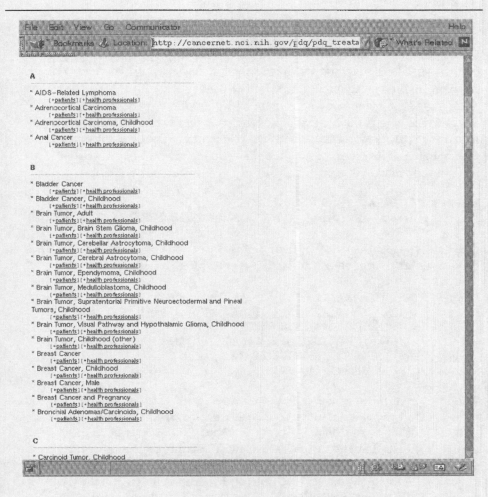

Fig. 6.2. List of cancer-related diseases.

the Web page in Figure 6.1 are not listed in the Web page in Figure 6.2. However, links related to "Larynx", "Melanoma", and so on are available in both Web pages. Hence in order to retrieve a complete list of treatment details of various types of cancer we need to exploit the link "treatment statement" and links related to different cancers in the Web page in Figure 6.1. In order to express this query, we need:

- A starting point for the search (Web page at rex.nci.nih.gov/PATIENTS/ SITES_TYPES.html); and
- to scan the pages accessible from the starting page by following links having the specific characteristics as described above.

Therefore

1. We search for a path in the Web hypertext structure, beginning at the Web page at `rex.nci.nih.gov/PATIENTS/SITES_TYPES.html` and ending at a page containing the keyword "treatment" by following only hypertext links that satisfy the specific characteristics as described above. Such a hypertext path can be expressed in the coupling query by the connectivity $x\langle(ef)|(gh)\rangle y$. Here x, y are node type identifiers and e, f, g, and h are link type identifiers.

2. An instance of x is the first vertex of the path and it corresponds to the page at `rex.nci.nih.gov/PATIENTS/SITES_TYPES.html`. The coupling query allows the mapping of specific pages to a node type identifier. This is written in the form of a predicate:

$$p_{1_1}(x) \equiv \text{METADATA::x[url] EQUALS}$$
$$\text{"}http://rex[.]nci[.]nih[.]gov/PATIENTS/SITES\_TYPES[.]html\text{"}$$

3. The link type identifiers e, f, g, and h must satisfy the above conditions. These conditions are expressed as the following predicates.

$p_{1_3}(f) \equiv \text{STRUCTURE::f[A] EXISTS\_IN "}body.p\text{"}$
$p_{1_4}(e) \equiv \text{CONTENT::e[A] NON-ATTR\_ENCL "}Treatment\ Statements\text{"}$
$p_{1_5}(h) \equiv \text{CONTENT::h[A] ATTR\_CONT}$
$\qquad \text{"}\{ \ (href,\ MATCH(:BEGIN\_WORD:\ +\ treat.*\ +\ ;END\_WORD:)\}\text{"}$
$p_{1_6}(g) \equiv \text{STRUCTURE::g SATISFIES "}A\text{"}$
$p_{1_7}(g) \equiv \text{STRUCTURE::g[A] EXISTS\_IN "}table(.\%)+.p\text{"}$

The first predicate specifies that the instances of f exist in a paragraph contained in the **body** element of the source documents. The next predicate specifies that the anchor text of instances of e is *Treatment Statements*. The predicate $p_{1_5}(h)$ says that the instances of h must contain the element A having an attribute labeled `href`. The value of `href` must match the regular expression *treat.**. That is, the target URL of the hyperlinks must contain the string "treat". The last two predicates indicate that g is a link type identifier and specifies that instances of g exist in a paragraph contained in the `table` elements of the source documents. Note that similar to the node type identifier, specific hyperlinks are mapped to a link type identifier.

4. The last vertex y must contain the keyword "treatment" anywhere in the document and is expressed by the predicate:

$$p_{1_2}(y) \equiv \text{CONTENT::y[html(.\%)+] NON-ATTR\_CONT}$$
$$\text{":BEGIN\_WORD: + }treatment\text{ + :END\_WORD:"}$$

5. In order not to overload the `rex.nci.nih.gov` HTTP server, we limit the time taken for the search. The search stops after 20 minutes and returns the result retrieved so far. Also we make sure that all the documents retrieved by the search belong to the NCI Web site. This is done by defining the following *coupling query predicates.*

$q_1(G_1) \equiv \text{COUPLING\_QUERY::}G_1\text{.time EQUALS "}20\ min\text{"}$
$q_2(G_1) \equiv \text{COUPLING\_QUERY::}G_1\text{.host EQUALS "}rex.nci.nih.gov\text{"}$

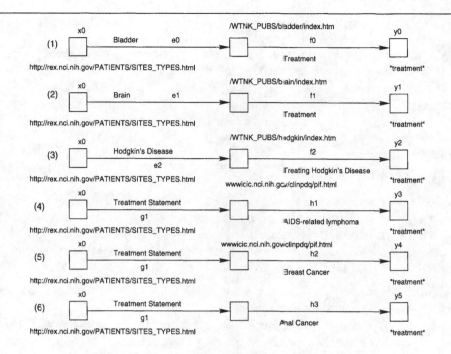

Fig. 6.3. Results of the query in Example 6.1.

The query is then expressed as

Example 6.1. Let the coupling query be $G_1 = \langle X_{n_{1q}}, X_{\ell_{1q}}, C_{1q}, P_{1q}, Q_{1q} \rangle$

$$X_{n_{1q}} = \{x, y\}$$
$$X_{\ell_{1q}} = \{e, f, g, h\}$$
$$C_{1q} \equiv x\langle (ef)|(gh)\rangle y$$

$P_{1q} = \{p_1, p_2, p_3, p_4, p_5, p_6, p_7\}$, where

$p_{1_1}(x) \equiv$ METADATA::x[url] EQUALS
    "$http://rex[.]nci[.]nih[.]gov/PATIENTS/SITES\_TYPES[.]html$"
$p_{1_2}(y) \equiv$ CONTENT::y[html(.%)+] NON-ATTR_CONT
    "$:BEGIN\_WORD: + treatment + :END\_WORD:$"
$p_{1_3}(f) \equiv$ STRUCTURE::f[A] EXISTS_IN "$body.p$"
$p_{1_4}(e) \equiv$ CONTENT::e[A] NON-ATTR_ENCL "$Treatment\ Statements$"
$p_{1_5}(h) \equiv$ CONTENT::h[A] ATTR_CONT
    "$\{(href, MATCH(:BEGIN\_WORD: + treat.* + :END\_WORD:)\}$"
$p_{1_6}(g) \equiv$ STRUCTURE::g SATISFIES "A"
$p_{1_7}(g) \equiv$ STRUCTURE::g[A] EXISTS_IN "$table(.%)+.p$"

and $Q_{1q} = \{q_1, q_2\}$, where

$q_1(G_1) \equiv$ COUPLING_QUERY::G_2.time EQUALS "$20\ min$"
$q_2(G_1) \equiv$ COUPLING_QUERY::G_1.host EQUALS "$rex.nci.nih.gov$"

The set of query results is shown in Figure 6.3.

6.2 Coupling Query

We now formally introduce the notion of a *coupling query*. We begin by describing a model of information on the Web. Next we introduce the components of a coupling query for expressing various query conditions. In Section 6.2.3, we formally define a coupling query. In Section 6.2.4, we discuss two flavors of the coupling query; *canonical* and *noncanonical*. Finally, we present the conditions for a canonical coupling query to be *valid* in Section 6.2.5.

6.2.1 The Information Space

The WWW involves a large number of information spaces ranging from simple files to complex service providers that are distributed over the Internet. In order to formally deal with information, we need to define a conceptually unified information space against which users can formulate queries. This information space must capture the following features of the Web:

- **Information content:** The information space must include the information content and some metadata information.
- **Hypertext structure:** In a hypertext environment, the organization of documents conveys information. The information space must reflect the graph structure of the hypertext in order to allow for the search of hypertext structural information.

We view the WWW as a directed graph. The entire graph topology is unknown but can be partly deduced by navigating the Web. The vertices and edges of the graph are defined by every possible WWW navigation activity.

We assume that the WWW is deterministic [102]. By this, we mean that the WWW structure, content, and programs (i.e., CGI scripts) are static and that programs are deterministic and time independent. This is clearly a simplification of the WWW. However, it allows us to assume that the WWW does not change during the execution of a query. The following definition captures the hypertext structure of WWW accessible information.

Definition 6.2. *A **WWW Graph** $G(WWW) = (V, E)$ is a pair where V and E are sets of node and link objects on the Web and $E \subseteq V \times V$. Each edge $e \in E$ is a hyperlink from a node object $v \in V$ to $u \in V$ such that there is a link object from a node object v to*

- *any node object corresponding to a file accessible by clicking on a valid hyperlink in v;*
- *any node object corresponding to the data returned by filling a form in v; and*
- *the default error HTML message (Error 404) obtained by clicking on an invalid hyperlink in v.* ∎

Observe that the previous definition captures a simplified model of the actual WWW. This is done for the sake of simplicity. Our model can be easily extended to include data accessible through protocols other than `http` and more complex HTML constructs such as `frames`. Although we do not discuss the querying and processing of HTML forms in this book, our model can be extended to handle them.

6.2.2 Components

A coupling query consists of the five components:

- A set of node and link type identifiers X_n and X_ℓ, respectively, where each element in X_n or X_ℓ is a nominal identifier of a set of node or link objects. Each nominal identifier in X_n or X_ℓ represents a set (possibly empty) of documents or hyperlinks retrieved from the Web. Each identifier is either bound or free;
- A set of predicates P on the node and link type identifiers to express the conditions defined by a user that must be satisfied by the relevant documents and hyperlinks of the corresponding identifiers;
- A set of connectivities C to express the hyperlink structure the relevant documents must satisfy with respect to the user's query; and
- A set of conditions Q on the coupling query to control the execution of the query for retrieving relevant data.

We now elaborate on these components. Note that we do not elaborate on predicates since we have already discussed them in Chapter 4.

Node and Link Type Identifiers

The components X_n and X_ℓ are used to nominally identify the set of node and link objects, respectively, sharing common properties. They also represent nodes and links that are not bound by any common characteristics. We give some examples of X_n and X_ℓ below to get the reader familiar with these components:

$$X_n = \{\texttt{x, y, z}\}$$
$$X_n = \{\texttt{x, y, z, \#}\}$$
$$X_\ell = \{\texttt{e, f, -}\}$$

The first expression says that some of the nodes retrieved by the query can be represented by node types x, y and z. Each of the identifiers represents a set of node objects that share one or more common properties related to the metadata, content, or structure of these nodes. These properties are expressed by predicates in P defined on these node type identifiers. The next expression specifies that some of the nodes retrieved by the query can be represented by the node type identifiers x, y, and z. The common properties of remaining nodes are not known and thus are represented by the symbol "#". Finally, the last expression indicates that some of the hyperlinks of the nodes retrieved by the query can be represented by the link type identifiers e, f, and -. Similar to the node objects, the common properties of the links represented by e and f are expressed by the predicates on e and f, i.e., P_e and P_f. Properties of some of the links are not known and these links are collectively represented as "-".

Connectivities

We have introduced the notion of a connectivity in Chapter 5. A coupling query may contain a set of simple or complex connectivities. They are used to specify that the hyperlinked structure of a set of relevant documents must conform to this connectivity constraint in order to match the query. Since we have elaborated on a connectivity element in the preceding chapter, we do not discuss this here. Instead, we show with examples how a set of connectivities is defined in a coupling query and its implications. Consider the following connectivities.

$$C_1 \equiv x\langle e\rangle y \wedge x\langle g\rangle z \wedge y\langle h\rangle w$$
$$C_2 \equiv x\langle ef?\rangle y \vee x\langle gh\rangle z \vee x\langle e\rangle b$$
$$C_3 \equiv x\langle e\{1,2\}\rangle y \wedge x\langle f\{2,3\}\rangle z$$

The first set of connectivities C_1 specifies that node objects of type x are connected to node objects of type y and z via links of type e and g, respectively. Furthermore, instances of y must be connected to documents of type w via hyperlinks of type of h. C_2 specifies that the hyperlink structure of documents satisfying the coupling query must conform to any one of the structures:

- node objects of type x are connected to node objects of type y via the links of type e, followed by optional links of type f; or
- node objects of type x are connected to those of type z through links of type g followed by links of type h; or
- node objects of type x are connected to those of type b via links of type e.

Finally, the last set of connectivities C_3 specifies that the node objects of type x are connected to node objects of type y and z via at most two hyperlinks of type e and at least two and at most three links of type f, respectively. Observe that C_1 contains simple connectivities only, whereas C_2 and C_3 contain complex connectivities. Moreover, these connectivity elements may be in conjunction or disjunction with one another.

Coupling Query Predicates

This is the last component of a coupling query. A *coupling query predicate* is defined over a coupling query and is used to impose *conditions* on how a coupling query executes. A predicate over a coupling query consists of the components: *query attribute*, *operator*, and *value* for imposing various constraints over coupling queries. Let q be a coupling query predicate. If G is a coupling query, then the following is the form of a predicate on G.

$$q(G) \equiv [\texttt{COUPLING\_QUERY}::G.\texttt{query\_attribute op "}V\texttt{"}]$$

where

- `query_attribute` is an *attribute* associated with a coupling query. We elaborate on this in the section below;
- `op` represents relational operators such as `EQUALS` to test equality and `LT` and `GT` to test the "less than" and "greater than" relationship;
- V is a regular expression over the ASCII character set; and
- G is the argument of q and represents the coupling query.

Withholding details of the components for the moment, the following are examples of coupling query predicates:

$q(G) \equiv$ COUPLING_QUERY::G.polling_frequency EQUALS "*30 days*"
$q(G) \equiv$ COUPLING_QUERY::G.number_of_tuples LT "*100*"

The first predicate specifies that the coupling query G should be executed periodically every 30 days. The last predicate specifies that the query G must stop executing once the number of web tuples retrieved from the Web exceeds 100. We now elaborate on *query attributes*.

Query Attributes

The notion of predicates introduced in Chapter 4 is used to impose constraints on node or link type identifiers. However, they fail to impose conditions on the properties associated with the execution of a web query. *Query attributes* [15] are a set of attributes associated with a coupling query over which one may impose additional constraints. Currently, query attributes may have any one of the following values.

- Polling_frequency: It is used to periodically execute a coupling query based on a specified time interval.
- Host: It is used to restrict the host of the nodes to a particular Web site.
- Number_of_tuples: This attribute is used to specify the total number of query results retrieved by a coupling query.
- Total_nodes: It is used to control the number of instances of a specified node type identifier in query results.
- Host_tuples: It is used to specify the constraint on the number of query results retrieved from *each* relevant Web site in query results.
- Host_nodes: It is used to specify the constraint on the number of instances of a specified node type identifier in *each* relevant Web site.
- Broken_link_mode: It is used to specify whether results of a coupling query should include web tuples containing broken links.
- Form_mode: It is used to specify if the results of a coupling query should include web tuples containing *hyperlink-free forms*.

Polling Frequency

The attribute polling frequency is used to enforce a coupling query to be executed periodically. An ordinary coupling query is evaluated over the current state of the WWW; the results are then stored in a web table. An example of an ordinary web query is "find a list of sideeffects and uses of drugs for various diseases." In contrast, a *polling* coupling query is a coupling query that repeatedly scans the Web for new results based on some given criteria. An example of a polling web query is "every 15 days, find a list of sideeffects and uses of drugs for various diseases." The polling frequency indicates the time at which the Web sources are to be polled. The polling frequency implies a sequence of time instants which we call *polling times*.

Host

Sometimes it is necessary to restrict the execution of a web query to a particular host, e.g., `rex.nci.nih.gov`. The execution of a web query only follows the links inside a web server. Naively, it may seem that this may be achieved by imposing constraints on the URL for each node type identifier in the coupling query. For instance, the following predicates can be used to impose a constraint on the metadata of each node type identifier in the coupling query.

$$p(x) \equiv \texttt{METADATA::} x \texttt{[url.server] EQUALS } \textit{"rex[.].nci[.]nih[.]gov"}$$

However, this is not a pragmatic solution due to the following reasons.

- It is repetitious and clumsy to define the same predicate on each node type identifier in the coupling query.
- It may not be possible to impose predicates on the host of all the nodes that are relevant to a query simply because there may exist free node type identifiers in the coupling query. For instance, consider a coupling query containing a connectivity of the form $x\langle-\{1,5\}\rangle y$. That is, the node and link type identifiers between x and y are free. The hosts of the nodes between the instances of x and y cannot be controlled by imposing predicates on the node type identifiers as it is not clear ahead of time the number of nodes between x and y (there may be at most five nodes).

Thus we restrict the execution of a web query to a particular host by imposing predicates on the coupling query itself in lieu of specifying predicates on the node type identifiers in the coupling query. The coupling query predicate is imposed on the attribute `host` to achieve this. For instance, the coupling query predicates q_2 in Example 1 specify that all the nodes traversed by the coupling query G_1 must belong to the host `rex.nci.nih.gov`.

Number of Tuples

Unlike a conventional database, one may wish to restrict the number of instances returned by a coupling query or the time taken to execute a query for the following reasons:

- The execution time of a coupling query depends on many factors such as the number of instances satisfying the coupling query, the existence of free node or link type identifiers in the coupling query, the *complexity* of the query, network traffic, locality cost [131], etc. The combined effect of these factors can adversely affect the time taken to retrieve the query results from the Web.
- In a conventional database, a user may wish to determine the complete results for his needs. For example, a user may wish to find details of all the employees whose salary is more than 50K. However, this computation of complete results may not always be necessary in the context of the Web. A user may not be looking for complete results of a query but a portion of it sufficient to satisfy her needs. For instance, suppose we wish to determine the treatments of AIDS from the Web. There are numerous sites that provide information related to

the treatment of AIDS. However, the information from different sites overlaps as there is a finite set of treatment procedures for AIDS. Thus retrieving all documents related to the treatment of AIDS may not be meaningful to a user. A user may only download a small portion of those documents that are sufficient for information related to the treatment for AIDS.

The query attributes `number_of_tuples`, `total_nodes`, `host_tuples`, `time`, and `host_nodes` discussed next are used to provide the flexibility to control the execution time of a query. In this section, we discuss `number_of_tuples`. In the subsequent sections we discuss the remaining attributes.

The attribute `number_of_tuples` restricts the search to a certain number of returned web tuples. If the specified number of tuples is exceeded, the search stops. For instance,

$$q(G) \equiv \text{COUPLING\_QUERY}::G.\texttt{number\_of\_tuples LT "}100\text{"}$$

The above predicate specifies that the coupling query should stop executing as the number of web tuples reaches 100.

Total Nodes

Note that the coupling query attribute `number_of_tuples` indirectly affects the number of instances of node type identifiers. However, the user does not know ahead of time the precise number of instances of each node type identifier. Sometimes it may be necessary to control these instances of node type identifiers. For example, suppose instances of node type identifier d in a coupling query are pages containing treatment-related information for a particular disease, say AIDS. As mentioned earlier, there may exist thousands of pages in the Web containing information related to treatments for AIDS that satisfy the predicate defined on d. A user may wish to limit the number of web tuples returned by a query by specifying the maximum number of instances of d to be retrieved. If the specified number of instances is exceeded, the execution of the coupling query stops. The attribute `total_nodes` is used to control the total number of instances of a node type identifier. Let $G = \langle X_n, X_\ell, C, P, Q \rangle$ be a coupling query. Then the syntax of the coupling query predicate containing the `total_nodes` attribute is given below, where $x \in X_n$ and

$$q(G) \equiv \text{COUPLING\_QUERY}::G.\texttt{(total\_nodes::}x\texttt{) op "V"}$$

The node type identifier whose total number of instances is to be controlled is specified by the identifier x and is separated from the query attribute `total_nodes` by the symbol "::". An example of such a coupling query predicate is given below.

$$q(G) \equiv \text{COUPLING\_QUERY}::G.\texttt{(total\_nodes::}d\texttt{) LT "}100\text{"}$$

The above predicate specifies that the coupling query G stop executing when the number of instances of d reaches 100.

Host Nodes and Host Tuples

A coupling query may return relevant sets of documents from one or more Web sites. Although the attributes `number_of_tuples` and `total_nodes` may be used to limit the number of results of a query, they have *some* limitations. When a coupling query retrieves information from a single Web site (that is, all nodes in the query result belong to the same Web site), the attributes `number_of_tuples` and `total_nodes` may provide the user flexibility to control the instances of the query result. However, when a coupling query retrieves results from multiple heterogeneous Web sites these query attributes are not always the most efficient way of controlling the number of instances retrieved from *each* Web site. These attributes are useful in controlling the total number of web tuples or node instances but they are not an accurate mechanism for controlling the number of web tuples and node instances from each Web site. Note that this problem does not arise when the query results contain information from a single Web site only. We elaborate this with the following examples.

Suppose a coupling query retrieves web tuples from three Web sites, say h_1, h_2, and h_3. Suppose we wish to control the number of instances retrieved from each Web site. For instance, we wish to retrieve a maximum of 50 tuples from each of these three Web sites. That is, the total number of tuples retrieved from h_1, h_2, and h_3 will be less than 150. However, the predicate

$$q(G) \equiv \texttt{COUPLING\_QUERY::}G.\texttt{number\_of\_tuples LT "150"}$$

may retrieve 150 tuples from h_1 and no tuples from h_2 and h_3. It may also retrieve 50 tuples from h_1, 100 from h_2, and none from h_3. Similarly, if we wish to control the instances of a node type identifier, say d for each Web site, then the attribute `total_node` may not be the most efficient way of doing it. Suppose from each Web site h_1, h_2, and h_3 we wish to gather at most 20 instances of d. Thus the maximum number of instances of d in the query results from these three Web sites must not exceed 60. The coupling query predicate used to impose this constraint is as follows.

$$q(G) \equiv \texttt{COUPLING\_QUERY::}G.\texttt{(total\_nodes::}d\texttt{) LT "60"}$$

However, the coupling query may retrieve 60 instances of d from h_1 and none from h_2 and h_3. It may also retrieve 30, 25, and 5 instances of d from h_1, h_2, and h_3 respectively.

In order to resolve the above limitation for query results containing tuples or nodes from multiple Web sites we introduce coupling query predicates containing the attributes `host_tuples` and `host_nodes`. These attributes are used to control the number of web tuples and specified node objects from each Web site, respectively. The syntax of the coupling query predicate involving `host_tuples` is

$$q(G) \equiv \texttt{COUPLING\_QUERY::}G.\texttt{host\_tuples SATISFIES "V"}$$

where $V = n$, where n is an integer, i.e., 100, 200, etc., or it is of the form $V = \{(h_1\ \texttt{op}_1\ n_1), (h_2\ \texttt{op}_2\ n_2), \ldots, (h_k\ \texttt{op}_k\ n_k)\}$, where h_i is a string and indicates host name, n_i is an integer, and $\texttt{op}_i$ is a relational operator such as $=, \leq, \geq, >, <$. Note that $V = n$ specifies that each Web site should satisfy the constraint imposed by the coupling query predicate. Some examples of coupling query predicates containing host_tuples attribute are

$$q(G) \equiv \text{COUPLING\_QUERY::} G.\text{host\_tuples SATISFIES } \text{"50"}$$
$$q(G) \equiv \text{COUPLING\_QUERY::} G.\text{host\_tuples SATISFIES}$$
$$\text{"} (ntu.edu.sg \leq 30, \ nus.edu.sg \leq 20) \text{"}$$

The first predicate indicates that the number of tuples from each Web site must not exceed 50 and the second predicate specifies that the number of web tuples from the Web sites ntu.edu.sg and nus.edu.sg must not exceed 30 and 20, respectively.

Similarly, the syntax of a coupling query predicate containing the attribute host_nodes is

$$q(G) \equiv \text{COUPLING\_QUERY::} G.(\text{host\_nodes::} x) \text{ SATISFIES "V"}$$

where $x \in X_n$, $p(x) \in P$, $X_n \in G$, and the syntax of V is identical to that in predicates containing host_tuples. Some examples of this type of coupling query predicate are

$$q(G) \equiv \text{COUPLING\_QUERY::} G.(\text{host\_nodes::} d) \text{ SATISFIES } \text{"20"}$$
$$q(G) \equiv \text{COUPLING\_QUERY::} G.(\text{host\_nodes::} d) \text{ SATISFIES}$$
$$\text{"} (ntu.edu.sg \leq 20, \ nus.edu.sg \leq 10) \text{"}$$

The first predicate indicates that the number of instances of d from each Web site must not exceed 20 and the second predicate specifies that the number of instances of d from the Web sites ntu.edu.sg and nus.edu.sg must not exceed 20 and 10, respectively.

Time

The attribute time enables us to restrict the processing of a web query to a specified amount of time. When the time reaches its limit, the execution stops and returns the web tuples found thus far. For instance, consider Example 6.1. The predicate q_1 specifies that the coupling query G_1 will be executed for 20 minutes only.

Broken Link Mode

While traversing the Web, the execution of a coupling query may often encounter "Document Not Found" error (Error 404); (also called *broken links*). A broken link prevents a query from traversing further. Hence it may seem that whenever a coupling query encounters a broken link it should ignore the corresponding nodes and links as they do not satisfy the coupling query. However, including broken links in the web tuples has the following advantages.

- Existence of relevant Web sites: If the results of a query do not contain tuples containing broken links, the user will not be aware of the existence of the corresponding Web site or Web pages that may provide useful information. Note that the broken link does not necessarily indicate that the Web site does not exist anymore. It may indicate that the address of the Web site has changed or it is temporarily removed from the Web or it may also suggest that the value of the HRE attribute of the link may contain typographical errors. Thus awareness of the user about the existence of the Web site may result in inspection of neighboring documents or modification of the coupling query by the user to locate the valid address of this Web site. However, if the query result ignores web tuples containing broken links then it may not be possible for a user to modify his query to locate the valid addresses of the Web sites or Web documents simply because he is not aware of it.

- **Appropriateness of Web sites for relevant information:** Identifying a number of broken links in a query result also helps us to determine the currency of relevant Web site(s) with respect to the information for which the user is looking. For instance, suppose we wish to retrieve information I from a set of Web sites. If the query results contain large numbers of web tuples that have encountered broken links then it may suggest that the Web sites considered for retrieving I may not be the "best" collection of sources for information related to I. Note that a user may only be able to determine these issues if she is aware of the existence of web tuples containing broken links in the query result.

- **Determining currently unavailable information using polling coupling query:** Observe that a broken link may occur if a Web document or Web site is temporarily removed from the Web. That is, it may not be available at time t_1, but may be globally accessible at time t_2, where $t_2 > t_1$. If we allow web tuples containing broken links in the query results then a user may be able to modify the query and execute it periodically to retrieve the set of relevant documents that were not previously available. However, a user may not be aware of this information if web tuples containing broken links are disregarded in query results. Thus he may not find the need to reexecute the query periodically to retrieve those relevant web tuples that previously contained broken links.

The attribute `broken_link_mode` is used in the coupling query predicate to provide the flexibility to materialize web tuples containing broken links. The value of such an attribute is set to `"on"` if we wish to retrieve web tuples that encountered broken links. On the other hand, the `"off"` mode will not retrieve and materialize in the web table those web tuples that encountered a 404 error. By default, the `broken_link_mode` is set to `"off"`. We illustrate this with an example given below.

Example 6.3. Assume that there is a Web site at `http://www.get-a-life.com` that identifies and categorizes online information into different directories, such as "Art & Entertainment", "Games", "Sports", "Health", etc., to help users retrieve relevant information easily. Specifically, the site provides information related to the treatment of AIDS from the web page at `http://www.get-a-life.com/health/`. Typically, there is a link labeled "Diseases & Conditions" in this page that links to a web page containing information about various diseases. From this page one can probe further by following the links related to AIDS to get a list of various sites providing information about various AIDS issues. Suppose a user wishes to find all documents from the web page at `http://www.get-a-life.com/health/` containing details of treatment of AIDS, based on the following known facts.

- From the home page at `http://www.get-a-life.com/health/` there is a link labeled "Diseases & Conditions" that connects to a web page containing information related to diseases.
- In this page, there is a link labeled "AIDS" that takes one to a page containing a list of various sites that provide AIDS-related information.

Furthermore, the query result must include web tuples that have encountered broken links. The coupling query may be formulated as follows.

Let the coupling query be $G_2 = \langle X_{n_{2q}}, X_{\ell_{2q}}, C_{2q}, P_{2q}, Q_{2q} \rangle$, where $X_{n_{2q}} = \{a, b, c, d, \#\}$, $X_{\ell_{2q}} = \{e, f, g, h, \text{-}\}$, $C_{2q} \equiv k_{2_1} \wedge k_{2_2} \wedge k_{2_3} \wedge k_{2_4}$, where $k_{2_1} \equiv a\langle e\rangle b$, $k_{2_2} \equiv b\langle f\rangle c$, $k_{2_3} \equiv c\langle g(\text{-})\rangle\{0,4\}\rangle\#$, $k_{2_4} \equiv \#\langle h\{1,5\}\rangle d$, and $P_{2q} = \{p_{2_1}, p_{2_2}, p_{2_3}, p_{2_4}, p_{2_5}, p_{2_6}, p_{2_7}, p_{2_8}\}$, where

$p_{2_1}(a) \equiv$ METADATA::a[url] EQUALS
    "$http://www[.]get\text{-}a\text{-}life[.]com/health/$"
$p_{2_2}(b) \equiv$ CONTENT::b[title] NON-ATTR_ENCL "$Health\ Information$"
$p_{2_3}(c) \equiv$ CONTENT::c[body.(%)*] NON-ATTR_CONT
    ":BEGIN_WORD: + $AIDS$ + :END_WORD:"
$p_{2_4}(d) \equiv$ CONTENT::d[html.(%)+] NON-ATTR_CONT
    ":BEGIN_WORD: + $treatment$ + :END_WORD:"
$p_{2_5}(e) \equiv$ CONTENT::e[A] NON-ATTR_ENCL "$Diseases\ \&\ Conditions$"
$p_{2_6}(f) \equiv$ CONTENT::f[A] NON-ATTR_ENCL "$AIDS$'
$p_{2_7}(g) \equiv$ CONTENT::g[A] NON-ATTR_CONT "(?= .*($AIDS$).*)"
$p_{2_8}(h) \equiv$ CONTENT::h[A] NON-ATTR_CONT
    ":BEGIN_WORD: + $Treatment$ + :END_WORD:"

and $Q_2 = \{q_{2_1}\}$, where

$q_{2_1}(G_2) \equiv$ COUPLING_QUERY::G_2.broken_link_node EQUALS "on"

The query result is shown in Figure 6.4.   ∎

Observe that the last web tuple in Figure 6.4 enables us to identify that the link `AIDS/HIV` is a broken link as it fails to connect to the Web site of *Mining Company*. If we do not retrieve this web tuple then we will not know of the existence of the *Mining Company* web site. Recall that if the `broken_link_mode` is set to "off" then the coupling query will retrieve all but the last web tuple in Figure 6.4. Furthermore, another advantage of this feature is that if the Web site of *Mining Company* is temporarily removed from the Web, then the user may modify the coupling query G_2 and execute it periodically to retrieve treatment-related information from the *Mining Company* Web site when it is available globally again.

Form Mode

While traversing the Web, the execution of a coupling query may often encounter Web pages containing forms. A query may encounter the following two types of Web pages containing forms.

- Hyperlink-free form: A Web page containing a form with no local or global hyperlinks to other Web pages is called a *hyperlink-free form*. For instance, the Web page in Figure 2.3 contains a form. But it does not have any local or global hyperlinks that enable us to navigate further from this document.

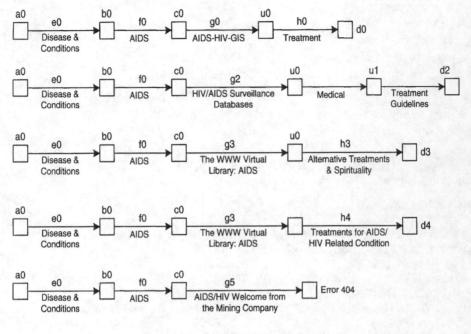

Fig. 6.4. Results of the query.

- **Nonhyperlink-free form:** A Web page containing a form as well as hyperlinks to other Web documents is called a *nonhyperlink-free form*. For instance, the Web page in Figure 2.4 contains a form for entering a query and also contains various clickable hyperlinks such as "Home", "Frequently Asked Questions", etc. that point to different Web documents.

Observe that a nonhyperlink-free form does not hinder a query from navigating further from the hyperlinks contained in the page to determine the satisfiability of the coupling query. However, this is not true for hyperlink-free forms. To elaborate further, consider the Web page in Figure 2.3. A query fails to navigate further from this Web page as it is a hyperlink-free form. Consequently, a web tuple containing a hyperlink-free form may not satisfy a coupling query due to navigational failure. Thus it may seem that whenever a coupling query encounters a hyperlink-free form it should ignore the corresponding web tuple from the query results. However, not including web tuples that encountered hyperlink-free forms in the query result has *some* disadvantages. If the query result ignores web tuples containing hyperlink-free forms then the user will not be aware of the existence of the corresponding nodes that may provide relevant information. The information is in Web pages that are generated by programs given user inputs (in the forms) and are therefore not accessible to crawling. In order to retrieve data from such documents one has to be aware of the existence of these hyperlink-free forms. Thus query results that include web tuples containing hyperlink-free forms enable us to further manipulate these forms to harness relevant information.

We impose a predicate on the attribute form_mode of the coupling query for retrieving web tuples containing hyperlink-free forms. If the form_mode is "on" then the coupling query will retrieve web tuples containing hyperlink-free forms. Otherwise, the "off" mode will ignore web tuples that encounter these forms. By default, we set the value to "off". An example of a coupling query predicate containing the form_mode attribute is given below.

$$q(G) \equiv \texttt{COUPLING\_QUERY}::G.\texttt{form\_mode EQUALS } "on"$$

Validity of Coupling Query Predicates

In the preceding section, we have discussed how to control execution of a coupling query using a set of coupling query predicates. We now highlight the *validity conditions* associated with coupling query predicates. Note that although a coupling query contains a set of coupling query predicates, any arbitrary set of coupling query predicates does not represent a valid coupling query. The predicates must satisfy certain *conditions* for a coupling query to be valid. We discuss these conditions now.

The criteria for validity checking in the context of coupling query predicates are as follows.

- Coupling query predicates must not contradict the predicates defined over node and link objects.
- The set of coupling query predicates must be able to coexist. That is, a predicate must not contradict the constraints imposed on the execution of the query by other coupling query predicates.

We now identify the conditions for checking the above criteria. We begin with the first criterion, i.e., contradiction of predicates on node and link objects. We first define a few terms for our exposition. If q is a coupling query predicate then $attr(q)$, $val(q)$, and $op(q)$ represent the query attribute, value, and predicate operator of q, respectively. Similarly, if $p(x)$ is a predicate on the identifier x then $qual(p)$, $attr\_path(p)$, $op(p)$, and $val(p)$ represent the predicate qualifier, attribute path expression, predicate operator, and value of the predicate, respectively.

Let x be a node type identifier in a coupling query G representing a set of documents and $p(x) \equiv \texttt{METADATA}::x\texttt{[url.server] EQUALS "www[.]ntu[.]edu[.]sg"}$ be a predicate on x. Then the instances of x must belong to the Web site at www.ntu.edu.sg. Now suppose $q_1(G)$ and $q_2(G)$ are two coupling query predicates in the query such that $q_1(G) \equiv \texttt{COUPLING\_QUERY}::G\texttt{[host] EQUALS}$ "www.nus.edu.sg" and $q_2(G) \equiv \texttt{COUPLING\_QUERY}::G\texttt{[host\_node}::x\texttt{] SATISFIES}$ "www.nus.edu.sg < 20". Observe that $q_1(G)$ specifies the host of all the nodes retrieved by the query must belong to www.nus.edu.sg which contradicts $p(x)$. Furthermore, $q_2(G)$ specifies that the number of instances of x that belong to the site www.nus.edu.sg should be less than 20. In fact, this predicate does not make any sense as the instances of x belong to different Web sites. Hence such types of contradicting predicates are not allowed in a coupling query. Formally, the following condition must be satisfied by the query.

Condition 6.1 *Let $x \in X_n$ and $p(x)$ be a predicate on x such that $qual(p) =$* METADATA, $attr\_path(p) =$ url.server, $op(p) =$ EQUALS, *and $val(p) = V$. Then there cannot be a coupling query predicate $q \in Q$ that satisfies any one of the following conditions.*

- $attr(q) =$ host, $op(q) =$ EQUALS, *and $val(q) \neq V$,*
- $attr(q) =$ host_nodes *and $id(q) = x$, where $id(q)$ denotes the node type identifier in the value of q.* ∎

The next condition ensures that the set of coupling query predicates can coexist. That is, they do not contradict each other. Consider two predicates q_1 and q_2 in a coupling query. If the query attribute of q_1 is number_of_tuples then the query attribute of q_2 cannot be total_nodes. This is because q_1 restricts the number of query results retrieved from the Web and hence there is no need to restrict the number of total nodes in the query result. Similarly, if the query attribute of q_1 is time then other attributes such as total_nodes and number_of_tuples to restrict the number of query results are superfluous. Moreover, having all these query attributes in the predicates may make q_1 and q_2 contradict each other. That is, if q_1 is satisfied then q_2 is never satisfied. Based on a similar notion the attributes host, host_nodes, and host_tuples cannot coexist in a set of coupling query predicates.

Condition 6.2 *Let q_1 and q_2 be two coupling query predicates in G. Then these conditions must be true:*

- *if $attr(q_1) =$ number_of_tuples then $attr(q_2) \neq$ total_nodes,*
- *if $attr(q_1) =$ time then $attr(q_2) \notin \{$number_of_tuples, total_nodes$\}$ for $op(q_1) = op(q_2) =$ EQUALS, and*
- *if $attr(q_1) =$ host then $attr(q_2) \notin \{$host_nodes, host_tuples$\}$.* ∎

6.2.3 Definition of Coupling Query

We now formally define a coupling query. Note that although a coupling query consists of five components as described in the preceding section, any arbitrary set of node and link type identifiers, connectivities, and predicates does not represent a valid coupling query. The following conditions must be satisfied by the components of a coupling query.

Conditions on Node and Link Type Identifiers

The conditions outlined below must be satisfied by the X_n and X_ℓ components of the coupling query.

- The set of node type identifiers X_n is always nonempty and must contain at least one bound node type identifier. That is, $X_n \neq \emptyset$.
- The identifiers used to represent node objects in the coupling query must be nominally dissimilar to those used to represent link objects. That is, the components X_n and X_ℓ must not overlap; i.e., $X_n \cap X_\ell = \emptyset$.

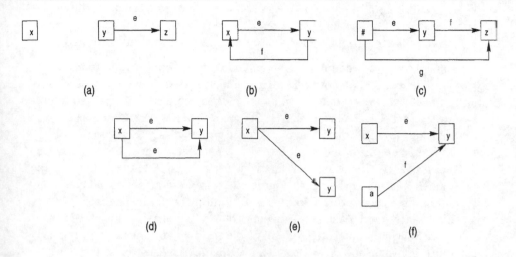

Fig. 6.5. Graphical representation of invalid coupling queries.

Conditions on Connectivities

We now identify the constraints imposed on the set of connectivities in a coupling query.

- The set of node and link type identifiers in the collection of connectivities must match the set of node and link type identifiers specified in the components of X_n and X_ℓ.
- The next condition specifies the only case when a coupling query may not contain any connectivities. This is possible only when the set of node objects is represented by a single node type identifier. In this case, the predicate set is nonempty as the node type identifier cannot be a free type identifier.
- If C_1 and C_2 represent two conjunctive connectivity sets in the coupling query and $C_1 \vee C_2$, then C_1 and C_2 must not contain same set of connectivities.

Condition on Predicates

Finally, the predicate set in a coupling query must satisfy the following condition.

- The argument of each predicate in the predicate set must be a node or link type identifier in X_n or X_ℓ.

Topological Conditions on the Coupling Query

A coupling query can be visualized as a directed graph. Recall from Chapter 5 that a connectivity can be visualized as a directed, connected acyclic graph. As a coupling query contains a set of connectivities, it can also be visualized as a directed graph, where a vertex and an edge of the graph are labeled by a node and link type identifier respectively, and a set of predicates, if any, on these identifiers. Formally, let k_1, k_2, ... , k_n be a set of connectivities in a coupling query G. Furthermore, to simplify formulation of a coupling query and for its efficient computation we pose certain constraints on the graphical form of a coupling query as outlined below.

- The graphical view of a coupling query must be a directed, connected acyclic graph. This indicates that not only each connectivity in a coupling query is a connected DAG, but also that the union of all the connectivities in a coupling query must also be a connected DAG. We do not allow a coupling query to be disconnected as such queries may not be *computable* [2]. For instance, Figure 6.5(a) is an example of a disconnected graph and hence does not represent a valid coupling query. Also we do not allow cycles in a coupling query in order to simplify the evaluation of the query. Figure 6.5(b) represents an invalid coupling query containing a cycle. It may seem that forbidding cycles in a coupling query would significantly hinder the expressiveness of a web query. This is indeed true as cycles are very common in the Web. Web sites may specifically be designed to distribute information across pages, and provide extensive links to lead the user back and forth across these pages. In fact, proper usage of cycles in a Web site is considered to be one of the important features for good Web site design. Hence, to address this problem we follow a two-level approach. At the first level, we use an acyclic coupling query to gather relevant documents from the Web and materialize them in our web warehouse. In the second level, we use the *web select* operation to impose cyclic constraints on the materialized query results. We discuss this in detail in Section 8.3.
- The graphical representation of a coupling query must have a single source vertex. That is, there must be only one vertex with zero in-degree. We disregard queries with multiple source vertices to simplify formulation and evaluation of coupling queries. Figure 6.5(f) is an example of an invalid query with multiple source vertices.
- The source vertex of the query must always be bound. That is, the node type identifier in the query representing the source vertex must always be associated with a set of nontrivial predicates defined over it. This is to ensure *computability* of the query (discussed later). Figure 6.5(c) is an example of an invalid query with a free source vertex.
- The labels of two edges in the graph are identical only if the start and end vertices of each edge are not identical to one another. Hence the query in Figure 6.5(d) is invalid.
- The labels of two vertices in the graph can be identical only if the labels of the incoming edges and their start vertices are not identical. The query in Figure 6.5(e) is invalid because of the violation of this rule.

Based on the above features, a coupling query can be formally defined as follows.

Definition 6.4. [Coupling Query] *A* **coupling query** *is a 5-tuple* $G = \langle X_n, X_\ell, C, P, Q \rangle$, *where* X_n *is a set of node type identifiers,* X_ℓ *is a set of link type identifiers,* C *is a set (possibly empty) of connectivities defined over* X_n *and* X_ℓ, *P is a set of predicates defined over* X_n *and* X_ℓ, *and* Q *is a set (possibly empty) of coupling query predicates such that the following conditions are true.*

- $X_n \neq \emptyset$, $P \neq \emptyset$, $X_n \cap X_\ell = \emptyset$;
- If $|X_n| = 1$, then $X_\ell = \emptyset$, $C = \emptyset$ and $P \neq \emptyset$;
- Let X_{nc} and $X_{\ell c}$ be the set of node and link type identifiers in C, respectively. Then $X_{nc} = X_n$ and $X_{\ell c} = X_\ell$;
- There must not exist connectivity set $C_a \equiv k_{a1} \wedge k_{a2} \wedge \cdots \wedge k_{an}$ and $C_b \equiv k_{b1} \wedge k_{b2} \wedge \cdots k_{bn}$ such that $C_a \vee C_b$ and $k_{ax} = k_{bx} \ \forall \ 0 < x \leq n$;
- Let $p(x) \in P$. Then $x \in (X_n \cup X_\ell)$;
- Let $G(C)$ be the graphical representation of C. Then $G(C)$ must be a directed, connected acyclic graph with a single source vertex. Furthermore, let x be the identifier of the source vertex in $G(C)$. Then there must exist a nontrivial predicate $p(x) \in P$. ∎

In Section 6.3, we illustrate coupling queries with examples.

6.2.4 Types of Coupling Query

A coupling query is categorized into two types: *canonical* and *noncanonical*. This categorization is based on the type of connectivities in the query and their relationship with one another. We elaborate on this further.

Canonical Coupling Query

We say that a coupling query is *canonical* if it contains a set (possibly empty) of simple connectivities in DNF. For example, if $G = \langle X_n, X_\ell, C, P, Q \rangle$, $C \equiv C_1 \vee C_2$, where $C_1 \equiv k_1 \wedge k_2$, $C_2 \equiv k_3$ $k_1 \equiv x\langle e \rangle y$, $k_2 \equiv y\langle j \rangle z$, and $k_3 \equiv x\langle e \rangle z$, then G is a canonical coupling query.

Definition 6.5. [Canonical Coupling Query] *Let* $G = \langle X_n, X_\ell, C, P, Q \rangle$ *be a coupling query. Then G is* **canonical** *if* $C = \emptyset$ *or* $C \equiv C_1 \vee C_2 \vee \cdots \vee C_r$ *for* $r > 0$ *and* $C_i \equiv k_{i1} \wedge k_{i2} \wedge \cdots \wedge k_{is}$ *where* k_{ij} *is a simple connectivity* $\forall \ 0 < j \leq s$ *and* $\forall$ $0 < i \leq r$. *Each C_i is called a* **conjunctive connectivity set**. ∎

Based on the above definition of a canonical coupling query, we classify canonical queries into the following five types. Let $G_c = \langle X_n, X_\ell, C, P, Q \rangle$ be a canonical coupling query. Then

- **Type 1:** G_c does not contain any connectivities. That is, $|X_n| = 1$, $X_\ell = \emptyset$ and $C = \emptyset$. Note that this is the simplest form of coupling query;
- **Type 2:** G_c contains a single simple connectivity. That is, $|X_n| = 2$, $|X_\ell| = 1$, $C \equiv k$ where k is a simple connectivity;
- **Type 3:** G_c contains more than one simple connectivity and these connectivities are in conjunction. That is, $C \equiv k_1 \wedge k_2 \wedge \cdots \wedge k_r$, where k_i is a simple connectivity for all $1 < i \leq r$;
- **Type 4:** G_c contains more than one simple connectivity and these connectivities are in disjunction. That is, $C \equiv k_1 \vee k_2 \vee \cdots \vee k_r$, where k_i is a simple connectivity for all $1 < i \leq r$;
- **Type 5:** G_c contains more than one simple connectivity and these connectivities are in DNF. That is, $C \equiv C_1 \vee C_2 \vee \cdots \vee C_r$, where C_i is a conjunctive connectivity set for all $1 < i \leq r$.

Noncanonical Coupling Query

A *non-canonical coupling query*, on the other hand, may contain simple or complex connectivities and these connectivities may not be in DNF. For instance, if $C \equiv k_1 \wedge k_2$, $k_1 \equiv x\langle e|f\rangle y$, and $k_2 \equiv y\langle g\rangle z$, then G is a non-canonical coupling query. This is because k_1 is a complex connectivity.

We classify noncanonical queries into the following four types. Let $G_{nc} = \langle X_n, X_\ell, C, P, Q \rangle$ be a noncanonical coupling query. Then

- **Type 1:** G_{nc} contains a single complex connectivity. That is, $|X_n| = 2$, $X_\ell \neq \emptyset$, $C \equiv k$, where k is a complex connectivity;
- **Type 2:** G_{nc} contains more than one connectivity and at least one of them is complex. Furthermore, these connectivities are in conjunction. That is, $C \equiv k_1 \wedge k_2 \wedge \cdots \wedge k_r$, where k_i is complex for $1 < i \leq r$;
- **Type 3:** G_{nc} contains more than one connectivity and at least one of them is complex. Furthermore, these connectivities are in disjunction. That is, $C \equiv k_1 \vee k_2 \vee \cdots \vee k_r$, where k_i is complex for $1 < i \leq r$;
- **Type 4:** G_{nc} contains more than one simple or complex connectivity and these connectivities are in conjunction and in disjunction to one another.

Note that a user may specify any form of coupling query to harness relevant documents from the Web. We illustrate canonical and noncanonical coupling queries with examples in Section 6.3. For brevity, different types of canonical and noncanonical coupling queries are denoted as G_c^t or G_{nc}^t, respectively, where $0 < t \leq 5$ and indicates G_c or G_{nc} is of Type t.

6.2.5 Valid Canonical Coupling Query

A *valid* canonical coupling query is necessary for generating *web schemas* of a set of web tuples retrieved from the Web (we discuss this in Chapter 7). Moreover, this form is also necessary for *global web coupling* operations (we elaborate on this in Chapter 8). Informally, a canonical coupling query is valid if each conjunctive connectivity set in the query represents a directed connected acyclic graph with a single source vertex. Hence a canonical query must satisfy the following conditions.

Directed Connected Graph with Single Source Vertex

Each conjunctive connectivity set must represent a directed connected graph with a single source vertex. We illustrate this condition with an example. Consider C_1 to be a conjunctive connectivity set in a canonical coupling query. Let $k_1 \equiv a\langle e\rangle b$ be a connectivity in C_1. Then there must exist another connectivity of the form $a\langle f\rangle z$, $x\langle f\rangle b$, or $x\langle f\rangle a$ in C_1 if the number of simple connectivities in C_1 is more than one. Furthermore, if a represents the source vertex, then $x\langle f\rangle b$ or $x\langle f\rangle a$ cannot exist in C_1. Also the node type identifier represented by the source vertex must be bound.

Acyclic Condition on Connectivities

Each conjunctive connectivity set must represent an acyclic graph. Hence if $x\langle e\rangle y$ is a connectivity in C_i, then there must not exist another connectivity $y\langle f\rangle x$ in C_i. It is observed that these two connectivities create a cycle. Second, if $k_1 \equiv x\langle e\rangle y$ is a connectivity such that there exists another connectivity $k_5 \equiv z\langle f\rangle x$, then this may result in a cycle if k_1 is connected to k_5 through a set of connectivities (say k_2, k_3, and k_4).

Acyclic Conditions on Predicates

Next we discuss conditions on predicates in a coupling query for ensuring the query to be acyclic in nature. We first illustrate the conditions with an example. Let x and y be two node type identifiers such that $|P_x| > 1$ or $|P_y| > 1$, $p_1(x) \in P_x$, $p_1(y) \in P_y$, and

$$p_1(x) \equiv \texttt{METADATA::x[url] EQUALS "http://www[.]druginfonet[.]com"}$$
$$p_2(y) \equiv \texttt{METADATA::y[url] EQUALS "http://www[.]druginfonet[.]com"}$$

or there exists a comparison predicate as given below.

$$p(x,y) \equiv \texttt{METADATA::x[url] IS\_EQUAL y[url]}$$

Note that in this case, the query may contain a cyclic component if any one of the following conditions is not satisfied.

- If x and y belong to a conjunctive connectivity set C_i, then x and y must represent two adjacent identifiers. That is, if x and y are adjacent node type identifiers, then instances of x and y represent identical documents connected by an interior link. Consequently, there must exist a simple connectivity $x\langle\ell\rangle y$ in C_i to express adjacency of these node type identifiers.
- Otherwise, neither x nor y exists in C_i. That is, if $x \in C_i$ and $y \in C_j$, then $i \neq j$; i.e., C_i and C_j represent two conjunctive connectivity sets and $C_i \vee C_j$. Hence C_i and C_j do not generate cyclic graphs.

Formally, a valid canonical coupling query is defined as follows.

Definition 6.6. [Valid Canonical Coupling Query] *Let $G_c = \langle X_n, X_\ell, C, P, Q\rangle$ be a canonical coupling query where $C \equiv C_1 \vee C_2 \vee \cdots \vee C_r$. Then G_c is* **valid** *if the following conditions are true.*

1. *Let k_{ij} and $k_{i(j+1)}$ be two simple connectivities in C_i for $0 < i \leq r$. Then any one of the following must be true: (1) $lnode(k_{ij}) = rnode(k_{i(j+1)})$; (2) $rnode(k_{ij}) = rnode(k_{i(j+1)})$; and (3) $lnode(k_{ij}) = lnode(k_{i(j+1)})$. Also the last two equalities are mutually exclusive. Furthermore, if the second equality is true, then $j > 1$.*

2. *Let k_{ij} be a connectivity in C_i, then there must not exist $k_{i(j+n)}$ such that $lnode(k_{ij}) = rnode(k_{i(j+n)}) \ \forall \ 0 < n \leq s$,*

3. *$lnode(k_{ij}) \neq rnode(k_{is})$ is true for all $0 < s \leq n$ and $j \neq s$ only if $j = 1$,*

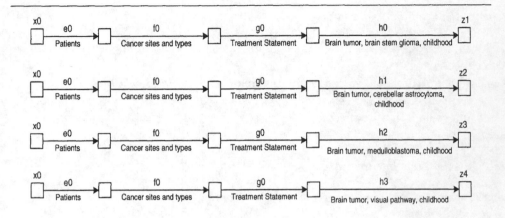

Fig. 6.6. Results of the query in Example 6.8.

4. *Let $(x, y) \in X_n$ and $(x, y) \exists C_i$. Then the following predicates are not valid if there does not exist $k \equiv x\langle \ell \rangle y$ in C_i for $0 < i \leq r$:*
   - *if $p_x(x)$ and $p_y(y)$ are two comparison-free predicates, then $attr\_path(p_x) = attr\_path(p_y) = \texttt{url}$, $qual(p_x) = qual(p_y) = \texttt{METADATA}$, $op(p_x) = op(p_x) = \texttt{EQUALS}$, and $val(p_x) = val(p_y)$, where $val(p_x)$ and $val(p_y)$ do not contain regular expressions;*
   - *If $p(x, y)$ is a comparison predicate on x and y, then $p(x, y) \equiv \texttt{METADATA::x[url] IS\_EQUAL y[url]}$.*
5. *There must exist a non-trivial predicate $p \in P$, where $arg(p) = lnode(k_{i1})$ $\forall$ $0 < i \leq r$,*
6. *Let C_a and C_b be two conjunctive connectivity sets. Then one of them must be true: $lnode(k_{a1}) = lnode(k_{b1})$, $lnode(k_{a1}) = lnode(k_{bj})$, or $lnode(k_{a1}) = rnode(k_{bj})$, where $j \neq 1$,*
7. *If $k \equiv x\langle \ell \rangle x$ is a connectivity in G_c, then the link type of the identifier ℓ must be defined in P.* ∎

6.3 Examples of Coupling Queries

As a coupling query is defined by a user, the structure and content of a coupling query depend on the factors: the information a user wishes to retrieve from the Web, and the user's level of knowledge of the content and structure of the Web site(s) containing the relevant information.

In a coupling query, the user specifies the five components X_n, X_ℓ, C, P, and Q. We now illustrate with examples the formulation of coupling queries. We begin with a noncanonical coupling query. Note that in this section, we provide multiple examples of coupling queries as we use these queries in the remaining portion of the book to illustrate various issues.

6.3.1 Noncanonical Coupling Query

Recall that we classified a noncanonical coupling query into four types, i.e., Types 1 to 4, based on the number of connectivities and their relationship with one another. We illustrate these types with examples.

Type 1-Noncanonical Coupling Query

Example 6.7. Consider the query in Section 6.1.2. Recall that a user wishes to retrieve information related to the treatment of different types of cancer from the NCI Web site. The query may be expressed by the noncanonical coupling query as depicted in Example 6.1. Observe that G_1 contains a single complex connectivity and hence belongs to the Type 1 category.   ∎

Example 6.8. Suppose we wish to retrieve information related to different forms of brain tumors from the Web site of NCI at `rex.nci.nih.gov` knowing that from the Web page at `http://rex.nci.nih.gov/SQUAREFIELD3.htm` one may follow the links labeled "patients" and then the links "Cancer sites and type" and "treatment statements", respectively, to reach a Web page containing a list of links for cancer-related disease. To formulate this query using a coupling query, a user needs to specify each component of the query. The formal representation of the coupling query may be as follows.

Let the coupling query be $G_2 = \langle X_{n_{2q}}, X_{\ell_{2q}}, C_{2q}, P_{2q}, Q_{2q} \rangle$

$$X_{n_{2q}} = \{x, z\}$$
$$X_{\ell_{2q}} = \{e, f, g, h\}$$
$$C_{2q} \equiv x \langle efgh \rangle z$$

$p_{2_1}(x) \equiv$ `METADATA::x[url]` EQUALS
    "*http://rex[.]nci[.]nih[.]gov/SQUAREFIELD3[.]html*"
$p_{2_2}(z) \equiv$ `CONTENT::z[title]` NON-ATTR_CONT
    ":BEGIN_WORD: + *tumou?r* + :END_WORD:"
$p_{2_3}(f) \equiv$ `CONTENT::f[A]` NON-ATTR_ENCL "*Cancer Sites and types*"
$p_{2_4}(e) \equiv$ `CONTENT::e[A]` NON-ATTR_ENCL "*Patients*"
$p_{2_5}(g) \equiv$ `CONTENT::g[A]` NON-ATTR_ENCL "*Treatment Statements*"
$p_{2_6}(h) \equiv$ `CONTENT::h[A]` NON-ATTR_CONT
    ":START_STR: + *brain tumou?r* + :END_STR:"

and $Q_{2q} = \{q_1\}$, where

$q_1(G_2) \equiv$ `COUPLING_QUERY::`G_2`.host` EQUALS "*rex.nci.nih.gov*"

Similar to the previous example, this query is also an example of a noncanonical coupling query of Type 1. The results of the query are shown in Figure 6.6.   ∎

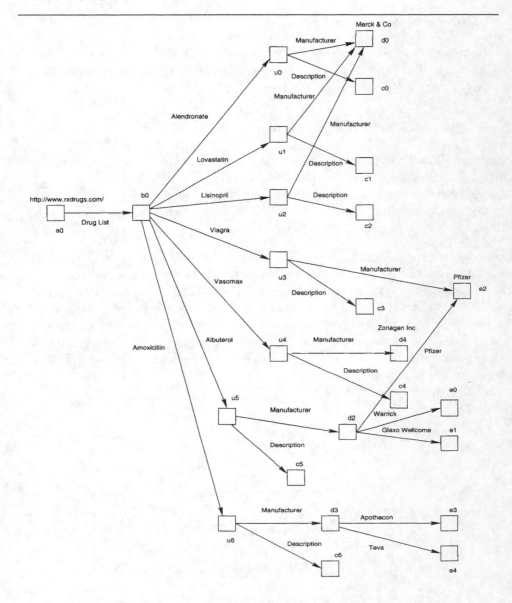

Fig. 6.7. Website at www.rxdrugs.com on 15th January, 2000.

Type 2-Noncanonical Coupling Query

We now illustrate a Type 2 noncanonical coupling query. The next two examples also illustrate the usage of partial knowledge in a coupling query.

Example 6.9. Assume that there is a Web site at `http://www.rxdrugs.com/` which provides information related to various drugs used for diseases. As with most of the sites in the WWW, the structure and content of this site change with time. For instance, the structures of the site on **15th January, 2000** and **15th February,**

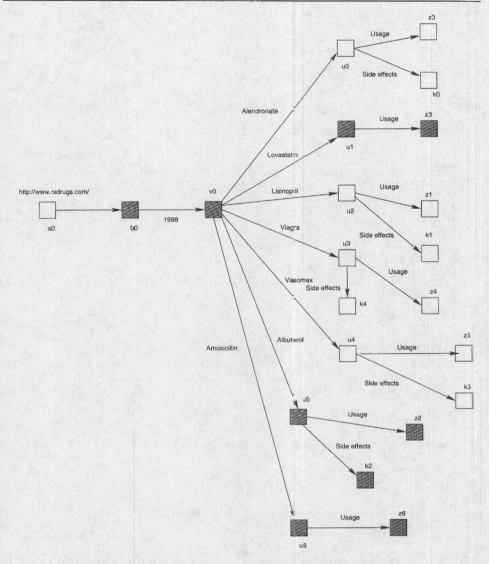

Fig. 6.8. Website at www.rxdrugs.com or 15th February, 2000.

2000 are shown in Figures 6.7 and 6.8. The pattern boxes indicate pages that have undergone modification during this time period. Suppose a user wishes to find descriptions and manufacturers of various drugs on 15th January, 2000 from this Web site. The user may specify the following noncanonical coupling query of Type 2. Let $G_{3q} = \langle X_{n_{3q}}, X_{\ell_{3q}}, C_{3q}, P_{3q}, Q_{3q} \rangle$, where

$$X_{n_{3q}} = \{a, b, c, d\}$$
$$X_{\ell_{3q}} = \{n, -_1, -_2\}$$
$$C_{3q} \equiv k_{3_1} \wedge k_{3_2} \wedge k_{3_3}$$

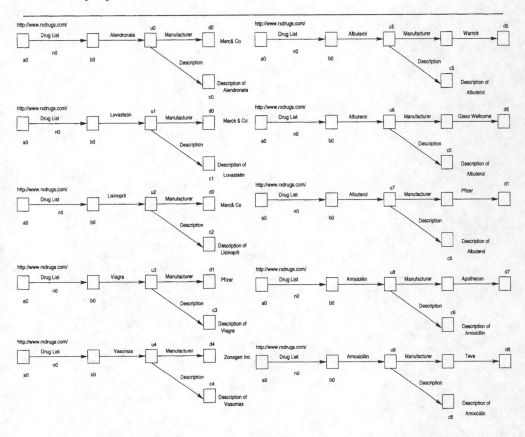

Fig. 6.9. Partial view of web table 'Drugs-Manufacturer'.

where

$$k_{3_1} \equiv a\langle n\rangle b$$
$$k_{3_2} \equiv b\langle -_1\{1,3\}\rangle c$$
$$k_{3_3} \equiv b\langle -_2\{1,3\}\rangle d$$

and $P_{3q} = \{p_{3_1}, p_{3_2}, p_{3_3}, p_{3_4}, p_{3_5}, p_{3_6}\}$, where

$p_{3_1}(a) \equiv$ `METADATA::a[url] EQUALS "http://www[.]rxdrugs[.]com/"`

$p_{3_2}(b) \equiv$ `CONTENT::b[html.body.title] NON-ATTR_CONT`
`":BEGIN_STR: + Drug List + :END_STR:"`

$p_{3_3}(c) \equiv$ `CONTENT::c[html.body.title] NON-ATTR_CONT`
`":BEGIN_WORD: + Description + :END_WORD:"`

$p_{3_4}(d) \equiv$ `CONTENT:: d[html.body.title] NON-ATTR_CONT`
`":BEGIN_WORD: + Manufacturer + :END_WORD:"`

$p_{3_5}(n) \equiv$ `CONTENT:: n[A] NON-ATTR_CONT`
`":BEGIN_STR: + Drug List + :END_STR:"`

$p_{3_6}(a) \equiv$ `METADATA::a[date] EQUALS "2nd January, 2000"`

and $Q_{3q} = \emptyset$. The set of results retrieved by this query is shown in Figure 6.9. ∎

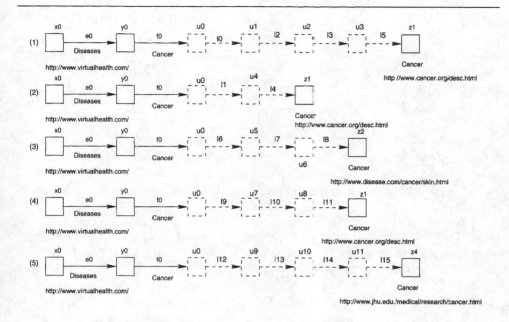

Fig. 6.10. Web tuples of "Cancer".

Example 6.10. Assume that the Web site at `http://www.virtualhealth.com/` integrates disease-related information from various Web sites. Suppose a user wishes to integrate cancer-related information from this Web site and store it in a *web table* labeled Cancer. The user specifies the query to couple cancer-related information by providing a coupling query $G_4 = \langle X_{n4}, X_{\ell 4}, C_4, P_4, Q_4 \rangle$, where

$$X_{n4} = \{x, y, z\}$$
$$X_{\ell 4} = \{e, f, -\}$$

and $C_4 \equiv x\langle e \rangle y \wedge y\langle f\text{-}\{1,4\}\rangle z$ and $P_4 = \{p_{4_1}, p_{4_2}, p_{4_3}, p_{4_4}, p_{4_5}\}$, where

$p_{4_1}(x) \equiv$ METADATA::x[url] EQUALS "$http://www[.]virtualhealth[.]com$"

$p_{4_2}(y) \equiv$ CONTENT::y[html(.%)+] NON-ATTR_CONT
"":BEGIN_WORD: + *cancer* + :END_WORD:"

$p_{4_3}(e) \equiv$ CONTENT::e[A] NON-ATTR_CONT
"BEGIN_WORD + *disease* + END_WORD"

$p_{4_4}(f) \equiv$ CONTENT::f[A] NON-ATTR_CONT
"BEGIN_WORD + *cancer* + END_WORD"

$p_{4_5}(z) \equiv$ CONTENT::z[title] NON-ATTR_CONT
"":BEGIN_WORD: + *cancer* + :END_WORD:"

and $Q_4 = \emptyset$. The set of results retrieved by this query is shown in Figure 6.10. ∎

Type 3-Noncanonical Coupling Query

Example 6.11. Consider the Type 1 noncanonical coupling query in Example 6.7. This can also be expressed as a noncanonical Type 3-coupling query by expressing the connectivity as a set of complex connectivities in disjunction. The formal representation of the query is as follows. Let the coupling query be $G_5 = \langle X_{n_{5q}}, X_{\ell_{5q}}, C_{5q}, P_{5q}, Q_{5q} \rangle$ where $X_{n_{5q}} = \{x, y\}$, $X_{\ell_{5q}} = \{e, f, g, h\}$, $C_{5q} \equiv k_{5_1} \vee k_{5_2}$, $k_{5_1} \equiv x\langle ef \rangle y$, $k_{5_2} \equiv x\langle gh \rangle y$, $P_{5q} = P_{1q}$, and $Q_{5q} = Q_{1q}$. ∎

Type 4-Noncanonical Coupling Query

Next, we provide an example of a noncanonical Type 4-coupling query. Note that a coupling query is noncanonical if it satisfies either of the conditions: (1) it contains complex connectivities, or (2) the set of simple connectivities in the query is not in DNF. Therefore we illustrate these two types of noncanonical Type 4-coupling query.

Example 6.12. Consider the coupling query in Example 6.1. This can be expressed as a noncanonical Type 4-coupling query by reducing the complex connectivity into sets of simple connectivities that are not in DNF. The formal representation of the query is as follows. Let the canonical coupling query be $G_6 = \langle X_{n_{6q}}, X_{\ell_{6q}}, C_{6q}, P_{6q}, Q_{6q} \rangle$, where $X_{n_{6q}} = \{x, y, \#_1, \#_2\}$, $X_{\ell_{6q}} = \{e, f, g, h\}$, $C_{6q} \equiv k_1 \vee k_2 \wedge k_3 \vee k_4$, where $k_1 \equiv x\langle e \rangle \#_1$, $k_2 \equiv x\langle g \rangle \#_2$, $k_3 \equiv \#_2\langle h \rangle y$, and $k_4 \equiv \#_1\langle f \rangle y$, $P_{6q} = P_{1q}$, and $Q_{6q} = Q_{1q}$. ∎

Example 6.13. Consider the Web page at www.druginfonet.com/maninfo.htm (Figure 2.1) which provides a list of addresses, email addresses, links, and telephone numbers of many pharmaceutical manufacturing companies. Each link related to a company connects to the Web site of the particular company. Suppose we wish to retrieve information about various products of the company "Alliance Laboratories" at www.allp.com. Note that this Web site uses individual product names as anchors of hyperlinks to describe their products (i.e., "Liquivent", "Flogel", and so on). Also observe that each product name contains the symbol of encircled R. Note that in HTML this symbol is expressed by the special character &reg. Hence this query may be expressed as $G_7 = \langle X_{n_{7q}}, X_{\ell_{7q}}, C_{7q}, P_{7q}, Q_{7q} \rangle$, where $X_{n_{7q}} = \{x, y, \#_1\}$, $X_{\ell_{7q}} = \{e, g, t\}$, $C_{7q} \equiv C_a \vee C_b \vee C_c \vee C_d \vee C_e \vee C_f \vee C_g$, where

$$C_a \equiv x\langle eg\text{-}\rangle y \quad C_b \equiv x\langle eg \rangle y \wedge y\langle t \rangle \#_1$$
$$C_c \equiv x\langle e \rangle y \wedge y\langle gt \rangle \#_1 \quad C_d \equiv x\langle e \rangle y \wedge y\langle g \rangle y \wedge y\langle t \rangle \#_1$$
$$C_e \equiv x\langle eg \rangle y \wedge y\langle t \rangle y \quad C_f \equiv x\langle e \rangle y \wedge y\langle gt \rangle y$$
$$C_g \equiv x\langle e \rangle y \wedge y\langle g \rangle y \wedge y\langle t \rangle y$$

$P_{7q} = \{p_{7_1}, p_{7_2}, p_{7_3}, p_{7_4}, p_{7_5}, p_{7_6}, p_{7_7}\}$, where

$p_{7_1}(x) \equiv$ METADATA::x[url] EQUALS
      "*http://www[.]druginfonet[.]com/maninfo[.]htm*"
$p_{7_2}(y) \equiv$ CONTENT::y[html(.%)+] NON-ATTR_CONT
      ":BEGIN_WORD: + *products?* + :END_WORD:"
$p_{7_3}(e) \equiv$ CONTENT::e[A(.%)*] NON-ATTR_ENCL "Alliance Laboratories"
$p_{7_4}(g) \equiv$ CONTENT::g[A(.%)*] CONT "MATCH(.*&reg + :END_STR:)"
$p_{7_5}(g) \equiv$ METADATA::g[link_type] EQUALS "*local*"
$p_{7_6}(t) \equiv$ METADATA::t[link_type] EQUALS "*local*"
$p_{7_7}(e) \equiv$ METADATA::e[link_type] EQUALS "*global*"

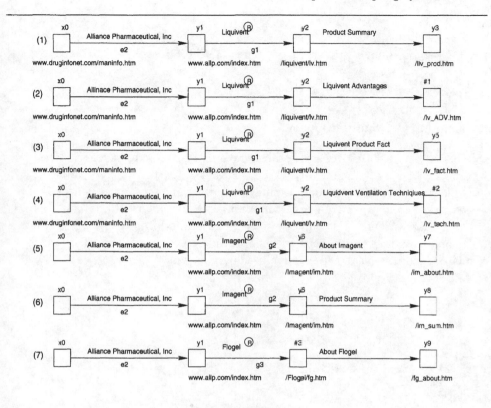

Fig. 6.11. Query results.

and $q_1(G_7) \equiv$ COUPLING_QUERY::G_7.number_of_tuples LT "20". Observe that C_a, C_b, C_c, C_e, and C_f contain complex connectivities. Hence this is an example of a non-canonical Type 4-coupling query.

6.3.2 Canonical Coupling Query

We now illustrate with examples valid canonical coupling queries. Recall that canonical coupling queries can be classified into Types 1 to 5. We illustrate Types 3 to 5 only.

Type 3-Canonical Coupling Query

Example 6.14. Consider the noncanonical Type 1-coupling query in Example 6.3. This query can be expressed in canonical form $G_8 = \langle X_{n_{8q}}, X_{\ell_{8q}}, C_{8q}, P_{8q}, Q_{8q} \rangle$ by *reducing* the complex connectivity into a set of simple connectivities as follows.

$$X_{n_{8q}} = \{x, \#_1, \#_2, \#_3, z\}$$
$$X_{\ell_{8q}} = \{e, f, g, h\}$$
$$C_{8q} \equiv k_{8_1} \wedge k_{8_2} \wedge k_{8_3} \wedge k_{8_4}$$

where

$$k_{8_1} \equiv x\langle e\rangle \#_1 \ k_{8_2} \equiv \#_1 \langle f\rangle \#_2 \ k_{8_3} \equiv \#_2 \langle g\rangle \#_3 \ k_{8_4} \equiv \#_3 \langle h\rangle z$$

$P_{8q} = P_{2q}$, and $Q_{8q} = Q_{2q}$.   ∎

Type 4-Canonical Coupling Query

Example 6.15. Consider the disease database Web page at `www.pedianet.com/news/illness/disease/disease.htm` (Figure 2.5). The purpose of this database is to provide information on various pediatric disorders. This page contains a list of diseases linked to another Web page containing detailed information about the respective diseases (Figure 2.5). Suppose we wish to find information about those "diseases" or "syndromes" that result in some sort of body "pain." This query may be formulated as a canonical Type 4-coupling query as shown below.

Let $G_9 = \langle X_{n_{9q}}, X_{\ell_{9q}}, C_{9q}, P_{9q}, Q_{9q}\rangle$, where

$$\begin{aligned} X_{n_{9q}} &= \{a, b\} \\ X_{\ell_{9q}} &= \{u, v\} \\ C_{9q} &\equiv k_{9_1} \vee k_{9_2} \end{aligned}$$

where $k_{9_1} \equiv a\langle u\rangle b$ and $k_{9_2} \equiv a\langle v\rangle b$ and $P_{9q} = \{p_{9_1}, p_{9_2}, p_{9_3}, p_{9_4}\}$, where

$p_{9_1}(a) \equiv$ METADATA::a[url] EQUALS
        "*http://www[.]pedianet[.]com/news/illness/disease/disease[.]htm*"
$p_{9_2}(b) \equiv$ CONTENT::b[html(.%)+] NON-ATTR_CONT
        ":BEGIN_STR: + *pain* + :END_STR:"
$p_{9_3}(u) \equiv$ CONTENT::u[A] NON-ATTR_CONT "
        :BEGIN_WORD: + *syndrome* + :END_WORD:"
$p_{9_4}(v) \equiv$ CONTENT::v[A] NON-ATTR_CONT
        ":BEGIN_WORD: + *disease* + :END_WORD:"

and $Q_{9q} = \emptyset$. Observe that this query is an example of a canonical Type 4-coupling query as k_{9_1} and k_{9_2} are simple connectivities in disjunction to each other.   ∎

Type 5 Canonical Coupling Query

Example 6.16. Consider the noncanonical coupling query in Example 6.11. This can be expressed as a canonical query by reducing the complex connectivities into sets of simple connectivities in DNF. The formal representation of the query is as follows. Let the canonical coupling query be $G_{10} = \langle X_{n_{10q}}, X_{\ell_{10q}}, C_{10q}, P_{10q}, Q_{10q}\rangle$, where $X_{n_{10q}} = \{x, y, \#_1, \#_2\}$, $X_{\ell_{10q}} = \{e, f, g, h\}$, $C_{10q} \equiv C_a \vee C_b$, $C_a \equiv x\langle e\rangle \#_1 \wedge \#_1 \langle f\rangle y$, $C_b \equiv x\langle g\rangle \#_2 \wedge \#_2 \langle h\rangle y$, $P_{10q} = P_{1q}$, and $Q_{10q} = Q_{1q}$. Notice that this is an example of a canonical Type 5-coupling query as all the connectivities are simple and are in DNF.   ∎

Example 6.17. Similarly, consider the query in Example 6.13. This query can also be formulated using a canonical Type 5-coupling query. Let the canonical coupling query be $G_{11} = \langle X_{n_{11q}}, X_{\ell_{11q}}, C_{11q}, P_{11q}, Q_{11q} \rangle$, where $X_{n_{11q}} = \{x, y, \#_1, \#_2, \#_3\}$, $X_{\ell_{11q}} = \{e, g, t\}$, $C_{11q} \equiv C_a \vee C_b \vee C_c \vee C_d \vee C_e \vee C_f \vee C_g$, where

$$C_a \equiv x\langle e\rangle\#_1 \wedge \#_1\langle g\rangle\#_2 \wedge \#_2\langle t\rangle y \qquad C_b \equiv x\langle e\rangle\#_1 \wedge \#_1\langle g\rangle y \wedge y\langle t\rangle\#_3$$
$$C_c \equiv x\langle e\rangle y \wedge y\langle g\rangle\#_2 \wedge \#_2\langle t\rangle\#_3 \qquad C_d \equiv x\langle e\rangle y \wedge y\langle g\rangle y \wedge y\langle t\rangle\#_3$$
$$C_e \equiv x\langle e\rangle\#_1 \wedge \#_1\langle g\rangle y \wedge y\langle t\rangle y \qquad C_f \equiv x\langle e\rangle y \wedge y\langle g\rangle\#_2 \wedge \#_2\langle t\rangle y$$
$$C_g \equiv x\langle e\rangle y \wedge y\langle g\rangle y \wedge y\langle t\rangle y$$

$P_{11q} = P_{7q}$, and $Q_{11q} = Q_{7q}$. Observe that the connectivities are expressed as a set of simple connectivities in DNF. Hence this is an example of a canonical Type 5-coupling query.   ∎

6.4 Valid Canonical Query Generation

In this section, we discuss how to transform a coupling query specified by a user to a *valid* canonical coupling query. Such a transformed form of canonical query has some major applications: First, it is used as input for the global web coupling operation for retrieving relevant data from the Web. We discuss this in detail in Chapter 8. Second, a valid canonical coupling query provides the framework for generating *web schema*(s) for the data retrieved from the Web.

6.4.1 Outline

The valid canonical coupling query generation process can be best explained by dividing it into the following two phases: the *canonical query generation phase* and the *validity checking phase*. We outline these phases now. In the following subsections we elaborate on these phases in turn.

Canonical Query Generation Phase:

This phase takes as input the coupling query formulated by the user and transforms it into a canonical form. Note that if the coupling query is in a canonical form, then it is not necessary to transform it. Hence input to this phase is a noncanonical coupling query $G_{nc} = \langle X_n, X_\ell, C, P, Q \rangle$ and output is the canonical form of G_{nc}; i.e., $G_c = \langle X'_n, X'_\ell, C', P, Q \rangle$, where $C' \equiv C_1 \vee C_2 \vee \cdots \vee C_r$, $X_n \subseteq X'_n$, and $X_\ell \subseteq X'_\ell$.

Validity Checking Phase:

This phase determines whether the canonical query is valid (satisfies the conditions in Definition 6.6). If not, then the query may contain disconnected or cyclic components. In this case this phase eliminates the invalid components of the query and transforms it to a valid form autonomously or by human intervention.

6.4.2 Phase 1: Coupling Query Reduction

In this phase we transform a noncanonical form of coupling query into a canonical form. We discuss how to reduce a user-specified noncanonical form of coupling query of Types 1 to 4 into canonical forms.

To transform any noncanonical coupling query $G_{nc} = \langle X_n, X_\ell, C, P, Q \rangle$ to a canonical form $G_c = \langle X'_n, X'_\ell, C', P', Q \rangle$ the following steps need to be performed.

- Reduce the set of connectivities C into a set of simple connectivities in DNF (denoted as C'). Note that this reduction involves transformation of complex connectivities into simple form.
- Identify the set of node and link type identifiers in C' and generate the set of node and link type identifiers X'_n and X'_ℓ, respectively, of G_c. Note that the complex connectivities in C are compact expressions for specifying connectivity involving a set of node and link type identifiers. Hence reduction of these complex connectivities into simple form generates additional node or link type identifiers that need to be incorporated in X'_n or X'_ℓ, respectively.
- Finally, the components P and Q of G_{nc} are assigned as the corresponding components of G_c without any modification. This is because the reduction of connectivities in DNF form does not affect the predicates and coupling query predicates of G_{nc}. It only affects the components X_n, X_ℓ, and C as described above.

Observe that the major step in reducing a noncanonical coupling query to its canonical form is to convert the set of connectivities in G_{nc} to a set of simple connectivities in DNF. Subsequent generation of X'_n, X'_ℓ and the other components is straightforward. Hence in the following discussion we describe the reduction of C to C' for noncanonical coupling queries of Types 1 to 4. Specifically, we show that any non-canonical coupling query can be reduced to its canonical form. We begin with non-canonical coupling queries of Types 1 and 2. To facilitate our exposition we define a few terms. Let k be a connectivity. Then the function $simple(k)$ reduces k, if it is in complex form, into a set of simple connectivities in DNF as described in Chapter 5 (Proposition 5.1). Otherwise, if k is simple, then it returns the connectivity itself. Formally,

$$simple(k) = \begin{cases} C_1 \vee \cdots \vee C_n & \text{if } k \text{ is complex} \\ k & \text{otherwise} \end{cases}$$

where $C_i \equiv k_{i1} \wedge k_{i2} \wedge \cdots \wedge k_{ir}, \ \forall \ 0 < i \leq n$, and k_{ij} are simple connectivities. Furthermore, if C represents a set of simple connectivities in DNF, then $node(C)$ and $link(C)$ return all the node and link type identifiers in C, respectively. Finally, the function $Transform(G_{nc})$ takes as input a noncanonical coupling query and returns as output the canonical form of the query (if possible).

Reduction of Noncanonical Type 1- and 2-Coupling Queries

In a noncanonical Type 1 or 2-coupling query one or more connectivities are in complex form. Also recall from Chapter 5, any complex connectivity can be reduced to a set of simple connectivities in DNF. Hence each complex connectivity in C of G_{nc} can be replaced by a set of simple connectivities in DNF. Observe that such a set of simple connectivities may be in conjunction with another set of simple connectivities in the coupling query. Consequently, these simple connectivities can be further reduced to a set of simple connectivities that are in DNF. For instance, consider the noncanonical Type 1-coupling query G_1 in Example 6.1. This query can be reduced to its canonical form G_{10} as shown in Example 6.16. Observe that the connectivities in G_{10} are all simple and in DNF. We now show formally that any noncanonical Type 1- or 2-coupling query can be reduced to a canonical form of Type 3 or 5.

Proposition 6.18. *Let G_{nc}^t be a noncanonical coupling query, where $t \in [1, 2]$. Then, $G_c^y = \mathrm{Transform}(G_{nc}^t)$, where $y \in [3, 5]$.* ∎

Proof. Let $C \equiv k_1 \wedge k_2 \wedge \cdots \wedge k_r$, where k_i is a complex connectivity for $0 < i \leq r$. Let the function $Reduce(C)$ take as input a set of connectivities and return a set of simple connectivities in DNF. We show that $Reduce(C)$ results in a set of simple connectivities in DNF where C is the connectivity component in a noncanonical coupling query of Type 1 or 2.

$$
\begin{aligned}
Reduce(C) &\equiv Reduce(k_1 \wedge k_2 \wedge \cdots \wedge k_r) \\
&\equiv simple(k_1) \wedge simple(k_2) \wedge \cdots \wedge simple(k_r) \\
&\equiv (C_{11} \vee C_{12} \vee \cdots \vee C_{1n1}) \wedge (C_{21} \vee C_{22} \vee \cdots \vee C_{2n2}) \cdots \quad (6.1)
\end{aligned}
$$

In the above equation each complex connectivity is reduced to a set of simple connectivities in DNF based on Proposition 5.1. The simple connectivities are unchanged. Finally, Equation (6.1) can be reduced to a set of simple connectivities in DNF using the distributive property of logical connectives; i.e.,

$$
Reduce(C) \equiv C_1' \vee C_2' \vee \cdots \vee C_k'
$$

Hence, any noncanonical Type 1 or 2 coupling query can be reduced to a canonical coupling query (Type 3 or 5). ∎

Reduction of Noncanonical Type 3-Coupling Query

The reduction of a noncanonical Type 3-coupling query to a canonical coupling query is similar to that discussed for AND-coupling queries. A noncanonical Type 3-coupling query contains one or more complex connectivities that are in disjunction to each other or to a simple connectivity. Since a complex connectivity can be transformed to a set of simple connectivities in DNF, the noncanonical form of Type 3-coupling query can be reduced to a canonical form of Type 5. The formal proof of reduction of connectivities of a noncanonical query to a set of simple connectivities in DNF is as follows.

Proposition 6.19. *Let G_{nc}^3 be a noncanonical coupling query of Type 3. Then $G_c^5 = \mathrm{Transform}(G_{nc}^3)$.* ∎

Proof. Let $C \equiv k_1 \vee k_2 \vee \cdots \vee k_r$, where k_j is a complex connectivity for $0 < i \leq r$. We show that $Reduce(C)$ results in a set of simple connectivities in DNF.

$$
\begin{aligned}
Reduce(C) &\equiv Reduce(k_1 \vee k_2 \vee \cdots \vee k_r) \\
&\equiv simple(k_1) \vee simple(k_2) \vee \cdots \vee simple(k_r) \\
&\equiv (C_{11} \vee C_{12} \vee \cdots \vee C_{1n1}) \vee (C_{21} \vee C_{22} \vee \cdots \vee C_{2n2}) \cdots \quad (6.2)
\end{aligned}
$$

In the above equation each complex connectivity is reduced to sets of simple connectivities in DNF based on Proposition 5.1. The simple connectivities are unchanged. Hence any noncanonical Type 3-coupling query can be reduced to a canonical coupling query of Type 5. ∎

Reduction of Noncanonical Type 4-Coupling Query

Finally, we discuss the reduction of a noncanonical Type 4-coupling query into its canonical form. Recall that a Type 4-coupling query may be noncanonical for the following reasons. First, the connectivities in the query are all simple but they are not in DNF. For example, a query containing the connectivity $C \equiv ((x\langle e\rangle y \vee x\langle z\rangle k) \wedge y\langle s\rangle t) \wedge t\langle -\rangle q$ is an example of such a noncanonical Type 4-coupling query. Second, there may exist one or more complex connectivities in the coupling query. Hence we discuss how to reduce these two categories of noncanonical Type 4-coupling queries into their canonical form. We begin our discussion by introducing some terms that we subsequently use.

Let $K = \{k_1, k_2, k_3, \ldots, k_n\}$ be a set of simple connectivities. Then $con(K) \equiv k_1 \wedge k_2 \wedge \cdots \wedge k_n$ and $dis(K) \equiv k_1 \vee k_2 \vee \cdots \vee k_n$, where $n > 0$ and $n > 1$ for $con(K)$ and $dis(K)$, respectively. That is, $con(K)$ and $dis(K)$ denote sets of simple connectivities in conjunction and disjunction, respectively.

Category 1: Noncanonical Type 4-Coupling Query with Simple Connectivities

The set of simple connectivities in this type of G_{nc} can be nested. At the lowest level of nesting, the connectivities can take any of the following forms.

- Case 1: $con(K_1) \vee con(K_2)$. For example, $((x\langle e\rangle y \wedge y\langle f\rangle z) \vee (x\langle f\rangle g)) \wedge y\langle f\rangle t$.
- Case 2: $dis(K_1) \wedge dis(K_2)$. For example, $((x\langle e\rangle y \vee x\langle f\rangle z) \wedge (x\langle f\rangle g \vee x\langle r\rangle g)) \wedge z\langle f\rangle t$.
- Case 3: $con(K_1) \vee dis(K_2)$. For example, $((x\langle e\rangle y \wedge y\langle f\rangle z) \vee (x\langle f\rangle g \vee x\langle r\rangle g)) \wedge y\langle f\rangle t$.
- Case 4: $dis(K_1) \wedge con(K_2)$. For example, $((x\langle e\rangle y \vee x\langle f\rangle z) \wedge (x\langle f\rangle g)) \wedge y\langle f\rangle t$.

Consequently, to reduce the set of connectivities in G_{nc} it is imperative to transform any of the above four cases to a set of simple connectivities in DNF at every level of nesting. Hence the steps for reduction of the connectivities in a noncanonical Type 4-coupling query of Category 1 type are as follows.

1. Reduce the set of connectivities that can take any of the above four forms in the lowest level of nesting into a set of simple connectivities in DNF, i.e, $con(K_1) \vee con(K_2) \vee \cdots \vee con(K_n)$.
2. These reduced sets of connectivities will again be in disjunction or in conjunction with another set of simple connectivities in the next level. These connectivities can again be expressed as any of the four forms and consequently reduced to DNF.

3. The above steps are repeated until the highest level of the nested expression is reduced to DNF.

We illustrate the above steps with an example. Consider the connectivity $C \equiv ((x\langle e\rangle y \vee x\langle z\rangle k) \wedge y\langle s\rangle t) \wedge t\langle -\rangle q$. Observe that at the lowest level of nesting the connectivities are of type Case 4; i.e., $dis(K_1) \wedge con(K_2)$. This can be reduced to the following set of simple connectivities in DNF: $(x\langle e\rangle y \wedge y\langle s\rangle t) \vee (x\langle z\rangle h \wedge y\langle s\rangle t))$. This expression is in conjunction with the connectivity $t\langle -\rangle q$ in the next level of nesting. Hence this can again be reduced to a set of simple connectivities in DNF: $((x\langle e\rangle y \wedge y\langle s\rangle t \wedge t\langle -\rangle q) \vee (x\langle z\rangle h \wedge y\langle s\rangle t \wedge t\langle -\rangle q))$.

Observe that the key issue in the reduction of simple connectivities to DNF lies in the ability to reduce any of the four cases into DNF. Next we provide the formal proof that it is indeed possible to reduce any of these cases to a set of simple connectivities in DNF.

Proposition 6.20. *Let $con(K)$ and $dis(K)$ represent a set of simple connectivities in conjunction and disjunction, respectively. Then the following expressions can be reduced to a set of simple connectivities in DNF: (1) $con(K_1) \vee con(K_2)$; (2) $dis(K_1) \wedge dis(K_2)$; (3) $dis(K_1) \vee con(K_2)$; and (4) $dis(K_1) \wedge con(K_2)$.* ∎

Proof. Let $con(K_1) \equiv a_1 \wedge a_2 \wedge \cdots \wedge a_n$ and $con(K_2) \equiv b_1 \wedge b_2 \wedge \cdots \wedge b_r$ for $(n,r) > 0$. Let $dis(K_1) \equiv a_1 \vee a_2 \vee \cdots \vee a_n$ and $dis(K_2) \equiv b_1 \vee b_2 \vee \cdots \vee b_r$ for $(n,r) > 1$. Then the first expression (Case 1) can be reduced as follows.

$$Reduce(con(K_1) \vee con(K_2)) \equiv (a_1 \wedge a_2 \wedge \cdots \wedge a_n) \vee (b_1 \wedge b_2 \wedge \cdots \wedge b_r)$$

This is already in DNF. Hence Case 1 can be reduced to a set of simple connectivities in DNF. Next consider Case 2, i.e., the second expression in the above proposition. This case can be reduced by using the distributive property of logical connectivities as shown below.

$$\begin{aligned} Reduce(dis(K_1) \wedge dis(K_2)) &\equiv (a_1 \vee a_2 \vee \cdots \vee a_n) \wedge (b_1 \vee b_2 \vee \cdots \vee b_r) \\ &\equiv (a_1 \wedge b_1) \vee (a_1 \wedge b_2) \vee (a_1 \wedge b_3) \cdots \vee (a_n \wedge b_r) \end{aligned}$$

The above equation is in canonical form. Hence Case 2 connectivities can be reduced to DNF. Consider now the third expression, i.e., Case 3.

$$\begin{aligned} Reduce(dis(K_1) \vee con(K_2)) &\equiv (a_1 \vee a_2 \vee \cdots \vee a_n) \vee (b_1 \wedge b_2 \wedge \cdots \wedge b_r) \\ &\equiv (a_1) \vee (a_2) \vee \cdots \vee (a_n) \vee (b_1 \wedge b_2 \wedge \cdots \wedge b_r) \end{aligned}$$

Observe that this expression is in DNF. Finally, consider the reduction of the last case.

$$\begin{aligned} Reduce(dis(K_1) \wedge con(K_2)) &\equiv (a_1 \vee a_2 \vee \cdots \vee a_n) \wedge (b_1 \wedge b_2 \wedge \cdots \wedge b_r) \\ &\equiv (b_1 \wedge b_2 \wedge \cdots \wedge b_r \wedge a_1) \\ &\quad \vee (b_1 \wedge b_2 \wedge \cdots \wedge b_3 \wedge a_2) \vee \cdots \vee \\ &\quad (b_1 \wedge \cdots \wedge b_r \wedge a_n) \end{aligned}$$

Hence all four cases can be reduced to a set of simple connectivities in DNF. ∎

Next we elaborate on the reduction of the second category of noncanonical Type 4-coupling queries, i.e., coupling queries containing complex connectivities.

Category 2: Noncanonical Type 4-Coupling Query Containing Complex Connectivities

To facilitate our discussion we classify those noncanonical queries into three types based on the nature of the complex connectivities in the query. Let G_{nc} be a noncanonical Type 4-coupling query. Then

- **Class 1:** C contains complex connectivities of Case 1 only as described in Chapter 5;
- **Class 2:** C contains complex connectivities of any type except Case 1;
- **Class 3:** C contains Case 1 and any remaining types of complex connectivities.

The steps for reducing a Category 2 noncanonical coupling query are as follows.

1. Reduce the complex connectivities into a set of simple connectivities in DNF as specified by Proposition 5.1 in Chapter 5.
2. The reduced connectivities are in any of the four forms described in Category 1. Therefore the problem is now reduced to the reduction of a noncanonical query containing simple connectivities. Hence execute the steps described in Category 1 to generate a set of simple connectivities in DNF.

Note that the key step in the reduction process is to convert the complex connectivities into simple form. The subsequent steps are similar to those of the first category. We now discuss the reduction of complex connectivities in detail. The connectivities in G_{nc} of Classes 1 and 2 may contain complex connectivities that may exist in any of the following six forms. Let k_c be a complex connectivity of Class 1 or 2. Then k_c may occur in any of the following ways.

- Case 1: $k_c \vee con(K)$. For example, $x\langle efg\rangle y \vee (x\langle r\rangle z \wedge z\langle f\rangle t)$.
- Case 2: $k_c \vee dis(K)$. For example, $x\langle ef|g\rangle y \vee (x\langle r\rangle z \vee x\langle f\rangle t)$.
- Case 3: $k_c \wedge con(K)$. For example, $x\langle ef\{1,3\}\rangle y \wedge (x\langle r\rangle z)$.
- Case 4: $k_c \wedge dis(K)$. For example, $x\langle efg\rangle y \wedge (x\langle r\rangle z \vee x\langle f\rangle t)$.
- Case 5: $k_{c1} \wedge k_{c2}$. For example, $x\langle ef\rangle y \wedge y\langle rs\rangle z$.
- Case 6: $k_{c1} \vee k_{c2}$. For example, $x\langle e|f\rangle y \vee x\langle e\{1,3\}\rangle t$.

For a coupling query of Class 3, there are two additional possible cases.

- Case 7: $k_{c1} \wedge k_{c2}$ where k_{c1} is a complex connectivity of Case 1 type and k_{c2} is of a type other than Case 1. For example, $x\langle ef\rangle y \wedge y\langle r|s\rangle z$.
- Case 8: $k_{c1} \vee k_{c2}$ where k_{c1} and k_{c2} are of the above types. For example, $x\langle e|f\rangle y \vee x\langle eg\rangle t$.

We now show that all the above cases can be reduced to one or more of the four cases as described in Category 1. Clearly, if this is possible, then any combination of connectivities in G_{nc} can always be reduced to a set of simple connectivities in DNF.

Proposition 6.21. *Let C be a set of connectivities containing one or more complex connectivities in a noncanonical Type 4-coupling query. Then C can be reduced to a set of simple connectivities in DNF.* ∎

Proof. To prove the above proposition we show that the eight cases identified for the three classes of noncanonical coupling query can be reduced to the four cases described in Proposition 6.20. Hence based on Proposition 6.20, these connectivities can be further reduced to a set of simple connectivities in DNF. We begin with the reduction of Case 1. If G_{nc} is of Class 1, then

$$Reduce(k_c \vee con(K)) \equiv (k_1 \wedge k_2 \wedge \cdots \wedge k_n) \vee (b_1 \wedge b_2 \wedge \cdots \wedge b_r)$$

This is already in canonical form. If G_{nc} is of Class 2, then

$$Reduce(k_c \vee con(K)) \equiv con(k_{c1}) \vee con(k_{c2}) \vee \cdots \vee con(k_{cn}) \vee (b_1 \wedge b_2 \wedge \cdots \wedge b_r)$$

This is also in canonical form. Now consider Case 2. If G_{nc} belongs to Class 1 then,

$$Reduce(k_c \vee dis(K)) \equiv (k_1 \wedge k_2 \wedge \cdots \wedge k_n) \vee dis(K)$$
$$\equiv con(k_c) \vee dis(K)$$

Hence the above expression can be reduced to Case 3 in Category 1. If G_{nc} is of Class 2 then,

$$Reduce(k_c \vee dis(K)) \equiv con(k_{c1}) \vee con(k_{c2}) \vee \cdots con(k_{cn}) \vee dis(K)$$

The above expression is equivalent to Cases 1 and 3 of Category 1. Next, for Case 3 and G_{nc} of Class 1,

$$Reduce(k_c \wedge con(K)) \equiv (k_1 \wedge k_2 \wedge \cdots \wedge k_n) \wedge con(K)$$
$$\equiv con(k_c) \wedge con(K)$$
$$\equiv con(k_c \wedge K)$$

This is already in canonical form. Next, if G_{nc} is of Class 2, then

$$Reduce(k_c \wedge con(K)) \equiv (con(k_{c1}) \vee con(k_{c2}) \vee \cdots \vee con(k_{cn})) \wedge con(K)$$
$$\equiv (con(k_{c1}) \wedge con(K)) \vee (con(k_{c2}) \wedge con(K))$$
$$\vee \cdots \vee (con(k_{cn}) \wedge con(K))$$
$$\equiv con(k_{c1} \wedge K) \vee con(k_{c2} \wedge K) \vee \cdots \vee con(k_{cn} \wedge K)$$

Next, we consider reduction of Class 1 and 2 coupling queries of Case 4. For Class 1,

$$Reduce(k_c \wedge dis(K)) \equiv (k_1 \wedge k_2 \wedge \cdots \wedge k_n) \wedge dis(K)$$
$$\equiv con(k_c) \wedge dis(K)$$

The above expression is of Case 4 in Category 1. Next, if G_{nc} belongs to Class 2, then

$$Reduce(k_c \wedge dis(K)) \equiv con(k_{c1}) \vee con(k_{c2}) \vee \cdots \vee con(k_{cn}) \wedge dis(K)$$
$$\equiv (con(k_{c1}) \wedge dis(K)) \vee (con(k_{c2}) \wedge dis(K))$$
$$\vee \cdots (con(k_{cn}) \wedge dis(K))$$

Clearly, the above equation is of Case 4 and hence can be reduced to a set of simple connectivities in DNF. Next, consider Case 5. For Class 1,

$$Reduce(k_{c1} \wedge k_{c2}) \equiv con(k_{c1}) \wedge con(k_{c2})$$
$$\equiv con(k_{c1} \wedge k_{c2})$$

This is already in canonical form. Next, for Class 2,

$$Reduce(con(k_{c1}) \wedge con(k_{c2})) \equiv (con(k_{c11}) \vee con(k_{c12}) \vee \cdots \vee con(k_{c1n})) \wedge (con(k_{c21})$$
$$\vee con(k_{c22}) \vee \cdots)$$
$$\equiv (con(k_{c11}) \wedge con(k_{c21})) \vee (con(k_{12}) \wedge con(k_{c22})) \vee \cdots$$
$$\equiv con(k_{c11} \wedge k_{c21}) \vee con(k_{c12} \wedge k_{c22}) \vee \cdots$$

Note that the above expression is of Case 1 in Category 1. Hence it can be reduced to a set of simple connectivities in DNF.

Similarly, reductions of Case 6 for Classes 1 and 2 are shown below.

$$Reduce(k_{c1} \vee k_{c2}) \equiv con(k_{c1}) \vee con(k_{c2})$$

$$Reduce(con(k_{c1}) \vee con(k_{c2})) \equiv$$
$$(con(k_{c11}) \vee con(k_{c12}) \vee \cdots$$
$$con(k_{c1n})) \vee (con(k_{c21}) \vee con(k_{c22}) \vee \cdots)$$

Observe that both expressions are reduced to Case 1 in Category 1. Finally, we consider the two cases, i.e., Cases 7 and 8 for Class 3 coupling query. For Case 7 the reduction is as follows.

$$Reduce(k_{c1} \wedge k_{c2}) \equiv (con(k_{c11}) \vee con(k_{c12}) \vee \cdots \vee con(k_{c1n})) \wedge con(k_{c2})$$
$$\equiv (con(k_{c11}) \wedge con(k_{c2})) \vee (con(k_{c12}) \wedge con(k_{c2}))$$
$$\vee \cdots \vee (con(k_{c1n}) \wedge con(k_{c2}))$$
$$\equiv con(k_{c11} \wedge k_{c2}) \vee con(k_{c12} \wedge k_{c2}) \vee \cdots \vee con(k_{c1n} \wedge k_{c2})$$

Next, for Case 8,

$$Reduce(k_{c1} \vee k_{c2}) \equiv con(k_{c11}) \vee con(k_{c12}) \vee \cdots \vee con(k_{c1n}) \vee con(k_{c2})$$

Observe that both Cases 7 and 8 are reducible to Case 1 of Category 1. Hence all the cases in this category can be reduced to a set of simple connectivities in DNF. ∎

Therefore, based on Propositions 6.20 and 6.21, we can say that any noncanonical Type 4-coupling query can be reduced to a Type 5 canonical coupling query.

Proposition 6.22. *Let G_{nc}^4 be a noncanonical coupling query of Type 4 category. Then $G_c^5 = \text{Transform}(G_{nc}^4)$.* ∎

To summarize, based on the above discussion it is clear that any noncanonical coupling query can be reduced to a canonical coupling query. Consequently, the following theorem holds.

Theorem 6.23. *Any noncanonical coupling query can be reduced to its canonical form.* ∎

Proof. The proof is straightforward and can be deduced from Propositions 6.18, 6.19, and 6.22. ∎

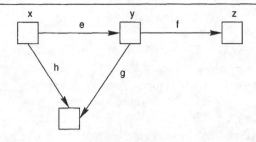

Fig. 6.12. Example of Phase 3.

6.4.3 Phase 2: Validity Checking

Finally, in this phase the canonical coupling query generated from the previous phase is inspected to determine if it represents a valid query. That is, if the query conforms to Definition 6.6 in Section 6.2.4. For each conjunctive connectivity set in the canonical query, the conditions in Definition 6.6 are checked, that is, whether each conjunctive connectivity set represents a directed, connected acyclic graph with a single source vertex. If one of these conditions is violated, then G_c is not a valid query and it requires further refinement. In that case, the invalid conjunctive connectivity set is either eliminated from the coupling query autonomously or the query is modified by the user so that it satisfies the validity conditions in Definition 6.6. Specifically, if an invalid canonical coupling query $G_c = \langle X_n, X_\ell, C, P, Q \rangle$ is modified autonomously, then the following steps are executed.

- Remove each invalid conjunctive connectivity set C_i from C in G_c.
- For each C_i, the corresponding node and link type identifiers that do not occur in C_j where $j \neq i$ and $0 < j \leq n$, are removed from X_n and X_ℓ, respectively.
- The predicates defined over these identifiers, if any, are also removed from P.

We illustrate this phase with an example given below. Consider a noncanonical coupling query containing the following connectivities $C \equiv (x\langle e\rangle y \vee x\langle h\rangle w) \wedge (y\langle f\rangle z \vee y\langle g\rangle w)$. The graphical representation of the query is shown in Figure 6.12. Observe that pictorially it is a directed connected acyclic graph with a single source vertex. This query can be transformed into a canonical form as shown below.

$$C \equiv ((x\langle e\rangle y \vee x\langle h\rangle w) \wedge y\langle f\rangle z) \vee ((x\langle e\rangle y \vee x\langle h\rangle w) \wedge y\langle g\rangle w)$$
$$\equiv (x\langle e\rangle y \wedge y\langle f\rangle z) \vee (y\langle f\rangle z \wedge x\langle h\rangle w) \vee (x\langle e\rangle y \wedge y\langle g\rangle w) \vee (x\langle h\rangle w \wedge y\langle g\rangle w)$$

Observe that the second conjunctive connectivity set represents a disconnected graph. Furthermore, the fourth conjunctive connectivity set represents a graph with multiple source vertices. Hence this query is not valid.

6.5 Coupling Query Formulation

By default, a coupling query is formulated in text form. It may also be formulated graphically. The textual representation of the query is called *coupling text* and the pictorial representation of a coupling query is called a *coupling graph*.

In coupling text, the user specifies the five components X_n, X_ℓ, C, P, and Q in textual form. Coupling text is a flexible query formulation mechanism and can be used to specify any meaningful query. In the remaining portion of this book we use coupling text and coupling query interchangeably. Example 6.1 is an example of coupling text.

Next we describe the second mechanism for formulating coupling queries, i.e., *coupling graphs*. We begin by defining a coupling graph. Then we discuss different types of coupling graphs a user may wish to draw. Next we discuss the limitations associated with coupling graphs in expressing different forms of queries. Finally, in Section 6.5.4 we introduce the notion of a *hybrid graph* in order to resolve these limitations. Also note that, unless explicitly stated otherwise, a canonical coupling query indicates a valid canonical query.

6.5.1 Definition of Coupling Graph

Informally, a coupling graph is a directed, connected acyclic graph. This mechanism enables a user to specify a coupling query by drawing a graph. The label of vertices of the graph are node type identifiers and predicates, if any, defined over these identifiers. The labels of the edges of the graph are link type identifiers and predicates on these link type identifiers (if any). The predicates are specified by clicking on the vertices and edges. The edges between the vertices specify the connectivity constraints. The set of coupling query predicates is specified by clicking on the entire coupling graph.

A coupling graph is used to express queries containing simple connectivities only. We justify the reasons behind this. Recall that complex connectivity is a compact mechanism when expressed in text form for expressing a set of simple connectivities that are in conjunction or in disjunction to one another. Thus coupling text containing complex connectivities enables a user to specify a query tersely without having the overhead of expressing all possible forms of simple connectivities. However, this advantage of complex connectivities in coupling text cannot be realized when formulating the query using a coupling graph. Essentially, a complex connectivity condenses a set of node and link type identifiers into a single expression. Such capability cannot be realized when drawing a graph. To express the connectivities one has to draw all the edges and vertices. For instance, to express the connectivity $x\langle(ef)|(gh)\rangle y$ using a coupling graph, the user has to draw all the vertices and edges as shown in Figure 6.15(b). This is equivalent to specifying all the simple connectivities that $x\langle(ef)|(gh)\rangle y$ represents. Hence there is no additional advantage in allowing a user to draw a complex connectivity. For this reason we do not allow users to specify queries containing complex connectivities using a coupling graph. We believe coupling text is the best mechanism to express queries containing complex connectivities. Formally, the definition of a coupling graph is as follows.

Definition 6.24. [**Coupling Graph**] *A* **coupling graph** $G_{cg} = (V_q, E_q)$ *for a query* $G = \langle X_n, X_\ell, C, P, Q \rangle$ *is a connected acyclic digraph with single source vertex, where*

- *C is a set of simple connectivities;*
- V_q *is a finite set of vertices. A vertex* v_q *is labeled by a node type identifier* $id(v_q) \in X_n$ *and a set (possibly empty) of predicates* $P_n \subseteq P$ *on the node type identifier. Furthermore,* $V_q = V(k_1) \cup V(k_2) \cup \cdots \cup V(k_n)$, *where* $k_1, k_2, \ldots, k_n$ *are connectivities in* C, $G(k_i) = (V(k_i), E(k_i)) \; \forall \; 0 < i \leq n$;
- E_q *is a finite set of directed edges such that* $E_q = E(k_1) \cup E(k_2) \cup \cdots \cup E(k_n)$. *An edge* e_q *is labeled by the link type identifier* $id(e_q) \in X_\ell$ *and a set (possibly empty) of predicates* $P_\ell \subseteq P$;
- $g : E_q \to V_q \times V_q$ *is a function such that* $g(e_q) = (v_{q_1}, e_q, v_{q_2})$ *if and only if there exists a simple connectivity* $id(v_{q_1}) \langle \; id(e_q) \; \rangle \; id(v_{q_2})$ *in* C. ∎

6.5.2 Types of Coupling Graph

We classify coupling graphs into three categories, i.e., *AND-coupling graph*, *OR-coupling graph*, and *AND/OR-coupling graph*. We elaborate on these three types of coupling graph.

AND-Coupling Graph

In an *AND-coupling graph* all the edges are AND'd together. It is used to express pictorially a coupling query containing a set of simple connectivities in conjunction to one another (canonical queries of Types 2 and 3). Formally, let $G_{cg} = (V_q, E_q)$ be a coupling graph. Then G_{cg} is an AND-coupling graph if $e_{qi} \in E_q$ and $e_{qj} \in E_q$ and $e_{qi} \wedge e_{qj} \; \forall \; 0 < i, j \leq |E_q|$ and $i \neq j$. Note that the graphical representation of the canonical form of coupling text (of Types 2 and 3) is identical to the corresponding AND-coupling graph. For example, Figures 6.13(a), (b) and (c) are examples of AND-coupling graphs expressing the sets of simple connectivities $(x\langle e\rangle\#_1 \wedge \#_1\langle f\rangle\#_2 \wedge \#_2\langle g\rangle\#_3 \wedge \#_3\langle h\rangle y)$, $(x\langle e\rangle\#_1 \wedge \#_1\langle f\rangle y \wedge x\langle g\rangle\#_2 \wedge \#_2\langle h\rangle y)$, and $(a\langle f\rangle b \wedge a\langle g\rangle c \wedge a\langle h\rangle d \wedge b\langle k\rangle\#_1 \wedge c\langle m\rangle\#_2)$, respectively.

OR-Coupling Graph

An *OR-coupling graph* is used to pictorially formulate coupling queries in which the connectivities are simple and are in disjunction to one another. In an *OR-coupling graph* all the edges are OR'd together. Note that an OR-coupling graph cannot be linear as it requires at least two outgoing or incoming edges to be OR'd together. Furthermore, as we only allow coupling graphs with a single source vertex, OR-coupling graphs must not have more than one vertex with no incoming edges. Consequently, OR-coupling graphs pictorially represent queries containing a set of

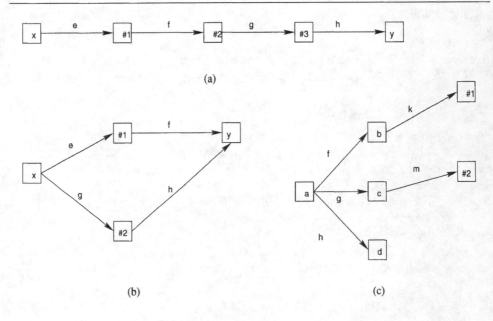

Fig. 6.13. AND-coupling graphs.

simple connectivities having identical source identifiers. Moreover, these connectivities must generate a directed, connected acyclic graph. As we disregard formulation of noncanonical coupling queries using coupling graphs, an OR-coupling graph is a pictorial representation of a canonical form of Type 4-coupling text. Formally, let $G_{cg} = (V_q, E_q)$ be a coupling graph. Then G_{cg} is an OR-coupling graph if $e_{qi} \in E_q$, $e_{qj} \in E_q$, $e_{qi} \vee e_{qj} \; \forall \; 0 < i, j \leq |E_q|$, and $i \neq j$. Observe that the depth of an OR-graph is always equal to one. This is because each simple connectivity represents a path of length one. Hence a set of simple connectivities in disjunction represents a graph having depth one. For example, Figures 6.14(a), (b), and (c) are examples of OR-coupling graphs expressing connectivities $(x\langle e \rangle y \vee x\langle f \rangle z \vee x\langle g \rangle w \vee x\langle h \rangle v)$, $(a\langle u \rangle b \vee a\langle v \rangle b)$, and $(x\langle e \rangle \# \vee x\langle f \rangle \# \vee x\langle g \rangle d)$, respectively.

AND/OR-Coupling Graph

Informally, an AND/OR-coupling graph represents coupling queries in which the connectivities are in conjunction as well as in disjunction to one another. We first define the notion of *AND-edges* and *OR-edges* in order to elaborate on this type of coupling graph. In a coupling graph, an edge (v_1, e, v_2) is an *AND-edge* if the out-degree and in-degree of v_1 and v_2, respectively, are equal to one. For example, in Figure 6.15(a) edges (y, f, a) and (z, h, b) are AND-edges. Otherwise, the edge is called an *OR-edge*. For instance, in Figure 6.15(a) the out-degree of vertex x is two. Hence edges (x, e, y) and (x, g, z) are OR-edges. Now we define an AND/OR-coupling graph. Let $G_{cg} = (V_q, E_q)$ be a coupling graph. Then G_{cg} is an AND/OR graph if either of the following conditions is true.

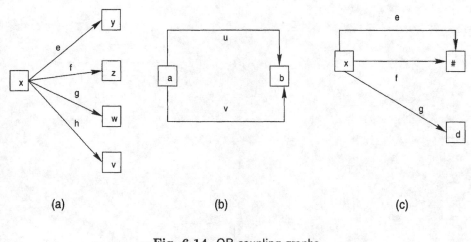

(a)   (b)   (c)

Fig. 6.14. OR-coupling graphs.

- If all edges are OR-edges then the depth of the graph must be greater than one. This is because if the depth is equal to one then the graph is an OR-coupling graph.
- G_{cg} must contain AND- and OR-edges.

The significance of the above restriction regarding the definition of an AND/OR-coupling graph is best understood in Section 6.5.3.

Note that in an AND/OR-coupling graph all the outgoing or incoming OR-edges to a vertex are OR'd together. Furthermore, connectivities in each level in the graph are AND'd together with the connectivities in the next level. For example, Figure 6.15 shows a set of AND/OR-coupling graphs. In this figure, AND and OR-edges are shown by thick and thin arrows, respectively. In Figure 6.15(a), the edges e and g are OR-edges and f and h are AND-edges. Hence it expresses a coupling query with the following connectivities, $(x\langle e\rangle y \wedge y\langle f\rangle a) \vee (x\langle g\rangle z \wedge z\langle h\rangle b)$. Similarly, Figure 6.15(b) is the pictorial representation of the canonical coupling text in Example 6.16. Note that in this case all edges are OR-edges. Figure 6.15(c) expresses a query with the following connectivities, $x\langle e\rangle y \vee (x\langle f\rangle a \wedge a\langle i\rangle c) \vee (x\langle g\rangle z \wedge z\langle h\rangle a \wedge a\langle i\rangle c) \vee (x\langle g\rangle z \wedge z\langle k\rangle b) \vee x\langle j\rangle b$. Similarly, Figures 6.15(d) and (e) express the connectivities: $(x\langle m\rangle y \wedge y\langle o\rangle a) \vee (x\langle m\rangle y \wedge y\langle p\rangle b) \vee (x\langle m\rangle y \wedge y\langle q\rangle c \wedge c\langle t\rangle e)$ $\vee (x\langle m\rangle y \wedge y\langle q\rangle c \wedge c\langle s\rangle d) \vee (x\langle n\rangle z \wedge z\langle r\rangle c \wedge c\langle s\rangle d) \vee (x\langle n\rangle z \wedge z\langle r\rangle c \wedge c\langle t\rangle e)$ and $(x\langle e\rangle y \wedge y\langle f\rangle z \wedge x\langle g\rangle a \wedge a\langle h\rangle b \wedge b\langle j\rangle c) \vee (x\langle m\rangle z \wedge z\langle g\rangle a \wedge a\langle h\rangle b \wedge b\langle j\rangle c) \vee (x\langle k\rangle a \wedge a\langle h\rangle b \wedge b\langle j\rangle c) \vee (x\langle e\rangle y \wedge y\langle f\rangle z \wedge z\langle p\rangle b \wedge b\langle j\rangle c) \vee (x\langle e\rangle y \wedge y\langle h\rangle a \wedge a\langle h\rangle b \wedge b\langle j\rangle c)$, respectively.

An AND/OR-coupling graph can be used to pictorially represent *some types* of canonical coupling text of Type 5, but not all. This is due to the inherent limitations of drawing an AND/OR-coupling graph to represent a unique coupling query. We discuss this issue in detail in the next subsection.

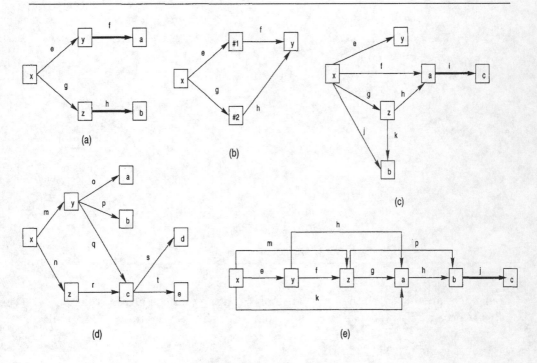

Fig. 6.15. AND/OR-coupling graphs.

6.5.3 Limitations of Coupling Graphs

In the preceding sections we have described how to draw a canonical coupling query using a coupling graph. In this section we explore the limitations of coupling graphs in expressing canonical coupling queries compared to their textual counterparts. In particular, we provide an answer to the following question. Let G be a coupling query. Then, is it possible to express G by a coupling graph? That is, we explore the issue of whether it is always possible to express any valid coupling query using a coupling graph.

Criteria

We first identify the criteria that are important in determining the limitations of a coupling graph compared to its textual counterpart. Recall that predicates in a coupling query facilitate imposing constraints on metadata, content, or structure of nodes and links. Furthermore, the ability to specify predicates in a coupling text and a coupling graph is the same. Whatever predicates can be expressed in textual form in a coupling text can also be expressed graphically in a coupling graph. Hence the predicates do not play a pivotal role in differentiating the expressiveness of these two types of query mechanisms. For similar reasons, coupling query predicates do not influence the differences between the expressiveness of coupling text and coupling graphs.

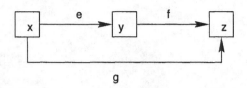

Fig. 6.16. Limitations of OR-coupling graph.

However, the connectivities in a coupling query play a major role in the context of expressive power of coupling text and coupling graphs. This is because coupling text allows us to express both simple and complex connectivities and enables us to impose explicitly how these connectivities are associated with one another. Consequently, it is possible to express the hyperlink structure precisely in a coupling text. On the other hand, the usage of connectivities in a coupling graph is restricted due to *certain limitations* of drawing a query. As a matter of fact, a coupling graph can only express simple connectivities. Furthermore, as we show, a coupling graph does not provide the flexibility to express any combination of disjunctive relationships in a set of simple connectivities. This has a direct impact on the expressiveness of a coupling graph. In the following sections, we discuss the effect of connectivities on coupling graphs.

Limitations

In this section, we discuss the limitations of the three types of coupling graphs compared to their textual counterparts. We begin with the AND-coupling graph.

AND-Coupling Graph

Edges in an AND-coupling graph represent a set of simple connectivities AND'd together. This is equivalent to a set of simple connectivities in conjunction to one another in a canonical form of Type 2- or 3-coupling text. Hence the expressiveness of the AND-coupling graph is equivalent to the canonical form of Types 2- and 3-coupling text. Any query that can be expressed by canonical form of Type 2- or 3-coupling text can also be formulated using an AND-coupling graph.

OR-Coupling Graph

An OR-coupling graph represents a set of simple connectivities in disjunction with one another. This is equivalent to the canonical form of Type 4-coupling text. Observe that each connectivity in the coupling query must represent a path from the source vertex to a leaf vertex in the OR-coupling graph. Hence an OR-coupling graph cannot express those simple connectivities that represent a path other than those between the source vertex and leaf vertices in the graphical representation of the connectivities. We elaborate on this with an example. Consider the connectivities $C \equiv k_1 \vee k_2 \vee k_3$, where $k_1 \equiv x\langle e \rangle y$, $k_2 \equiv y\langle f \rangle z$, and $k_3 \equiv x\langle g \rangle z$.

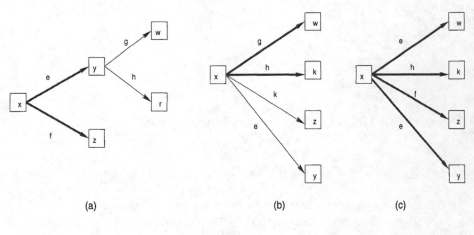

Fig. 6.17. Case 1.

A query containing these connectivities can be expressed by a canonical form of Type 4-coupling text. The graphical representation of this query is shown in Figure 6.16. However, this query cannot be composed using an OR-coupling graph. This is because k_2 represents a path between an interior vertex and a leaf vertex in Figure 6.16. Typically, an OR-coupling graph is only capable of expressing simple connectivities with identical source identifiers. If all the source identifiers are not identical in the connectivities then there may exist a connectivity that does not represent a path between the source and leaf vertex. Consequently, we may conclude that the expressiveness of an OR-coupling graph is not equivalent to that of the canonical form of Type 4-coupling text.

Condition 6.3 *Let $C \equiv k_1 \vee k_2 \vee \cdots \vee k_n$ be a set of simple connectivities in a valid canonical coupling query G_c^4. Then G_c^4 cannot be expressed by an OR-coupling graph if* $\mathrm{lnode}(k_i) \neq \mathrm{lnode}(k_j)$ *for $0 < (i, j) \leq n$ and $i \neq j$.* ∎

AND/OR-Coupling Graph

We now identify the limitations of AND/OR-coupling graphs and illustrate them with examples. Within this context we justify the reasons for the restrictive definition of an AND/OR-coupling graph as highlighted in Section 6.5. We begin with the first limitation.

Case 1

Recall that in an AND/OR-coupling graph each path from the source vertex to a leaf vertex represents a conjunctive connectivity set in the coupling query. In other words, if $C \equiv C_1 \vee C_2 \vee \cdots \vee C_n$ is a set of connectivities in a coupling query G and if G_{cg} is the AND/OR-coupling graph of G then $C_1, C_2, \ldots, C_n$ represent such paths in G_{cg}. This indicates that an AND/OR-coupling graph fails to express a set of connectivities that can be visualized as a nonlinear structure, i.e., a tree or

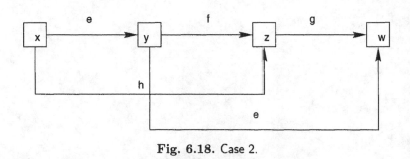

Fig. 6.18. Case 2.

a graph. For instance, an AND/OR-coupling graph cannot express the following connectivities, $C_3 \equiv C_{31} \vee C_{32}$, where $C_{31} \equiv x\langle e\rangle y \wedge x\langle f\rangle z \wedge y\langle g\rangle w$ and $C_{32} \equiv x\langle e\rangle y \wedge x\langle f\rangle z \wedge y\langle h\rangle r$. Similarly, it cannot express $C_4 \equiv C_{41} \vee C_{42}$, where $C_{41} \equiv x\langle g\rangle w \wedge x\langle h\rangle k \wedge x\langle f\rangle z$ and $C_{42} \equiv x\langle e\rangle y \wedge x\langle g\rangle w \wedge x\langle h\rangle k$. Observe that C_{31}, C_{32}, C_{41} and C_{42} can be visualized as trees.

One may argue that the above limitation arises because of the restrictive definition of the AND/OR-coupling graph. That is, in an AND/OR-coupling graph if a vertex has more than one incoming or outgoing edge then these edges are OR'd together. We only allow an edge $e = (v_1, \ell, v_2)$ to be an AND-edge if the out-degree and in-degree of v_1 and v_2, respectively, are equal to one. However, in order to accommodate the ability to express tree- or graph-structured connectivities using an AND/OR-coupling graph it is imperative to allow AND-edges for vertices with more than one incoming or outgoing edge. It may seem that by relaxing the definition of an AND/OR-coupling graph it may be possible to resolve this limitation. For example, consider the graph in Figure 6.17(a). Let edges with identifiers e and f be AND-edges in lieu of OR-edges. Then C_3 in the above example can be expressed by this AND/OR-coupling graph. Similarly, the coupling graph in Figure 6.17(b) may be used to express the connectivities C_4.

Although it may seem that the resolution of this problem lies in the relaxation of the definition of AND and OR-edges, this is not the case. Consider the connectivities $C_5 \equiv C_{51} \vee C_{52}$, where $C_{51} \equiv x\langle e\rangle w \wedge x\langle h\rangle k$ and $C_{52} \equiv x\langle f\rangle z \wedge x\langle e\rangle y$. The coupling graph of a query involving C_5 is shown in Figure 6.17(c). However, since all the edges are AND-edges, this graph actually expresses $(x\langle e\rangle w \wedge x\langle h\rangle k \wedge x\langle f\rangle z \wedge x\langle e\rangle y)$. This connectivity constraint cannot be expressed even by relaxing the definition of AND-edges. Hence allowing such a flexible definition of AND-edges may generate an AND/OR-coupling graph that may not represent the intended connectivities when transformed to its textual form. Due to this problem, we disallow AND-edges from vertices whose in-degree or out-degree is more than one.

Condition 6.4 *Let $G_c^5 = \langle X_n, X_\ell, C, P, Q\rangle$ be a valid canonical form of Type 5-coupling text where $C \equiv C_1 \vee C_2 \vee \cdots \vee C_r$. Let $G(C_i) = (V_i, E_i)$ be the graphical representation of C_i for $0 < i \leq r$. Then G_c^5 cannot be composed using an AND/OR-coupling graph if $G(C_i)$ is a tree or graph where $|V_i| > 2$.* ∎

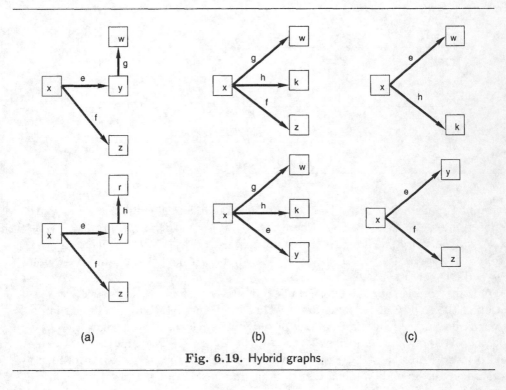

Fig. 6.19. Hybrid graphs.

Case 2

This shortcoming is similar to the one discussed in the context of an OR-coupling graph. An AND/OR-coupling graph, similar to an OR-coupling graph cannot express connectivity that represents a path in the graph other than those from the source vertex to leaf vertices. For example, consider the connectivities $C_6 \equiv C_{61} \vee C_{62} \vee C_{63}$ where $C_{61} \equiv x\langle e\rangle y \wedge y\langle f\rangle z \wedge z\langle g\rangle w$, $C_{62} \equiv x\langle h\rangle z \wedge z\langle g\rangle w$, and $C_{63} \equiv y\langle e\rangle w$. The graphical representation of these connectivities is shown in Figure 6.18. Observe that a query containing these connectivities cannot be expressed using an AND/OR-coupling graph. This is because C_{63} represents a path from an interior vertex to a leaf vertex in Figure 6.18.

Condition 6.5 *Let $G_c^5 = \langle X_n, X_\ell, C, P, Q\rangle$ be a valid canonical form of Type 5-coupling text where $C \equiv C_1 \vee C_2 \vee \cdots \vee C_r$. Let $C_i \equiv k_{i1} \wedge k_{i2} \wedge \cdots \wedge k_{iq}$ for all $0 < i \leq r$. Let $x = \mathrm{lnode}(k_{ij})$, $0 < j \leq q$ such that $x \neq \mathrm{rnode}(k_{is}) \ \forall \ 0 < s \leq q$ and $s \neq j$. Then G_c^5 cannot be expressed by an AND/OR-coupling graph if there exist C_t such that $y = \mathrm{lnode}(k_{tj})$, $y \neq lnode(k_{ts})$, and $y \neq x$, $t \neq i$.* ∎

6.5.4 Hybrid Graph

We now introduce the notion of a *hybrid graph* to resolve the limitations of OR and AND/OR-coupling graphs discussed in the preceding section. Informally, a *hybrid* graph is composed by drawing a p-connected coupling graph for $p > 1$ such that

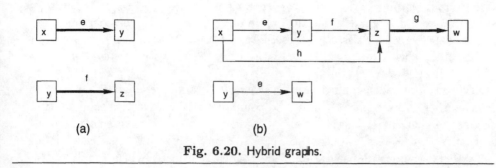

Fig. 6.20. Hybrid graphs.

- Each *connected component*[1] is an AND, OR, or AND/OR-coupling graph. Each connected component in the hybrid graph is a set of vertices such that all vertices in the set are connected from the source vertex (reachable by some path);
- The connected components are in disjunction to one another; and
- If $G_i = (V_i, E_i)$ and $G_j = (V_j, E_j)$ are two connected components then $V_i \cap V_j \neq \emptyset$.

For example, Figure 6.19(a) represents a hybrid graph with two connected components consisting of AND-coupling graphs. This hybrid graph represents the connectivities C_3 as depicted in Case 1 in the preceding section. Next we illustrate with examples how hybrid graphs can be used to resolve the shortcomings of drawing an OR or AND/OR-coupling graph.

Resolution of Case 1

An AND-coupling graph can express connectivities that can be visualized as trees or graphs. Hence the limitations discussed in Case 1 of the AND/OR-coupling graph can be eliminated by drawing a hybrid graph containing an AND-coupling graph. For instance, consider the connectivities C_3 and C_4 of Case 1 in Section 6.5.3. Queries containing these connectivities can be expressed by the hybrid graphs in Figures 6.19(a) and (b), respectively. Observe than these graphs are 2-connected graphs where all the components are AND-coupling graphs. Furthermore, in each hybrid graph the AND-coupling graphs are in disjunction to one another. Similarly, the query containing the connectivities C_5 can be expressed by the hybrid graph in Figure 6.19(c).

Resolution of Case 2

We consider the case that is a limitation for both OR-coupling graphs and AND/OR-coupling graphs. Consider the query containing the connectivity C in

---

[1] Traditionally, given a graph $G = (V, E)$, where V is a set of vertices (of size n) and E is a set of edges (of size m), the connected components of G are the sets of vertices such that all vertices in each set are mutually connected (reachable by some path), and no two vertices in different sets are connected. However, in this book we do not consider this notion in this context.

an OR-coupling graph as discussed earlier. This query can be formulated using a 2-connected hybrid graph as shown in Figure 6.20(a). Similarly, consider the query containing the connectivities C_6 as described in Case 2. This can be expressed by a 2-connected hybrid graph as depicted in Figure 6.20(b). Notice that it consists of an AND/OR and an AND-coupling graph.

Observe that in all the above cases the connected components are in disjunction to one another. Also, a pair of connected components always shares some vertices with identical identifiers. This is because if G_i and G_j are two connected components such that $V_i \cap V_j = \emptyset$ then G_i and G_j can be expressed by two distinct coupling graphs. Hence there is no need to express G_i and G_j using a hybrid graph.

6.6 Coupling Query Results

We now discuss the results of a valid coupling query. Within this context, we identify the *conformity conditions* a set of documents and hyperlinks must satisfy to match a coupling query.

Informally, the result of a coupling query is a set of directed, connected acyclic graphs containing node and link objects. These graphs are called *web tuples*. Intuitively, a web tuple t is a subgraph of $G(WWW)$ (recall from Section 6.2) and the set of documents and hyperlinks in t satisfies the connectivities and predicates defined in a query. For instance, each directed connected graph in Figures 6.3 and 6.11 is an example of a web tuple.

Definition 6.25. [Web Tuple] *Let* $G(WWW) = (V, E)$ *be the WWW graph. Then* $t = \langle N(t), L(t) \rangle$ *is a* **web tuple**, *where* $N(t) = \{n_i(t)|1 \leq i \leq n\}$ *and* $N(t) \subseteq V$ *is the set of nodes with* n *number of nodes in the web tuple.* $L(t) = \{\langle n_r(t), n_s(t) \rangle |1 \leq r, s \leq n\}$, $L(t) \subseteq E$ *is the set (possibly empty) of directed links, where each link is a directed 2-tuple* $\langle n_r(t), n_s(t) \rangle$, *denoted simply as* $\ell_{rs}(t)$. ∎

Note that in the above definition we do not specify that the web tuple must be connected and acyclic. This is because, as we show in Chapter 8, disconnected or cyclic web tuples may be generated while manipulating web tuples locally using a set of algebraic operators.

Given a web tuple t and a coupling query G, we now identify the conditions that t must satisfy in order to conform to G. We first discuss the conformity condition of a conjunctive connectivity set. As we shown, the coupling query conformity condition can be expressed in terms of conformity conditions of a set of conjunctive connectivity sets. Let $k \equiv x\langle\ell\rangle y$ be a simple connectivity. Given such a set of simple connectivities in CNF, say C, and a set of documents D in a web tuple t, t will conform to C (denoted by $t \dashv C$) if there exist a pair of documents in D that conform to each simple connectivity in C. Formally,

Definition 6.26. [Conformity Condition of Conjunctive Connectivity Set] *Given a web tuple* $t = \langle N(t), L(t) \rangle$ *and a set of simple connectivities* $C \equiv k_1 \wedge k_2 \wedge \cdots \wedge k_r$, *let* D *be the set of documents represented by* $N(t)$; *i.e.,* $|D| \leq |N(t)|$. *Then*

t **conforms** to C, denoted by $t \dashv C$ if and only if $D_1 \dashv k_1 \wedge D_2 \dashv k_2 \wedge D_3 \dashv k_3 \cdots \wedge D_r \dashv k_r$, where $D = D_1 \cup D_2 \cup \cdots \cup D_r$ and $|L(t)| = r$. If k_i and k_j are connected, then $D_i \cap D_j \neq \emptyset \; \forall \; 0 < (i,j) \leq r$. ∎

We now use the above definition to describe coupling query conformity conditions. A coupling query can be of two forms: either it may contain only a single node type identifier and no link type identifiers or it may contain a set of node and link type identifiers. Moreover, for the latter case the query must be a directed, connected acyclic graph. Also any coupling query can be expressed in canonical form. If the query contains only a single node type identifier, then a web tuple t conforms to the query if it contains a single node object that satisfies the predicates defined on the node type identifier. Otherwise, the web tuple must satisfy the connectivity constraints specified in the query. Recall that the connectivities in a valid canonical coupling query are in DNF; i.e., $C \equiv C_1 \vee C_2 \vee \cdots \vee C_n$, where C_k is a conjunctive connectivity set for all $0 < k \leq n$. Therefore the set of documents in a web tuple will satisfy C if they conform to any one of the conjunctive connectivity sets. For example, a web tuple containing a set of documents D satisfies the connectivity $k \equiv x\langle (ef)|(gh)\rangle y$ if the documents satisfy either of the conjunctive connectivity sets, $C_1 \equiv (x\langle e\rangle \texttt{\#}_1 \wedge \texttt{\#}_1 \langle f\rangle y)$ or $C_2 \equiv (x\langle g\rangle \texttt{\#}_2 \wedge \texttt{\#}_2 \langle h\rangle y)$. Formally, the query conformity conditions can be expressed as follows.

Definition 6.27. [**Coupling Query Conformity**] Let $t = \langle N(t), L(t)\rangle$ be a web tuple and $G_c = \langle X_n, X_\ell, C, P, Q\rangle$ be a canonical coupling query. Let D be the set of documents in t. Then t **conforms** to G_c, denoted by $t \dashv G_c$, if either of the following conditions is true.

1. If $X_\ell = \emptyset$, then for $x \in X_n$ there must exist a document $d \in D$ such that $P_x(d) = \texttt{true}$. Furthermore, $|D| = 1$.
2. If $X_\ell \neq \emptyset$, then $t \dashv C_i$ for $0 < i \leq n$, where $C \equiv C_1 \vee C_2 \vee \cdots \vee C_n$, $C_j \equiv k_{j_1} \wedge k_{j_2} \wedge \cdots \wedge k_{j_v}$, where k_{j_v} is a simple connectivity $\forall \; 0 < j \leq n$. ∎

Hence the results of a coupling query can be defined as follows.

Definition 6.28. [**Coupling Query Results**] The **result** of a valid canonical coupling query $G_c = \langle X_n, X_\ell, C, P, Q\rangle$ is the set $\{t | t$ is a subgraph of $G(WWW)$ and $t \dashv G_c\}$. ∎

In the next chapter, we show how a set of web tuples is materialized in a web table by generating the web schema(s) of the web tuples.

6.7 Computability of Valid Coupling Queries

In the preceding sections, we have discussed in detail various issues related to coupling queries and described how to generate a valid canonical coupling query. We also discussed the results of a coupling query, i.e., web tuples. In this section, we explore the notion of computability in the context of coupling queries in WHOWEDA. Our discussion is based on the pioneering work by Abiteboul et al. in [2] on the

computable and *eventually computable* queries in the context of the Web. We use
this framework to explore the computability issues of coupling queries. We begin by
classifying coupling queries into two types, i.e., *browser* and *browse/search* coupling
queries. As we show, this classification is based on the types of web queries in [2] that
are computable by the *browser* and *browse/search machines*. Finally, we discuss the
computability of these two types of coupling queries.

6.7.1 Browser and Browse/Search Coupling Queries

We define two types of coupling queries, *browser* and *browse/search*, and express
the computability of coupling queries with respect to these. Informally, the predicate on the identifier represented by the source vertex of a browser coupling query
must specify the value of the URL of its instances. For instance, the examples
of coupling queries in this chapter are all browser coupling queries. Formally, let
$G = \langle X_n, X_\ell, C, P, Q \rangle$ be a coupling query and $x \in X_n$ be the identifier of the
source vertex. Then G is a browser coupling query if there exists a metadata predicate $p(x) \in P$ such that $attr_path(p) = $ URL, $op(p) = $ EQUALS, and $val(p)$ is a
URL. Observe that such queries only access the portion of the Web reachable from
the URL of an instance of the source vertex. This is an example of controlling the
computation of a Web query. We next prove a result that confirms the central role
of the computation of browser coupling queries in the context of the Web.

Theorem 6.29. *All browser coupling queries are computable.*   ∎

Proof. We use the results in [2] to prove the above theorem. Observe that browser
coupling queries are navigational queries and are implementable by browsers. In
particular, the browser coupling queries are based on specifications of paths from
the source object (an instance of the source vertex) using regular expressions. Also,
we do not allow cycles and negation in coupling queries. Furthermore, the depth
of traversal is finite and fixed by the connectivities in the query. Therefore, based
on [2], all such queries are computable by a browser machine. In addition, every
generic and computable Web query is browser computable [2]. Hence, based on
these results, we can conclude that all browser coupling queries are computable. ∎

Next we define *browse/search* coupling queries. In this case, the predicate on
the identifier represented by the source vertex of a browser coupling query must
not specify the value of the URL. Hence the predicates on the source vertex can
be any nontrivial metadata, content, or structural predicates specifying syntactic
characteristics. Formally, let $G = \langle X_n, X_\ell, C, P, Q \rangle$ be a coupling query and $x \in X_n$
be the identifier of the source vertex. Then G is a browser/search coupling query if
there does not exist a metadata predicate $p(x) \in P$ such that $attr_path(p) = $ URL,
$op(p) = $ EQUALS, and $val(p)$ is an URL. Observe that this type of coupling query is
an augmentation of the browser coupling queries. A predicate on the start vertex is
essentially a selection operation on all Web objects [2]. Such a selection operation
is essentially a search operation in search engines. In general, a search triggers an
eventually computable subquery, whose results may be infinite. Hence such queries
can be handled by the browse/search machine. The following result specifies the
computability of browse/search coupling queries.

Theorem 6.30. *All browse/search coupling queries are (eventually) computable.* ∎

Proof. We again use the results in [2] to prove the above result. All coupling queries are directed, connected acyclic graphs and disallow negation. A browse/search coupling query simulates the computation of a query using a browse/search machine. Therefore browse/search coupling queries are (eventually) computable by a browse/search machine. Furthermore, a generic Web query is eventually computable if and only if it is eventually computable by a browse/search machine [2]. Consequently, all browse/search coupling queries are eventually computable.   ∎

Since the browser and browse/search coupling queries are the only two types of queries in WHOWEDA for retrieving Web data, based on the above two results we can say the following.

Theorem 6.31. *All coupling queries are (eventually) computable.*   ∎

6.8 Recent Approaches for Querying the Web

In this section, we compare our notion of coupling queries with existing Web query mechanisms. We focus on high-level similarities and differences between existing systems and our work. A detailed description of these systems is presented in Chapter 2. A summary of the comparison is given in Table 6.1.

Similar to coupling queries, WebSQL materializes a portion of the Web in two relations by navigating from known URLs and path regular expressions are used to describe this navigation. However, unlike connectivities in coupling queries, WebSQL fails to impose complex disjunctive query conditions. Furthermore, WebSQL does not provide a mechanism for controlling execution of web queries similar to coupling query predicates. Unlike coupling queries, WebSQL also fails to express queries based on the internal structure of Web documents. Finally, as WebSQL represents Web data in virtual relations, the topological structures of query results are lost once they are materialized. In WHOWEDA, the topological structure is preserved by materializing coupling query results in the form of web tuples.

Konopnicki and Shmueli [101, 102] proposed a high-level querying system called the W3QS for the WWW whereby users may specify content and structure queries on the WWW and maintain the results of queries as database views of the WWW. The queries in W3QL are expressed as directed multigraphs. Although W3QL allows users to specify queries based on partial knowledge using the notion of *unbounded length paths*, it is not as expressive as coupling queries. In fact, W3QL is restrictive in expressing disjunctive queries. It also does not provide a mechanism to express connectivities compactly. Furthermore, the expressive power of W3QL with respect to content and structural queries is restrictive compared to coupling queries due to limited exploitation of the internal structure of Web documents. Also, it does not support imposition of constraints on tag attributes in Web documents. Query results in W3QL are expressed as an HTML table. The table contains the URLs of the WWW nodes and WWW links' strings that satisfy the query, organized in rows. Due to this flattening of query results, the topological structure of the query result

System	Query HTML	Query XML	Querying hyper-links	Sub-page Querying	Partial knowledge	Querying tags, tag attributes	Control query exec.	Preserve result structure
Coupling Query	Yes	Yes	Yes	Yes	Yes	Yes	Yes	Yes
W3QS	Yes	No	Limited	Limited	Limited	No	No	No
WebSQL	Yes	No	Limited	No	No	No	No	No
WebLog	Yes	No	Limited	No	No	No	No	No
NetQL	Yes	No	Limited	Limited	Limited	No	Yes	No
FLORID	Yes	No	Limited	Limited	Limited	No	No	No
ARANEUS	Yes	No	Limited	Limited	Limited	No	No	No
WebOQL	Yes	No	Limited	Yes	Yes	No	No	Yes
Lorel	No	Yes	Not HTML link	Yes	Yes	Yes	No	Yes
XML-QL	No	Yes	Not HTML link	Yes	Yes	Yes	No	Yes
YAT$_L$	No	Yes	Not HTML link	Yes	Yes	Yes	No	Yes

Table 6.1. Comparison of web query systems.

is lost. However, unlike coupling queries, W3QL allows the user to query forms. Also the multigraph allows queries involving multiple source vertices and cycles. We believe that these additional features of W3QL can easily be incorporated in coupling queries.

WebOQL [6] is a functional language, but queries are couched in the familiar select-from-where form. It allows users to navigate, query and restructure graphs of trees and is capable of accommodating lack of knowledge of the structure of the data to be queried and potential irregularities, or even lack of explicit structure, in these data, which are common issues in the context of the Web. Hence WebOQL supports some of the features in coupling queries. However, WebOQL does not provide a mechanism to control the execution of web queries similar to coupling query predicates. Also query results in WebOQL are expressed as a collection of hypertrees, whereas, results of coupling query results are materialized as web tuples.

WebLog [106] provides a declarative interface for querying as well as restructuring (the language is logic-based). Similar to coupling queries, it accommodates partial knowledge the user may have on the information being queried. FLORID (**F-LO**gic **R**easoning **I**n **D**atabases) [93, 122] is a prototype implementation of the deductive and object-oriented formalism F-logic [97]. FLORID has been extended to provide a declarative semantics for querying the Web. The proposed extension allows extraction and restructuring of data from the Web. However, both these languages suffer from similar limitations as discussed above.

NetQL [119] follows the approach of structure-based queries; however, it attempts to overcome the problems unsolved by WebSQL, W3QS, and WebLog. First, a novel approach to mine information from Web pages is presented so that queries involving information or structures inside pages can be issued. Second, various methods are provided to control the complexity of query processing. This is similar to coupling query predicates in our query. However, similar to other query mechanisms NetQL does not exploit disjunctive query conditions. Also the expressive power of this query language in terms of structure and content of Web data is restrictive compared to coupling queries. For instance, NetQL does not include a notion similar to attribute path expression to impose constraints on specific portions of Web documents.

The Araneus Project [7] addressed the issue of views in the Web context. It introduced a language called ULIXES that allows us to express and evaluate queries over a Web site. It implemented a *navigational algebra* [129] over nested structures. The notion of *navigational expressions* is used as a means to express a set of navigations, i.e., paths through pages in a site, along which selections, projections, and joins can be performed to select data of interest and return a set of tuples. Unlike coupling queries which allow us to specify regular path expressions, ULIXES is only capable of expressing queries with simple path expressions without recursion. This limits the expressive power of ULIXES in comparison with our coupling query. Next, ULIXES is based on page-schemes used to model the structure of a Web site. Hence, in order to use ULIXES, one has to be familiar with the Web site structure to generate the scheme of the site. This limits the usage of ULIXES as a user may not always be aware of the Web site structure. Our coupling query is capable of querying a Web site based on partial or zero knowledge by making use of regular link path expressions in connectivities and regular attribute path expressions in the predicates. Finally, query results of ULIXES are flattened into a relational view and hence the topological structure of the data instances is lost.

Recently, a few XML query languages have been proposed by the database community: XML-QL [67], Lorel [84], and YAT$_L$ [58, 59]. These languages are specifically used for XML data and support powerful features for querying such data. Our coupling query is capable of querying both HTML as well as XML data. One important difference is that these languages manipulate and query XML data at the subpage level and provide data restructuring facilities. They are also capable of querying based on the order of the document. The coupling query, on the other hand, at this point of time does not support data restructuring facilities. Query results in our web warehouse are always represented as a set of web tuples. Moreover, we do not manipulate documents at the subpage level. We also do not support queries based on the order of XML documents. We believe that these features can be incorporated in the future (see Chapter 12) to enhance the expressive power of coupling queries.

6.9 Summary

In this chapter, we described the query mechanism in WHOWEDA for harnessing relevant documents from the Web. We expressed a web query in the form of a coupling query. We illustrated with examples how to formulate coupling queries. Within this context, we introduced two types of coupling queries, canonical and noncanonical. Finally, we discussed how to transform a noncanonical coupling query into canonical form. We also discussed the results of a coupling query, i.e., web tuples. Finally, we showed that all coupling queries are (eventually) computable. In Chapter 7, we show how a valid canonical coupling query is used to generate the schema(s) of a set of web tuples. In Chapter 8 we show how to evaluate a valid canonical coupling query to retrieve relevant documents from the Web that match the query.

7

Schemas for Warehouse Data

Traditionally, a schema provides a structural summary of its data instances. In this chapter, we introduce the notion of a *web schema* to model instances of warehouse data in the context of WHOWEDA. A web schema provides certain types of information. First, it specifies some of the common properties shared by the documents and hyperlinks in the web table with respect to not only their structure, but also their metadata and content. Second, a web schema(s) summarizes the hyperlink structure of these documents in the web table. For brevity, a schema means a web schema (unless explicitly stated otherwise). Also note that in the rest of the book a canonical coupling query implies a valid canonical query (unless explicitly stated otherwise).

We begin by discussing related research in the field of schema generation for semistructured data. Next we provide an overview of the notion of a web schema in WHOWEDA. Finally, we discuss the importance of web schemas in the web warehouse in Section 7.1.4. In Section 7.2, we discuss the concept of a web schema in detail. We begin by describing the components of a web schema. We formally define a web schema and discuss different types of schema, i.e., *complex* and *simple* web schemas. Next we reintroduce the notion of web tuples in a different flavor. In the previous chapter, web tuples are defined as results of evaluation of a coupling query on the Web. We extend the notion of web tuples by expressing them as instances of a web schema. Within this context, we define the conditions for *schema conformity*. Finally, we describe *web tables*. Next, Sections 7.3 to 7.8 discuss the procedure to generate web schemas for data in the web warehouse. Sections 7.3 to 7.6 elaborate on the generation of web schemas for data resulting from the evaluation of a coupling query. Section 7.7 describes the formal algorithm for generation of a simple schema set. Section 7.8 presents the procedure to generate web schemas for web tuples generated by local web operations. In the last section, we conclude by summarizing our discussion on web schemas.

7.1 Preliminaries

In this section, we first present some of the recent approaches in generating schemas for semistructured data and describe how our approach differs from these approaches. Next, we provide an overview of the notion of web schemas in WHOWEDA. Finally, in Section 7.1.4, we discuss the importance of a web schema in the context of a web warehouse.

7.1.1 Recent Approaches for Modeling Schema for Web Data

Web query systems such as W3QS [101, 102], WebSQL [131], NetQL [119], Florid, [122] and WebLog [106] do not exploit the notion of schemas of Web data. WebSQL is based on a relational model and contains two virtual relations, Document and Anchor. The attributes of these relations are simple such as URL, modif, base, and so on, and do not provide any structural or content summary of the data retrieved from the Web. Similarly, W3QS uses the notion of multigraphs for modeling Web data and does not provide any facility to generate the schema of Web data. Query languages such as WebLog and Florid are based on rules and do not provide any rules to specify the metadata, content, and structural summary of Web data.

However, there has been recent work on schemas for semistructured data. For example, Buneman et al. [42] discussed schemas for graph-structured databases. A formal definition of a *graph schema* is given, along with an algorithm to determine whether a database conforms to a specific schema. Schema ordering, subsumption, and equivalence are also discussed. This work is presented with a more traditional view of a schema. Optimization and browsing functionality depend on having a database (or at least fragments of the database) conform to an explicitly specified schema.

Milo and Zohar in [133] use schema information for semistructured data translation. The authors implemented the TRANSCM translation system, and describe the architecture and functionalities. Translation from source to target formats is achieved by (1) importing data from the source to a middleware model, (2) translating it to another middleware representation that better fits the target structure, and then (3) exporting the translated data to the target system. In this process, schema information is extensively used. Source and target formats are each represented in a common schema language; then a correspondence between the source and target schemas is specified. Once such correspondence is established, translation becomes an automatic process: data from the source are imported to the common data model and are typed, i.e., matched to their schema, thus their components are associated with appropriate schema elements. Next, the schema correspondence is used for translation of the data to the target structure, where each component is translated according to its type. Then data are exported to the target.

In [10], the authors elaborate on the theoretical foundations of the schema model in [133]. This paper presents two schema definition languages, SCMDL and VSCMDL, and illustrates their expressive power. In SCMDL, a schema is a set of type definitions. The definition of a type (schema element) has two parts: a regular expression describing the possible sequences of children that a node can have and a part containing attributes that describe properties of a node. Three of these are Boolean flags that determine if instance data nodes of this type are ordered, can be referenced from other nodes, and can be the root of the data graph (instance of the schema). The fourth attribute is a unary predicate that determines the possible labels of data nodes of this type. Next the authors presented motivation for augmenting the basic language SCMDL with the notions of "virtual nodes" and "types", and showed that these extend the expressive power. The authors also investigated the complexity of significant problems regarding schemas and instances, showing that in many cases they can be solved efficiently. An important contribution of this approach is the extension of the semistructured data model to support order, both in the data and in the schema level.

The closest to the model in [10] is YAT [58], supporting order and an expressive schema language. The schema language is similar to SCMDL and uses regular expressions. But YAT does not support virtual types. While the *instantiation* mechanism provides a notion of matching data to a schema, it does not provide any explicit type assignment to instance nodes as in SCMDL. However, YAT offers subtyping which is not offered by SCMDL.

DataGuides [85] is cast in the context of the Lore system [1]. It is an OEM graph G that corresponds to an OEM database D, such that every distinct label path from the root of D appears exactly once as a path from the root of G, and every label path from the root of G has at least one matching label in D. In this context, the authors specify the definition of a *strong* DataGuide, which allows us to store annotations, such as statistics and sample values, with each label path in the DataGuide. The definition of a strong DataGuide is based on *target sets*. The target set of a path is the set of all objects reachable via that path. In a strong DataGuide, each DataGuide object corresponds to the target set of all label paths that reach the DataGuide object. Two label paths in the DataGuide point to the same DataGuide object if and only if the target set of both label paths is exactly the same in the original database. There exists exactly one strong DataGuide for any database. The algorithm presented in [85] creates a strong DataGuide by performing a depth-first exploration of the database.

In [86] Goldman and Widom relax the notion of DataGuides to *approximate DataGuides* to address the limitations on performance traps. To elaborate further, for a tree-shaped database, DataGuide construction is linear in space and time with respect to the size of the database. For a general graph, however, the algorithm is exponential in the worst case. Particularly for cyclic databases, DataGuide construction is prohibitively expensive. The authors introduce an *approximate* DataGuide (ADG) which provides an approximate summary of the database and is much cheaper to compute. An ADG drops the requirement that all DataGuide paths must exist in the original database.

Nestorov et al. [138] present a work on the extraction of implicit structure in semistructured data modeled in the style of [1] as a directed labeled graph. They show that data can be typed using the greatest fixpoint semantics of monadic Datalog programs. Within this context, they assert that it is imperative to allow some *defects* when objects are typed. To achieve this, an algorithm for *approximate* typing of semistructured data is proposed. By approximate typings, the authors mean an object does not have to fit its type definition precisely. The authors describe the methods for the approximate typing of semistructured data in stages. The gist of the first stage is to assign *every* object to a single *home type*. They use the minimal number of home types such that every object fits its home *perfectly* (with no *defects*). In the second stage, the authors address the optimization problem of reducing the number of types, thus having objects that fit their home types with some defect, while incurring a lower cumulative defect. The third and the final stage of the schema extraction method is about recasting the original data within the chosen types.

7.1.2 Features of Our Web Schema

Our approach differs from these works in the following ways.

Content, Metadata ,and Structural Summary

Traditionally, a schema provides a structural summary of the data it binds. However, we believe that to expedite query formulation and evaluation in a web warehouse, a structural summary of a set of Web documents is not enough. Query formulation and evaluation can be performed efficiently if some of the content and metadata properties shared by the Web documents and hyperlinks are highlighted in the schema. Although structural summary of XML documents may enable us to speculate on the content of XML data due to the usage of meaningful user-defined tags, such may not be the case for HTML documents. HTML tags are not used for describing the data segment enclosed in them and hence a structural summary of HTML pages is not very useful in subsequent query evaluation and formulation. Furthermore, capturing a summary of the hyperlink structure of a set of Web documents also helps to formulate meaningful queries in the warehouse. Consequently, a *web schema* provides certain types of information. First, it specifies some of the common properties shared by the documents and hyperlinks in the *web table* with respect to not only their structure, but also their metadata and content. Second, a web schema(s) summarizes the hyperlink structure of these documents. For instance, given a set of documents, the web schema(s) may specify that the titles of all these documents contain the keyword "genetic disorder". It may also specify that these documents belong to the Web site at `www.ninds.nih.gov` and contain the tags `symptom`, `treatment`, and `drugs` inside the tag `disease`. Also, a web schema may specify that a set of documents containing the keyword "genetic disorder" is directly linked to a set of documents having the tags `drugs` and `side effects` via a set of hyperlinks whose labels contain the keyword "drugs".

Reverse Approach for Schema Generation

We take a *reverse* approach in generating a web schema. The standard database paradigm in schema generation involves first creating a schema to describe the structure of the database and then populating that database through the interface provided by the schema. A schema is then used to decide whether some new data fit the schema or whether a query is legal against the set of data. Hence a schema is defined before the query. In our approach, a web schema is defined from a coupling query. The results of such a query are a set of directed graphs called web tuples stored in a *web table*. We justify this reverse approach now. If a web schema is defined by a user ahead of time, the structure, content, and rigidity of a web schema depend on the following factors: the information a user wishes to retrieve from the Web, and the user's level of knowledge of the content and structure of the Web site(s) containing the relevant data. However, this conventional approach is not feasible for these reasons.

- As mentioned earlier, it is unrealistic to assume from the user complete knowledge about the content and structure of Web pages in Web sites. The user knows what she is looking for, but she may not have a clear idea of how to express her needs. This is primarily because one may not necessarily know anything about the architecture of a given site, anything about the structure used to represent the data, or how the desired information is represented in the source. Thus a web schema generated by a user may contain very *loose* structure. Such a schema does not represent the *best* schema for the data it binds.
- Even if a user is successful in finding the schema of a set of documents by browsing the Web site(s) manually, it is not a realistic approach. For a reasonably small size of web documents, browsing the set of documents for information of schema is a feasible option. However, browsing a document set of significant size is a tedious and inefficient way of determining the schema of the data. This problem may be minimized by specifying a coupling query based on partial knowledge of the data of interest and then generating the schema of the data from the query and the query results (web tuples) autonomously.

Express Free Nodes and Links

Due to the unstructured and irregular nature of the Web, there may exist a set of documents or links in the query result (web tuples) whose common characteristics are not known ahead of time, or they simply may not share any similar properties. Moreover, there may also exist a collection of documents and links that does not share any common characteristics with respect to their connectivities with one another or other documents. Such documents and links are called free documents and links. Our web schema is flexible enough to represent these documents and links and how they are connected to one another.

Maintenance of Web Schemas

The dynamic nature of the Web further aggravates the problem of using traditional schema generation techniques. As new Web data are added frequently to its sources, we may find a schema is incomplete or inconsistent. Consequently, DataGuides [85, 86], are recomputed, or incrementally updated, when the data change. In WHOWEDA, a set of web schemas is associated with each web table. These schemas are not incrementally updated as the web tables are not modified. We justify the reasons behind this in Section 7.2.4. Hence the maintenance of web schemas is less complicated compared to DataGuides.

Schema for HTML and XML Documents

Recent approaches of schema generation for semistructured data [10, 42, 85, 133, 138] focus on generating schemas for XML-like documents. These approaches are useful for documents having user-defined tags. However, as mentioned earlier, the structural summary provided by these approaches may not be always helpful for HTML documents. Our notion of *web schema* is *generic*. That is, it can be used for both HTML and XML documents.

7.1.3 Summary of Our Methodology

In this section, we provide an overview of the notion of schema in the context of our web warehouse. The various issues are detailed in subsequent sections. In WHOWEDA, a *web schema* is used to summarize the characteristics of a set of interlinked documents. Informally, a web schema consists of four components: sets of *node* and *link type identifiers* to represent a collection of node and link objects, respectively, a set of *simple connectivities* defined over these node and link type identifiers to express the interlinked structure of the documents, and a set of *predicates* to express the common characteristics of some of the nodes and links with respect to their metadata, textual content, or structure. A web schema can be of two types: *complex* or *simple*. A complex web schema contains a set of simple connectivities in DNF, whereas, in a simple web schema, the set (possibly empty) of simple connectivities is in conjunction to each other.

Instances of a web schema are also called web tuples. In WHOWEDA, web tuples are generated (1) by retrieving a set of Web documents from the Web that matches a user's coupling query using a *global web coupling* operation [29, 121], and (2) by manipulating web tuples stored in the web warehouse using a set of web algebraic operators to generate a new set of web tuples. Hence the schemas of these two types of web tuples are generated (1) by manipulating the coupling query of the globally coupled Web data, and (2) by manipulating the schemas of the input web tuples during local operations to generate a new set of web schemas for resultant web tuples. The first mechanism of schema generation, from the coupling query, consists of several stages. The gist of the first stage is to transform the coupling query specified by the user to a simple or complex web schema by eliminating all coupling query predicates defined over it and *refining* the set of predicates defined over the node and link type identifiers. Note that if the transformation generates a simple web schema, then all the remaining stages are ignored. In the second stage, we convert the complex web schema that may result from the first phase into a set of simple web schemas. The third and final stage of our method associates each schema with a set of web tuples. In this context, we *prune* the set of simple web schemas in order to eliminate *noisy* web schemas (schemas that do not bind any web tuples) and impose a restriction that a web tuple must be bound by one and only one simple web schema. We discuss these stages in detail in Sections 7.4 to 7.6.

The second method of schema generation, by manipulating schemas of web tuples participating in local web operations, consists of only two stages. This is because the schemas of the web tuples stored locally in web tables are already in simple form and therefore the first two steps of the previous method are ignored. In this case, the first stage generates a set of simple schemas by manipulating the set of input web schemas depending on the specific algebraic operations and *query conditions*. The next stage then *prunes* these schemas to create the final set of simple schemas and associates them with the resultant web tuples. Note that the pruning process is similar to that of the previous method. We discuss this method of generating schema in Section 7.8.

7.1.4 Importance of Web Schema in a Web Warehouse

We now discuss the benefits realized by the use of web schemas in a web warehouse. Beyond its use to define the structure of a set of data in the warehouse, a web schema serves two important functions. It helps the user in query formulation and aids the query processor for efficient execution of the query. We elaborate on these two functions.

Query Formulation

A web schema enables the user to understand the partial structure and content of a set of instances of the schema materialized in the form of web tuples and form a meaningful query over it. Without a schema this task becomes significantly harder as the user does not know the structure and content of underlying data and this impedes his efforts to formulate reasonable queries. Although it may be possible to manually browse a small set of web tuples to formulate queries, in general forming a meaningful query when a large number of web tuples exist is difficult without a schema or some kind of summary information of the underlying data.

Query Evaluation

A web schema also facilitates efficient query processing in the web warehouse. A query processor relies on the schema to devise efficient plans for computing query results. It uses information available in the schema to prune the search. Note that a lack of information about the structure and content of the data in the warehouse can cause a query processor to resort to exhaustive searches. We illustrate this with an example given below.

Suppose we wish to combine treatment information of neurological disorders which is stored in two web tables. Assume that the query processor needs to perform a *web join* operation on the instances of node type identifiers y and b in these web tables to gather this information. Disregarding the details of *web join* for the moment, intuitively it is an operation to concatenate two web tuples over identical nodes having the same URL and content. Also, for the moment ignore the existence of schema in the warehouse. Thus, in order to perform a web join operation, the query processor has to compare each instance of y to the instances of b to determine if they have identical URLs and content. However, if there exist schemas of these two web tables, then it may be possible for the query processor to restrict its search for identical nodes by inspecting the schemas. The query processor may evaluate the predicates (defined in the schemas) associated with y and b before evaluating the instances of y and b. Suppose the predicates on y and b are as follows:

$$p_1(y) \equiv \text{CONTENT::y[title] NON-ATTR\_CONT ":START\_STR: +}$$
$$\textit{neurological disorders} \text{ + :END\_STR:"}$$
$$p_2(b) \equiv \text{CONTENT::b[title] NON-ATTR\_ENCL "}\textit{Treatment}\text{"}$$

From these predicates it is clear that the instances of y and b cannot be identical as the titles of the instances of y and b are not the same. Consequently, web tuples containing instances of y and b cannot be joined over these identifiers and the joined web table will return no web tuples. Note that the query processor can efficiently determine the result of the web join operation without operating on the web tuples.

Observe that the importance of a web schema in query formulation and query evaluation depends on the quality or *goodness* of the schema (the quality of non-trivial information provided by the schema). Thus a very "weak" or low quality schema may not provide much help in query evaluation and formulation. For example, suppose in the above example the predicates defined on b and y are

$$p_1'(y) \equiv \text{CONTENT::y[title] NON-ATTR\_CONT ":START\_STR: +}$$
$$\textit{neurological disorders} \text{ + :END\_STR:"}$$
$$p_2'(b) \equiv \text{CONTENT::b[title] NON-ATTR\_CONT ":BEGIN\_WORD: +}$$
$$\textit{Treatment} \text{ + :END\_WORD:"}$$

These predicates do not guarantee that the URL and content of instances of b and y are not identical. Hence these predicates do not aid the query processor in determining if the web tuples can be joined over the instances of b and y by inspecting the schemas alone. It has to inspect each instance of b and y to determine whether the web tuples can be joined.

Note that a web schema may not always aid in query formulation and evaluation as it is not always possible to provide a complete summary of a set of web tuples. But having a web schema is certainly advantageous in some situations, rather than having no structural and content summary of warehouse data instances.

7.2 Web Schema

In this section, we elaborate on the notion of web schemas. We begin by formally introducing the concept of a web schema. Next, we categorize web schemas into two types, i.e., *simple* and *complex* web schemas. In Section 7.2.3, we discuss the notion of web tuples in the context of a web schema. Finally, we conclude this section by describing the notion of a *web table*.

7.2.1 Definition

A web schema consists of four components: sets of node and link type identifiers, a set of simple connectivities, and a set of predicates. The notions of node and link type identifiers and predicates are identical to those discussed in the context of a coupling query in the previous chapter. Similar to coupling queries, web schemas cannot have any arbitrary collection of these four components. Specifically, the following conditions must be satisfied by the components of a web schema.

Conditions on Node and Link Type Identifiers

The conditions outlined below must be satisfied by the X_n and X_ℓ components of a web schema.

- The set of node type identifiers X_n is always nonempty.
- The identifiers used to represent node objects in a web schema must be nominally dissimilar to those used to represent link objects. That is, the components X_n and X_ℓ must not overlap.

Conditions on Connectivities

We now identify the constraints imposed on the set of connectivities in a web schema.

- A web schema contains only simple connectivities and these connectivities must be in DNF or in CNF. Recall that in a coupling query, the connectivities may be in simple or complex form and they may not be in DNF.
- The set of node and link type identifiers in the collection of connectivities must match with the set of node and link type identifiers specified in the components of X_n and X_ℓ.
- If C_1 and C_2 represent two conjunctive connectivity sets in a web schema and $C_1 \vee C_2$, then C_1 and C_2 must not contain the same set of connectivities.

Condition on Predicates

Finally, the predicate set in a web schema must satisfy the following condition.

- The argument of each predicate in the predicate set must be a node or link type identifier in X_n or X_ℓ.

Based on the above features, a web schema can be formally defined as follows.

Definition 7.1. [Web Schema] *A **web schema** is a 4-tuple $S = \langle X_n, X_\ell, C, P \rangle$ where X_n is a set of node type identifiers, X_ℓ is a set (possibly empty) of link type identifiers, C is a set (possibly empty) of simple connectivities in DNF defined over X_n and X_ℓ, and P is a set (possibly empty) of predicates defined over X_n and X_ℓ such that the following conditions are true.*

- $X_n \cap X_\ell = \emptyset$;
- *If $X_\ell = \emptyset$ then $C = \emptyset$. Otherwise, $C \equiv C_1 \vee C_2 \vee \cdots \vee C_r$, where $r > 0$, $C_i \equiv k_{i1} \wedge k_{i2} \wedge \cdots \wedge k_{is}$ is a conjunctive connectivity set such that $k_{ia} \neq k_{ib} \ \forall a \neq b$ and $0 < (a, b) \leq s$;*
- *Let X_{nc} and $X_{\ell c}$ be the set of node and link type identifiers, respectively, in C. Then $X_{nc} \subseteq X_n$ and $X_{\ell c} \subseteq X_\ell$;*

- *There must not exist conjunctive connectivity sets $C_a \equiv k_{a1} \wedge k_{a2} \wedge \cdots \wedge k_{an}$ and $C_b \equiv k_{b1} \wedge k_{b2} \wedge \cdots \wedge k_{bn}$ such that $k_{ax} = k_{bx} \ \forall \ 0 < x \leq n$ and $0 < (a,b) \leq r$;* ∎

In Section 7.4, we illustrate web schemas with examples.

Similar to a coupling query, a web schema contains a set of connectivities. Hence a web schema can also be visualized as a directed graph. However, based on the above definition, the graphical structure of a schema is different from the structure of a coupling query. Recall that a coupling query is a directed connected acyclic graph with a single source vertex. The source vertex in a coupling query always represents a bound node type identifier. However, a web schema can be a disconnected cyclic graph having multiple source vertices. Also, one of the source vertices of a web schema may represent a free node type identifier. Such features are possible for a web schema because of the different types of manipulation of web tables in the web warehouse. For instance, a *web project* operation may generate a disconnected schema. Furthermore, a schema may also be cyclic. This may happen if we are interested in *selecting* those web tuples from a web table where each of these tuples contains a node that links back to any one of the predecessor nodes. We discuss these issues in detail in the next chapter.

7.2.2 Types of Web Schema

Web schemas are categorized into two types: *complex* and *simple* web schemas. This categorization is based on the relationships of simple connectivities in a schema with each other. We say that a web schema is *complex* if it contains a set of simple connectivities in DNF. As we show, a complex schema can only be generated from a valid canonical coupling query. Hence the features of a valid canonical coupling query are also incorporated in a complex web schema.

Definition 7.2. [Complex Web Schema] *Let $S = \langle X_n, X_\ell, C, P \rangle$ be a web schema. Then S is **complex** if the following conditions are true.*

- *$C \equiv C_1 \vee C_2 \vee \cdots \vee C_r$ for $r > 1$;*
- *Let X_{nc} and $X_{\ell c}$ be the set of node and link type identifiers in C. Then $X_{nc} = X_n$ and $X_{\ell c} = X_\ell$;*
- *Let k_{ij} and $k_{i(j+1)}$ be two simple connectivities in C_i for $0 < i \leq r$. Then any one of the following must be true: (1) $lnode(k_{ij}) = rnode(k_{i(j+1)})$, (2) $rnode(k_{ij}) = rnode(k_{i(j+1)})$, and (3) $lnode(k_{ij}) = lnode(k_{i(j+1)})$. Also the last two equalities are mutually exclusive. Furthermore, if the second equality is true, then $j > 1$;*
- *Let k_{ij} be a connectivity in C_i. Then, there must not exist $k_{i(j+n)}$ such that $lnode(k_{ij}) = rnode(k_{i(j+n)}) \ \forall \ 0 < n \leq t$;*
- *$lnode(k_{ij}) \neq rnode(k_{is})$ is true for all $0 < s \leq n$ and $j \neq s$ only if $j = 1$.*
- *Let C_a and C_b be two conjunctive connectivity sets. Then any one of the following must be true: $lnode(k_{a1}) = lnode(k_{b1})$, $lnode(k_{a1}) = lnode(k_{bj})$, or $lnode(k_{a1}) = rnode(k_{bj})$, where $j \neq 1$.* ∎

Observe that the definition of a complex web schema is similar to that of the valid canonical coupling query.

A simple web schema, on the other hand, contains only a set (possibly empty) of simple connectivities where each connectivity is in conjunction to another. That is, S is simple if it contains a set of simple connectivities k_1. Note that a simple web schema cannot be further decomposed. A simple schema is the simplest form of web schema. Formally, a simple web schema can be defined as follows.

Definition 7.3. [Simple Web Schema] *Let $S = \langle X_n, X_\ell, C, P \rangle$ be a web schema. Then S is* **simple** *if $C = \emptyset$ or $C \equiv k_1 \wedge k_2 \wedge \cdots \wedge k_n$, where k_i is a simple connectivity $\forall\ 0 < i \le n$. Furthermore, the following conditions may be true.*

- *Let X_{nc} be the set of node type identifiers in C. Then there may exist $x \in X_n$ such that $x \notin X_{nc}$.*
- *There may exist $(x, y) \in X_n$ such that there does not exist a connectivity k in C where $lnode(k) = x$ and $rnode(k) = y$.*
- *Let k_i be a connectivity in C. Then there may exist $k_{(i+r)}$ such that $lnode(k_i) = rnode(k_{i+r})$ for $0 < r \le n$.* ∎

Observe that based on the above definition, a simple web schema may be a disconnected cyclic graph having multiple source vertices. As we show later, a simple web schema may be generated from a coupling query or during manipulation of web tables locally using a set of web algebraic operators.

7.2.3 Schema Conformity

Recall from Section 6.6 in Chapter 6, a web tuple is a directed graph consisting of a set of node and link objects that are instances of node and link type identifiers in a coupling query, respectively. Furthermore, web tuples are the result of evaluation of a coupling query on the Web. Specifically, we discussed the conformity conditions of a web tuple with respect to a coupling query. In this case, a web tuple must be a directed connected acyclic graph with a single source vertex. We now discuss conformity conditions of a web tuple with respect to a web schema.

Recall that unlike a coupling query, a web schema may be a directed disconnected cyclic graph with multiple source vertices. Hence additional conformity conditions need to be developed for a tuple to satisfy a web schema. As a simple web schema may be a disconnected cyclic graph with multiple source vertices, the web tuple satisfying such a schema must also be a disconnected cyclic graph. Specifically, a web schema may be structurally classified into the following types.

- **Type 1:** A schema S may contain a set of node type identifiers that are not connected to each other. That is, S is a simple schema where $X_\ell = \emptyset$, $C = \emptyset$, and $X_n \neq \emptyset$.
- **Type 2:** S may be visualized as a directed connected graph where $C \equiv C_1 \vee C_2 \vee \cdots \vee C_r$ for $r > 0$. In this case, the node type identifiers in S are connected to each other by a set of link type identifiers. Note that in this case, S can be simple or complex.
- **Type 3:** S is disconnected and contains more than one connected component. Furthermore, each connected component contains at least two node type identifiers. That is, $X_\ell \neq \emptyset$, $X_n \neq \emptyset$, and $C \neq \emptyset$. Note that in this case, S is a

simple web schema. For example, $S = \langle X_n, X_\ell, C, P \rangle$ where $X_n = \{x, y, a, b\}$, $X_\ell = \{e, f\}$, and $C \equiv x\langle e \rangle y \wedge a\langle f \rangle b$.

- **Type 4:** Finally, this type is a combination of the above three types. S is a p-connected graph for $p > 1$ and there exists at least one component in S consisting of only a single node type identifier. For example, $S = \langle X_n, X_\ell, C, P \rangle$, where $X_n = \{x, y, z, a, b\}$, $X_\ell = \{e, f\}$, and $C \equiv x\langle e \rangle y \wedge a\langle f \rangle b$.

Informally, a web tuple t *conforms* to a schema S if the set of documents and hyperlinks in t satisfies the connectivities and predicates defined in S. A web tuple t must satisfy one of the four types of web schema identified above. We now discuss the *conformity conditions* for each type of web schema.

- A web tuple t satisfies a web schema S of Type 1 if t contains a set of documents such that each document is an instance of a node type identifier in X_n. Also, all the node type identifiers specified in X_n must have an instance in t.
- The conformity condition for a Type 2 web schema is similar to the conformity condition of a coupling query. Since $C \equiv C_1 \vee C_2 \vee \cdots \vee C_r$ for $r > 0$, a web tuple t conforms to S if t satisfies any one of the conjunctive connectivity sets C_i; i.e., $t \dashv C_i$. Observe that t may satisfy more than one conjunctive connectivity set. For example, a web tuple t satisfies the connectivity $C \equiv C_1 \vee C_2$ where $C_1 \equiv x\langle e \rangle \text{\#}_1 \wedge \text{\#}_1 \langle f \rangle y$ and $C_2 \equiv x\langle g \rangle \text{\#}_2 \wedge \text{\#}_2 \langle h \rangle y$ if t satisfies any one of the simple connectivities $(x\langle e \rangle \text{\#}_1 \wedge \text{\#}_1 \langle f \rangle y)$ or $(x\langle g \rangle \text{\#}_2 \wedge \text{\#}_2 \langle h \rangle y)$.
- Note that for this type of schema $C \equiv k_1 \wedge k_2 \wedge \cdots \wedge k_r$. Let p be the number of connected components in S. Since each connected component contains more than one node type identifier, they are expressed by C. Therefore C can be decomposed to p connected graphs $C \equiv C_1 \wedge C_2 \wedge \cdots \wedge C_p$, where $C_i \equiv k_1 \wedge k_2 \wedge \cdots \wedge k_s$ for $s < r$. Observe that C_i represents a set of connectivities in C that generated a directed connected graph. For example, consider the schema in the definition of Type 3 schemas described above. Here the number of connected components is two. Hence C can be decomposed into C_1 and C_2 where $C_1 \equiv x\langle e \rangle y$ and $C_2 \equiv a\langle f \rangle b$. Hence a tuple satisfies S if t can be decomposed into p connected components such that they conform to the connected components in C, i.e., $C_1, C_2, \ldots, C_p$, respectively. This indicates that the number of connected components of t should be identical to that of C, i.e., p.
- Finally, in this case, we decompose $S = \langle X_n, X_\ell, C, P \rangle$ into two schemas S_1 and S_2 of the above three types. To elaborate further, let $S_1 = \langle X_{n1}, X_{\ell 1}, C_1, P_1 \rangle$ and $S_2 = \langle X_{n2}, X_{\ell 2}, C_2, P_2 \rangle$. Let X_{nc} and $X_{\ell c}$ denote the set of node and link type identifiers in C, respectively. Then $X_{n1} = X_{nc}$, $X_{\ell 1} = X_{\ell c}$, $C_1 = C$, and $P_1 \subseteq P$. Also, $X_{n2} = X_n - X_{nc}$, $X_{\ell 2} = \emptyset$, $C_2 = \emptyset$, and $P_2 \subseteq P$. For instance, consider the schema in the definition of Type 4 schemas described above. Here $X_{nc} = \{x, y, a, b\}$ and $X_{\ell c} = \{e, f\}$. Then S can be decomposed into S_1 and S_2 where $X_{n1} = \{x, y, a, b\}$, $X_{n2} = \{z\}$, $X_{\ell 1} = \{e, f\}$, $X_{\ell 2} = \emptyset$, $C_1 = C$, and $C_2 = \emptyset$. Observe that S_1 is a schema of Type 2 or 3 and S_2 is a schema of Type 1. Therefore, a web tuple t satisfies S if it can be decomposed into two parts t_1 and t_2 such that t_1 and t_2 conform to S_1 and S_2, respectively.

Formally schema conformity can be defined as follows.

Definition 7.4. [Schema Conformity] *Let* $t = \langle N(t), L(t) \rangle$ *be a web tuple and* $S = \langle X_n, X_\ell, C, P \rangle$ *be a web schema. Then* t **conforms** *to* S, *denoted by* $t \dashv S$, *if any one of the following conditions is true.*

1. *If* $X_\ell = \emptyset$, *then for each bound node type identifier* $x_b \in X_n$ *there must exist a document* $d \in N(t)$ *such that* $p_d(x_b) = \mathrm{true}$ *and for each free node type identifier* $x_f \in X_n$ *there exists an arbitrary document* d *in* t.
2. *If* S *is of Type 2, then* $t \dashv C_j$ *for* $0 < j \le n$, *where* $C \equiv C_1 \vee C_2 \vee \cdots \vee C_n$ *and* $C_j \equiv k_{j_1} \wedge k_{j_2} \wedge \cdots \wedge k_{j_v}$, *where* k_{j_v} *is a simple connectivity.*
3. *If* S *is of Type 3, then let* $C \equiv C_1 \wedge C_2 \wedge \cdots \wedge C_p$ *where* p *denotes the number of connected components in* S *and* $C_j \equiv k_{j_1} \wedge k_{j_2} \wedge \cdots \wedge k_{j_v}$ *represents a connected component* $\forall\ 0 < j \le p$. *Then* $t \dashv S$ *if* t *can be decomposed into* p *connected components* $t_1, t_2, \ldots, t_p$, *where* $t_i = \langle N(t_i), L(t_i) \rangle$, $N(t_i) \subset N(t)$, $L(t_i) \subset L(t)$, *and* $t_1 \dashv C_1 \wedge t_2 \dashv C_2 \cdots \wedge t_p \dashv C_p$.
4. *If* S *is a Type 4 schema, and* S_1 *and* S_2 *are the decomposed schemas, then* t *can be decomposed into two components* t_1 *and* t_2 *such that* $t_1 \dashv S_1$ *and* $t_2 \dashv S_2$. ∎

7.2.4 Web Table

In a web warehouse, a set of web tuples satisfying a schema is stored in a web table. The notion of a web table is somewhat analogous to its relational counterpart. It binds together data instances that satisfy conditions defined by a set of simple web schemas. However, a web table, unlike its relational counterpart, may have one or more schemas to bind the set of web tuples. Informally, a web table W consists of the following: the *name* of the web table, a set of simple web schemas $\mathcal{S}$, and a set of web tuples T bound by these web schemas. Each simple web schema $S_i \in \mathcal{S}$ binds a set of web tuples $T_i \subseteq T$. The pair (S_i, T_i) is collectively called a *partition* (denoted by U). Note that a partition may contain a web schema that does not bind any web tuples; i.e., $T_i = \emptyset$. Such a partition is called a *noisy partition* and S_i is called a *noisy schema*. Formally,

Definition 7.5. [Partition] *A* **partition** *is a pair* $U = \langle S, T \rangle$ *where* S *is a simple web schema and* T *is a set of web tuples. If* $t_i \in T$, *then* $t_i \dashv S\ \forall\ 0 < i \le |T|$. *If* $T_i = \emptyset$, *then* U *is called a* **noisy partition** *and* S_i *is called a* **noisy schema**. ∎

Notice that a web table can be realized as a set of partitions, denoted as $\mathcal{U} = \{U_1, U_2, \ldots, U_n\}$. Also observe that a web table is associated with a set of simple web schemas but not with complex schemas. In the web warehouse, a complex web schema binding a set of web tuples T is *decomposed* and *pruned* into a set of simple web schemas before assigning them as the schema(s) of the web table containing T. In Sections 7.5 and 7.6 we elaborate on this in detail.

Definition 7.6. [Web Table] *A* **web table** *is a 2-tuple* $W = \langle N, \mathcal{U} \rangle$, *where* N *is the name of the web table and* $\mathcal{U}$ *is a set of partitions where* $U_i \in \mathcal{U}$, $U_i = \langle S_i, T_i \rangle$ $\forall\ 0 < i \le |\mathcal{U}|$. *Also* $\mathcal{U} = \langle \mathcal{S}, T \rangle$, *where* $\mathcal{S} = \{S_1, S_2, \ldots, S_{|\mathcal{U}|}\}$ *and* $T = T_1 \cup T_2 \cup \cdots \cup T_{|\mathcal{U}|}$. ∎

Observe that as a set of simple web schemas is always associated with a web table, the generation of a set of simple web schemas is associated with the generation of a web table. In WHOM, a web table can be generated primarily in two ways.

- A web table is constructed by retrieving a set of interlinked documents from the Web using the *global web coupling* operator. Global web coupling is an operation for retrieving a set of interlinked documents from the Web that satisfies a user's coupling query.
- A web table may also be created locally by manipulating existing web tables using different web algebraic operators. We elaborate on this in Chapter 8.

We now discuss some issues related to the modification of web tables. In WHOWEDA, a web table is not updated; i.e., no web tuples are inserted, deleted, or modified. The only deletion occurs when we wish to delete the entire web table. In a relational database, insertion, deletion, or update of a tuple in a relation is driven by the schema of the relation. A tuple can only be inserted or updated if and only if it strictly adheres to the schema of the relation. This assumption is reasonable in the traditional environment as the schema of the relation is relatively stable, rigid, and does not change frequently. However, allowing the update, deletion, or insertion of web tuples in a web table based on the conventional approach has some serious disadvantages as discussed below.

The change of structure and content of Web data is much more frequent than relational data. A consequence of this property is that a relevant web tuple may not be inserted in a web table simply because it does not satisfy the previously generated schema of the web table. One may argue that the insertion of web tuples may be possible by modifying the set of web schemas. However, such an operation has some major repercussions. First, the schema may have to be modified frequently due to frequent changes to Web data. Frequent modification of a web schema to incorporate new data may adversely affect the quality or *goodness* of the existing web schema. Consequently, modification of a web schema incurs overheads in maintaining the goodness of the schemas. Second, some of the existing web tuples may not satisfy the modified web schemas anymore. Moreover, web tuples may now satisfy more than one schema. Hence web table modification may result in generating a new set of schemas for all the web tuples again. As a result, the maintenance overhead of web schemas and web tuples is high. Note that such problems do not arise in relational databases as the schema of a relation is rigidly and completely defined and data are forced to comply to the schema. However, due to the very nature of Web data, such enforcement is not feasible.

The second issue is the manipulation of historical Web data. One of the objectives of our web warehouse is to be able to store and manipulate historical data to facilitate data analysis over broad vistas of data over time. The historical data are generated due to changes to the Web. Web pages replace their antecedent, usually leaving no trace of the previous document. These rapid and often unpredictable changes to the information create a new problem of detecting, representing, and querying these changes. Note that this is a challenging problem because information sources on the Web are autonomous and typical database approaches based on triggering mechanisms are not applicable. Moreover, these information sources typically do not keep track of historical information in a format that is accessible to an outside user [50]. These changes are reflected in the warehouse in the form of insertion, deletion, and updates of previous versions of web tuples. However, if we delete or modify the previous versions of a web tuple, then there is no way to retrieve these versions again for further analysis. Hence data once deleted or updated are completely lost. If we wish to query these changes by comparing their snapshots at different instances of time, then we need to store different versions of modified web tuples. Hence it is convenient to store different snapshots of web tuples in different web tables and use a set of algebraic operators to manipulate them [19].

7.3 Generation of Simple Web Schema Set from Coupling Query

In this section, we give an overview of how a set of simple web schemas is generated for a set of web tuples resulting from the evaluation of a coupling query. In the subsequent sections we discuss this procedure in detail.

When data for the warehouse are retrieved from the Web, the generation of a set of simple web schema for these data instances can most easily be described as consisting of the following three steps:

- *Valid Canonical Coupling Query to Schema Transformation Phase:* In this phase, a simple or complex web schema is generated from a valid canonical coupling query without inspecting the content or structure of the web tuples. If the schema is simple, then it is assigned as the schema of the web table containing the set of web tuples. Otherwise, the phases below are followed.
- *Complex Schema Decomposition Phase:* The complex web schema from the canonical coupling query to schema transformation phase is decomposed into a set of simple web schemas in this phase. This process is called *complex schema decomposition* and is discussed in detail in Section 7.5.
- *Schema Pruning Phase:* In this phase, the set of simple web schemas generated from the schema decomposition process is associated with corresponding web tuples and *pruned*. Those web schemas that do not bind any web tuple are removed and each web tuple is bound by only one web schema. Note that in this phase, the pruning operation is performed by inspecting the set of web tuples. At the end of this phase, a web table is constructed by generating a set of partitions $\mathcal{U}$. We discuss this in detail in Section 7.6.

7.4 Phase 1: Valid Canonical Coupling Query to Schema Transformation

In this section, we discuss the first phase of the schema generation process. Specifically, we show how to create the components of a simple or complex web schema from a valid canonical coupling query. We call this process the *valid canonical coupling query to schema transformation phase*. Hereafter, a coupling query means a canonical coupling query (unless explicitly stated otherwise). Intuitively, the components X_n, X_ℓ, C, and P of the schema are generated from the corresponding components of the coupling query. However, these components of the schema may not be exactly identical to the corresponding components in the coupling query. This is because some of the components of a web schema are *influenced* by the set of coupling query predicates associated with the coupling query. We elaborate on this later in this section. We begin by introducing some terminology.

The coupling query predicates in a coupling query can be categorized into two types: *schema-independent predicates* and *schema-influencing predicates*. The coupling query predicates that are *schema-independent* do not influence the components of the web schema generated from this query. For instance, the predicates on the attributes `time`, `total_nodes`, and `number_of_tuples` control the number of web tuples to be retrieved from the Web. Furthermore, a predicate on `polling_frequency` periodically executes a query. On the other hand, coupling queries containing *schema-influencing predicates* influence the components of the schema. For instance, the predicate on the attribute `host` is referred to as a schema-influencing predicate.

7.4.1 Schema from Query Containing Schema-Independent Predicates

A web schema does not indicate the number of web tuples it binds. Hence the components of a web schema generated from a coupling query are not influenced by the coupling query predicates if they contain only schema-independent predicates. Consequently, the components X_n, X_ℓ, C and P of the query are directly assigned as the corresponding components of the web schema. Note that the web schema can either be simple or complex depending on the connectivities in the canonical query. If all the connectivities are simple and in conjunction, then the transformation will result in a simple web schema. Otherwise, the transformation will generate a complex web schema. Formally;

Definition 7.7. *Let T be a set of web tuples retrieved by the canonical coupling query $G_c = \langle X_n, X_\ell, C, P, Q \rangle$. Let Q be a set (possibly empty) of schema-independent predicates. Then, the web schema of T is $S = \langle X_{n_s}, X_{\ell_s}, C_s, P_s \rangle$ where $X_{n_s} = X_n$, $X_{\ell_s} = X_\ell$, $C_s = C$ and $P_s = P$. S is* **simple** *if $C \equiv k_1 \wedge k_2 \wedge \cdots \wedge k_n$ and k_i is simple connectivity $\forall\ 0 < i \leq n$. Otherwise, S is a* **complex** *web schema.* ∎

Example 7.8. Consider the canonical query G_{11} in Example 6.17. Note that the coupling query predicate in this query is a schema-independent predicate. Thus, based on Definition 7.7, the schema of the web tuples in Figure 6.11 is $S_1 = \langle X_{n_{s1}}, X_{\ell_{s1}}, C_{s1}, P_{s1} \rangle$, where $X_{n_{s1}} = X_{n_{11q}}$, $X_{\ell_{s1}} = X_{\ell_{11q}}$, $C_{s1} = C_{11q}$, and $P_{s1} = P_{11q}$. Furthermore, as C_{s1} represent sets of simple connectivities in DNF, S_{s1} is a complex web schema. ∎

7.4.2 Schema from Query Containing Schema-Influencing Predicates

We now discuss how to create the web schema when the coupling query contains schema-influencing predicates. Specifically, we explain how to generate a web schema from a coupling query containing a coupling query predicate on the attribute host.

A coupling query predicate $q(G)$ over the attribute host is of the form: $q(G) \equiv$ COUPLING_QUERY::G.host EQUALS "V" where V is a host name. Recall that a coupling query may contain free node type identifiers in X_n to represent nodes that cannot be characterized by a set of common properties. We discuss the effect of the coupling query predicates on the components of web schema in the presence and absence of free node type identifiers. We first show how to generate the web schema when the coupling query $G_c = \langle X_n, X_\ell, C, P, Q \rangle$ does not contain any free node type identifiers.

Case 7.9. Observe that the predicate on host constrains all the nodes in the set of retrieved web tuples to represent documents stored in the host V. However, this characteristic may not be captured by the set of predicates defined on the node type identifiers in the coupling query. Thus, while generating the web schema from the coupling query, the set of predicates defined on these node type identifiers must be extended to incorporate the property related to the host of the nodes in the web tuples. Moreover, as the coupling query does not contain any free node type identifiers, the components X_{n_s}, X_{ℓ_s}, and C_s of the web schema are identical to the corresponding components of the coupling query. That is, $X_{n_s} = X_n$, $X_{\ell_s} = X_\ell$, and $C_s = C$.

The component P_s of the web schema may not be identical to the predicates in the coupling query. P_s must capture the constraints on the host of the nodes in the web tuples. Thus P must be modified to incorporate these additional constraints. Specifically, the host names of Web documents are captured by the metadata attribute server in WHOM. Thus P_s must include the following type of predicate imposed on each bound node type identifier $x \in X_n$: $p(x) \equiv$ METADATA::x[url.server] EQUALS "V". In order to achieve this, we follow the steps shown below.

- Determine a set of predicates $P_n \subseteq P$ such that each predicate $p \in P_n$ is of either of the following forms, $p(x) \equiv$ METADATA::x[url] EQUALS".*V.*" or $p(x) \equiv$ METADATA::x[url.server] EQUALS "V", where $x \in X_n$ and V is the value of the coupling query predicate over the query attribute host. Let $arg(P_n)$ denote the set of arguments of predicates in P_n.
- Let $P_{suf} \subseteq P$ represent a set of metadata predicates where the suffix of the attribute path expression of each predicate in P_{suf} is equal to geo_location, domain name, or host name.
- Generate a set of predicates P_h where each predicate is of the following form, $p(y) \equiv$ METADATA:: y[url.server] EQUALS "V", where $y \in X_n$ is the nominal identifier of a bound node type identifier in X_n and $y \notin arg(P_n)$.
- The set of predicates P_s of the web schema is the union of $(P - P_{suf})$ and P_h. That is, $P_s = (P - P_{suf}) \cup P_h$.

Case 7.10. We now show how to generate the web schema when the coupling query contains free node type identifiers. Recall that each free node type identifier represents a set of arbitrary nodes. As all nodes retrieved by the coupling query belong to a particular host defined by the coupling query predicate, it is possible to impose constraints on the metadata attribute `server` of the instances of free node type identifiers in the web tuples. Thus, while generating the web schema from this coupling query, the free node type identifiers are transformed into bound node type identifiers by imposing constraints on the metadata of their instances. Consequently, this requires modification of the content of X_n and C of the coupling query while transforming it into the web schema. We now outline the procedure to generate the web schema (denoted by $S = \langle X_{n_s}, X_{\ell_s}, C_s, P_s \rangle$) from the coupling query. The steps for creating the components X_{n_s}, X_{ℓ_s}, C_s, and P_s are as follows.

1. Determine a set of node predicates P_n and P_{suf} as described in Case 1.
2. Generate a set of predicates P_h as described in Case 1.
3. For each conjunctive connectivity set C_i for $0 < i \leq n$ and $C \equiv C_1 \vee C_2 \vee \cdots \vee C_n$, perform the following.
   a) Replace each free node identifier in C_i, i.e., #$_1$, #$_2$, ..., #$_r$, with a bound node type identifier b_j for $0 < j \leq r$ such that $b_j \notin X_n$. Each set of such modified simple connectivities is denoted as C_i'.
   b) Compute $X_{n_i} = X_{n_i}' \cup \{b_1, b_2, \ldots, b_r\}$ where X_{n_i}' is a set of bound node type identifiers in X_n; i.e., $X_{n_i}' \subseteq X_n$.
   c) Generate a predicate set $P_i = \bigcup_{j=1}^r p_i(b_j)$ where $p_i(b_j) =$ METADATA:: b_j[url.`server`] EQUALS "V" and $b_j \in X_{n_i}$.
4. The set of node type identifiers of S is given by $X_{n_s} = \bigcup_{i=1}^n X_{n_i}$. Observe that the free node type identifiers are replaced by bound node type identifiers in X_{n_s}.
5. The set of link type identifiers X_{ℓ_s} of S is identical to X_ℓ. That is, $X_{\ell_s} = X_\ell$.
6. The set of connectivities C_s is given as $C_s \equiv C_{mod} \vee C_{nmod}$, where $C_{mod} \equiv C_1' \vee C_2' \vee \cdots \vee C_k'$ are sets of modified connectivities, where $0 < k \leq n$ and $C_{nmod} \equiv C_1 \vee C_2 \vee \cdots \vee C_r$ are sets of unmodified connectivities in C and $0 < r \leq n$.
7. The set of predicates P_s is given as $P_s = ((P - P_{suf}) \cup P_h) \bigcup_{i=1}^n P_i$.

Example 7.11. Consider the coupling query G_{10} in Example 6.16. Observe that this coupling query has a coupling query predicate Q_{10q} that imposes conditions on the query attribute `host` as follows. $q_1(G_{10}) \equiv$ COUPLING_QUERY:: G_{10}.`host` EQUALS "*rex.nci.nih.gov*". Notice that $X_{n_{10q}}$ contains free node type identifiers #$_1$ and #$_2$. Thus the schema (denoted as $S_{s2} = \langle X_{n_{s2}}, X_{\ell_{s2}}, C_{s2}, P_{s2} \rangle$) generated from the coupling query is based on the above case and is shown below.

1. From Step (1) of Case 2, $P_n = p_{1_1}(x)$ and $P_{suf} = \emptyset$. Hence, after Step (2), $P_h = \{p_{1_2}'\}$ where $p_{1_2}'(y) \equiv$ METADATA:: y[url.`server`] EQUALS "*rex[.]nci[.]nih [.]gov*".
2. As $C_{10q} \equiv C_a \vee C_b$, $i = 2$. After executing Step (3) twice we get $C_{10q}' \equiv C_a' \vee C_b'$, where $C_a' \equiv x\langle e\rangle a \wedge a\langle f\rangle y$ and $C_b' \equiv x\langle g\rangle b \wedge b\langle h\rangle y$, where a and b replace the free node type identifiers #$_1$ and #$_2$, respectively. Hence

$X_{n_1} = \{x, y, a\}$, $X_{n_2} = \{x, y, b\}$, $P_1 = \{p_1(a)\}$ and $P_2 = \{p_2(b)\}$, where $p_1(a) \equiv$ METADATA::a[url.server] EQUALS "rex[.]nci[.]nih[.]gov" and $p_2(b) \equiv$ METADATA::b[url.server] EQUALS "rex[.]nci[.]nih[.]gov".

3. After Steps (4) to (7), we get the components of the schema: $X_{n_{s2}} = X_{n_1} \cup X_{n_2}$ $= \{x, y, a, b\}$, $X_{\ell_{s2}} = X_{\ell_{10q}}$, $C_{s2} \equiv C_a \vee C_b$, where $C_a = C'_a$, $C_b = C'_b$, and $P_{s2} = P_{10q} \cup P_h \cup \{p_1(a), p_2(b)\}$. Notice that the schema is a complex one as the connectivities are in DNF. ∎

7.5 Phase 2: Complex Schema Decomposition

In this section we discuss the second phase of the schema generation process, that is, how to decompose a complex web schema to a set of simple web schemas. We define this phase as the *complex schema decomposition phase*. We begin by motivating this phase. Next we discuss the process of generating a set of simple web schemas from a complex web schema. Finally, we identify the limitations of this phase.

7.5.1 Motivation

It may seem that the schema generated from the canonical coupling query is good enough to be the schema of a web table W. This is of course true if the schema is simple in nature. In this case all the web tuples in W satisfy the schema and the hyperlink structure of each web tuple conforms to the set of simple connectivities in the schema. However, if a complex schema is assigned as the schema of the web table, then it may have serious implications on subsequent query evaluation and on schema generation during local web operations. Due to these implications we decompose a complex schema into a set of simple schemas. We elaborate on these two factors now.

Query Evaluation

Without a set of simple schemas, it may not always be possible to expedite subsequent query evaluation on web tables. We elaborate on this with an example given below.

Example 7.12. Consider the complex web schema S_{s1} in Example 7.8 and the set of web tuples it binds as depicted in Figure 6.11. Observe that the first, third, fifth, and sixth web tuples in Figure 6.11 satisfy the conjunctive connectivity set C_g. However, they do not conform to any other conjunctive connectivity sets. On the other hand, the second and fourth web tuples conform to C_d and the last web tuple conforms to C_f only.

Suppose a user wishes to determine those web tuples in Figure 6.11 that satisfy the connectivity and predicate: $C_q \equiv x\langle\epsilon\rangle y \wedge y\langle g\rangle y \wedge y\langle t\rangle y$ and $p_q(t) \equiv$ CONTENT::t[A] NON-ATTR_CONT ":BEGIN_WORD: - *product* + :END_WORD:". Observe that the schema in Example 7.8 does not aid in identifying the set of web tuples that are to be inspected to evaluate the above query. Hence the query processor needs to inspect all web tuples (Figure 6.11) to determine those that are relevant. One may argue that efficient query evaluation may also be possible by using an indexing mechanism on the node and link type identifiers to identify relevant web tuples for further query processing. However, this may not always be true. For instance, indexing on the node and link type identifiers will return all the web tuples in Figure 6.11 as these identifiers appear in all the tuples.

Now suppose we have *decomposed* the complex schema into the following set of simple schemas.

1. $S_a = \langle X_{n_a}, X_{\ell_a}, C_a, P_a \rangle$ where $X_{n_a} = \{x, y, \#_1, \#_2\}$, $X_{\ell_a} = \{e, g, t\}$, and $P_a = P_{s1}$.
2. $S_b = \langle X_{n_b}, X_{\ell_b}, C_b, P_b \rangle$ where $X_{n_b} = \{x, y, \#_1, \#_3\}$, $X_{\ell_b} = \{e, g, t\}$, and $P_b = P_{s1}$.
3. $S_c = \langle X_{n_c}, X_{\ell_c}, C_c, P_c \rangle$ where $X_{n_c} = \{x, y, \#_2, \#_3\}$, $X_{\ell_c} = \{e, g, t\}$, and $P_c = P_{s1}$.
4. $S_d = \langle X_{n_d}, X_{\ell_d}, C_d, P_d \rangle$ where $X_{n_d} = \{x, y, \#_3\}$, $X_{\ell_d} = \{e, g, t\}$, and $P_d = P_{s1}$.
5. $S_e = \langle X_{n_e}, X_{\ell_e}, C_e, P_e \rangle$ where $X_{n_e} = \{x, y, \#_1\}$, $X_{\ell_e} = \{e, g, t\}$, and $P_e = P_{s1}$.
6. $S_f = \langle X_{n_f}, X_{\ell_f}, C_f, P_f \rangle$ where $X_{n_f} = \{x, y, \#_2\}$, $X_{\ell_f} = \{e, g, t\}$, and $P_f = P_{s1}$.
7. $S_g = \langle X_{n_g}, X_{\ell_g}, C_g, P_g \rangle$ where $X_{n_g} = \{x, y\}$, $X_{\ell_g} = \{e, g, t\}$, and $P_g = P_{s1}$.

Observe that the web tuples that conform to C_q must satisfy the set of connectivities C_g in S_g. Hence the query can be evaluated efficiently if only the first, third, fifth, and sixth web tuples (tuples bound by S_g) are inspected in lieu of all the web tuples in Figure 6.11 (Web tuples bound by S_g are identified by a *schema pruning* operation discussed in the next section). Notice that the first, third, and the sixth web tuples satisfy the above query. ∎

Subsequent Schema Generation

If a single complex schema is assigned to a web table, then it may not always be possible to generate the schema of a resultant web table during certain local web operations. For instance, if the input web tables in a web join operation contain complex schemas, then in certain cases they may fail to generate a unique schema for the joined web tuples. However, this limitation is resolved if the input web tables contain a set of simple schemas. Specifically, a set of simple schemas simplifies the schema generation process during any web algebraic operation. It gives us the flexibility to generate a set of schemas for any web table that may result from a web operation in WHOWEDA.

7.5.2 Discussion

The complex schema decomposition process takes as input a complex web schema S and generates as output a set of simple web schemas, i.e., $S_1, S_2, \ldots, S_r$, where r is the number of conjunctive connectivity sets. Observe that if S is a simple schema, then S is not decomposed further and the process returns the original web schema S as output. Each of these simple schemas S_i binds a subset of web tuples in T having identical hyperlink structure. The identification of such web tuples is performed in the next phase (Section 7.6). Therefore, if $C_1, C_2, \ldots, C_r$ are the conjunctive connectivity sets in S, then S can be decomposed into r simple schemas $S_1, S_2, \ldots, S_r$ having connectivities $C_1, C_2, \ldots, C_r$, respectively. For instance, the complex schema in Example 7.8 can be decomposed to a set of simple schemas as shown in Example 7.12. Similarly, the complex web schema in Example 7.11 can be decomposed into the simple schemas S_x and S_y as shown below.

Example 7.13. (1) $S_x = \langle X_{n_x}, X_{\ell_x}, C_x, P_x \rangle$, where $X_{n_x} = \{x, y, a\}$, $X_{\ell_x} = \{e, f\}$, $C_x = C_a$ and $P_x = P_{s2} - \{p_{45}(h), p_{46}(g), p_{47}(g), p_2(b)\}$ and (2) $S_y = \langle X_{n_y}, X_{\ell_y}, C_y, P_y \rangle$, where $X_{n_y} = \{x, y, b\}$, $X_{\ell_y} = \{g, h\}$, $C_y = C_b$ and $P_y = P_{s2} - \{p_{43}(f), p_{44}(e), p_1(a)\}$. ∎

Definition 7.14. [**Complex Schema Decomposition**] *Let $S = \langle X_n, X_\ell, C, P \rangle$ be a complex web schema where $C \equiv C_1 \vee C_2 \vee \cdots \vee C_r$. Then $\mathcal{S} = \mathbf{decompose}(S)$ where* **decompose** *is the complex schema decomposition operation, $\mathcal{S} = \{S_1, S_2, \ldots, S_r\}$ such that $S_i = \langle X_{n_i}, X_{\ell_i}, C_i, P_i \rangle \ \forall \ 0 < i \leq r$, where $X_{n_i} \cap X_n \neq \emptyset$, $X_{\ell_i} \cap X_\ell \neq \emptyset$, and $P_i \subseteq P$.* ∎

7.5.3 Limitations

The complex schema decomposition process generates a set of simple schemas such that each schema can be used to bind a set of web tuples with identical hyperlink structure. It does not inspect the web tuples to generate the simple schemas. As a result, it does not identify the set of web tuples bound by each simple schema. Also, the structure of the simple or complex web schema depends completely on the structure and content of the coupling query. Note that this has serious implications on the "quality" of schemas generated for the web table. Due to the irregular structure of the Web and the partial or imprecise knowledge of a user, simple schemas generated from the coupling query may not be the *best* set of schemas to bind the set of web tuples. The set of simple schemas may contain noisy schemas, i.e., schemas that do not bind any web tuples. For instance, the simple schemas S_a, S_b, S_c, and S_e in Example 7.12 do not bind any web tuple in Figure 6.11. Furthermore, a web tuple may satisfy more than one simple web schema. Not all simple schemas generated from the canonical coupling query can be rigid enough to bind only a distinct set of web tuples. This is because while evaluating a coupling query, we only check if a web tuple satisfies any one of the conjunctive connectivity sets. However, some of these web tuples may satisfy more than one such conjunctive connectivity set. To elaborate further, let $C \equiv C_1 \vee C_2 \vee \cdots \vee C_r$ be the connectivities in a canonical coupling query G. Then it is possible that $t \dashv C_1 \wedge t \dashv C_2 \wedge \cdots t \dashv C_k$ for $k \leq r$. Consequently, t will be bound by the schemas $S_1, S_2, \ldots, S_k$.

Because of these reasons the complex schema decomposition process may generate a large number of simple schemas. At the worst case the number of simple schemas can be more than the total number of web tuples. This adversely affects query evaluation and formulation. In the next section, we describe the *schema pruning* phase to address these limitations.

7.6 Phase 3: Schema Pruning

In this section, we discuss the final phase of schema generation, *schema pruning*. We begin by discussing the objectives of the schema pruning process. Next we introduce some terms related to web schemas that we use to explain the schema pruning process. Then, in Section 7.6.3, we informally introduce the schema pruning operation by illustrating a few examples. Finally, Sections 7.6.4 to 7.6.6 elaborate on the schema pruning operation in detail.

7.6.1 Motivation

The set of simple schemas generated by the complex schema decomposition process certainly aids in efficient query evaluation. However, we cannot conclude that this set of simple schemas represents the best possible set of schemas for the web table. This is because of the shortcomings of the schema decomposition process as discussed in Section 7.5.3. The *schema pruning* operation enables us to resolve these shortcomings and takes us one step closer to the generation of the best set of simple schemas for the web table. Consequently, the schema pruning process serves several important purposes. First, it identifies the set of web tuples bound by each simple schema. Recall that the schema decomposition process only generates a set of simple schemas. It does not relate each of these schemas to the corresponding set of web tuples. Second, it eliminates noisy schemas. Next, it ensures that the number of web schemas binding the web tuples does not exceed the total number of web tuples in the web table. Lastly, it ensures that each web tuple is bound by only one simple web schema.

Note that the phenomenon of pruning schemas does not arise in relational databases. This is because relational design is guided by the presence or absence of functional dependencies. Hence the generation of relational schemas is performed ahead of data and data instances strictly adhere to the data. Furthermore, each relational table has one schema and is adhered to by all the tuples in that table. There is no need to bind the tuples in a relation with more than one relational schema. Also there is no necessity for the relational schema to be pruned as all data instances strictly conform to the data. However, such luxury is not applicable for Web data by their very nature lack the consistency, stability and structure implied by these assumptions. Moreover, the web schema is not guided by the analogous notion of functional dependencies, but is generated from the user's query. It may not always be possible to define a rigid relationallike schema from Web data. The noise introduced by human perception of the content and the structure of relevant Web data needs to be minimized in the web schema. Hence, it is important to prune the set of simple web schemas generated from the complex schema decomposition process.

7.6.2 Classifications of Simple Schemas

We now introduce the notion of *identical*, *equivalent*, *inclusive*, and *intersecting* web schemas that we use in the later portion of the book.

Let $S_1 = \langle X_{n_1}, X_{\ell_1}, C_1, P_1 \rangle$ and $S_2 = \langle X_{n_2}, X_{\ell_2}, C_2, P_2 \rangle$ be two simple schemas. Let T_1 and T_2 be the set of web tuples bound by these schemas, respectively. Then

- S_1 and S_2 are *identical*, denoted as $S_1 = S_2$, if $P_1 = P_2$ and $C_1 = C_2$;
- S_1 and S_2 are *equivalent*, denoted as $S_1 \equiv S_2$, if $T_1 = T_2$ and $S_1 \neq S_2$;
- S_1 is *inclusive* to S_2, denoted by $S_1 \subset S_2$, if $T_1 \subset T_2$;
- S_1 is *intersecting* to S_2, denoted by $S_1 \cap S_2$, if $T_1 \cap T_2 \neq \emptyset$ and S_1 and S_2 are not inclusive.

We now illustrate these types of schemas with some examples.

Example 7.15. Consider the disease database Web page at `www.pedianet.com/news/illness/disease/disease.htm`. The purpose of this database is to provide information on various pediatric disorders. This page contains a list of diseases that are linked to another Web page containing detailed information about the respective diseases (Figure 2.5). Suppose we wish to find information about those diseases related to bacterial infection in the colon that result in "diarrhea" or some sort of body or abdominal "pain." Hence, the links in the Web page at `www.pedianet.com/new/illness/disease/disease.htm` may contain the keyword "colitis". These links may connect to pages that may contain the keywords "diarrhea" or "pain". Figure 7.1 depicts the set of web tuples satisfying this query. The set of simple web schemas for these web tuples is shown below.

- $S_1 = \langle X_{n1}, X_{\ell 1}, C_1, P_1 \rangle$, where $X_{n1} = \{x, y\}$, $X_{\ell 1} = \{e\}$, $C_1 \equiv x\langle e \rangle y$, and $P_1 = \{p_{11}, p_{12}, p_{13}\}$, where

$p_{11}(x) \equiv$ METADATA::x[url] EQUALS
          "*www[.]pedianet[.]com/news/illness/disease/disease[.]htm*"
$p_{12}(e) \equiv$ CONTENT::g[A] NON-ATTR_CONT
          "*:BEGIN_WORD: + colitis + :END_WORD:* "
$p_{13}(y) \equiv$ CONTENT::y[html(.%)+] NON-ATTR_CONT
          "*:BEGIN_WORD: + diarrhea + :END_WORD:* "

- $S_2 = \langle X_{n2}, X_{\ell 2}, C_2, P_2 \rangle$ where $X_{n2} = \{x, z\}$, $X_{\ell 2} = \{e\}$, $C_2 \equiv x\langle e \rangle z$, and $P_2 = \{p_{11}, p_{12}, p_{21}\}$, where

$$p_{21}(z) \equiv \text{CONTENT::z[html(.\%)-] NON-ATTR\_CONT}$$
$$\text{"}\textit{:BEGIN\_WORD: + pain + :END\_WORD:}\text{ "}$$

Note that symptoms of all diseases related to bacterial infection in the colon include both pain and diarrhea. Hence all the web tuples in Figure 7.1 are bound by both S_1 and S_2; i.e., S_1 and S_2 are equivalent.∎

Example 7.16. Reconsider the Web site in Example 7.15. Suppose we wish to find information about all "chronic" or "persistent" diseases. Figure 7.2(a) depicts the set of web tuples satisfying this query. The set of simple web schemas for these web tuples is shown below.

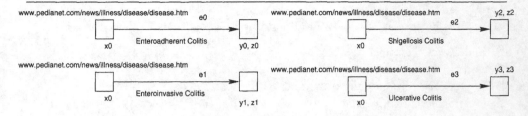

Fig. 7.1. Examples of equivalent schemas.

- $S_1 = \langle X_{n1}, X_{\ell 1}, C_1, P_1 \rangle$, where $X_{n1} = \{x, \#_1\}$, $X_{\ell 1} = \{e\}$, $C_1 \equiv x\langle e \rangle \#_1$, and $P_1 = \{p_{11}, p_{12}\}$, where

  $p_{11}(x) \equiv$ METADATA::x[url] EQUALS
      "*www[.]pedianet[.]com/news/illness/disease/disease[.]htm*"
  $p_{12}(e) \equiv$ CONTENT::e[A] NON-ATTR_CONT
      ":BEGIN_WORD: + *persistent* + :END_WORD:"

- $S_2 = \langle X_{n2}, X_{\ell 2}, C_2, P_2 \rangle$, where $X_{n2} = \{x, \#_2\}$, $X_{\ell 2} = \{f\}$, $C_2 \equiv x\langle f \rangle \#_2$, and $P_2 = \{p_{11}, p_{22}\}$, where

  $p_{22}(f) \equiv$ CONTENT::f[A] NON-ATTR_CONT
      ":BEGIN_STR: + *chronic* + :END_STR:"

Observe that S_1 binds the last web tuple in Figure 7.2(a) and S_2 binds all the web tuples. Therefore, S_1 and S_2 are inclusive. ∎

Example 7.17. Suppose we wish to find information about diseases related to bacterial infection in the colon. Hence the links may contain the strings "entero" or "colitis". Figure 7.2(b) depicts the set of web tuples satisfying this query. The set of simple web schemas for these web tuples is shown below.

- $S_1 = \langle X_{n1}, X_{\ell 1}, C_1, P_1 \rangle$, where $X_{n1} = \{x, \#_1\}$, $X_{\ell 1} = \{g\}$, $C_1 \equiv x\langle g \rangle \#_1$, and $P_1 = \{p_{11}, p_{12}\}$, where

  $p_{12}(g) \equiv$ CONTENT::g[A] NON-ATTR_CONT
      ":BEGIN_WORD: + MATCH(entero.*) + :END_WORD: "

- $S_2 = \langle X_{n2}, X_{\ell 2}, C_2, P_2 \rangle$, where $X_{n2} = \{x, \#_2\}$, $X_{\ell 2} = \{h\}$, $C_2 \equiv x\langle h \rangle \#_2$, and $P_2 = \{p_{11}, p_{22}\}$, where

  $p_{22}(h) \equiv$ CONTENT::h[A] NON-ATTR_CONT
      ":BEGIN_WORD: + *colitis* + :END_WORD: "

Observe that S_1 binds the first three web tuples in Figure 7.2(b) and S_2 binds the first two and last two web tuples. As the first two web tuples are bound by both the schemas, S_1 and S_2 are intersecting. ∎

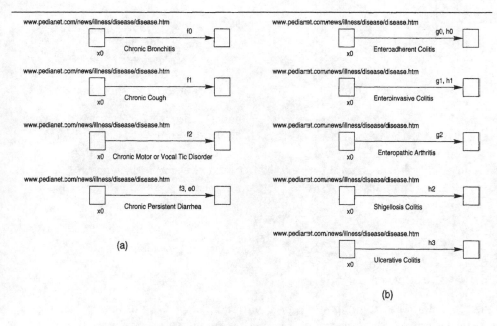

Fig. 7.2. Examples of Cases 2 and 3.

7.6.3 Schema Pruning Process

The set of simple schemas S and web tuples T are provided as input to the schema pruning process and the output is a set of *nonoverlapping* partitions U. These partitions represent the resultant web table. This process can be best discussed by the following phases.

1. *Preprocessing Phase:* In this phase, we eliminate some of the noisy simple schemas in S without matching the schemas with the web tuples.
2. *Matching Phase:* In this phase, we generate a set of partitions containing non-noisy simple web schemas by eliminating the remaining noisy schemas from S by comparing them with the web tuples.
3. *Nonoverlapping Partitioning Phase:* Finally, in this phase, we transform the *overlapping* partitions into a set of *nonoverlapping* partitions. In this phase, equivalent, inclusive, or intersecting schemas are converted to a set of distinct web schemas binding a distinct set of web tuples.

We now illustrate these phases informally with some examples. In Sections 7.6.4 to 7.6.6 we elaborate on these phases.

Example 7.18. Consider the set of simple schemas in Example 7.13. Notice that the schema S_x binds the first three web tuples in Figure 6.3. The simple schema S_y binds the last three web tuples. Hence, after performing the schema pruning operation, we have the following set of partitions $U = \{U_x, U_y\}$, where

1. $U_x = \langle S_x, T_x \rangle$, where $T_x = \{t_1, t_2, t_3\}$;
2. $U_y = \langle S_y, T_y \rangle$, where $T_y = \{t_4, t_5, t_6\}$.

Observe that in this example there do not exist any noisy schemas as both of the simple schemas bind a set of web tuples. Hence the set of simple schemas of the web table (consisting of web tuples $t_1, t_2, \ldots, t_6$) are S_x and S_y. That is, $W = \langle N, \mathcal{U} \rangle$ where $\mathcal{U} = \{U_x, U_y\}$. Furthermore, as S_x and S_y are not equivalent, inclusive, or intersecting, the non-overlapping partitioning phase is ignored in this case.   ∎

Example 7.19. Consider the set of simple schemas in Example 7.12. Notice that the schema S_d binds the second and fourth web tuples in Figure 6.11. On the other hand, the simple schemas S_f and S_g bind the last web tuple, and the first, third, fifth, and sixth web tuples, respectively. Notice that the simple schemas S_a, S_b, S_c, and S_e do not bind any web tuples. These simple schemas are noisy schemas. The schema pruning process first eliminates these noisy simple schemas. That is, $W = \langle N, \mathcal{U} \rangle$, where $P = \{U_d, U_f, U_g\}$, where

1. $U_d = \langle S_d, T_d \rangle$, where $T_d = \{t_2, t_4\}$;
2. $U_f = \langle S_f, T_f \rangle$, where $T_f = \{t_7\}$;
3. $U_g = \langle S_g, T_g \rangle$, where $T_g = \{t_1, t_3, t_5, t_6\}$.   ∎

Next we illustrate the nonoverlapping partitioning phase. Observe that in the above two examples there is no need to perform non-overlapping partitioning as the set of web schemas binds distinct sets of web tuples.

Example 7.20. Consider the equivalent schemas S_1 and S_2 in Example 7.15. The partitions $U_1' = \langle S_1, T_1 \rangle$ and $U_2' = \langle S_2, T_2 \rangle$, where $T_1 = T_2 = \{t_1, t_2, t_3, t_4\}$ are *overlapping*. After the nonoverlapping partitioning operation the overlapping partitions are reduced to the nonoverlapping partition: $U_1 = \langle S_{eq}, T_1 \rangle$, where $S_{eq} = \langle X_{n_{eq}}, X_{\ell_{eq}}, C_{eq}, P_{eq} \rangle$, $X_{n_{eq}} = \{x, w\}$, $X_{\ell_{eq}} = X_{\ell 1}$, $C_{eq} \equiv x\langle e \rangle w$, and $P_{eq} = P_1 \cup \{p_{11}, p_{12}, p_{21}', p_{13}'\}$, where

$$p_{21}'(w) \equiv \texttt{CONTENT::w[html(.\%)+] NON-ATTR\_CONT}$$
$$\texttt{":BEGIN\_WORD: + } \textit{pain} \texttt{ + :END\_WORD: "}$$
$$p_{13}'(w) \equiv \texttt{CONTENT::w[html(.\%)+] NON-ATTR\_CONT}$$
$$\texttt{":BEGIN\_WORD: + } \textit{diarrhea} \texttt{ + :END\_WORD: "}$$ ∎

7.6.4 Phase 1: Preprocessing Phase

In the preprocessing phase, we look for noisy simple schemas without comparing the simple schemas and the web tuples. To achieve this we perform the following steps to identify and filter out some of the noisy simple schemas from S. (1) Identify the set of bound node and link type identifiers in S that do not have any instance in T. (2) Identify the schemas whose *connectivity size* does not match with any *fragment size* of the tuples in T. Informally, the *connectivity size* of a simple schema S is the total number of connectivities in S. That is, if $S = \langle X_n, X_\ell, C, P \rangle$, where $C \equiv k_1 \wedge k_2 \wedge k_3 \wedge \cdots \wedge k_r$, then the connectivity size of S is r. On the other hand, the *fragment size* of a web tuple t represents the total number of distinct *tuple fragments* in t. By *tuple fragment* we mean a path in t containing only two nodes and a single link between them. For instance, the fragment size of the first tuple in Figure 6.11 is three and the tuple fragments are $x_0 \langle e_2 \rangle y_1$, $y_1 \langle g_1 \rangle y_2$, and $y_2 \langle -_1 \rangle y_3$.

At the end of the preprocessing phase, we get a modified set of simple schemas by eliminating some of the noisy simple schemas from S. We now justify the reasons for performing these two steps in the preprocessing phase. Recall that the bound node and link objects in a tuple set must be instances of the set of bound node and link type identifiers in S, respectively. A schema containing a bound identifier x is noisy if T does not contain any instance of x.

Observation 7.1 *Let x be a bound node or link type identifier in a simple web schema $S_i \in S$. Let T be a set of web tuples. Then S_i is a noisy schema if there does not exist any instance of x in T.* ∎

Now consider the second step. The connectivity size of each simple schema must be identical to the fragment size of the tuple $t \in T$ that satisfies this schema. We exploit this fact to identify some of the noisy schemas in S. S_i is noisy if T does not contain any web tuple with fragment size L_i.

Observation 7.2 *Let L_i be the connectivity size of a simple web schema $S_i \in S$. Then S_i is a noisy schema if there does not exist a web tuple $t \in T$ such that the fragment size of t is L_i.* ∎

Based on this criterion, we sort the web tuples in T based on their fragment size. Let L_s be the set of connectivity sizes of the simple schemas in S. Let L_t be the set of fragment sizes of the web tuples in T. Then $L_n = L_s - L_t$ represents the set of connectivity sizes of the noisy simple schemas. Therefore, for each $\ell \in L_n$ we eliminate the corresponding noisy simple schemas from S.

7.6.5 Phase 2: Matching Phase

In the matching phase we generate the partitions containing nonnoisy simple schemas. We know that at the end of the preprocessing phase, some of the noisy simple schemas may be removed from S. In the matching phase, we eliminate the remaining noisy simple schemas by comparing web tuples and simple schemas. However, given a simple schema $S_i \in S$, we do not match S_i with any arbitrary web tuple, but only with tuples t_j whose fragment sizes are identical to the connectivity size of S_i. This is because if S_i and t_j have different sizes, then t_j will never conform to S_i. Finally, we eliminate those simple schemas in S that do not match with any web tuple. The result is a set of nonnoisy simple schemas. For each of these simple schemas we generate the corresponding partition. The partition is then appended in $\mathcal{U}$.

7.6.6 Phase 3: Nonoverlapping Partitioning Phase

Due to the nature of web schema, a web tuple may be bound by more than one simple schema. Let $U_1 = \langle S_1, T_1 \rangle$ and $U_2 = \langle S_2, T_2 \rangle$ be two partitions in $\mathcal{U}$. Then it may be possible that $T_1 \cap T_2 \neq \emptyset$. That is, some of the web tuples in T_1 or T_2 satisfy the schemas S_1 and S_2. We call such partitions *overlapping*. In nonoverlapping partitioning phases we modify the overlapping partitions, i.e., U_1 and U_2, to generate a set of *nonoverlapping* partitions $U' = \{U'_1, U'_2, \cdots, U'_n\}$ such that $T_k \cap T_r = \emptyset$ for all $0 < (k, r) \leq n$ and $k \neq r$.

There can be three possible cases for overlapping partitions as shown below.

- **Case 1:** The set of web tuples in T_1 and T_2 are identical, i.e., $T_1 = T_2$, but the schemas are not identical. That is, $S_1 \equiv S_2$.
- **Case 2:** T_1 is contained in T_2; i.e., $T_1 \subset T_2$. That is, $S_1 \subset S_2$.
- **Case 3:** Some of the web tuples in T_1 but not all are contained in T_2. That is, S_1 and S_2 are intersecting web schemas.

Next for each of the above cases, we show how to generate a set of nonoverlapping partitions.

Case 1: In this case all the web tuples in S_1 must satisfy S_2 and vice versa. This indicates that the hyperlink structure of the web tuples T_1 specified by C_1 is identical to those of T_2 specified by C_2. Similarly, the set of predicates P_1 satisfied by T_1 must be satisfied by T_2 and vice versa. Moreover, the number of node and link type identifiers in S_1 and S_2 must be identical. Hence we can conclude that the partitions $U_1 = \langle S_1, T_1 \rangle$ and $U_2 = \langle S_2, T_2 \rangle$ can be replaced by the partition $U_{eq} = \langle S_{eq}, T_{eq} \rangle$, where S_{eq} is generated by *combining* S_1 and S_2 and $T_{eq} = T_1 = T_2$. Observe that in this case, the two partitions are reduced to a single partition. We now outline the steps for generating the resultant simple web schema.

- From T we first generate two sets A and B. Each element in A is a pair $\langle n_1, n_2 \rangle$, whereof n_1 is a node type identifier in S_1 and n_2 is the corresponding identifier in S_2 as determined from the web tuples. Similarly, B represents a set of pairs of link type identifiers. Note that n_1 and n_2 may be identical. For instance, for the web tuples in Example 7.20 (Figure 7.1) $A = \{(x, x), (y, z)\}$. Instances of x in S_1 are represented by the same nominal identifier in S_2 and instances of y in S_1 are represented by the identifier z in S_2. For Example 7.20, $B = \{(e, e)\}$.
- Next, from A we identify those pairs in which the nominal identifiers are not identical. Let (a, b) be such pair. Also, let a be an identifier in S_1, b be the identifier of S_2, and $a \neq b$. Note that there can be three cases: both identifiers are bound, one identifier is free, and both identifiers are free. We ignore the third case as it does not affect the resultant schema in any way. For the first case these steps are followed.
  1. Retrieve all the predicates in P_1 and P_2 whose arguments are a and b, respectively, and modify the arguments to a new identifier $d \notin (X_n \cup X_\ell)$ and store the predicates in a set P'. For instance, in Example 7.20, (y, z) is such a pair in U. Hence we modify the argument of predicates on y and z ($p_{13}(y)$, $p_{21}(z)$) to w ($p'_{13}(w)$, $p'_{21}(w)$) and store it in P'.
  2. Remove predicates on a from P_1.
  3. Eliminate a from X_{n1} and insert d in X'_n.
  4. Identify the connectivities in C_1 whose source or target node type identifier is a and replace a with d and insert in the set C'. Mark these connectivities in C_1. For instance, $x\langle e \rangle y$ in Example 7.20 is modified to $x\langle e \rangle w$.

For the second case, we ignore the case when the identifier in S_2, b, is free. If the identifier in S_1, a, is free, these steps are followed.

  1. Eliminate a from X_{n1} and insert the identifier of S_2, b, in X'_n.

2. Identify the connectivities in C_1 whose source or target node type identifier is a and replace a with b and insert it in the set C'. Mark these connectivities in C_1.

3. Identify the predicates in P_2 whose argument is b and insert them in the set P'.

- Similarly we generate the sets X'_ℓ, C', and P' for the set of pairs of link type identifiers in B. We remove all the marked connectivities from C_1.

- Finally, we generate the components of the resultant web schema as follows. $X_{n_{eq}} = X_{n1} \cup X'_n$, $X_{\ell_{eq}} = X_{\ell 1} \cup X'_\ell$, $C_{eq} \equiv C_1 \wedge C'$, and $P_{eq} = P_1 \cup P'$.

Case 2: If $S_1 \subset S_2$, then some of the web tuples in T_2 also satisfy the schema S_1. That is, the web tuples T_2 can be subdivided into two distinct sets of web tuples, $(T_2 - T_1)$ and T_1. The $(T_2 - T_1)$ web tuples satisfy only the schema S_2 and web tuples T_1 satisfy both S_1 and S_2. Hence the partitions U_1 and U_2 can be first reduced to the partitions: $U'_1 = \langle S_1, T_1 \rangle$, $U'_2 = \langle S_2, T_1 \rangle$, and $U'_3 = \langle S_2, T_2 - T_1 \rangle$. Observe that in U'_1 and U'_2 the schemas belong to Case 1. Hence, U'_1 and U'_2 can be combined to a single partition as described in Case 1. Therefore the partitions U_1 and U_2 can be replaced by two nonoverlapping partitions U_{r1} and U_{r2}, where $U_{r1} = \langle S_{eq}, T_1 \rangle$ and $U_{r2} = U'_3$. We illustrate this with an example.

Example 7.21. Consider Example 7.16. Observe that S_1 binds the last web tuple in Figure 7.2(a) and S_2 binds all the web tuples. Therefore S_1 and S_2 are inclusive and the partitions $U'_1 = \langle S_1, T_1 \rangle$ and $U'_2 = \langle S_2, T_2 \rangle$, where $T_1 = \{t_1, t_2, t_3, t_4\}$ and $T_2 = \{t_4\}$ are overlapping. After the nonoverlapping partitioning operation the overlapping partitions will be reduced to the following nonoverlapping partitions.

1. $U_1 = \langle S_{eq}, T_1 \rangle$, where $T_1 = \{t_4\}$ and $S_{eq} = \langle X_{n_{eq}}, X_{\ell_{eq}}, C_{eq}, P_{eq} \rangle$, $X_{n_{eq}} = X_{n1}$, $X_{\ell_{eq}} = \{s\}$, $C_{eq} \equiv x\langle s \rangle \#_1$, and $P_{eq} = (P_1 - p_{12}) \cup \{p'_{12}, p'_{22}\}$, where

$$p'_{22}(s) \equiv \texttt{CONTENT::s[A] NON-ATTR\_CONT}$$
$$\texttt{":BEGIN\_STR: + } chronic \texttt{ + :END\_STR:"}$$
$$p'_{12}(s) \equiv \texttt{CONTENT::s[A] NON-ATTR\_CONT}$$
$$\texttt{":BEGIN\_WORD: + } persistent \texttt{ + :END\_WORD:"}$$

2. $U_2 = \langle S_2, T_2 \rangle$, where $T_2 = \{t_1, t_2, t_3\}$.

Note that S_{eq} is generated from S_1 and S_2. ∎

Case 3: Finally, consider the third case. Some of the web tuples in T_1 and T_2 are identical. Therefore the web tuples T_1 and T_2 can be subdivided into three distinct sets of web tuples: $T_1 \cap T_2$, $(T_1 - (T_1 \cap T_2))$, and $(T_2 - (T_1 \cap T_2))$. Observe that the web tuples $(T_1 \cap T_2)$ satisfy both S_1 and S_2. Web tuples $[T_1 - (T_1 \cap T_2)]$ satisfy only S_1, and $[T_2 - (T_1 \cap T_2)]$ satisfies only S_2. Hence the partitions U_1 and U_2 can be replaced by the following partitions: $U'_1 = \langle S_1, T_1 \cap T_2 \rangle$, $U'_2 = \langle S_2, T_1 \cap T_2 \rangle$, $U'_3 = \langle S_1, T_1 - (T_1 \cap T_2) \rangle$, and $U'_4 = \langle S_2, T_2 - (T_1 \cap T_2) \rangle$.

Observe that in U'_1 and U'_2 the schemas S_1 and S_2 are of Case 1, as the web tuples $T_1 \cap T_2$ satisfy both schemas. Hence U'_1 and U'_2 can be combined to a single partition $U_{r1} = \langle S_{eq}, T_1 \cap T_2 \rangle$. Therefore, for Case 3, the partitions U_1 and U_2 are transformed to the three nonoverlapping partitions: $U_{r1} = \langle S_{eq}, T_1 \cap T_2 \rangle$, $U_{r2} =$

$\langle S_1, T_1 - (T_1 \cap T_2) \rangle$, and $U_{r3} = \langle S_2, T_2 - (T_1 \cap T_2) \rangle$. We illustrate this case with an example given below.

Example 7.22. Consider the schemas in Example 7.17. The overlapping partitions are reduced to the following three nonoverlapping partitions.

1. $U_1 = \langle S_{eq}, T_1 \cap T_2 \rangle$ where $S_{eq} = \langle X_{n_{eq}}, X_{\ell_{eq}}, C_{eq}, P_{eq} \rangle$, $X_{n_{eq}} = X_{n1}$, $X_{\ell_{eq}} = \{s\}$, $C_{eq} \equiv x\langle s \rangle \#_1$, and $P_{eq} = (P_1 - p_{12}) \cup \{p'_{22}, p'_{12}\}$, where

$$p'_{22}(s) \equiv \texttt{CONTENT::s[A] NON-ATTR\_CONT}$$
$$\texttt{":BEGIN\_WORD: + colitis + :END\_WORD: "}$$
$$p_{12}(s) \equiv \texttt{CONTENT::s[A] NON-ATTR\_CONT}$$
$$\texttt{":BEGIN\_WORD: + MATCH(entero.*) + :END\_WORD: "}$$

2. $U_2 = \langle S_1, T'_1 \rangle$, where $T'_1 = \{t_1, t_2, t_3\} - \{t_1, t_2\} = \{t_3\}$.
3. $U_3 = \langle S_2, T'_2 \rangle$, where $T'_2 = \{t_1, t_2, t_4, t_5\} - \{t_1, t_2\} = \{t_4, t_5\}$.

Note that S_{eq} is generated from S_1 and S_2. ∎

After the nonoverlapping partitioning phase we get a set of simple schemas S where each schema binds a distinct set of web tuples. That is, for any two partitions $U_1 = \langle S_1, T_1 \rangle$ and $U_2 = \langle S_2, T_2 \rangle$, $T_1 \cap T_2 = \emptyset$. This implies that if there are n web tuples in the web table, i.e., $|T_1 \cup T_2 \cup \cdots \cup T_n| = n$, then there can be at most n schemas. Recall that after the complex schema decomposition phase, the number of schemas generated may be greater than the number of web tuples in the web table. The schema pruning operation enables us to reduce the number of simple schemas.

Definition 7.23. [**Schema Pruning**] *Let $S = \{S_1, S_2, S_3, \ldots, S_r\}$ be a set of simple web schemas and T be a set of web tuples bound by these web schemas. Then $\mathcal{U} = \text{prune}(S, T)$, where prune defines the schema pruning operation, $\mathcal{U} = \{U_1, U_2, \ldots, U_k\}$, $U_i = \langle S_i, T_i \rangle \, \forall \, 0 < i \leq k$, $k \leq r$, $T_i \subseteq T$, $T_1 \cup T_2 \cup \cdots \cup T_k = T$, $T_i \neq \emptyset$, and $T_i \cap T_j = \emptyset \, \forall \, 0 < (i, j) \leq k$, and $i \neq j$.* ∎

7.7 Algorithm Schema Generator

We now provide the algorithm for generating a set of simple web schemas to bind the web tuples generated by the global web coupling operation. We focus on high-level procedures of the algorithm, deferring detailed discussion to the later portion of the section that presents our techniques in detail. Figure 7.3 provides the pseudo-code for the algorithm. It takes as input a canonical coupling query G, the name of the web table N, and a set of web tuples retrieved from the Web (denoted as *tupleSet* in the algorithm) and generates a web table containing *tupleSet* and a set of simple web schemas. The construct **GenerateSchemaFromQuery** transforms the canonical coupling query to a complex or simple web schema. Note that this step is performed without inspecting the web tuples. Next, if the generated schema is a complex type then Step (7) is executed and the schema is converted into a set of simple schemas each of which binds a distinct set of web tuples. In this step the schema decomposition and pruning is performed. This procedure is encapsulated

---

Input: Canonical coupling query G, Name N, Set of web tuples *tupleSet.*
Output: Web table $W = \langle N, \mathcal{U} \rangle$.

(1) $S = \textbf{GenerateSchemaFromQuery}(G)$ /* Figure 7.4 */;
(2)   if $(S = \langle X_n, X_\ell, C, P \rangle$ is simple) {
(3) $U = \langle tupleSet, S \rangle$;
(4)   Append U in $\mathcal{U}$;
(5)   }
(6)   else {
(7) $\mathcal{U} = \textbf{Partition}(S, tupleSet)$; /* Figure 7.5 */
(8)   }
(9)   Return $W = \langle N, \mathcal{U} \rangle$;

Fig. 7.3. Pseudocode for the algorithm Schema Generator.

in the construct **Partition** and is discussed later If the schema generated from Step (1) is simple then Steps (2) to (5) are executed. The schema and the tuple set are directly inserted in the partition set $\mathcal{U}$. Note that in this case the schema is not decomposed and pruned. Finally, the output of **Schema Generator**, is a set of non-overlapping partitions $\mathcal{U}$, and the name of the table N which is returned in the form of web table W.

7.7.1 Pruning Ratio

Before describing the details of the algorithm of schema generation, we introduce the notion of *pruning ratio* which we use in our subsequent discussion. Each simple web schema generated during the schema decomposition process binds a set of web tuples (possible empty) in the web table. The *pruning ratio* computes the number of web tuples bound by a simple schema compared to the total number of web tuples in the web table. Formally, let T be the set of web tuples in the web table. Let $T_i \subseteq T$ be the set of web tuples bound by the simple web schema S_i. Then the pruning ratio, denoted by $\mathcal{R}$, is defined as: $\mathcal{R} = |T_i|/|T|$. For example, consider the schema S_x in Example 7.13. It binds three web tuples out of six web tuples. Hence $\mathcal{R}_x = 3/6 = 0.5$. Similarly, the pruning ratio of S_d in Example 7.12 is $\mathcal{R}_d = 2/7 = 0.28$. Observe that for a noisy simple schema, the pruning ratio is equal to zero as it does not bind any web tuples. On the other hand, if a web table is bound by only one schema then the pruning ratio is equal to 1. Hence the value of the pruning ratio of a web schema varies between 0 to 1.

Let us now explore the implications of the pruning ratio. Let a complex schema binding a set of web tuples T be reduced to a set of simple web schemas S_1, S_2, S_3, ..., S_r by the schema decomposition process. Let $\mathcal{R}_1$, $\mathcal{R}_2$, ..., $\mathcal{R}_r$ be the pruning ratios of these web schemas. Then,

$$\mathcal{R}_1 + \mathcal{R}_2 + \cdots + \mathcal{R}_r = \frac{|T_1|}{|T|} + \frac{|T_2|}{|T|} + \cdots + \frac{|T_r|}{|T|}$$

$$= \frac{|T_1| + |T_2| + \cdots + |T_r|}{|T|} \tag{7.1}$$

Observe that the numerator in the above equation is equal to $|T|$ only if the web tuples T_1, T_2, ... , T_r do not overlap. That is, $T_i \cap T_j = \emptyset$ for all $0 < i, j \leq r$. For instance, consider the simple web schemas in Example 7.12. The pruning ratios of these schemas are as follows: $\mathcal{R}_a = 0$, $\mathcal{R}_b = 0$, $\mathcal{R}_c = 0$, $\mathcal{R}_d = 0.28$, $\mathcal{R}_e = 0$, $\mathcal{R}_f = 1/7 = 0.14$, and $\mathcal{R}_g = 4/7 = 0.58$. Since none of the web tuples bound by the schemas S_d, S_f, and S_g overlaps, $\mathcal{R}_a + \mathcal{R}_b + \cdots + \mathcal{R}_g = 1$. Hence, when a set of simple web schemas binds a nonoverlapping set of web tuples, then summation of their pruning ratio is always equal to 1.

Now consider the case when one or more web tuples bound by these web schemas overlaps. That is, a web tuple $t \in T$ may be bound by one or more web schemas. In that case, $|T_1| + |T_2| + \cdots + |T_r| > |T|$. Hence, from the above equation, the sum of the values of the pruning ratios is always greater than 1; i.e., $\mathcal{R}_1 + \mathcal{R}_2 + \cdots + \mathcal{R}_r > 1$. As we show later the set of web schemas needs to be pruned further when $\sum_{i=1}^{r} \mathcal{R}_i > 1$ such that the set of web schemas generated binds distinct sets of web tuples, i.e., $\sum_{i=1}^{r} \mathcal{R}_i = 1$. Also observe that if $\sum_{i=1}^{r} \mathcal{R}_i > 1$, then there must exist a pair of simple web schemas, S_1 and S_2, such that S_1 and S_2 are equivalent, inclusive, or intersecting.

Now let us explore the implications of the number of simple web schemas on the pruning ratio. Observe that the schema decomposition operation can generate n simple web schemas where $n > 1$. Now consider the case when $n > |T|$. That is, the number of simple web schemas generated by the schema decomposition process is greater than the total number of web tuples in the web table. In this case one of the following must be true. (1) Some of the simple web schemas are noisy web schemas as they do not bind any web tuples. (2) A web tuple may be bound by more than one simple web schemas.

However, when $n \leq |T|$, then the above conditions may not necessarily be true. Observe that the preprocessing and matching phases eliminate noisy simple schemas. Hence, after these two phases the pruning ratio of all the simple schemas is nonzero. Next, if the sum of the pruning ratio of the set of nonnoisy simple schemas is greater than one then there must exist at least a pair of schemas that are inclusive, equivalent, or intersecting. That is, there exist overlapping partitions. Next, if the sum of the pruning ratios of the simple schemas resulted from the matching phase is greater than one then the nonoverlapping partitioning phase modifies the equivalent, inclusive, or intersecting schemas to web schemas binding distinct sets of web tuples. At the end of the nonoverlapping partitioning phase, the sum of pruning ratios of the simple web schemas is equal to 1.

7.7.2 Algorithm of GenerateSchemaFromQuery

We now present the algorithm for transforming a canonical coupling query to a web schema. The pseudocode for the algorithm is shown in Figure 7.4. It takes as input a coupling query $G = \langle X_n, X_\ell, C, P, Q \rangle$ and returns as output a web schema $S = \langle X_{n_s}, X_{\ell_s}, C_s, P_s \rangle$.

Input: Coupling query $G = \langle X_n, X_\ell, C, P, Q \rangle$.

Output: Web schema $S = \langle X_{n_s}, X_{\ell_s}, C_s, P_s \rangle$.

(1)   Generate a set of schema-independent predicates Q_1 from Q ;

(2)   Generate a set of schema-influencing predicates Q_2 from Q;

(3)   if $(|Q_2| = \emptyset)$ {

(4) $X_{n_s} = X_n$;

(5) $X_{\ell_s} = X_\ell$;

(6) $C_s = C$;

(7) $P_s = P$;

(8)   }

(9)   else {

(10)   Compute $C \equiv C_1 \vee C_2 \vee \ldots \vee C_n$;

(11)   for $(i = 1 \ to \ |Q_2|)$ {

(12)   if $(\mathbf{attr}(Q_2[i]) = \mathbf{host})$ {

(13)   Generate P_n and P_{suf};

(14)   Generate P_h such that $P_h \cap P_n = \emptyset$;

(15)   for $(j = 1 \ to \ r)$ {

(16)   if (free node identifier exist in C_j) {

(17) $N_j = \mathbf{GenerateIdentifiers}(C_j, X_n)$;

(18) $C'_j = \mathbf{ReplaceConn}(C_j, N_j)$;

(19) $P_j = \mathbf{GeneratePredicates}(N_j)$;

(20)   Insert P_j in P'_s;

(21)   Insert N_j in X'_{n_s};

(22)   }

(23)   else

(24) $C'_j = C_j$;

(25) $C_s = \vee^n_{j=1} C'_j$;

(26)   }

(27)   }

(28)   }

(29) $X_{n_s} = X'_{n_s} \cup X_n$;

(30) $X_{\ell_s} = X_\ell$;

(31) $P_s = (P - P_{suf}) \cup P_h \cup P'_s$;

(32) }

(33) Return $S = \langle X_{n_s}, X_{\ell_s}, C_s, P_s \rangle$;

Fig. 7.4. Pseudocode of GenerateSchemaFromQuery.

The algorithm first categorizes the coupling query predicates into schema-independent and schema-influencing predicates (denoted by Q_1 and Q_2, respectively, in the algorithm) as shown in Steps (1) and (2). If there do not exist any schema-influencing predicates then the components X_n, X_ℓ, C, and P of G are assigned as the corresponding components of the schema S (Steps (3) to (8)). Otherwise, for each schema-influencing predicate (denoted by $Q_2[i]$) Steps (9) to (35) are executed. The connectivity C is reduced to a set of simple connectivities in DNF (Step 10).

Next, if the query attribute of the predicate is host then the Steps (12) to (27) are executed first. If a set of simple connectivities (C_j) contains free node type identifiers then the Steps (17) to (21) are executed. Transformation of free node type identifiers to bound node identifiers (denoted by the symbol X'_{n_s} in the algorithm) and modification of the connectivities (as described in Section 7.4) are performed in these steps. Specifically, the construct **GenerateIdentifiers** transforms the free node type identifiers in C_j to bound identifiers. The construct **ReplaceConn** then converts the connectivity set C_j to a set of simple connectivities containing bound node type identifiers by replacing the free node type identifiers with the nominal identifiers in N_j. Finally, the construct **GeneratePredicates** creates predicates on these node type identifiers by imposing constraints on the server value (as described in the previous section). If the connectivity set C_j does not contain any free node type identifiers then Step (24) is executed. Finally, Steps (29) to (32) generate the X_{n_s}, X_{ℓ_s}, and P_s components of the web schema.

7.7.3 Algorithm for the Construct Partition

We now present the complete algorithm for the construct **Partition**. The pseudocode for the algorithm is shown in Figure 7.5. In the algorithm, we combine the three phases discussed in the previous section. Given a complex schema S and a set of web tuples T, our algorithm generates a set of nonoverlapping partitions $\mathcal{U}$. It starts with an empty set of partitions $\mathcal{U}$ and appends each partition as it proceeds. When the algorithm terminates, we will have transformed the complex schema and the web tuples into a set of nonoverlapping partitions containing simple schemas.

Intuitively, the complex schema S is decomposed into a set of simple schemas and each such simple schema S_i is matched against the web tuples in W by the algorithm. If there exists a web tuple that conforms to the simple schema then S_i is included as a nonnoisy simple schema and the algorithm generates the partition by identifying the set of web tuples that are bound together by S_i. However, comparing each possible pair of simple schema and web tuples to identify a set of partitions can have a significant impact on the total cost of the schema generation process rendering this algorithm impractical. A practical solution to this problem is to minimize the number of comparisons by subdividing the algorithm into the preprocessing phase and the matching phase. We describe the implementation of each phase in turn.

Steps (3) to (8) in the algorithm are based on the principle of Observation 1 in Section 7.6.4. Observe that a tuple may conform to a simple schema if the tuple contains instances of all the node type identifiers in the simple schema. Based on this notion, the algorithm first identifies those node and link type identifiers that exist in S but not in the tuple set T. It first determines the set of bound node and link type identifiers in the tuple set and the schema using the constructs **BoundNodeTypeSet** and **BoundLinkTypeSet** (Steps (3) to (6)). Then Steps (7) and (8) compute sets of node and link type identifiers that do not have any instances in T.

Input: A complex web schema $S = \langle X_n, X_\ell, C, P \rangle$ and set of web tuples T.
Output: A set of nonoverlapping partitions $\mathcal{U}$

(1)   Initialize a partition set $\mathcal{U}$;
(2)   Initialize $temp = -1$ and $ratio = 0$;
(3) $X_{n_w} = \mathbf{BoundNodeTypeSet}(T, X_n)$;
(4) $X_{\ell_w} = \mathbf{BoundLinkTypeSet}(T, X_\ell)$;
(5) $X_{n_s} = \mathbf{BoundNodeTypeSet}(X_n)$;
(6) $X_{\ell_s} = \mathbf{BoundLinkTypeSet}(X_\ell)$;
(7) $X_n' = X_{n_s} - X_{n_w}$;
(8) $X_\ell' = X_{\ell_s} - X_{\ell_w}$;
(9)   Sort C based on connectivity size of each C_i where $0 < i \leq r$;
(10)   Let $C \equiv C_1 \vee C_2 \vee \ldots \vee C_r$;
(11) $L_t = \mathbf{Sort}(T)$;
(12)   for $(i = 1 \ to \ r)$ {
(13) $X_{n_i} = \mathbf{GetNodeTypeIds}(C_i)$;
(14)   if $(X_{n_i} \cap X_n' \neq \emptyset)$
(15)   Ignore C_i;
(16)   else {
(17) $S_i = \mathbf{GenerateSimpleSchema}(C_i, X_n, X_\ell, P)$; /* Figure 7.6 */
(18)   Get size L_i of S_i;
(19)   if $(temp \neq -1 \ or \ L_i \neq temp)$ {
(20)   if $(temp \neq -1 \ and \ temp \neq L_i)$ {
(21)   if $(ratio > 1)$ {
(22) $P_k = \mathbf{NonoverlappingPartition}(P_k)$; /* Figure 7.8 */
(23)   Insert P_k in $\mathcal{U}$;
(24)   Remove elements from P_k;
(25)   }
(26) $ratio = 0$;
(27)   }
(28)   Get tuples $T_l \subseteq T$ whose size $L_i \in L_z$;
(29)   }
(30) $T_i = \mathbf{Match}(S_i, T_l)$; /* Figure 7.7 */
(31)   if $(|T_i| \neq 0)$ {
(32)   Insert $\langle S_i, T_i \rangle$ in P_k;
(33) $ratio = \frac{|T_i|}{|T|} + ratio$;
(34) $temp = L_i$;
(35)   }
(36)   else
(37)   Remove S_i; /* Noisy schema */
(38)   }
(39)   } /* End of for loop */
(40)   Return $\mathcal{U}$;

Fig. 7.5. Pseudocode for Partition.

Next, the sets of simple connectivities in C and the web tuples T are sorted based on their connectivity size using the construct **Sort**. The purpose of sorting is based on Observation 3 in Section 7.6.4. Note that a web tuple conforms to a simple schema if the fragment sizes are identical. Hence we sort the tuples and connectivities to identify those schemas whose connectivity size does not match with any tuples. Observe that L_t in Step (11) represents a set of fragment sizes of the tuples in T. Then, for each set of simple connectivities C_i, the Steps (13) to (38) are executed as follows.

- Step (13) retrieves the set of node type identifiers in C_i and stores them in X_{n_i}. The condition in Step (14) checks if any of the elements in X_{n_i} also occur in X'_n. Recall that X'_n represents those node type identifiers whose instances do not occur in T. Hence if the condition in Step (14) is evaluated true then none of the web tuples in T satisfies the connectivity C_i. Therefore we ignore C_i. Observe that the conformity checking of tuples that may match C_i is performed without comparing the contents of the web tuples.
- If the condition in Step (14) is evaluated false then the Steps (17) to (37) are executed. First, the algorithm generates the simple schema with connectivity C_i. The procedure is encapsulated in the construct **GenerateSimpleSchema** (Step (18)) and is elaborated below.

Algorithm for the Construct `GenerateSimpleSchema`

The pseudocode for the algorithm is shown in Figure 7.6. It takes as input a set of simple connectivities $C_i \in C$ in the complex web schema $S = \langle X_n, X_\ell, C, P \rangle$, and X_n, X_ℓ, and P components of S and returns as output a simple web schema $S_s = \langle X_{n_s}, X_{\ell_s}, C_s, P_s \rangle$.

For a set of simple connectivities C_i for $0 < i \leq r$, the algorithm executes the Steps (2) to (20). It first identifies the set of node and link type identifiers in C_i (denoted by X_{n_s} and X_{ℓ_s}, respectively, in the algorithm) using the constructs **GetNodeTypeIds** and **GetLinkTypeIds**, respectively. These constructs take as input a set of simple connectivities in CNF, i.e., C_i. **GetNodeTypeIds** returns as output the set of node type identifiers in these connectivities. On the other hand, the construct **GetLinkTypeIds** determines the set of link type identifiers in C_i.

Next, for each node and link type identifier in X_{n_s} and X_{ℓ_s} respectively the predicates defined on these identifiers are identified from P and stored in P_s (Steps (4) to (19)). Observe that free node and link type identifiers are ignored in these steps as these identifiers do not have any predicate defined on them in the web schema S. Specifically, the procedure to retrieve predicates of a node or link type identifier from P is encapsulated in the construct **GetPredicates**. It takes as input a node or link type identifier and predicate set P and returns as output a set of predicates $P_j \subseteq P$ that is defined over j.

- Note that in the algorithm in Figure 7.5 the variable *temp* is used to monitor the connectivity size of the simple schemas. The variable *ratio* is used to compute the pruning ratios of a set of simple schemas with identical connectivity size and

> **Input:** Set of simple connectivities C_i, set of node and link type identifiers X_n and X_ℓ, Set of predicates P;
> **Output:** Simple schema $S_s \langle X_{n_s}, X_{\ell_s}, C_s, P_s \rangle$
>
> (1)   Initialize $S_s = \langle X_{n_s}, X_{\ell_s}, C_s, P_s \rangle$;
> (2) $X_{n_s} = \mathbf{GetNodeTypeIds}(C_i)$;
> (3) $X_{\ell_s} = \mathbf{GetLinkTypeIds}(C_i)$;
> (4)   for $(j = 1 \ to \ |X_{n_s}|)$ {
> (5)   if $(X_{n_s}[j]$ is not free type) {
> (6) $P_j = \mathbf{GetPredicates}(X_{n_s}[j], \ P)$;
> (7)   Insert P_j into P_s;
> (8)   }
> (9)   else
> (10)   ;
> (11) }
> (12) for $(k = 1 \ to \ |X_{\ell_s}|)$ {
> (13)   if $(X_{\ell_s}[k]$ is not free type) {
> (14) $P_k = \mathbf{GetPredicates}(X_{\ell_s}[k], \ P)$;
> (15)   Insert P_k into P_s;
> (16)   }
> (17)   else
> (18)   ;
> (19) }
> (20) Return $S_s = \langle X_{n_s}, X_{\ell_s}, C_s, P_s \rangle$;

Fig. 7.6. Pseudocode for **GenerateSimpleSchema**.

is initially set to 0. Consider Step (19) now. Initially, *temp* is set to -1. Hence the connectivity size of schema S_i, denoted by $L_i > 0$, is never equal to *temp* when the step is executed for the first time. Therefore this step is evaluated true as *temp* $\neq L_i$.

- Next the condition in Step (20) is evaluated. Observe that when this condition is evaluated for the first time it is always false as *temp* $\neq -1$ and *temp* $\neq L_i$ can never be true at the same time. However, as we show, it is only evaluated true when the set of connectivities with identical connectivity size has been already inspected by the algorithm. For the time being, we consider that the condition is evaluated false. Therefore Steps (21) to (27) are ignored and Step (28) is executed. It retrieves the set of tuples $T_\ell \subseteq T$ whose fragment sizes are the same as that of the connectivity size of the schema S_i, i.e., L_i. Note that as the tuples T are sorted based on their fragment sizes the algorithm can retrieve tuples with fragment size L_i efficiently. Note that it is necessary for the connectivity size of the simple schema and tuples to be identical in order to minimize the number of comparisons of schemas and tuples to determine if

---

Input: A simple schema $S = \langle X_n, X_\ell, C, P \rangle$ and tuple set T_ℓ.
Output: A set of matched tuples T_m.

(1)   Initialize $flag = 0$, T_m;
(2)   for $(i = 1 \ to \ |T_\ell|)$ {
(3) $flag = \textbf{ConnConformity}(C, t_i)$;
(4)   if $(flag = 1)$ {
(5) $flag = \textbf{PredConformity}(P, t_i)$;
(6)   if $(flag = 1)$
(7)   Insert t_i in T_m;
(8)   }
(9) $flag = 0$;
(10)   }
(11)   Return T_m;

Fig. 7.7. Pseudocode for **Match**.

the schemas are nonnoisy. The matching phase is performed by the construct **Match** and is discussed below.

Algorithm for the Construct Match

The algorithm takes as input a simple schema S and a set of tuples T_ℓ whose fragment sizes are identical to that of the connectivity size of the schema and returns a set of tuples (possibly empty) $T_m \subseteq T_\ell$ that conforms to the schema S. The pseudocode of the algorithm is shown in Figure 7.7.

For each tuple in T_ℓ the Steps (3) to (9) are executed. For each tuple t_i the algorithm first checks if it satisfies the connectivity constraints. This is performed by the construct **ConnConformity** in Step (3). It returns 1 if the tuple satisfies the connectivity constraints; otherwise it returns 0. Next, Step (4) is evaluated true only if the tuple t_i satisfies C. Then the algorithm checks if t_i satisfies the predicates P using the construct **PredConformity**(P, t_i). If it does then the construct returns 1; otherwise it returns 0. Finally, if the value of the variable $flag$ is 1 then the t_i satisfies both the connectivity and predicate constraints. Hence it satisfies the schema S. Consequently, t_i is stored in T_m. Once all the tuples are inspected the algorithm returns T_m.

• If the matching operation returns a nonempty set of tuples, i.e., $|T_i| \neq 0$, then Steps (31) to (35) are executed. Otherwise, S_i is a noisy schema and is ignored (Step 37). For $|T_i| \neq 0$, the partition $\langle S_i, T_i \rangle$ is inserted in the partition set P_k. Note that P_k is used to represent a set of partitions where each schema in the partition has identical connectivity size. Next, Step (33) computes the pruning ratio and adds it to the total ratios of the schemas with connectivity size L_i. Finally, *temp* is assigned the size L_i in Step (34).

- Observe that the subsequent execution of the loop indicates that the condition in Step (19) is always evaluated false until all the schemas with identical connectivity size L_i are generated (as C is sorted based on connectivity size). Hence Steps (20) to (29) are ignored for all simple schemas with identical connectivity size. Note that for schemas with identical connectivity size we first find the non-noisy schemas and the set of tuples they bind. We also compute the pruning ratio for these schemas. Once all the schemas and tuples with size L_i are inspected the algorithm may perform the nonoverlapping partitioning operation. In this case the conditions in Steps (19) and (20) are both evaluated true. This operation is encapsulated in the construct **nonoverlappingPartition** and is shown in Figure 7.8. We now elaborate on this.

To perform the nonoverlapping partitioning operation it is necessary to determine whether there exist overlapping partitions in $\mathcal{U}_k$. Recall that two partitions are overlapping if the schemas are equivalent, inclusive, or intersecting. This is possible only if the connectivity sizes of the two schemas are identical and the connectivities of these schemas are identical. The algorithm uses this notion to perform the nonoverlapping partitioning operation.

Observe that $\mathcal{U}_k$ contains a set of partitions, possibly overlapping, where the connectivity size of all the schemas is $L_s(k)$. Note that a pair of partitions in $\mathcal{U}_k$ may overlap if the sum of the pruning ratios of the schemas in $\mathcal{U}_k$ is greater than 1. Hence Step (21) in Figure 7.5 checks this condition. If it is, then there exist overlapping partitions in $\mathcal{U}_k$. The algorithm then proceeds to identify and replace these overlapping partitions with nonoverlapping ones (Steps 1 to 16) in Figure 7.8.

Algorithm for the Construct NonoverlappingPartition

In order to determine potential overlapping partition pairs in $\mathcal{U}_k$, the algorithm identifies pairs of partitions with identical connectivities (Step (1)). Observe that the algorithm performs this in order to minimize the number of comparisons between the partitions. This stems from the fact that overlapping partitions must have identical connectivities. The set of partition pairs with identical connectivities is denoted as $\mathcal{U}_c$ in the algorithm. Note that $\mathcal{U}_c = \{(U_1, U_2), (U_3, U_4), \ldots, (U_{n_1}, U_n)\}$ such that for each pair (U_i, U_j) $C_i = C_j$, where $U_i \in \mathcal{U}_k$ and $U_j \in \mathcal{U}_k$ $\forall$ i, j such that $0 < (i, j) \leq n$. Also note that at this point $\mathcal{U}_c$ contains a pair of partitions that may or may not be overlapping. Hence the algorithm determines if a pair in $\mathcal{U}_c$ is overlapping. If it is then the pair of partitions is transformed to nonoverlapping partitions. Note that the evaluation of the three cases discussed in Section 7.6 is performed here. Next the set of nonoverlapping partition pairs is inserted in $\mathcal{U}_k$. Then in Step (8) the algorithm computes the sum of the pruning ratios of the modified set of partitions $\mathcal{U}_k$ with size L_i. If the ratio is equal to 1 then all the partitions in $\mathcal{U}_k$ are nonoverlapping and the algorithm exits from the for loop and appends $\mathcal{U}_k$ in $\mathcal{U}$. Last, it returns the modified $\mathcal{U}_k$.

Input: A set of partitions $\mathcal{U}_k$.
Output: A set of nonoverlapping partitions.

(1)   Get set of partition pairs with identical connectivity $\mathcal{U}_c$ from $\mathcal{U}_k$;
(2)   if $(|\mathcal{U}_c| \neq 0)$ { /* Overlapping partitions may exist */
(3)   for $(i = 1\ to\ |\mathcal{U}_c|)$ {
(4)   if $(\mathcal{U}_{ci}$ is overlapping partition pairs) {
(5)   Remove $\mathcal{U}_{ci}$ from $\mathcal{U}_k$;
(6)   Perform nonoverlapping partitioning on $\mathcal{U}_{ci}$;
(7)   Insert $\mathcal{U}_{ci}$ in $\mathcal{U}_k$;
(8)   Compute $ratio = \frac{|T_1|}{|T_\ell|} + \frac{|T_2|}{|T_\ell|} + \ldots + \frac{T_{|\mathcal{U}_k|}}{|T_\ell|}$;
(9)   if $(ratio = 1)$
(10)   Exit from the loop;
(11)   }
(12)   }
(13)   }
(14)   else
(15)   The partitions are nonoverlapping;
(16)   Return $\mathcal{U}_k$;

Fig. 7.8. Pseudocode for **NonoverlappingPartition**.

- Finally, the algorithm **Schema Generator** terminates once all nonnoisy simple schemas are identified and a set of nonoverlapping partitions is generated to bind all the web tuples in T.

7.8 Web Schema Generation in Local Operations

When a web table is generated locally by manipulating existing web table(s), the procedure of schema generation of the resultant web table is *distinct* from that discussed in the previous sections. Since the schemas of the input web table(s) are already transformed from the coupling queries and pruned when they are coupled from the Web, the canonical coupling query to schema transformation phase and the complex schema decomposition phase are ignored in this process. Hence the nonoverlapping partition generation process consists of the two phases: *schema generation* and *schema pruning*. We now discuss these phases.

7.8.1 Schema Generation Phase

In this phase, the schema(s) and the set of resultant web tuples are generated first by manipulating the schema(s) and web tuples of the input web tables based on the *query conditions* and type of operation to be performed. The procedure for generating schemas of the resultant web table varies with the type of web operation.

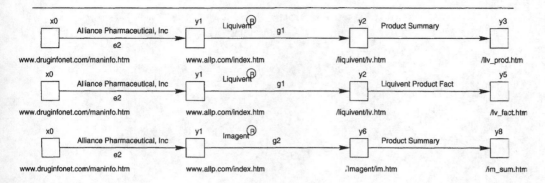

Fig. 7.9. Selected web tuples in Example 7.24.

We illustrate the generation of web schemas and corresponding resultant web tuples with an example.

Example 7.24. Consider the web table in Example 7.19 (Figure 6.11). The set of web schemas associated with the web table is S_d, S_f, and S_g. Suppose a user wishes to determine those web tuples that satisfy the following connectivities and predicate,

$$C_s \equiv C_{s_1} \vee C_{s_2} \vee C_{s_3}$$

where

$$C_{s_1} \equiv x\langle e\rangle y \wedge y\langle g\rangle y \wedge y\langle t\rangle \#_3$$
$$C_{s_2} \equiv x\langle e\rangle y \wedge y\langle g\rangle \#_2 \wedge \#_2\langle t\rangle y$$
$$C_{s_3} \equiv x\langle e\rangle y \wedge y\langle g\rangle y \wedge y\langle t\rangle y$$

and

$$p_s(t) = \texttt{CONTENT::t[A] NON-ATTR\_CONT}$$
$$\texttt{":BEGIN\_WORD: } + \textit{product} + \texttt{ :END\_WORD:"}$$

This operation is performed by the *web select* operation. The set of web tuples satisfying the above conditions is shown in Figure 7.9. The web schemas to bind these web tuples are generated by manipulating the set of simple web schemas of the input web table and are given below.

1. $S_{sd} = \langle X_{n_{sd}}, X_{\ell_{sd}}, C_{sd}, P_{sd}\rangle$ where $X_{n_{sd}} = \{x, y, \#_3\}$, $X_{\ell_{sd}} = \{e, g, t\}$, $C_{sd} = C_{s_1}$, and $P_{sd} = P_d \cup \{p_s(t)\}$.
2. $S_{sf} = \langle X_{n_{sf}}, X_{\ell_{sf}}, C_{sf}, P_{sf}\rangle$ where $X_{n_{sf}} = X_{n_f}$, $X_{\ell_{sf}} = \{e, g, t\}$, $C_{sf} = C_{s_2}$, and $P_{sf} = P_f \cup \{p_s(t)\}$.
3. $S_{sg} = \langle X_{n_{sg}}, X_{\ell_{sg}}, C_{sg}, P_{sg}\rangle$ where $X_{n_{sg}} = \{x, y\}$, $X_{\ell_{sg}} = \{e, g, t\}$, $C_{sg} = C_{s_3}$, and $P_{sg} = P_g \cup \{p_s(t)\}$. ∎

```
        Input:  A set of partitions P_k.
        Output:  Partitions P_d containing distinct schemas.

(1)     for (i = 1 to |P_k|) {
(2)         Get A_i = ⟨S_i, T_i⟩;
(3)         for (j = i + 1 to |P_k|) {
(4)             Get A_j = ⟨S_j, T_j⟩;
(5)             if (|X_{n_i}| = |X_{n_j}| and |X_{ℓ_i}| = |X_{ℓ_j}|) {
(6)                 if (C_i = C_j and P_i = P_j) {
(7)                     T_i = T_i ∪ T_j;
(8)                         Remove A_j from P_k;
(9)                 }
(10)            }
(11)            else
(12)                ;
(13)        }
(14)        Move A_i to P_d;
(15)    }
(16)    Return P_d;
```

Fig. 7.10. Pseudocode for distinct schema phase.

7.8.2 Schema Pruning Phase

Once the set of simple schemas and web tuples is computed from schemas and tuples of input web table(s), it may be necessary to prune these simple web schemas. The schema pruning phase is similar to that described in Section 7.6. At the end of this phase, a set of nonoverlapping partitions is generated to represent the resultant web table. Observe that if the output of the schema generation phase is only a single simple web schema, then there is no need to perform the schema pruning operation as all the web tuples in the resultant web table are bound by this schema.

However, when the schema generation process ejects more than one simple web schema, then it may be necessary to prune this set of web schemas by inspecting the resultant web tuples. Note that the schema pruning operation described earlier has to be augmented to check the existence of identical web schemas in the collection of simple web schemas. Recall that in our previous discussion we do not perform checking for identical web schemas in the pruning operation. This is because identical schemas are never generated from a coupling query. However, such assumptions may not hold for web tables generated by local web operation. For instance, sets of distinct web schemas may become identical after removal of some of the node or link type identifiers by a local web operation (*web project*). Hence the schema pruning process for local web operation consists of the following four phases: preprocessing, matching, distinct schema, and nonoverlapping partitioning phase. Note that the preprocessing, matching, and nonoverlapping partitioning phases are the same as described earlier. Hence we do not elaborate on this further. Instead, we illustrate this with an example.

Example 7.25. Consider the set of simple schemas in Example 7.24. Notice that the schema S_{sf} binds all web tuples in Figure 7.9. On the other hand, the simple schemas S_{sd} and S_{sg} do not bind any web tuples (noisy web schemas). Hence we have the following set of partitions after performing the schema pruning operation.

1. $U_{sf} = \langle S_{sf}, T_{sf} \rangle$, where $T_{sf} = \{t_1, t_2, t_3\}$, where t_1, t_2, and t_3 are the web tuples in Figure 7.9.

The web table containing these web tuples is bound by the schema S_{sf}. That is, $W = \langle N, \mathcal{U} \rangle$, where $\mathcal{U} = \{U_{sf}\}$. Observe that as the noisy schema elimination generates only one web schema, there is no need to perform distinct schema and nonoverlapping partitioning phases. ∎

We now describe the *distinct schema phase*. Note that if two web schemas are identical, then the following must be true: the size of X_n and X_ℓ for the schemas should be identical and the sizes of predicate sets and connectivities must be identical. That is, the schemas must have the same connectivity size. We use this concept to minimize the number of comparisons between the connectivities and predicates of the set of simple schemas to determine identical schemas. The pseudocode for the algorithm for distinct schema phase is shown in Figure 7.10. Note that this algorithm may be executed after Step (20) in the algorithm in Figure 7.5. The reason behind this is that after execution of this step the algorithm generates a set of partitions P_k in which all schemas have identical length. Hence this reduces the total number of comparisons required to identify identical schemas. Next, for each partition in $\mathcal{P}_k$, the Steps (2) to (15) in Figure 7.10 are executed. The algorithm first retrieves a partition and for the remaining partitions it compares if the sizes of the set of node and link type identifiers of the simple schemas are identical (Step (5)). If it is then the algorithm checks if the sets of connectivities and predicates are identical in Step (6). If the condition is evaluated true then the schemas S_i and S_j in the partitions A_i and A_j are identical and the corresponding sets of tuples T_i and T_j are combined in a single set. Then one of the partitions containing duplicate schema is removed from $\mathcal{P}_k$. We defer the example of the distinct schema phase to Chapter 8.

7.9 Summary

In this chapter, we introduced the notion of web schemas to model instances of warehouse data in the context of WHOWEDA. Informally, our web warehouse can be conceived of as a collection of web tables. A web table contains sets of web tuples and simple web schemas. A web schema provides two types of information: it specifies some of the common properties shared by the documents and hyperlinks in the web table with respect to not only their structure, but also their metadata and content; and a web schema(s) summarizes the hyperlink structure of these documents in the web table.

Web schemas in WHOWEDA are generated (1) by manipulating the coupling query and (2) by manipulating the schemas of the input web table(s) during local operations to generate a new set of web schemas for the resultant web table. In the former case, a simple or complex web schema is generated first from a valid canonical coupling query. In the next stage, the complex web schema is decomposed into a set of simple web schemas. These two stages are performed without inspecting the web tuples. Finally, in the last stage the set of simple web schemas is pruned by inspecting the hyperlink structure of the web tuples.

WHOM-Algebra

In this chapter, we focus on how web tables are generated by the *global web coupling* operation and are further manipulated in the web warehouse by a set of *web algebraic operators*. The web algebra provides a formal foundation for data representation and manipulation for the web warehouse. We begin by identifying different types of manipulation that are possible in the web warehouse. In the subsequent sections, we introduce a set of web operators to perform these tasks.

8.1 Types of Manipulation

Algebraic operations in WHOWEDA can be broadly categorized into the following set of operations.

- *Extraction:* This operation extracts a set of web tuples from the Web that satisfy a coupling query. This is the first step to populate the web warehouse. It retrieves relevant data from the Web. This operation is performed by the *global web coupling* operation and is described in Section 8.2.
- *Selection:* This operation involves choosing a set of web tuples in a web table based on metadata, content, or structural properties of the document or hyperlinks. As a simple example, consider the web table in Figure 7.2(a) in Chapter 7. Say that we are interested in finding out if there are diseases in the web tuples that are related to "air pollution." The resultant web tuples will look like the set of web tuples in Figure 8.1. This operation is performed by the *web select* operator and is discussed in Section 8.3.
- *Reduction:* We may wish to drop or eliminate a set of nodes from the web tuples of a web table that we no longer consider relevant. For example, consider the web table in Figure 6.10. Suppose we wish to eliminate all nodes between the instances of y and z. The resultant web tuples are shown in Figure 8.2. This operation is performed by the *web project* operator and is discussed in Section 8.4.
- *Combination:* In a web warehouse, we may wish to combine multiple web tables based on different conditions. For instance, we may wish to combine web tuples

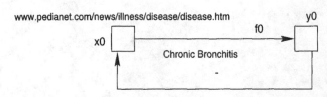

Fig. 8.1. Tuple of selected table.

of the web tables in Figures 6.3 and 6.10 into a single web table since they both contain information about cancer. Web tuples in the resultant web table are a union of the web tuples in the two input web tables. This operation is performed by the *web union* operator and is discussed in Section 8.9. Another way of combining web tuples in different web tables is by *joining* them based on certain *conditions*. For example, consider the web tables Drugs-Manufacturer and Drugs-Usage in Figures 6.9 and 8.19. We may wish to concatenate the tuples over identical nodes (same documents) that are instances of a and x in these web tables. The set of resultant tuples may look like those in Figure 8.20.

8.2 Global Web Coupling

Global web coupling enables a user to retrieve a set of interlinked documents satisfying a coupling query, regardless of the locations of the documents in the Web. To initiate global web coupling, a user specifies a coupling query. The result of such user-driven coupling is a set of related documents in the form of a web tuple materialized in a web table.[1]

8.2.1 Definition

The global web coupling operator Γ takes in a coupling query G and returns a web table $W = \langle N, \mathcal{U} \rangle$ containing a set of web tuples T extracted from the WWW satisfying the query and a set of simple web schemas $\mathcal{S}$ generated from G. That is, $W = \Gamma(G)$. Each web tuple matches a portion of the WWW satisfying the conditions described in the query. This related set of web tuples is coupled and stored in a web table along with a set of simple web schemas. Each web tuple in the web table is structurally identical to the query of the table. For example, consider the query in Example 6.1 in Chapter 6. The set of web tuples generated from the global web coupling operation is shown in Figure 6.3. The set of schemas of these web tuples is depicted in Example 7.13 in Chapter 7.

---

[1] A portion of this section appeared in [29, 121].

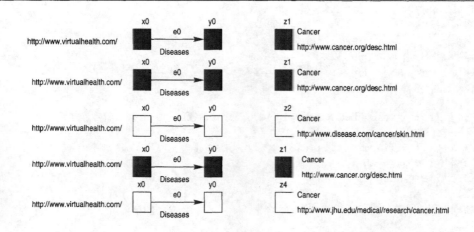

Fig. 8.2. Web table after projecting node instances between y and z.

8.2.2 Global Web Coupling Operation

The global web coupling operation may be best described by the following four phases, the *query formulation*, *valid canonical query generation*, *web tuples generation*, and *web table generation phase*. We briefly describe each of these phases.

- *Query formulation phase:* In this phase, a user specifies a coupling query. Since we have described the query formulation mechanism in detail in Chapter 6, we do not elaborate on this any further.
- *Valid canonical query generation phase:* The coupling query formulated in the previous phase is given as input in this phase and a valid canonical form of the query is generated. We have described the detailed procedure of valid canonical coupling query generation in Chapter 6. Hence we do not elaborate on this anymore.
- *Web tuples generation phase:* A valid canonical query is given as input to this phase and a set of web tuples that conforms to the query is retrieved from the Web.
- *Web table generation phase:* Finally, if the preceding phase returns a nonempty set of web tuples, then the web table is created in this phase to materialize these web tuples along with a set of simple web schemas. Note that the simple web schemas are generated from the canonical coupling query itself. Hence the input to this phase is a set of web tuples (nonempty) T, the valid canonical coupling query G, and the name N of the web table, and the output is a web table $W = \langle N, \mathcal{U} \rangle$. Note that we have already described the generation of a web table and its schemas from a canonical query in Chapter 7. Hence we do not discuss this any further.

```
       Input:  Coupling query G, Name N.
       Output:  Web table W = ⟨N, P⟩.

(1)    if (G is a coupling graph)
(2)        G_t = TransformToCouplingText(G); /* Section 6.4 in Chapter 6 */
(3)    else
(4)        ;
(5)    G_c = ReduceToCanonical(G_t); /* Section 6.4 in Chapter 6 */
(6)    if (G_t is valid) {
(7)        T = GenerateTuples(G_t); /* Figure 8.4 */
(8)        if (|T| = 0)
(9)            return;
(10)       else {
(11)           W = GenerateWebTable(G_t, T, N); /* Figure 7.3 */
(12)           return W;
(13)       }
(14)   }
(15)   else
(16)       Refine G_t; /* Chapter 6 */
```

Fig. 8.3. Pseudocode for the global web coupling operation.

8.2.3 Web Tuples Generation Phase

In this section we elaborate on the third phase of the global web coupling operation, i.e., the web tuples generation phase. The algorithm for the global web coupling operation is shown in Figure 8.3. In this algorithm we assume that the set of coupling query predicates is empty in a coupling query; i.e., $Q = \emptyset$. Our evaluation technique can be augmented to incorporate evaluation of coupling query predicates. In this section, we elaborate on the construct **GenerateTuples** in Step (7) in Figure 8.3.

The procedure to generate a set of web tuples that satisfies the coupling query can be classified into three stages: *finding the source vertex*, *matching documents in the Web*, and *cleaning up invalid node objects*. We elaborate on each of these stages.

Finding the Source Vertex

The first step in this phase is to identify the source vertex in the coupling query. Recall that a coupling query has a single source vertex with zero in-degree. This source vertex is the starting point of navigating the Web for matching documents that satisfy the query.

Matching Documents in the Web

If a source node's URL is known (for browser coupling queries) then the corresponding document is retrieved. Otherwise, for browse/search coupling queries a set of documents satisfying the predicates on the source vertex is retrieved. In the retrieval process, existing search engines are used to obtain the set of WWW documents corresponding to start node(s) whose URL(s) are unknown. Note that we may not want to rely on a single search engine to identify the initial documents as it may not have a good index of the WWW documents that are of our interest. Therefore we can widen the range of documents from different search engines that better match the search conditions in the coupling query. The search engine we have experimented with is METAFind (http://www.metafind.com). It is chosen because it submits keyword search requests to a few popular search engines such as AltaVista, Lycos, and WebCrawler simultaneously. The results obtained from METAFind are formatted into a single page. This simplifies the task of having to visit all result pages.

When a set of documents for a node type identifier (say x) is obtained, each document is analyzed as follows. A parser extracts hyperlinks from the document. These links are checked against the search conditions specified on the out-edge(s) of x. If a hyperlink satisfies the condition on an out-edge $\ell = (x, y)$, then the document corresponding to the node type identifier y (which is adjacent to x) will be examined next. Note that if y is a free node type identifier then all the documents reached from an instance of x by following the specified hyperlinks will be considered for inspection.

The pseudocode of the algorithm for generating the set of web tuples is shown in Figure 8.4. Before the matching begins, some initializations are performed. The source vertex is determined and a connection is established with the proxy server in order to retrieve Web documents. Then matching begins. First, a set of Web document(s) is retrieved from the WWW. If a URL has been defined for the start node, only one document will be retrieved. The retrieved document(s) for the start node is then processed and stored.

With the start node identified, we may traverse the graph to identify and match WWW documents corresponding to each node type identifier and satisfying the search conditions defined on it in terms of predicates. A breadth-first or depth-first traversal may be used. For each start document obtained, the coupling query will be traversed once. The algorithm for traversal is shown in Figure 8.5. The starting document is provided by the calling module. Together with the traversal order, the algorithm retrieves documents from the WWW that satisfy the coupling query. With the initial set of starting documents, it begins by evaluating links in the documents. The algorithm checks whether a document has more than one outlink; if so, it ensures that all the outlink conditions are satisfied before it proceeds. If the current document corresponds to a terminating identifier in the coupling query, then all the links from it are removed. A terminating node is identified as one with zero out-degree. If the current evaluation results in an empty set of links, the document will be deleted as an indication that it does not satisfy the coupling query. Otherwise, the URL of the links will be inserted into a pool that holds the URLs of all subsequent documents to be evaluated. Before inserting a URL into the pool, a check is also performed to ensure that the URL has not been visited in the traversal.

The algorithm returns a set of Web documents that satisfy the coupling query. An empty set indicates a failed traversal. With this set of Web documents, a cleanup

---

Inputs :   Canonical coupling query G_t

Output :   Set of web tuples T
Variables : S,R,Z := set of materialized node instances
              K := set of node type identifiers of G_t in order of traversal

(1) $startNodeId = \textbf{GetStartNode}(G_t)$;
(2)   K = **GetTraversalOrder**($startNodeId$, G_t);
(3)   S = **GetNodeset**($startNodeId$);
(4)   for $(s = 1\ to\ n)$ {
(5)   R = **TraverseQuery**(G_t, **K**, S_s); /* Figure 8.5 */
(6) $R_0 = \textbf{Cleanup}(\ \textbf{R},\ S_s)$; /*Figure 8.6 */
(7)   for $(z = 1\ to\ n)$ {
(8) $R_z = \textbf{Cleanup}(\ R_{z-1}\ )$; /Figure 8.6 */
(9)   }
(10)   if $(R_n \neq \emptyset)$
(11)   StoreNodes(R_n, T)
(12)   }
(13)   return T;

Fig. 8.4. Algorithm of **GenerateTuples**.

module (see below) is invoked to remove invalid links in the documents. An invalid link arises as a result of retrieving an invalid document corresponding to that link. For example, suppose a document D has three links that satisfy some edge conditions. In the course of evaluating the target document of the link, only two out of the three links satisfy the edge conditions. Therefore an invalid link is present in document D, and it should be removed. The `dfsTuple` construct is invoked for each initial document in the multiple start nodes case. Eventually, the algorithm finds a set of WWW documents for the coupling query and stores them in the form of web tuples.

Cleaning Up Invalid Node Objects

After traversing through all the nodes in a coupling query, a preliminary set of web tuples (graph instances) is formed. However, these tuples are not stored immediately during the traversal since we do not know whether any links of a document would still be valid after the evaluation. Therefore a second traversal is performed to determine the valid documents that can be formed into a tuple. The traversal is now performed in a depth-first manner. The algorithm is shown in Figure 8.6.

This module uses a recursive approach to determine whether the links in each document lead to another valid document. If the link points to an invalid or deleted document, the link is removed. If this results in an empty set of links and the document is not a terminating document, the document will be marked for deletion. Since the action is recursive, it will replicate the removal of links and nodes all the way to the starting point. That is, if there is a valid node for the beginning of a

```
Inputs :      Coupling query G_t
              L := set of links in G_t
              s := source vertex of G_t
              K := a set of vertices of G_t in order of traversal


Output :   R
Variables : E,R := set of materialized node instances

(1)     for (i = 1 to n) {
(2)         E = GetNodeSet( K_i);
(3)         for (j = 1 to m) {
(4)             if (outdegree( K_i) > 1) {
(5)                 Evaluate E_j on all outlinks;
(6)                 if (∃ a link that fails)
(7)                     E = E - {E_j};
(8)             }
(9)             if (outdegree( K_i ) = 0) {
(10)                Remove all links in E_j;
(11)                R = r ∪ {E_j};
(12)            }
(13)            for (k = 1 to p) {
(14)                if (LeftHandSideOf( L_k ) = K_i){
(15)                    Evaluate E_j on L_k;
(16)                    if (|E_j| = 0)
(17)                        E = E - {E_j};
(18)                    else {
(19)                        Add url of links to URLPool;
(20)                        R = R ∪ {E_j};
(21)                    }
(22)                }
(23)            }
(24)        }
(25)    }
(26)    if (K = ∅)
(27)        R = ∅
(28)    Return R;
```

Fig. 8.5. Coupling query traversal algorithm.

web query, but a valid node does not exist for the ending node in the web query, all the nodes coupled will be removed and this will result in an empty tuple set.

8.2.4 Limitations

Although global web coupling provides an attractive mechanism for harnessing relevant Web data, it also has some limitations. When the user specifies a browser coupling query then the URL of the source node is specified in the query. In such

```
Inputs :     s := materialized node instance
             R := set of materialized node instances
             K := set of materialized node instances processed by this function

Output :     status
Variables :  N := materialized node instance
             status := boolean variable
```

```
(1)    if (outdegree( s ) = 0) {
(2)        K = K ∪ {s};
(3)        status = true;
(4)    else if( s ∈ K)
(5)        status = true;
(6)    else
(7)        status = false;
(8)    }
(9)    if (status = true) {
(10)       Let L be linkset of s;
(11)       for(i = 1 to n) {
(12)           Let N be the node pointed by L_i;
(13)           if (state(N) = valid) {
(14)               K = K ∪ {N};
(15)               if (Cleanup( N ) = false) {
(16)                   L = L - {L_i};
(17)               }
(18)           }
(19)       }
(20)       if (L = ∅) {
(21)           K = K - {N};
(22)           status = false;
(23)       }
(24)       else
(25)           status = true;
(26)   }
```

Fig. 8.6. Algorithm for cleaning up of nodes.

a situation the global web coupling operation can directly start navigating through the relevant documents starting from the specified Web page. However, when a user specifies a browse/search coupling query then the global web coupling operation resorts to the search engines for retrieving a set of start nodes. Consequently, the limitations of search engines affect the selection of start nodes for further traversal. Note that at this point of time the search engines primarily support content-based keyword searches. Some of the search engines, as discussed in Chapter 2, support some form of metadata-based search. Hence the predicate set on the source vertex of the coupling query must not contain any structural predicates as these predicates cannot be evaluated using conventional search engines.

Even if we impose content and metadata predicates on the source node type identifier, there is always additional processing required to find the valid set of documents. To elaborate further, when a content predicate is imposed then the value of the predicate may be used to perform a keyword-based search using a conventional search engine. However, the set of documents returned by the query needs to be inspected further to check whether the value of the predicate occurs in a particular location of the page as specified by the attribute path expression in the predicate. Moreover, if the value of the predicate contains regular expressions then the search engines may not be capable of performing an efficient search simply because they do not support searches based on complex regular expressions. Based on the above reasons not all types of predicates on the source node type identifier can be evaluated by the global web coupling operation. Note that such problems do not arise in subsequent evaluations of nodes as we do not need to resort to search engines to determine instances of remaining node type identifiers. Of course, we believe that with the advent of XML, search facilities based on the structure of Web pages and complex regular expressions will be a reality in the near future.

8.3 Web Select

In the preceding section, we have described the global web coupling operation for retrieving a set of relevant data from the Web in the form of web tuples and materializing them in a web table. In the following sections we discuss the operators for manipulating these web tables. In this section, we discuss the *web select* operation. We begin with identifying different selection criteria. Then we formally define the web select operator. Next we explore *selection conditions* for the web select operation. Then we discuss how to express selection conditions using a *selection schema*. Finally, we discuss how to generate the selected web table.

8.3.1 Selection Criteria

Given a set of web tuples in a web table, the objective of the web select operation is to extract a subset of those web tuples that satisfy some additional *constraints*. These constraints are imposed using predicates and connectivities. Since a web tuple is a directed graph, the *criteria* on which the web select operation extracts a web tuple is that a subgraph of the tuple must conform to the imposed constraints. These selection criteria are as follows:

Criteria Defined on Node Type Identifiers

Let X_n be the set of node type identifiers in a web table W. Then a user may wish to impose additional constraints on one or more of these identifiers by specifying predicates over these identifiers. Consequently, all the web tuples in W that contain the instances of these identifiers are inspected to determine if they satisfy the specified conditions.

Criteria Based on Link Type Identifiers

Similar to node type identifiers, we may wish to select web tuples based on certain characteristics of the hyperlinks. Such a condition is specified on the corresponding link type identifiers.

Criteria Defined on Connectivities

Observe that the above conditions for selection are based on imposing conditions on the metadata, content, or structure of the nodes and links in a web table. These conditions do not impose constraints on the hyperlink structure of the web tuples. To express constraints on the web tuples such that they satisfy additional hyperlink structure, it is necessary to express conditions on the connectivities in the set of schemas of the web table. Example 7.24 in Chapter 7 is an example of such selection constraints.

8.3.2 Web Select Operator

The `select` operation on a web table extracts web tuples from a web table satisfying certain conditions. However, since the schema(s) of web tables is more complex than that of relational tables, selection conditions have to be expressed as predicates on node and link type identifiers, as well as connectivities of web tuples as highlighted in the preceding subsection. The `web select` operation augments some of the schema(s) of web tables by incorporating new conditions into the schema(s). Thus it is different from its relational counterpart.

Formally, we define web select as follows. $W_s = \sigma_\Phi(W)$, where σ is the select operator, $W = \langle N, \mathcal{P} \rangle$, and Φ is called the *selection condition*. Informally, the *selection condition* consists of two components: a set of simple schemas, denoted by M, and a *selection schema* $\Re$. Formally, a selection condition on a web table $W = \langle N, \mathcal{P} \rangle$, where $\mathcal{P} = \langle \mathcal{S}, T \rangle$ is a 2-tuple $\Phi = \langle M, \Re \rangle$, where $M \subseteq \mathcal{S}$, $M \neq \emptyset$, and $\Re = \langle X_{pn}, X_{p\ell}, C_r, P_r \rangle$. We now elaborate on these two components.

8.3.3 Simple Web Schema Set

The first component M specifies the set of tuples in W that is to be evaluated against the *selection schema*. M represents a subset of the set of simple schemas in W. Only those tuples in W that are bound by the schemas in M are evaluated by the web select operation. By default, M is set to $\mathcal{S}$ (the set of all schemas in W). Observe that in relational select we do not specify the schema of the relation in the selection condition. This is because a relation always has a single schema and the tuples rigidly adhere to the schema. However, such is not the case in a web table. As mentioned earlier, a web table may have more than one simple schema and a web tuple may satisfy any one of them. Hence when we perform a web select operation, we may not always wish to perform it on all the web tuples but only on some of the tuples that conform to a certain set of schemas in W. Furthermore, given two simple schemas S_1 and S_2 in W, the set of node or link type identifiers in

S_1 and S_2 may share some common identifiers. For instance, let a be an identifier in S_1 and S_2. Suppose we wish to select tuples that satisfy the connectivities in S_1 and some additional constraints on a as defined by the *selection schema*. If we disallow specification of the schema set M in the selection condition then the web select operation will select tuples that are bound by the schemas S_1 or S_2.

The second component, the selection schema $\Re$, expresses the hyperlink structure and metadata, content, or structural conditions the nodes and links of a web tuple must satisfy in order to be a tuple in the selected web table. In the next section we elaborate on the selection schema.

8.3.4 Selection Schema

We now elaborate on the selection schema. We first discuss the components of a selection schema. In the next subsection, we present the conditions a web tuple must satisfy in order to *conform* to a selection condition.

Components

Selection schemas, denoted by $\Re = \langle X_{pn}, X_{p\ell}, C_r, P_r \rangle$, consist of four components: a set of pairs of node type identifiers X_{pn}, a set of pairs of link type identifiers $X_{p\ell}$, a set of simple connectivities C_r in DNF, and a set of predicates P_r. We elaborate on these components in turn.

Set of Pairs of Node Type Identifiers.

Let $W = \langle N, \mathcal{P} \rangle$ be a web table where $\mathcal{P} = \langle \mathcal{S}, T \rangle$. Let $\Phi = \langle M, \Re \rangle$ be the selection condition where $\Re = \langle X_{pn}, X_{p\ell}, C_r, P_r \rangle$. The set of pairs of node type identifiers X_{pn} represents the set of node type identifiers over which some selection constraints are imposed. For each pair, the identifier on the left-hand side represents a node type identifier in W. The identifier on the right-hand side represents a bound node type identifier that may or may not occur in W. The significance of the pair is that it specifies that certain conditions are imposed on the node type identifier on the left-hand side and this identifier is nominally identified in $\Re$ by the identifier on the right-hand side. To elaborate further, let (l, r) be a pair in X_{pn}. Then l must be an identifier in X_n, where $X_n = X_{n1} \cup X_{n2} \cup \ .. \cup X_{n|\mathcal{S}|}$. That is, l is a node type identifier in W. Note that l can be bound or free. If l is bound then r must be equal to l. This is because in $\Re$ the bound node identifiers in W are not nominally modified while imposing constraints over them. Note that l may be the argument of a set of predicates defined in P_r. However, if l is free then r must be bound and cannot be identical to l. This is because imposing predicates on a free identifier transforms it into a bound identifier. Some examples of X_{pn} are as follows.

$$\{(x, x), (y, y)\}$$
$$\{(\#_1, a), (\#_2, b), (\#_3, b)\}$$

The first expression specifies that the selection constraints are imposed on the node type identifiers x and y in the input web table. Since these identifiers are bound the nominal identifier remains unchanged in the selection schema. However, in the second expression, selection constraints are imposed on the free node type identifiers $\#_1$, $\#_2$, and $\#_3$ in W. Hence the nominal identifiers are now replaced by the bound node type identifiers a and b in $\Re$. Observe that two different free identifiers may be replaced by an identical bound identifier. This is because we may wish to impose identical constraints on these two free identifiers. Formally, let $X_{pn} = \{(l_{n1}, r_{n1}), (l_{n2}, r_{n2}), \ldots, (l_{nk}, r_{nk})\}$. Then $l_{ni} \in (X_{n1} \cup X_{n2} \cup \ldots \cup X_{n|S|})$ $\forall$ $i \in [1, k]$. If l_{ni} is bound then $r_{ni} = l_{ni}$. If l_{ni} is free then r_{ni} is bound and $r_{ni} \neq l_{ni}$. Furthermore, it is possible to have two pairs, (l_{n1}, r_{n1}) and (l_{n2}, r_{n2}), such that $r_{n1} = r_{n2}$ and $l_{n1} \neq l_{n2}$. We denote the sets of all left and right node type identifiers in X_{pn} as $left(X_{pn})$ and $right(X_{pn})$, respectively. In the next section, we use these symbols to discuss the algorithm for the web select operation.

Set of Pairs of Link Type Identifiers

The set of pairs of link type identifiers are similar to X_{pn}. In this case $X_{p\ell} = \{(l_{\ell 1}, r_{\ell 1}), (l_{\ell 2}, r_{\ell 2}), \ldots, (l_{\ell k}, r_{\ell k})\}$, where $l_{\ell i} \in (X_{\ell 1} \cup X_{\ell 2} \cup \ldots \cup X_{\ell|S|})$ $\forall$ $i \in [1, k]$ or $l_{\ell i} = \emptyset$. Note that, unlike X_{pn}, $X_{p\ell}$ allows the left link type identifier in a pair to be null. Such a pair of link type identifiers is only specified when a user wishes to select web tuples that have additional links between two existing nodes. In this case the link is represented by a new type identifier. As such an identifier did not exist in the original web table, the left-hand side of the pair is set to null. Similar to X_{pn}, if $l_{\ell i}$ is a free link type identifier then $l_{\ell i} \neq r_{\ell i}$ and $r_{\ell i}$ is bound. Furthermore, two pairs $(l_{\ell 1}, r)$ and $(l_{\ell 2}, r)$ can coexist in $X_{p\ell}$ if $l_{\ell 1} \neq l_{\ell 2}$. Also, if $(\emptyset, r) \in X_{p\ell}$ then r can be bound or free. However, if $(l, r) \in X_{p\ell}$ where l is bound or free then r is always bound. Observe that in X_{pn}, r is always bound, but such is not always the case for X_{pl}. For example, the following are valid sets of pairs of link type identifiers in the selection schema.

$$\{(\mathsf{e}, \mathsf{e}), (\emptyset, \mathsf{f})\}$$
$$\{(\text{-}_1, \mathsf{e}), (\emptyset, \text{-}_3)\}$$

The first expression specifies that the selection constraints are imposed on the link type identifier e in the input web table. Since this identifier is bound, the nominal identifier remains unchanged in the selection schema. Also there is the new link type identifier f between two node type identifiers in W (the node type identifiers are specified in the *connectivity component*). In the second expression, selection constraints are imposed on the free node type identifier -_1 in W. Hence the nominal identifier is now replaced by the bound node type identifier e. Furthermore, similar to the previous expression there is a new link type identifier -_3. Observe that in this case the new link type identifier is free.

Observe that the components X_{pn} and $X_{p\ell}$ are different from the corresponding components X_n and X_ℓ in a web schema. X_n and X_ℓ contain only sets of node and link type identifiers whereas X_{pn} and $X_{p\ell}$ contain pairs of these identifiers. Also, X_n is a nonempty set whereas X_{pn} can be an empty set in $\Re$. Later we justify the need to specify pairs of identifiers in the selection schema.

Set of Simple Connectivities

The set of simple connectivities C_r is in DNF in the selection schema. These connectivities express the hyperlink structure of the node type identifiers involved in the web select operation. Let $k = x\langle \ell \rangle y$ be a connectivity C_r. Then there must exist selection constraints on x, ℓ, or y in the form of predicates. That is, $x \in left(X_{pn})$, $y \in left(X_{pn})$, or $\ell \in (left(X_{p\ell}) \cup right(X_{p\ell}))$. Note that specifying a set of simple connectivities is not always mandatory in $\Re$. Hence the set of connectivities in $\Re$ may be empty. However, if there exists $(\emptyset, b) \in X_{p\ell}$ then there must exist a connectivity k in C_r such that $link(k) = b$. This is to represent the location of the new link type identifiers in selected web tuples. The identifier b represents the instances of the new link objects in the selected web tuples. Hence there must exist k to express the pair of nodes in the tuples connected by a link of type b. Note that due to the nature of connectivities there is a constraint on k containing the new link type identifier. If $link(k) = b$ then $rnode(k) \neq lnode(k)$. That is, the left and right node type identifiers cannot be identical. For instance, consider the web table in Example 7.18. Suppose we specify a new link type identifier in the select condition as $y\langle s \rangle y$. This is ambiguous due to the existence of more than one identifier of type y in the connectivities of the schemas. It does not clearly specify which pair of nodes an instance of t must connect.

Set of Predicates

The set of predicates P_r in $\Re$ specifies the additional metadata, content, or structural constraints imposed on the web tuples. The existence of predicates on the node and link type identifiers over which selection constraints have been defined depends on the nature of the identifiers in X_{pn} or $X_{p\ell}$. First, if (a, a) is a pair in X_{pn} or $X_{p\ell}$ then there must exist a set of predicates $P_a \subseteq P_r$ such that for each $p_a \in P_a$, $arg(p_a) = a$. Clearly, as a is a bound identifier in W, $\Re$ must contain a set of predicates to capture the additional constraints imposed on a. Second, if (l, r) is a pair such that l is free then there may not be any predicate on r in the selection schema. When $r \in X_n$ then there may not be any additional predicates in P_r as the predicates on r defined in the schemas of the input web tables may be imposed on l. However, if $r \notin X_n$ then there must be a set of predicates defined over r in the selection schema. Finally, if $(\emptyset, b) \in X_{pi}$ then there must exist a predicate set $P_b \in P_r$ if b is bound and $b \notin X_\ell = (X_{\ell 1} \cup X_{\ell 2} \cup \ldots \cup X_{\ell |S|})$. If $b \in X_\ell$ then there may not exist any predicate. Lastly, if b is free then obviously there cannot be any predicate in P_r whose argument is b.

Naively, it may seem that specifying the left node and link type identifiers in X_{pn} and $X_{p\ell}$ is superfluous. That is, the selection constraints can be expressed by specifying only sets of node and link type identifiers and corresponding connectivities involving these identifiers. The equivalence of node and link type identifiers in $\Re$ and $S_i \in S$ can be established by inspecting the connectivities in C_r and matching them against the connectivities C_i in S_i. For example, suppose $C \equiv x\langle e \rangle \#_1 \wedge \#_1 \langle f \rangle y$ is a set of connectivities of a web table. Suppose we wish to select those web tuples in this web table that satisfy some conditions defined on the node type identifier $\#_1$. If we ignore explicit specification of node type identifiers over which selection constraints are defined, i.e., $\#_1$, then the selection schema will contain only a set of node type identifiers in lieu of a set of pairs of identifiers. Let the components of the selection schema be $X_{pn} = \{s\}$, $X_{p\ell} = \emptyset$, $C_r \equiv x\langle e \rangle s$, and $P_r = \{p(s)\}$. Observe that from this schema it is easy to determine that s represents the identifier $\#_1$ by matching the connectivity $x\langle e \rangle s$ against C. Hence specifying $X_{pn} = \{(\#_1, s)\}$ is superfluous. However, this may not always be true. We depict a situation when such equivalence mapping is not practical.

Consider a web table with connectivity $C \equiv x\langle -_1 \rangle \#_1 \wedge \#_1 \langle -_2 \rangle \#_2 \wedge \#_2 \langle -_3 \rangle \#_3 \wedge \#_3 \langle -_4 \rangle y$. Suppose the selection schema over this web table is $X_{pn} = \{a, b\}$, $X_{p\ell} = \{e\}$, $C_r \equiv a\langle e \rangle b$, and $P_r = \{p(a), p(b), p(e)\}$. Note that in this case $a\langle e \rangle b$ can be mapped to $\#_1 \langle -_2 \rangle \#_2$ in C. It can also be mapped to $\#_2 \langle -_3 \rangle \#_3$. The selection schema does not precisely specify this. In order to specify this condition it is necessary for the user to specify additional connectivities in C_r so that C_r can be uniquely mapped to C. For instance, if we say $C_r \equiv x\langle -_1 \rangle a \wedge a\langle e \rangle b$ then it is clear a, b, and e are equivalent to the identifiers $\#_1$, $\#_2$, and $-_2$, respectively. This may be easily determined for schemas with lesser numbers of connectivities, but as the size of the connectivity grows in the input web table such precise specification requires significant cognitive overhead. However, if we specify $X_{pn} = \{(\#_1, a), (\#_2, b)\}$ and $X_{p\ell} = \{(-_2, e)\}$ then it is clear that we are referring to the connectivity $\#_1 \langle -_2 \rangle \#_2$ in C. Hence we believe that specifying sets of pairs of node and link type identifiers in the selection schema simplifies the imposition of selection constraints. We now illustrate selection schemas with a few examples.

Example 8.1. We begin with a simple example of a selection schema. Consider the web table in Example 7.18. The set of web tuples of this table is depicted in Figure 6.3. Suppose we wish to select those web tuples in Figure 6.3 in which the instance of y contains the keyword "delirium". Such a selection condition on the node type identifier y can be expressed by the following selection schema. Let $\Re = \langle X_{pn}, X_{p\ell}, C_r, P_r \rangle$ be the selection schema such that $X_{pn} = \{(y, y)\}$, $X_{p\ell} = \emptyset$, $C_r \equiv \emptyset$ and $P_r = \{p(y)\}$ where

$$p(y) \equiv \texttt{CONTENT::y[html(.\%)+]\ NON-ATTR\_CONT}$$
$$\texttt{":BEGIN\_WORD: + delirium + :END\_WORD:"}$$

Observe that in this case the selection constraints are imposed on the node type identifier only. ∎

Example 8.2. Consider the query in Example 7.24. Such a selection criterion on the link type identifier t can be expressed by the selection condition $\Phi = \langle M, \Re \rangle$, where $M = \{S_d, S_f, S_g\}$ and $\Re = \langle X_{pn}, X_{p\ell}, C_r, P_r \rangle$, where $X_{pn} = \emptyset$, $X_{p\ell} = \{(t, t)\}$, $C_r \equiv \emptyset$, and $P_r = \{p(t)\}$, where

$$p(t) \equiv \texttt{CONTENT::t[A]\ NON-ATTR\_CONT\ ":BEGIN\_WORD: + product + :END\_WORD:"}$$

Observe that in this case the selection constraint is imposed on a link type identifier. ∎

Example 8.3. Consider the web table in Example 7.21. The set of web tuples of this table is depicted in Figure 7.2(a). Observe that the web table has two simple web schemas S_{eq} and S_2. S_{eq} binds the first three web tuples in Figure 7.2(a) and the schema S_2 binds the last web tuple. Suppose we wish to select those web tuples that satisfy the following conditions.

- Instances of $\#_1$ and $\#_2$ must contain the keyword "air pollution" as a list item.
- There must exist a link from an instance of $\#_1$ and $\#_2$ to a node object of type x.

These constraints can be expressed by the following selection schema. Let $\Re = \langle X_{pn}, X_{p\ell}, C_r, P_r \rangle$ be the selection schema such that $X_{pn} = \{(\#_1, y), (\#_2, y)\}$, $X_{p\ell} = \{(\emptyset, -)\}$, $C_r \equiv y\langle - \rangle x$, and $P_r = \{p(y)\}$, where

$$p(y) \equiv \texttt{CONTENT::y[html(.\%)+.ul.li] NON-ATTR\_CONT}$$
$$\texttt{":BEGIN\_STR: + air pollution + :END\_STR:"}$$

Observe that in this case, the selection constraints are imposed on the node and link type identifiers, and connectivities. The selected web table consists of a single web tuple as shown in Figure 8.1. ∎

8.3.5 Selection Condition Conformity

Finally, we discuss the *conformity* of a selection condition. That is, given a selection condition Φ, what are the constraints a web tuple t in a web table W must satisfy to conform to the selection condition. Let $\Phi = \langle M, \Re \rangle$ be the selection condition where $\Re = \langle X_{pn}, X_{p\ell}, C_r, P_r \rangle$. Let $W = \langle N, \mathcal{P} \rangle$ be a web table. Let $t \in T$ be a web tuple in W, where $T = T_1 \cup T_2 \cup \ldots \cup T_{|\mathcal{P}|}$, $U_i \in \mathcal{P}$, and $U_i = \langle S_i, T_i \rangle$. Let $t \in T_i$. Then t conforms to Φ, denoted by $t \dashv \Phi$, if the following conditions are true.

1. S_i must be an element in M; i.e., $S_i \in M$. Note that this condition checks whether the schema of the tuple t is specified in M.
2. The schema S_i must *conform* to the selection schema $\Re$. We say that $S_i = \langle X_{ni}, X_{\ell i}, C_i, P_i \rangle$ conforms to $\Re = \langle X_{pn}, X_{p\ell}, C_r, P_r \rangle$, denoted by $S_i \dashv \Re$, if any one of the following conditions is true.
   - $X_{ni} \cap left(X_{pn}) \neq \emptyset$;
   - $X_{\ell i} \cap left(X_{p\ell}) \neq \emptyset$;
   - If $\exists k = n_1 \langle \ell \rangle n_2$ in C_r s.t $(\emptyset, \ell) \in X_{p\ell}$ then there exist $(n_1, n_2) \in X_{ni}$.
   Observe that this condition checks if the hyperlink structure of the schema S_i matches the structure of selection schema $\Re$.
3. t conforms to a simple schema $S_{sj} \in \mathcal{S}_s$, i.e., $t \dashv S_{sj}$, where $\mathcal{S}_s$ is a set of simple web schemas generated by integrating $\Re$ with S_i and $0 < j \leq |\mathcal{S}_s|$.

In the next section we show how these three conditions are used to generate the selected web table.

8.3.6 Select Table Generation

In this section we show how to generate the selected web table. We first provide a brief overview of the table generation process. Then we formally describe the algorithm for generating the web tuples and schemas of the selected web table.

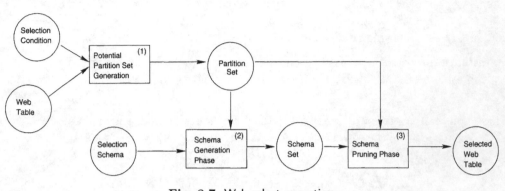

Fig. 8.7. Web select operation.

Overview

Given a selection condition $\Phi = \langle M, \Re \rangle$ and a web table $W = \langle N, \mathcal{P} \rangle$, the web select operation generates a web table $W_s = \langle N_s, \mathcal{P}_s \rangle$ by extracting a set of web tuples $T_s \subseteq T$ in W that satisfy Φ. This process of generation of the selected web table can be best described by the following three phases: the *potential partition set generation*, *schema generation*, and *schema pruning phase*. We now describe each of these phases in turn. Figure 8.7 depicts the schematic overview of these phases.

Potential Partition Set Generation Phase

This phase takes as input the selection condition Φ and the web table $W = \langle N, \mathcal{P} \rangle$ and returns as output a set of partitions $\mathcal{P}' \subseteq \mathcal{P}$. The objective of this phase is to identify those partitions in W that may contain tuples conforming to Φ.

Recall that a web table consists of a set of partitions $\mathcal{P}$. Each partition $U_i \in \mathcal{P}$ consists of a simple web schema S_i and a set of web tuples T_i that conform to S_i. Hence, to extract a subset of web tuples from W, it is judicious to first identify the set of potential partitions in W that may contain the selected web tuples, instead of directly inspecting all the web tuples in W to determine those that conform to Φ. Note that the identification of the potential partition set can be performed by inspecting the schemas only (without looking into the web tuples). This is possible because tuples in a partition U_i may satisfy the selection condition only if the S_i conform to $\Re$ but not necessarily vice versa.

This phase can be explained in stages, beginning with the identification of the *solution space* of the potential partition set. By solution space, we mean the set of partitions in W from which the potential partition set is selected. When $M = \mathcal{S}$, the solution space is all the partitions in W, i.e., $\mathcal{P}$. However, when $M \neq \mathcal{S}$ then the set of partitions in W that constitute the solution space are the ones whose schema $S_i \in M$. Hence partitions containing the schemas in M form the solution space. Subsequently, the identification of the potential partition set is performed by inspecting only the partitions whose schemas are in M. Also note that the identification of the solution space implies the satisfaction of the first conformity condition in Section 8.3.5. The second stage of this phase is the selection of a set of potential partitions from the solution space that may contain web tuples that satisfy the selection schema. Specifically, this stage checks the second conformity condition in Section 8.3.5. For each schema S_i in the solution space we determine whether it conforms to $\Re$ by evaluating the conditions in Section 8.3.5. If $S_i \dashv \Re$, then the partition is inserted into the potential partition set $\mathcal{P}'$.

Observe that at this point we have only identified a set of partitions $\mathcal{P}'$ in $\mathcal{P}$ that may contain web tuples that satisfy the selection condition. However, this does not necessarily indicate that each partition contains such tuples. There may exist a partition in which none of the tuples satisfies Φ. However, the set of tuples in W conforming to Φ is definitely contained in these partitions. Formally, let $\mathcal{P}' \in \mathcal{P}$ be the potential set of partitions such that the web schema S_i' in each partition $U_i' \in \mathcal{P}'$ conforms to $\Re$, $S_i' \dashv \Re$, and $T_s \subseteq T'$, where $T' = T_1' \cup T_2' \cup \ldots T_{|\mathcal{P}'|}'$ and for each $t_s \in T_s$ the following is true; $t_s \dashv \Phi$.

Note that at the end of this phase the partitions $\mathcal{P}'$ conform to the first two conditions in Section 8.3.5. That is, each schema in $\mathcal{P}'$ is contained in M and conforms to the selection schema $\Re$.

Schema Generation Phase

This phase is executed only if the set of potential partitions $\mathcal{P}'$ is nonempty. In this phase we generate the set of *possible* schemas of the selected web table by combining the selection schema $\Re$ with the schemas in $\mathcal{P}'$. In this phase the partition set $\mathcal{P}'$ generated in the preceding phase is given as input along with the selection schema $\Re$. The output of this phase is a nonempty set of simple web schemas S_s' generated by combining $\Re$ with S_i' for $i \leq |\mathcal{P}'|$. Observe that the generation of S_s' does not involve inspection of web tuples in $\mathcal{P}'$. Also note that a simple schema S_i' in a partition $U_i' \in \mathcal{P}'$, when combined with $\Re$ may generate more than one simple web schema. This is because the set of connectivities in $\Re$ may be in DNF. Hence each set of connectivities in conjunction with each other will generate a simple web schema. Consequently, the number of simple schemas generated during this phase may be greater than the size of the partition set $\mathcal{P}'$. That is, $|S_s'| \geq |\mathcal{P}'|$.

Also notice that some of the simple schemas in S_S' may be noisy; i.e., they may not bind any web tuples. This is because the simple schemas are generated by inspecting the schemas in $\mathcal{P}'$ only, not by comparing the web tuples with the selection schema. We elaborate on the procedure of generating the set of simple schemas in the next subsection. Formally, let $U_i' = \langle S_i', T_i' \rangle$ be a partition in $\mathcal{P}'$. Then the schema generation phase generates a set of simple schemas $S_{si}' \subseteq S_s'$ by combining S_i' with $\Re \ \forall \ i \in [1, |\mathcal{P}'|]$. At the end of this phase we get a set of simple web schemas $S_s' = S_{s1}' \cup S_{s2}' \cup \ldots \cup S_{s|\mathcal{P}'|}'$.

Observe that this phase is similar to the schema decomposition process discussed in Chapter 7. Recall that in the schema decomposition process a complex web schema is decomposed to a set of simple web schemas. In this case a simple web schema while combining with the selection schema is decomposed into a set of simple web schemas. Both these phases are performed without looking at the data instances, i.e., web tuples.

Schema Pruning Phase

Finally, in this phase we construct the partitions of the selected web table. This phase is identical to the schema pruning operation described in Chapter 7. Hence we do not discuss this in detail. It takes as input the set of simple web schemas S'_s generated in the preceding phase along with the partitions $\mathcal{P}'$ and produces as output the web table containing the set of schemas $S_s \subseteq S'_s$ and web tuples $T_s \subseteq T'$ by eliminating noisy schemas and reducing overlapping partitions to non-overlapping ones. Observe that each web tuple $t_s \in T_s$ satisfies the selection condition Φ and conforms to a schema in S_s. Formally, this phase generates a web table $W_s = \langle N_s, \mathcal{P}_s \rangle$ such that $U_{si} \in \mathcal{P}_s$, $U_{si} = \langle S_{si}, T_{si} \rangle \ \forall \ i \in [1, |\mathcal{P}_s|]$, where $S_{si} \in S'_s$, $T_{si} \subseteq T'$. Observe that this phase evaluates the last conformity condition in Section 8.3.5; i.e., $t \dashv S_{si}$.

Next, we discuss the formal algorithm of the web select operation.

Algorithm Select

Given the selection condition $\Phi = \langle M, \Re \rangle$ where $\Re = \langle X_{pn}, X_{p\ell}, C_r, P_r \rangle$ and web table $W = \langle N, \mathcal{P} \rangle$ as input, the algorithm Select generates a web table $W_s = \langle N_s, \mathcal{P}_s \rangle$ by extracting tuples from W that satisfy Φ. The algorithm Select combines all the three phases discussed in the preceding section to create the selected web table. It scans the relevant set of partitions (partitions containing the schemas in M) once to identify the potential partition set and generates the partitions of the selected web table. Note that the generation of partitions involves creation of schemas of W_s and extraction of web tuples from W. The pseudocode for the algorithm is shown in Figure 8.8. We first elaborate on these steps to highlight the implementation of the three phases and then illustrate the execution of this algorithm with an example.

Steps (1) to (4) in Figure 8.8 first generate the sets of node and link type identifiers involved in the web select operation by inspecting the selection schema $\Re$. Let L_n and L_ℓ be the sets of node and link type identifiers over which certain selection constraints are imposed. Specifically, L_n represents the set of node type identifiers in X_{pn} that are on the left-hand side in each pair. Recall that the left identifier in each pair in X_{pn} represents the node type identifiers over which some selection constraints are imposed. Similarly, L_ℓ contains the link type identifiers in $X_{p\ell}$ that occur on the left-hand side of each pair. Note that L_ℓ excludes all pairs in $X_{p\ell}$ whose left identifier is null, i.e., pairs that represent the specification of new link type identifiers. Finally, the set L_{link} denotes link type identifiers that are new and N_{link} is a set of pair of node type identifiers where each pair is connected by a link type identifier in L_{link}. To elaborate further, if a is a new link type identifier such that $(\emptyset, a) \in X_{p\ell}$ and $x\langle a \rangle y$ is a connectivity in C_r, then a is stored in L_{link} and (x, y) is inserted in N_{link}.

Next the algorithm proceeds to identify a potential partition set from W. To determine whether a partition $U_i \in \mathcal{P}$ is to be included in the potential partition set, each partition in W that contains a schema in M is inspected (Steps (5) to (9)). A partition $U_i = \langle S_i, T_i \rangle$ is included in the potential partition set if there is an

Input: Selection condition $\Phi = \langle M, \Re \rangle$ where $\Re = \langle X_{pn}, X_{p\ell}, C_r, P_r \rangle$,
Web table $W = \langle N, \mathcal{P} \rangle$, selected table name N_s.
   Output: Selected web table $W_s = \langle N_s, \mathcal{P}_s \rangle$.

(1)   Let $L_n = \{l_{n1}, l_{n2}, \ldots, l_{n|X_{pn}|}\}$ where $l_{ni} \in left(X_{pn}) \ \forall \ i \in [1, |X_{pn}|]$
(2)   Let $L_\ell = \{l_{\ell 1}, l_{\ell 2}, \ldots, l_{\ell t}\}$ where $l_{\ell i} \in left(X_{p\ell})$ for $i \in [1, |X_{p\ell}|]$
(3)   Let $L_{link} \subseteq right(X_{p\ell})$ s.t for each $\ell \in L_{link}$ there $\exists \ (\emptyset, \ell) \in X_{p\ell}$;
(4)   Let $N_{link} \subseteq X_n$ s.t for each $(n_1, n_2) \in N_{link}$ there $\exists \ n_1'\langle \ell \rangle n_2' \in C_r$ and $\ell \in L_{link}$
        s.t $n_v = n_v'$ if $(l, n_v) \notin X_{pn}$ and $n_v = l$ otherwise for $v \in [1, 2]$;
(5)   for $(i = 1$ to $|M|)$ {
(6)   Let $S_i \in M$ and $U_i = \langle S_i = \langle X_{ni}, X_{\ell i}, C_i, P_i \rangle, T_i \rangle$ where $U_i \in \mathcal{P}$;
(7) $L_{ni} = X_{ni} \cap L_n$; /* Potential Partition Set Generation Phase */
(8) $L_{\ell i} = X_{\ell i} \cap L_\ell$;
(9) $N_i = N_{link} \cap X_{ni}$;
(10)   if $(L_{ni} \neq \emptyset$ or $L_{\ell i} \neq \emptyset$ or $N_i \neq \emptyset)$ {
(11)   Let $C_r \equiv C_{r1} \vee C_{r2} \vee \ldots \vee C_{rj}$;
(12)   if $(j > 0)$ /* Schema Generation Phase */
(13) $S_{si} = \mathbf{GenerateSchemaSet}(\Re, L_{ni}, L_{\ell i}, L_{link})$; /* Figure 8.9 */
(14)   else { /* When no connectivity is specified in $\Re$ */
(15)   Let R_{ni} is a set of node type identifiers s.t each $r \in R_{ni}$ satisfies
                       $(l, r) \in X_{pn}$ where $l \in L_{ni}$;
(16)   Let $R_{\ell i}$ is a set of link type identifiers s.t each $r \in R_{\ell i}$ satisfies
                       $(\ell, r) \in X_{p\ell}$ where $\ell \in L_{\ell i}$;
(17) $X_{ns_i} = (X_{ni} - L_{ni}) \cup R_{ni}$;
(18) $X_{\ell s_i} = (X_{\ell i} - L_{\ell i}) \cup R_{\ell i}$;
(19)   for $(a = 1$ to $|C_i|)$ { /* Connectivity set generation */
(20)   if $((lnode(k_a) \in L_{ni}) \wedge (\exists \ r_n$ s.t. $(lnode(k_a), r_n) \in X_{pn}))$
(21)   Replace $lnode(k_a)$ with r_n;
(22)   if $((rnode(k_a) \in L_{ni}) \wedge (\exists \ r_n$ s.t. $(rnode(k_a), r_n) \in X_{pn}))$
(23)   Replace $rnode(k_a)$ with r_n;
(24)   if $((link(k_a) \in L_{\ell i}) \wedge (\exists \ r_\ell$ s.t. $(link(k_a), r_\ell) \in X_{p\ell}))$
(25)   Replace $link(k_a)$ with r_ℓ;
(26)   insert k_a in C_{si};
(27)   }
(28)   for $(b = 1$ to $|X_{ns_i} \cup X_{\ell s_i}|)$ { /* Predicate set generation. */
(29)   if $(x_b \in (X_{ns_i} \cup X_{\ell s_i})$ is bound) {
(30)   Generate predicate set P_b where for each $p_b \in P_b$, $p_b \in (P_i \cup P_r)$
                               and $arg(p_b) = x_b$;
(31)   Insert P_b in P_{si};
(32)   }
(33)   }
(34)   Insert $S_{s_i} = \langle X_{ns_i}, X_{\ell s_i}, C_{si}, P_{si} \rangle$ in S_{si};
(35)   }
(36) $\mathcal{P}_{si} = \mathbf{Partition}(S_{si}, T_i)$; /* Schema Pruning Phase */
(37)   Insert $\mathcal{P}_{si}$ in $\mathcal{P}_s$;
(38)   }
(39)   else
(40)   ; /* This partition does not contain any selected tuple */
(41)   }
(42)   Return $W_s = \langle N_s, \mathcal{P}_s \rangle$;

Fig. 8.8. Algorithm Select.

overlap between the node and link type identifiers in S_i (X_{ni} and $X_{\ell i}$) with those in L_n, L_ℓ, or N_{link}. Steps (7) to (9) in Figure 8.8 compute these overlaps (denoted by L_{ni}, $L_{\ell i}$, and N_i, respectively). If any one of these sets of identifiers is not empty then it indicates that there exists a type identifier in S_i which is involved in the web select operation (Step 10). If so, then the algorithm proceeds to generate the set of simple schemas by combining S_i with $\Re$ (Steps (11) to (35)).

The generation of these simple schemas involves inspection of connectivities C_r in $\Re$. If the selection schema $\Re$ does not contain any connectivity then the simple schema is generated simply by replacing the node and link type identifiers in S_i with the corresponding identifiers in R_{ni} and $R_{\ell i}$ (Steps (14) to (34)). Also the node and link type identifiers in C_i are replaced (Steps (19) to (25)). Note that in this case there is no new connectivity added since $C_r \equiv \emptyset$. Finally, the set of predicates for the simple schema is generated by combining the predicates in $\Re$ and P_i (Steps (28) to (33)). Note that only those predicates in $\Re$ whose arguments are in X_{ns_i} or $X_{\ell s_i}$ are considered. Finally, the schema $S_{s_i} = \langle X_{ns_i}, X_{\ell s_i}, C_{si}, P_{si} \rangle$ is inserted in the schema set $\mathcal{S}_{si}$.

However, if $\Re$ contains a set of simple connectivities in DNF, i.e., $C_r \equiv C_{r1} \vee C_{r2} \vee \ldots \vee C_{rj}$, then one or more simple web schemas may generate while integrating in S_i and $\Re$. The steps to create these schemas are encapsulated in the construct **GenerateSchemaSet**. The pseudocode of this construct is depicted in Figure 8.9.

The generation of the potential set of simple schemas involves the following steps. First, it is necessary to determine if each set of conjunctive connectivities in C_r can be mapped to a set of simple connectivities in C_i. Since the connectivities in C_r may contain new link or node type identifiers, it is necessary to check if each conjunctive connectivity in C_r matches a connectivity structure in C_i. This is achieved by replacing the new identifier in C_r with its corresponding old value (Steps (3) to (17) in Figure 8.9). Then the algorithm checks whether the set of connectivities generated (denoted as C_{tmp}) is contained in C_{ra}; i.e., $C_{tmp} \subseteq C_{ra}$ (Step (23)). Note that connectivities in C_{ra} that contain link type identifiers in L_{link} are ignored in C_{tmp}. For such link type identifiers the corresponding pair of node type identifiers connecting each link type identifier is stored in N_{tmp}. Now a conjunctive connectivity set in C_r matches C_i if $C_{tmp} \subseteq C_i$ and the pairs N_{tmp} are contained in X_{ni} (Step (23)). If so then the components of the schema S_{si} are generated (Steps (24) to (35)) and inserted in the schema set $\mathcal{S}_{si}$. After the termination of the outer for loop in Figure 8.9, the algorithm generates a set of simple schemas $\mathcal{S}_{si}$ by integrating $\Re$ and S_i which may bind a set of web tuples in T_i.

Finally, the schema pruning process begins to generate a set of nonoverlapping partitions of the selected web table (Steps (36) and (37)). Since we have described the algorithm for schema pruning in Chapter 7, we do not elaborate this any further. We augment the algorithm to prune a set of simple schemas and a set of web tuples with identical fragment size. The outer for loop in Figure 8.8 is executed for each schema in M and finally the selected web table is generated at the termination of this for loop.

Input: Selection schema $\Re$ where $\Re = \langle X_{pn}, X_{p\ell}, C_r, P_r \rangle$, simple schema S_i, sets of node and link type identifiers L_{ni}, $L_{\ell i}$ and set of new link type identifiers L_{link}.
Output: Set of simple web schemas S_{si}.

```
(1)    Let C_r ≡ C_{r1} ∨ C_{r2} ∨ ... ∨ C_{rj};
(2)    for (a = 1 to j) { /* Each set of conjunctive connectivities */
(3)        for (b = 1 to |C_{ra}|) { /* Simple connectivities in each set */
(4)            Insert lnode(k_b), rnode(k_b) in N_b;
(5)            Insert link(k_b) in L_b;
(6)            if ((lnode(k_b) ∉ L_{ni}) ∧ (∃ l s.t. (l, lnode(k_b)) ∈ X_{pn} and l ∈ L_{ni}))
(7)                Replace lnode(k_b) with l;
(8)            if ((rnode(k_b) ∉ L_{ni}) ∧ (∃ l s.t. (l, rnode(k_b)) ∈ X_{pn} and l ∈ L_{ni}))
(9)                Replace rnode(k_b) with l;
(10)           if (link(k_b) ∉ L_{ℓi}) ∧ (∃ℓ s.t (ℓ, link(k_b)) ∈ X_{pℓ})) {
(11)               if (ℓ = ∅) {
(12)                   Insert (n_1, n_2) in N_{tmp} s.t (n_1, lnode(k_b)) ∈ X_{pn} or n_1 ∈ X_{ni}
                       and (n_2, lnode(k_b)) ∈ X_{pn} or n_2 ∈ X_{ni}
(13)                   flag = 1;
(14)               }
(15)               else if (∃ ℓ s.t. (ℓ, link(k_b)) ∈ X_{pℓ} and ℓ ∈ L_{ℓi})
(16)                   Replace link(k_b) with ℓ;
(17)           }
(18)           if (flag = 0)
(19)               Insert k_b in connectivity set C_{tmp};
(20)           else
(21)               flag = 0;
(22)       }
(23)       if (C_{tmp} ⊆ C_i and N_{tmp} ⊆ X_{ni}) {
(24)           C' = C_i − C_{tmp};
(25)           for (d = 1 to |C'|) {
(26)               Execute steps (20) to (25) of Figure 8.8;
(27)               Insert lnode(k_d), rnode(k_d) in N_b;
(28)               Insert link(k_d) in L_b;
(29)           }
(30)           C_{si} ≡ C' ∧ C_r; /* Generation of schema components */
(31)           X_{ns_i} = N_b;
(32)           X_{ℓs_i} = L_b;
(33)           Generate P_{si} by executing steps (28) to (33) of Figure 8.8;
(34)           Insert S_{si} = ⟨X_{ns_i}, X_{ℓs_i}, C_{si}, P_{si}⟩ in S_{si};
(35)       }
(36)   } /* End of for loop */
(37)   Return S_{si};
```

Fig. 8.9. Algorithm for **GenerateSchemaSet**.

Example 8.4. Consider the web table in Figure 7.2(a) in Chapter 7. The schemas S_{eq} and S_2 of the web table are depicted in Example 7.21. Consider the selection condition in Example 8.3. The steps to generate the selected web table based on this selection condition are as follows.

1. From Steps (1) to (4) in Figure 8.8, we get the sets: $L_n = \{\#_1, \#_2\}$, $L_\ell = \{\emptyset\}$, $L_{link} = \{\text{-}\}$, and $N_{link} = \{(x, \#_1), (x, \#_2)\}$.

2. Since $M = \{S_{eq}, S_2\}$ the for loop in Step (5) is executed twice. For $i = 1$, $U_1 = \langle S_{eq}, T_1 \rangle$, where $T_1 = \{t_4\}$, $X_{n1} = \{x, \#_1\}$, $X_{\ell 1} = \{s\}$, and $C_1 \equiv x\langle s \rangle \#_1$.

3. Therefore, after executing Steps (7) to (9), we get $L_{n1} = \{x, \#_1\} \cap \{\#_1, \#_2\} = \{\#_1\}$, $L_{\ell 1} = \emptyset$, and $N_i = \{x, \#_1\}$.

4. Since $L_{n1} \neq \emptyset$ and $N_1 \neq \emptyset$, the if condition in Step (10) is evaluated true and the Steps (11) to (35) are executed.

5. As $C_r \equiv y\langle\text{-}\rangle x$, $j = 1$. Therefore the condition in Step (12) is true and Step (13) is executed. Consequently, the algorithm in Figure 8.9 is executed as follows.

   a) As $j = 1$, the for loop in Step (2) is executed once. Again as $|C_{r1}| = 1$, the inner for loop is executed once too. After Steps (4) and (5), we get $N_b = \{x, y\}$ and $L_b = \{\text{-}\}$.

   b) Since $rnode(k_1) = x$, $lnode(k_1) = y$, $lnode(k_1) \notin L_{n1}$. Furthermore, $(\#_1, y) \in X_{pn}$ and $\#_1 \in L_{n1}$. Therefore the condition in Step (6) is evaluated true and Step (7) is executed. Thus after Step (7) $k_1 \equiv \#_1\langle\text{-}\rangle x$.

   c) Since $link(k_1) = \{\text{-}\}$ and $(\emptyset, \text{-}) \in X_{p\ell}$, the condition in Step (10) is evaluated true. Furthermore, as $\ell = \emptyset$, Steps (12) and (13) are executed. Consequently, $n_1 = \#_1$, $n_2 = x$. Therefore $N_{tmp} = \{\#_1, x\}$ and $flag = 1$.

   d) Since $flag = 1$, Step (21) is executed. Therefore $flag = 0$ and $C_{tmp} = \emptyset$.

   e) As $C_{tmp} \equiv \emptyset$ and $N_{tmp} = X_{n1}$, the condition in Step (23) is true and Steps (24) to (35) are executed.

   f) After Step (24), $C' \equiv \{x\langle s \rangle \#_1\} - \emptyset \equiv x\langle s \rangle \#_1$.

   g) The for loop in Step (25) is executed once as $d = 1$. As $k_1 \equiv x\langle s \rangle \#_1$, then $lnode(k_1) = x$, $rnode(k_1) = \#_1$, and $link(k_1) = s$. As $(\#_1, y) \in X_{pn}$, Step (22) in Figure 8.8 is evaluated true. Therefore $k_1 \equiv x\langle s \rangle y$.

   h) Therefore after Step (26) in Figure 8.9, $C' \equiv x\langle s \rangle y$.

   i) After the execution of Step (29), we get $N_b = \{x, y\}$ and $L_b = \{\text{-}, s\}$.

   j) Finally, the Steps (31) to (34) are executed to generate the schema $S_{s1} = \langle X_{ns_1}, X_{\ell s_1}, C_{s1}, P_{s1} \rangle$, where $X_{ns_1} = \{x, y\}$, $X_{\ell s_1} = \{s, \text{-}\}$, $C_{s1} \equiv x\langle s \rangle y \wedge y\langle\text{-}\rangle x$, and $P_{s1} = P_{eq} \cup \{p(y)\}$. S_{s1} is inserted in the schema set $\mathcal{S}_{s1}$ and returned.

6. Finally, the Steps (36) and (37) in Figure 8.8 are executed to generate the partition. S_{s1} is a noisy schema as t_4 does not conform to S_{s1} (the instance of $\#_1$ does not contain the string "air pollution"). Hence $\mathcal{P}_{s1} = \emptyset$.

7. Similarly, the for loop in Step (5) of Figure 8.8 is executed again for $S_2 = \langle X_{n2}, X_{\ell 2}, C_2, P_2 \rangle$. After the execution, we get the partition $\mathcal{P}_{s2} = \{U_1 = \{S_{s2}, T_{s2}\}$, where $X_{ns_2} = \{x, y\}$, $X_{\ell s_2} = \{\text{-}, s\}$, $C_2 \equiv x\langle s \rangle y \wedge y\langle\text{-}\rangle x$, and $P_{s2} = P_2 \cup \{p(y)\}$ and $T_{s2} = \{t_1'\}$ where t_1' is generated from the first web tuple t_1 in Figure 7.2(a) (it satisfies the schema S_{s2}); (Figure 8.1). Therefore $\mathcal{P}_s = \{\mathcal{P}_{s2}\}$.

8. The selected web table, denoted as $W_s = \langle N_s, \mathcal{P}_s \rangle$, consists of a single web tuple as shown in Figure 8.1. ∎

8.4 Web Project

Although it seems that it is advantageous to couple related information from the Web using the global web coupling operator, in many cases it may also couple irrelevant information. The existence of irrelevant information increases the size of the resultant web table. This adversely affects the storage and subsequent query processing cost of coupled Web data. The *web project* operation is used to eliminate these irrelevant nodes from the web table. It extracts portions of a web tuple in a web table satisfying certain conditions. Analogous to its relational counterpart, a web project operator is used to eliminate one or more node objects from a set of web tuples in a web table. It is used to isolate data of interest, allowing subsequent queries to run over smaller, perhaps more structured, Web data. We discuss this operator in detail now.

8.4.1 Definition

Given a web table $W = \langle N, \mathcal{U} \rangle$ and *project condition* τ, a web project on W computes a new web table $W_p = \langle N_p, \mathcal{U}_p \rangle$ containing some of the nodes of W. Formally, we define the web project as $W_p = \pi_\tau(W)$, where π is the web project operator and $\tau = \langle M, P_c \rangle$ is the project condition. The first component of τ, i.e., M, is similar to that in the selection condition in the web select operation. It specifies the set of tuples in W that are to be considered for the web project operation. M represents a subset of the set of simple schemas in W. Only those tuples in W that are bound by the schemas in M are evaluated by the web project operation. By default, M is set to S (the set of all schemas in W). The second component P_c is called *projection attributes* and specifies the set of nodes that are to be eliminated from the input web tuples. We discuss P_c in detail in the next section.

Note that, unlike relational project, the web project operation does not remove duplicate web tuples automatically. The projected collection of web tuples may contain identical web tuples. In this case, it is called a *web bag*. A web bag may be used in WHOWEDA to discover different types of knowledge from the user's query results (discussed in Chapter 11). The *web distinct* operator is used to eliminate duplicate web tuples from a web table. It removes all but one occurrence of a web tuple from a web table. We discuss web distinct in Section 8.5. Furthermore, in web project we specify the node type identifiers to be eliminated in the project conditions, as opposed to relational project, where we specify the attributes to be projected from a relation.

8.4.2 Projection Attributes

Projection attributes are expressed as node and link type identifiers and/or connectivities between the node type identifiers. A user may explicitly specify any combination of the five projection attributes discussed below to initiate a web project operation. Note that unless otherwise stated explicitly, M is assumed to be the set of all schemas in the input web table.

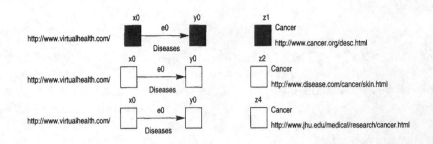

Fig. 8.10. Web table after removal of duplicate tuples.

Set of Node Type Identifiers

This is the most straightforward projection attribute. A user may specify a set of node type identifiers whose instances she may wish to eliminate from the web table. After the web project operations, the set of predicates and connectivities involving these node type identifiers is removed from the schema(s) of the projected web table. Moreover, the set of link type identifiers whose start or terminal is one of these node type identifiers is eliminated from the resultant schema(s). The projected web tuples contain only those instances of node type identifiers that are not included in the specified set. We specify this attribute by NODE_TYPE. The value of this attribute is a set of node type identifiers.

Start and End Bound Node Type Identifiers

A user may wish to eliminate all instances of node type identifiers between the instances of two bound node type identifiers. Specifying a projection attribute in this form has the following advantages.

- It is a more compact way of specifying a set of successive node type identifiers. Rather than specifying each individual node type identifier whose instances are to be eliminated, it is more compact to specify the start and end identifiers of these successive node identifiers.
- Due to the irregular structure of web schemas of a web table it may not always be possible to specify individual node type identifiers that are to be eliminated. This is because these identifiers may be free or they may not occur in all schemas of a web table. In such a situation, it is advantageous to specify the projection attributes using the notion of start and end node type identifiers. Instances of all node type identifiers between these two identifiers are eliminated from the projected web table.

We specify such projection attributes using START_NODE_TYPE and END_NODE_TYPE. The value of each of these attributes is a node type identifier. We illustrate this projection attribute with the following example.

Example 8.5. Consider the query in Example 6.10. The results (a set of web tuples) are stored in the web table Cancer as shown in Figure 6.10. The sets of web schemas for the web tuples in Cancer are as follows.

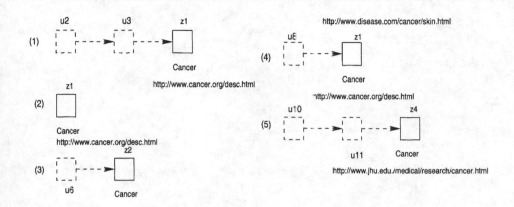

Fig. 8.11. Query results.

1. $S_a = \langle X_{n_a}, X_{\ell_a}, C_a, P_a \rangle$, where $X_{n_a} = \{x, y, z, \#_1, \#_2\}$, $X_{\ell_a} = \{e, f, -_1, -_2\}$, $C_a \equiv k_{a1} \wedge k_{a2} \wedge k_{a3} \wedge k_{a4}$, where $k_{a1} \equiv x\langle e\rangle y$, $k_{a2} \equiv y\langle f\rangle\#_1$, $k_{a3} \equiv \#_1\langle -_1\rangle\#_2$, $k_{a4} \equiv \#_2\langle -_2\rangle z$, and $P_a = P_1$.

2. $S_b = \langle X_{n_b}, X_{\ell_b}, C_b, P_b \rangle$, where $X_{n_b} = \{x, y, z, \#_1, \#_2, \#_3\}$, $X_{\ell_b} = \{e, f, -_1, -_2, -_3\}$, $C_b \equiv k_{b1} \wedge k_{b2} \wedge k_{b3} \wedge k_{b4} \wedge k_{b5}$, where $k_{b1} \equiv x\langle e\rangle y$, $k_{b2} \equiv y\langle f\rangle\#_1$, $k_{b3} \equiv \#_1\langle -_1\rangle\#_2$, $k_{b4} \equiv \#_2\langle -_2\rangle\#_3$, $k_{b5} \equiv \#_3\langle -_3\rangle z$, and $P_b = P_1$.

3. $S_c = \langle X_{n_c}, X_{\ell_c}, C_c, P_c \rangle$, where $X_{n_c} = \{x, y, z, \#_1, \#_2, \#_3, \#_4\}$, $X_{\ell_c} = \{e, f, -_1, -_2, -_5, -_4\}$, $C_c \equiv k_{c1} \wedge k_{c2} \wedge k_{c3} \wedge k_{c4} \wedge k_{c5} \wedge k_{c6}$, where $k_{c1} \equiv x\langle e\rangle y$, $k_{c2} \equiv y\langle f\rangle\#_1$, $k_{c3} \equiv \#_1\langle -_1\rangle\#_2$, $k_{c4} \equiv \#_2\langle -_2\rangle\#_3$, $k_{c5} \equiv \#_3\langle -_4\rangle\#_4$, $k_{c6} \equiv \#_4\langle -_5\rangle z$, and $P_c = P_1$.

Observe that the web tuples bound by S_a, S_b, and S_c are $\{t_2\}$, $\{t_3, t_4\}$, and $\{t_1, t_5\}$, respectively.

Suppose we wish to eliminate the nodes between the instances of y and z. This can be performed by the web project operation and the projection attribute/value is expressed as: START_NODE_TYPE $= \{y\}$ and END_NODE_TYPE $= \{z\}$. The set of web tuples resultant from the project operation is shown in Figure 8.2. Observe that in each web tuple the nodes between instances of y and z are eliminated from the result tuple. The schema of this set of web tuples, denoted as $S_p = \langle X_{n_p}, X_{\ell_p}, C_p, P_p \rangle$, is generated by manipulating the schemas of the web table **Cancer** as follows; $X_{n_p} = \{x, y, z\}$, $X_{\ell_p} = \{e\}$, $C_p \equiv x\langle e\rangle y$, and $P_p = P_1 - \{p_4(f)\}$. The projected web table (Figure 8.2) after the partition refinement operation consists of a single partition as follows.

- $U_p = \langle S_p = \langle X_{n_p}, X_{\ell_p}, C_p, P_p \rangle, T_p \rangle$, where $X_{n_p} = \{x, y, z\}$, $X_{\ell_p} = \{e\}$, $C_p \equiv k_{a_1}$, $P_p = \{p_1, p_2, p_3, p_5\}$, and $T_p = \{t_{p1}, t_{p2}, t_{p3}, t_{p4}, t_{p5}\}$. ∎

Node Type Identifier and Depth

In the previous attribute we have seen that we can specify conditions to eliminate a set of nodes between two instances of specified node type identifiers. Note that

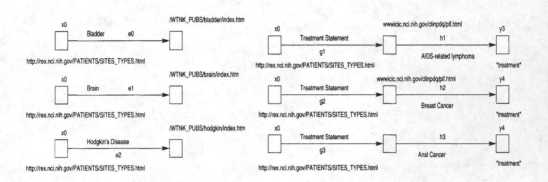

Fig. 8.12. Projected tuples.

the number of nodes between the specified instances of start and end node type identifiers may vary in different web tuples. Furthermore, we may not always wish to eliminate all these nodes but only some of them. We illustrate this with an example. Consider the web table **Cancer** in Figure 6.10. Suppose we wish to eliminate the nodes of type x and y, and also the first two free nodes in each web tuple. The projected web tuples are shown in Figure 8.11. Observe that the nodes following the free nodes may be free or bound of type z. For instance, the node following the first two free nodes in the second web tuple is of type z. However, for the remaining web tuples the following nodes are free. Hence it is not possible to use the START_NODE_TYPE and END_NODE_TYPE attributes to impose the specified projection attribute. In this case, we specify the attribute using the following attribute pair, START_NODE_TYPE or END_NODE_TYPE and DEPTH. The values of the attributes START_NODE_TYPE and END_NODE_TYPE are node type identifiers specifying the start or end node type identifier and the value of DEPTH is an integer that specifies the set of nodes to be eliminated within a certain depth of links from the specified node type identifier.

Example 8.6. In the above example, the projection attribute/value may be expressed as (START_NODE_TYPE = x, DEPTH = 3). The set of partitions generated from the web project operation is given below.

1. $U_{a1} = \langle S_{a1}, T_{a1} \rangle$, where $S_{a1} = \langle X_{n_{a1}}, X_{\ell_{a1}}, C_{a1}, P_a \rangle$, $X_{n_{a1}} = \{z\}$, $X_{\ell_{a1}} = \emptyset$, $C_{a1} = \emptyset$, and $P_{a1} = \{p_5\}$ and $T_{a1} = \{t_2\}$.
2. $U_{b1} = \langle S_{b1}, T_{b1} \rangle$, where $S_{b1} = \langle X_{n_{b1}}, X_{\ell_{b1}}, C_{b1}, P_{b1} \rangle$, $X_{n_{b1}} = \{z, \#_3\}$, $X_{\ell_{b1}} = \{-_3\}$, $C_{b1} \equiv \#_3\langle -_3 \rangle z$, and $P_{b1} = \{p_5\}$ and $T_{b1} = \{t_3, t_4\}$.
3. $U_{c1} = \langle S_{c1}, T_{c1} \rangle$, where $S_{c1} = \langle X_{n_{c1}}, X_{\ell_{c1}}, C_{c1}, P_{c1} \rangle$, $X_{n_{c1}} = \{z, \#_3, \#_4\}$, $X_{\ell_{c1}} = \{-_3, -_4\}$, $C_{c1} \equiv \#_3\langle -_3 \rangle \#_4 \wedge \#_4 \langle -_4 \rangle z$, and $P_{c1} = \{p_5\}$ and $T_{c1} = \{t_1, t_5\}$. ∎

Set of To-Link Type Identifiers

It is not always possible to specify node type identifiers that are to be eliminated from the projected web table simply because it may trigger elimination of instances of relevant node type identifiers. For instance, consider the web table in Example 7.18 of Chapter 7. If these web tuples are materialized in a web table then the schemas of the web table are as shown below.

1. $S_r = \langle X_{n_r}, X_{\ell_r}, C_r, P_r \rangle$, where

$$X_{n_r} = \{x, y, \#_1\},$$
$$X_{\ell_r} = \{e, f\},$$

$C_r \equiv k_{r1} \wedge k_{r2}$, where

$$k_{r1} \equiv x\langle e \rangle \#_1$$
$$k_{r2} \equiv \#_1 \langle f \rangle y$$

and $P_r = \{p_1, p_2, p_3, p_4\}$.

2. $S_t = \langle X_{n_t}, X_{\ell_t}, C_t, P_t \rangle$, where

$$X_{n_t} = \{x, y, \#_1\},$$
$$X_{\ell_t} = \{g, h\},$$

$C_t \equiv k_{t1} \wedge k_{t2}$, where

$$k_{t1} \equiv x\langle g \rangle \#_1$$
$$k_{t2} \equiv \#_1 \langle h \rangle y$$

and $P_t = \{p_1, p_2, p_5, p_6, p_7\}$.

Observe that the schema S_r binds the first three web tuples in Figure 6.3 and the remaining web tuples are bound by S_t.

Suppose we wish to eliminate those instances of y pointed to by links of type f. That is, we wish to eliminate the instances of y in the first three tuples in Figure 6.3. In this case, one may specify the projection attribute/value as TO_LINK_TYPE = $\{f\}$. The set of projected web tuples is shown in Figure 8.12. Observe that if we specify the projection attribute/value as NODE_TYPE = $\{y\}$, then the instances of y pointed to by links of type h will also be eliminated which is not desirable. However, we may prevent such elimination by specifying $M = \{S_x\}$, but in certain cases this may not be sufficient. Hence we allow users to specify link type identifiers that link to a set of node type identifiers which are to be eliminated by the web project operation. Such an attribute is specified using TO_LINK_TYPE. The value of this attribute is a set of link type identifiers. We illustrate this with an example.

Example 8.7. Consider the web project operation in the above example. In this case, one may specify the project condition as TO_LINK_TYPE = $\{f\}$. The set of projected web tuples is shown in Figure 8.12. Observe that the first three web tuples do not contain any instances of y and the last three web tuples are not modified during the project operation. The schemas of the web tuples, denoted by $S_{\pi r}$ and $S_{\pi t}$, are generated from S_r and S_t and are given below.

1. $S_{\pi r} = \langle X_{n_{\pi r}}, X_{\ell_{\pi r}}, C_{\pi r}, P_{\pi r} \rangle$, where $X_{n_{\pi r}} = \{x, \#_1\}$, $X_{\ell_{\pi r}} = \{e\}$, $C_{\pi r} \equiv x\langle e \rangle \#_1$, and $P_{\pi r} = P_r - \{p_2, p_3\}$.

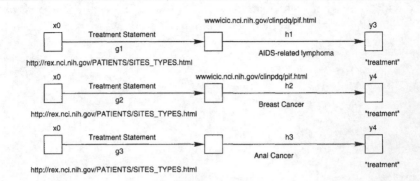

Fig. 8.13. Projected table.

2. $S_{\pi t} = \langle X_{n_{\pi t}}, X_{\ell_{\pi t}}, C_{\pi t}, P_{\pi t} \rangle$, where $X_{n_{\pi t}} = X_{n_t}$, $X_{\ell_{\pi t}} = X_{\ell_t}$, $C_{\pi t} = C_t$, and $P_{\pi t} = P_t$.

We discuss how the projected schemas and web tuples are generated in Section 8.4.3.   ∎

Set of From-Link Type Identifiers

Similar to the projection attribute involving to-link type identifiers, we may eliminate those instances of node type identifiers where one of the outgoing links is of the specified type. That is, if the specified link type identifier is ℓ, then according to this projection attribute nodes where one of the outgoing links is of type ℓ is eliminated by the web project operation. The motivation for such a projection attribute is similar to that of to-link type identifiers. We specify this attribute using FROM_LINK_TYPE. The value of this attribute is a set of link type identifiers.

Example 8.8. Reconsider the set of web tuples in Figure 6.3. Suppose we wish to eliminate the first three web tuples. Note that it is not possible to specify the node type identifiers in project condition as it will eliminate all the nodes in Figure 6.3. In this case, we can specify the project condition as TO_LINK_TYPE = $\{f\}$ and FROM_LINK_TYPE = $\{e, f\}$. The set of projected web tuples is shown in Figure 8.13. Observe that the first three web tuples in Figure 6.3 do not appear in the result. The schema of the projected web table is given as: $S_{\pi} = \langle X_{n_{\pi}}, X_{\ell_{\pi}}, C_{\pi}, P_{\pi} \rangle$, where $X_{n_{\pi}} = X_{n_t}$, $X_{\ell_{\pi}} = X_{\ell_t}$, $C_{\pi} = C_t$, and $P_{\pi} = P_t$. Observe that the schema S_r is ignored in the result as the tuples bound by this schema are removed by the web project operation.   ∎

8.4.3 Algorithm for Web Project

In this section, we develop the algorithm for creating a projected web table. Given a web table and a project condition, the algorithm generates the set of web tuples in the projected result and a set of schemas of these web tuples by *modifying* the web tuples and schemas of the input web table. Our algorithm starts with an empty projected web table and appends schemas and web tuples to the projected table as it proceeds. When the algorithm terminates, we will have a web table or web bag that satisfies the project condition. The set of constructs used by the algorithm is shown in Table 8.1.

Outline of the Algorithm

The algorithm is most easily described as consisting of two phases: the *partition generation* and *partition pruning phase*. We describe each phase in turn. In the next section, we provide a formal treatment of the algorithm.

Partition Generation Phase

In this phase the set of partitions for the projected web table or web bag is generated. It takes as input a web table and a project condition and ejects as output a collection of partitions that satisfy the project condition. As generation of partitions involves schema and web tuple generation for the projected web table, we therefore classify this phase into the following subphases.

1. *Schema Generation Phase:* Recall that a web table contains a set of simple schemas. Furthermore, each simple schema binds a set of web tuples. The set of schemas of the projected web table is generated from these canonical schemas. Observe that the structure of the web schemas depends on the projection criteria. Based on the projection criteria there are several cases that are to be considered for generating the set of resultant schemas as shown below.
   - *Case 1:* All node type identifiers of the input simple schema are to be eliminated. That is, if X_{n_p} denotes the set of node type identifiers after eliminating the node type identifiers in the input schema then $X_{n_p} = \emptyset$.
   - *Case 2:* Some of the node type identifiers of the input simple schema are eliminated but not all. That is, $X_{n_2} \subset X_n$, where X_n is a set of node type identifiers in the input schema.
   - *Case 3:* None of the node type identifiers is eliminated from the input simple schema. This indicates that the schema of the set of web tuples remains unchanged after the web project operation. Hence in this case $X_{n_p} = X_n$.

   Each simple schema in the input web table must satisfy any one of these three cases. Moreover, as we show later the implementation techniques for the construction of projected schemas and corresponding web tuples depend on these cases. The output of this phase is a set of simple schemas that bind the set of projected web tuples.
2. *Web Tuples Generation Phase:* In this phase, the web tuples of the projected web table or web bag are constructed from the input web tuples. For each input simple schema S_i the corresponding set of web tuples (denoted as T_i) is retrieved. Then, based on the projected schema S_{p_i} generated from S_i, T_i is modified. Observe that this modification depends on the above three cases as follows.

Construct name	Input	Output	Function
GetProjectNodeTypeIds	S_i (optional), P_c	X_n	For a given P_c, it identifies those node type identifiers whose instances are to be eliminated from the web tuples bound by S_i
GetProjectLinkTypeIds	X_n, X_ℓ, C	X_ℓ	Identifies the set of link type identifiers that are to be eliminated from the tuple set bound by S_i
GetProjectNodeIds	T, X_n	Node ids of some nodes in T	Identifies identifier of those nodes in web tuples that are instances of the node type identifiers
GetProjectLinkIds	T, X_ℓ	Link ids of some links in T	Identifies identifier of those links in web tuples that are instances of the link type identifiers
GetTupleNodeIds	Web tuple t	Node id set	Returns the identifiers of the set of nodes in t
GetTupleLinkIds	Web tuple t	Link id set	Returns the identifiers of the set of links in t
GetPredicatesOnType	P, X_n or X_ℓ	$P_x \subseteq P$	Returns those predicates in P whose arguments are the bound node or link identifier
GetPredicates	P, X_n or X_ℓ	$P_x \subseteq P$	Returns those predicates in P whose arguments are the bound node or link identifiers
GetLeftIdentifier	C, X_n	$C_\ell \subset C$	Generates a set of connectivities C_ℓ where $c \in C_\ell$ such that $\text{lnode}(c) \in X_n$ $\forall\, 0 < i \leq |C_\ell|$
GetRightIdentifier	C, X_n	$C_r \subset C$	Generates a set of connectivities C_r where $c \in C_r$ such that $\text{rnode}(c) \in X_n$ $\forall\, 0 < i \leq |C_r|$

Table 8.1. Constructs used in the algorithm.

- If the projected schema S_{p_i} is a result of Case 1 as described above then all the nodes in the web tuples T_i are eliminated. Hence T_i does not appear in the resultant web table.
- If it is a result of Case 2 then web tuples of the projected web table or web bag are generated by eliminating some of the nodes in T_i that satisfy the projection constraints. A modified set of web tuples T_{p_i} containing fewer nodes compared to those in T_i but the same number of web tuples appears in the resultant web table.
- For Case 3, as none of the instances of node type identifiers in the input schema are eliminated during the project operation, the set of web tuples T_i remains unchanged and is inserted in the projected web table without any modification in the projected web table.

At the end of the partition generation phase we have a set of partitions containing a collection of web schemas and a collection of web tuples. Note that the partition generation phase may create identical, equivalent, or inclusive web schemas. Hence it is required to refine the set of web schemas and corresponding web tuples generated by the project operation. This is performed by the partition pruning phase.

Partition Pruning Phase

A web project operation may create identical, equivalent, or inclusive web schemas. In the partition pruning phase, we transform these schemas into a set of distinct web schemas that binds a distinct collection of web tuples. Note that we do not perform elimination of noisy web schemas in this phase as the web project operation never generates noisy web schemas. The procedure to refine the partitions is has been discussed in detail in Section 7.8 of Chapter 7. Hence we do not discuss this further.

Web Table Construction

We now present the complete algorithm to compute the projected web table or web bag satisfying some project condition. In the algorithm, we combine the two phases described above into one scan on the input web table W. In particular, we elaborate on the algorithm for implementing the partition generation phase. The algorithm for the partition pruning phase was already discussed in Section 7.8 of Chapter 7. Hence we do not elaborate it further. Instead we illustrate the partition pruning operation with an example.

The pseudocode for the algorithm is shown in Figure 8.14. It takes as input a web table $W = \langle N, \mathcal{P} \rangle$ and a project condition $\tau = \langle M, P_c \rangle$ and creates a projected web table or web bag $W_p = \langle N_p, \mathcal{P}_p \rangle$. Steps (1) and (2) in Figure 8.14 identify the set of node type identifiers whose instances are to be removed from the input web table. If the projection attribute P_c contains only bound node type identifiers then for each simple schema of W Steps (4) to (27) are executed. Step (5) checks if P_c contains bound node type identifiers only. The variable X_{n_p} stores the set of such bound node type identifiers. If X_{n_p} is empty it indicates that P_c may

---

Input: Project condition $\tau = \langle M, P_c \rangle$, Web table $W = \langle N, \mathcal{P} \rangle$, projected table name N_p.
Output: Projected web table or web bag $W_p = \langle N_p, \mathcal{P}_p \rangle$.

(1)   if (P_c contains bound node type identifiers)
(2) $X_{n_p} = \mathbf{GetProjectNodeTypeIds}(P_c)$;
(3)   Let $M = \{S_1, S_2, \ldots, S_r\}$ where $U_i = \langle S_i, T_i \rangle$, $U_i \in \mathcal{P} \ \forall \ 0 < i \le r$;
(4)   for ($i = 1 \ to \ |M|$) {
(5)   if ($|X_{n_p}| = 0$)
(6) $X'_{n_p i} = \mathbf{GetProjectNodeTypeIds}(P_c, \ S_i)$;
(7)   else
(8) $X'_{n_p i} = X_{n_p}$;
(9) $X'_{\ell_p i} = \mathbf{GetProjectLinkTypeIds}(X'_{n_p i}, X_{\ell_i}, C_i)$;
(10) $X_{n_p i} = X_{n_i} - X'_{n_p i}$;
(11) $X_{\ell_p i} = X_{\ell_i} - X'_{\ell_p i}$;
(12)   if ($X_{n_p i} \ne X_{n_i}$) {
(13)   if ($|X_{n_p i}| > 0$) {
(14) $C_{pi} = \mathbf{ModifyConn}(C_i, \ X_{n_p i})$; /* Figure 8.17 */
(15) $P_{pi} = \mathbf{GeneratePredicates}(P_i, \ X_{n_p i}, \ X_{\ell_p i})$; /* Figure 8.16 */
(16) $T_{pi} = \mathbf{GenerateTuples}(T_i, \ S_{pi})$; /* Figure 8.15 */
(17) $U_{pi} = \langle S_{pi}, T_{pi} \rangle$;
(18)   Insert U_{pi} in $\mathcal{P}_p$;
(19)   }
(20)   else
(21)   ;
(22)   else {
(23) $S_{pi} = S_i$;
(24) $T_{pi} = T_i$;
(25) $U_{pi} = \langle T_{pi}, S_{pi} \rangle$;
(26)   Insert U_{pi} in $\mathcal{P}_p$;
(27)   }
(28)   }
(29)   if ($|\mathcal{P}_p| > 1$)
(30) $\mathcal{P}_p = \mathbf{PrunePartition}(\mathcal{P}_p)$;
(31)   Return $W_p = \langle N_p, \mathcal{P}_p \rangle$;

Fig. 8.14. Algorithm for constructing the projected web table or web bag.

contain free node type identifiers. If so then Step (6) is executed and the set of node type identifiers in S_i that are to be eliminated based on P_c is computed using the construct **GetProjectNodeTypeIds**. The resultant set of projected node type identifiers is stored in $X'_{n_p i}$. Otherwise, if X_{n_p} is nonempty (indicating the eliminated node type identifiers are bound only) then X_{n_p} is assigned to $X'_{n_p i}$. Note that $X'_{n_p i}$ represents a set of node type identifiers whose instances are to be eliminated from the tuple set T_i bound by the schema S_i. Next the algorithm identifies the corresponding set of link type identifiers (denoted as $X'_{\ell_p i}$ in Step (9)) that are to be eliminated. The construct **GetProjectLinkTypeIds** computed this by inspecting the connectivities C_i of S_i and $X'_{n_p i}$.

Once $X'_{n_p i}$ and $X'_{\ell_p i}$ are computed the algorithm proceeds to generate the set of node and link type identifiers in the projected web schema S_{pi} (Steps (10) and

Input: Simple projected schema S_p, Web tuples T.
Output: Projected web tuples T_p.

(1) $N_p = \textbf{GetProjectNodeIds}(T, X_{n_p})$;
(2) $L_p = \textbf{GetProjectLinkIds}(T, X_{\ell_p})$;
(3)   for $(i = 1\ to\ |T|)$ {
(4) $N_i = \textbf{GetTupleNodeIds}(t_i)$;
(5) $L_i = \textbf{GetTupleLinkIds}(t_i)$;
(6) $N_{pi} = N_p \cap N_i$;
(7) $L_{pi} = L_p \cap L_i$;
(8) $t_{pi} = \textbf{ConstructTuple}(N_{pi}, L_{pi}, C_{pi})$;
(9)   Append t_{pi} in T_p;
(10)   }
(11)   Return T_p;

Fig. 8.15. Algorithm of **GenerateTuples**.

(11)). Based on the three cases discussed previously, the algorithm generates the set of projected web tuples T_{pi} and schema S_{pi} from the simple schema S_i and the set of web tuples T_i. Steps (13) to (19) compute the projected web tuples and their schema if Case 2 is true. Specifically, Steps (14) and (15) generate connectivities and the predicate set of S_{pi} and Step (16) produces the projected web tuples. The procedure for these steps is encapsulated in the constructs **ModifyConn** and **GeneratePredicates**, respectively, and is discussed in detail later. Finally, the partition U_{pi} is generated and is inserted in $\mathcal{P}_p$ (Steps (17) and (18)).

Steps (19) and (20) implement Case 1. As all instances of node type identifiers are eliminated, the set of web tuples T_i and its schema S_i are ignored and are not inserted in the projected web table. Finally, Steps (22) to (27) implement Case 3. Since none of the instances of node type identifiers X_{n_i} are eliminated the schema and tuples S_i and T_i remain unchanged in the projected web table (depicted by Steps (23) and (24)). Hence the partition U_{pi} is inserted in $\mathcal{P}_p$.

Once all the partitions are generated, Steps (30) and (31) prune the collection of partitions by transforming the identical, equivalent, or inclusive web schemas into a set of distinct web schemas. These steps are encapsulated in the construct **PrunePartition**. The detailed procedure of this construct is described in Section 7.8 of Chapter 7.

Algorithm of GeneratePredicates Construct

Generation of a predicate set for a projected schema is straightforward. It takes as input the projected set of node and link type identifiers $X_{n_{pi}}$ and $X_{\ell_{pi}}$, respectively and the predicate set P_i of input simple schema S_i, and returns as output the predicate set P_{pi} for the schema S_{pi}. The pseudocode for the algorithm is shown in Figure 8.16.

The predicates on bound node type identifiers are computed by executing Steps (1) to (8). The free node type identifiers in $X_{n_{pi}}$ are ignored and the set of predicates on each bound identifier is retrieved from P_i and inserted in P_{pi}. This is executed until the predicates of all bound node type identifiers in $X_{n_{pi}}$ are inserted in P_{pi}. The predicates on bound link type identifiers are similarly identified and are shown in Steps (9) to (16).

Algorithm of ModifyConn Construct

The **ModifyConn** construct is used to generate the connectivity set of a projected simple schema. The pseudocode is shown in Figure 8.17. It takes as input a set of simple connectivities C and a set of node type identifiers X_{n_p} which are to be eliminated from the projected schema and returns as output the set of connectivities C_p of the projected web schema. The algorithm first identifies those simple connectivities in C whose left node type identifier is an element of X_{n_p} and stores them in the set C_ℓ. Next, these connectivities are removed from C as the left node type identifiers are to be eliminated after the project operation. Then the set of connectivities whose right node type identifier is an element in X_{n_p} are identified from the remaining connectivities in C and eliminated. The resultant set of connectivities represents the connectivity set of the projected web schema.

Algorithm of GenerateTuples Construct

The pseudocode for generating the projected web tuples bound by a projected simple schema is shown in Figure 8.15. It takes as input the projected schema S_p and a set of web tuples T which are bound by the schema S of the input partition and returns as output a set of projected web tuples T_p bound by S_p.

First, all instances of projected node and link type identifiers are computed from T by identifying the instances of each node and link type identifiers in $X_{n_{pi}}$ and $X_{\ell_{pi}}$, respectively. Steps (1) and (2) in the algorithm in Figure 8.15 compute these instances using the constructs **GetProjectNodeIds** and **GetProjectLinkIds**, respectively. Steps (3) to (10) then generate the projected web tuple collection by iterating through the web tuples T. For each tuple in T, the set of node and link objects is identified. Then only those nodes and links that match with the nodes and links in N_p and L_p, respectively, are stored in the sets N_{pi} and L_{pi}. Note that these are the nodes and links that are to be present in the projected tuple. Finally, the resultant web tuples are constructed by matching the nodes in N_{pi} and L_{pi} with the schema S_p using the construct **ConstructTuples**.

Next we illustrate with examples the execution of the algorithm in Figure 8.14.

Example 8.9. Consider the web project operation in Example 8.5. We outline the steps executed by the algorithm to generate the projected web table in Figure 8.10.

1. Since $P_c = \{(\text{START\_NODE\_TYPE} = y, \text{END\_NODE\_TYPE} = z)\}$, the condition in Step (1) in Figure 8.14 is not satisfied. Hence, after Step (2), $X_{n_p} = \emptyset$.
2. As the web table Cancer contains three simple schemas, after Step (3) we get $M = \{S_a, S_b, S_c\}$.
3. Since $|M| = 3$, the for loop in Step (4) is executed three times. For $i = 1$, $S_1 = S_a$, and $|X_{n_p}| = 0$. Therefore after Step (6) we get $X'_{n_{p1}} = \{\#_1, \#_2\}$.

Input: Predicate set P, Node type identifier set X_{n_p}, Link type identifier set X_{ℓ_p}.
Output: Predicate set P_p of projected web table.

(1)   for $(i = 1\ to\ |X_{n_p}|)$ {
(2)   if $(X_{n_p i}$ is free)
(3)   ;
(4)   else {
(5) $P_i = \textbf{GetPredicatesOnType}(P, X_{n_p i})$;
(6)   Insert P_i in P_p;
(7)   }
(8)   }
(9)   for $(j = 1\ to\ |X_{\ell_p}|)$ {
(10)   if $(X_{\ell_p j}$ is free)
(11)   ;
(12)   else {
(13) $P_j = \textbf{GetPredicatesOnType}(P, X_{\ell_p i})$;
(14)   Insert P_j in P_p;
(15)   }
(16)   }
(17)   Return P_p;

Fig. 8.16. Algorithm **GeneratePredicates**.

Input: Set of connectivities C, set of node type identifiers X_n.
Output: Modified set of connectivities C_p.

(1) $C_\ell = \textbf{GetLeftIdentifier}(C, X_n)$;
(2) $C' \equiv C - C_\ell$;
(3) $C_r = \textbf{GetRightIdentifier}(C', X_n)$;
(4) $C_p \equiv C' - C_r$;
(5)   Return C_p;

Fig. 8.17. Algorithm of **ModifyConn**.

4. Next Step (9) is executed to identify the set of link type identifiers that are to be eliminated; i.e., $X'_{\ell_{p1}} = \{f, \text{-}_1, \text{-}_2\}$.

5. Steps (10) and (11) generate the set of node and link type identifiers of the projected schema (created from S_a). That is, after execution of these steps $X_{n_{pa}} = \{x, y, z, \#_1, \#_2\} - \{\#_1, \#_2\} = \{x, y, z\}$, and $X_{\ell_{pa}} = \{e, f, \text{-}_1, \text{-}_2\} - \{f, \text{-}_1, \text{-}_2\} = \{e\}$.

6. Since $X_{n_p} \neq X_{n_{pa}}$ and $|X_{n_{pa}}| > 0$, Steps (14) to (18) are executed (Case 2). Step (14) generates the connectivity set of the projected schema based on the algorithm in Figure 8.17 as shown below.

   • Observe that the set of connectivities in S_a that contains $\#_1$ and $\#_2$ as left node type identifiers is k_{a_3} and k_{a_4}. Hence, after Step (1) in Figure 8.17, we get $C_\ell = \{k_{a_3}, k_{a_4}\}$.

   • After Step (2), $C' = \{k_{a_1}, k_{a_2}, k_{a_3}, k_{a_4}\} - \{k_{a_3}, k_{a_4}\} = \{k_{a_1}, k_{a_2}\}$.

- Finally, execution of Steps (5) and (6) of Figure 8.17 results in the following. $C_r = \{k_{a_2}\}$ and $C_m = \{k_{a_1}, k_{a_2}\} - \{k_{a_2}\} = \{k_{a_1}\}$. Note that C_m is the resultant connectivity in the projected schema.

7. Step (15) in Figure 8.14 generates the set of predicates of the projected web schema by executing the algorithm in Figure 8.16. Note that $X_{n_{pa}} = \{x, y, z\}$ and $X_{\ell_{pa}} = \{e\}$. Therefore, after executing Steps (1) to (8), we get $P_{n_a} = \{p_1, p_2, p_5\}$. Executing Steps (9) to (16) we get $P_{\ell_a} = \{p_4\}$. Therefore the set of predicates for the projected web schema from S_a is $P_{p_a} = \{p_1, p_2, p_4, p_5\}$.

8. Next, the set of projected web tuples from the web tuples bound by S_a is computed by executing the steps in Figure 8.15 as shown below. Observe that S_a binds the web tuple t_2 in Figure 6.10. Therefore $T_1 = \{t_2\}$ in the algorithm.
   - After Steps (1) and (2) in Figure 8.14 we get $N_p = \{u_0, u_4\}$ and $L_p = \{f_0, \ell_1, \ell_4\}$.
   - Since $|T_1| = 1$, the for loop in Step 3 is executed once. For Steps (4) and (5), $N_1 = \{x_0, y_0, z_1, u_0, u_4\}$ and $L_1 = \{e_0, f_0, \ell_1, \ell_4\}$.
   - After Steps (6) and (7) we get $N_{p_1} = \{u_0, u_4\}$ and $L_{p_1} = \{f_0, \ell_4, \ell_1\}$.
   - Lastly, Step (8) constructs the projected web tuple as shown in Figure 8.10 (second tuple) and inserts it in T_p.

9. Finally, the partition $U_{p_a} = \langle S_{p_a}, T_{p_a} \rangle$ is generated.

10. The for loop is executed similarly for the schemas S_b and S_c. After the for loop we get the set of partitions $\mathcal{P}_p = \{U_{p_a}, U_{p_b}, U_{p_c}\}$, where:
   a) $U_{p_a} = \langle S_{p_a} = \langle X_{n_{pa}}, X_{\ell_{pa}}, C_{pa}, P_{pa} \rangle, T_{p_a} \rangle$, where $X_{n_{pa}} = \{x, y, z\}$, $X_{\ell_{pa}} = \{e\}$, $C_{pia} \equiv k_{a_1}$, $P_{pa} = \{p_1, p_2, p_3, p_5\}$, and $T_{pa} = \{t_{p2}\}$;
   b) $U_{p_b} = \langle S_{p_b} = \langle X_{n_{pb}}, X_{\ell_{pb}}, C_{pb}, P_{pb} \rangle, T_{p_b} \rangle$, where $X_{n_{pb}} = \{x, y, z\}$, $X_{\ell_{pb}} = \{e\}$, $C_{pib} \equiv k_{a_1}$, $P_{pb} = \{p_1, p_2, p_3, p_5\}$, and $T_{pb} = \{t_{p3}, t_{p4}\}$;
   c) $U_{p_c} = \langle S_{p_c} = \langle X_{n_{pc}}, X_{\ell_{pc}}, C_{pc}, P_{pc} \rangle, T_{p_c} \rangle$, where $X_{n_{pc}} = \{x, y, z\}$, $X_{\ell_{pc}} = \{e\}$, $C_{pic} \equiv k_{a_1}$, $P_{pc} = \{p_1, p_2, p_3, p_5\}$, and $T_{pc} = \{t_{p1}, t_{p5}\}$.

11. Finally, the above partitions are refined by the algorithm in Figure 7.5. Observe that S_{p_a}, S_{p_b}, and S_{p_c} are identical web schemas. The steps for refinement are illustrated in Figure 7.10 in Chapter 7. Hence we do not elaborate on this further. The projected web bag after the partition refinement operation consists of a single partition as follows.
   - $U_p = \langle S_p = \langle X_{n_p}, X_{\ell_p}, C_p, P_p \rangle, T_p \rangle$, where $X_{n_p} = \{x, y, z\}$, $X_{\ell_{pi}} = \{e\}$, $C_{pi} \equiv k_{a_1}$, $P_p = \{p_1, p_2, p_3, p_5\}$, and $T_p = \{t_{p1}, t_{p2}, t_{p3}, t_{p4}, t_{p5}\}$. ∎

Example 8.10. Consider the web project operation in Example 8.8. Here $P_c = \{\text{TO\_LINK\_TYPE} = e, \text{FROM\_LINK\_TYPE} = \{e, f\}\}$. We elaborate on how the projected web table is generated by executing the steps of the algorithm in Figure 8.14.

1. The condition in Step (1) is not true in this case and therefore after Step (3) we have $X_{n_p} = \emptyset$ and $M = \{S_x, S_y\}$.
2. As $M = 2$, the for loop in Step (4) is executed twice. Since $|X_{n_p}| = 0$, after Step (6) we have $X'_{n_{p1}} = \{x, y, \#_1\}$.
3. After Step (9), $X'_{\ell_{p1}} = \{e, f\}$.

4. Hence the sets of node and link type identifiers for the projected schema are
   $X_{n_{p1}} = \{x, y, \#_1\} - \{x, y, \#_1\} = \emptyset$ and $X_{\ell_{p1}} = \{e, f\} - \{e, f\} = \emptyset$.
5. Note that as $X_{n_{p1}} \neq X_{n_x}$ and $|X_{n_{p1}}| = 0$, Steps (20) and (21) are executed
   (Case 1). Hence the schema S_x is ignored in the projected web table result.
6. Similarly, the for loop is executed once again for the schema S_y. As $X_{n_p} = \emptyset$
   after Step (6) we have $X'_{n_{p2}} = \emptyset$.
7. After Step (9), $X'_{\ell_{p2}} = \emptyset$.
8. Hence the sets of node and link type identifiers in the projected schema generated from S_y remain unchanged; i.e., $X_{n_{p2}} = \{x, y, \#_1\}$ and $X_{\ell_{p2}} = \{e, f\}$.
9. Note that as $X_{n_x} = X_{n_{p2}}$, the condition in Step (12) is evaluated false and
   Steps (22) to (27) are executed (Case 3). Therefore $S_{p2} = S_y$ and $T_{p2} = T_y = \{t_4, t_5, t_6\}$.
10. The set of partitions generated after the execution of the for loop is $\mathcal{P}_p = \{U_{p_y} = \langle S_{p2}, T_{p2} \rangle\}$.
11. As the web project operation generates only one partition, there is no need to
    refine the partition. Hence Step (30) is ignored. ∎

8.5 Web Distinct

As discussed in the preceding section a web project operation may generate a web
bag. The *web distinct* operator is used to eliminate duplicate web tuples from a web
bag. It removes all but one occurrence of a web tuple from a web table. Note that
we do not remove the duplicate web tuples automatically during the web project
operation as web bags are useful in knowledge discovery in the web warehouse
[21, 26, 23, 24] (discussed in Chapter 11). Hence we define a separate operator
to perform the duplicate elimination task and decouple it from the web project
operation. Formally, the web distinct operator is expressed as follow. $W_d = \Delta(W_b)$,
where Δ is the web distinct operator, W_b is a web table or web bag, and W_d is a web
table with distinct web tuples. For example, consider the web table in Figure 8.2.
The first, second, and fourth web tuples (denoted by t_1, t_2 and t_4) are identical,
i.e., $t_1 = t_2 = t_4$. Therefore this is a web bag. Hence any two web tuples can be
eliminated by the web distinct operation. After duplicate elimination the projected
web table is depicted in Figure 8.10. Note that the schema(s) of the projected web
table remains unchanged during duplicate elimination.

We now describe the algorithm for the web distinct operation. Observe that
after the web project operation a set of partitions is generated. These partitions
may represent a web table with distinct web tuples or a web bag. Moreover, after
the partition pruning process, $S_i \neq S_j$ for all $0 < (i, j) \leq |S|$ and $i \neq j$ where S is
a set of web schemas in the projected web table or web bag. Furthermore, for all
sets of web tuples in the partition $T_i \cap T_j = \emptyset$ for all $i \neq j$. This has the following
implications.

- If the projected web table is a web bag then each set of duplicate web tuples
  must be bound by a single web schema. There cannot exist cases where duplicate
  web tuples are bound by more than one web schema.

Input: Web table or Web bag $W_b = \langle N, \mathcal{P} \rangle$.
Output: Distinct web table $W_d = \langle N, \mathcal{P} \rangle$.

(1)   Initialize a map $M = \langle j, Q \rangle$ where j is a tuple identifier
       and Q is a set of (url, date) pair;
(2)   for $(i = 1 \ to \ |\mathcal{P}|)$ {
(3)   Retrieve tuple set T_i bound by S_i
(4)   for $(j = 1 \ to \ |T_i|)$
(5)   Insert j and Q_j (key) in the map M where $q = \langle \ell, d \rangle$, $q \in Q_j$;
(6)   if $(|M| < |T_i|)$
(7)   Remove t_j from T_i such that j is not in M;
(8)   Erase elements from M;
(9)   }
(10)   Return $W_d = \langle N, \mathcal{P} \rangle$;

Fig. 8.18. Algorithm of web distinct.

- Moreover, if D is a collection of identical web tuples and S_d is the web schema then there must exist a partition $U = \langle S_d, T \rangle$, where $D \subseteq T$. That is, each identical tuple set belongs to a single partition. The web tuples in an identical web tuple set cannot exist in different partitions.

Based on the above issues, in order to implement the web distinct operation we need to check each partition separately for identifying and eliminating duplicate web tuples. There is no need to compare the tuples of one partition to those of others to eliminate identical web tuples. The algorithm for the web distinct operation is shown in Figure 8.18. Note that we use a map container M to store for each partition the tuple identifier j and a set of URL and last modification date pairs (denoted by Q) of the nodes in tuple t_j. We use Q as the key for the map. Note that duplicate web tuples in a partition will have the same key; hence if data from one of the duplicate web tuples are already inserted in M then data from other identical tuples cannot be inserted in M. If there exist duplicate tuples in a partition then the size of M must be less than the number of elements in the tuple set T of the partition (Step (6)). We identify the identical tuple identifiers from M and eliminate the corresponding web tuples from the partition as shown in Step (7). This procedure is repeated for all the partitions in the web bag.

8.6 Web Cartesian Product

Like its relational counterpart, a *web cartesian product*, denoted by $\times$, is a binary operation that combines two web tables by concatenating a web tuple of one web table with a web tuple of another. If W_i and W_j are web tables with n and m web tuples, respectively, the resulting web table W created by web cartesian product consists of $n \times m$ web tuples. The schemas of the resultant table are generated from the input web schemas. This process has been discussed in Chapter 7.

8.7 Web Join

There has been considerable research on the join operation in relational databases [135]. It is one of the fundamental operations in relational databases for relating information from two or more relations. In addition, joins are one of the most expensive operations that a relational database system performs. There has also been increasing research effort to extend the concept of a join to support nontraditional data, including temporal data and spatial objects. We also see that research interest in data models and query languages for Web data has intensified recently [79]. In particular, there is an increasing effort to combine related Web data using the notion of join [1, 67]. For instance, the join operation is used in XML-QL [67] to combine information collected from different portions of documents, which is necessary to merge information from multiple documents. It uses the same variable binding for character data in a tag element for causing a join between two data sources. Lorel [1] uses an explicit equality predicate on character data to perform the join. Note that the issue of join in the context of Web data is more challenging than the corresponding problem for relational join due to the irregularity and incompleteness of data in the World Wide Web. In this section, we discuss the *web join* operation in WHOWEDA [30, 18, 19].

8.7.1 Motivation and Overview

The web join operator is used to combine two web tables by *joining* a web tuple of one table with a web tuple of the other table. The basic idea of web join is as follows. Given two web tables W_1 and W_2, two web tuples $t_a \in W_1$ and $t_b \in W_2$ can be joined into a single web tuple t_{ab} if and only if there exists at least one node (*joinable node*) in each tuple that is *identical* to the other. Thus the joined web table, denoted as W_{12}, has one web tuple for each pair of web tuples from W_1 and W_2 that contains joinable nodes. Note that by identical nodes we indicate Web documents that are identical in content and structure.

Intuitively, a web join serves several important functions. First, a web join can be used to relate information from two web tables. Second, this information can be stored in a separate web table and can be used for future queries. One of the objectives of a web join is to capitalize on the reuse of retrieved data from the WWW in order to reduce the execution time of queries. Note that the resultant web table may also be derived directly from the World Wide Web. But materializing a web table created by joining two web tables provides fast access to data compared to deriving the same information from the WWW. Finally, if a web warehouse maintains several materialized web tables created by joining web tables, the query optimizer can use these materialized tables when optimizing arbitrary queries, even when the queries do not mention the web tables. Without a join operator, all of these tasks become significantly time consuming and expensive.

We illustrate the web join operation with an example given below. Note that the significance of a web join perhaps can be best realized when some of the information in a Web site is no longer available due to changes to the Web site.

Example 8.11. Assume that the results of the query in Example 6.9 are materialized in a web table labeled **Drugs-Manufacturer** (Figure 6.9). Let us consider some
modifications to the Web site at `www.rxdrugs.com/` introduced in Example 6.9 in
Chapter 6. First, on **20th January, 2000**, the Web page denoted by b_0 in Figure 6.7
is changed. Now it contains links to the top 200 drugs for each year starting from
1995. On the same day, information related to "manufacturer" of various drugs
is no longer considered suitable for the Web site, and the corresponding links are
removed (links labeled "manufacturer" from the documents u_0, u_1, and so on in
Figure 6.7). Finally, on **10th February, 2000** the structure of the links and documents
related to drugs "Albuterol" and "Amoxicillin" are modified. Moreover, the links
related to side effects of the drug "Lovastatin" are removed. The resulting modified
representation of the Web site is shown in Figure 6.8, with modified documents
highlighted by patterned boxes.

Suppose on **15th February, 2000**, the user wishes to find descriptions, side effects,
and usage as well as manufacturers' descriptions of the top 200 drugs for the year
1998. Although it is possible to retrieve the description, side effects, and usage of
drugs from the modified Web site, information related to the manufacturers of drugs
has been removed from `http://www.rxdrugs.com/`. Thus the only way to retrieve
this information is to first download the side effects, and usage of the top 200 drugs
from this Web site and then manually identify those drugs in **Drugs-Manufacturer**
(related to manufacturers and description of drugs) that match with the top 200
list of drugs. However, this method is tedious, irritating, and frustrating. Thus we
need a mechanism to combine such related information. Note that some of this
information may no longer be available for retrieval from the Web. Hence the user
needs to perform the following steps to execute this query.

- First, specify a coupling query to retrieve information related to a list of drugs,
  their side effects, and uses, and materialize this information in the web table
  Drugs-Usage. The coupling query may be expressed as follows.
  Let the formal representation of the query be $G_j = \langle X_{n_j}, X_{\ell_j}, C_j, P_j, Q_j \rangle$, where

$$X_{n_j} = \{x, y, z, k, \#\}$$
$$X_{\ell_j} = \{r, s, {}_{-1}, {}_{-2}\}$$
$$C_j \equiv k_{j_1} \wedge k_{j_2} \wedge k_{j_3} \wedge k_{j_4}$$

where

$$k_{j_1} \equiv x\langle r\rangle y \qquad\qquad k_{j_2} \equiv y\langle s\rangle\#$$
$$k_{j_3} \equiv \#\langle {}_{-1}\{1,3\}\rangle z \qquad k_{j_4} \equiv \#\langle {}_{-2}\{1,3\}\rangle k$$

and $P_j = \{p_{j_1}, p_{j_2}, p_{j_3}, p_{j_4}, p_{j_5}, p_{j_6}, p_{j_7}\}$, where

$p_{j_1}(x) \equiv$ `METADATA::x[url]` `EQUALS` `"http://www[.]rxdrugs[.]com/"`
$p_{j_2}(y) \equiv$ `CONTENT::y[html.body.title]` `NON-ATTR_CONT`
   `":BEGIN_STR: + Drug List + :END_STR:"`
$p_{j_3}(z) \equiv$ `CONTENT::z[html.body.title]` `NON-ATTR_CONT`
   `":BEGINWORD: + Usage + :END_WORD:"`
$p_{j_4}(k) \equiv$ `CONTENT::k[html.body.title]` `NON-ATTR_CONT`
   `":BEGIN_STR: + side effects + :END_STR:"`

$p_{j_5}(s) \equiv$ CONTENT::s[A] NON-ATTR_CONT
        ":BEGIN_STR: + 1998 + :END_STR:"
$p_{j_6}(r) \equiv$ CONTENT::r[A] NON-ATTR_CONT
        ":BEGIN_STR: + Drug List + :END_STR:"
$p_{j_7}(x) \equiv$ METADATA::x[date] EQUALS "2nd January, 2000"

Figure 8.19(b) depicts the partial view of the tuples in Drugs-Usage. Observe that due to a change in the Web site, the side effects and uses of drugs "Lovastatin" and "Amoxicillin" are not materialized in Drugs-Usage. This is because the inter-linked documents related to these drugs (shown by pattern boxes in Figure 6.8) do not satisfy the coupling query.

- Then perform a web join on the web tables Drugs-Manufacturer (Figure 6.9) and Drugs-Usage.

We elaborate further on the second step. Observe that the information related to the descriptions and manufacturers of various drugs and also their side effects and usage are already materialized in tables Drugs-Manufacturer (Figure 6.9) and Drugs-Usage. Thus the query can be computed from these two web tables. In WHOWEDA, we can perform this computation using the web join operator. In particular, a web join concatenates web tuples in the web tables over the identical instances of the *joinable node type identifiers* (a and x in this case). A portion of the joined web table is shown in Figure 8.20. The black boxes in Figure 8.20 refer to identical nodes over which concatenation of the web tuples is performed, respectively. Each web tuple in the joined web table contains information related to the description, side effects, usage of drugs, and details of manufacturers of these drugs. ∎

8.7.2 Concept of Web Join

In this section, we begin by introducing some terms that we use to explain the web join operation. Then we formally define the web join operator.

Terminology

Join Condition

Intuitively, a *join condition* is specified by the user to indicate the sets of web tuples and nodes in the input web tables over which the web join operation may be performed. Let $W_1 = \langle N_1, U_1 \rangle$ and $W_2 = \langle N_2, U_2 \rangle$ be two web tables participating in a web join. Then the join condition consists of two components: a set of simple web schemas M and a set (possibly empty) of pairs of node type identifiers X_j. The first component, i.e., M, is similar to that discussed in Section 8.3. It specifies the set of tuples in W_1 and W_2 that are to be considered for the web join operation. By default, M is set to $(S_1 \cup S_2)$ (set of schemas in W_1 and W_2).

The second component X_j is a set of pairs of node type identifiers in W_1 and W_2. A user may specify a set of node type identifier pairs based on which web join operation is to be performed. Given two web tuples, the web join operation is

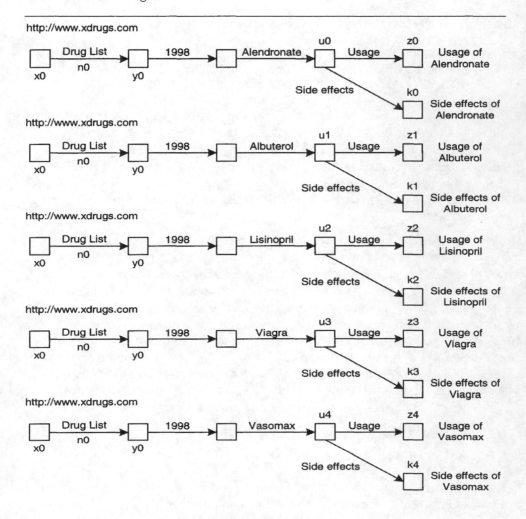

Fig. 8.19. Partial view of web tuples in " Drugs-Usage".

performed by evaluating instances of the specified node type identifiers to determine if they are *joinable* (discussed later). Note that the identifiers in each pair belong to the web tables W_1 and W_2 respectively. To elaborate further, let $(l, r) \in X_j$ be a pair. Then $l \in X_{n1}$ and $r \in X_{n2}$, where X_{n1} and X_{n2} are the sets of node type identifiers in W_1 and W_2, respectively. Note that when $X_j = \emptyset$, then all nodes in web tuples bound by the schemas in M are considered to determine if the tuples are joinable.

Formally, the join condition $\Psi = \langle M, X_j \rangle$ on W_1 and W_2 is a pair, where $M \subseteq (\mathcal{S}_1 \cup \mathcal{S}_2)$ and $M \neq \emptyset$ and X_j is a set of pairs of node type identifiers such that for each pair $(l, r) \in X_j$, $l \in X_{n1}$, and $r \in X_{n2}$. For example, consider **Drug-Manufacturer** and **Drug-Usage**. Suppose we wish to join these web tables over node

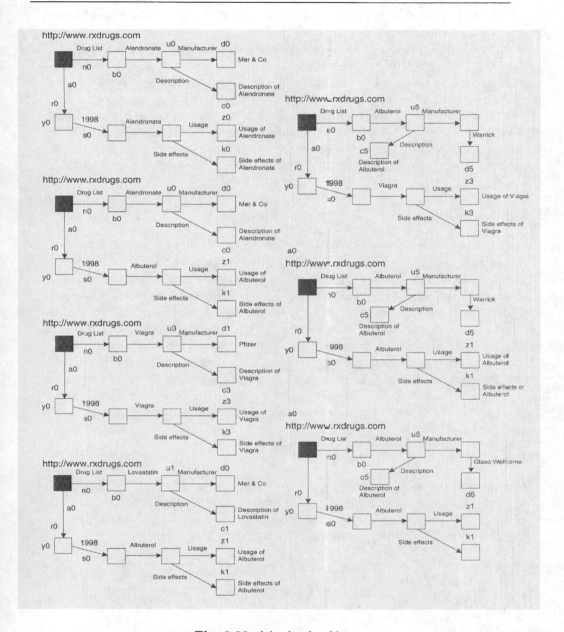

Fig. 8.20. Joined web table.

type identifiers x and a. Then M represents the set of schemas in these two web tables and $X_j = \{(a, x)\}$.

If (l_1, r_1) and (l_2, r_2) are two pairs in X_j such that $(l_1, l_2) \in X_{n1_a}$ and $(r_1, r_2) \in X_{n2_b}$, then $l_1 \neq l_2$ and $r_1 \neq r_2$, where X_{n1_a} and X_{n2_a} are components of schemas S_{a1} and S_{2b} in W_1 and W_2, respectively. That is, a node type identifier in a web schema in W_1 cannot be paired with more than one node type identifier in a schema in W_2. For example, let (a, b) and (x, y) be node type identifiers in schemas S_1 and S_2 in W_1 and W_2, respectively. Then $\{(a, x), (a, y)\} \subseteq X_j$ or $\{(a, x), (b, x)\} \subseteq X_j$ does not hold. Note that X_j here indicates that an instance of a is joinable to multiple nodes. That is, if t_1 and t_2 are two web tuples bound by schemas S_1 and S_2, respectively, then an instance of a in t_1 is joinable with instances of x and y in t_2. Similarly, an instance of x is joinable with instances of a and b, respectively. We do not allow this type of join condition in WHOWEDA. However, $\{(a, x), (a, y)\}$ can exist in X_j only if x and y are contained in two different schemas in W_2. That is, $(x, y) \notin X_{n2_k}$. In this case t_1 and t_2 can be joined over instances of a and x or a and y but not both.

Identical Nodes

Recall that a node represents a Web document. In WHOWEDA two nodes n_1 and n_2 are *identical*, denoted as $n_1 = n_2$, if the URL and last modification date of n_1 is identical to that of n_2. Note that we consider the last modification date of Web documents to determine if they are identical. This is necessary because in WHOWEDA a Web document or node in two web tables having different *coupling times* (time of retrieval of corresponding Web documents from the Web) may not be identical in content even though they have identical URLs. For instance, consider the documents at `http://www.rxdrugs.com/`, denoted by a_0 and x_0, in **Drugs-Manufacturer** and **Drugs-Usage**. The coupling times of these web tables are 15th January, 2000 and 15th February, 2000, respectively. Although the URLs are identical, the content of a_0 is different in these two web tables due to the modification of a_0 during this time period.

Joinable Nodes

Informally, joinable nodes are nodes participating in a web join. Let $n_l(t_a)$ and $n_r(t_b)$ be two nodes in web tuples t_a and t_b of W_1 and W_2, respectively. Let these nodes be instances of node type identifiers l and r, respectively. Then $n_l(t_a)$ and $n_r(t_b)$ are joinable nodes if they satisfy the following conditions.

- $n_l(t_a) = n_r(t_b)$;
- If $X_j \neq \emptyset$, then $(l, r) \in X_j$;
- $l \in X_{ni}$ and $r \in X_{nk}$ where $S_i = \langle X_{ni}, X_{\ell i}, C_i, P_i \rangle$, $S_k = \langle X_{nk}, X_{\ell k}, C_k, P_k \rangle$, and $(S_i, S_k) \in M$.

For example, consider the first web tuples of **Drugs-Manufacturer** and **Drugs-Usage** in Figures 6.9 and 8.19. Nodes a_0 and x_0 are instances of node type identifiers a and x respectively. Let $X_j = \{(a, x)\}$. Based on the predicates on a and x as defined in Examples 6.9 and 8.11, instances of a and x are identical as they refer to the same Web document at `www.rxdrugs.com` where the last modification date of the document is "2nd January, 2000". Hence nodes a_0 and x_0 are joinable nodes. Node type identifiers x and a are called *joinable node type identifiers*.

Observe the significance of X_j in the context of joinable nodes. If X_j is disregarded, then web join operations do not explicitly specify any conditions over type identifiers of the joinable nodes. Hence two nodes are joinable if they are identical. Consequently, any pair of web tuples sharing identical nodes can be joined. Given two input web tables, a web join is performed autonomously without human instruction or interaction. However, since a web join between two web tuples can be based on different nodes in input web tuples, different types of composite information may be generated sometimes by an unguided, autonomous web join. This may lead to a loss of useful information or it may lead to the existence of irrelevant information in the joined web table. Thus, to minimize an unguided web join operation, a user may explicitly specify a pair of node type identifiers in X_j.

Dangling Nodes

Nodes that do not participate in the web join process (are not joinable) are called dangling nodes. Formally, let W_1 and W_2 be two web tables participating in a web join. Let J_1 be the set of joinable nodes of W_1 with respect to W_2. Then a node n in W_1 is a dangling node if $n \notin J_1$.

Dangling Web Tuples

The notion of dangling web tuples is similar to its counterpart in relational databases. Web tuples in either input web table that do not participate in the web join are called dangling web tuples. Formally, let $n_r(t_a)$ and $n_s(t_b)$ be two nodes. Then $t_a \in W_1$ and $t_b \in W_2$ are dangling web tuples if and only if $n_r(t_a) \notin J_1$, $n_s(t_b) \notin J_2 \ \forall \ 0 < r \leq |N(t_a)|$, and $0 < s \leq |N(t_b)|$, where $N(t_a)$ and $N(t_b)$ denote the sets of nodes in web tuples t_a and t_b, respectively.

Web Join Operator

The web join operator is used to combine two web tables by *joining* a web tuple of one table with a web tuple of another table whenever there exist joinable nodes. Let $t_a \in W_1$ and $t_b \in W_2$ be two web tuples. Then these tuples are joinable if there exists at least one node in t_a that is joinable to a node in t_b. Formally, let $t_a \in W_1$, $t_b \in W_2 \ \forall \ 0 < a \leq |W_i|$, and $0 < b \leq |W_j|$. Let $n_r(t_a)$ and $n_s(t_b)$ be two nodes in t_a and t_b, respectively. Then t_a and t_b are joinable if $n_r(t_a)$ and $n_s(t_b)$ are joinable nodes. Note that $(n_r(t_a), n_s(t_b))$ are called a joinable node pair.

Once we have determined that a pair of web tuples is joinable, the joined web tuple consists of nodes and links integrated from input web tuples. We materialize the joined web tuple in a separate web table. As one of the joinable nodes in each joinable node pair is superfluous (because they are identical), we remove one of them from the joined web tuple. For example, consider the first web tuples of **Drugs-Manufacturer** and **Drugs-Usage** in Figures 6.9 and 3.19. Since the nodes x_0 and a_0 are joinable nodes, the tuples are joinable. The first web tuple in Figure 8.20 is the joined web tuple of these two web tuples. Note that we remove one of the joinable nodes, i.e., a_0, from the joined web tuple. In other words, the joined web tuple t_{ab} contains nodes and links from web tuples t_a and t_b and is made up of two parts; those nodes in t_a and t_b that do not participate in the web join (dangling nodes) and their corresponding links, and one of the joinable nodes from each joinable node pair of t_a or t_b and their corresponding links.

Hence, to perform a web join on web tables W_1 and W_2, a pair of web tuples is selected, one from each web table, and all pairs of nodes are evaluated to determine if there exist joinable nodes. If there exist joinable nodes in a pair of web tuples then the web tables are joinable. Formally, two web tables W_1 and W_2 are joinable if $t_a \in W_1$ and $t_b \in W_2$ are joinable, where $0 < a \leq |W_1|$, $0 < b \leq |W_2|$. We express a web join between two W_1 and W_2 as follows: $W_{wj} = W_1 \bowtie_\Psi W_2$ where $\Psi = \langle M, X_j \rangle$ is the join condition.

Intuitively, it may seem that there exists some similarity between the concept of relational join and web join. However, the notion of a web join in WHOWEDA differs from a relational join in two major ways: a web join deals with unstructured or semistructured data derived from the Web, not relational data; and a relational join is identified by schemas of participating relations, as opposed to a web join which *may not* always be determined from web schemas of input web tables. We elaborate on this issue later in Section 8.7.4.

Example 8.12. Consider Drug-Manufacturer and Drug-Usage resulting from the coupling queries in Examples 6.9 and 8.11. These two web tables can be represented as follows. Let $W_m = \langle \text{Drug} - \text{Manufacturer}, \mathcal{P}_{dm} \rangle$ be the web table Drug-Manufacturer, where $\mathcal{P}_{dm} = \{U_{dm1}, U_{dm2}\}$ and

- $U_{dm1} = \langle S_{m1} = \langle X_{nm1}, X_{\ell m1}, C_{m1}, P_{m1} \rangle, T_{m1} \rangle$, $X_{nm1} = \{a, b, c, d, \#_1\}$, $X_{\ell m1} = \{n, \text{-}_1, \text{-}_2, \text{-}_3\}$, $C_{m1} \equiv a\langle n \rangle b \wedge b\langle \text{-}_1 \rangle \#_1 \wedge \#_1\langle \text{-}_2 \rangle d \wedge \#_1\langle \text{-}_3 \rangle c$, $P_{m1} = P_{4q}$, and $T_{m1} = \{t_1, t_2, t_3, t_4, t_5\}$;
- $U_{dm2} = \langle S_{m2} = \langle X_{nm2}, X_{\ell m2}, C_{m2}, P_{m2} \rangle, T_{m2} \rangle$, $X_{nm2} = \{a, b, c, d, \#_1, \#_2\}$, $X_{\ell m2} = \{n, \text{-}_1, \text{-}_3, \text{-}_4, \text{-}_5\}$, $C_{m2} \equiv a\langle n \rangle b \wedge b\langle \text{-}_1 \rangle \#_1 \wedge \#_1\langle \text{-}_4 \rangle \#_2 \wedge \#_2\langle \text{-}_5 \rangle d \wedge \#_1\langle \text{-}_3 \rangle c$, $P_{m2} = P_{4q}$, and $T_{m2} = \{t_6, t_7, t_8, t_9, t_{10}\}$.

Similarly, let $W_u = \langle \text{Drug} - \text{Usage}, \mathcal{P}_{du} \rangle$ be the web table Drug-Usage, where $\mathcal{P}_{du} = \{U_{du1}\}$, where

- $U_{du1} = \langle S_{u1} = \langle X_{nu1}, X_{\ell u1}, C_{u1}, P_{u1} \rangle, T_{u1} \rangle$, $X_{nu1} = \{x, y, z, k, \#_1, \#_2\}$, $X_{\ell u1} = \{r, s, \text{-}_1, \text{-}_2, \text{-}_3\}$, $C_{u1} \equiv x\langle r \rangle y \wedge y\langle s \rangle \#_1 \wedge \#_1\langle \text{-}_1 \rangle \#_2 \wedge \#_2\langle \text{-}_2 \rangle z \wedge \#_2\langle \text{-}_3 \rangle k$, $P_{u1} = P_j$, and $T_{u1} = \{t_1, t_2, t_3, t_4, t_5\}$.

Let $\Psi = \langle M, X_j \rangle$ be the join condition where M is the set of schemas in these two web tables and $X_j = \{(a, x)\}$. Then these two web tables are joinable since there exist joinable nodes a_0 and x_0 in each pair of tuples in W_m and W_u. Performing a web join on these web tables creates a joined web table (Figure 8.20). Due to space limitations, we only show a partial view of the joined web table. This web join operation will generate a web table containing the partitions: $\mathcal{P}_{wj} = \{U_{wj1}, U_{wj2}\}$, where

- $U_{wj1} = \langle S_{j1} = \langle X_{nj1}, X_{\ell j1}, C_{j1}, P_{j1} \rangle, T_{j1} \rangle$, $X_{nj1} = \{x, b, c, d, y, z, k, \#_1, \#_2, \#_3\}$, $X_{\ell j1} = \{n, r, s, \text{-}_1, \text{-}_2, \text{-}_3, \text{-}_6, \text{-}_7, \text{-}_8\}$, $C_{j1} \equiv x\langle n \rangle b \wedge b\langle \text{-}_6 \rangle \#_3 \wedge \#_3\langle \text{-}_7 \rangle d \wedge \#_3\langle \text{-}_8 \rangle c \wedge x\langle r \rangle y \wedge y\langle s \rangle \#_1 \wedge \#_1\langle \text{-}_1 \rangle \#_2 \wedge \#_2\langle \text{-}_2 \rangle z \wedge \#_2\langle \text{-}_3 \rangle k$, $P_{j1} = (P_{4q} \cup P_j) - \{p_1(a), p_7(a)\}$, and $T_{j1} = \{t_1, t_2, t_3, t_4, \ldots\}$ (Figure 8.20);

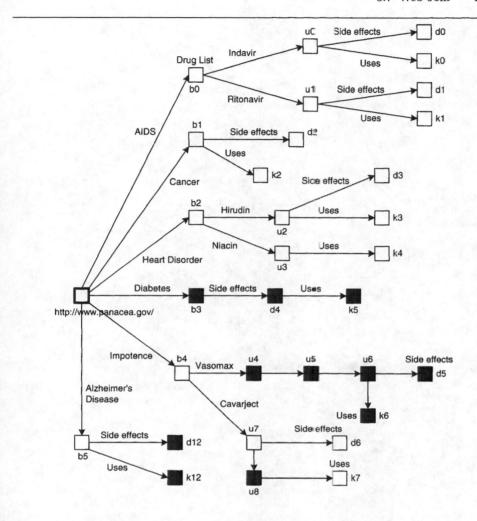

Fig. 8.21. Web site on 15th January, 2001.

- $U_{wj2} = \langle S_{j2} = \langle X_{nj2}, X_{\ell j2}, C_{j2}, P_{j2}\rangle, T_{j2}\rangle, X_{nj2} = \{x, b, c, d, y, z, k, \#_1, \#_2, \#_3, \#_4\}$, $X_{\ell j2} = \{n, r, s, \text{-}_1, \text{-}_2, \text{-}_3, \text{-}_6, \text{-}_9, \text{-}_{10}, \text{-}_{11}\}$, $C_{j2} \equiv x\langle n\rangle b \wedge b\langle \text{-}_6\rangle \#_3 \wedge \#_3\langle \text{-}_9\rangle \#_4 \wedge \#_4\langle \text{-}_{10}\rangle d \wedge \#_4\langle \text{-}_{11}\rangle c \wedge x\langle r\rangle y \wedge y\langle s\rangle \#_1 \wedge \#_1\langle \text{-}_1\rangle \#_2 \wedge \#_2\langle \text{-}_2\rangle z \wedge \#_2\langle \text{-}_3\rangle k$, $P_{j2} = (P_{4q} \cup P_j) - \{p_1(a), p_7(a)\}$, and $T_{j2} = \{t_5, t_6, t_7\}$.

The construction details of the joined schemas and tuples are explained in Section 8.7.4. ∎

The previous example illustrates a web join operation when a set of pairs of node type identifiers is specified by the user. The next example illustrates a web join operation when no such constraint is imposed on the join operation; i.e., $X_j = \emptyset$.

Example 8.13. Assume that there is a Web site at http://www.panacea.gov/ that provides information related to drugs used for various diseases. For instance, the

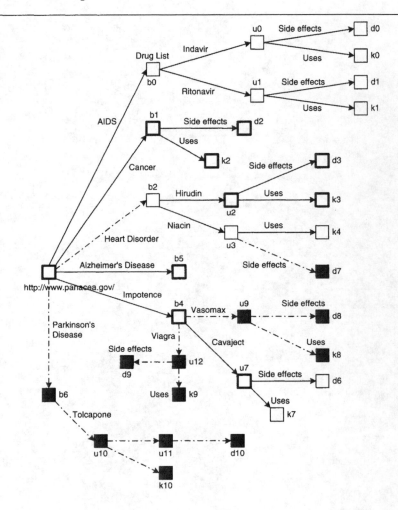

Fig. 8.22. Web site on 15th February, 2001.

structure of the site as of **15th January, 2001** is shown in Figure 8.21. We can see that the Web page at **http://www.panacea.gov/** (denoted by a_0) contains a list of diseases. From this list, each link of a particular disease points to a Web page (denoted by b_0, b_1, b_2, etc. for various drugs) containing a list of drugs used for treatment of the disease. For example, the link labeled "AIDS" in the Web page at **http://www.panacea.gov/** points to a document (denoted by b_0) containing the list of drugs (i.e., "Indavir", "Ritonavir", etc.) used against AIDS. From the hyperlinks associated with each drug, one can probe further to find documents (denoted by u_0, u_1, etc.) containing a list of various issues related to a particular drug, i.e., "description", "manufacturers", "clinical pharmacology", "uses", "side effects", "warnings", etc. From the hyperlinks associated with each issue, one can retrieve details of these issues for a particular drug. Note that in Figures 8.21

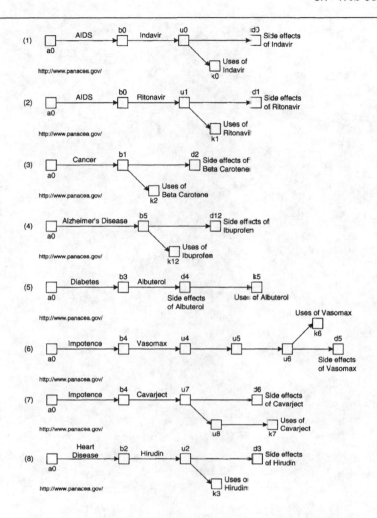

Fig. 8.23. Partial View of web table "Drugs".

and 8.22, we only show the links related to "uses" and "side effects" of drugs to simplify visualization.

Let us consider some modifications to this Web site on 15th February, 2001 as shown in Figure 8.22. The black boxes, the grey boxes, and the boxes with thick boundaries in this figure depict the addition of new documents, deletion of existing documents, and modification of existing documents, respectively. Furthermore, the dashed dotted arrows indicate the addition, deletion, or modification of hyperlinks. Observe the modification of the link structure of "Impotence". Previously, the information related to "Vasomax", a drug used against "Impotence" was provided by the Web site at http://www.pfizer.com/ (Web pages u_4, u_5, u_6, d_5, and k_6 in Figure 8.21 belong to the Web site at http://www.pfizer.com/). That is, the link labeled as "Vasomax" in b_4 in Figure 8.21 was a global link. Now this information

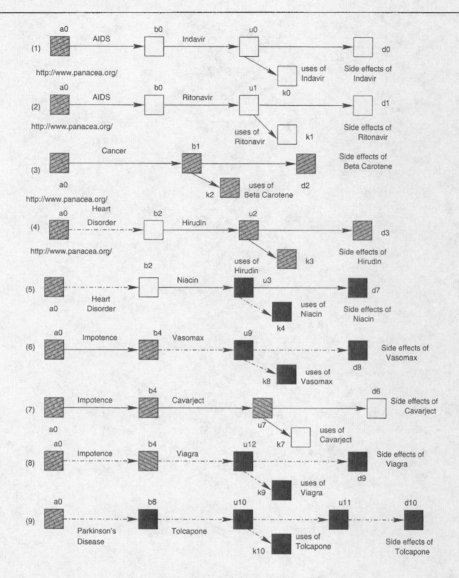

Fig. 8.24. Partial View of "New Drugs"

is provided locally by `http://www.panacea.gov/` and the structure of interlinked documents is modified as shown in Figure 8.22 (documents u_9, d_8, and k_8).

Suppose on 15th January, 2001, a user wishes to find out periodically (say every 30 days) information related to side effects and uses of drugs for various diseases. The query can be expressed as follows. Let $G = \langle X_n, X_\ell, C, P, Q \rangle$, where

$$X_n = \{a, b, d, k\}$$
$$X_\ell = \{-\}$$
$$C \equiv k_1 \wedge k_2 \wedge k_3$$

where

$$k_1 \equiv a\langle\text{-}\rangle b$$
$$k_2 \equiv b\langle\text{-}\{1,6\}\rangle d$$
$$k_3 \equiv b\langle\text{-}\{1,3\}\rangle k$$

and $P = \{p_1, p_2, p_3, p_4\}$, where

$p_1(a) \equiv$ METADATA::a[url] EQUALS "$http://www.panacea.gov$"
$p_2(b) \equiv$ CONTENT::b[html.body.title] NON-ATTR_CONT "$drug\ List$"
$p_3(k) \equiv$ CONTENT::k[html.body.title] NON-ATTR_CONT " $uses$ "
$p_4(d) \equiv$ CONTENT::d[html.body.title] NON-ATTR_CONT "$side\ effects$ "

and $Q \equiv q_1$, where

$q_1(G) \equiv$ COUPLING_QUERY::G.polling_frequency EQUALS "$30\ days$"

At polling time 15th January, 2001, the global web coupling operation retrieves a set of interlinked documents and materializes them in the form of a web table called Drugs as depicted in Figure 8.23. Each web tuple in the table contains information about side effects and uses of a drug indicated for a particular disease. Before polling time 15th February, 2001, the Web site at http://www.panacea.gov/ is modified as depicted earlier. Therefore, on 15th February, the result New Drugs (Figure 8.24) of the polling coupling query contains the relevant changes that have occurred during this period. These two web tables can be represented as follows. Let $W_d = \langle$Drugs$, \mathcal{P}_d\rangle$ be the web table Drugs, where $\mathcal{P}_d = \{U_{d1}, U_{d2}, U_{d3}, U_{d4}, U_{d5}\}$, where

- $U_{d1} = \langle S_{d1} = \langle X_{nd1}, X_{\ell d1}, C_{d1}, P_{d1}\rangle, T_{d1}\rangle$, $X_{nd1} = \{a, b, d, k, \#_1\}$, $X_{\ell d1} = \{\text{-}_1, \text{-}_2, \text{-}_3, \text{-}_4\}$, $C_{d1} \equiv a\langle\text{-}_1\rangle b \wedge b\langle\text{-}_2\rangle\#_1 \wedge \#_1\langle\text{-}_3\rangle d \wedge \#_1\langle\text{-}_4\rangle k$, $P_{d1} = P_{5q}$, and $T_{d1} = \{t_1, t_2, t_8\}$.
- $U_{d2} = \langle S_{d2} = \langle X_{nd2}, X_{\ell d2}, C_{d2}, P_{d2}\rangle, T_{d2}\rangle$, $X_{nd2} = \{a, b, d, k\}$, $X_{\ell d2} = \{\text{-}_1, \text{-}_5, \text{-}_{13}\}$, $C_{d2} \equiv a\langle\text{-}_1\rangle b \wedge b\langle\text{-}_5\rangle d \wedge b\langle\text{-}_{13}\rangle k$, $P_{d2} = P_{5q}$, and $T_{d2} = \{t_3, t_4\}$.
- $U_{d3} = \langle S_{d3} = \langle X_{nd3}, X_{\ell d3}, C_{d3}, P_{d3}\rangle, T_{d3}\rangle$, $X_{nd3} = \{a, b, d, k\}$, $X_{\ell d3} = \{\text{-}_1, \text{-}_5, \text{-}_6\}$, $C_{d3} \equiv a\langle\text{-}_1\rangle b \wedge b\langle\text{-}_5\rangle d \wedge d\langle\text{-}_6\rangle k$, $P_{d3} = P_{5q}$, and $T_{d3} = \{t_5\}$.
- $U_{d4} = \langle S_{d4} = \langle X_{nd4}, X_{\ell d4}, C_{d4}, P_{d4}\rangle, T_{4d}\rangle$, $X_{nd4} = \{a, b, d, k, \#_1, \#_2, \#_3\}$, $X_{\ell d4} = \{\text{-}_1, \text{-}_2, \text{-}_7, \text{-}_8, \text{-}_9, \text{-}_{10}\}$, $C_{d4} \equiv a\langle\text{-}_1\rangle b \wedge b\langle\text{-}_2\rangle\#_1 \wedge \#_1\langle\text{-}_7\rangle\#_2 \wedge \#_2\langle\text{-}_8\rangle\#_3 \wedge \#_3\langle\text{-}_9\rangle d \wedge \#_3\langle\text{-}_{10}\rangle k$, $P_{d4} \equiv P_{5q}$, and $T_{d4} = \{t_6\}$.
- $U_{d5} = \langle S_{d5} = \langle X_{nd5}, X_{\ell d5}, C_{d5}, P_{d5}\rangle, T_{d5}\rangle$, $X_{nd5} = \{a, b, d, k, \#_1, \#_4\}$, $X_{\ell d5} = \{\text{-}_1, \text{-}_2, \text{-}_3, \text{-}_{11}, \text{-}_{12}\}$, $C_{d5} \equiv a\langle\text{-}_1\rangle b \wedge b\langle\text{-}_2\rangle\#_1 \wedge \#_1\langle\text{-}_3\rangle d \wedge \#_1\langle\text{-}_{11}\rangle\#_4 \wedge \#_4\langle\text{-}_{12}\rangle k$, $P_{d5} = P_{5q}$, and $T_{d5} = \{t_7\}$.

Similarly, let $W_{nd} = \langle$NewDrugs$, \mathcal{P}_{nd}\rangle$ be the web table New Drugs, where $\mathcal{P}_{nd} = \{U_{nd1}, U_{nd2}, U_{nd3}\}$ and

- $U_{nd1} = \langle S_{nd1}, T_{nd1}\rangle$ where $S_{nd1} = S_{d1}$ and $T_{nd1} = \{t_1, t_2, t_4, t_5, t_6, t_7, t_8\}$.
- $U_{nd2} = \langle S_{nd2}, T_{nd2}\rangle$ where $S_{nd2} = S_{d2}$ and $T_{nd2} = \{t_3\}$.
- $U_{nd3} = \langle S_{nd3} = \langle X_{nd3}, X_{\ell d3}, C_{nd3}, P_{nd3}\rangle, T_{nd3}\rangle$, $X_{nd3} = \{a, b, d, k, \#_1, \#_2\}$, $X_{\ell nd3} = \{\text{-}_1, \text{-}_2, \text{-}_3, \text{-}_4, \text{-}_5\}$, $C_{nd3} \equiv a\langle\text{-}_1\rangle b \wedge b\langle\text{-}_2\rangle\#_1 \wedge \#_1\langle\text{-}_3\rangle\#_2 \wedge \#_2\langle\text{-}_4\rangle d \wedge \#_1\langle\text{-}_5\rangle k$, $P_{nd3} = P_{5q}$, and $T_{nd3} = \{t_9\}$.

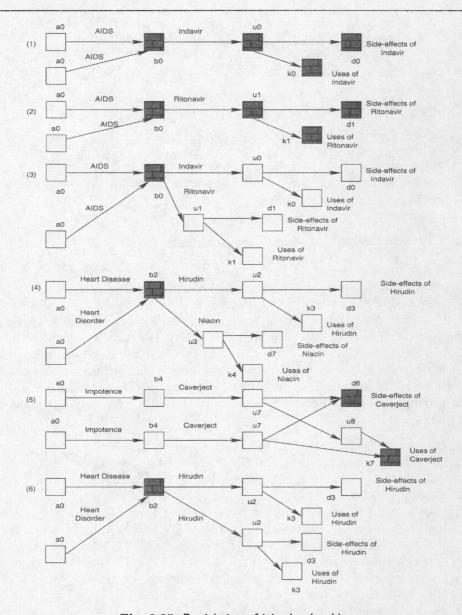

Fig. 8.25. Partial view of joined web table.

Let $\Psi = \langle M, X_j \rangle$ be the join condition where M is the set of schemas in these two web tables and $X_j = \emptyset$. Then these two web tables are joinable since there exist joinable nodes (identical nodes). The nodes b_0, u_0, d_0, and k_0 in the first web tuple in **Drugs** are identical to those in the first web tuple in **New Drugs** as these nodes remain unchanged during the transition. The set of joinable node id pairs

is $J = \{(b_0, b_0), (b_2, b_2), (u_0, u_0), (u_1, u_1), (d_0, d_0), (\bar{c}_1, d_1), (d_6, d_6), (k_0, k_0), (k_1, k_1),$
$(k_7, k_7)\}$. (We show how to compute these joinable nodes in the next section.)
Hence the joinable node type identifiers in **Drugs** and **New Drugs** are $b, d, k, \#_1$. The
joined web tuple generated by concatenating these two web tuples over the nodes b_0,
u_0, d_0, and k_0 is shown in Figure 8.25 (the first web tuple). Similarly, the second
joined web tuple in Figure 8.25 is the result of joining the second web tuples in
Drugs and **New Drugs**. The third joined web tuple is generated by joining the first
web tuple in **Drugs** to the second web tuple in **New Drugs** over the node b_0, and
so on. Observe that the third, fourth, fifth, and sixth web tuples in **Drugs** do not
participate in the web join process as the nodes in these web tuples are not identical
to any nodes in **New Drugs**.

Observe that the sets of partitions in **Drugs** and **New Drugs** containing joinable
tuples are U_{d1}, U_{d5}, and U_{nd1}, respectively. Hence the join operation between these
two web tables will result in joining partitions U_{d1} and U_{d5} with U_{nd1}. Specifically,
web tuples t_1, t_2, and t_8 in U_{d1} are joinable tuples with web tuples t_1, t_2, t_4 and t_5
in U_{nd1}. The joined web tuples are shown in Figure 8.25 (all tuples except the fifth
one). The sets of partitions to represent these partitions are as follows.

1. $U_{wj1} = \langle S_{wj1}, T_{wj1} \rangle$, where $X_{nj1} = \{a, z, b, \#_1, k, d\}$, $X_{\ell j1} = \{-_1, -_2, -_3, -_4, -_6\}$,
$C_{j1} = z\langle -_6 \rangle b \wedge b\langle -_2 \rangle \#_1 \wedge \#_1\langle -_3 \rangle d \wedge \#_1\langle -_4 \rangle k \wedge a\langle -_1 \rangle b$, $P_{j1} = P_{5q} \cup \{p_7\}$, and
$T_{wj1} = \{t_{j1}, t_{j2}\}$, where

$$p_7(z) \equiv \texttt{METADATA::z[url] EQUALS "http //www[.]panacea[.]gov/"}$$

2. $U_{wj2} = \langle S_{wj2}, T_{wj2} \rangle$ where $X_{nj2} = \{a, b, \#_1, \#_3, k, d, x, y, z\}$, $X_{\ell j2} = \{-_1, -_2, -_3, -_4, -_6, -_7, -_8, -_9\}$, $C_{j2} = a\langle -_1 \rangle b \wedge b\langle -_2 \rangle \#_1 \wedge \#_1\langle -_3 \rangle d \wedge \#_1\langle -_4 \rangle k \wedge z\langle -_6 \rangle b \wedge b\langle -_9 \rangle \#_3 \wedge$
$\#_3\langle -_7 \rangle x \wedge \#_3\langle -_8 \rangle y$, $P_{j2} = P_{5q} \cup \{p_7, p_8, p_9\}$, and $T_{wj2} = \{t_{j3}, t_{j4}, t_{j6}\}$, where

$$p_8(y) \equiv \texttt{CONTENT::y[html.body.title] NON-ATTR\_CONT}$$
$$\texttt{" :BEGIN\_WORD: + } uses \texttt{ + :END\_WORD:"}$$
$$p_9(x) \equiv \texttt{CONTENT::x[html.body.title] NON-ATTR\_CONT}$$
$$\texttt{":BEGIN\_STR: + } side\ effects \texttt{ + :END\_STR:"}$$

Similarly, the web tuple t_7 in U_{d5} is joinable with the web tuple t_7 in U_{nd1}. The
joined web tuple is shown in Figure 8.25 (fifth web tuple). The partition containing
the joined web tuple is shown below.

1. $U_{wj3} = \langle S_{wj3}, T_{wj3} \rangle$, where $X_{nj3} = \{a, b, \#_1, \#_4, k, d, w, z\}$, $X_{\ell j3} = \{-_1, -_2, -_3, -_4, -_6, -_7, -_9, -_{11}, -_{12}\}$, $C_{j3} = a\langle -_1 \rangle b \wedge b\langle -_2 \rangle \#_1 \wedge \#_1\langle -_3 \rangle d \wedge \#_1\langle -_4 \rangle k \wedge z\langle -_6 \rangle w \wedge$
$w\langle -_9 \rangle \#_3 \wedge \#_3\langle -_7 \rangle d \wedge \#_3\langle -_{11} \rangle \#_4 \wedge \#_4\langle -_{12} \rangle k$, $P_{j3} = P_{5q} \cup \{p_9\}$, and $T_{wj3} = \{t_{j5}\}$,
where

$$p_9(w) \equiv \texttt{CONTENT::w[html.body.title] NON-ATTR\_CONT}$$
$$\texttt{":BEGIN\_STR: + } drug\ List \texttt{ + :END\_STR:"}$$

The construction details of the joined web table are explained in Section 8.7.4. The
joined web table can be represented by the partition set $\mathcal{P}_j = \{U_{wj1}, U_{wj2}, U_{wj3}\}$.
Observe that the joinable partitions U_{d1} and U_{nd1} in **Drugs** and **New Drugs** result in
two joined partitions U_{jd1}, U_{jd2}. However, in the previous example (when $X_j \neq \emptyset$)
each pair of partitions generates a single joined partition.   ∎

Input: Web table name N_j, join condition $\Psi = \langle M, X_j \rangle$,
web tables $W_1 = \langle N_1, \mathcal{P}_1 \rangle$ and $W_2 = \langle N_2, \mathcal{P}_2 \rangle$.
Output: Joined web table $W_j = \langle N_j, \mathcal{P}_j \rangle$.

(1) $(J, I) = \mathbf{JoinExistence}(W_1, W_2, \Psi)$; /* Figure 8.27 */
(2)   if $(J = \emptyset)$
(3)   return; /* Tables are not joinable */
(4)   else
(5) $W_j = \mathbf{JoinConstruction}(W_1, W_2, J, I, \Psi)$;
(6)   Return $W_j = \langle N_j, \mathcal{P}_j \rangle$;

Fig. 8.26. Algorithm of web join.

Web Join Process

The web join process [18] can be decomposed into two phases.

Join Existence Phase

Given two web tables W_1 and W_2 and a join condition Ψ, we determine if these web tables are joinable by identifying the joinable nodes in W_1 and W_2. If joinable nodes cannot be determined then these two web tables are not joinable. This process is called *join existence*. In the next section we discuss this process.

Join Construction Phase

If W_1 and W_2 are joinable then the joinable nodes are used to construct the joined web table and its schema(s). This process is called *join construction*. We discuss this in Section 8.7.4.

The complete algorithm for web join is shown in Figure 8.26. We first define some symbols to facilitate our discussion of the web join process. Let $W_1 = \langle N_1, \mathcal{P}_1 \rangle$ and $W_2 = \langle N_2, \mathcal{P}_2 \rangle$ be two web tables participating in a web join. Let $\mathcal{P}_i = \langle S_i, T_i \rangle$ for $i \in [1, 2]$ such that $S_i = \langle X_{ni}, X_{\ell i}, C_i, P_i \rangle$ where $X_{ni} = X_{ni_1} \cup X_{ni_2} \cup \ldots \cup X_{ni_{|\mathcal{P}_i|}}$, $X_{\ell i} = X_{\ell i_1} \cup X_{\ell i_2} \cup \ldots \cup X_{\ell i_{|\mathcal{P}_i|}}$, $C_i \equiv C_{i1} \vee C_{i2} \vee \ldots \vee C_{i|\mathcal{P}_i|}$, $P_i = P_{i1} \cup P_{i2} \cup \ldots \cup P_{i|\mathcal{P}_i|}$. Let $\Psi = \langle M, X_j \rangle$ be the join condition and $W_{12} = W_1 \bowtie_\Psi W_2$.

8.7.3 Join Existence Phase

Given two web tables, the join existence process determines if these tables are joinable by computing the joinable nodes and their corresponding type identifiers in these tables. The join existence process is driven by the type of join condition Ψ specified by the user. If $X_{pj} \neq \emptyset$, then the join existence process may be decomposed into the following steps.

1. Identify the existence of joinable nodes by inspecting the schemas of the input web tables.

2. Identify the set of node type identifiers in X_{pj} whose instances are not joinable nodes by inspecting the schemas of the input web tables.

3. Note that due to the very nature of the web schema, it may not be possible to identify the identifiers of all joinable nodes by inspecting the schemas of W_1 and W_2 only. Hence the last step is to identify the remaining set (possibly empty) of joinable nodes by inspecting the web tuples of W_1 and W_2.

However, if $\Psi = \emptyset$ [34] then the joinable nodes are identified by comparing pairs of nodes in the web tuples of W_1 and W_2. In this process the inspection of the schemas to determine some of the joinable nodes is ignored. The joinable nodes are determined directly by comparing the nodes in the input web tables. Specifically, the URLs and last modification dates are compared to determine identical nodes.

In this section, we begin by addressing how to identify some of the joinable nodes by inspecting the schemas of W_1 and W_2. In order to identify the existence of joinable nodes from the web schemas, they must satisfy some *joinability conditions*. In this section, we determine these conditions. Note that if these web schemas do not satisfy any one of the joinability conditions, then we cannot identify joinable nodes in a web tuple from the schemas. Next, we discuss the conditions the schemas must satisfy in order to identify the dangling nodes. Finally, we discuss the complete algorithm of the join existence phase.

Joinability Conditions

We first introduce some terms to facilitate our exposition. We denote the argument, predicate qualifier, attribute path expressions, predicate operator and value of a predicate $p(x)$ as $arg(p)$, $qual(p)$, $attr\_path(p)$, $op(p)$, and $val(p)$, respectively. Also, if $k \equiv x\langle e\rangle y$ then $\mathrm{lnode}(k) = x$, $\mathrm{rnode}(k) = y$, and $\mathrm{link}(k) = e$.

Joinability conditions may be based on the *node predicates* and/or the *link predicates*. The predicate on a node type identifier as defined in the schema is called a *node predicate*. For example, the predicate $p_{j_1}(x)$ in Example 8.11 is a node predicate on the node type identifier x. Similarly, the predicate on a link type identifier as defined in the schema is called a *link predicate*.

Conditions Based on the Node Predicates

In order to facilitate computation of the joinable nodes from the node predicates of the schemas S_i and S_j, the condition given below must be satisfied. Unless otherwise stated, predicates in this section imply metadata predicates.

Condition 8.6 *Let p_{i_1} and p_{i_2} be two node predicates on x in the schema S_i. Similarly, let p_{j_1} and p_{j_2} be two node predicates y in the schema S_j. Then the instances of x and y are joinable nodes if the* url *and* last modification date *of x and y are identical. That is,*

$$\arg(p_{i_1}) = \arg(p_{i_2}),\ \arg(p_{j_1}) = \arg(p_{j_2}),$$
$$\mathrm{attr\_path}(p_{i_1}) = \mathrm{attr\_path}(p_{j_1}) = \texttt{url},$$
$$\mathrm{attr\_path}(p_{i_2}) = \mathrm{attr\_path}(p_{j_2}) = \texttt{date},$$
$$\mathrm{op}(p_{i_1}) = \mathrm{op}(p_{j_1}) = \texttt{EQUALS},\ \mathrm{op}(p_{i_2}) = \mathrm{op}(p_{j_2}) = \texttt{EQUALS},$$
$$\mathrm{val}(p_{i_1}) = \mathrm{val}(p_{j_1}),\ \text{and}\ \mathrm{val}(p_{i_2}) = \mathrm{val}(p_{j_2}).$$

The joinable node type identifiers are $\mathrm{arg}(p_{i_1})$ *and* $\mathrm{arg}(p_{j_1})$. ∎

Example 8.14. Consider the following predicates in Examples 6.9 and 8.11.

$p_{i_1}(a) \equiv$ METADATA::a[url] EQUALS "http://www[.]rxdrugs[.]com/"
$p_{i_6}(a) \equiv$ METADATA::a[date] EQUALS "2nd January, 2001"
$p_{j_1}(x) \equiv$ METADATA::a[url] EQUALS "http://www[.]rxdrugs[.]com/"
$p_{j_7}(x) \equiv$ METADATA::x[date] EQUALS "2nd January, 2001"

$$\mathrm{arg}(p_{i_1}) = \mathrm{arg}(p_{i_6}) = a,\ \mathrm{arg}(p_{j_1}) = \mathrm{arg}(p_{j_7}) = x,$$
$$\mathrm{attr\_path}(p_{i_1}) = \mathrm{attr\_path}(p_{j_1}) = \mathtt{url},$$
$$\mathrm{attr\_path}(p_{i_6}) = \mathrm{attr\_path}(p_{j_7}) = \mathtt{date},$$
$$\mathrm{op}(p_{i_1}) = \mathrm{op}(p_{j_1}) = \mathtt{EQUALS},\ \mathrm{op}(p_{i_6}) = \mathrm{op}(p_{j_7}) = \mathtt{EQUALS},$$
$$\mathrm{val}(p_{i_1}) = \mathrm{val}(p_{j_1}) = \mathtt{http://www.rxdrugs.com/},$$
$$\text{and } \mathrm{val}(p_{i_6}) = \mathrm{val}(p_{j_7}) = \mathtt{2nd\ January,\ 2001}.$$

Thus instances of the node type identifiers a and x are joinable nodes based on Condition 8.6. ∎

Conditions Based on the Node and Link Predicates

Let k_i and k_j be two simple connectivities in the schemas S_i and S_j, respectively. Let, p_{i_1} and p_{j_1} be two link predicates and let p_{i_2} and p_{j_2} be two node predicates. Then the instances of $\mathrm{lnode}(k_i)$, $\mathrm{lnode}(k_j)$, $\mathrm{rnode}(k_i)$ and $\mathrm{rnode}(k_j)$ are joinable nodes if one or more of the following conditions holds.

Condition 8.7 *The* source_url *of the link type identifiers e and f of k_i and k_j, respectively are identical and the last modification dates of the node type identifiers* $\mathrm{lnode}(k_i)$ *and* $\mathrm{lnode}(k_j)$ *are identical; i.e.,*

$$\mathrm{arg}(p_{i_2}) = \mathrm{lnode}(k_i),\ \mathrm{arg}(p_{j_2}) = \mathrm{lnode}(k_j),$$
$$\mathrm{arg}(p_{i_1}) = e,\ \mathrm{arg}(p_{j_1}) = f,$$
$$\mathrm{attr\_path}(p_{i_1}) = \mathrm{attr\_path}(p_{j_1}) = \mathtt{source\_url},$$
$$\mathrm{attr\_path}(p_{i_2}) = \mathrm{attr\_path}(p_{j_2}) = \mathtt{date},$$
$$\mathrm{op}(p_{i_1}) = \mathrm{op}(p_{j_1}) = \mathtt{EQUALS},\ \mathrm{op}(p_{i_2}) = \mathrm{op}(p_{j_2}) = \mathtt{EQUALS},$$
$$\mathrm{val}(p_{i_1}) = \mathrm{val}(p_{j_1}),\ \text{and } \mathrm{val}(p_{i_2}) = \mathrm{val}(p_{j_2}). \blacksquare$$

To elaborate further, both the link type identifiers e and f exist in the same Web document with identical last modification dates, since the source_url of these links and the modification dates of these documents are identical. Thus $\mathrm{lnode}(k_i)$ and $\mathrm{lnode}(k_j)$ are joinable node type identifiers.

Condition 8.8 *The* target_url *of the link type identifiers g and h of k_i and k_j, respectively, are identical and the last modification dates of the node type identifiers* $\mathrm{rnode}(k_i)$ *and* $\mathrm{rnode}(k_j)$ *are identical; i.e.,*

$$\arg(p_{i_2}) = \text{rnode}(k_i), \ \arg(p_{j_2}) = \text{rnode}(k_j),$$
$$\arg(p_{i_1}) = g, \ \arg(p_{j_1}) = h,$$
$$\text{attr\_path}(p_{i_1}) = \text{attr\_path}(p_{j_1}) = \textbf{target\_url},$$
$$\text{attr\_path}(p_{i_2}) = \text{attr\_path}(p_{j_2}) = \textbf{date},$$
$$\text{op}(p_{i_1}) = \text{op}(p_{j_1}) = \textbf{EQUALS}, \ \text{op}(p_{i_2}) = \text{op}(p_{j_2}) = \textbf{EQUALS},$$
$$\text{val}(p_{i_1}) = \text{val}(p_{j_1}), \ \text{and val}(p_{i_2}) = \text{val}(p_{j_2}).$$

Like the previous condition, since **target_url** *of g and h is identical, both the link type identifiers g and h reference the same web documents (identical last modification dates) denoted by* $\text{rnode}(k_i)$ *and* $\text{rnode}(k_j)$, *respectively. Thus the instances of* $\text{rnode}(k_i)$ *and* $\text{rnode}(k_j)$ *are joinable nodes.* ∎

Condition 8.9 *The* source_url *of the link type identifiers e and the* target_url *of the link type identifier g of* k_i *and* k_j, *respectively, are identical and the last modification dates of the node type identifiers* $\text{lnode}(k_i)$ *and* $\text{rnode}(k_j)$ *are identical; i.e.,*

$$\arg(p_{i_2}) = \text{lnode}(k_i), \ \arg(p_{j_2}) = \text{rnode}(k_j),$$
$$\arg(p_{i_1}) = e, \ \arg(p_{j_1}) = g,$$
$$\text{attr\_path}(p_{i_1}) = \textbf{source\_url}, \ \text{attr\_path}(p_{j_1}) = \textbf{target\_url},$$
$$\text{attr\_path}(p_{i_2}) = \text{attr\_path}(p_{j_2}) = \textbf{date},$$
$$\text{op}(p_{i_1}) = \text{op}(p_{j_1}) = \textbf{EQUALS}, \ \text{op}(p_{i_2}) = \text{op}(p_{j_2}) = \textbf{EQUALS},$$
$$\text{val}(p_{i_1}) = \text{val}(p_{j_1}), \ \text{and val}(p_{i_2}) = \text{val}(p_{j_2}).$$

To elaborate further, since the source_url *of e and* target_url *of g are identical, the URL and the last modification date of the web document (*$\text{lnode}(k_i)$*) containing the link e is identical to the URL and last modification date of the Web document (*$\text{rnode}(k_j)$*) referenced by the link g. Thus the instances of* $\text{lnode}(k_i)$ *and* $\text{rnode}(k_j)$ *are joinable nodes.* ∎

Let p_{i_1} be a link predicate and let p_{i_2}, p_{j_1} and p_{j_2} be three node predicates. Then, the set of joinable node type identifiers can be identified from S_i and S_j if one or more of the following conditions holds.

Condition 8.10 *The* url *of the node type identifier x and the* target_url *of the link type identifier g are identical and the last modification date* date *of x is identical to that of* $\text{rnode}(k_j)$. *That is, the URL and date of the Web document referenced by the link type identifier g, i.e.,* $\text{rnode}(k_j)$, *are identical to the URL and date of x. Formally,*

$$\arg(p_{i_1}) = g, \ \arg(p_{i_2}) = \text{rnode}(k_j),$$
$$\arg(p_{j_1}) = x, \ \arg(p_{j_2}) = x,$$
$$\text{attr\_path}(p_{i_1}) = \textbf{target\_url}, \ \text{attr\_path}(p_{j_1}) = \textbf{url},$$
$$\text{attr\_path}(p_{i_2}) = \text{attr\_path}(p_{j_2}) = \textbf{date},$$
$$\text{op}(p_{i_1}) = \text{op}(p_{j_1}) = \textbf{EQUALS}, \ \text{op}(p_{i_2}) = \text{op}(p_{j_2}) = \textbf{EQUALS},$$
$$\text{val}(p_{i_1}) = \text{val}(p_{j_1}), \ \text{and val}(p_{i_2}) = \text{val}(p_{j_2}).$$

The joinable node type identifiers are x and $\mathrm{rnode}(k_j)$.   ∎

Condition 8.11 *The* url *of the node type identifier x and the* source_url *of the link type identifier f are identical and the last modification date* date *of x is identical to that of* $\mathrm{lnode}(k_j)$. *That is, similar to the previous condition, the URL and date of the Web document containing the link type identifier f, i.e.,* $\mathrm{lnode}(k_j)$, *are identical to the URL and date of x. Formally,*

$$\arg(p_{i_1}) = f,\ \arg(p_{i_2}) = \mathrm{lnode}(k_j),$$
$$\arg(p_{j_1}) = x,\ \arg(p_{j_2}) = x,$$
$$\mathrm{attr\_path}(p_{i_1}) = \mathtt{source\_url},\ \mathrm{attr\_path}(p_{j_1}) = \mathtt{url},$$
$$\mathrm{attr\_path}(p_{i_2}) = \mathrm{attr\_path}(p_{j_2}) = \mathtt{date},$$
$$\mathrm{op}(p_{i_1}) = \mathrm{op}(p_{j_1}) = \mathtt{EQUALS},\ \mathrm{op}(p_{i_2}) = \mathrm{op}(p_{j_2}) = \mathtt{EQUALS},$$
$$\mathrm{val}(p_{i_1}) = \mathrm{val}(p_{j_1}),\ \text{and}\ \mathrm{val}(p_{i_2}) = \mathrm{val}(p_{j_2}).$$

The joinable node type identifiers are x and $\mathrm{lnode}(k_j)$.   ∎

We illustrate some of these conditions with an example.

Example 8.15. Let us consider some modifications of the schemas in Example 8.12. Suppose we have the following predicates.

$p_{i_1}(n) \equiv$ METATDATA::n[source_url] EQUALS "http://www[.]rxdrugs[.]com/"
$p_{i_2}(a) \equiv$ METADATA::a[date] EQUALS "2nd January, 2001"
$p_{j_1}(r) \equiv$ METADATA::r[source_url] EQUALS "http://www[.]rxdrugs[.]com/"
$p_{j_2}(x) \equiv$ METADATA::x[date] EQUALS "2nd January, 2001"

Since $k_i \equiv a\langle n\rangle b$ and $k_j \equiv x\langle r\rangle y$, $\mathrm{lnode}(k_i) = a$ and $\mathrm{lnode}(k_j) = x$.

$$\arg(p_{i_1}) = n, \arg(p_{i_2}) = a,\ \arg(p_{j_1}) = r, \arg(p_{j_2}) = x,$$
$$\mathrm{attr\_path}(p_{i_1}) = \mathrm{attr\_path}(p_{j_1}) = \mathtt{source\_url},$$
$$\mathrm{attr\_path}(p_{i_2}) = \mathrm{attr\_path}(p_{j_2}) = \mathtt{date},$$
$$\mathrm{op}(p_{i_1}) = \mathrm{op}(p_{j_1}) = \mathtt{EQUALS},\ \mathrm{op}(p_{i_2}) = \mathrm{op}(p_{j_2}) = \mathtt{EQUALS},$$
$$\mathrm{val}(p_{i_1}) = \mathrm{val}(p_{j_1}) = \mathtt{http}://\mathtt{www.rxdrugs.com}/,$$
$$\text{and}\ \mathrm{val}(p_{i_2}) = \mathrm{val}(p_{j_2}) = \text{2nd January, 2001}.$$

Thus the node type identifiers a and x are joinable based on Condition 8.7.

Now consider the following set of predicates.

$p_{i_1}(a) \equiv$ METADATA::a[url] EQUALS "http://www[.]rxdrugs[.]com/"
$p_{i_2}(a) \equiv$ METADATA::a[date] EQUALS "2nd January, 2001"
$p_{j_1}(r) \equiv$ METADATA::r[source_url] EQUALS "http://www[.]rxdrugs[.]com/"
$p_{j_2}(x) \equiv$ METADATA::x[date] EQUALS "2nd January, 2001"

$$\arg(p_{i_1}) = \arg(p_{i_2}) = a,\ \arg(p_{j_1}) = r, \arg(p_{j_2}) = x,$$
$$\text{attr\_path}(p_{i_1}) = \text{url}, \text{attr\_path}(p_{j_1}) = \text{source\_url},$$
$$\text{attr\_path}(p_{i_2}) = \text{attr\_path}(p_{j_2}) = \text{date},$$
$$\text{op}(p_{i_1}) = \text{op}(p_{j_1}) = \text{EQUALS},\ \text{op}(p_{i_2}) = \text{op}(p_{j_2}) = \text{EQUALS},$$
$$\text{val}(p_{i_1}) = \text{val}(p_{j_1}) = \text{http} : //\text{www.rxdrugs.com/},$$
$$\text{and } \text{val}(p_{i_2}) = \text{val}(p_{j_2}) = \text{2nd January, 2001.}$$

Thus the node type identifiers a and x are joinable based on Condition 8.11. ∎

Conditions Specifically for Multijoinable Node Type Identifiers

We have seen that at least one of the above conditions has to be satisfied to identify the joinable node type identifiers by inspecting S_i and S_j of W_i and W_j. We now introduce a condition applicable only to a join involving more than one joinable node type identifier. This condition is valid only when we have determined at least a pair of joinable node type identifiers satisfying any one of the above conditions. It cannot determine joinable node type identifiers unless at least one pair of joinable node type identifiers has already been determined. Let $\text{lnode}(k_i)$ and $\text{lnode}(k_j)$ be joinable node type identifiers. Furthermore, let $\text{rnode}(k_i)$ and $\text{rnode}(k_j)$ be the node type identifiers adjacent to $\text{lnode}(k_i)$ and $\text{lnode}(k_j)$, respectively. Finally, let e and f be the link type identifiers between these adjacent node type identifiers. Then the instances of $\text{rnode}(k_i)$ and $\text{rnode}(k_j)$ are joinable nodes if the following condition is true:

Condition 8.12 *The* link_type *of link type identifiers e and f of k_i and k_j respectively, are identical and equal to* interior; *i.e.,* $\arg(p_i) = e$, $\arg(p_j) = f$, $\text{attr\_path}(p_i) = \text{attr\_path}(p_j) = \text{link\_type}$, $\text{op}(p_i) = \text{op}(p_j) = \text{EQUALS}$, $\text{val}(p_i) = \text{val}(p_j) = \text{interior}.$ ∎

Here $\text{rnode}(k_i)$ and $\text{rnode}(k_j)$ are joinable node type identifiers since the URLs and last modification dates of the Web documents (i.e., $\text{lnode}(k_i)$ and $\text{lnode}(k_j)$) containing the links e and f are identical to the Web documents (i.e., $\text{rnode}(k_i)$ and $\text{rnode}(k_j)$) referenced by these links.

Example 8.16. Consider the web schemas in Example 8.12. Suppose the node type identifiers a and x are joinable. Let the link predicates of link type identifier n and r be:

$$p_i(n) \equiv \text{METADATA}::\text{n[link\_type] EQUALS "interior"}$$
$$p_j(r) \equiv \text{METADATA}::\text{r[link\_type] EQUALS "interior"}$$

Clearly, the instances of b and y are joinable nodes based on Condition 8.12. Note that if a and x are not joinable node type identifiers, the joinability of the instances of b and y cannot be determined by inspecting these predicates alone. ∎

Nonjoinability Conditions

In the preceding section we have identified the conditions a pair of simple schemas must satisfy in order to identify some of the joinable nodes by inspecting the schemas only. In this section we discuss *conditions* a pair of simple schemas must satisfy to identify those nodes in W_1 and W_2 that cannot be joinable.

Conditions Based on the Node Predicates

In order to facilitate computation of the nonjoinable nodes from the node predicates of the schemas S_i and S_j, the condition given below must be satisfied. The first condition is applicable only for HTML documents.

Condition 8.13 *Let p_{i_1} and $p_{j,1}$ be two content predicates on the node type identifiers x and y in the schemas S_i and S_j, respectively. Then the instances of x and y are nonjoinable nodes if the* title *of the instances of x and y is not identical. That is,*

$$\text{attr\_path}(p_{i_1}) = c_1.c_2.\ldots.c_n \text{ where } c_n = \text{title},$$
$$\text{attr\_path}(p_{j_1}) = d_1.d_2.\ldots.d_r \text{ where } d_r = \text{title},$$
$$\text{op}(p_{i_1}) = \text{op}(p_{j_1}) = \text{NON} - \text{ATTR\_ENCL},$$
$$\text{val}(p_{i_1}) \neq \text{val}(p_{j_1}) \text{ or } \text{val}(p_{i_1}) \text{ does not match with } \text{val}(p_{j_1}).$$

The nonjoinable node type identifiers are $\arg(p_{i_1})$ and $\arg(p_{j_1})$. ∎

Example 8.17. Consider the following predicates.

$$p_i(b) \equiv \text{CONTENT::b[html.body.title] NON-ATTR\_ENCL "Side effects"}$$
$$p_j(y) \equiv \text{CONTENT::y[title] NON-ATTR\_ENCL "Usage"}$$

$$\arg(p_{i_1}) = b, \ \arg(p_{j_1}) = y,$$
$$\text{attr\_path}(p_{i_1}) = \text{html.body.title}, \ \text{attr\_path}(p_{j_1}) = \text{title},$$
$$\text{op}(p_{i_1}) = \text{op}(p_{j_1}) = \text{NON} - \text{ATTR\_ENCL},$$
$$\text{val}(p_{i_1}) = \text{Side effects}, \ \text{and} \ \text{val}(p_{j_1}) = \text{Usage}.$$

Thus instances of the node type identifiers b and y are nonjoinable nodes based on Condition 8.13. ∎

Conditions Based on the Node or Link Predicates

The next condition involves determination of the nonjoinable node type identifiers by inspecting the node or link predicates.

Condition 8.14 *Let p_i and p_j be two metadata predicates in the schemas S_i and S_j, respectively such that $\arg(p_i) = x$, $\arg(p_j) = y$, and any one of the following conditions is true.*

1. $\text{attr\_path}(p_i) = \text{attr\_path}(p_j)$ *or* $\text{attr\_path}(p_i)$ *is a suffix of* $\text{attr\_path}(p_j)$, $\text{attr\_path}(p_i) = \text{attr\_path}(p_j) \neq \texttt{link\_type}$, *or* $(p_i) = \text{op}(p_j) = \texttt{EQUALS}$ *and* $\text{val}(p_i) \neq \text{val}(p_j)$ *or* $\text{val}(p_i)$ *does not match with* $\text{val}(p_j)$.

2. $\text{attr\_path}(p_i)$ *is a prefix or infix of* $\text{attr\_path}(p_j)$, $\text{attr\_path}(p_i) = \text{attr\_path}(p_j) \neq \texttt{link\_type}$, $\text{op}(p_i) = \text{op}(p_j) = \texttt{EQUALS}$ *and* $\text{val}(p_j)$ *is not contained in* $\text{val}(p_j)$.

Then the following conditions are true.

- *If p_i and p_j are node predicates, then $\arg(p_i)$ and $\arg(p_j)$ are nonjoinable node type identifiers.*
- *If p_i and p_j are link predicates such that $link(k_i) = x$ and $link(k_j) = y$, then*
  - *If $\text{attr\_path}(p_i)$ and $\text{attr\_path}(p_j)$ are on* `source_url`, *then* $\text{lnode}(k_i)$ *and* $\text{lnode}(k_j)$ *are not joinable node type identifiers;*
  - *If $\text{attr\_path}(p_i)$ and $\text{attr\_path}(p_j)$ are on* `target_url`, *then* $\text{rnode}(k_i)$ *and* $\text{rnode}(k_j)$ *are not joinable node type identifiers;*
  - *If $\text{attr\_path}(p_i)$ and $\text{attr\_path}(p_j)$ are on* `source_url` *and* `target_url`, *then* $\text{lnode}(k_i)$ *and* $\text{rnode}(k_j)$ *are not joinable node type identifiers.*
- *If p_i and p_j are node and link predicates such that $link(k_j) = y$, then*
  - $\arg(p_i)$ *and* $\text{lnode}(k_j)$ *are nonjoinable if* $\text{attr\_path}(p_i)$ *and* $\text{attr\_path}(p_j)$ *are on* `url` *and* `source_url`, *respectively;*
  - $\arg(p_i)$ *and* $\text{rnode}(k_j)$ *are nonjoinable if* $\text{attr\_path}(p_i)$ *and* $\text{attr\_path}(p_j)$ *are on* `url` *and* `target_url`, *respectively;* ∎

We illustrate some of these conditions with an example:

Example 8.18. Let us consider some modifications of the web schemas in Example 8.12. Suppose we have the following predicates

$p_{i_1}(x) \equiv \texttt{METATDATA::x[url.server] EQUALS "www[.]rxdrugs[.]com"}$
$p_{j_1}(y) \equiv \texttt{[METADATA::y[server] EQUALS "www[.]rxlist[.]com"}$

Observe that the attribute path expression of p_{j_1} is a suffix of the attribute path expression of p_{i_1} and $\text{val}(p_{i_1}) \neq \text{val}(p_{j_1})$. As p_{i_1} and p_{j_1} are node predicates, based on the first condition, (x, y) are nonjoinable node type identifiers. This is obvious as the instances of these two node type identifiers reside in different servers.

Now consider the following sets of link predicates.

$p_{i_1}(n) \equiv \texttt{METADATA::n[source\_url] EQUALS "http://www[.]rxdrugs[.]com/"}$
$p_{j_1}(r) \equiv \texttt{METADATA::r[source\_url.server.domain] EQUALS "edu"}$

In this case,

$\arg(p_{i_1}) = n, \ \arg(p_{j_1}) = r,$

$\text{attr\_path}(p_{i_1}) = \texttt{source\_url}, \text{attr\_path}(p_{j_1}) = \texttt{source\_url.server.domain},$

$\text{op}(p_{i_1}) = \text{op}(p_{j_1}) = \texttt{EQUALS},$

$\text{val}(p_{i_1}) = \texttt{http}://\text{www.rxdrugs.com/}, \text{ and } \text{val}(p_{j_1}) = \texttt{edu}.$

Here $\text{attr\_path}(p_{i,1})$ is the prefix of $\text{attr\_path}(p_{j,1})$ and the value of p_{j_1} is not contained in p_{i_1}. Therefore, based on the second condition in Condition 8.14, the node type identifiers a and x are nonjoinable. ∎

Conditions Based on the Joinable or Nonjoinable Node Type Identifiers

We have seen that at least one of the above conditions has to be satisfied to identify the nonjoinable node type identifiers by inspecting S_i and S_j of W_i and W_j. We now introduce two conditions applicable only when we have determined at least a pair of joinable or nonjoinable node type identifiers satisfying any one of the preceding conditions. It cannot determine nonjoinable node type identifiers unless at least one pair of joinable or nonjoinable node type identifiers has already been determined. Let lnode(k_i) and lnode(k_j) be node type identifiers. Furthermore, let rnode(k_i) and rnode(k_j) be the node type identifiers adjacent to lnode(k_i) and lnode(k_j), respectively. Finally, let e and f be the link type identifiers between these adjacent node type identifiers. Then the following conditions hold.

Condition 8.15 *Let* lnode(k_i) *and* lnode(k_j) *be nonjoinable node type identifiers. Then the instances of the node type identifiers* rnode(k_i) *and* rnode(k_j) *are not joinable if the following condition is true,* $\arg(p_i) = e$, $\arg(p_j) = f$, attr_path(p_i) = attr_path(p_j) = link_type, op(p_i) = op(p_j) = EQUALS, val(p_i) = val(p_j) = interior. *Here* rnode(k_i) *and* rnode(k_j) *are non-joinable node type identifiers since the URLs and last modification dates of the Web documents (i.e., lnode(k_i) and lnode(k_j)) containing links e and f are identical to the Web documents (i.e., rnode(k_i) and rnode(k_j)) referenced by these links.* ∎

Example 8.19. Consider the web schemas in Example 8.12. Suppose the node type identifiers a and x are nonjoinable. Let the link predicates of link type identifiers n and r be:

$$p_i(n) \equiv \texttt{METADATA::n[link\_type] EQUALS "interior"}$$
$$p_j(r) \equiv \texttt{METADATA::r[link\_type] EQUALS "interior"}$$

Clearly, the instances of b and y are nonjoinable nodes based on Condition 8.15. Note that if a and x are not nonjoinable node type identifiers, then the nonjoinability of the instances of b and y cannot be determined by inspecting these predicates alone. ∎

Condition 8.16 *Let* lnode(k_i) *and* lnode(k_j) *be joinable node type identifiers such that the* link_type *of the link type identifiers e and f of k_i and k_j, respectively, are identical and equal to* local *or* global; *i.e.,* $\arg(p_i) = e$, $\arg(p_j) = f$, attr_path(p_i) = attr_path(p_j) = link_type, op(p_i) = op(p_j) = EQUALS, val(p_i) = val(p_j) = global|local. *Then* lnode(k_i) *and* rnode(k_j), *and* lnode(k_j) *and* rnode(k_i) *are nonjoinable. Furthermore, if* val(p_i) = local, val(p_j) = global, *then* rnode(k_i) *and* rnode(k_j) *are nonjoinable.* ∎

Example 8.20. Consider the previous example again. Suppose the node type identifiers a and x are joinable. Let the link predicates of the link type identifiers n and r be:

$$p_i(n) = \texttt{METADATA::n[link\_type] EQUALS "local"}$$
$$p_j(r) = \texttt{METADATA::r[link\_type] EQUALS "global"}$$

Input: Web tables $W_1 = \langle Z_1, \mathcal{U}_1 \rangle$, $W_2 = \langle Z_2, \mathcal{U}_2 \rangle$ and join condition $\Psi = \langle M, X_{pj} \rangle$.
Output: Set of joinable nodes J, set of pairs of joinable node identifiers I.

(1) Let $M_1 \subseteq M$ s.t $\forall\ S_k \in M_1$, $S_k \in \mathcal{S}_1$ where $0 < k \le |M_1|$;
(2) Let $M_2 \subseteq M$ s.t $\forall\ S_k \in M_2$, $S_k \in \mathcal{S}_2$ where $0 < k \le |M_2|$;
  /* Joinable nodes from schemas */
(3) $\mathcal{S}_{temp1} = \textbf{FindJoinableSchemas}(M_1, left(X_{pj}))$ /* Figure 8.28 */
(4) $\mathcal{S}_{temp2} = \textbf{FindJoinableSchemas}(M_2, right(X_{pj}))$; /* Figure 8.28 */
(5) for ($a = 1$ to $\mathcal{S}_{temp1}$) {
(6)   for ($b = 1$ to $\mathcal{S}_{temp2}$) {
(7) $(X'_{nj}, X'_{pj}) = \textbf{SchemaJoinability}(S_a, S_b, X_{pj})$, $X'_{nj} \subseteq X_{pj}$, $X'_{pj} \subseteq X_{pj}$
          and $X'_{pj} \cap X'_{nj} = \emptyset$;
(8)   if ($X'_{nj} \ne \emptyset$)
(9)   /* Partitions $U_a = \langle S_a, T_a \rangle \in \mathcal{U}_1$ and $U_b = \langle S_b, T_b \rangle \in \mathcal{U}_2$
          does not participate in join */;
          /* Joinable nodes from web tuples */
(10)   else {
(11) $X = X_{pj} - X'_{pj}$;
(12)   Let J_a represents set of node ids of identifiers X'_{pj};
(13) $N_1 = \textbf{GetAllNodeIds}(U_a,\ left(X))$; /* Returns a set of identifier
          of all the instances of nodes of type $x \in left(X)$ in U_a */
(14) $N_2 = \textbf{GetAllNodeIds}(U_b,\ right(X))$;
(15) $(J_b, I) = \textbf{ComputeJoinableNodes}(N_1, N_2, W_1, W_2)$; /* Figure 8.29 */
(16) $J = J_a \cup J_b$;
(17)   }
(18)   }
(19)}
(20) $I = X_{pj}$;
(21) return (J, I);

Fig. 8.27. Algorithm of join existence.

Clearly, the instances of b and x are nonjoinable nodes based on Condition 8.16. Similarly, the instances of a and y are nonjoinable. Also, the instances of b and y are nonjoinable. ∎

Algorithm for Join Existence

We now describe the algorithm for computing the joinable nodes and their corresponding type identifiers in the join existence phase. The pseudocode of this algorithm is given in Figure 8.27.

The algorithm takes as input the web tables W_1 and W_2 and the join condition $\Psi = \langle M, X_{pj} \rangle$, and returns as output the set of joinable node ids (possibly empty) and the corresponding node type identifiers, respectively, in W_1 and W_2 (denoted by J and I). First the algorithm identifies the set of schemas (Steps (1) and (2))

Input: Set of schemas M, Set of node type identifiers X;
Output: Set of schemas $\mathcal{S}_{temp}$.

(1)   for $(a = 1\ to\ M)$ {
(2)   Let $S_a = \langle X_{na}, X_{\ell a}, C_a, P_a \rangle$;
(3)   if $(X \subseteq X_{na})$
(4)   Insert S_a in $\mathcal{S}_{temp}$;
(5)   }
(6)   return $\mathcal{S}_{temp}$;

Fig. 8.28. Algorithm of **FindJoinableSchemas**.

in W_1 and W_2 involved in the join (denoted as M_1 and M_2 in the algorithm). The algorithm computes J and I based on the join condition. In this case the set of joinable node type identifiers is specified in Ψ.

Identify Joinable Nodes from Schemas

Note that not all identical nodes in W_1 and W_2 are joinable. The identical nodes must be instances of the identifiers in X_{pj} and must be in the partitions bound by the schemas in M to be joinable. Hence, to compute the joinable nodes we first scan the partitions in W_1 and W_2 having schemas in M to identify those partitions that contain the joinable node type identifiers (Steps (3) and (4)). Let $left(X_{pj})$ and $right(X_{pj})$ denote the set of node type identifiers in the left-hand side and right-hand side of each pair in X_{pj}, respectively. Then the construct **Find-JoinableSchema** (in Steps (3) and (4)) identifies the set of schemas in W_1 and W_2 (denoted by $\mathcal{S}_{temp1}$ and $\mathcal{S}_{temp2}$) that contain the identifiers in $left(X_{pj})$ and $right(X_{pj})$, respectively. The pseudocode of the algorithm is shown in Figure 8.28. Once the schemas containing the joinable node type identifiers are identified, Steps (5) to (9) compare each possible pair of simple web schemas in $\mathcal{S}_{temp1}$ and $\mathcal{S}_{temp2}$ to check if the pairs of joinable node type identifiers satisfy any one of the joinability and nonjoinability conditions discussed earlier. This comparison is encapsulate in the construct **SchemaJoinability** in Step (7). It returns a pair of sets of the node type identifiers X'_{pj} and X'_{nj} respectively. X'_{pj} denotes the set of pairs of node type identifiers whose instances are joinable nodes as determined by evaluating the joinability conditions against the pair of schemas. Note that $X'_{pj} \subseteq X_{pj}$. The set X'_{nj} denotes the set of pairs of joinable node type identifiers in X_{pj} whose instances cannot be joined as they satisfy one of the nonjoinability conditions. Note that if $X'_{nj} = \emptyset$, then the tuples bound by the schemas are joinable. Otherwise, they are not joinable as the instances of at least one pair of type identifiers in X_{pj} are not joinable. This condition is evaluated in Step (8). If $X'_{nj} = \emptyset$, then Steps (11) to (16) are executed to identify the joinable nodes. Observe that as the instances of each pair in X'_{pj} (denoted as J_a in the algorithm) are joinable, it is not necessary to compare the URLs and dates of these nodes. For the remaining pairs of joinable

---

Input: Web tables $W_1 = \langle Z_1, U_1 \rangle$, $W_2 = \langle Z_2, U_2 \rangle$, set of node ids N_1 and N_2.
Output: Set of joinable nodes J, set of pairs of joinable node type identifiers I.

(1) $D = N_1 \cap N_2$;
(2)   for $(a = 1 \ to \ |D|)$ {
(3)   Get node $n_a \in D$ and $n_a \in W_1$;
(4)   Get node $n_a \in D$ and $n_a \in W_2$;
(5)   if $(\text{date}(n_a \in W_1) = \text{date}(n_a \in W_2))$ {
(6)   Insert n_a is J; /* n_a is joinable */
(7)   Insert the identifiers (x_{a1}, x_{a2}) in I;
(8)   }
(9)   }
(10)   return (J, I);

Fig. 8.29. Algorithm of joinable node and identifiers computation.

node type identifiers, denoted as X, joinable nodes are computed by the construct **ComputeJoinableNodes** (Step (15)).

Identify Joinable Nodes from the Web Tuples

To identify the joinable nodes from the web tuples, we need to compare the contents of the nodes. However, comparing the contents and structure of each possible pair of Web pages represented by the nodes in W_1 and W_2 can have significant impact on the total cost and the query response time for large web tables to render the web join impractical. A practical solution to this problem is to first subdivide the set of nodes in each web table into a disjoint and smaller subset D containing ids of nodes that occur in W_1 as well as in W_2 (Step (1) in Figure 8.29). In WHOWEDA, each node object has an identifier called the *node id*. Two nodes have identical node ids if the URLs of these nodes are identical. Thus each element in D is the identifier of a node that exists in W_1 and W_2. However, as nodes with identical URLs in different web tables may not always be identical in their contents, for each node id $n_a \in D$ the algorithm retrieves the last modification date of n_a in W_1 and W_2. If the dates are identical (Step (5) in Figure 8 29), then the nodes represented by n_a in W_1 and W_2 are identical and are considered joinable nodes. In that case the algorithm inserts n_a in J. Observe that in this case we do not compare the Web pages corresponding to the node ids in D to identify joinable nodes. Also, the algorithm retrieves the corresponding node type identifiers of n_a in W_1 and W_2 (say x_{a1} and x_{a2}) and inserts them in I (Step (7) in Figure 8.29). Finally, the pair (J, I) is returned by the algorithm.

8.7.4 Join Construction Phase When $X_{pj} \neq \emptyset$

Join construction is the process of deriving a joined web table from two web tables. In the previous section, we showed how to determine the joinable nodes and

Input: Web table name Z_j, join condition $\Psi = \langle M, X_{pj} \rangle$, Set of joinable node ids J, Set of pairs of joinable node type identifiers I, and web tables $W_1 = \langle Z_1, \mathcal{U}_1 \rangle$ and $W_2 = \langle Z_2, \mathcal{U}_2 \rangle$.
Output: Joined web table $W_j = \langle Z_j, \mathcal{U}_j \rangle$.

(1)   Let $M_1 \subseteq M$ s.t $\forall S_k \in M_1, S_k \in \mathcal{S}_1$ where $k \leq |M_1|$;
(2)   Let $M_2 \subseteq M$ s.t $\forall S_k \in M_2, S_k \in \mathcal{S}_2$ where $k \leq |M_2|$;
(3) $\mathcal{U}_1' = \mathbf{SelectJoinablePartition}(W_1, J, left(I), M_1)$; /* Figure 8.31 */
(4) $\mathcal{U}_2' = \mathbf{SelectJoinablePartition}(W_2, J, right(I), M_2)$; /* Figure 8.31 */
(5)   if $(\mathcal{U}_1' = \emptyset \vee \mathcal{U}_2' = \emptyset)$
(6)   Return $W_j = \langle N_j, \mathcal{U}_j \rangle$ where $\mathcal{U}_j = \emptyset$;
(7)   else
(8) $\mathcal{U}_j = \mathbf{GenerateJoinPartition}(\mathcal{U}_1', \mathcal{U}_2', X_{pj})$; /* Figure 8.32 */
(9)   Return $W_j = \langle N_j, \mathcal{U}_j \rangle$;

Fig. 8.30. Algorithm of join construction.

their type identifiers from the input web tables. In this section, we discuss how to construct the joined web table when $X_{pj} \neq \emptyset$.

We begin by giving a brief overview of the join construction process when $X_{pj} \neq \emptyset$. Then we identify different structures of the joined web schemas. We also introduce the concept of *disambiguation* of the node and link type identifiers which we are going to use in the process of construction of the joined web schema. Next we describe the procedure to construct the joined schemas and the web tuples. The pseudocode for the join construction algorithm is given in Figure 8.30.

Overview

Given two web tables $W_1 = \langle N_1, \mathcal{U}_1 \rangle$ and $W_2 = \langle N_1, \mathcal{U}_2 \rangle$, and the join condition $\Psi = \langle M, X_{pj} \rangle$, the following steps are performed in the join construction phase to generate the joined web table.

1. Identify the set of partitions $\mathcal{U}_1' \subseteq \mathcal{U}_1$ and $\mathcal{U}_2' \subseteq \mathcal{U}_2$, where $\mathcal{S}_1' \subseteq M$, $\mathcal{S}_2' \subseteq M$ and each partition $U_i \in \mathcal{U}_1'$ and $U_j \in \mathcal{U}_2'$ contains the joinable node type identifiers as specified in X_{pj} (Steps (3) and (4) in Figure 8.30).

2. For each pair of partitions $U_1 = \langle S_i, T_i \rangle$ and $U_j = \langle S_j, T_j \rangle$ generate the joined schema S_{ij} from S_i and S_j based on the joinable node type identifiers in X_{pj}

3. Construct joined web tuples by concatenating each pair of tuples in T_i and T_j over the instances of the joinable node type identifiers. Such a set of joined web tuples is denoted as T_{ij} (Steps (1) to (10) in Figure 8.32).

4. Generate the joined partition $\mathcal{U}_{ij} = \langle S_{ij}, T_{ij} \rangle$.

5. Prune the joined partition $\mathcal{U}_{ij}$ if necessary and insert it into the joined web table W_{wj} (Step (22) in Figure 8.32).

Input: Web table $W = \langle Z, \mathcal{U} \rangle$, Joinable node id set J,
Joinable node type identifier set X and simple web schema set M.
Output: Partition $\mathcal{U}'$;

(1)   for $(i = 1 \ to \ |M|)$ {
(2)   Let $S_i \in M$ and $U_i = \langle S_i = \langle X_{ni}, X_{\ell i}, C_i, F_i \rangle, T_i \rangle$ where $U_i \in \mathcal{U}$;
(3)   if $(X \cap X_{ni} \neq \emptyset)$ {
(4)   for $(a = 1 \ to \ |T_i|)$ {
(5)   Get tuple t_a;
(6) $tupleNodeIdSet[a] = \mathbf{GetTupleNodeIds}(t_a);$/* Node ids in t_a */
(7)   if $(tupleNodeIdSet[a] \cap J \neq \emptyset)$
(8)   Store tuple t_a in temporary tuple pool T_i'; /* Joinable web tuple* /
(9)   else
(10) t_a is not joinable;
(11)   }
(12)   if $(T_i' \neq \emptyset)$ {
(13) $U_i' = \langle S_i, T_i' \rangle$;
(14)   Insert U_i' in $\mathcal{U}'$;
(15)   }
(16)   }
(17)   }
(18)   Return $\mathcal{U}'$;

Fig. 8.31. Algorithm **SelectJoinablePartition**.

6. Repeat the above four steps for each pair of partitions in $\mathcal{U}_1'$ and $\mathcal{U}_2'$.

In the subsequent sections we elaborate on the above steps. Specifically, we discuss Steps (2) to (5) in detail. That is, given two partitions $U_i = \langle S_i, T_i \rangle$ and $U_j = \langle S_j, T_j \rangle$ in the web tables W_i and W_j (containing joinable node type identifiers), we show how to construct the joined partition $U_{ij} = \langle S_{ij}, T_{ij} \rangle$, showing how to construct the joined schema S_{ij} and a set of joined web tuples T_{ij}.

Anatomy of the Joined Web Schema

Based on the number of node type identifiers in the input web schemas participating in the join process, we can classify the joined schema as follows.

- *Single-node joined schema:* When only one node type identifier in a web schema participates in the join, the joined schema is called a single-node joined schema. For example, the joined schemas in Example 8.12 are single-node joined schemas since only one node type identifier from each input schema (a and x from Drugs-Manufacturer and Drugs-Usage respectively) participates in the join process.

- *Multinode joined schema:* When more than one node type identifier in a web schema participates in the web join, the joined schema is called a multinode

```
Input: Set of pairs of identifiers X_pj and partitions U'_1 and U'_2.
Output: Joined partitions U_j.

(1)      for (i = 1 to |U'_1|) {
(2)          Let U'_i = ⟨S'_i, T'_i⟩;
(3)          for (h = 1 to |T'_i|) {
(4)              Get tuple t_h;
(5)              for (d = 1 to |U'_2|) {
(6)                  Let U'_d = ⟨S'_d, T'_d⟩;
(7)                  for (b = 1 to |T'_d|) {
(8)                      Get tuple t_b;
(9)                      t_hb = JoinTuples(t_h, t_b, J); /*Section 8.7.4 */
(10)                     Insert t_hb in T_hb;
(11)                 }
(12)                 if (X_pj ≠ ∅) {
(13)                     if (T_hb ≠ ∅) {/* S_hb is not a noisy schema */
(14)                         S_hb = GenerateSchema(S'_i, S'_d, X_pj); /* Section 8.7.4 */
(15)                         U_hb = ⟨S_hb, T_hb⟩;
(16)                         U_hb = PrunePartition(U_hb); /* Section 8.7.5 */
(17)                         Insert U_hb in U_j;
(18)                     }
(19)                 }
(20)             }
(21)         }
(22)     }
(23)     Return U_j;
```

Fig. 8.32. Algorithm of **GenerateJoinPartition**.

joined schema. There can be at most three possible cases for each pair of joinable node type identifiers in each schema for a multinode joined schema. These cases depend on the locus of the joinable node type identifiers (position of the joinable node type identifiers relative to each other) in each schema. Let us elaborate further. Let (x, y) and (a, b) be one of the pairs of joinable node type identifiers in S_i and S_j. Then there can be at most three possible ways these node type identifiers can be joined with each other. We discuss these three cases. The significance of identifying these cases is that the locus of the joinable node type identifiers influences the link type identifier set, connectivities, and predicates of the joined schema. In each case, we use the web schemas in Example 8.12 for illustration. We modify this schema by changing the joinable node type identifiers to aid our illustration.

Case 8.21. Adjacent-adjacent joinable node type identifiers: Let the pair of joinable node type identifiers of **Drugs-Manufacturer** and **Drugs-Usage** be (a, x) and (b, y). Then it is clear that the joinable node type identifiers in each schema

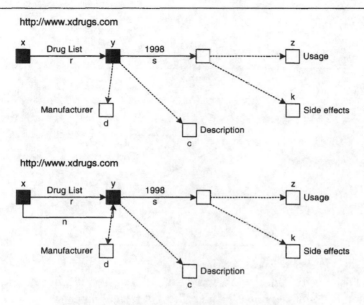

Fig. 8.33. Adjacent-adjacent multinode join.

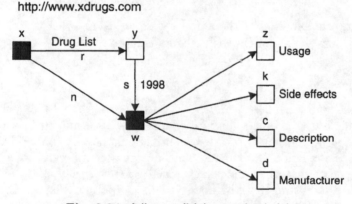

Fig. 8.34. Adjacent-disjoint multinode join.

are adjacent to each other. The pictorial representation of the joined schema is shown in Figure 8.33.

Case 8.22. Adjacent-disjoint joinable node type identifiers: Let the free node type identifier $\#_1$ in Example 8.12 be modified to a bound node type identifier w. Furthermore, let us modify the pairs of joinable node type identifiers to (a, x) and (b, w). Observe that only the joinable node type identifiers of Drugs-Manufacturer are adjacent to each other. We refer to these as adjacent-disjoint joinable node type identifiers. The pictorial representation of the joined schema is shown in Figure 8.34.

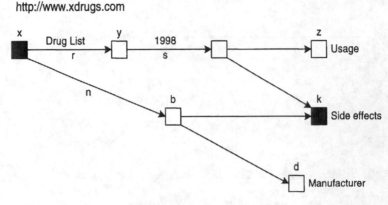

Fig. 8.35. Disjoint-disjoint multinode join.

Case 8.23. Disjoint-disjoint joinable node type identifiers: Consider the case when the pairs of joinable node type identifiers of **Drugs-Manufacturer** and **Drugs-Usage** are (a, x) and (c, k). Observe that none of the joinable node type identifiers of **Drugs-Manufacturer** and **Drugs-Usage** are adjacent. We refer to these as disjoint-disjoint joinable nodes. The joined schema is shown in Figure 8.35.

Note that any combination of the above cases can occur when the number of joinable node type identifiers in each schema is more than two.

Disambiguation

Given two simple web schemas S_i and S_j in partitions U_i and U_j of web tables W_1 and W_2, some of the node and link type identifiers in S_i and S_j may be nominally identical to one another or to other identifiers in the web table. This is due to the fact that the creation of the node and link type identifiers for one web table is independent of the other. Since the joined schema is derived from S_i and S_j, it is necessary to ensure that the node and link type identifiers in the joined schema be nominally distinct. The process of deriving nominally distinct node and link type identifiers for the joined schema is called *disambiguation*. The objective of the disambiguation process is to ensure that the node type identifiers in X_{n_i} of S_i (in web table W_1) are nominally distinct from the node type identifiers in X_{n2} (set of node type identifiers in W_2), and that the link type identifiers in X_{ℓ_i} are nominally distinct from the link type identifiers in $X_{\ell 2}$ (set of link type identifiers in W_2). Formally, it is necessary to disambiguate the nodes or link type identifiers if either of these conditions is true: $X_{n_i} \cap X_{n2} \neq \emptyset$ or $X_{\ell_i} \cap X_{\ell 2} \neq \emptyset$. We denote the disambiguation process by the symbol $\oplus$. Thus the process of disambiguating the node and link type identifiers is denoted by $X_{n_i} \oplus X_{n2}$, and $X_{\ell_i} \oplus X_{\ell 2}$, respectively. During disambiguation, for each pair of node or link type identifiers that are identical to each other, we replace any one of their occurrences with another type identifier that is nominally distinct. After disambiguation $X_{n_i} \cap X_{n2} = \emptyset$ and $X_{\ell_i} \cap X_{\ell 2} = \emptyset$.

Next we discuss the construction of the joined schema and web tuples from the joinable partitions U_i and U_j. As mentioned earlier, this construction is repeated for all pairs of joinable partitions in the input web tables.

Construction of the Joined Schema

We construct the schema of the joined partition by *integrating* the schemas of the input partitions U_i and U_j. We show how to determine each of the four components of S_{ij}. The construct **GenerateSchema** in Step (14) in Figure 8.32 encapsulates the construction details discussed below.

Determining the Node Type Identifier Set of the Joined Schema

The node type identifiers in X_{n_i} and X_{n_j} can either be nominally distinct or there may exist at least one pair of node type identifiers from X_{n_i} and X_{n2} that are identical to each other. If the node type identifiers are all nominally distinct, then the node type identifier set of the joined schema is given by either of the following. $X_{n_{ij}} = (X_{n_i} \cup X_{n_j}) - left(X_{pj})$ or $X_{n_{ij}} = (X_{n_i} \cup X_{n_j}) - right(X_{pj})$.

Otherwise, it is necessary to disambiguate the identical node type identifiers. The disambiguation process is performed in steps. First, the set of joinable node type identifiers $(left(X_{pj})$ or $right(X_{pj}))$ is removed from the node type identifier set of the schema S_i or S_j. Let $X'_{n_i} = X_{n_i} - left(X_{pj})$ and $X'_{n_j} = X_{n_j} - right(X_{pj})$. Finally, we determine the node type identifier set $X_{n_{ij}}$ of the joined schema by disambiguating X'_{n_i} and X_{n2} or X'_{n_j} and X_{n1} and then combining it with X_{n_j} or X_{n_i}, respectively. Formally, the set of node type identifiers of the joined schema is given by either $X_{n_{ij}} = ((X'_{n_i} \bigoplus X_{n2}) \cup X_{n_j})$ or $X_{r_{ij}} = ((X'_{n_j} \bigoplus X_{n1}) \cup X_{n_i})$.

Example 8.24. Consider the partitions U_{dm1} and U_{du1} of **Drug-Manufacturer** and **Drug-Usage** in Example 8.12. From the join condition it is evident that the node type identifiers a and x in these partitions are joinable. Also $X_{n1} = \{a, b, c, d, \#_1, \#_2\}$ and $X_{n2} = \{x, y, z, k, \#_1, \#_2\}$. Furthermore, $X_{nm1} = \{a, b, c, d, \#_1\}$ and $X_{nu1} = \{x, y, z, k, \#_1, \#_2\}$. Observe that the node type identifiers X_{nm1} and X_{n2} or X_{nu1} and X_{n1} are not nominally distinct; i.e., $X_{nm1} \cap X_{n2} = \{\#_1\}$ and $X_{nu1} \cap X_{n1} = \{\#_1, \#_2\}$. Hence it is necessary to disambiguate one of these sets of node type identifiers. Following the steps mentioned above, we first remove the joinable node type identifier set from X_{nm1}; i.e., $X'_{n_i} = \{a, b, c, d, \#_1\} - \{a\} = \{b, c, d, \#_1\}$. We then disambiguate the node type identifier sets X'_{n_i} and X_{n2}. We change one of the node type identifiers in each identical node pair to a nominally distinct type identifier. For example, we change $\#_1$ to $\#_3$. Then the node type identifier set of the joined schema is $X_{n_{ij}} = ((\{b, c, d, \#_1\} \bigoplus \{x, y, z, k, \#_1, \#_2\}) \cup \{x, y, z, k, \#_2, \#_1\}) = \{b, c, d, \#_3\} \cup \{x, y, z, k, \#_2, \#_1\} = \{b, c, d, x, y, z, k, \#_1, \#_2, \#_3\}$. ∎

Determining the Link Type Identifier Set of the Joined Schema

The set of link type identifiers of the joined schema depends on the number of joinable node type identifiers in each schema and their relative locii. Previously, we classified the joined schema into single-node and multinode joined schemas depending on the number of joinable node type identifiers in each schema. We now determine the link type identifier set for each type of joined schema.

Link set for single-node joined schema: Similar to node type identifiers, the link type identifiers in X_{ℓ_i} or X_{ℓ_j} are either nominally distinct or there exists at least one pair of link type identifiers in X_{ℓ_i} or X_{ℓ_j} that are nominally identical to some identifiers in $X_{\ell 2}$ or $X_{\ell 1}$, respectively. If the type identifiers are all distinct, the link type identifier set of the joined schema is $X_{\ell_{ij}} = X_{\ell_i} \cup X_{\ell_j}$. Otherwise, we disambiguate the nominally identical link type identifiers. In that case, the link type identifier set of the joined schemas is $X_{\ell_{ij}} = ((X_{\ell_i} \bigoplus X_{\ell 2}) \cup X_{\ell_j})$.

Example 8.25. Consider the link type identifier sets $X_{\ell m1}$ and $X_{\ell u1}$ in Example 8.12. The link type identifiers in $X_{\ell m1}$ and $X_{\ell u1}$ are not nominally distinct with respect to the link type identifiers in Drug-Manufacturer and Drug-Usage. Here $X_{\ell 1} = \{n, -_1, -_2, -_3, -_4, -_5\}$ and $X_{\ell 2} = \{r, s, -_1, -_2, -_3\}$. Therefore $X_{\ell m1} \cap X_{\ell 2} = \{-_1, -_2, -_3\}$ and $X_{\ell u1} \cap X_{\ell 1} = \{-_1, -_2, -_3\}$. Hence it is necessary to disambiguate these sets of link type identifiers. Following the steps mentioned above, we change one of the link type identifiers in each identical link pair to a nominally distinct type identifier. For example, we change $-_1, -_2$ and $-_3$ to $-_6, -_7,$ and $-_8$, respectively. Then the link type identifier set of the joined schema is $X_{\ell_{ij}} = ((\{n, -_1, -_2, -_3\} \bigoplus \{r, s, -_1, -_2, -_3\}) \cup \{r, s, -_1, -_2, -_3\}) = \{n, -_6, -_7, -_8\} \cup \{r, s, -_1, -_2, -_3\} = \{n, r, s, -_1, -_2, -_3, -_6, -_7, -_8\}$. Note that $X_{\ell_{ij}}$ is identical to the link type identifier set in Example 8.12. ∎

Link set for multinode joined schema: For multinode joined schemas, the position of the joinable node type identifiers relative to one another in each schema influences the link type identifier set of the joined schema. Let us recall the three cases of multinode joined schemas as described before. We determine the link type identifier set of the joined schema for each case.

- *Adjacent-adjacent joinable node type identifiers (Case 8.21):* The joinable node type identifiers in each schema in this case are adjacent to each other. To elaborate further, refer to Figure 8.33. Node type identifiers a, b and x, y are joinable node type identifiers in the schemas S_i and S_j, respectively, and each pair of these node type identifiers is adjacent to the other. The link type identifiers (adjacent link type identifiers) between a, b and x, y are n and r, respectively. In this case, the link set of the joined schema is constructed based on the following rules.
  - Let (a, x) and (b, y) be the joinable node type identifiers such that $a\langle n\rangle x$ and $b\langle r\rangle y$. Let P_n and P_r denote the sets of predicates on n and r, respectively. If $P_n = P_r$ or $P_n = P_r = \emptyset$ then we remove any one of the adjacent link type identifiers from the link type identifier set of the joined schema; i.e., we remove n or r (Figure 8.33(a)). Formally, if L_i and L_j represent the sets of adjacent link type identifiers in S_i and S_j, then the link type identifier set of the joined schema when the link type identifiers are all nominally distinct is given by either: $X_{\ell_{ij}} = (X_{\ell_i} \cup X_{\ell_j}) - L_i$ or $X_{\ell_{ij}} = (X_{\ell_i} \cup X_{\ell_j}) - L_j$.
  - Otherwise, if $P_n \neq P_r$ then we do not remove the adjacent link type identifiers from the joined schema (Figure 8.33(b)). This is because removal of

such an identifier will imply removal of the predicates associated with that link type identifier. Since $P_n \neq P_r$, removal of the predicates P_n or P_r will result in the loss of some information about the instances of the links in the nodes of type a or b. Hence, in this case, the set of link type identifiers is given as $X_{\ell_{ij}} = X_{\ell i} \cup X_{\ell j}$.

If the link type identifiers in the input schemas are not distinct, then we disambiguate them. The process of disambiguation is similar to that followed in determining the node type identifier set of the joined schema. First, the set of adjacent link type identifiers (L_i or L_j) is removed, if necessary, from the link type identifier set of S_i or S_j, respectively. (Note that we either remove L_i from X_{ℓ_i} or L_j from X_{ℓ_j} but not both.) Finally, we disambiguate X'_{ℓ_i} and X_{ℓ_j} or X'_{ℓ_j} and X_{ℓ_i}, where $X'_{\ell_i} = X_{\ell_i} - L_i$ and $X'_{\ell_j} = X_{\ell_j} - L_j$. Thus the set of link type identifiers of the joined schema is given by either $X_{\ell_{ij}} = ((X'_{\ell_i} \bigoplus X_{\ell 2}) \cup X_{\ell_j})$ or $X_{\ell_{ij}} = ((X'_{\ell_j} \bigoplus X_{\ell 1}) \cup X_{\ell_i})$. If we do not remove the adjacent link type identifier then $X_{\ell_{ij}} = ((X_{\ell_i} \bigoplus X_{\ell 2}) \cup X_{\ell_j})$.

- *Adjacent-disjoint joinable node type identifiers (Case 8.22) and disjoint-disjoint joinable node type identifiers (Case 8.23):* In these cases, there exists at least one pair of joinable node type identifiers that are not adjacent to each other (Figures 8.34 and 8.35). The link type identifier set of the joined schema when the link type identifiers are all nominally distinct is $X_{\ell_{ij}} = X_{\ell_i} \cup X_{\ell_j}$. Otherwise, the set of identical link type identifiers is disambiguated and the link type identifier set of the joined schema is $X_{\ell_{ij}} = ((X_{\ell_i} \bigoplus X_{\ell 2}) \cup X_{\ell_j})$.

Example 8.26. Consider the link type identifier sets $X_{\ell m1} = \{n, -_1, -_2, -_3\}$ and $X_{\ell u1} = \{r, s, -_1, -_2, -_3\}$ in the joined schema in Example 8.12. If a, b and x, y are the joinable node type identifiers (Case 8.21), then the link type identifier set of the joined schema is given by $X_{\ell_{ij}} = (((\{n, -_1, -_2, -_3\} - \{n\}) \bigoplus \{r, s, -_1, -_2, -_3\}) \cup \{r, s, -_1, -_2, -_3\}) = \{r, s, -_6, -_7, -_8\}$ or $X_{\ell_{ij}} = (((\{r, s, -_1, -_2, -_3\} - \{r\}) \bigoplus \{n, -_1, -_2, -_3\}) \cup \{n, -_1, -_2, -_3\}) = \{n, s, -_6, -_7, -_8\}$ (Figure 8.33(a)). Observe that in this case, we remove the adjacent link type identifier r as $P_n = P_r$. ∎

Determining the Connectivities of the Joined Schema

The set of connectivities of the joined schema depends on the number of joinable node type identifiers in each schema and their relative position to one another in the schema. Similar to the determination of the link type identifier set (as described above), we first determine the connectivities for the single-node joined schema and then proceed to determine the connectivity set for the multinode joined schema. First, we introduce some terms to facilitate our exposition. Let $C_i(join)$ and $C_j(join)$ denote the set of *join connectivities* of S_i and S_j, respectively. By join connectivities we mean simple connectivities in C_i and C_j that contain joinable node type identifiers. For example, consider the schemas in Example 8.12. Here the connectivities $a\langle n \rangle b$ and $x\langle r \rangle y$ are join connectivities as a and x are joinable node type identifiers. Clearly, $C_i(join) \subseteq C_i$ and $C_j(join) \subseteq C_j$. Furthermore, let $C'_i = C_i - C_i(join)$ and $C'_j = C_j - C_j(join)$.

Set of connectivities for single-node joined schema: Our approach to determine the connectivities of a single-node joined schema is as follows.

1. Identify the set of joined connectivities $C_i(join)$ and $C_j(join)$ for the input schemas S_i and S_j, respectively.

2. Identify those connectivities in $C_i(join)$ and $C_j(join)$ that satisfy the following condition: If $x\langle\ell\rangle y$ is in the joined connectivity set, then $x \notin X_{n_{ij}}$ or $y \notin X_{n_{ij}}$ where $X_{n_{ij}}$, is the node type identifier set of the joined schema.

3. Replace the joinable node type identifiers in these connectivities with the joinable node type identifiers of the other schema. We denote the modified join connectivity set (after replacement) as $C_i(join)'$ or $C_j(join)'$. For example, $C_i(join) = \{a\langle n\rangle b\}$ and after replacement $C_i(join)' = \{x\langle n\rangle b\}$ as $a \notin X_{n_{ij}}$.

4. If the node and link type identifiers are not nominally distinct, replace any one of the identical type identifiers in C_i and $(C_j(join)' \cup C_j')$ or C_j and $(C_i(join)' \cup C_i')$ with the disambiguated value.

5. Finally, the connectivities C_{ij} of the joined schema are given by either $C_{ij} \equiv C_i \wedge (C_j(join)' \cup C_j')$ or $C_{ij} \equiv C_j \wedge (C_i(join)' \cup C_i')$.

Set of connectivities for multinode joined schema: For a multinode joined schema, the position of the joinable node type identifiers relative to each other in each schema influences the connectivities of the joined schema. We determine the connectivities for the three cases of multinode joined schema.

- *Adjacent-adjacent joinable node type identifiers (Case 8.21):* Our approach to determine the connectivities for the multinode joined schema when there exists at least one pair of joinable node type identifiers in each schema that are adjacent to one another is as follows.

  1. Identify the set of joined connectivities $C_i(join)$ and $C_j(join)$ for the input schemas S_i and S_j, respectively.

  2. Remove those connectivities in $C_i(join)$ or $C_j(join)$ that satisfy the following conditions.
     a) If $x\langle\ell\rangle y$ is in the joined connectivity set and $x \neq y$, then x and y must be joinable node type identifiers and $\ell \notin X_{\ell_{ij}}$.

     b) $x \notin X_{n_{ij}}$ and $y \notin X_{n_{ij}}$ where $X_{n_{ij}}$ is the node type identifier set of the joined schema. We denote the modified join connectivity set (after removal) as $C_i(join)'$ or $C_j(join)'$.

  3. If the node and link type identifiers are not nominally distinct, replace any one of the identical type identifiers in C_i and $(C_j(join)' \cup C_j')$ or C_j and $(C_i(join)' \cup C_i')$ with the disambiguated value.

  4. Finally, the connectivities C_{ij} of the joined schema are given by either $C_{ij} \equiv C_i \wedge (C_j(join)' \cup C_j')$ or $C_{ij} \equiv C_j \wedge (C_i(join)' \cup C_i')$.

- *Adjacent-disjoint joinable node type identifiers (Case 8.22) and disjoint-disjoint joinable node type identifiers (Case 8.23):* The procedure for determining the connectivities of the joined schema is similar to that for single-node join.

Example 8.27. Consider the connectivities C_{m1} and C_{u1} in Example 8.12. If we consider Example 8.12 to be the joined schema, then it is a single-node joined schema.

Clearly, $C_i(join) = \{a\langle n\rangle b\}$, $C_j(join) = \{x\langle r\rangle y\}$, $C_i' \equiv \{b\langle{-1}\rangle\#_1, \#_1\langle{-2}\rangle d, \#_1\langle{-3}\rangle c\}$. Moreover, $C_i(join)' = \{x\langle n\rangle b\}$. Furthermore, the node and link type identifiers are not all distinct. Thus connectivities of the joined schema are

$$C_j \bigoplus (C_i(join)' \cup C_i')$$
$$= \{x\langle r\rangle y, y\langle s\rangle\#_1, \#_1\langle{-1}\rangle\#_2, \#_2\langle{-2}\rangle z, \#_2\langle{-3}\rangle k\} \bigoplus (\{x\langle n\rangle b\} \cup \{b\langle{-1}\rangle\#_1, \#_1\langle{-2}\rangle d, \#_1\langle{-3}\rangle c\})$$
$$= \{x\langle r\rangle y, y\langle s\rangle\#_1, \#_1\langle{-1}\rangle\#_2, \#_2\langle{-2}\rangle z, \#_2\langle{-3}\rangle k\} \bigoplus \{x\langle n\rangle b, b\langle{-1}\rangle\#_1, \#_1\langle{-2}\rangle d, \#_1\langle{-3}\rangle c\})$$
$$= \{x\langle r\rangle y, y\langle s\rangle\#_1, \#_1\langle{-1}\rangle\#_2, \#_2\langle{-2}\rangle z, \#_2\langle{-3}\rangle k, x\langle n\rangle b, b\langle{-6}\rangle\#_3, \#_3\langle{-7}\rangle d, \#_3\langle{-8}\rangle c\}$$

These are identical to the connectivities in Example 8.12. ∎

Determining the Predicates of the Joined Schema

Let $P_i(join)$ and $P_j(join)$ be the set of predicates of S_i and S_j, respectively, whose arguments are a joinable node type identifier. Our approach to the determination of the predicates of the joined schema is as follows.

1. Identify the set of join predicates $P_i(join)$ and $P_j(join)$ for S_i and S_j, respectively.

2. Compute $P_i' = P_i - P_i(join)$ and $P_j' = P_j - P_j(join)$.

3. Disambiguate the arguments of the predicates in P_i' and P_j' with their corresponding new nominal identifiers. Let $P_d = P_i' \bigoplus P_j'$. If the identifiers are nominally distinct then $P_d = P_i'$.

4. Combine the predicates of P_d and P_j'. That is, $P_u = P_d \cup P_j'$.

5. Remove predicate p from P_u where $arg(p) \notin X_{\ell_{ij}}$. Denote the modified set of predicates as P_u'.

6. Let $P_{ai} \subseteq P_i(join)$ be the set of predicates on a joinable node type identifier a; i.e., $arg(p_i) = a$ for predicate p_i in P_{ai}. Let $P_{bj} \subseteq P_j(join)$ be the set of predicates on the node type identifier b where $(a\ b) \in X_{pj}$. That is, $arg(p_j) = b$ for predicate p_j in P_{bj}. Then

   a) If $P_{ai} = P_{bj}$ remove the predicates P_{bj} from $P_j(join)$. Note that removal of these predicates does not result in any loss of information. Ignore the next three steps;

   b) Otherwise, identify those predicates $P_{bj}' \subseteq P_{bj}$ that are not identical to any of the predicates in P_{ai}. These predicates capture constraints that are not captured by the predicates in P_i;

   c) Replace $arg(p_j')$ for each predicate in P_{bj}' with $arg(p_i)$. This ensures that additional information provided by P_j is not lost during the construction of the joined schema;

   d) Remove the identical predicates, i.e., $P_{bj} - P_{bj}'$, from $P_j(join)$.

7. Perform the above steps for all predicates in $P_i(join)$ and $P_j(join)$.

8. We denote the modified predicate set as $P_j(join)'$.

9. Finally, the predicate set P_{ij} of the joined schema is given by one of the following, $P_{ij} = P'_u \cup P_i(join) \cup P_j(join)'$.

Example 8.28. Consider the predicate sets $P_{m1} = \{p_{i_1}, p_{i_2}, p_{i_3}, p_{i_4}, p_{i_5}, p_{i_6}\}$ and $P_{u1} = \{p_{j_1}, p_{j_2}, p_{j_3}, p_{j_4}, p_{j_5}, p_{j_6}, p_{j_7}\}$ in Example 8.12. When the joinable node type identifiers are a and x, the join predicates of S_i and S_j are $P_i(join) = \{p_{i_1}, p_{i_6}\}$ and $P_j(join) = \{p_{j_1}, p_{j_7}\}$, respectively. Hence $P'_i = \{p_{i_2}, p_{i_3}, p_{i_4}, p_{i_5}\}$ and $P'_j = \{p_{j_2}, p_{j_3}, p_{j_4}, p_{j_5}, p_{j_6}\}$. Since the bound node type identifiers are all nominally distinct, $P_d = P'_i$ (Step (3)). Consequently, $P_u = \{p_{i_2}, p_{i_3}, p_{i_4}, p_{i_5}, p_{j_2}, p_{j_3}, p_{j_4}, p_{j_5}, p_{j_6}\}$ (Step (4)). Furthermore, as this is a single-node join $P'_u = P_u$ (Step (5)). Also, as the predicates on x are identical to those on a, the set of predicates on a is removed from $P_i(join)$ based on Step (6(a)). Hence $P_i(join)' = \{p_{i_2}, p_{i_3}, p_{i_4}, p_{i_5}\}$. Hence the predicate set of the joined schema is $P_{ij} = \{p_{i_2}, p_{i_3}, p_{i_4}, p_{i_5}, p_{j_1}, p_{j_2}, p_{j_3}, p_{j_4}, p_{j_5}, p_{j_6}, p_{j_7}\}$ or $P_{ij} = \{p_{i_1}, p_{i_2}, p_{i_3}, p_{i_4}, p_{i_5}, p_{i_6}, p_{j_2}, p_{j_3}, p_{j_4}, p_{j_5}, p_{j_6}\}$. ∎

Joined Web Tuples Generation

Once the construction of the joined schema is finished, we proceed to construct the joined web tuples from the web tuples in partitions U_i and U_j. A joined web tuple is created by *integrating* a pair of input web tuples. The structure of the web tuples in the joined partition must be identical to that of the joined schema. The node and link objects in the web tuples of the joined partition satisfy the connectivities and predicates in the joined schema. The steps for creating the set of joined web tuples from the web tuples T_i and T_j are as follows. The construct **JoinTuples** in Step (9) in Figure 8.32 encapsulates the construction details discussed below.

- For each web tuple $t_k \in T_i$ do the following.
  1. Get tuple $t_r \in T_j$.

  2. For each pair of joinable node type identifiers in X_{pj} do the following.
     a) Let $(x_1, x_2) \in X_{pj}$, $x_1 \in X_{ni}$, and $x_2 \in X_{nj}$. Then get instances of x_1 and x_2 in t_k and t_r (denoted as I_1 and I_2, respectively) such that $I_1 \subseteq J$ and $I_2 \subseteq J$.

     b) Let $I = I_1 \cup I_2$ represent the set of pairs of joinable nodes in t_k and t_r that are instances of x_1 and x_2. That is, $left(I) \subseteq I_1$ and $right(I) \subseteq I_2$. Then, for each pair of joinable nodes, say $(n_1(t_k), n_2(t_r)) \in I$, do the following.
        i. If $x_1 \in X_{n_{ij}}$ and $x_2 \notin X_{n_{ij}}$, then get the set of incoming and outgoing links to $n_2(t_r)$ in t_r (denoted as L_{in} and L_{out}, respectively).

        ii. Remove $n_2(t_r)$.

        iii. Set the target id of the links in L_{in} to the URL of $n_1(t_k)$.

        iv. Set the source id of the links in L_{out} to the URL of $n_1(t_k)$.

        v. Let t'_{kr} represent the concatenated tuple. Repeat the above three steps on t'_{kr}.

c) Let t'_{kr} represent the web tuple after concatenating the joinable nodes by the above step. We now check whether there exist joinable node type identifiers in S_{ij} that are adjacent to one another (Case 1).

d) Let D be the set of pairs of joinable node type identifiers in S_i and S_j that are adjacent to one another. Then, for each pair $(x, y) \in D$, we do the following.

   – Let L denote the set of links in t'_{kr}, where the source and target ids of each link are instances of x and y, respectively.

   – Let $L_{ad} \subseteq X_{\ell_{ij}}$ be the set of adjacent link type identifiers between x and y.

   – Remove those links $L' \subseteq L$ in t'_{kr} whose type identifiers are not in L_{ad}. This is to ensure that the joined web tuples match the joined schema and the adjacent link type identifiers that are ignored in S_{ij} are removed from t'_{kr}.

e) The modified concatenated web tuple t'_{kr} (denoted as t_{kr}) represents the joined web tuple and is inserted in T_{ij}.

For example, consider the partitions U_{dm1} and U_{du1} in Example 8.12. The joinable node type identifiers are a and x. The joined partition U_{ij} is constructed by concatenating a web tuple of U_i with a web tuple of U_j over the joinable node type identifiers as shown in Figure 8.20. Observe that the five web tuples in T_{m1} are joined with the five web tuples in T_{u1} resulting in 25 joined web tuples. Four of these web tuples are depicted in Figure 8.20 (first four web tuples). All these web tuples are bound by the joined schema S_{j1}.

8.7.5 Joined Partition Pruning

The joined partition generated by the above process may be required to be pruned under *certain conditions*. We now discuss these conditions. The pruning of a joined partition may result in the creation of one or more distinct partitions. The construct **PrunePartition** in Step (16) in Figure 8.32 encapsulates the two conditions discussed below.

Case 1:

Informally, the first condition states that it is necessary to prune the joined schema if one of the joinable node type identifiers in the input schema has an outgoing link type identifier, say e, such that one of the predicates on e is on the link type of e and the value of the predicate is `interior`. We illustrate this condition with an example and explain why it is necessary to prune the joined partition. Let $U_1 = \langle S_1, T_1 \rangle$ and $U_2 = \langle S_2, T_2 \rangle$ be two partitions participating in the web join where $X_{n1} = \{x, y\}$, $X_{\ell 1} = \{e, f\}$, $C_1 \equiv x\langle e \rangle x \wedge x\langle f \rangle y$, and $p(e) \in P_1$, where $attr\_path(p(e))$ = `link_type` and $val(p(e))$ *contains* `interior`. That is, the value of $p(e)$ may be either of the following: `interior|local` or `interior|global`. Furthermore, let $X_{n2} = \{a, z\}$, $X_{\ell 2} = \{n\}$, and $C_2 \equiv a\langle n \rangle z$. The pictorial representations of the schemas are shown in Figure 8.36.

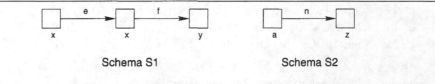

Schema S1   Schema S2

Fig. 8.36. Schemas of the two partitions.

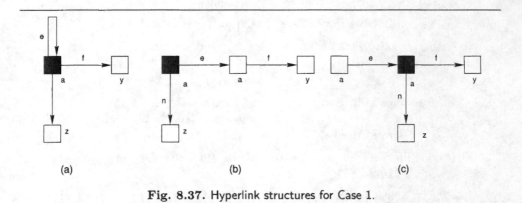

(a)   (b)   (c)

Fig. 8.37. Hyperlink structures for Case 1.

Let (x, a) be the pair of joinable node type identifiers in X_{pj}. Then the node and link type identifiers and connectivity components of the joined schemas generated based on the steps described earlier are $X_{n_{12}} = \{a, y, z\}$, $X_{\ell_{12}} = \{e, f, n\}$, and $C_{12} \equiv a\langle e\rangle a \wedge a\langle f\rangle y \wedge a\langle n\rangle z$. Pictorially, this can be represented as in Figure 8.37. Observe that when an instance of e is an interior link then the node type identifiers in $x\langle e\rangle x$ are joinable nodes. In such cases it is better to represent the joined web tuples with the schema in Figure 8.37(a). However, when the link type is local or global then either of the node type identifiers in $x\langle e\rangle x$ can be joinable but not both. That is, either instance of left or right node type identifier x is joinable with the instance of a. Consequently, these joined web tuples can be bound by any one of the schemas in Figures 8.37(b) and 8.37(c). Hence the joined web tuples generated from T_1 and T_2 may contain web tuples that conform to any one of these three types of hyperlink structures. However, the distinction between these different hyperlink structures is not captured in the joined schema S_{12} as it is generated without inspecting the joined web tuples. Hence it is necessary to prune the joined partition by inspecting the link type of the instances of e in the joined web tuples. Formally, this condition can be expressed as follows.

Condition 8.17 *Let* $U_i = \langle S_i, T_i\rangle$ *and* $U_j = \langle S_j, T_j\rangle$ *be two partitions participating in the web join operation and let* $X_{pj} \neq \emptyset$ *and* $(a, x) \in X_{pj}$, *where* $a \in X_{ni}$ *and* $x \in X_{nj}$. *Then the joined partition* U_{ij} *generated from* U_i *and* U_j *needs to be pruned if* $x\langle e\rangle x$ *is a connectivity in* C_{wj} *where,* attr_path$(p(e)) = $ link_type *and* val$(p(e)) \in \{$"interior|local", "interior|global"$\}$. ∎

The joined partition pruning operation first decomposes the joined schema to the three types of joined schemas as discussed above. Next it removes the noisy

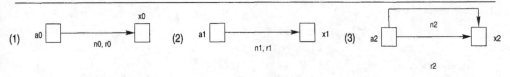

Fig. 8.38. Web tuples for Case 2.

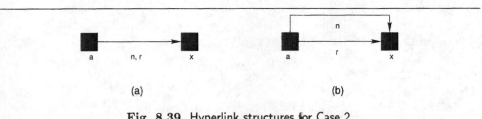

Fig. 8.39. Hyperlink structures for Case 2.

schemas from this set of decomposed schemas by inspecting the joined web tuples. For example, the joined schema S_{12} is first decomposed into the following three schemas.

- $S_{j1} = \langle X_{nj1}, X_{\ell j1}, C_{j1}, P_{j1} \rangle$, where $X_{nj1} = \{a, y, z\}$, $X_{\ell j1} = \{h, f, n\}$, $C_{j1} \equiv a\langle h \rangle a \wedge a\langle f \rangle y \wedge a\langle n \rangle z$, and $p(h) \in P_{j1}$, where

$$p(h) \equiv \texttt{METADATA::h[link\_type] EQUALS "interior"}$$

- $S_{j2} = \langle X_{nj2}, X_{\ell j2}, C_{j2}, P_{j2} \rangle$, where $X_{nj2} = \{a, y, z, w\}$, $X_{\ell j1} = \{g, f, n\}$, $C_{j2} \equiv a\langle g \rangle w \wedge w\langle f \rangle y \wedge a\langle n \rangle z$, $P_w = P_a$, and $p(g) \in P_{j2}$, where

$$p(g) \equiv \texttt{METADATA::g[link\_type] EQUALS "global|local"}$$

- $S_{j3} = \langle X_{nj3}, X_{\ell j3}, C_{j3}, P_{j3} \rangle$, where $X_{nj3} = \{a, y, z, w\}$, $X_{\ell j3} = \{g, f, n\}$, $C_{j3} \equiv a\langle g \rangle w \wedge a\langle f \rangle y \wedge a\langle n \rangle z$, $P_w = P_a$, and $p(g) \in P_{j3}$, where

$$p(g) \equiv \texttt{METADATA::g[link\_type] EQUALS "global|local"}$$

Next these decomposed schemas are pruned by eliminating the noisy schemas. This results in the generation of one or more joined partitions. Observe that in the above process the following modifications are considered to be the joined schemas while decomposing to a set of schemas: (1) the link type identifier e is replaced by the two identifiers g and h to represent interior and local or global links; (2) the joinable node type identifier a is replaced by a new node type identifier w when the link type is global or local in order to distinguish between the hyperlink structures in Figures 8.37(b) and 8.37(c).

Case 2:

We now discuss the second condition, when it is necessary to prune the joined partition. Informally, it is necessary to prune the joined partition if there exist joinable node type identifiers in each partition that are adjacent to each other and the predicates on the adjacent link type identifiers in these two partitions are not identical. We illustrate this condition with an example and explain why it is necessary to prune the joined partition. Let $U_1 = \langle S_1, T_1 \rangle$ and $U_2 = \langle S_2, T_2 \rangle$ be two partitions participating in the web join where $X_{n1} = \{x, y\}$, $X_{\ell 1} = \{n\}$, $C_1 \equiv x\langle n \rangle y$, and $P_1 = P_x \cup P_y \cup P_n$. Also let $X_{n2} = \{a, z\}$, $X_{\ell 2} = \{r\}$, $C_2 \equiv a\langle r \rangle z$, and $P_2 = P_a \cup P_z \cup P_r$. Furthermore, let (a, x) and (z, y) be the joinable node type identifiers and $P_n \neq P_r$. Observe that the joinable node type identifiers are adjacent to one another. The components of the joined schema generated by the above procedure are as follows. $X_{n12} = \{a, z\}$, $X_{\ell 12} = \{n, r\}$, $C_{12} \equiv a\langle n \rangle z \wedge a\langle r \rangle z$, and $P_{12} = \{P_a, P_x, P_n, P_r\}$. Note that as $P_n \neq P_r$, the adjacent link type identifiers n and r are both included in the joined schema.

Figure 8.38 depicts the joined web tuples. Observe that the instances of n and r in the first two web tuples are identical. That is, the link satisfies both the predicates on n and r. However, in the third web tuple, the links satisfying P_n and P_r are distinct. Hence these two types of web tuples may be represented by two distinct schemas as shown in Figure 8.39. Hence it is necessary to prune the joined partition. Formally, the condition can be expressed as follows.

Condition 8.18 *Let $U_i = \langle S_i, T_i \rangle$ and $U_j = \langle S_j, T_j \rangle$ be two partitions participating in the web join operation and let $\{(a, x), (b, y)\} \subseteq X_{pj}$, where $(a, b) \in X_{ni}$ and $(x, y) \in X_{nj}$. Then the joined partition U_{ij} generated from U_i and U_j needs to be pruned if $a\langle e \rangle b$ and $x\langle f \rangle y$ are connectivities in C_i and C_j, respectively, and $P_e \neq P_f$,* ∎

We now show how to decompose the joined partition into one or more partitions by inspecting the joined web tuples. Observe that the first two web tuples can be bound by the schema in Figure 8.39(a) as the link between the instances of a and z can be represented by a single link type identifier by combining the predicates on n and r. However, for the third web tuple the joined schema S_{12} is required to bind it as there exist two distinct instances of adjacent link type identifiers. Hence the joined partition may be reduced into the following two partitions.

- $U_{j1} = \langle S_{j1}, T_{j1} \rangle$, where $S_{j1} = \langle X_{nj1}, X_{\ell j1}, C_{j1}, P_{j1} \rangle$, where $X_{nj1} = \{a, z\}$, $X_{\ell j1} = \{s\}$, $C_{j1} \equiv a\langle s \rangle z$ and $P_s \subseteq P_{j1}$, where P_s includes the predicates on n and r in S_1 and S_2, and $T_{j1} = \{t_1, t_2\}$.

- $U_{j2} = \langle S_{j2}, T_{j2} \rangle$, where $S_{j2} = S_{12}$ and $T_{j2} = \{t_3\}$.

8.7.6 Join Construction Phase When $X_j = \emptyset$

In this section we discuss the construction of a joined web table and its schemas when the joinable node type identifiers are not specified by the user; i.e., $X_j = \emptyset$. Recall that in this case the web tuples participating in the web join must be bound by a schema in M and must contain identical nodes. Similarly to the previous sections we first provide an overview of the join construction phase and then describe the procedure to create the joined web table.

There are some issues when $X_j = \emptyset$ that set apart the join construction process compared to when $X_j \neq \emptyset$. We identify these issues first.

- Let $U_i = \langle S_i, T_i \rangle$ and $U_j = \langle S_j, T_j \rangle$ be two partitions in W_1 and W_2 where $S_i \in M$ and $S_j \in M$. To determine whether the tuples bound by these partitions are joinable it is necessary to identify joinable nodes in T_i and T_j. Observe that as $X_j = \emptyset$, it is not always possible to identify node type identifiers of all joinable nodes in T_i and T_j by inspecting S_i and S_j. Recall that when $X_j \neq \emptyset$, we may identify the potential joinable partitions by determining whether X_j is contained in S_i and S_j.

- Second, a pair of partitions may generate more than one joined schema from S_i and S_j to bind the joined web tuples resulting from the partitions. For instance, consider the partitions U_{d1} and U_{nd1} in Drugs and New Drugs in Example 8.13. The join operation on these partitions results in the generation of two joined partitions U_{wj1} and U_{wj2} to bind the five joined web tuples created during this process as shown in Example 8.13. Observe that the joinable nodes for each pair of tuples in these partitions do not belong to the same pair of node type identifiers in S_i and S_j. Hence two partitions U_i and U_j participating in the web join may generate at most $|T_i| \times |T_j|$ schemas to bind all the joined web tuples resulting from the join operation. Formally, let $U_i = \langle S_i, T_i \rangle$ and $U_j = \langle S_j, T_j \rangle$ be two partitions in W_1 and W_2 participating in the web join and $X_j = \emptyset$. Let $\mathcal{P}_j$ represent the set of joined partitions resulting from U_i and U_j. Then $0 \leq |\mathcal{P}_j| \leq |T_i| \times |T_j|$. Note that in the previous case, i.e., $X_j \neq \emptyset$, the join operation between two partitions may result in the generation of more than one joined partition only if the joined schema satisfies either Condition 8.17 or 8.18. Otherwise, the join operation always yields a single joined partition.

- Finally, if t_i and t_j are two joinable web tuples then it is possible for a node of type x to be joinable with more than one node of different type identifiers, that is, if $n_1(t_i)$ and $n_2(t_j)$ are nodes in t_i are of type x_1 and x_2 and $n_3(t_j)$ is a node in t_j of type x_3. Then it is possible for $n_3(t_j)$ to be joinable with both $n_1(t_i)$ and $n_2(t_i)$. Note that such a case is not possible when $X_j \neq \emptyset$ since we do not allow specification of a set of pairs of joinable node type identifiers sharing some common identifiers.

Overview

Our method of generating the joined web table when $X_j = \emptyset$ is different from that described in the previous section. Unlike when $X_j \neq \emptyset$, we first generate a joined web tuple from a pair of joinable tuples in partitions U_i and U_j and then create a joined schema to bind the joined web tuple. We perform this operation for all pairs of joinable tuples in the input partitions. Once the set of joined partitions is generated, we prune the partition by *combining* partitions with duplicate joined schemas into a single partition. This is repeated for all possible pairs of joinable partitions in the input web tables. Formally, given two web tables $W_1 = \langle N_1, \mathcal{P}_1 \rangle$ and $W_2 = \langle N_1, \mathcal{P}_2 \rangle$, and a join condition $\Psi = \langle M, X_j \rangle$ where $X_j = \emptyset$, the following steps are performed in the join construction phase to generate the joined web table.

1. Identify the sets of partitions $\mathcal{P}'_1 \subseteq \mathcal{P}_1$ and $\mathcal{P}'_2 \subseteq \mathcal{P}_2$ where $S'_1 \subseteq M$, $S'_2 \subseteq M$ and each partition $U_i \in \mathcal{P}'_1$ and $U_j \in \mathcal{P}'_2$ contains web tuples with joinable nodes (Steps (3) and (4) in Figure 8.30).

2. Let T_i and T_j be the set of web tuples in U_i and U_j. Then determine the possible pairs of tuples in T_i and T_j which are joinable to each other. Let $T_i' \subseteq T_i$ and $T_j' \subseteq T_j$ denote such sets of web tuples.

3. For each pair of tuples (t_k, t_r), $t_k \in T_i'$, $t_r \in T_j'$ generate the joined web tuple t_{kr} by joining these tuples over the joinable nodes (Steps (1) to (10) in Figure 8.32).

4. Generate a joined schema S_{ij} from S_i and S_j to bind t_{kr} (Step (12) in Figure 8.32).

5. Create a partition $U_k = \langle S_{ij}, t_{kr} \rangle$ (Step (13) in Figure 8.32).

6. Insert U_k in a partition collection $\mathcal{P}_{ij}'$ (Step (14) in Figure 8.32).

7. Repeat Steps (3) to (6) for all pairs of web tuples in T_i' and T_j'.

8. Combine partitions in $\mathcal{P}_{ij}'$ having identical schemas into a single partition (Step (27) in Figure 8.32).

9. Repeat the above Steps (2) to (8) for each pair of partitions in $\mathcal{P}_1'$ and $\mathcal{P}_2'$.

In the subsequent sections we elaborate on the above steps. Specifically, we discuss Steps (3) to (8) in detail. That is, given two partitions $U_i = \langle S_i, T_i \rangle$ and $U_j = \langle S_j, T_j \rangle$ in W_1 and W_2 containing joinable nodes, we show how to construct the set of joined partitions $\mathcal{P}_{ij}$.

Construction of the Joined Web Tuples

Given two joinable web tuples $t_k \in T_i$ and $t_r \in T_j$ in the partitions U_i and U_j, we describe the steps to construct the joined web tuple t_{kr}. This step is repeated for all pairs of joinable tuples in T_i and T_j. The construct **JoinTuples** in Figure 8.32 encapsulates the construction details of the joined web tuple. Recall that a joinable node in t_r of type x may be joinable with multiple nodes in t_k having distinct node type identifiers. Hence we categorize the join construction process into two types to facilitate our discussion. Category 1 represents the scenario when the joinable tuples t_k and t_r do not contain joinable nodes that may be joined with more than one node having distinct identifiers. Category 2, on the other hand, represents joinable tuples containing these types of joinable nodes. We begin with category 1.

Category 1

Observe that this case emulates the joined web tuple construction procedure for $X_j \neq \emptyset$. The only difference is that the joinable nodes are not restricted by their type identifiers as specified in X_j. Hence the steps for such a tuple construction are as follows.

1. Identify a set of pairs of joinable nodes in t_k and t_r (denoted by J_t).

2. For each pair of joinable nodes $(n_1(t_k), n_2(t_r)) \in J_t$, execute the Steps 2(b)(1) to 2(b)(5) as discussed in the joined web tuple construction process when $X_j \neq \emptyset$.

3. Let t_{kr}' represent the joined web tuples after concatenating the joinable nodes in t_k and t_r. Let D denote the set of pairs of joinable nodes in $t_{kr'}$ that are adjacent to each other.

4. For each $(n_1(t_k), n_2(t_r)) \in D$, let L denote the set of links between n_1 and n_2. Then remove those links in L of t_{kr}' that are duplicates. This is to ensure that we do not represent identical links between two nodes multiple times in t_{kr}'.

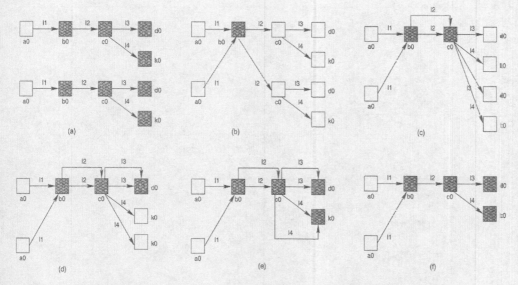

Fig. 8.40. Category 1 joined tuple construction in Example 8.29.

5. The modified t'_{kr} (denoted as t_{kr}) represents the joined web tuple.

Example 8.29. Consider the partitions U_{d1} and U_{nd1} in Example 8.13 and the web tuples denoted by t_1 in these two partitions (the first tuples in Figures 8.23 and 8.24). The joined web tuple of these two web tuples is shown in Figure 8.25 (the first web tuple). We now elaborate on how this web tuple is constructed. Observe that the pairs of joinable nodes in these two tuples are $(b_0, b_0), (u_0, u_0), (d_0, d_0)$, and (k_0, k_0). Hence the for loop in Step (2) is executed four times and the structure of the concatenated tuple at the end of each loop is shown in Figures 8.40(b) to 8.40(e). At the end of this step, we get a joined web tuple as shown in Figure 8.40(e). Since the joinable nodes in Figure 8.40(e) are adjacent to each other, $D = \{(b_0, u_0), (u_0, d_0), (u_0, k_0)\}$ after executing Step (3). Furthermore, the pair of links between each adjacent joinable node is identical. Hence we remove any one of these links from each adjacent joinable node pair in Figure 8.40(e). Consequently, the joined web tuple takes the form shown in Figure 8.40(f) (also identical to the first web tuple in Figure 8.25). ∎

Category 2

Note that in this case the tuples t_r contain at least one joinable node that can be joined with multiple nodes having distinct node type identifiers in t_k. The steps for constructing the joined web tuple are as follows.

1. Identify the set of pairs of joinable nodes in t_k and t_r (denoted by J_t).
2. Let $J_m \subseteq J_t$ be a set of pairs of joinable nodes that represent the joinability of a single node with multiple instances of different node type identifiers. That is, if $(n(t_k), n_2(t_r)) \in J_m$ and $(n(t_k), n_4(t_r)) \in J_m$ then type identifiers of

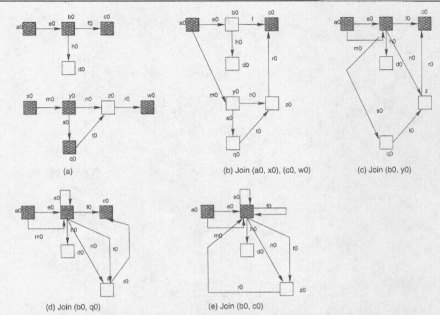

(a)

(b) Join (a0, x0), (c0, w0)

(c) Join (b0, y0)

(d) Join (b0, q0)

(e) Join (b0, c0)

Fig. 8.41. Category 2 joined web tuple construction in Example 8.30.

$n_2(t_k)$ and $n_4(t_r)$ are not identical for all pairs in J_m. For instance, $J_m = \{(y, a), (y, b), (z, q), (z, r), (z, t)\}$.

3. Then $J' = J_t - J_m$ represents a pair of joinable nodes of Category 1. For each pair of joinable nodes in J' execute the Steps 2(b)(1) to 2(b)(5) as discussed in the joined tuple construction in Section 8.7.4. Note that the result of this step is a concatenated web tuple (denoted by t'_{kr}).

4. Let $(x, y) \in J_m$ then replace y with ℓ if there exist $(\ell, y) \in J'$. This is because once ℓ and y are concatenated then the node labeled y does not exist anymore in t'_{kr}. Hence any subsequent concatenation on y indicates concatenation of the node labeled ℓ. Let the modified J_m be denoted J'_m.

5. Next we concatenate nodes in J'_m. Let x be a node in t_r and N_x represent a set of nodes in t_k that are joinable to x. Note that J'_m contains a set of such pairs of joinable nodes for each x. That is, $x \in left(J'_m)$ and $N_x \subseteq right(J'_m)$. For each $x \in left(J'_m)$ we perform the following steps to t'_{kr}.

   a) Get the set of incoming and outgoing links from $n(t_r) \in right(J_m)$ in t_r (denoted as L_{in} and L_{out}, respectively).
   b) Remove $n(t_r)$.
   c) Set the target id of the links in L_{in} to the URL of x in t'_{kr}.
   d) Set the source id of the links in L_{out} to the URL of x in t'_{kr}.

6. Execute Steps 2(c) to 2(e) of joined web tuple construction in Section 8.7.4.

Example 8.30. Consider the two web tuples in Figure 8.41(a). Let (a_0, x_0), (b_0, y_0), (b_0, q_0), (b_0, w_0), and (c_0, w_0) be joinable nodes. Let the type identifiers be $(a, x), (b, y), (b, q), (b, w)$, and (c, w). Observe that the node b_0 is joinable with multiple nodes y_0, q_0, and w_0. Hence $J_m = \{(b_0, y_0), (b_0, q_0), (b_0, w_0)\}$ and $J' = \{(a_0, x_0), (c_0, w_0)\}$. Then after Step (3) we get the joined web tuple in Figure 8.41(b). Next the set J_m is modified to J'_m as in Step (4). Observe that the node w_0 in $(b_0, w_0) \in J_m$ also exists in $(c_0, w_0) \in J'$. Hence, (b_0, w_0) is replaced by (b_0, c_0). Therefore $J'_m = \{(b_0, y_0), (b_0, q_0), (b_0, c_0)\}$. Next, the nodes in J'_m are concatenated based on Step (5). The concatenation of each pair of nodes is shown in Figures 8.41(c) to 8.41(e). Finally, at the end of the construction process the joined web tuple takes the form as shown in Figure 8.41(e). Observe that the joined web tuple may contain loops and cycles. ∎

Construction of the Joined Web Schema

Once the joined web tuples are generated from the web tuples in U_i and U_j, we proceed to create the set of joined schemas to bind these joined web tuples. The steps discussed below are encapsulated in the construct **GenerateSchema** (Step (12)) in Figure 8.32. The structure of the joined schema of a web tuple depends on the set of pairs of joinable node type identifiers whose instances are joinable nodes in the web tuples. That is, a set of joined web tuples may be represented by a single joined schema if the set of pairs of joinable nodes in each tuple belongs to the same pair of node type identifiers in S_i and S_j. We now describe the steps for generating the joined schema for a joined web tuple. We begin with tuples of Category 1.

Category 1

The steps for creating the joined schema of a joined web tuple are as follows.

1. Identify the set of pairs of joinable nodes (J_t) in t_k and t_r that generate the joined tuple t_{kr}.
2. For each $(n_1(t_k), n_2(t_r)) \in J_t$ identify the type identifiers of $n_1(t_k)$ and $n_2(t_r)$ in X_{ni} and X_{nj} (say x_1 and x_2) and insert $(x_1 \in X_{ni}, x_2 \in X_{nj})$ in X_{jt}.
3. At this point we have a set of pairs of joinable node type identifiers (similar to X_j) and schemas S_i and S_j. Hence we may construct the four components of S_{ij} by following the steps described in Section 8.7.4.
4. If S_{ij} satisfies either of the Conditions 8.17 or 8.18 then S_{ij} is modified based on the discussion of pruning joined partitions in Section 8.7.4 so that t_{kr} conforms to S_{ij}. Note that as S_{ij} binds only a single web tuple it is not necessary to decompose S_{ij} into multiple schemas as done during the pruning operation for $X_j \neq \emptyset$. Rather, we modify S_{ij} based on the pruning conditions so that $t_{kr} \dashv S_{ij}$.

We now illustrate the joined schema construction with an example given below.

Example 8.31. Consider the joined web tuple in Example 8.29. The schema of this web tuple is constructed from the schemas S_{d1} and S_{nd1} in Example 8.13. Observe that $J_t = \{(b_0, b_0), (u_0, u_0), (d_0, d_0), (k_0, k_0)\}$. Hence the set of pairs of joinable node type identifiers is $X_{jt} = \{(b, b), (\#_1, \#_1), (d, d), (k, k)\}$. Next, the joined schema is constructed best on the procedure described in Section 8.7.4. Since the type identifiers in S_{d1} and S_{nd1} are not nominally distinct, it is necessary to disambiguate them. Therefore $X'_{n_i} = X_{nd1} - \{b, \#_1, d, k\} = \{a\}$. Furthermore, $X_{n2} = \{a, b, c, d, \#_1, \#_2\}$. Consequently, $X'_{n_i} \bigoplus X_{n2} = \{z\}$. Hence the set of node type identifiers in the joined schema is given as $X_{n_{wj1}} = \{z, a, b, c, d, \#_1\}$. Next the set of link type identifiers is generated. Note that the joinable node type identifiers are adjacent to each other and the adjacent links are all bound by free link type identifiers. Therefore $L_i = \{-_2, -_3, -_4\}$, $X'_{\ell i} = \{-_1\}$, $X'_{\ell i} \bigoplus X_{\ell 2} = \{-_1\} \bigoplus \{-_1, -_2, -_3, -_4, -_5, -_{13}\} = \{-_6\}$. Therefore, the set of link type identifiers in the joined schemas is $\{-_6\} \cup \{-_1, -_2, -_3, -_4\} = \{-_1, -_2, -_3, -_4, -_6\}$. Finally, the set of connectivities and predicates can be computed by following the steps in Section 8.7.4, respectively.   ∎

Category 2

We now show how to construct the schema of the joined web tuple of Category 2, that is, tuples in which a single node is joinable with multiple nodes having distinct type identifiers. The procedure to generate the joined schema is as follows.

1. Identify the set of pairs of joinable nodes (J_t) in t_k and t_r that generate the joined tuple t_{kr}.
2. For each $(n_1(t_k), n_2(t_r)) \in J_t$ identify the type identifiers of $n_1(t_k)$ and $n_2(t_r)$ in X_{ni} and X_{nj} (say x_1 and x_2) and insert $(x_1 \in X_{ni}, x_2 \in X_{nj})$ in X_{jt}.
3. Compute $J_m \subseteq J_t$ and for each pair of nodes in J_m generate the corresponding pair of node type identifiers and store it in X_m.
4. Compute $X' = X_{jt} - X_m$.
5. At this point we have a set of pairs of joinable node type identifiers X' (similar to X_j) and schemas S_i and S_j. Hence we construct the four components of a temporary joined schema S_{temp} by following the steps described in Section 8.7.4.
6. Modify X_m to X'_m such that it contains a pair of node type identifiers of each pair of joinable nodes in J'_m.
7. Next we remove those node type identifiers in $X_{n_{temp}}$ that are involved in the join over multiple node type identifiers. Hence $X'_{n_{temp}} = X_{n_{temp}} - (right(X'_m) \cup left(X'_m))$.
8. Similarly, we remove those node predicates in P_{temp} that are defined over the node type identifiers in X'_m. Hence $P'_{temp} = P_{temp} - P_x$, where for each $p \in P_x$ $arg(p) \in (left(X'_m) \cup right(X'_m))$.
9. For each $x \in left(X'_m)$ do the following.
   a) Generate a nominally distinct identifier, say n.
   b) Insert n in $X'_{n_{temp}}$.
   c) Let R_x be the set of right identifiers in X'_m such that for each $r \in R_x \ \exists$ $(x, r) \in X'_m$.
   d) Replace the arguments of the predicates on the identifiers in X'_m with n and insert these predicates in P'_{temp}.
   e) Replace all x and R_x in C_{temp} with n.
10. Generate the joined schema S_{kr} where $X_{n_{kr}} = X'_{n_{temp}}$, $X_{\ell_{kr}} = X_{\ell_{temp}}$, $C_{kr} = C_{temp}$, and $P_{kr} = P'_{temp}$.

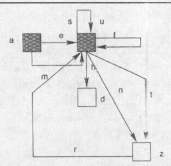

Fig. 8.42. Schema of joined web tuple in Example 8.30.

11. If S_{ij} satisfies either Condition 8.17 or 8.18, the S_{ij} is modified based on the discussion of pruning joined partitions in Section 8.7.4 so that t_{kr} conforms to S_{ij}. Note that as S_{ij} binds only a single web tuple it is not necessary to decompose S_{ij} into multiple schemas as done during the pruning operation for $X_j \neq \emptyset$.

Example 8.32. Consider the web tuples in Figure 8.41(a). Let the schemas of these web tuples be as follows.

- $S_1 = \langle X_{n1}, X_{\ell 1}, C_1, P_1 \rangle$, where $X_{n1} = \{a, b, c, d\}$, $X_{\ell 1} = \{e, f, h\}$, $C_1 \equiv a\langle e\rangle b \wedge b\langle f\rangle c \wedge b\langle h\rangle d$, and $P_1 = P_a \cup P_b \cup P_c \cup P_d \cup P_e \cup P_f \cup P_h$.
- $S_2 = \langle X_{n2}, X_{\ell 2}, C_2, P_2 \rangle$, where $X_{n2} = \{x, y, z, w, q\}$, $X_{\ell 2} = \{m, n, r, s, t\}$ $C_2 \equiv x\langle m\rangle y \wedge y\langle n\rangle z \wedge z\langle r\rangle w \wedge y\langle s\rangle q \wedge q\langle t\rangle z$, and $P_2 = P_x \cup P_y \cup P_z \cup P_w \cup P_q \cup P_m \cup P_n \cup P_r \cup P_s \cup P_t$.

Based on Example 8.30, $J_m = \{(b_0, y_0), (b_0, q_0), (b_0, w_0)\}$, $J' = \{(a_0, x_0), (c_0, w_0)\}$, and $J'_m = \{(b_0, y_0), (b_0, q_0), (b_0, c_0)\}$. Hence after Step(6) we get $X'_m = \{(b, y), (b, q), (b, c)\}$ and $X' = \{(a, x), (c, w)\}$. Hence Step (7) generates the following temporary joined schema, $S_{temp} = \langle X_{n_{temp}}, X_{\ell_{temp}}, C_{temp}, P_{temp} \rangle$, where $X_{n_{temp}} = \{a, b, c, d, y, z, q\}$, $X_{\ell_{temp}} = \{m, n, r, s, t, e, f, h\}$ $C_{temp} \equiv a\langle e\rangle b \wedge b\langle f\rangle c \wedge b\langle h\rangle d \wedge a\langle m\rangle y \wedge y\langle n\rangle z \wedge z\langle r\rangle c \wedge y\langle s\rangle q \wedge q\langle t\rangle z$, and $P_{temp} = (P_1 \cup P_2) - (P_x \cup P_w)$. After Steps (7) and (8) $X'_{n_{temp}} = \{a, d, z\}$ and $P'_{temp} = P_{temp} - (P_b \cup P_y \cup P_c \cup P_q)$.

Next, as $left(X'_m) = \{b\}$ the for loop in Step (9) is executed once. Suppose u denotes a new node type identifier. Then after Step (10) we get the following joined schema, $S_{ij} = \langle X_{n_{ij}}, X_{\ell_{ij}}, C_{ij}, P_{ij} \rangle$, where $X_{n_{ij}} = \{a, d, z, u\}$, $X_{\ell_{temp}} = \{m, n, r, s, t, e, f, h\}$ $C_{ij} \equiv a\langle m\rangle u \wedge u\langle n\rangle z \wedge z\langle r\rangle u \wedge u\langle s\rangle u \wedge u\langle t\rangle z \wedge a\langle e\rangle u \wedge u\langle f\rangle u \wedge u\langle h\rangle d$, and $P_{ij} = P'_{temp} \cup P_u$. Observe that P_u combines the predicates on the identifiers b, c, y, and q. The pictorial representation of the joined schema is shown in Figure 8.42. ∎

Joined Partition Pruning

Once a set of joined partitions is generated, we prune the partitions if necessary. Note that in this case each partition consists of a single joined web tuple and its joined schema. To elaborate further, let $U_i = \langle S_i, T_i \rangle$ and $U_j = \langle S_j, T_j \rangle$ be the joinable partitions. The join construction process will generate a set of joined partitions $\mathcal{P}_{ij}$ where the number of partitions $n \leq |T_i| \times |T_j|$. Each of these partitions binds a single joined web tuple. Hence the number of partitions is equal to the number of joined web tuples generated during this process. The set of partitions may share identical schemas if the sets of joinable node type identifiers for some tuples are identical. Consequently, in this situation it is necessary to prune the partitions in order to combine the partitions having identical schemas into a single partition. The pruning process is similar to that described in Section 8.4. Hence we do not elaborate on this further. Formally, it is necessary to prune the joined partition if the following condition is true.

Condition 8.19 *Let $\mathcal{P}_{ij}$ denote the set of joined partitions generated from $U_i = \langle S_i, T_i \rangle$ and $U_j = \langle S_j, T_j \rangle$ when $X_j = \emptyset$. Then it is necessary to prune $\mathcal{P}_{ij}$ if there exist partitions $(U_1, U_2) \in \mathcal{P}_{ij}$ such that $S_1 = S_2$.* ∎

8.8 Derivatives of Web Join

In this section, we discuss the derivatives of the basic web join operation. Some are direct derivatives of the web join; others are combinations of the web join and other web operations such as web select. For instance, σ-*web join* is a combination of web join followed by the web select operation and is used to eliminate irrelevant web tuples from a joined web table. The *outer web join* is used to identify dangling web tuples in the input web tuples. We discuss these two derivatives in detail.

8.8.1 σ-Web Join

The web join operation discussed in the previous sections enables us to combine information residing in two different web tables. However, in many cases the web join operation may also concatenate irrelevant information. For example, consider the joined web table in Figure 8.20. Observe that the second web tuple contains information related to the description and manufacturer of "Alendronate" and also the usage and side effects of "Albuterol". However, the information provided by this web tuple is superfluous since the first web tuple and the last two web tuples in Figure 8.20 have already captured the information related to the description, manufacturer, side effects, and usage of Alendronate and Albuterol, respectively. Furthermore, even though the manufacturer and description of the drug "Lovastatin" are stored in **Drugs-Manufacturer**, the side effects and uses of "Lovastatin" are not materialized in **Drugs-Usage** due to the change in the Web site structure. Hence only the manufacturer and description of "Lovastatin" are included in the joined table (in the fourth tuple along with "Albuterol"). The σ-web join is used to filter out these irrelevant web tuples containing superfluous or partial information. It is a combination of a web join operation followed by a web select based on some σ-*join selection condition* on the nodes and links in the joined web tuples. The selection conditions are used to filter out irrelevant joined web tuples. The web select operation is performed after the web join to eliminate those web tuples that do not satisfy these conditions. These conditions impose additional constraints on web tuples participating in the web join. Formally, we denote a σ-web join as follows. $W_{sj} = W_i \bowtie_{\{\Psi, \Omega\}} W_j$, where Ψ is the join condition and Ω denotes the σ-join selection condition. Ω expresses the hyperlink structure and metadata, content, or structural conditions the nodes and links of a joined web tuple must satisfy in order to be a tuple in the σ-joined web table. We elaborate on the *sigma-join selection condition* now.

Informally, Ω consists of three components; sets of pairs of node type identifiers in W_1 and W_2 denoted by X_{pn1} and X_{pn2}, respectively, sets of pairs of link type identifiers in W_1 and W_2 denoted by $X_{p\ell1}$ and $X_{p\ell2}$ sets of simple connectivities in DNF to impose selection conditions based on connectivities of W_1 and W_2 (denoted by C_1 and C_2, respectively), and a set of predicates to impose constraints on the node and link type identifiers. We elaborate on each of these components.

Sets of Pairs of Node Type Identifiers

The sets X_{pn1} and X_{pn2} represent the sets of node type identifiers in W_1 and W_2, respectively, over which some selection constraints are imposed in terms of predicates. For each pair in X_{pn1} or X_{pn2} the identifiers on the left-hand side represent a node type identifier in X_{n1} or X_{n2}, respectively. The identifier in the right-hand side represents a bound node type identifier that may or may not occur in X_{n1} or X_{n2}. Similar to the X_{pn} component in the selection schema $\Re$ (discussed earlier), the significance of the pair is that it specifies that certain conditions are imposed on the node type identifier on the left-hand side and this identifier is nominally identified in σ-joined tables by the identifier in the right-hand side. That is, let (l, r) be a pair in X_{pn_i} for $i \in [1, 2]$. Then l must be an identifier in X_{ni}; i.e., l is a node type identifier in W_i. Note that l may be bound or free. If l is bound then r must be equal to l. However, if l is free then r must be bound.

Sets of Pairs of Link Type Identifiers

These pairs are similar to the $X_{p\ell}$ component in the selection schema $\Re$ (discussed in Section 8.3). However, one important difference is that the link type identifier cannot be null in this case. In a σ-web join we do not impose constraints regarding the existence of instances of new link type identifiers in joined web tuples. The selection constraints are imposed only on the existing node and link type identifiers in W_1 and W_2. Formally, $X_{p\ell_i} = \{(l_{\ell1}, r_{\ell1}), (l_{\ell2}, r_{\ell2}), \dots, (l_{\ell k}, r_{\ell k})\}$, where $l_{\ell j} \in X_{\ell i}$ $\forall i \in [1, 2]$ and $l_{\ell i} \notin \emptyset$.

Sets of Simple Connectivities

The sets of simple connectivities in the σ-join selection condition are analogous to the corresponding component in the selection schema. In Ω a set (possibly empty) of simple connectivities for each input web table may be specified. These connectivities express the hyperlink structure of the node type identifiers involved in the σ-web join operation. Let $k \equiv x\langle\ell\rangle y$ be a connectivity in the set. Then there must exist selection constraints on x, ℓ, or y in the form of predicates. That is, $lnode(k) \in$

$(left(X_{pn_i}) \cup right(X_{pn_i}))$, $rnode(k) \in (left(X_{pn_i}) \cup right(X_{pn_i}))$, or $link(k) \in$ $(left(X_{p\ell_i}) \cup right(X_{p\ell_i}))$. Note that specifying a set of simple connectivities is not always mandatory in Ω. Unlike in the selection schema for a web select operation, connectivities in Ω do not express connectivity involving a new link type identifier. Consequently, there is no mandatory requirement to specify connectivity for these identifiers.

Set of Predicates

There may be three types of predicates in Ω. A set of predicates P_1 may be used to impose constraints on node and link type identifiers in W_1. Also, a set of predicates P_2 may be used to impose constraints on identifiers in W_2. Finally, a set of comparison predicates (denoted by P_{comp}) may be used to relate the identifiers in W_1 and W_2 based on certain conditions. Note that all these predicates impose additional metadata, content, or structural constraints on the joined web tuples. Also P_1 and P_2 may contain both comparison and comparison-free predicates.

Formally, a σ-join selection condition is a 3-tuple $\Omega = \langle \Re_1, \Re_2, P_{comp} \rangle$, where $\Re_1 = \langle X_{pn1}, X_{p\ell1}, C_1, P_1 \rangle$, $\Re_2 = \langle X_{pn2}, X_{p\ell2}, C_2, P_2 \rangle$, $left(X_{pni}) \subseteq X_{ni}$, $left(X_{p\ell i})$ $\subseteq X_{\ell i}$ for $i \in [1, 2]$, and for each predicate $p \in P_i$, $arg(p) \subseteq (right(X_{pni}) \cup$ $right(X_{p\ell i}))$ and for each $p_c \in P_{comp}$ $arg(p_c) = \{x, y\}$ s.t $x \in ((right(X_{pn1}) \cup$ $right(X_{p\ell1}))$ and $y \in ((right(X_{pn2}) \cup right(X_{p\ell2}))$. We now illustrate the σ-join selection condition with an example.

Example 8.33. Consider the web tables **Drug-Manufacturer** and **Drug-Usage**. Suppose we wish to perform a σ-web join on these two web tables. Suppose we wish to select those joined web tuples that satisfy the following selection condition. *The label of the outgoing link type identifier from the free node type identifier #$_1$ in W_2 must be identical to the label of the outgoing link type identifier from b in W_1.* This condition can be expressed by the following σ-join selection condition; $\Omega = \langle \Re_1, \Re_2, P_{comp} \rangle$, where $X_{pn1} = X_{pn2} = \emptyset$, $X_{p\ell1} = \{(\text{-}_1, h)\}$, $X_{p\ell2} = \{(\text{-}_1, g)\}$, $C_1 \equiv b\langle h \rangle$#$_1$, $C_2 \equiv$ #$_1\langle g \rangle$#$_2$, $P_1 = P_2 = \emptyset$, and $P_{comp} = \{p(h, g)\}$ where

$$p(h, g) \equiv \text{CONTENT::h[A] IS\_EQUAL g[A]}$$

Notice that $right(X_{p\ell1} = \{h\}$, $right(X_{p\ell2}) = \{g\}$, and $arg(p)$ in the above predicate contain the identifiers in $right(X_{p\ell1})$ and $right(X_{p\ell2})$. ∎

Algorithm of σ-Web Join

We now discuss formally the algorithm for performing a σ-web join. We first discuss the philosophy behind the algorithm. Observe that in a σ-web join, web tuples that satisfy the σ-join selection condition and join condition are joined together. Hence given two web tables W_1 and W_2, the join condition $\Psi = \langle M, X_j \rangle$ and the σ-join selection condition $\Omega = \langle \Re_1, \Re_2, P_{comp} \rangle$, the set of web tuples in W_1 and W_2 that participate in the σ-web join operation, must satisfy the following conditions.

- The sets of web tuples in W_1 and W_2 (say T_1' and T_2', respectively) must contain joinable nodes and satisfy the selection schemas $\Re_1$ and $\Re_2$, respectively.

Input: Web table name N_{sj}, σ-join selection condition $\Omega = \langle \Re_1, \Re_2, P_{comp} \rangle$, join condition $\Psi = \langle M, X_j \rangle$ and web tables $W_1 = \langle N_1, \mathcal{P}_1 \rangle$ and $W_2 = \langle N_2, \mathcal{P}_2 \rangle$.
Output: σ-joined web table $W_{sj} = \langle N_{sj}, \mathcal{P}_{sj} \rangle$.

```
(1)     (J, I) = JoinExistence(W₁, W₂, Ψ); /* Figure 8.27 */
(2)     if (J = ∅)
(3)         return; /* Tables are not joinable */
(4)     else {
(5)         Let M₁ ⊆ M s.t ∀ Sₖ ∈ M₁, Sₖ ∈ S₁ where k ≤ |M₁|;
(6)         Let M₂ ⊆ M s.t ∀ Sₖ ∈ M₂, Sₖ ∈ S₂ where k ≤ |M₂|;
(7)         P′₁ = SelectPartition(W₁, J, ℜ₁, M₁); /* Figure 8.44 */
(8)         P′₂ = SelectPartition(W₂, J, ℜ₂, M₂); /* Figure 8.44 */
(9)         if (P′₁ = ∅ ∨ P′₂ = ∅)
(10)            Return Wₛⱼ = ⟨Nₛⱼ, Pₛⱼ⟩ where Pₛⱼ = ∅;
(11)        else {
(12)            for (i = 1 to |P′₁|) {
(13)                Let U′ᵢ = ⟨S′ᵢ, T′ᵢ⟩;
(14)                for (j = 1 to |T′ᵢ|) {
(15)                    Get tuple tⱼ;
(16)                    for (d = 1 to |P′₂|) {
(17)                        Let U′_d = ⟨S′_d, T′_d⟩;
(18)                        for (b = 1 to |T′_d|) { /* Joined tuple construction */
(19)                            Get tuple t_b;
(20)                            if ((tⱼ and t_b satisfies P_comp) ∨ (P_comp = ∅)){
(21)                                t_jb = JoinTuples(tⱼ, t_b, J);
(22)                                Insert t_jb in T_jb;
(23)                            }
(24)                            else
(25)                                /* Tuples not joinable */
(26)                            if (Xⱼ = ∅) { /* Schema construction */
(27)                                S_jb = GenerateSchema(S′ᵢ, S′_d, t_jb, Ω);
(28)                                U_jb = ⟨S_jb, t_jb⟩;
(29)                                Insert U_jb in P_sj;
(30)                            }
(31)                        }
(32)                        if (Xⱼ ≠ ∅) { /* Schema construction */
(33)                            if (T_jb ≠ ∅) {
(34)                                S_jb = GenerateSchema(S′ᵢ, S′_d, Xⱼ, Ω);
(35)                                U_jb = ⟨S_jb, T_jb⟩;
(36)                                Insert U_jb in P_sj;
(37)                            }
(38)                            else
(39)                                /* S_jb is noisy schema */
(40)                        }
(41)                        else /* Xⱼ = ∅ */
(42)                            Remove identical schemas from P_sj;
(43)                    }
(44)                }
(45)            }
(46)        }
(47)    }
(48)    Return Wₛⱼ = ⟨Nₛⱼ, Pₛⱼ⟩;
```

Fig. 8.43. Algorithm of σ-web join.

- A pair of web tuples from T_1' and T_2' must satisfy the set of comparison predicates P_{comp}.

Based on the above requirement, the algorithm for a σ-web join is designed to first identify these types of web tuples from the input web tables before performing the web join. Observe that the set of tuples that satisfy the first condition can be identified by inspecting the web tuples independently in W_1 and W_2. However, to identify the pairs of web tuples that conform to the second condition it is necessary to inspect the pair of web tuples from the input web tables. Consequently, the algorithm is categorized into two stages: it selects those web tuples in W_1 and W_2 that contain joinable nodes and satisfy $\Re_1$ and $\Re_2$ by scanning the web tables; and it identifies pairs of tuples that satisfy P_{comp} from the selected set of web tuples and performs the web join operation. We now discuss this algorithm in detail.

Figure 8.43 depicts the pseudocode of the σ-web join algorithm. It takes as input two web tables $W_1 = \langle Z_1, \mathcal{P}_1 \rangle$ and $W_2 = \langle Z_2, \mathcal{P}_2 \rangle$, the join condition $\Psi = \langle M, X_j \rangle$, and the σ-join selection condition $\Omega = \langle \Re_1, \Re_2, P_{comp} \rangle$ and returns as output the σ-joined table $W_{sj} = \langle Z_{sj}, \mathcal{P}_{sj} \rangle$. Step (1) first determines if the web tables W_1 and W_2 are joinable based on the join condition Ψ. Since we have discussed this earlier (Figure 8.27), we do not elaborate on the join existence process any further. If this process returns a nonempty set of joinable nodes then Steps (4) to (48) are executed. Steps (5) and (6) identify the sets of schemas of W_1 and W_2 in M (denoted by M_1 and M_2 respectively). Then the construct **SelectPartition** in Steps (7) and (8) identifies the partitions in W_1 and W_2 (denoted by $\mathcal{P}_1'$ and $\mathcal{P}_2'$, respectively) that contain web tuples satisfying the first condition. It also enhances schemas of these partitions to incorporate the selection conditions expressed by $\Re_1$ and $\Re_2$. The pseudocode of this construct is depicted in Figure 8.44. We elaborate on this algorithm later.

Once the partitions $\mathcal{P}_1'$ and $\mathcal{P}_2'$ are generated the algorithm proceeds to identify pairs of web tuples in T_1' and T_2' that satisfy the predicates in P_{comp} and perform the join operation (Steps (12) to (48)). For each pair of tuples the algorithm checks if it satisfies P_{comp} (Step (20)). If it does then it creates a joined web tuple (Step (21)). The process of constructing the joined web tuple is identical to that discussed earlier. Hence we do not elaborate on this. The process of schema generation is encapsulated in the construct **GenerateSchema** and is similar to that described in the web join operation earlier. The only difference is that in this case the schemas of the joined web tuples are augmented by incorporating the predicates in P_{comp}. Observe that Steps (12) to (48) are similar to those discussed in Figure 8.32. The only difference is that the algorithm includes the condition to check whether a pair of tuples satisfies P_{comp} (Step (20)).

We now elaborate on the algorithm of the construct **SelectPartition** (Figure 8.44). Note that the objective of this construct is to identify those partitions in input web tables that have web tuples containing joinable nodes and satisfying the selection schema. Steps (1) to (5) in Figure 8.44 first generate the sets of node and link type identifiers involved in the σ-web join operation by inspecting the selection schema $\Re$ and predicate set P_{comp}. Let L_n and L_ℓ be the set of node and link type identifiers, respectively, over which certain selection constraints are imposed.

Input: Web table $W = \langle Z, \mathcal{P} \rangle$, Joinable node set J, $\Re = \langle X_{pn}, X_{p\ell}, C, P \rangle$,
Set of simple schemas M and predicate set P_{comp};
Output: Selected partition $\mathcal{P}'$;

(1) Let $L_n = \{l_{n1}, l_{n2}, \ldots, l_{nk}\}$ where $l_{ni} \in left(X_{pn})$ $\forall\, i \in [1, k]$
and $\exists\, (l_{ni}, r_{ni}) \in X_{pn}$, $(l_{nj}, r_{nj}) \in X_{pn}$ s.t $p(r_{ni}) \in P$ or $p(r_{ni}, r_{nj}) \in P$;

(2) Let $L_\ell = \{l_{\ell 1}, l_{\ell 2}, \ldots, l_{\ell t}\}$ where $l_{\ell i} \in left(X_{p\ell})$ for $i \in [1, |X_{p\ell}|]$
and $\exists\, (l_{\ell i}, r_{\ell i}) \in X_{p\ell}$, $(l_{\ell j}, r_{\ell j}) \in X_{p\ell}$ s.t $p(r_{\ell i}) \in P$ or $p(r_{\ell i}, r_{\ell j}) \in P$;

(3) if $(P_{comp} \neq \emptyset)$ {

(4)   Let $L_n' = \{l_{n1}', l_{n2}', \ldots, l_{nk}'\}$ where $l_{ni}' \in left(X_{pn})$ $\forall\, i \in [1, k]$
and $\exists\, (l_{ni}', r_{ni}') \in X_{pn}$, $(l_{nj}', r_{nj}') \notin X_{pn}$ s t $p(r_{ni}', r_{nj}') \in P_{comp}$;

(5)   Let $L_\ell' = \{l_{\ell 1}', l_{\ell 2}', \ldots, l_{\ell t}'\}$ where $l_{\ell i}' \in left(X_{p\ell})$ $\forall\, i \in [1, t]$
and $\exists\, (l_{\ell i}', r_{\ell i}') \in X_{p\ell}$, $(l_{\ell j}', r_{\ell j}') \notin X_{p\ell}$ s.t $p(r_{\ell i}', r_{\ell j}') \in P_{comp}$;

(6) }

(7) if $(L_n = \emptyset \land L_\ell = \emptyset)$

(8) $\mathcal{P}' = \textbf{SelectJoinablePartition}(W, M, J)$; /* Figure 8.31 */

(9) else {

(10)   for $(i = 1$ to $|M|)$ {

(11)   Let $S_i \in M$ and $U_i = \langle S_i = \langle X_{ni}, X_{\ell i}, C_i, P_i \rangle, T_i \rangle$ where $U_i \in \mathcal{P}$;

(12) $L_{ni} = X_{ni} \cap L_n$;

(13) $L_{\ell i} = X_{\ell i} \cap L_\ell$;

(14)   if $((L_{ni} \neq \emptyset \lor L_{\ell i} \neq \emptyset)$ {

(15)   if $(L_n' \neq \emptyset \lor L_\ell' \neq \emptyset)$ {

(16) $L_{ni}' = X_{ni} \cap L_n'$;

(17) $L_{\ell i}' = X_{\ell i} \cap L_\ell'$;

(18)   if $(L_{\ell i}' = \emptyset \land L_{ni}' = \emptyset)$

(19)   The tuples bound by S_i are not joinable;

(20)   else {

(21)   Steps (3) to (10) of Figure 8.31 are executed;

(22)   Steps (11) to (38) of Figure 8.8 are executed;

(23)   }

(24)   }

(25)   else {

(26)   Steps (3) to (10) of Figure 8.31 are executed;

(27)   Steps (11) to (38) of Figure 8.8 are executed;

(28)   }

(29)   }

(30)   else

(31)   The partition does not satisfy selection condition;

(32)   }

(33) }

(34) Return $\mathcal{P}'$;

Fig. 8.44. Algorithm **SelectPartition**.

Specifically, L_n represents the set of node type identifiers in X_{pn} that are on the left-hand side of each pair. Similarly, L_ℓ contains link type identifiers in $X_{p\ell}$ that occur on the left-hand side of each pair. Note that L_n and L_ℓ exclude all pairs in X_{pn} and $X_{p\ell}$ whose right identifiers are arguments of a predicate in P_{comp}. This is because satisfaction of P_{comp} can only be determined by inspecting web tuples from both W_1 and W_2 and not individual input tables. Specifically, those identifiers involved in P_{comp} are denoted by L'_n and L'_ℓ in the algorithm (Steps (4) and (5)), respectively.

Next the algorithm proceeds to identify the potential partition set from W. The condition in Step (7) determines whether constraints on web tuples are imposed only by the set of comparison predicates P_{comp}. In such cases $L_n = L_\ell = \emptyset$. If this condition is evaluated true then the joinable partitions are selected by only inspecting if the web tuples contain joinable nodes (Step (8)). Otherwise, Steps (9) to (32) are executed. These steps select the potential partitions by checking if the web tuples satisfy $\Re$ and contain joinable nodes. Since we have elaborated on the generation of such partitions in Section 8.3, we do not discuss this further. Also note that the algorithm in Figure 8.45 represents the modified construct **GenerateSchemaSet** in Figure 8.9. We modify it to address the selection constraints in a σ-web join operation. Note that this modification is based on the fact that in a σ-web join new link type identifiers are not specified in Ω to represent new instances of links in the joined web tuples.

Example 8.34. Consider the σ-join selection condition on Drug-Manufacturer and Drug-Usage in Example 8.33. The σ-web join operation will generate a web table containing the following partitions (Figure 8.46) $\mathcal{P}_{sj} = \{U_{sj1}, U_{sj2}\}$ where

- $U_{sj1} = \langle S_1 = \langle X_{n1}, X_{\ell 1}, C_1, P_1 \rangle, T_1 \rangle$, $X_{n1} = \{x, b, c, d, y, z, k, \#_1, \#_2, \#_3\}$, $X_{\ell 1} = \{n, r, h, g, s, \text{-}_7, \text{-}_2, \text{-}_3, \text{-}_8\}$, $C_1 \equiv x\langle n\rangle b \wedge b\langle h\rangle \#_3 \wedge \#_3\langle\text{-}_7\rangle d \wedge \#_3\langle\text{-}_8\rangle c \wedge x\langle r\rangle y \wedge y\langle s\rangle \#_1 \wedge \#_1\langle g\rangle \#_2 \wedge \#_2\langle\text{-}_2\rangle z \wedge \#_2\langle\text{-}_3\rangle k$, $P_1 = P_j \cup \{p(h, g)\}$, and $T_1 = \{t_1, t_2, t_3\}$ (Figure 8.46);
- $U_{sj2} = \langle S_2 = \langle X_{n2}, X_{\ell 2}, C_2, P_2 \rangle, T_2 \rangle$, $X_{n2} = \{x, b, c, d, y, z, k, \#_1, \#_2, \#_3, \#_4\}$, $X_{\ell 1} = \{n, r, h, g, s, \text{-}_9, \text{-}_{10}, \text{-}_3, \text{-}_2, \text{-}_{11}, \text{-}_7\}$, $C_2 \equiv x\langle n\rangle b \wedge b\langle h\rangle \#_3 \wedge \#_3\langle\text{-}_9\rangle \#_4 \wedge \#_4\langle\text{-}_{10}\rangle d \wedge \#_4\langle\text{-}_{11}\rangle c \wedge x\langle r\rangle y \wedge y\langle s\rangle \#_1 \wedge \#_1\langle g\rangle \#_2 \wedge \#_2\langle\text{-}_2\rangle z \wedge \#_2\langle\text{-}_3\rangle k$, $P_2 = P_j \cup \{p(h, g)\}$, and $T_2 = \{t_4, t_5, t_6\}$.

Observe that when the algorithm is executed on these web tables $L_n = L_\ell = L'_n = \emptyset$ and $L'_\ell = \{\text{-}_1\}$ for both input web tables. Hence the condition in Step (7) of Figure 8.44 is evaluated true and Step (8) is executed. Since instances of a and x occur in all web tuples in Drug-Manufacturer and Drug-Usage, all partitions of these web tables are returned by the construct **SelectJoinablePartition**.   ∎

8.8.2 Outer Web Join

The web tuples that do not participate in the web join operation (dangling web tuples) are absent from the joined web table. In certain situations [25, 19] it is necessary to identify the dangling web tuples from one or both input web tables. The outer web join operation enables us to identify them. Depending on whether the outer-joined web table must contain the nonparticipant web tuples from the first or second web tables, we define two kinds of outer web join: the *left-outer web join* and the *right-outer web join*, respectively. Formally, given two web tables W_1 and W_2, the left-outer web join and right-outer web join on these two web tables are denoted by $W_1 =\!\!\bowtie W_2$ and $W_1 \bowtie\!\!= W_2$, respectively, where the symbols $=\!\!\bowtie$

Input: Selection schema $\Re$ where $\Re = \langle X_{pn}, X_{p\ell}, C_r, P_r \rangle$, simple schema S_i, sets of node and link type identifiers L_{ni} and $L_{\ell i}$.

Output: Set of simple web schemas S_{si}.

(1)   Let $C_r \equiv C_{r1} \vee C_{r2} \vee \ldots \vee C_{rj}$;
(2)   for $(a = 1 \ to \ j)$ { /* Each set of conjunctive connectivities */
(3)   for $(b = 1 \ to \ |C_{ra}|)$ { /* Simple connectivities in each set */
(4)   if $((lnode(k_b) \notin L_{ni}) \wedge (\exists \ l \ \text{s.t.} \ (l, lnode(k_b)) \in X_{pn} \ \text{and} \ l \in L_{ni}))$ {
(5)   Replace $lnode(k_b)$ with l;
(6)   Insert $lnode(k_b)$ in N_b;
(7)   }
(8)   if $((rnode(k_b) \notin L_{ni}) \wedge (\exists \ l \ \text{s.t.} \ (l, rnode(k_b)) \in X_{pn} \ \text{and} \ l \in L_{ni}))$ {
(9)   Replace $rnode(k_b)$ with l;
(10)   Insert $rnode(k_b)$ in N_b;
(11)   }
(12)   if $(link(k_b) \in L_{\ell i}) \wedge (\exists \ell \ \text{s.t} \ (\ell, link(k_b)) \in X_{p\ell}) \ \text{and} \ \ell \in L_{\ell i}))$ {
(13)   Replace $link(k_b)$ with ℓ;
(14)   Insert $link(k_b)$ in L_b;
(15)   }
(16)   Insert k_b in connectivity set C_{tmp};
(17)   }
(18)   if $(C_{tmp} \subseteq C_i)$ {
(19) $C' \equiv C_i - C_{tmp}$;
(20)   for $(d = 1 \ to \ |C'|)$ {
(21)   Execute steps (20) to (25) of Figure 3.8;
(22)   Insert $lnode(k_d)$, $rnode(k_d)$ in N_b;
(23)   Insert $link(k_d)$ in L_b;
(24)   }
(25) $C_{si} \equiv C' \wedge C'_r$ where $C'_r \subseteq C_r$; /* Generation of schema components */
(26) $X_{ns_i} = (X_{ni} - L_{ni}) \cup N_b$;
(27) $X_{\ell s_i} = (X_{\ell i} - L_{\ell i}) \cup L_b$;
(28)   Generate P_{si} by executing steps (28) to (33) of Figure 8.8;
(29)   Insert $S_{si} = \langle X_{ns_i}, X_{\ell s_i}, C_{si}, P_{si} \rangle$ in S_{si};
(30)   }
(31)   } /* End of for loop */
(32)   Return S_{si};

Fig. 8.45. Algorithm **GenerateSchemaSet** for σ-web join.

and $\bowtie=$ correspond to the different flavors of outer web join. The resultant web table W_o for a left-outer or right-outer web join will contain the dangling web tuples from W_1 or W_2, respectively.

Although there exist similarities between the notion of outer web join and outer join in relational databases, the concept of outer web join differs from its relational counterpart in certain major ways. First, in an outer join, the resulting relation contains the dangling tuples as well as the tuples participating in the join operation. However, in an outer web join, we only extract the dangling web tuples as the resultant web table. Next, an outer join operation in a relational database is particularly useful in dealing with situations where there are null values in the join

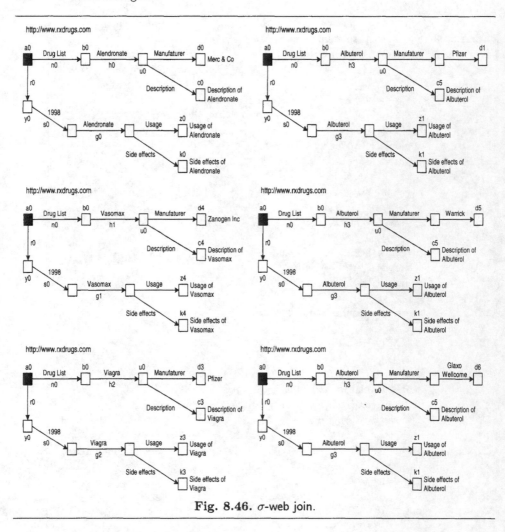

Fig. 8.46. σ-web join.

attributes of either relation. The outer web join is primarily used to detect web deltas in our web warehouse [25, 19] (discussed later).

Algorithm of Outer Web Join

The algorithm for outer web join takes as input two web tables W_1 and W_2 and a join condition Ψ, and returns as output a left or right outer web joined table W_o. The pseudocode for implementing this algorithm is given in Figure 8.49. The algorithm first identifies the joinable node ids J using the procedure explained earlier.

Once the joinable node ids of the input web tables are detected, the ids of the dangling nodes in W_1 or W_2 are computed. We denote the set of dangling node ids in W_1 or W_2 as $danglingNodeSet = N_1 - J$ or $danglingNodeSet = N_2 - J$, respectively.

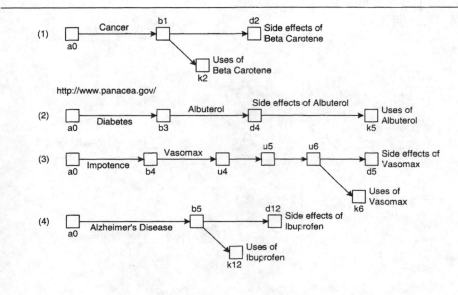

Fig. 8.47. Left outer web join.

To locate dangling web tuples in W_1 or W_2 for left or right outer web join, the algorithm examines the node ids in each web tuple in each partition of W_1 or W_2 to identify the existence of dangling nodes (Steps (10) to (19)). First, it retrieves the set of node ids in a web tuple t_k of W_1 or W_2 (Step (14)). Then the algorithm checks whether these node ids are dangling node ids (i.e., all the node ids are elements of *danglingNodeSet*) (Step (15)). If so, the web tuple t_k is a dangling web tuple and is inserted into the the tuple set T_{or}.

Once all web tuples in a partition U_r are inspected, the schema of the dangling web tuples is generated. If T_{or} is nonempty (Step (20)) then there must exist at least one dangling web tuple in the partition U_r. Furthermore, since a left or right outer web join operation extracts a subset of web tuples from W_1 or W_2, the web schemas of the outer joined web table will be identical to that of some of the schemas of W_1 or W_2 depending on the flavor of outer web join. Hence the schema of U_r, i.e., S_r, is assigned as the schema of the partition U_{or} of the outer joined web table (Step (21)). We illustrate the execution of left and right outer web join operations with an example.

Example 8.35. Consider the web tables **Drugs** and **New Drugs** in Figures 8.23 and 8.24, respectively. The web tuples in **Drugs** and **New Drugs**, which are associated with the side effects and uses of "Beta Carotene", a drug used for cancer (third web tuple), do not participate in the web join process as the content of all the nodes in the web tuple in **New Drugs** has changed with respect to those in **Drugs**. The link structure of the web tuple related to "Vasomax" has been modified after 15th January, 2001 and none of the nodes in this web tuple in **Drugs** are joinable to the corresponding web tuple in **New Drugs**. The web tuple related to "Alzheimer's Disease" in **Drugs** is not materialized again in **New Drugs** as the

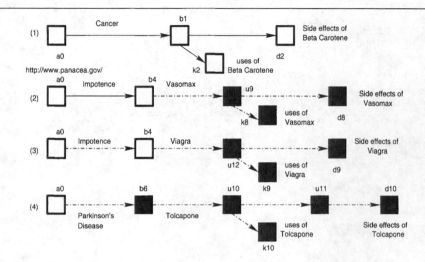

Fig. 8.48. Right outer web join.

new set of documents does not satisfy the coupling query anymore. Similarly, the web tuple containing documents related to "Diabetes" in **Drugs** has been removed from the Web site and is not materialized once again in **New Drugs**. These four web tuples in **Drugs** are dangling web tuples. Performing a left outer join on these two web tables enables us to identify these dangling web tuples (Figure 8.47).

The execution of the algorithm in Figure 8.49 (left outer web join) is as follows.

- Step (1) in Figure 8.49 is the same as described earlier. Hence we do not elaborate on this.

- Since we are performing a left outer web join operation, the condition in Step (2) is evaluated true and Steps (3) to (5) are executed. This operation is performed on **Drugs**. After Step (3), we get $danglingNodeSet = N_1 - J = \{a_0, b_1, b_3, b_4, b_5, u_2, u_4, u_5, u_6, u_7, u_8, d_2, d_3, d_4, d_5, d_2, k_2, k_3, k_5, k_6, k_{12}\}$.

- Next Steps (10) to (24) are executed. The for loop in Step (10) is executed five times as the number of partitions in **Drugs** is five (Example 8.13). It retrieves each web tuple from each partition. For $r = 1$, the first web tuple t_1 bound by U_{d1} is retrieved. After Step (14), $tupleNodeIdSet[1] = \{a_0, b_0, u_0, k_0, d_0\}$. After Step (15), $tupleNodeIdSet[1] \cap danglingNodeSet = \{a_0\}$ and is not equal to $tupleNodeIdSet[1]$. Consequently, the conditional statement is evaluated false. Hence Step (16) is ignored. The first tuple is not a dangling web tuple as it contains joinable nodes. Similarly, the second and eighth web tuples in **Drugs** (in partition U_{d1}) are ignored.

- Consider the second partition U_{d2} for $r = 2$. In this case, $T_2 = \{t_3, t_4\}$. For the third web tuple t_3, $tupleNodeIdSet[3] = \{a_0, b_1, d_2, k_2\}$ and $tupleNodeIdSet[3] \cap danglingNodeSet = \{a_0, b_1, d_2, k_2\}$ which is the same as $tupleNodeIdSet[3]$. Hence the if condition is evaluated true. Therefore Step (16) is executed and

Input: Web tables $W_1 = \langle N_1, \mathcal{P}_1 \rangle$ and $W_2 = \langle N_2, \mathcal{P}_2 \rangle$, Join condition Ψ.
Output: Left or right outer web joined table $W_c = \langle N_o, \mathcal{P}_o \rangle$.

(1) $(J, I) = \textbf{JoinExistence}(W_1, W_2, \Psi)$;
(2)   if (left outer web join is to be performed) {
(3) $danglingNodeSet = N_1 - J$;
(4)   Let temporary web table $W_t = W_1$;
(5)   }
(6)   else {
(7) $danglingNodeSet = N_2 - J$;
(8)   Let temporary web table $W_t = W_2$;
(9)   }
(10)   for $(r = 1$ to $|\mathcal{P}_t|)$ {
(11)   Let $U_r = \langle S_r, T_r \rangle$;
(12)   for $(k = 1$ to $|T_r|)$ {
(13)   Get tuple t_k;
(14) $tupleNodeIdSet[k] = \textbf{GetTupleNodeIds}(t_k)$;
(15)   if $(tupleNodeIdSet[k] \cap danglingNodeSet = tupleNodeIdSet[k])$
(16)   Store tuple t_k in T_{or};
(17)   else
(18) t_k is a joinable tuple;
(19)   }
(20)   if $(T_{or} \neq \emptyset)$ {
(21) $S_{or} = S_r$;
(22)   Insert $\mathcal{P}_{or} = \langle S_{or}, T_{or} \rangle$ in $\mathcal{P}_o$;
(23)   }
(24)   }
(25)   return $W_o = \langle N_o, \mathcal{P}_o \rangle$;

Fig. 8.49. Algorithm of outer web join.

the third web tuple is stored in T_{o2}. Similarly, the fourth tuple is a dangling web tuple and stored in T_{o2}.

- As $T_{o2} = \{t_3, t_4\}$, Steps (21) to (22) are executed. The schema of the partition U_{d2}, i.e., S_{d2}, is assigned as the schema of the dangling web tuples t_3 and t_4.
- Similarly, the fifth and sixth web tuples in Drugs are identified as dangling web tuples from the partitions U_{d3} and U_{d4} in Example 8.13. The resultant set of tuples in the left outer joined web table is shown in Figure 8.47.
- The left outer joined table can be represented as $W_{lo} = \langle N_{lo}, \mathcal{P}_{lo} \rangle$, where $\mathcal{P}_{lo} = \{U_{l1}, U_{l2}, U_{l3}\}$ and
  1. $U_{l1} = \langle S_{l1}, T_{l1} \rangle$, $S_{l1} = S_{d2}$, and $T_{l1} = \{t_3, t_4\}$;
  2. $U_{l2} = \langle S_{l2}, T_{l2} \rangle$, $S_{l2} = S_{d3}$, and $T_{l2} = \{t_5\}$;
  3. $U_{l3} = \langle S_{l3}, T_{l3} \rangle$, $S_{l3} = S_{d4}$, and $T_{l3} = \{t_6\}$.

Next we illustrate the execution of a right outer join operation. Consider the web table New Drugs. The last two web tuples dealing with "Viagra" and "Tolcapone" did not exist in the previous version as these drugs were added to the Web site after 15th January, 2001. Moreover, all the nodes in the web tuples related to "Vasomax" and "Beta Carotene" are modified. Thus these tuples are dangling web tuples.

Performing a right-outer web join on these two web tables enables us to identify these dangling web tuples in **New Drugs** (Figure 8.48).

The execution of the algorithm for a right outer join operation is similar to that of a left outer join. The only difference is that now it operates on **New Drugs**. Hence we illustrate the execution of the algorithm briefly. In this case, Steps (6) to (9) are executed and $danglingNodeSet = \{a_0, b_1, k_2, d_2, u_3, d_7, u_2, k_3, d_3, u_4, k_4, u_9, k_8, d_8, b_4, u_7, u_{12}, k_9, d_9, b_6, u_{10}, u_{11}, d_{10}, k_{10}\}$. Next, Steps (10) to (24) are executed three times. Consider the sixth web tuple, for $r = 1$. $tupleNodeIdSet[6] = \{a_0, b_4, u_9, d_8, k_8\}$. As $tupleNodeIdSet[6] \cap danglingNodeSet = \{a_0, b_4, u_9, d_8, k_8\}$, the conditional statement is evaluated true and the sixth web tuple is inserted in the right outer joined table. After execution of the for loop, the right outer joined table is created (Figure 8.48). The right outer joined table can be represented as $W_{ro} = \langle N_{ro}, \mathcal{P}_{ro} \rangle$ where $\mathcal{P}_{ro} = \{U_{r1}, U_{r2}, U_{r3}\}$ and

1. $U_{r1} = \langle S_{r1}, T_{r1} \rangle$, $S_{r1} = S_{nd1}$, and $T_{l1} = \{t_6, t_8\}$;
2. $U_{r2} = \langle S_{r2}, T_{r2} \rangle$, $S_{r2} = S_{nd2}$, and $T_{l2} = \{t_3\}$;
3. $U_{r3} = \langle S_{r3}, T_{r3} \rangle$, $S_{r3} = S_{nd3}$, and $T_{l3} = \{t_9\}$.

Observe that although the web tuple related to "Niacin" in **New Drugs** does not appear in **Drugs**, it is not a dangling web tuple as the node b_2 in this tuple is joinable with the corresponding node in the web tuple related to the drug "Hirudin" in **Drugs**. ∎

8.9 Web Union

The notion of a *web union* is similar to that of a set union. The union of two web tables results in web tuples from either of two tables satisfying any one of the schema in the input web tables. Since the web union is very similar to a set union we do not discuss this in detail in this book. Informally, the web union operation involves a *partition generation phase* followed by a *partition pruning* phase. Note that a web union operation may create identical, equivalent, or inclusive web schemas. Hence, in the partition pruning phase, we transform these schemas into a set of distinct web schemas that bind a distinct collection of unioned web tuples. Note that we do not perform elimination of noisy web schemas in this phase as the web union operation never generates noisy web schemas. We illustrate the web union operation with the following example.

Example 8.36. Consider the web tables in Examples 7.18 and 6.10. These web tables contain information about cancer. Suppose we wish to combine the web tuples of these two web tables into a single web table. This may be performed using the web union operator. The unioned web table contains all the web tuples from both web tables. The set of partitions of the unioned web table is identical to the set union of partitions of these two input web tables. Since all the partitions are distinct, it is not necessary to prune these partitions.

Web Algebra	Relational Algebra
Γ operator	–
σ operator	σ operator
π operator	π operator
Δ operator	–
$\cup$ operator	$\cup$ operator
$\bowtie$ operator	$\bowtie$ operator

Table 8.2. Web versus relational algebra.

8.10 Summary

The above set of operators on web objects forms a web algebra. A web algebra manipulates web tables as first-class objects; each operator accepts one or two web tables as input and produces a web table as output. A set of simple web schemas and web tuples are produced each time a web operator is applied. (We ignore trivial applications of operators whereby the output web table is the same as the input web table.) The **global web coupling** operator extracts web tuples from the Web. In particular, portions of the WWW are extracted when it is applied to the WWW. **web union** and **web join** are binary operators on web tables. **Web select** extracts a subset of web tuples from a web table. **Web project** removes some of the nodes from the web tuples in a web table. The **web distinct** operator removes duplicate web tuples from a web bag.

It is interesting to contrast the web algebra with relational algebra. In relational algebra, a relation is the first-class object of manipulation by relational operators. The **select** operator performs rowwise extraction of tuples from a relation. Its counterpart in web algebra is the **web select** operator which extracts a subset of web tuples from web tables. The **project** operator performs columnwise extraction of attributes from a relation. Its corresponding **web project** operator *projects* portions of web tuples from a web table. The other operators in both algebras are quite similar although their precise semantics are different. Unlike web operators, relational operators do not always produce a relation with a new schema; only certain operators such as **project** and **join** result in new schemas. Finally, a relation in relational databases always has a single schema, whereas a web table may have multiple simple web schemas to represent the web tuples.

9

Web Data Visualization

In the preceding chapters we have seen how to store web information in the form of a web table. This approach of storing web information in a web table has the following shortcomings.

- It has no ability to view the structural similarity or differences among the web tuples. It is not possible for a user to visualize how one web tuple in a web table is related to another.
- The set of web tuples in a web table may contain duplicate web documents. For example, suppose a user Bill wishes to find a list of drugs and their side effects on diseases from the WWW. This information may be provided by different web sites. In particular, assume there is a web site at http://www.panacea.org/ that provides drug-related information. The global web coupling operator [29, 121] can be applied to retrieve those sets of related documents that match the coupling query and materialize them in a web table called Side-effects. A small portion of the web tuple set is shown in Figure 9.1[1] Each web tuple in Side-effects contains information about the side effects of a drug on a disease. Observe that the documents at http://www.panacea.org/ (denoted by a_1) in all the web tuples in Figure 9.1 are identical. Similarly documents (denoted by b_1) in the first two web tuples are identical. Thus a web table may contain duplicate documents and there is no mechanism to provide a *coalesced view* of the set of web tuples. A coalesced view allows a user to browse a lesser number of directed connected graphs when locating information.
- It does not allow a user to group web tuples based on *related information content*, or *similar (or identical)* web sites. A user has to manually probe each web tuple to find this information. For example, the fifth, seventh, and eighth web tuples in Figure 9.1 deal with the side effects of the drug Beta Carotene. However, this information cannot be grouped together in our web table.
- The set of web tuples is materialized in web tables. There is no other materialized representation of these web tables. For example the collective view of these web tuples can be stored as a set of directed graphs having a lesser number of nodes

---

[1] The numbers on the left-hand side of all the figures related to web tables in this chapter are used to aid visualization and are not part of the web tuples.

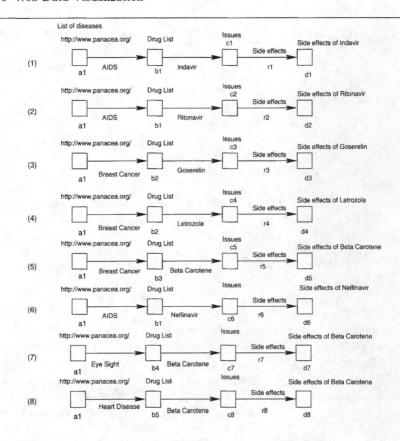

Fig. 9.1. Partial view of web tuples in "Side-effects".

or links as compared to the original web table. This can optimize the query, storage, and maintenance cost. However, this discussion is outside the scope of the book.

In this chapter, we introduce the following *data visualization operators* to resolve the above difficulties.

- **Web Nest**: Allows one to visualize relationships between web tuples in a web table. It provides an overview of the information space harnessed from the WWW and shows how this information is topically related.
- **Web Unnest**: Returns the original web tuples from a set of directed connected graphs created by the web nest operation.
- **Web Coalesce**: Coalesces duplicate nodes to reduce the size of the number of directed connected graphs in a web table. A coalesced web table is a set of condensed graphs and allows a user to browse a lesser number of graphs (web tuples).
- **Web Expand**: Expands a coalesced web table to recover the original set of web tuples.

- **Web Pack**: Groups a set of web tuples based on related (or similar) information content, and similar (or identical) web sites.
- **Web Unpack**: Returns the original set of web tuples from the packed web table.
- **Web Sort**: This operator sorts web tuples in *ascending* or *descending* order based on the total number of nodes or link types (*local*, *global*, or *interior*) in a web tuple.

These web operators take as input a set of web tuples of a web table and provide a different view of the tuples as output. This gives users the flexibility to view documents in different perspectives that are more meaningful. Formally, we illustrate data visualization operators and express them in a web query language.

9.1 Web Data Visualization Operators

A user may wish to view web tuples in different frameworks. In this section, we introduce some data visualization operators to add flexibility in viewing query results coupled from the WWW. Within this context, we provide the syntax for a web query involving data visualization operators. We also illustrate each operator with an example. In the next section, we discuss the formal algorithms of the data visualization operators. For simplicity, we assume in this chapter that a web table has a single web schema that binds all the web tuples. Formally, if $W = \langle N, \mathcal{U} \rangle$ is a web table then $\mathcal{U} = \{U\}$ where $U = \langle S, T \rangle$. Note that the visualization process can easily be extended to web tables with multiple web schemas.

9.1.1 Web Nest

Web tuples in a web table may be topically related. However, the relationship is not explicit from the way we store tuples in a web table. A visualization of this relationship gives an overview of the information space harnessed from the WWW and how this information is topically related. The **web nest** operator achieves this. It is an unary operator whose operand is a web table and whose output is a set of directed connected graphs condensed from the web table. Formally, let W be a web table. Then $G_n = \text{Nest}(W)$ where G_n is the set of condensed graphs.

Syntax of a Web Query Using Web Nest

The query in our model adopts a SQL-like syntax to facilitate a high-level web nest. The syntax for a web nest query is defined in a simplified BNF grammar ("[ ]" represents 0 or one occurrence and words in **typewriter** font represent keywords) as shown below.

$\langle WQL \rangle ::=$
    NEST $\langle web\_table\_name \rangle$
    [AS $\langle graph\_set\_name \rangle$]

- The "NEST $\langle web\_table\_name \rangle$" clause performs the web nest operation on the web table $\langle web\_table\_name \rangle$.

- " AS ⟨*graph_set_name*⟩" stores a set of directed connected graphs created after a web nest operation in ⟨*graph_set_name*⟩.

We now illustrate the web nest operation with an example. Note that in all the figures in the rest of this chapter we have eliminated the content descriptions of some of the nodes and links to simplify the figures.

Example 9.1. Consider the web table in Figure 9.1. Application of the web nest operator on the web table Side-effects will result in a directed connected graph as shown in Figure 9.2. The query for the web nest operation is shown below.

```
NEST Side-effects
AS   Nest_Side-effects
```

Note that in Figure 9.2 none of the instances of node type identifiers is replicated. The darkened boxes in the figure represent nodes over which web tuples are concatenated. The web nest operation provides an overview of the topical relationship of the web tuples in Side-effects. Furthermore, we may materialize the set of graphs as Nest_Side-effects. ∎

9.1.2 Web Unnest

The web unnest operator is a binary operator whose operand is a set of directed connected graphs and a set of web schemas, and the result is a web table satisfying the input web schemas. It performs the inverse function of the web nest operation. It returns the original web tuples of the web table from the set of graphs created by the web nest operation. Formally, let G_n be the set of directed connected graphs created by the web nest operation on web table W with schema S. Then $W = \text{Unnest}(G_n, S)$.

Syntax of a Web Query Using Web Unnest

The syntax for a web unnest query is given below.
⟨*WQL*⟩ ::=
    UNNEST ⟨*graph_set_name*⟩
    WITH SCHEMASET ⟨*schema_set*⟩
    TO ⟨*web_table_name*⟩

- The "UNNEST ⟨*graph_set_name*⟩" clause performs the web unnest operation on the set of graphs ⟨*graph_set_name*⟩.
- The "WITH SCHEMASET ⟨*schema_set*⟩" clause specifies the creation of web tuples from the ⟨*graph_set_name*⟩ satisfying the schemas ⟨*schema_set*⟩.
- The "TO ⟨*web_table_name*⟩" clause specifies returning the original web table ⟨*web_table_name*⟩.

We depict a web unnest with an example.

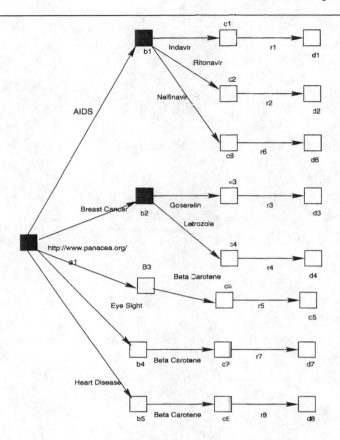

Fig. 9.2. Web nest operation.

Example 9.2. Consider the directed connected graph in Figure 9.2. The query to perform the web unnest operation on Nest_Side-effects is shown below.

```
UNNEST         Nest_Side-effects
WITH SCHEMASET Side-effects_schema
TO             Side-effects
```

This query will create the original web table Side-effects as shown in Figure 9.1. Note that it is not necessary for web tuples created by the web unnest operation to be in the same order as that of the original web table.   ∎

9.1.3 Web Coalesce

The set of web tuples in a web table may contain duplicate Web documents. For example, documents denoted by b_1 in the first two web tuples in Figure 9.1 are identical. The number of duplicate nodes (documents) increases with the number of outgoing links of each node that satisfies the coupling query. Thus the size of a web table is proportional to the number of outgoing links satisfying the schema in each node. For reasonably small sizes of web tables, browsing each web tuple

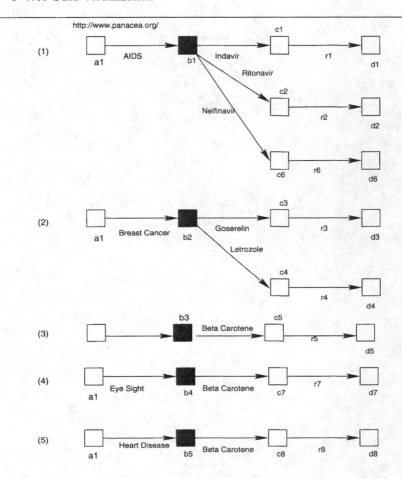

Fig. 9.3. Web coalesce operation on node type identifier b.

for information of interest is a feasible option. However, browsing web tables of significant size may be a tedious and inefficient way of locating information of interest. This problem may be minimized by coalescing duplicate nodes to reduce the size of the number of directed connected graphs in a web table. A coalesced web table results in a set of directed connected graphs and allows the user to browse fewer graphs (web tuples) compared to the original web table to locate desired information. To achieve this, we define the `web coalesce` operator. It takes a web table and a node type identifier as input and produces as output a set of directed connected graphs. It combines those web tuples in a web table that contains identical instances of the input node type identifier. Note that web coalesce is a specialization of the web nest operation. The web nest coalesces web tuples by removing all duplicate nodes, whereas a web coalesce operation coalesces a web table based on a node type identifier explicitly specified by a user.

Formally, let W be a web table with schema $S = \langle X_n, X_\ell, C, P \rangle$. Then the web coalesce operation on node type identifier $x \in X_n$ is defined as $G_c = \text{Coalesce}(W, x)$ where G_c is a set of directed graphs.

Syntax of a Web Query Using Web Coalesce

The syntax for a web query involving the web coalesce operation is shown below:
$\langle WQL \rangle ::=$
    COALESCE $\langle web\_table\_name \rangle$
    ON $\langle node\_type\_identifier \rangle$
    [AS $\langle graph\_set\_name \rangle$]

- The "COALESCE $\langle web\_table\_name \rangle$" clause performs the web coalesce operation on the web table $\langle web\_table\_name \rangle$.
- The "ON $\langle node\_type\_identifier \rangle$" clause performs the web coalesce operation on the node type identifier $\langle node\_type\_identifier \rangle$.
- " AS $\langle graph\_set\_name \rangle$" stores the set of directed connected graph created after a web coalesce operation in $\langle graph\_set\_name \rangle$.

We now illustrate a web coalesce with an example.

Example 9.3. Consider the web table in Figure 9.1. Suppose Bill wishes to coalesce the web tuples in Side-effects on node type identifier b so that he has to browse fewer directed graphs to find information related to side effects of various drugs for each disease. The query for the web coalesce operation on the node type identifier b in the web table Side-effects is shown below.

```
COALESCE Side-effects
ON        b
AS        Coalesce_Side-effects
```

This query will create a set of directed connected graphs as shown in Figure 9.2. The darkened boxes in the figure represent nodes over which the web coalesce is performed. Note that each graph describes side effects of various drugs for a particular disease. ∎

9.1.4 Web Expand

The **web expand** operator is a binary operator whose operand is a set of directed connected graphs and a web schema and the result is a web table satisfying the input web schema. It performs the inverse function of the web coalesce operation. It converts the set of coalesced tuples created by a web coalesce operation to the original web tuples of the web table. Formally, let G_c be the set of directed connected graphs created due to a web coalesce operation on web table W with schema $S = \langle X_n, X_\ell, C, P \rangle$. Then the web expand operation is defined as $W = \text{Expand}(G, S)$.

Syntax of a Web Query Using Web Expand

The syntax for a web expand query is given below.
⟨*WQL*⟩ ::=
   EXPAND ⟨*graph_set_name*⟩
   WITH SCHEMA ⟨*schema_name*⟩
   TO ⟨*web_table_name*⟩

- The "EXPAND ⟨*viewed_table_name*⟩" clause performs the web expand operation on the set of graphs ⟨*graph_set_name*⟩.
- The "WITH SCHEMA ⟨*schema_name*⟩" clause specifies the creation of web tuples from the ⟨*graph_set_name*⟩ satisfying the schema ⟨*schema_name*⟩.
- The "TO ⟨*web_table_name*⟩" clause specifies returning the original web table ⟨*web_table_name*⟩.

We now illustrate the syntax with an example.

Example 9.4. Consider the set of tuples created after a web coalesce operation on the node type identifier b in Figure 9.3. Suppose we materialize the set of graphs in Coalesce_Side-effects. The query for the web expand operation on Coalesce_Side-effects is shown below.

```
EXPAND      Coalesce_Side-effects
WITH SCHEMA Side-effects_schema
TO          Side-effects
```

This query will return the original web table Side-effects (Figure 9.1).   ∎

9.1.5 Web Pack

The web pack operator groups the web tuples in a web table based on *similar criteria*. It provides the flexibility to view web tuples containing *similar* nodes together. A user explicitly specifies the node type identifier and the criteria based on which web pack operation is performed. The criteria based on which packing of web tuples can be performed are given below.

- Host name: Web tuples containing instances of specified node type identifiers with identical host name are packed together.
- Domain name: Web tuples containing instances of specified node type identifiers with identical domain names (.com, .edu, .org, .gov, .net, .mil, etc.) are grouped together.
- Keyword content: Packing may be performed by grouping web tuples whose instances of specified node type identifiers contain user-specified keyword(s).

Note that in the case of packing based on keywords, the packed web table may contain duplicate web tuples since two different keywords may appear in the same node in a web tuple. Furthermore, tuples containing the keyword are displayed as top results and the remaining web tuples are pushed down in the packed web table. Formally, the web pack operation on node type identifier $x \in X_n$ is defined as $W_p = \text{Pack}(W, x, criteria)$, where W_p is the packed web table.

Syntax of a Web Query Using Web Pack

The syntax of web pack is as follows.
$\langle WQL \rangle ::=$

PACK $\langle web\_table\_name \rangle$
ON $\langle node\_type\_identifier \rangle$
[OR $\langle pack\_condition \rangle$]
[AS $\langle web\_table\_name \rangle$]

- The "PACK $\langle web\_table\_name \rangle$" clause performs the web pack operation on the web table $\langle web\_table\_name \rangle$.
- The "ON $\langle node\_type\_identifier \rangle$" clause performs the web pack operation on the node type identifier $\langle node\_type\_identifier \rangle$.
- The "FOR $\langle pack\_condition \rangle$" clause specifies the packing condition based on which the web pack operation is to be performed. The following packing conditions are supported in our query language.
  1. Host name.
     $\langle pack\_condition \rangle ::=$ host_name
  2. Domain name.
     $\langle pack\_condition \rangle ::=$ domain_name
  3. Set of keywords.
     $\langle pack\_condition \rangle ::= \langle keyword\_set \rangle$

Note that the set of keywords is explicitly specified by the user and may be in conjunctive and/or in disjunctive form.

- The "AS $\langle web\_table\_name \rangle$" clause stores the web table created after a web pack operation in $\langle graph\_set\_name \rangle$.

We now illustrate a web pack with an example.

Example 9.5. Continuing with the web table in Figure 9.1, suppose Bill wishes to group all the web tuples in Side-effects on node type identifier d that contains the keywords "Beta Carotene" or "Letrozole". The query for this web pack operation on the node type identifier d is shown below:

```
PACK Side-effects
ON   d
FOR  "beta carotene" OR "letrozole"
AS   Pack_Side-effects
```

The result of this query is shown in Figure 9.4. Note that the group of web tuples whose instance of node type identifier d contains the keyword "Beta Carotene" or "Letrozole" is displayed as top query results and the remaining web tuples in Side-effects are pushed down. The tuples whose instance of node type identifier d (the first four tuples) is filled with black are grouped together since they contain the keyword "Beta Carotene". The tuples whose instance of node type identifier d (fifth tuple) is filled with a pattern are grouped together because they contain the keyword "Letrozole". Note that the node d_4 contains both keywords. Thus the tuple containing d_4 is replicated (the first and fifth web tuples are identical) in the web table created after the web pack operation. ∎

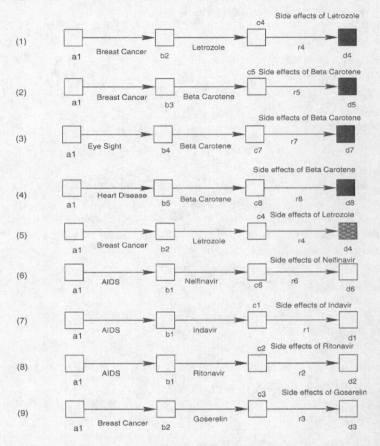

Fig. 9.4. Web pack operation on node type identifier d.

9.1.6 Web Unpack

The web unpack operator performs the inverse function of the web pack operation. Recall that the web pack operation on web table W may create duplicate web tuples when the packing is based on a set of keywords. The web unpack operator removes these replicated web tuples and returns the original web table. The order of the web tuples in the table created after a web unpack operation may not be identical to that of the original web table. It is worth mentioning that the web unpack operation is not useful if the packed web table does not contain duplicate web tuples. Formally, a web unpack on web table W is defined as $W = \mathtt{Unpack}(W_p)$, where W_p is the packed web table.

Syntax of a Web Query Using Web Unpack

The syntax for a web unpack query is given below.

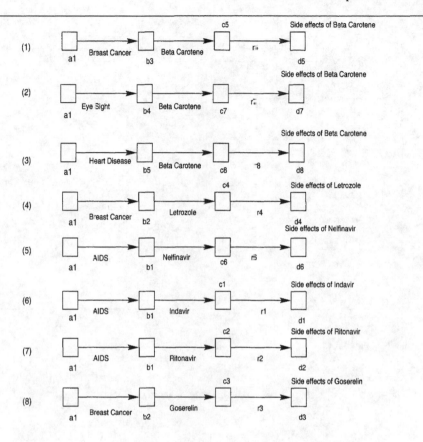

Fig. 9.5. Web unpack operation.

⟨WQL⟩ ::=
  UNPACK ⟨packed_table_name⟩
  TO ⟨web_table_name⟩

- The "UNPACK ⟨packed_table_name⟩" clause performs the web unpack operation on ⟨packed_table_name⟩.
- The "TO ⟨web_table_name⟩" clause specifies returning the original web table ⟨web_table_name⟩.

The following example illustrates the web unpack operation.

Example 9.6. Suppose we wish to perform a web unpack on Pack_Side-effects (Figure 9.4). The query is given below.

```
UNPACK Pack_Side-effects
TO     Side-effects
```

The result of this query will eliminate duplicate web tuples from Pack_Side-effects (Figure 9.5). Note that the web tuples in Figure 9.5 may not be in the same order as in the original web table Side-effects. ∎

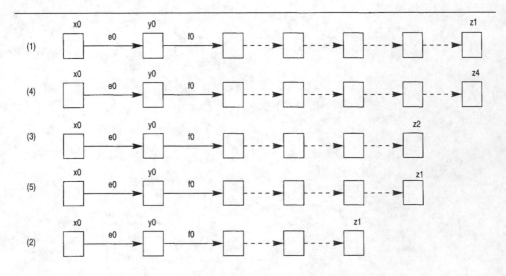

Fig. 9.6. Web sort operation.

9.1.7 Web Sort

The Web sort operator sorts web tuples based on given *conditions*. The conditions to sort the web tuples in a web table in ascending or descending order are given below:

- Total number of nodes in each web tuple;
- Total number of specified linktype (local, global, or interior) in each web tuple. This allows a user to measure the frequency of local, interior, and global links in the web tuples returned in response to her query.

Web sort enables us to rearrange the tuples in ascending or descending order based on the number of occurrences of local, global, or interior links in each tuple or the total number of nodes in each tuple. Formally, the web sort operation on a web table W with schema $S = \langle X_n, X_\ell, C, P \rangle$ is $W_s = \text{Sort}(W, \text{sort\_condition}, \text{order\_type})$ where *sort_condition* is the condition based on which sorting is performed and *order_type* specifies the ordering method (ascending or descending) of the sorted web tuples.

Syntax of a Web Query Using Web Sort

The syntax of a query involving a web sort operation is given below.
$\langle WQL \rangle ::=$
    SORT $\langle web\_table\_name \rangle$
    ON $\langle sort\_condition \rangle$
    [AS $\langle sorted\_table\_name \rangle$]
    ORDER BY $\langle ordering\_type \rangle$

- The "SORT ⟨web_table_name⟩" clause performs the web sort operation on the web table ⟨web_table_name⟩.
- The "ON ⟨sort_condition⟩" clause performs the web sort operation based on the sorting condition ⟨sort_condition⟩. The following sorting conditions are supported in our query language:
  1. Total number of nodes.
     ⟨sort_condition⟩::= node
  2. Total number of local link-type.
     ⟨sort_condition⟩::= local
  3. Total number of global link-type.
     ⟨sort_condition⟩::= global
  4. Total number of interior link-type.
     ⟨sort_condition⟩::= interior
- "AS ⟨sorted_table_name⟩" stores the sorted web table in ⟨sorted_table_name⟩.
- "ORDER BY ⟨ordering_type⟩" specifies the ordering method of the sorted web table. The following ordering types are supported in our query language.
  1. Ascending order.
     ⟨order_type⟩::= asc
  2. Descending order.
     ⟨order_type⟩::= desc

We now illustrate the syntax with an example.

Example 9.7. Reconsider the web table Cancer in Figure 6.10 containing information related to cancer. Suppose we wish to sort the web tuples in descending order based on the total number of nodes in each web tuple. The query is given below.

```
SORT      Cancer
ON        node
ORDER BY desc
```

The sorted web table is shown in Figure 9.6. Observe that the first and fourth web tuples have the maximum number of nodes, i.e., seven. Hence these web tuples are displayed at the top of the sorted web table in Figure 9.6 followed by the third and fifth web tuples (tuples containing six nodes) and the second web tuple (containing five nodes). ∎

9.2 Summary

In this chapter, we have motivated the need for the data visualization operators and introduced some operators such as web nest, web unnest, web coalesce, web expand, web pack, web unpack, and web sort that provide different flavors of visualizing web tables. The web nest and web coalesce operators are similar in nature. Both of these operators concatenate a set of web tuples over identical nodes and produce a set of directed graphs as output. The web pack and web sort operations produce a web table as output. The web pack operator enables us to group web tuples based on the domain name or host name of the instances of a specified node type identifier or the keyword set in these nodes. A web sort, on the other hand, sorts web tuples based on the total number of nodes or total number of local, global, or interior links in each tuple. Web unnest, web expand, and web unpack, however, perform the inverse functions of web nest, web coalesce, and web pack, respectively.

Detecting and Representing Relevant Web Deltas

10.1 Introduction

The Web offers access to large amounts of heterogeneous information and allows this information to change at any time and in any way. These rapid and often unpredictable changes to the information create a new problem of detecting and representing changes. This is a challenging problem because the information sources in the Web are autonomous and typical database approaches to detect changes based on triggering mechanisms are not usable. Moreover, these sources typically do not keep track of historical information in a format that is accessible to the outside user [50].

Recently, there has been increased research interest in detecting changes in structured and semistructured data [51, 52, 60]. In this chapter, we present a mechanism for detecting and representing changes in Web documents (henceforth referred to as *web deltas*) [25, 19] that are relevant to a user's query using two *web algebraic operators*, i.e., *web join* and *outer web join*, in the context of our web warehousing system called WHOWEDA (*Warehouse Of Web Data*) [13, 28]. Such a mechanism for detection and representation of web deltas may be used by the following types of web users. (1) *Web site administrators:* by scanning the changes, administrators will be sure whether the changes are consistent with any policies for content or format without having to review the entire set of pages at the same level of detail. (2) *Customers of e-commerce Web sites:* a user may wish to monitor new products, services, or auctions on e-commerce Web sites. (3) *Analysts for gathering competitive intelligence:* companies can monitor evolution of their competitors' Web sites to discover their new directions or offerings over a period of time that may influence their market positions. (4) *Developers of web mining applications:* by detecting and representing web deltas over broad vistas of time, our system can be used as the foundation for mining information related to trends, patterns, etc. (5) *Wireless users:* the ability to download or highlight only changes instead of a complete Web page can be a very desirable feature for wireless users using handheld devices.

Reconsider the web site at www.panacea.gov in Example 8.13. Suppose on 15th January, 2001, a user wishes to find out periodically (say every 30 days) information related to side effects and uses of drugs for various diseases and also changes to this information compared to its previous version. This query requires access to previous states of the Web site and a mechanism to detect these changes automatically, features that are not supported by the Web or the existing search engines. Thus we need a mechanism to compute and represent changes in the context of Web data.

10.1.1 Overview

The work on change detection and representation reported in this chapter has four key characteristics.

- **Relevant web deltas:** We focus on detecting *relevant* web deltas. In particular, our goal is to detect and represent web deltas that are relevant to a user's query, not any arbitrary web deltas.
- **Changes in interlinked Web documents**: Our focus is on detecting and representing relevant changes given old and new versions of a set of interlinked Web documents. In particular, we are interested in detecting those Web documents in a Web site that are added to or deleted from the site, or those documents no longer considered relevant to a user's query. We also want to identify a set of documents that have undergone content modification compared to their antecedent. Furthermore, we wish to determine how these modified Web documents are related to one another and to other relevant Web documents in the context of a user's query.
- **Web algebraic operators:** We present a mechanism for detecting and representing relevant web deltas using a set of *web algebraic operators*. These operators are applied on a sequence of Web data snapshots to infer changes.
- **Static Web pages:** Web documents that do not provide the last modification date, such as the output from Common Gateway Interface (CGI) scripts, are not considered in this chapter for change detection.

As Web data in our web warehouse consist of materialized views stored in the form of web tables, any changes to the relevant Web data are also reflected in the corresponding web tables. Consequently, in order to detect web deltas, we materialize the old and new versions of data in two web tables. Next we create a set of web tables by manipulating these input web tables using the web join and outer web join operators. Finally, we create a set of *delta web tables* by further manipulating the joined and outer joined web tables. Delta web tables encapsulate the changes that have occurred in the Web such as the addition, modification, or deletion of a set of Web documents in the context of a user's query.

The rest of the chapter is organized as follows. We discuss our work with respect to the existing work in change detection in Section 10.2. We formally introduce the problem of change detection and identify different types of change operation in Section 10.3. We show how to generate delta web tables containing web deltas in Section 10.4. The last section concludes this chapter.

10.2 Related Work

In recent years, several tools have become available to address the problem of determining when an HTML page has changed. URL-minder [139] runs as a service on the Web itself and sends an email when a page changes. However, the need to send URLs explicitly through a form is cumbersome and may not be a feasible option when there are a large number of URLs to track.

The AT&T Internet Difference Engine (AIDE) [71] is a system that finds and displays changes to pages on the World Wide Web. A tool called *HtmlDiff* highlights changes between versions of a page, and offers a graphical interface to view the relationship between pages over time. *HtmlDiff* automatically compares two HTML pages and creates a "merged" page to show the differences with special HTML markups. TopBlend [55] is an HTML differencing tool implemented in Java and significantly outperforms the old HtmlDiff in the most time-consuming jobs.

AIDE also supports recursive tracking and differencing of a page and its descendants. When recursion is specified, changes to the child pages are reported separately by default. A user may specify a number of operations in AIDE that include registering a URL including the degree of recursion through links to other pages, viewing textual differences between a pair of versions, viewing a graph showing the structure of a page, etc.

WebGUIDE (Web Graphical User Interface to a Difference Engine) [70] is another tool that supports recursive document comparison: users may explore the differences between the pages with respect to two dates. Differences between pages are computed automatically and summarized in a new HTML page, and the differences in link structure are shown via graphical representations. WebGUIDE is a combination of two tools, Ciao [56] and AIDE. With Ciao, the high-level structural differences are displayed as graphs that show the relationships between pages using colored nodes to indicate which pages have been modified. Using AIDE, the low-level textual differences are illustrated by marking changes between versions and modifying anchors to cause documents reached from that page to be annotated. WebGUIDE allows a user to issue queries for specific types of deltas.

The AIDE and WebGUIDE have certain limitations. First, we believe that specifying a set of URLs to track changes may not be feasible when there are a large number of URLs. Second, the recursion specification is restrictive. That is, it selects all the children of a specified document(s), whereas, in reality, a user may often be interested in only some of those links. On top of that, the user may wish to track changes of successive interlinked documents satisfying some hyperlinked structure. Such constraints cannot be specified in AIDE. Third, AIDE displays all the changes in the documents. In reality we may not be interested in all the changes but only some of these changes. Hence it is necessary to be able to query these changes rather than browsing them to find the relevant changes. This is extremely useful when the number of documents monitored is large.

In [148], the authors define a change detection problem for ordered trees, using insertion, deletion, and label-update as the edit operations. In [52], the authors discuss a variant of the change detection problem for ordered trees using subtree *moves* as an edit operation in addition to insertions, deletions, and updates, and present an efficient algorithm for solving it. They focus on the problem of detecting changes given the old and new versions of hierarchically structured data. The change detection problem for unordered trees is presented in [51]. The authors present efficient algorithms to detect changes in operations that move an entire subtree of nodes and that copy an entire subtree. More recently in [50], a *snapshot-delta* approach has been used for representing changes in semistructured data. The authors present a simple and general model called *DOEM* for representing changes and also present a language called *Chorel* for querying changes represented in *DOEM*. This model is founded on the OEM data model and the Lorel query language [1]. It uses *annotations* on the nodes and arcs of an OEM graph to represent changes. Intuitively, the set of annotations on a node or arc represents the history of that node or arc. An important feature of this approach is that it represents and queries changes directly as annotations on the affected area instead of representing them indirectly as the difference between database states. Furthermore, they describe the design and implementation of an application of change management called a *Query Subscription Service* (QSS). QSS can be used to notify subscribers of relevant changes in semistructured information sources.

DOEM was not specifically developed for the Web, and the model does not distinguish between graph edges that represent the connection between a document and one of its parts, and edges that represent a hyperlink from one Web document to another. We take a different approach as compared to [50, 52]. Our approach is specifically developed for finding changes to Web data. Rather than finding changes to the internal structure and content of Web documents, in this chapter we focus on identifying changes to a set of hyperlinked Web documents relevant to a user's query. Our approach can easily be extended to detect and represent changes to internal structure and content of Web documents.

The WebCQ system [118] is a prototype system for Web information monitoring and delivery. It provides a personalized notification of what and how Web pages of interest have been changed and a personalized summarization of Web page changes. Users' update monitoring requests are modeled as *continual queries* [117] on the Web. WebCQ has the same limitations as those of AIDE, described earlier.

Recently, the XML research community has recognized the importance of the change management problem and in [60], the authors have discussed change management in the context of XML data. Their approach to change management is based on tree-comparison. However, they do not address the problem of detecting changes to hyperlinked XML documents. Moreover, we only find changes that affect a user's query responses. However, in their approach, they find changes between any two given versions of XML data. Our approach can be extended for detecting and representing changes in XML data.

Finally, our approach is different from graph matching and isomorphic graph problems. A matching in a graph is a set of edges such that every vertex of the graph is on at most one edge in the set. Two graphs are isomorphic if one can label both graphs with the same labels so that every vertex has exactly the same neighbors in both graphs. Some of the related research on graph matching problems are [125, 153, 152]. In our approach, two nonisomorphic graphs may also join if some of the nodes are identical. Thus we focus more on the node content similarity rather than the structure of the graph.

10.3 Change Detection Problem

In this section, we first describe the change detection problem. Then we identify the basic *change operations* in WHOWEDA corresponding to the changes in the Web. Finally, we show how to represent these changes in the context of our web warehouse. For simplicity, we assume in this chapter that a web table has a single web schema that binds all the web tuples. Formally, if $W = \langle Z, \mathcal{U} \rangle$ is a web table then $\mathcal{U} = \{U\}$, where $U = \langle S, T \rangle$. Hence a web table can be denoted as $W = \langle Z, S, T \rangle$. Note that the change detection process can easily be extended to web tables with multiple web schemas.

10.3.1 Problem Definition

As changes in relevant Web data are reflected in the web tables, we can address the problem of detecting and representing changes to Web data in the context of such web tables. We first describe the problem informally using the example in Section 10.1. Recall from Section 10.1, a user wishes to find a list of drugs for various diseases, their side effects, and uses starting from the Web site at http://www.panacea.gov/. The user specifies a polling coupling query with polling times $t_1 = $ 15th January, 2001, $t_2 = $ 15th February, 2001. At polling time t_1, the global web coupling operation retrieves a set of interlinked documents and materializes them in the form of a web table called **Drugs** as depicted in Figure 8.23. Each web tuple in the table contains information about side effects and uses of a drug for a particular disease.

Before polling time t_2, the Web site at http://www.panacea.gov/ is modified as depicted in Section 10.1. Therefore, at t_2, the result **New Drugs** (Figure 8.24) of the polling coupling query contains the relevant changes that have occurred between times t_1 and t_2. Observe that in Figure 8.21 information related to the drug "Niacin" used for Heart diseases (documents u_3 and k_4) is not materialized in **Drugs** as it does not satisfy the coupling query. However, it is materialized in **New Drugs** as it satisfies the coupling query on **15th February** due to the addition of a document related to the sideeffects of "Niacin" (d_7) to the Web site at http://www.panacea.gov/. Notice that the web tuples related to Diabetes and Alzheimer's disease are not materialized in **New Drugs** due to the removal of documents b_3, d_4, k_5, d_{12}, and k_{12} from the Web site.

Given two such web tables **Drugs** and **New Drugs** containing the snapshots of two versions of relevant Web data, the problem of change detection is to find the set of web tuples containing nodes that are inserted into or deleted from **Drugs** or those nodes that are modified in **Drugs** to transform it into **New Drugs**. Note that these web tuples will reflect the changes to the Web site that are relevant to the user.

10.3.2 Types of Changes

Changes to the web tables are reflected in the individual web tuples in WHOWEDA. Consequently, the different types of change operations in WHOWEDA can be defined in terms of the following.

- **Insert Node**: Intuitively, the operation **Insert Node** creates a set of nodes N in a web tuple in the web table W. The nodes must be new; i.e., N must not have occured in W before. Note that N can be a new web tuple added to W or it can be a set of nodes inserted into an existing web tuple in W.
- **Delete Node**: This operation is the inverse of the **Insert Node** operation. It removes a set of nodes from W.
- **Update Node**: The operation **Update Node** modifies the contents of the nodes in a web tuple. By content modification of a node, we mean the textual contents or structure of the node may change or the attributes of the links embedded in the node may change.
- **Insert Link**: Intuitively, the operation **Insert Link** creates a set of links L in a web tuple in the web table W. The links must be new; i.e., L must not have occured in the web tuple before. Observe that in a web table a new link can occur in two ways: a new link may connect an existing node to a new node (in this case, the **Insert Link** results in a **Insert Node** operation), or a new link may connect to existing nodes in a web tuple (in this case, the **Insert Link** operation is equivalent to the **Update Node** operation as the source node of the link has to be modified in order to incorporate the new link). So we can express the **Insert Link** operation by the **Insert Node** or **Update Node** operations.
- **Delete Link**: It removes a set of links from W. Similar to **Insert Link**, in a web table deletion of a link may occur based on two cases. Removal of a link may remove the only link to an existing node. In this case, it is equivalent to the **Delete Node** operation. Second, a link may be deleted between two nodes that are connected by more than one link. In this case, this operation is essentially the **Update Node** operation. Therefore, we can express the **Delete Link** operation by the **Delete Node** or **Update Node** operations.
- **Update Link**: This operation involves modification of the anchor of a link. Hence it is essentially an **Update Node** operation.

10.3.3 Representing Changes

We define a structure called the *delta web table* for representing web deltas. Delta web tables encapsulate the relevant changes that have occurred in the Web with respect to a user's query. We define the following three types of delta web tables to represent the above types of change operations.

- Δ^+**-web table** (denoted as W_{Δ^+}): contains a set of tuples containing the new nodes inserted into W_1 for transforming it into W_2. Note that this web table represents the **Insert Node** operation.

- Δ^--**web table** (denoted as W_{Δ^-}): contains a set of tuples containing nodes deleted from W_1 as determined by the **Delete Node** operation that transforms W_1 to W_2. Note that the web tuples in W_{Δ^-} do not necessarily indicate that these sets of inter-linked Web documents are deleted from the Web site. These documents may still exist in the Web, however, they may no longer be relevant to the user's query due to modification of the content or interlinked structure of these pages.
- Δ^M-**web table** (denoted as W_{Δ^M}): contains a set of web tuples that represents the previous and current sets of nodes modified by the **Update Node** operation.

Definition 10.1. [Delta Web Tables] *Let* $W_1 = \langle Z_1, S_1, T_1 \rangle$ *and* $W_2 = \langle Z_2, S_2, T_2 \rangle$ *be two web tables generated by a polling coupling query* G *at time* t_1 *and* t_2. *Let* A, D, *and* U *be the sets of nodes added to, deleted from, and updated during* t_1 *and* t_2 *to transform* W_1 *to* W_2. *Then*

- $W_{\Delta^+} = \langle Z_{\Delta^+}, S_{\Delta^+}, T_{\Delta^+} \rangle$ *is called a* Δ^+-**web table** *where* $S_{\Delta^+} = S_2$, $T_{\Delta^+} \subseteq T_2$ *and for each web tuple* $w_i \in T_{\Delta^+}$, $\forall\, 0 < i \leq |T_{\Delta^+}|$ *there exists a node* $n(w_i)$ *such that* $n(w_i) \notin T_1$ *and* $n(w_i) \in A$;
- $W_{\Delta^-} = \langle Z_{\Delta^-}, S_{\Delta^-}, T_{\Delta^-} \rangle$ *is called a* Δ^--**web table** *where* $S_{\Delta^-} = S_1$, $T_{\Delta^-} \subseteq T_1$ *and for each web tuple* $w_i \in T_{\Delta^-}$, $\forall\, 0 < i \leq |T_{\Delta^-}|$ *there exists a node* $n(w_i)$ *such that* $n(w_i) \notin T_2$ *and* $n(w_i) \in D$;
- $W_{\Delta^M} = \langle Z_{\Delta^M}, S_{\Delta^M}, T_{\Delta^M} \rangle$ *is called a* Δ^M-**web table** *where* S_{Δ^M} *is generated from* S_1 *and* S_2 *and for each web tuple* $w_i \in T_{\Delta^M}$, $\forall\, 0 < i \leq |T_{\Delta^M}|$ *at least one of the following conditions must be true.*
  1. *If there exists a node* $n_1(w_i)$ *such that* $n_1(w_i) \in U$ *and* $n_1(w_i) \notin (D \cup A)$ *then there must exist a node* $n_2(w_i)$ *such that* $\mathtt{url}(n_1(w_i)) = \mathtt{url}(n_2(w_i))$ *and* $\mathtt{date}(n_1(w_i)) \neq \mathtt{date}(n_2(w_i))$.
  2. *If there exists a node* $n_3(w_i)$ *such that* $n_3(w_i) \notin U$ *then* $n_3(w_i) \in (D \cup A)$ *must be true. In this case, there must not exist a node* $n_4(w_i)$ *such that* $\mathtt{url}(n_3(w_i)) = \mathtt{url}(n_4(w_i))$.
  3. *If there exists a node* $n_4(w_i)$ *such that* $n_4(w_i) \notin (D \cup A \cup U)$ *then there must not exist another node* $n_5(w_i)$ *such that* $\mathtt{url}(n_4(w_i)) = \mathtt{url}(n_5(w_i))$. ∎

Typically, the delta web tables reflect the *net effect* of Web site modification; that is, they contain only the net result of successive modification of a set of relevant documents in the Web. Note that in most of the cases the size of these delta web tables will be much smaller than W_1 or W_2. Representing changes in the form of a set of delta web tables enables us to view the history of a web table as a combination of a single web table snapshot and a collection of delta web tables. We can obtain various states of a web table by starting with a single web table and applying some sequence of web deltas to it. Also, to minimize the storage cost we materialize only a single web table and a set of delta web tables in lieu of the various states of the web table.

Observe that the representation of web deltas using delta web tables are comparable to delta relations in the relational model. In a relational database, deltas usually are represented using delta relations. For a relation R, delta relations *inserted(R)* and *deleted(R)* contain the tuples inserted to and deleted from R, while delta relations *old-updated(R)* and *new-updated(R)* contain the old and new values of updated tuples [157]. Similarly, we store the Web documents that are added, deleted, or modified in Δ^+, Δ^- and Δ^M-web tables, respectively.

10.3.4 Decomposition of Change Detection Problem

The problem of detecting and representing changes can now be decomposed into parts.

1. Construction of the joined and outer joined web tables from W_1 and W_2. Since we have discussed this in Chapter 8, we do not elaborate on this further. Note that the web schemas of these joined web tables do not play a pivotal role in the web delta generation. Hence the construction of joined and outer joined web tables in this chapter ignores the schema generation process.
2. Use the joined and outer joined web tables to generate a set of delta web tables, i.e., W_{Δ^+}, W_{Δ^-} and W_{Δ^M}, containing web deltas. We discuss this in Section 10.4.

10.4 Generating Delta Web Tables

This section initiates a discussion on the algorithm to detect and represent different types of change operations using the web join and outer web join operations. We first briefly introduce various physical storage structures in WHOWEDA for storing Web objects. Then we describe the Algorithm *Delta* that generates a set of delta web tables to detect and represent web deltas.

10.4.1 Storage of Web Objects

In this section, we briefly introduce various physical storage structures in WHOWEDA for storing Web objects, i.e., nodes, links, Web documents, web tables, etc. We introduce three types of storage structures: the *warehouse node pool*, the *warehouse document pool*, and the *web table pool* for storing Web objects. The warehouse node pool contains distinct nodes from all web tables in our web warehouse. Each node represents a Web document stored in the warehouse document pool. The links in each Web document are stored in this pool along with the corresponding node. Furthermore, each node has an identifier called a *node id*. Note that the node id of a node is different from that of another node if their URLs are different. A node may have several *versions*. In order to distinguish between several versions of a node, each version of a node is identified by a unique *version id*. Note that each node id can have a set of version ids across different web tables. A node in our web warehouse can be uniquely identified by the pair (node id, version id).

The web tables are stored in the *web table pool*. Each web table in this pool is stored in three types of structures, i.e., the *table node pool*, the *web tuple pool*, and the *web schema pool*. For each distinct node and link object in a web table, we store certain attributes in the table node pool: the identifier that the node and the link represent in the web schema, node id and link id, version id and URL of the node, target node id, and label and link type of the link. Next we store the web tuples of a web table in the web tuple pool. For each tuple in this pool, we only store the ids of all the nodes and links belonging to that tuple. Finally, we store the web schemas and coupling query in the web schema pool. The reader may refer to [163, 162] for a detailed exposition on these storage structures.

10.4.2 Outline of the Algorithm

The algorithm for delta web table generation can be best described by the four phases: the *join tables generation phase*, the *delta node identification phase*, the *delta tuples identification phase*, and the *delta table generation phase*. We discuss these phases one by one.

Phase 1: Join Tables Generation Phase

This phase takes as input two web tables, new and old versions, and generates the joined, right outer joined and left outer joined web tables. For instance, after this phase the web tables in Figures 8.25, 8.47, and 8.48 are generated from Drugs and New Drugs.

The right outer join operation on W_1 and W_2 may create several categories of dangling web tuples: (1) Web tuples that are added to W_1 during the polling times t_1 and t_2 (these tuples may contain some new nodes and the contents of the remaining ones have been changed); (2) tuples in which all the nodes have undergone content modification; and (3) tuples in which some of the nodes are new and the contents of the remaining ones have changed but these tuples existed in W_1. For example, consider the web table in Figure 8.48. The last two web tuples belong to the first category. The first web tuple belongs to the second category and the second web tuple is an example of the third category.

The web join operation on W_1 and W_2 may contain these types of web tuples: (1) Web tuples in which all the nodes are joinable nodes (these tuples are the result of joining two versions of web tuples in W_1 and W_2 that have remained unchanged during t_1 and t_2); (2) Web tuples in which some of the nodes are joinable nodes and remaining nodes are the result of insertion, deletion, or modification operations during the transition; and (3) some of the nodes are joinable nodes and out of the remaining ones, some are the result of insertion, deletion, or modification, and the remaining ones are not joinable in this web tuple but have remained unchanged during the transition. That is, these nodes may be joinable nodes in some other joined web tuple(s). While generating delta web tables, the algorithm ignores the first category of web tuples in the joined web table as it does not reflect any changes. For instance, in the joined web table in Figure 8.25, all the web tuples are of the second and third categories. Specifically, the first two and the last three tuples contain nodes whose contents are modified. The fourth web tuple contains nodes whose contents are modified as well as a node k_4 which is inserted during t_1 and t_2. Finally, the fifth tuple contains a node u_8 which is deleted as well as a set of nodes that are modified. Hence these web tuples represent the second category. On the other hand, the third web tuple represents the third category. This is because a_0 represents a modified node and the nodes u_0, u_1, d_0, d_1, k_0, and k_1 are not joinable in this web tuple but they are joinable nodes in the first and second web tuples.

Similar to the right outer joined web table, the left outer joined table may contain these categories of web tuples: (1) Web tuples that are deleted from W_1 (these tuples do not occur in W_2); (2) tuples in which every node has undergone content modification; and (3) tuples in which some nodes are deleted from W_1 and remaining ones have been modified. The new and old versions occur in both tables in W_1 and W_2. For instance, the second and fourth web tuples in Figure 8.47 belong to the first category. The first and the third web tuples belong to the second and third categories, respectively.

Phase 2: Delta Nodes Identification Phase

In this phase, the nodes that are added, deleted or modified during t_1 and t_2 are identified. This phase takes as input the web tables W_1 and W_2 and the set of joinable nodes from the joined table and generates sets of nodes that are added, deleted, or modified during the time interval. Thus nodes that exist in W_2 but not in W_1 are the new nodes that are added to W_1. Similarly, nodes that only exist in W_1, but not in W_2 are the nodes that are removed from W_1. Furthermore, the nodes that are not joinable nodes, but exist in W_1 as well as W_2 are essentially the nodes that have undergone content modification during t_1 and t_2. For instance, $\{b_3, u_4, u_5, u_6, u_8, d_4, d_5, d_{12}, k_5, k_6, k_{12}\}$ are the ids of nodes that appear in Drugs but not in New Drugs. Hence these nodes were removed during transition. Similarly, $\{k_4, u_9, k_8, d_8, d_7, u_3, u_{12}, d_9, k_9, u_{10}, u_{11}, d_{10}, k_{10}\}$ are the ids of nodes that exist in New Drugs but not in Drugs. Hence these nodes were added during t_1 and t_2. Finally, the nodes with ids a_0, b_1, d_2, k_2, u_2, d_3, k_3, b_4, and u_7 appear in both web tables but are not joinable. Hence these nodes have undergone content modification.

Observe that at this point we have identified the nodes that are inserted, deleted, or modified during the transformation. Next the algorithm proceeds to determine how these nodes are related to each other and how they are associated with those nodes that have remained unchanged during t_1 and t_2.

Phase 3: Delta Tuples Identification Phase

In the delta tuples identification phase we are interested in identifying those web tuples containing nodes that are added, deleted, or modified during the transition. It should be clear that we are not simply identifying these web tuples as it can be done by inspecting W_1 and W_2 without performing any web join or outer web join operations. Our objectives are the following.

- In the case of added or deleted nodes, we are not simply interested in identifying tuples containing these nodes, but also how these nodes are linked to or related to the existing nodes (nodes that prevailed during the transition). Moreover, we wish to determine how the new or deleted nodes are related to each other.
- For nodes that have undergone content modification during the transition, we wish to determine how these nodes are linked to one another and to those nodes

that have remained unchanged. We also wish to present the old and new versions of the nodes in a single tuple so that a user can view them effectively. Finally, we wish to highlight the changes in the overall hyperlink structure due to the content modification.

To achieve this, we scan the joined and outer joined web tables. The delta tuples identification phase takes as input these web tables and the sets of nodes that are added, deleted, or modified. It returns as output sets of tuples containing nodes that are added, deleted, and modified respectively. In the remaining portion of this chapter, these sets are denoted as *insertTupleSet*, *deleteTupleSet*, and *updateTupleSet*, respectively. Observe that the nodes added during the transition can occur in the following tables.

- In the right outer joined table if the remaining nodes in a tuple containing the new nodes are modified and hence are not joinable. The second, third, and fourth web tuples in Figure 8.48 are examples of such tuples.
- In the joined web table if some of the nodes in the tuple containing new nodes have remained unchanged during the transition and hence are joinable. For instance, the fourth web tuple in Figure 8.25 is an example of such a web tuple where k_4, u_3, and d_7 are the new nodes and b_2 has remained unchanged during the transition and is therefore joinable.

Hence we need to scan the joined and right outer joined tables to identify the tuples containing nodes that are inserted during t_1 and t_2. Similarly, the nodes deleted during the transition may occur in the two web tables:

- In the left outer joined table if the remaining nodes in a tuple containing the deleted nodes are modified and hence are not joinable. The second, third, and fourth web tuples in Figure 8.47 are examples of such tuples;
- In the joined web table if some of the nodes in the tuple containing deleted nodes have remained unchanged during the transition and hence are joinable. For instance, the seventh web tuple in Figure 8.23 contains the node u_8 which is deleted. As the nodes d_6 and k_7 have remained unchanged during the transition, these nodes are joinable. The tuple containing this deleted node can be detected from the joined web table in Figure 8.25 (third web tuple).

Thus the algorithm scans the left outer joined and joined tables to retrieve the tuples containing deleted nodes. Finally, the nodes that are modified during the transition can be identified by inspecting all three web tables:

- Tuples in the left and right outer joined tables that do not contain any new or deleted nodes represent the old and new versions of these nodes, respectively. These web tuples do not occur in the joined table as all the nodes are modified. For instance, the first web tuples in Figures 8.47 and 8.48 are examples of such tuples;
- Tuples in the left and right outer joined tables that contain modified nodes as well as inserted or deleted nodes. Note that these modified nodes may not appear in the joined web table if no other joinable web tuples contain these modified nodes;

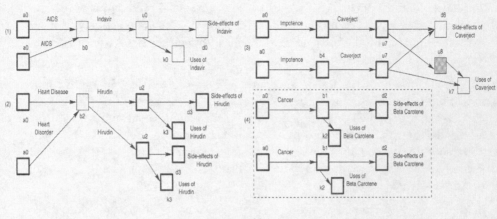

Fig. 10.1. Δ^M-web table.

- Tuples in the joined web tables where some of the nodes represent the old and new versions of these modified nodes. For instance, the first web tuple in Figure 8.25 contains the old and new versions of a_0.

Phase 4: Delta Web Tables Generation Phase

Finally, the three types of delta web tables are generated in this phase. It takes as input the three sets of tuples, i.e., *insertTupleSet*, *deleteTupleSet*, and *updateTupleSet*, generated in the previous phase, and generates the delta web tables from these sets. The procedure to generate these tables is straightforward. The tuples in *insertTupleSet* are stored in the Δ^+-web table. The tuples in *deleteTupleSet* and *updateTupleSet* are stored in the Δ^- and Δ^M-web tables, respectively.

Next we illustrate the generation of delta web tables informally with an example given below.

Example 10.2. Consider the two web tables Drugs and New Drugs in Figures 8.23 and 8.24. We would like to find the various change operations that transform Drugs into New Drugs. Changes may include inserting, deleting, and updating nodes in Drugs. For each type of change, we create the W_{Δ^+}, W_{Δ^-}, and W_{Δ^M} tables. We discuss the generation of each delta web table in turn. Figure 10.1 depicts the Δ^M-web table. The patterned boxes in this figure in each web tuple are the old and new versions of the nodes. For example, the second web tuple in Figure 10.1 contains the old and new versions of the nodes a_0, u_2, d_3, and k_3, along with the joinable node u_2 (the content of u_2 has remained unchanged during the transition). Each web tuple shows how the sets of modified nodes are related to one another and to the joinable nodes. Observe that the first four web tuples are extracted from the joined web table in Figure 8.25. The last web tuple (enclosed in a dotted box) is the result of the integration of two web tuples; one from the left outer joined web table in Figure 8.47 and another from the right outer joined table in Figure 8.48.

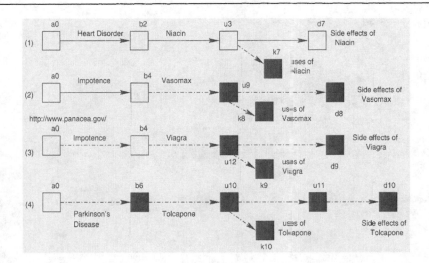

Fig. 10.2. Δ^+-web table.

Figure 10.2 illustrates the Δ^+-web table. The black boxes in each web tuple are the new nodes inserted into Drugs during 15th January, 2001 and 15th February, 2001. Similar to the Δ^M-web table, each web tuple in the Δ^+-web table shows how the new nodes are related to other relevant nodes in the web table. Note that the last three web tuples in Figure 10.2 are extracted from the right outer joined web table in Figure 8.48. However, as the node b_2 in the first web tuple is a joinable node, the new nodes k_4, u_3, and d_7 in this tuple are identified from the fourth web tuple of the joined web table in Figure 8.25.

Finally, Figure 10.3 depicts the Δ^--web table containing all the nodes that are deleted from Drugs. The last three web tuples are extracted from the web table in Figure 8.47. However, the tuple containing the deleted node u_8 is extracted from the fifth web tuple in the joined web table in Figure 8.25.

Observe that we do not materialize the joined web tuples containing new or deleted nodes in W_{Δ^+} and W_{Δ^-}, respectively. Instead, we extract the original web tuple containing these nodes from the joined web tuple and materialize them in W_{Δ^+} and W_{Δ^-}, respectively. ∎

10.4.3 Algorithm Delta

We now provide the formal algorithm for the four phases discussed in the previous section. We describe how, given two web tables W_1 and W_2 created by a polling global coupling operation at polling times t_1 and t_2, we compute a set of delta web tables corresponding to various types of changes to transform W_1 to W_2. The pseudocode for this algorithm is given in Figure 10.4. It takes as input two web tables $W_1 = \langle Z_1, S_1, T_1 \rangle$ and $W_2 = \langle Z_2, S_2, T_2 \rangle$ created by a coupling query Q at polling times t_1 and t_2, respectively. It returns as output a

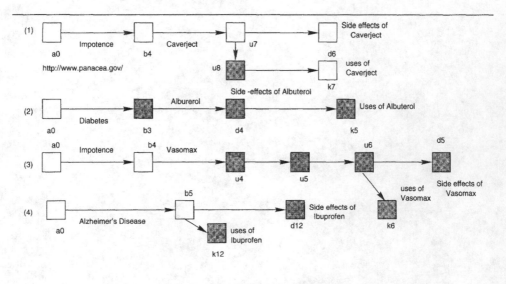

Fig. 10.3. Δ^+-web table.

set of delta web tables $W_{\Delta^+} = \langle Z_{\Delta^+}, S_{\Delta^+}, T_{\Delta^+}\rangle$, $W_{\Delta^-} = \langle Z_{\Delta^-}, S_{\Delta^-}, T_{\Delta^-}\rangle$, and $W_{\Delta^M} = \langle Z_{\Delta^M}, S_{\Delta^M}, T_{\Delta^M}\rangle$. The steps to generate these delta web tables are as follows.

Algorithm for Phases 1 and 2

Steps (1) to (4) implement the first phase of the algorithm and generate the joined and the right and the left outer joined web tables from W_1 and W_2 (Line (4)). In the algorithm, these web tables are denoted as W_j, W_{ro}, and $W_{\ell o}$, respectively. Steps (5) to (7) implement the second phase of the algorithm and identify the node ids added to W_1, node ids removed from W_1, and ids of the nodes that have undergone content modification during t_1 and t_2.

Algorithm of Phase 3

We now discuss the algorithm for implementing the delta web tuples identification phase. To determine the association of nodes (represented by the identifiers in *addNodeSet*, *delNodeSet*, and *updateNodeSet*) with each other and with other relevant nodes in W_1, we identify the web tuples in W_j, W_{ro}, and $W_{\ell o}$ containing these nodes and store them in the sets of web tuples denoted in the algorithm as *insertTupleSet*, *deleteTupleSet*, and *updateTupleSet*, respectively. Each element in *insertTupleSet* and *deleteTupleSet* is a web tuple containing nodes that are inserted into or deleted from W_1 during t_1 and t_2. Each element in *updateTupleSet* is an *integrated* web tuple containing old and new versions of the nodes that have undergone content modification. Note that these sets of web tuples encapsulate the various change operations introduced in Section 10.3.

Input: Web tables $W_1 = \langle Z_1, S_1, T_1 \rangle$, $W_2 = \langle Z_2, S_2, T_2 \rangle$.
Output: Delta web tables $W_{\Delta+} = \langle Z_{\Delta+}, S_{\Delta+}, T_{\Delta-} \rangle$, $W_{\Delta-} = \langle Z_{\Delta-}, S_{\Delta-}, T_{\Delta-} \rangle$
and $W_{\Delta M} = \langle Z_{\Delta M}, S_{\Delta M}, T_{\Delta M} \rangle$.

(1) $N_1 = $ **GetAllNodeIds**(W_1); /* Phase 1 */
(2) $N_2 = $ **GetAllNodeIds**(W_2);
(3) $J = $ **ComputeJoinableNodeIds**(N_1, N_2); /* Chapter 8 */
(4) $W_{12} = $ **GenerateResultTables**(N_1, N_2, W_1, W_2, J)
          where $W_{12} = \{W_{ro}, W_{lo}, W_j\}$;
(5) $delNodeSet = N_1 - N_2$; /* Ids of the nodes deleted from W_1 */
       /* Phase 2 */
(6) $addNodeSet = N_2 - N_1$; /* Ids of the nodes added to W_1 */
(7) $updateNodeSet = (N_1 - J - delNodeSet) \cup (N_2 - J - addNodeSet)$;
(8) $N_j = $ **GetAllNodeIds**(W_j); /* Phase 3 */
(9)   Let $K = updateNodeSet - (N_j - J)$;
(10)   Let $A = addNodeSet$;
(11)   Let $D = delNodeSet$;
(12)   Let $U = (N_j - J) \cap updateNodeSet$;
(13) $insertTupleSet = $ **DeltasFromRightOuter**$(A, K, W_{ro}, temp1, temp2)$;
       /* Figure 10.5 */
(14) $deleteTupleSet = $ **DeltasFromLeftOuter**$(D, K, W_{lo}, temp1, temp2)$;
(15)   if $(|A| = 0$ and $|D| = 0)$ {
          /* checks if all the inserted and deleted nodes are identified */
(16) $updateTupleSet = $ **DeltasFromJoin**(W_j, U, N_1, N_2);
          /* Figure 10.6 */
(17)   else
(18) $updateTupleSet = $ **DeltasFromJoin**$(A, D, U, W_j, insertTupleSet,$
          $deleteTupleSet)$; /* Figure 10.7 */
(19)   if $(|temp1| \neq 0)$
(20)   Insert into $updateTupleSet$ web tuples from $temp1$;
(21)   if $(|temp2| \neq 0)$
(22)   Insert into $updateTupleSet$ web tuples from $temp2$;
                /* Phase 4 */
(23) $W_{\Delta M} = $ **CreateDeltaM**$(updateTupleSet, W_1, W_2, S_{12}, updateNodeSet)$;
(24) $W_{\Delta+} = $ **CreateDeltaPlus**$(insertTupleSet, W_1, W_2, addNodeSet)$;
(25) $W_{\Delta-} = $ **CreateDeltaMinus**$(deleteTupleSet, W_1, W_2, delNodeSet)$;
(26)   return $W_{\Delta+}$, $W_{\Delta-}$ and $W_{\Delta M}$;

Fig. 10.4. Algorithm Delta.

Steps (8) to (22) in Figure 10.4 present the pseudocode for the delta web tuples identification phase. Step (9) computes those nodes that are updated during the transition but are not captured by the joined web table. The set K contains ids of those updated nodes that do not exist in N_j; i.e., K represents those updated nodes not present in W_j but in W_{ro} and $W_{\ell o}$. If n is a node in K, then n does not occur in W_j. That is, the tuple containing n is a dangling web tuple and consequently is ignored by the web join operation. That is, if n represents a node that has undergone an update during t_1 and t_2 then the web tuples containing n in W_1 and W_2 must be

Input: Right outer-joined table W_{ro}, set of added and updated node ids A and U respectively, temporary sets $temp1$ and $temp2$ to store tuples.
Output: Set of web tuples $insertTupleSet$ containing new nodes.

```
(1)     for (b = 1 to |W_ro|) { /* Case 1: Detecting web deltas from W_ro */
(2)         Get tuple w_b;
(3)         tupleNodeIdSet[b] = GetTupleNodeIds(w_b);
(4)         if (tupleNodeIdSet[b] ∩ A ≠ ∅) {
                /* w_b contains node(s) which were inserted during the transition */
(5)             Store w_b in insertTupleSet;
(6)             Insert (tupleNodeIdSet[b] ∩ A) in tempAddSet;
                    /* represents new nodes in w_b */
(7)             if (K ≠ ∅) {
                /* identify web tuples which contain modified nodes
                which are not present in the joined table */
(8)                 if (tupleNodeIdSet[b] ∩ K ≠ ∅)
(9)                     Insert w_b in temp2;
(10)            }
(11)        }
(12)        else
(13)            Store w_b in temp1; /* tupleNodeIdSet[b] ∩ A = ∅ */
(14)    }
(15)    A = A − tempAddSet; /* New nodes which are already
        identified are now removed from A */
(16)    return temp1, temp2, insertTupleSet, A, K;
```

Fig. 10.5. Algorithm for **DeltasFromRightOuter**(A, K, W_{ro}, $temp1$, $temp2$).

dangling web tuples. Otherwise, n must occur in the joined web table. As a result, the tuples containing n in W_1 and W_2 must be captured by the left and right outer joined web tables, respectively (W_{ro} and $W_{\ell o}$). If $K = \emptyset$, then all updated nodes are captured by the joined web table.

Next (Steps (10) and (11)) the sets of node ids of new and deleted nodes are copied to the sets A and D, respectively. This is because subsequently A and D need to be updated every time we identify new and deleted nodes while scanning the right and left outer joined web tables. However, we do not wish to modify the $addNodeSet$, $delNodeSet$, and $updateNodeSet$ since the algorithm is going to use them again to generate the delta web tables in Steps (23) to (25). Finally, U (Step (12)) represents those modified nodes that occur only in the joined web table W_j; i.e., $U \cap K = \emptyset$. Then Steps (13) and (14) scan the right and left outer joined web tables to identify the web tuples containing inserted, deleted, and updated (if any) nodes. We elaborate on these algorithms now.

Algorithm of DeltasFromRightOuter(A, K, W_{ro}, $temp1$, $temp2$) (Step (13) in Figure 10.4)

This algorithm takes as input the set of node ids that are added during the transition, i.e., A, the set K, the right outer joined web table W_{ro}, and two empty sets *temp*1 and *temp*2 to store *specific* web tuples. It returns as output a set of tuples containing the nodes that are inserted during t_1 and t_2, denoted by *insertTupleSet*, modified A and K, and *temp*1 and *temp*2 (possibly nonempty). Let us elaborate on the purpose of the tuple sets *temp*1 and *temp*2. The tuple set *temp*1 stores those web tuples in the right or left outer joined tables that do not contain any new or deleted nodes (Category 2 web tuples as discussed in the previous section). That is, the tuples in *temp*1 represent those web tuples in which all the nodes' contents are modified during the transition. For instance, *temp*1 will store the first web tuples in Figures 8.47 and 8.48. Recall that in *updateTupleSet*, the old and new versions of a web tuple are integrated and stored together. However, the right outer join operation only identifies the new version of the modified web tuple. The old version of the tuple can be extracted from the result of the left outer join operation. Thus the insertion of the web tuples containing modified nodes into *updateTupleSet* is deferred to the execution of the inspection of the left outer joined web table. Consequently, we store these tuples temporarily in *temp*1.

On the other hand, *temp*2 contains those tuples from the left or right outer joined tables containing the updated nodes not captured by the joined web table. That is, *temp*2 contains tuples from W_{ro} and W_{lo} where each tuple contains at least one node that is an element of K and some of the remaining nodes must be new or deleted nodes. Notice the differences between the tuples in *temp*1 and *temp*2. In *temp*1, all the nodes in each web tuple have undergone content modification. However, in *temp*2 each web tuple must contain at least one node that is added or deleted during the transition and remaining nodes must have undergone content modification. Also observe that $temp1 \cap temp2 = \emptyset$. Note that the nodes in a tuple in *temp*1 may also occur in K. However, they are not captured in *temp*2 because each web tuple in *temp*2 contains one or more new or deleted nodes. Specifically, *temp*2 enables us to capture the web tuples containing modified nodes that cannot be identified from the joined web tables. For similar reasons as explained in the case of *temp*1, we defer the insertion of these tuples in the *updateTupleSet*. The pseudocode of this algorithm is given in Figure 10.5.

Algorithm of DeltasFromLeftOuter(D, K, W_{lo}, *temp*1, *temp*2) (Step (14) in Figure 10.4)

Next the algorithm Delta inspects the left outer joined table $W_{\ell o}$ to identify the deleted or modified nodes. The pseudocode for this algorithm will be similar to Figure 10.5 and hence it is omitted.

Algorithm of DeltasFromJoin(W_j, U, N_1, N_2) (Step (16) in Figure 10.4)

Finally, the algorithm Delta in Figure 10.4 proceeds to inspect the joined web table W_j. If $A = D = \emptyset$, then the joined web table will only contain the updated nodes. Consequently, Step (16) is executed. Each joined web tuple in W_j is inspected to determine the existence of the old and new versions of the modified nodes. It may seem that each tuple containing dangling node(s)(nodes that are not joinable) may represent the old and new versions of the modified nodes. However, this assumption

Input: Joined table W_j, set of updated node ids U, N_1 and N_2.
Output: Modified $updateTupleSet$.

(1)   for $(a = 1$ to $|W_j|)$ {
(2)   Get tuple w_a;
(3) $tupleNodeIdSet[a] = \textbf{GetTupleNodeIds}(w_a)$;
(4)   Let $X = tupleNodeIdSet[a] \cap U$;
               /* Identify the relevant tuples in the input web tables which
               contain the updated nodes */
(5)   Retrieve node set $N_1(w_a)$ such that $N_1(w_a) \subseteq X$ and $N_1(w_a) \subset N_1$;
(6)   Retrieve node set $N_2(w_a)$ such that $N_2(w_a) \subseteq X$ and $N_2(w_a) \subset N_2$;
(7)   if $(X - (N_1(w_a) \cap N_2(w_a)) = \emptyset)$ {
               /* tuple contains only both the old and new version
               of the updated nodes */
(8)   Store w_a in $updateTupleSet$;
(9)   /* Category 2 type joined web tuple */
(10)   }
(11)   else
(12) w_a is ignored;
(13)   }
(14)   }
(15)   Return $updateTupleSet$;

Fig. 10.6. Algorithm of **DeltasFromJoin**(W_j, U, N_1, N_2).

is not true. Note that we are specifically interested in those joined web tuples that contain both the old and new versions of the updated nodes. Note that not all joined web tuples may satisfy this condition. For example, consider the joined web table in Figure 8.25. The fourth web tuple contains the dangling nodes u_2, k_3, d_3, etc. However, both the old and new versions of these nodes are missing in this tuple. Specifically, they exist in the last joined web tuple. Hence the last web tuple is inserted in $updateTupleSet$ but not the fourth web tuple. Observe that this condition is checked in Step (7) of the algorithm in Figure 10.6. For instance, for the last web tuple, $N_1(w_a) = \{a_0, u_2, d_3, k_3\}$, $N_2(w_a) = \{a_0, u_2, d_3, k_3\}$, and $X = \{a_0, u_2, d_3, k_3\}$. Hence $\{X - (N_1(w_a) \cap N_2(w_a))\} = \emptyset$ and the joined tuple is inserted in $updateTupleSet$. However, for the fourth web tuple, $N_1(w_a) = \{a_0, u_3, k_3, d_3\}$, $N_2(w_a) = \{a_0, u_3, d_7, k_4\}$, and $X = \{a_0, u_2, d_3, k_3\}$. Hence $\{X - (N_1(w_a) \cap N_2(w_a))\} = \{u_2, k_3, d_3\}$. Consequently, the condition is not satisfied (See Figure 10.6).

Algorithm of DeltasFromJoin(A, D, U, W_j, $insertTupleSet$, $deleteTupleSet$) (Step (18) in Figure 10.4)

If all the new or deleted nodes are not identified after scanning W_{ro} and $W_{\ell o}$ then $|A| \neq 0$ or $|D| \neq 0$. Hence in that case Step (18) in Figure 10.4 is executed. The pseudocode for the construct **DeltasFromJoin** is given in Figure 10.7. Note that in this case the algorithm is not only looking for the web tuples containing the

Input:Joined table W_j, set of added, deleted and updated node ids A, D and U respectively, *deleteTupleSet, insertTupleSet.*
Output: Modified *deletedTupleSet, insertTupleSet, updateTupleSet* .

```
(1)     for (a = 1 to |Wj|) {
(2)         Get tuple wa;
(3)         tupleNodeIdSet[a] = GetTupleNodeIds(wa);
(4)         Let Y = tupleNodeIdSet[a] − (tupleNodeIdSet[a] ∩ J);
(5)         if ((Y ≠ ∅) or (Y ∩ A ≠ ∅) or (Y ∩ D ≠ ∅)){
(6)             Retrieve node set N1(wa) such that N1(wa) ⊆ Y and N1(wa) ⊂ N1;
(7)             Retrieve node set N2(wa) such that N2(wa) ⊆ Y and N2(wa) ⊂ N2;
(8)             if (Y − (N1(wa) ∩ N2(wa)) = ∅) {
(9)                 Store wa in updateTupleSet;
(10)            }
(11)            else {
(12)                if ((Y − (N1(wa) ∩ N2(wa))) ⊂ A ∪ D) {
                        /* checks if the remaining dangling nodes are actually
                        new or deleted nodes. */
(13)                    Extract w2 ∈ W2 from wa; /* Original web tuple in W2
                        which is in wa is extracted */
(14)                    Extract w1 ∈ W1 from wa;
(15)                    Insert wa in updateTupleSet;
(16)                    Insert w1 or w2 to deleteTupleSet or insertTupleSet;
(17)                }
(18)                else {
(19)                    if (A ∩ [Y − (N1(wa) ∩ N2(wa))] ≠ ∅)
(20)                        Insert w2 in insertTupleSet;
(21)                    if (D ∩ [Y − (N1(wa) ∩ N2(wa)) ≠ ∅)
(22)                        Insert w1 in deleteTupleSet;
(23)                }
(24)                A = A − (A ∩ [Y − (N1(wa) ∩ N2(wa))]);
(25)                D = D − (D ∩ [D − (N1(wa) ∩ N2(wa))]);
(26)            }
(27)        }
(28)        else
(29)            wa is ignored;
(30)    }
(31)    Return insertTupleSet, deleteTupleSet, updateTupleSet;
```

Fig. 10.7. Algorithm of **DeltasFromJoin**(A, D, U, W_j, *insertTupleSet, deleteTupleSet*).

updated nodes but also those web tuples containing the new or deleted nodes. We elaborate on these steps now. Note that Steps (2) to (10) are similar to the previous steps. Steps (12) to (25) are executed if not all the dangling nodes in w_a represent the new and old versions of the nodes. We explain these steps with examples. Consider the fifth web tuple in Figure 8.25. Here $Y = \{a_0, b_4, u_7, u_8\}$ and $N_1(w_5) = N_2(w_5) = \{a_0, b_4, u_7\}$. Hence $Y - (N_1(w_5) \cap N_2(w_5)) = \{u_8\}$. Hence the condition in Step (8) is evaluated false. As u_8 represents a deleted node, $u_8 \in D$. The condition in Step (12) is evaluated true. We insert the tuple in *updateTupleSet* and extract the seventh web tuple in **Drugs**. Observe that the seventh web tuple in **Drugs** contains u_8 which is deleted during transition. Finally, we insert this tuple in the *deleteTupleSet*.

At this point the web tuples containing the new nodes k_4, u_3, and d_7 in the joined web table (fourth joined tuple) have not been identified yet. Note that for this web tuple $Y = D - (N_1(w_4) \cap N_2(w_4)) = \{u_2, k_3, d_3, k_4, u_3, d_7\}$. Also, $Y \subset A$ or $Y \subset D$ is not satisfied. Consequently, the condition in Step (12) is evaluated false. In order to identify this node, Steps (18) to (23) are executed. The condition in Step (19) is satisfied by Y as $Y \cap A = \{k_4, u_3, d_7\}$. Hence Step (20) is executed and the original web tuple (fifth web tuple in **New Drugs**) is retrieved and inserted in *insertTupleSet*. If $Y \cap D \neq \emptyset$, then Step (22) is executed and the original web tuple from W_1 is retrieved and inserted in *deleteTupleSet*. Steps (24) and (25) update A and D by removing those ids that are already used to identify the web tuples.

We have now identified all the web tuples containing the new or deleted nodes. We have also identified some of the tuples containing the updated nodes. The remaining tuples containing the updated nodes are identified from *temp1* and *temp2* (Steps (19) to (22) in Figure 10.4). The web tuples in *temp1* representing the old and new versions of the modified nodes are inserted in *updateTupleSet* as a single web tuple. For instance, the first web tuples in Figures 8.47 and 8.48 are contained in *temp1*. These two web tuples are combined and inserted as a single web tuple (represented by the fourth web tuple in Figure 10.1). Similarly, the new and old versions of the web tuples in *temp2* are determined and inserted in *updateTupleSet*. After Step (22) in Figure 10.4, the algorithm generates three sets, *insertTupleSet*, *deleteTupleSet*, and *updateTupleSet* representing the web tuples that contain all the relevant nodes that are inserted, deleted, or updated.

Algorithm of Phase 4

Next the algorithm proceeds to create the delta web tables, i.e., W_{Δ^+}, W_{Δ^-}, and W_{Δ^M} from *insertTupleSet*, *deleteTupleSet*, and *updateTupleSet* (Steps (23) to (25) in Figure 10.4). We describe the construction of the Δ^M-web table here. As the construction of the Δ^+ and Δ^--web tables is straightforward, we do not discuss this in detail in this chapter.

The algorithm first materializes each web tuple in *updateTupleSet* in the web tuple pool of W_{Δ^M}. Then it retrieves the node objects (old and new versions) from the table node pools of W_1 and W_2 for each node id in *updateNodeSet* and materializes these nodes in the table node pool of W_{Δ^M}. Observe that in the table node pool of W_{Δ^M} we only materialize nodes that have undergone content modification. However, in the web tuple pool of W_{Δ^M} we materialize the node ids of the joinable nodes in addition to the identifiers of the modified nodes. This is because each tuple in the web tuple pool contains not only the old and new versions of the modified nodes but also how these nodes are related to other nodes that have remained unchanged during t_1 and t_2. Finally, the schemas of the joined web table and the outer joined web table are *manipulated* to generate the schema of W_{Δ^M}. As mentioned earlier, we do not discuss it in this chapter.

The creation of the Δ^+ and Δ^- web tables are quite similar to that of the Δ^M-web table. The only difference is that the tuples are created from *insertTupleSet* and *deleteTupleSet*, respectively, and the schemas of W_{Δ^+} and W_{Δ^-} are identical to the web schema of W_1 or W_2.

10.5 Conclusions and Future Work

In this chapter, we have formally defined the change detection problem in the web warehouse context. To solve this problem, we have presented algorithms that are based on representing two versions of Web data as web tables and manipulating these web tables using a set of web algebraic operators for detecting changes. We have represented the web deltas in the form of delta web tables. We have implemented algorithms for computing and representing changes in Web data relevant to a user's query.

As ongoing work, we are addressing the following issues. (1) Analytical and empirical studies of the algorithms for generating the delta web tables. We wish to perform experiments to evaluate the performance of the algorithms. We are also investigating the scalability issues in this context. (2) Currently, the delta web tables contain tuples where only some of the nodes represent the insertion, deletion, or update operations during the transition. This is because we wish to show how these nodes are related to one another and to other nodes that have remained unchanged during the transition. Therefore we need a mechanism to distinguish between the modified, new, or deleted nodes in each delta web table. We are currently building a data model over our warehouse data model to allow *annotation* on the affected nodes to represent these changes. (3) As we represent the web deltas in the form of web tables, these tables can be further manipulated using the existing set of web operators and queried. We are designing and implementing a powerful query language for the change management system in the context of our web warehouse. (4) We intend to implement a *change notification mechanism* in WHOWEDA similar to one proposed in [50]. We intend to support various subscription services such as allowing changes to be detected, queried, and reported whenever a user is interested. (5) Design of an event-condition-action trigger language for WHOWEDA based on the ideas from the change detection system.

Knowledge Discovery Using Web Bags

11.1 Introduction

Sets and *bags* are closely related structures. When a set is allowed to have multiple occurrences of an element, it is called a bag or multiset [151]. While a set of tuples (i.e., a relation) is a simple, natural model of data as they might appear in a database, commercial systems are rarely if ever based purely on sets. In some situations, relations as they appear in database systems are permitted to have duplicate tuples. For example, the "select distinct" construct and the "select average of column" constructs of SQL can be better explained if bags instead of sets are used. While sets have been studied intensively by the database community, relational bags have recently received attention [151] for the following reasons.

- Allowing relations to be bags rather than sets expedites operational speed. For example, when we perform a projection, allowing the resulting relation to be a bag lets us work with each tuple independently. Note that allowing the result as bags, although larger in size, leads to faster computation.
- Having relations as bags eliminates the cost of duplicate removal from the relations.
- Permitting bags as results saves time in subsequent relational operations such as union.

Recently, there has been increased research interest in data models and query languages for Web data [79]. However, we are not aware of any work that addresses the concept of bags in the context of Web data. As shown, this issue is more challenging than the corresponding problem for relational bags due to the irregularity and incompleteness of data in the World Wide Web. In this chapter, we introduce the concept of bags in the context of a *web warehouse*. Specifically, our motivation is to describe how *web bags* can be used to discover different types of knowledge such as *visible nodes*, *luminous nodes*, and *luminous paths* with respect to a user's query. In the next section, we briefly highlight the shortcomings of existing search engines and contemporary web query systems with respect to discovering useful knowledge from the results returned by a query.

11.1.1 Motivation

Given the high rate of growth of the volume of data available on the WWW, locating information of interest in such an anarchic setting becomes a more difficult process every day. Thus there is the recognition of the pressing need for effective and efficient tools for information consumers, who must be able to easily locate and manipulate information in the Web. The current approach for locating information of interest mostly depends on browsing or sending a keyword or a combination of keywords to search engines. These approaches to locating information have the following shortcomings. Note that these shortcomings are not meant to be exhaustive. Our intention is to highlight only those shortcomings addressed in this chapter.

1. While web browsers fully exploit hyperlinks among web pages, most of the search engines (except Google) have so far made little progress in exploiting link information. Not only do most search engines fail to support queries on the Web utilizing link information, they also fail to return link information as part of a query's result.
2. From the query's result returned by search engines, a user may wish to locate the most *visible* Web sites [36] or documents for reference, that is, sites or documents that can be reached by many paths (high fan in). The significance of visible web documents or sites is that it enables us to identify popular web documents or sites for a given query. Visible documents for a query are those documents that can be reached by many different paths. Presently, one may only do so manually by visiting the documents in the query result, following each link in the web documents, and then downloading the visible documents as files on user's hard disk for future reference. Nevertheless, this method is tedious due to the large volume of results returned by search engines.
   Note that engines such as Google [39] use a combination of *relevance* and *quality* metrics [68] in ranking the responses to user queries. Quality metrics typically use link information to distinguish frequently referred pages from less visible ones.
3. Reversing the concept of visibility, a user may wish to locate the most *luminous* Web sites [36] or documents for reference, that is, web sites or documents that have the most number of outgoing links. Luminous documents or web sites define a document's or a site's exposure to other related web documents or sites. Thus *luminosity* is a measure of a web site's or web document's connectivity to different web documents or web sites. Currently, one may locate this information by manually visiting each Web document.
4. Current search engines fail to measure efficiently the *intersite connectivity* of web documents or sites. By web connectivity, we mean how richly connected is a web document or web site from/to other offsite servers. We may determine the richness by measuring the intersite connectivity of visible or luminous documents. Intersite connectivity helps us to determine if the visibility or luminosity of these documents is due to links from local servers or from offsite URLs. The importance of intersite connectivity is that it enables us to quantify the popularity of a web document to other sites.

5. Furthermore, a user may wish to find the most traversed path for a particular query result. This is important since it helps the user to identify the set of most popular interlinked Web documents that are traversed frequently to obtain the query result. Presently, one may only do so by visiting each document in the search result and comparing link information. This method is time consuming due to the quantity of results returned by search engines.

6. Over a period of time, there will be large collections of Web documents created by the user. As each of these collections exists simply as a set of files on the user's system, there is no convenient and systematic way to manage and discover useful knowledge from them.

Researchers in the area of the WWW have emphasized the importance of resolving the limitations of present search engines [6, 101, 106, 131]. However, most of the existing web query processing systems [79] do not address all the issues raised above with respect to discovering useful knowledge from query results.

11.1.2 Overview

Informally, a web bag is a web table containing multiple occurrences of *identical web tuples* [17]. A web bag may be created by eliminating some of the nodes from web tuples of a web table using the web project operator. Recall from Chapter 8, a web project operator is used to isolate data of interest, allowing subsequent queries to run over smaller, perhaps more structured web data. Unlike its relational counterpart, a web project operator does not eliminate *identical* web tuples autonomously. Thus the projected web table may contain identical web tuples (web bag). The duplicate elimination process is initiated explicitly by a user. As we show in Section 11.4, autonomous duplicate elimination may hinder the possibility of discovering useful knowledge from a web table. This is due to the fact that this knowledge can be discovered from web bags. The following example briefly illustrates the notion of a web project and web bag.

Example 11.1. Reconsider the project operation in Example 8.5. Note that the user now wishes to eliminate all instances of node type identifiers or nodes between y and z from each web tuple in the web table Cancer. This is performed by the web project operator and the resultant web table is shown in Figure 8.2. The first, second, and fourth web tuples in the figure are now identical (URL and connectivity of instances of node type identifiers in each web tuple are *identical* to those of another web tuple) and thus they form a web bag. The significance of the web bag indicates that the document at http://www.cancer.org/desc.html can be reached from http://www.virtualhealth.com/ by three different paths. A user may explicitly initiate the elimination of duplicate tuples (first and the second tuples in this case). The web table created after the removal of identical web tuples is shown in Figure 8.10. ∎

There are a number of new challenges related to web bags due to the richer nature of the WHOM data model which handles unstructured data. For example, what exactly is a web bag in WHOM? How are web bags created in WHOM? Is there is a need to materialize web bags? If we do, then what are the advantages? What is the usefulness of web bags from the perspective of information provided to users? In this chapter, we address some of these challenges. In particular, the contributions of this chapter are as follows.

- We motivate and develop the problem of discovering visible nodes, luminous nodes and luminous paths in the context of a user's query result.
- We formally introduce and define the concept of a web bag in a web warehouse. To the best of our knowledge, this is the first work on the concept of a web bag.
- We discuss the usefulness of different types of knowledge that may be garnered from a web warehouse using web bags. We also provide formal algorithms to discover this knowledge using a web bag.

The rest of the chapter is organized as follows. We present related research in the area of visible and luminous web sites in Section 11.2. We introduce the concept of a web bag in Section 11.3. In Section 11.4, we discuss the usefulness of different types of knowledge that may be harnessed using web bags in our web warehouse and illustrate their algorithms with examples. We formally discuss the knowledge discovery query language associated with web bags and examine the general philosophies that influence the design of such a query language in the context of web bags. In the last section, we conclude the chapter with some directions for future research.

11.2 Related Work

The visibility and luminosity of a Web page or web site can also be viewed from two perspectives—its *relevance* to a specific information need such as a user query, and its absolute *quality* irrespective of particular user requirements. Relevance metrics [110, 164] relate to the similarity of Web pages with *driving queries* using a variety of models for performing the comparison. Quality metrics typically use link information to distinguish frequently referred pages from less visible ones. For instance, the authors in [36, 161] have ranked various web sites based on the number of links to or from these web sites. However, as we show, the quality metrics discussed here are more sophisticated than simple in-degree counts.

Specifically, recent work in Web search such as PageRank [39], Authorities/Hubs [98] and Hyperinformation content [126] has demonstrated that the quality of a web page is dependent on the hyperlink structure in which it is embedded. Link structure analysis is based on the notion that a link from a page p to page q can be viewed as an endorsement of q by p, and as some form of positive judgement by p of q's content.

Two important types of techniques in link-structure analysis are *cocitation*-based schemes and *random walk*-based schemes. The main idea behind cocitation-based schemes is the notion that when two pages p_1 and p_2 both point to some page q, it is reasonable to assume that p_1 and p_2 share a mutual topic of interest. Likewise, when p links to both q_1 and q_2, it is probable that q_1 and q_2 share some mutual topic. On the other hand, random walk-based schemes model the Web (or part of it) as a graph where pages are nodes and links are edges, and apply some *random walk model* to the graph. Pages are then ranked by the probability of visiting them in the modeled random walk. We now discuss some of these metrics.

11.2.1 PageRank

The PageRank R_i of a page i having in-degree n can be defined in terms of the PageRank of each of the n neighboring pages and their out-degrees. Let us denote by j $(1 \leq j \leq n)$, the index of neighboring pages that point to i and by X_j the out-degree of page j. Then for a fixed parameter d in $[0,1]$ the PageRank R_i of i is given as

$$R_i = (1 - d) + d \sum_{j=1}^{n} \frac{R_j}{X_j} \tag{11.1}$$

We refer to d $(0 \leq d \leq 1)$ as the damping factor for the calculation of PageRank. Intuitively a page has a high PageRank if there are many pages that point to it or if there are some pages with high PageRank that point to it. Therefore, PageRank is a characteristic of the Web page itself: it is higher if more Web pages link to this page, as well as if these Web pages have high PageRank. Consequently, important Web pages help to make other Web pages important.

The PageRank may also be considered as the probability that a *random surfer* visits the page. A random surfer who is given a web page at random, keeps clicking on links, without hitting the "back" button but eventually gets bored and starts from another random page. The probability that the random surfer visits a page is its PageRank. The damping factor d in $R(p)$ is the probability at each page that the random surfer will get bored and request another random page.

The PageRank is used as one component of the Google search engine [39], to help determine how to order the pages returned by a web search query. The score of a page with respect to a query in Google, is obtained by combining the position, font, and capitalization information stored in *hitlists* (the IR score) with the PageRank measure. User feedback is used to evaluate search results and adjust the ranking functions. Cho et al. [57] describe the use of PageRank for ordering pages during a crawl so that the more important pages are visited first. It has also been used for evaluating the quality of search engine indexes using random walks [91]. However, PageRank has the problem of *Link Sink*. Link Sink occurs when page a and page b point to each other but have no links to other pages. If page a is pointed to by an external page, during the iteration of PageRank, the loop accumulates the weight and never distributes the weight to other pages. This causes the oscillation of the algorithm and the algorithm cannot converge.

11.2.2 Mutual Reinforcement Approach

A method that treats hyperlinks as conferrals of authority on pages for locating relevant, authoritative WWW pages for a broad topic query was introduced by Kleinberg in [98]. He suggested that web page importance should depend on the search query being performed. This model is based on a mutually reinforcing relationship between *authorities*—pages that contain a lot of information about a topic, and *hubs*—pages that link to many related authorities. That is, each page should have a separate *authority* rating based on the links going to the page and *hub* rating based on the links going from the page. Kleinberg proposed first using a text-based web search engine to get a Root Set consisting of a short list of web pages relevant to a given query. Second, the Root Set is augmented by pages that link to pages in the Root Set, and also pages linked from pages in the Root Set, to obtain a larger Base Set of web pages. If N is the number of pages in the final Base Set, then the data of Kleinberg's algorithm consist of an $N \times N$ adjacency matrix A, where $A_{ij} = 1$ if there are one or more hypertext links from page i to page j; otherwise $A_{ij} = 0$.

Authority and hub weights can be used to enhance Web search by identifying a small set of high quality pages on a broad topic [47, 48]. Pages related to a given page p can be determined by finding the top authorities and hubs among pages in the vicinity of p [66]. The same algorithm has also been used for finding densely linked communities of hubs and authorities [83].

One of the limitations of Kleinberg's [98] *mutual reinforcement principle* is that it is susceptible to the *Tightly Knit Communities* (TKC) effect. The TKC effect occurs when a community achieves high scores in link-analysis algorithms even as sites in the TKC are not authoritative on the topic, or pertain to just one aspect of the topic. A striking example of this phenomenon is provided by Cohn and Chang [62]. They use Kleinberg's Algorithm with the search term "jaguar", and converge to a collection of sites about the city of Cincinnati! They found out that the cause of this is a large number of online newspaper articles in the *Cincinnati Enquirer* that discuss the Jacksonville Jaguars football team, and all link to the same *Cincinnati Enquirer* service pages.

An important difference between Kleinberg's algorithm and PageRank is that PageRank is query-independent, whereas hubs and authorities depend heavily on the subject in which we are interested. In PageRank all pages on the Web are ranked on their *intrinsic* value, regardless of topic. Hence, whenever a query is made, PageRank must be combined with query-specific measures to determine the relative importance in a given context. On the other hand, instead of globally ranking pages, hubs and authorities assign ranks that are specific to the query in which we are interested.

11.2.3 Rafiei and Mendelzon's Approach

Generalizations of both PageRank and authorities/hubs models for determining the topics on which a page has a reputation are considered by Rafiei and Mendelzon [146]. In the one-level influence propagation model of PageRank, a surfer performing a random walk may jump to a page chosen uniformly at random with probability d *or* follow an outgoing link from the current page. Rafiei and Mendelzon introduce into this model, topic-specific surfing and parameterize the step of the walk at which the rank is calculated. Given that N_t denotes the number of pages that address topic t, the probability that a page p will be visited in a random jump during the walk is

d/N_t if p contains t and zero otherwise. The probability that the surfer visits p after n steps, following a link from page q at step $n-1$ is $((1-d)/O(q))R^{n-1}(q,t)$, where $O(q)$ is the number of outgoing links in q and $R^{n-1}(q,t)$ denotes the probability of visiting q for topic t at step $n-1$. The stochastic matrix containing pairwise transition probabilities according to the above model can be shown to be aperiodic and irreducible, thereby converging to stationary state probabilities when $n \to \infty$. In the two-level influence propagation model of authorities and hubs [98], outgoing links can be followed *directly* from the current page p, or *indirectly* through a random page q that has a link to p.

11.2.4 SALSA

Lempel and Moran [111] propose the Stochastic Approach for Link Structure Analysis (SALSA). This approach is based upon the theory of Markov Chains, and relies on the stochastic properties of random walks[1] performed on a collection of sites. Like Kleinberg's algorithm, SALSA starts with a similarly constructed Base Set. It then performs a random walk by alternately (a) going uniformly to one of the pages that links to the current page, and (b) going uniformly to one of the pages linked to by the current page. The authority weights are defined to be the stationary distribution of the two-step chain doing first step (a) and then (b), while the hub weights are defined to be the stationary distribution of the two-step chain doing first step (b) and then (a).

SALSA does not have the same *mutually reinforcing structure* that Kleinberg's algorithm does. The relative authority of sites within a connected component is determined from local links, not from the structure of the component. Also, in the special case of a single component, SALSA can be viewed as a one-step truncated version of Kleinberg's algorithm [35]. Furthermore, Kleinberg ranks the authorities based on the structure of the entire graph, and tends to favor the authorities of tightly knit communities. SALSA ranks the authorities based on their popularity in the immediate neighborhood, and favors various authorities from different communities. Specifically, in SALSA, the TKC effect is overcome through random walks on a bipartite web graph for identifying authorities and hubs. It has been shown that the resulting Markov chains are ergodic[2] and high entries in the stationary distributions represent sites most frequently visited in the random walk. If the web graph is weighted, the authority and hub vectors can be shown to have stationary distributions with scores proportional to the sum of weights on incoming and outgoing edges, respectively. This result suggests a simpler calculation of authority/hub weights than through the mutual reinforcement approach.

---

[1] According to [146], a *random walk* on a set of states $S = \{s_1, s_2, \ldots, s_n\}$, corresponds to a sequence of states, one for each step of the walk. At each step, the walk switches to a new state or remains in the current state. A random walk is *Markovian* if the transition at each step is independent of the previous steps and only depends on the current state.

[2] A *Markov chain* is simply a sequence of state distribution vectors at successive time intervals, i.e., $\langle \Pi^0, \Pi^1, \ldots, \Pi^n \rangle$. A Markov chain is *ergodic* if it is possible to go from every state to every other state in one or more transitions.

11.2.5 Approach of Borodin et al.

Borodin et al. proposed a set of algorithms for hypertext link analysis in [35]. We highlight some of these algorithms here. The authors proposed a series of algorithms based on minor modification of Kleinberg's algorithm to eliminate its previously mentioned errant behavior. They proposed an algorithm called the *Hub-Averaging-Kleinberg Algorithm* which is a hybrid of the Kleinberg and SALSA algorithms as it alternated between one step of each algorithm. It does the authority rating updates just like Kleinberg (giving each authority a rating equal to the sum of the hub ratings of all the pages that link to it). However, it does the hub rating updates by giving each hub a rating equal to the average of the authority ratings of all the pages to which it links. Consequently, a hub is better if it links to only *good* authorities, rather than linking to both good and bad authorities. Note that it shares the following behavior characteristics with the Kleinberg algorithm. If we consider a full bipartite graph, then the weights of the authorities increase exponentially fast for Hub-Averaging (the rate of increase is the square root of that of Kleinberg's algorithm). However, if one of the hubs points to a node outside the component, then the weights of the component drop. This prevents the Hub-Averaging algorithm from completely following the drifting behavior of Kleinberg's algorithm [35]. Hub-Averaging and SALSA also share a common characteristic as the Hub-Averaging algorithm tends to favor nodes with high in-degree. Namely, if we consider an isolated component of one authority with high in-degree, the authority weight of this node will increase exponentially faster [35].

The authors also proposed two different algorithms called *Hub-Threshold* and *Authority-Threshold* that modify the "threshold" of Kleinberg's algorithm. The *Hub-Threshold algorithm* is based on the notion that a site should not be considered a good authority simply because many hubs with very poor hub weights point to it. When computing the authority weight of the ith page, the Hub-Threshold algorithm does not take into consideration all hubs that point to page i. It only considers those hubs whose hub weight is at least the average hub weight over all the hubs that point to page i, computed using the current hub weights for the nodes.

The *Authority-Threshold algorithm*, on the other hand, is based on the notion that a site should not be considered a good hub simply because it points to a number of "acceptable" authorities; rather, to be considered a good hub it must point to some of the best authorities. When computing the hub weight of the ith page, the algorithm counts those authorities that are among the top K authorities, based on the current authority values. The value of K is passed as a parameter to the algorithm.

Finally, the authors also proposed two algorithms based on the Bayesian network approach, namely, the *Bayesian Algorithm* and *Simplified Bayesian Algorithm*, as opposed to the more common algebraic/graph theoretic approach. They experimentally verified that the *Simplified Bayesian Algorithm* is almost identical to the SALSA algorithm and has at least 80% overlap on all queries. On the other hand, the *Bayesian algorithm* appears to resemble both the Kleinberg and the SALSA behavior, leaning more towards the first. It has higher intersection numbers with Kleinberg than with SALSA.

Note that the above approaches do not focus on addressing the issue of determining visibility or luminosity of a web document and luminous paths with respect to user's query result in a warehousing environment. This is important because one may only be interested in popular web documents relevant to this query. Thus identification of a set of visible or luminous web sites may not be useful.

11.3 Concept of Web Bag

We have introduced the notion of web bag informally in Chapter 8. In this section, we formally define the concept of a web bag and discuss some properties associated with web bags. First, we introduce the concept of *equal* or *identical tuples* which we use to define a web bag.

Definitions

First, we formally define identical link sets in a web tuple t.

Definition 11.2. [Linkset Equality] *Let* $t_i = \langle N(t_i), L(t_i) \rangle$ *and* $t_j = (N(t_j), L(t_j))$ *be two web tuples in a web table* W. *Let* $url(n_k(t))$ *denote the URL of node* $n_k(t)$. *The set of links* $L(t_i)$ *and* $L(t_j)$ *is* **equal** *or* **identical**, *denoted by* $L(t_i) = L(t_j)$, *if* $|L(t_i)| = |L(t_j)|$ *and for each* $\ell_{pq}(t_i) \in L(t_i)$, *there exist* $\ell_{rs}(t_j) \in L(t_j)$ *such that* $url(n_p(t_i)) = url(n_r(t_j))$ *and* $url(n_q(t_i)) = url(n_s(t_j))$ ∎

Next we formally define the concept of identical web tuples.

Definition 11.3. [Tuple Equality] *Given a web table* W, *two web tuples* $t_i, t_j \in W$, *where* $t_i = \langle N(t_i), L(t_i) \rangle$, $t_j = \langle N(t_j), L(t_j) \rangle$ *are* **equal** *or* **identical**, *denoted by* $t_i = t_j$, $\forall i \neq j$, $0 < i, j \leq |W|$ *if* $N(t_i) = N(t_j)$ *and* $L(t_i) = L(t_j)$. ∎

We illustrate the above definition with an example below:

Example 11.4. Consider the collection of web tuples in Figure 8.2. The first (denoted by t_1) and second (denoted by t_2) web tuples are equal because $N(t_1) = N(t_2)$ (the URLs of the nodes in each set are www.virtualhealth.com/, www.virtualhealth.com/diseases/ and www.cancer.org/desc.html), $L(t_1) = L(t_2) = \{(x_0, y_0)\}$. ∎

Now we formally define the concept of a web bag. Recall that a bag is different from a set in that it is sensitive to the number of times an element occurs in it while a set is not.

Definition 11.5. [Web Bag] *A web table* W_b *is a* **web bag** *if and only if there exist* $t_i, t_j \in W_b$ *such that* $t_i = t_j$. ∎

A web bag may contain different collections of identical web tuples. We call each collection of such identical web tuples a *multiplet*. A web bag may have one or more multiplets. Note that a multiplet is a special type of bag in which all the web tuples are identical.

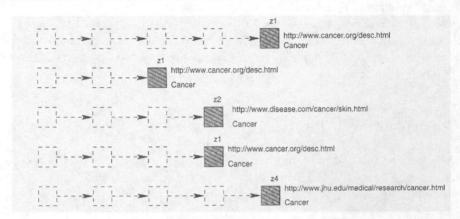

Fig. 11.1. Web table after projection.

Definition 11.6. [**Multiplet**] *A collection of web tuples M_b is a* **multiplet** *if and only if $t_1 = t_2 = t_3 = \cdots = t_{|M_b|}$, where $t_i \in M_b$, $1 \leq i \leq |M_b|$.* ∎

We use $\langle\{\ldots,\ldots\}\rangle$ brackets to identify a multiplet.

Example 11.7. Consider the collection of web tuples in Figure 8.2. The first, second, and fourth web tuples (denoted by t_1, t_2, and t_4) are identical; i.e., $t_1 = t_2 = t_4$. Thus the collection may be considered as a web bag and $\langle\{t_1, t_2, t_4\}\rangle$ forms a multiplet. ∎

Properties

In this section, we discuss some properties associated with web bags. A web bag may be created by eliminating some nodes from the web tuples of a web table using the web project operator. Thus the occurrence of a web bag depends on the set of node(s) eliminated from each input web tuple. However, it is not always true that eliminating node(s) from each web tuple in the input web table will result in the creation of a web bag.

Example 11.8. Consider Example 11.1. If we eliminate all the nodes between y and z from each web tuple in **Cancer**, a web bag is created since the first, second, and the fourth web tuples are identical (Figure 8.2). However, if we eliminate x and y as shown in Figure 6.10, the projected web table is not a web bag since each web tuple in Figure 11.1 is distinct. ∎

The next property deals with a condition for the creation of a web bag. A web bag may be created if the number of web tuples of W_p is less than the total number of web tuples in the input web table W.

Property 11.9. Let $W_b = \pi_{P_c}(W)$ and $W_p = Distinct(W_b)$, where P_c is a set of project conditions. Then W_b is a web bag if and only if $0 < |W_p| < |W|$. ∎

The next property states that the minimum number of identical web tuples in a multiplet must be two. The number of multiplets that may be created due to a web project operation is finite and varies between 0 and $|W|/2$. This is because the number of identical web tuples in a multiplet must at least be two. Thus the maximum number of multiplets created after any project condition on W is $|W|/2$ (each multiplet has two identical web tuples).

Property 11.10. Let M be the set of multiplets in W_b that may be created after a project operation on W. Let $\mathsf{count}(M_b)$ be defined as the number of times a web tuple occurs as an element in the multiplet M_b. For example, in Figure 8.2 there is only one multiplet with three identical web tuples, i.e., $\mathsf{count}(M_b) = 3$. Then the following are true.

- $\sum_{i=1}^{|M|} \mathsf{count}(\mathsf{M}_{b_i}) \leq |W_b|$,
- $0 \leq |M| \leq |W|/2$ ∎

11.4 Knowledge Discovery Using Web Bags

In the previous section we have seen that a web project operation may result in a web bag. In this section, we discuss the usefulness of storing identical web tuples. In particular, we discuss how a knowledge discovery process may proceed to find different types of knowledge such as *visibility*, *luminosity* of nodes, and *luminous paths* using web bags in a web warehouse. Note that the removal of identical web tuples may eliminate the possibility of discovering these types of knowledge from a web table.

We begin by defining some terms that we use in the knowledge discovery process. Then we elaborate on the different types of knowledge that may be discovered using web bags and illustrate with examples the algorithm of each type of knowledge to be discovered. Next we examine the general principles that influence the design of a knowledge discovery query in a web warehouse. Finally, we present an SQL-like syntax adopted by our query language to facilitate high-level knowledge discovery in the web warehouse. For simplicity, we assume in this chapter that a web table has a single web schema that binds all the web tuples. Formally, if $W = \langle N, \mathcal{U} \rangle$ is a web table then $\mathcal{U} = \{U\}$, where $U = \langle S, T \rangle$. Note that the knowledge discovery process can easily be extended to web tables with multiple web schemas.

11.4.1 Terminology

- **Threshold**: A knowledge discovery task in a web warehouse may need to specify a set of thresholds to control its knowledge discovery process by constraining the search for useful information. Different types of knowledge may require different kinds of thresholds. A threshold indicates that there should exist at least some reasonably substantial evidence of a pattern in the web table to warrant its presentation. The threshold is explicitly specified by the user and the value varies between 0 and 1.

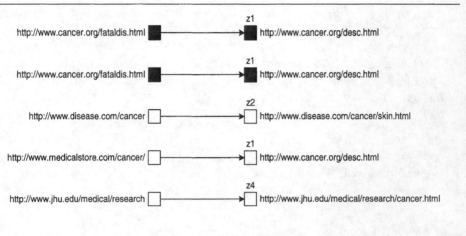

Fig. 11.2. Web table W_v.

- **Intersite connectivity**: When we think of Web connectivity, we are more interested in intersite linkages. Intersite connectivity enables us to quantify the site connectivity of a node in a web table. Formally, let x be a node in W and h_x denote the host name x. Let H be a bag of host names of all nodes in W that have direct links to/from x. Furthermore, let C_h be the number of times h_x appears in H. The inter-site connectivity, denoted as I is given as $I = 1 - C_h/|H|$.
- **Source node**: The start node type identifier(s) of a schema for a web table is defined as the source node. These identifiers cannot be the target identifiers in the connectivity set of the schema.
- **Sink node**: The terminal node type identifier(s) of a schema is defined as the sink node. These identifiers cannot be the source identifiers in the connectivity set of the schema.

11.4.2 Visibility of Web Documents and Intersite Connectivity

Suppose the result of a query Q is stored in web table W. The visibility of a web document D in a web table W measures the number of different web documents in W that have links to D. We call such documents visible nodes since they are the most visible in the web table as they are linked by a large number of distinct nodes. The significance of a visible node D is that the document D is relatively more important compared to other documents or nodes in W (since D is linked from many other web documents) for the query Q.

In a web table, each node type identifier may have a set of visible nodes. All of these may not be useful to the user. Thus we explicitly specify in a query the node type identifier based on which visible nodes are to be discovered. Moreover, we specify a threshold value (varying between 0 to 1) called the *visibility threshold* to control the search for visible nodes. The visibility threshold indicates that there should exist at least some reasonably substantial evidence of the visibility of instances of the specified node type identifier in the web table to warrant the

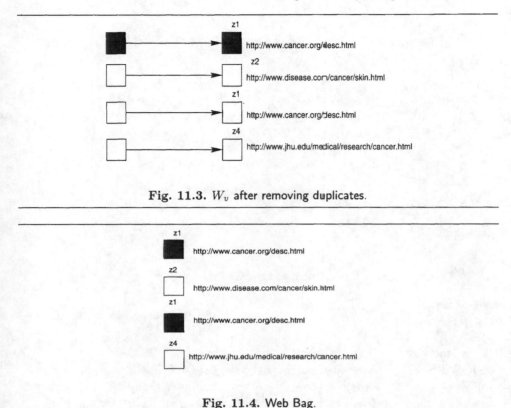

Fig. 11.3. W_v after removing duplicates.

Fig. 11.4. Web Bag.

presentation of visible nodes. This threshold is explicitly specified by a user. We now give the formal definition of visible nodes:

Definition 11.11. [**Visible Node**] *Let x be a node type identifier of web table W with schema $S = \langle X_n, X_\ell, C, P \rangle$, $x \in X_n$. Let x_i be an instance of x. Furthermore, let $N_{in}(i)$ be the number of distinct nodes (instances with distinct URLs) in W containing a link to x_i and let $N_{max} > 1$ and $N_{min} > 1$ be the maximum and minimum number of incoming links to instances of x in W respectively. Then the* **node visibility** *of x_i, denoted as α_i, is given by the following formula.*

$$\alpha_i = \begin{cases} \left(1 - K_1 \times \log_e \frac{N_{max}}{N_{in}(i)}\right) & \text{if } \frac{N_{max}}{N_{in}(i)} < e \text{ and } N_{in}(i) > 1 \\ 0 & \text{if } N_{in}(i) = 1 \\ \left(K_2 - 0.1 \log_e \frac{N_{max}}{N_{in}(i)}\right) & \text{if } \frac{N_{max}}{N_{in}(i)} \geq e \text{ and } N_{in}(i) > 1 \end{cases}$$

where e is an exponential constant and K_1, K_2, and K are constants such that $K = \frac{N_{max}}{N_{min}} + \delta$, $K_1 = 1.1 - 0.1 \log_e K$, and $K_2 = 1.1 - K_1$, where $0 < \delta < 1$. x_i is a **visible node** *of x if $\alpha_i \geq \epsilon_v$, where $0 \leq \epsilon_v \leq 1$ is the visibility threshold.* ∎

Note that we introduce the constants K_1 and K_2 to normalize α_i so that its value varies between 0 and 1 (i.e., $0 \leq \alpha_i \leq 1$). For a given web table and specified node type identifier, N_{max} and N_{min} are always constant. Thus the variability of

---

Input: Web table W, node type identifier x, visibility threshold ϵ_v.
Output: Visible node set V.

(1)   Initialize web table W_v;
(2)   Let $W_v = \textbf{CreateWv}(W, x)$; /* Figure 11.6 */
(3) $W_v = \textbf{Distinct}(W_v)$;
(4) $W_b = \textbf{WebProject}(W_v, x_{-1})$;/* Figure 8.14*/
(5)   if (W_b is a web bag)
(6) $V = \textbf{CreateVisibleNodeSet}(W_b, \epsilon_v)$; /* Figure 11.7 */
(7)   else
(8)   Visible node set does not exist;
(9)   Return V;

Fig. 11.5. Algorithm to determine visible nodes.

α_i depends on $N_{in}(i)$ only and its value increases as $N_{in}(i)$ increases. Note that the ratio $(N_{max}/N_{in}(i)) \geq 1$, and in practice the ratios $N_{max}/N_{in}(i)$ and N_{max}/N_{min} will not be too large for a given web table.

We now discuss how a web bag enables us to discover visible nodes of a specified node type identifier x in a web table W for a given visibility threshold ϵ_v. We first create a web table W_v by projecting the instances of x and all nodes that have links to any instances of x (see Figure 11.2). We eliminate any duplicate tuples in W_v to ensure that the incoming URLs to each instance of node type identifier x are distinct (see Figure 11.3). Then we eliminate the nodes linked to x in W_v and store the result in W_b. W_b may be a web bag since some of the instances of node type identifier x may be identical (identical URLs). Each multiplet in W_b indicates that the instance of a node type identifier x is pointed to by more than one node in W. The number of distinct nodes linked to an instance of x depends on the size of the multiplet containing that instance. For each multiplet in the web bag (Figure 11.5), we compute the node visibility α_i using the formula in Definition 11.11. Note that $N_{in}(i)$ is equal to the size of the multiplet containing x_i. The larger the size of a multiplet, the higher is the value of α_i. The visible nodes of x with visibility threshold ϵ_v are determined by comparing each α_i with ϵ_v. If for a multiplet $\alpha_i \geq \epsilon_v$ then the node x_i in the multiplet is considered as a visible node of x for threshold ϵ_v. Note that the set of visible nodes thus obtained may change with the change in the visibility threshold ϵ_v. We now discuss in detail the procedure to determine visible nodes and intersite connectivity. The formal representation of the algorithm for visible nodes is depicted in Figures 11.5 through 11.7.

Determination of Visible Nodes and Intersite Connectivity

Let x be a node type identifier in W with web schema $S = \langle X_n, X_\ell, C, P \rangle$, where $x \in X_n$ and x is not a source node type identifier. Then the x_{-1} node denotes all

Input: Web table W, node type identifier x.
Output: Web table W_v.

(1)   Let $N_p = \textbf{GetProjectNodeIds}(P_c)$;
(2)   Let $N_x = \textbf{GetNodeIds}(x)$;
(3)   Let $N_{x-1} = \textbf{GetNodeIds}(x_{-1})$;
(4)   for $(i = 1\ to\ |W|)$ {
(5) $T_n(i) = \textbf{GetTupleNodeIds}(t_i)$;
(6)   Let $D = T_n(i) \cap N_{x-1}$;
(7)   if $(|D| = 1)$ {
(8) $N_p(i) = T_n(i) \cap N_p$;
(9) $N_v(i) = T_n(i) - N_p(i)$; /* Ids of the nodes in the W_v */
(10) $L_v(i) = \textbf{GetLinkIds}(N_v(i))$;
(11)   Store $N_v(i)$ and $L_v(i)$ in the tuple file of W_v;
(12)   }
(13)   else {
(14)   for $(j = 1\ to\ |D|)$ {
(15) $N_p(i) = T_n(i) \cap N_p$;
(16) $projectNodeIdSet = T_n(i) - N_p(i)$;
(17) $N_v(i) = projectNodeIdSet - \hat{}(T_n(i) \cap N_{x-1}) - D[j])$;
(18) $L_v(i) = \textbf{GetLinkIds}(N_v(i))$;
(19)   Store $N_v(i)$ and $L_v(i)$ in the tuple file of W_v;
(20)   }
(21)   }
(22)   }
(23)   Return W_v;

Fig. 11.6. Algorithm for **CreateWv**(W, x).

nodes in the web table W that have links to the instances of x. Note that a web tuple in a web table may have more than one x_{-1} node because a web tuple may have more than one inbound link to an instance of x. The determination of visible node instances for a given node type identifier in a web table is as follows.

Input:

1. Web table W with schema $S = \langle X_n, X_\ell, C, P \rangle$,
2. Node type identifier $x \in X_n$ and x is not a source node,
3. Visibility threshold ϵ_v.

Output:

1. A set V of visible nodes that are instances of x,
2. Intersite connectivity I_j of each visible node instances of x.

Method

The visible nodes for x are determined as follows.

1. **Creation of web table W_v.** Create a web table W_v where each web tuple contains distinct instances of node x and x_{-1}, using the input web table W (Steps (2) in Figure 11.5). The construction of the web table is as follows. The formal algorithm for creating W_v is depicted in Figure 11.6.
   - Eliminate all nodes except x and x_{-1} from each web tuple in W using the web project operator. The elimination of these nodes is performed by the construct **GetProjectNodeIds(P_c)** in Figure 11.6 (Step (1)).
   - From the collection of projected web tuples, for each web tuple, if the number of x_{-1} nodes is $n > 1$, create n distinct web tuples containing nodes x and x_{-1}. If there are no web tuples with $n > 1$ x_{-1} nodes then avoid this step. This procedure is depicted in Steps (4) to (22) in Figure 11.6. The algorithm, for each web tuple t_i, identifies the instances of x_{-1} (denoted as D in Figure 11.6). In case there is more than one instance of x_{-1} in t_i (if $|D| > 1$) it creates $|D|$ distinct web tuples (Steps (14) to (20)).
   - Eliminate duplicate web tuples from the collection of web tuples and store the resultant set of web tuples in W_v. This is to ensure that the incoming URLs of node type identifier x are distinct. That is, if there are m web tuples in the collection after the elimination of identical web tuples then there are m distinct x_{-1} nodes in the web table W that has links to x. This step is performed by the construct **Distinct(W_v)** in Figure 11.5 (Step (3)).

2. **Creation of the collection of nodes x.** Create a collection of nodes x from W_v as follows (Step(4) in Figure 11.5).
   - Eliminate node x_{-1} from each web tuple in W_v using the web project operator.
   - Store the collection of nodes x in W_b. Note that each node in W_b corresponds to a web tuple.

3. **Checking the existence of a web bag.** Check if the collection of web tuples in W_b is a web bag (Step (5) in Figure 11.5). The following steps determine this.
   - Compare the URL of each node in W_b with that of other nodes to identify if the URLs are identical.
   - If all the nodes in W_b are distinct (no duplicate URLs) then there are no visible nodes for x in W. The rest of the steps are ignored.
   - If there exist nodes with identical URLs then W_b is a web bag.
   The remaining steps are encapsulated in the construct **CreateVisibleNodeSet(W_b, ϵ_v)** in Figure 11.7.

4. **Creation of multiplets.** Let there be k collections of identical nodes in W_b. Store each collection in a multiplet M_{b_i}, $i = 1, 2, \ldots, k$.

5. **Computation of node visibility.** For each multiplet M_{b_i} in the web bag, compute the node visibility, denoted as α_i, using the formula in Definition 11.11. Note that $N_{in}(i) = count(M_{b_i})$. Thus node visibility is calculated by replacing $N_{in}(i)$ with $count(M_{b_i})$ in the formula defined in Definition 11.11.

6. **Determination of visible nodes.** The visible nodes of x with threshold ϵ_v are determined by the following steps.

- If $\alpha < \epsilon_v$ then the node is not a visible node for the threshold ϵ_v.
- Otherwise, obtain one of the nodes (visible node) from M_{b_i} and store it in the visible node set V.

Steps (2) to (11) in Figure 11.7 give the formal description of the above two steps.

7. **Determination of intersite connectivity.** Now determine the intersite support for each visible node in V.
   - For each element in V, perform the following steps.
   - Determine the host name (denoted by H_{x_i}) of the node v_j, where $v_j \in V$ and $0 < j \leq |V|$.
   - Determine the nodes x_{-1} corresponding to v_j from W_v.
   - Determine the host names of the set of x_{-1} nodes from their URLs and store the host names in a bag H_{x-1}.
     The above two steps are encapsulated in the construct **InNodeURLs**(v_k) where $v_k \in V$ as shown in Step (14) in Figure 11.7.
   - Count the number of times H_{x_i} appears in H_{x-1}. The intersite connectivity I_j is given by: $I_j = 1 - C_h/|H_{x-1}|$, where C_h is the number of times H_{x_i} appears in H_{x-1} (Steps (15) to (24) in Figure 11.7).

The following example illustrates the execution of the algorithm for visible nodes on the scenario of Example 11.18.

Example 11.12. Consider the web table Cancer in Figure 6.10. Suppose we wish to find the visible nodes for node type identifier z in this web table. In particular, we consider only those nodes with a visibility threshold greater than or equal to 0.8. The procedure for determining visible nodes is as follows.

1. Figure 11.3 shows the projected web table W_v after eliminating all the nodes except instances of z and nodes x_{-1} with respect to instances of z from each web tuple in the web table Cancer (Figure 6.10). Note that one of the duplicate web tuples (first and second web tuples in Figure 11.2) is eliminated from W_v.
2. Next project the x_{-1} nodes from W_v and the resultant collection of tuples is shown in Figure 11.4.
3. Since the first tuple (denoted as t_1) and third tuple (denoted as t_3) in Figure 11.4 are identical (having identical URLs http://www.cancer.org/ desc.html) the collection of tuples in Figure 11.4 is a web bag.
4. Create the multiplet $M_{b_1} = \langle\{t_1, t_3\}\rangle$.
5. count(M_{b_1}) $= N_{in}(1) = 2$, $N_{max} = |M_{max}(W_b)| = 2$. Thus $N_{max}/N_{in}(1) = 2/2 = 1$ i.e., $N_{max}/N_{in}(1) < e$. The node visibility of z_1 is given by the following equation (Definition 11.11): $\alpha_1 = \left(1 - K_1 \log_e \frac{N_{max}}{N_{in}(1)}\right) = \left(1 - K_1 \log_e \frac{2}{2}\right) = 1$.
6. Since the visibility threshold $\epsilon_v = 0.8$, a visible node exists for node type identifier z ($\alpha_1 > \epsilon_v$).
7. The visible node set $V = \{$www.cancer.org/desc.html$\}$.
8. For the above visible node $H_{x_1} = \{$www.cancer.org/$\}$. From the web table W_v, $H_{x-1} = \{$www.cancer.org/, www.medicalstore.com/$\}$. Thus $C_h = 1$, $|H_{x-1}| = 2$. The intersite connectivity for the visible node is $I_1 = 1 - 1/2 = 0.5$.

```
Input: Web table $W_b$, $\epsilon_v$.
Output: Set of visible nodes $V$.

(1)      Let $|M| = m$ be the number of multiplets;
(2)      for $(j = 1$ $to$ $m)$ {
(3)          Compute node visibility $\alpha_j$ for $M_{b_j}$;
(4)              if $(\alpha_j < \epsilon_v)$
(5)                  ; /* The node is not visible */
(6)              else {
(7)                  Retrieve a node for an id in $M_{b_j}$;
(8)                  Store the node in $V$;
(9)              }
(10)      }
(11)  }
          /* Determination intersite connectivity of visible nodes */
(12)  for $(k = 1$ $to$ $|V|)$ {
(13)          Determine the host-name $H_x(k)$ of $v_k \in V$;
(14)          Get $H_{x-1}(k) = \mathbf{InNodeURLs}(v_k)$;
(15)          for $(g = 1$ $to$ $|H_{x-1}(k)|)$ {
(16)              if $(H_x = H_{x-1}(k)(g))$ {
(17)                  counter = counter + 1;
(18)              }
(19)              else
(20                   ;
(21)          }
(22)          Compute $I_h(k) = 1 - \frac{counter}{|H_{x-1}(k)|}$;
(23)          Store $I_h(k)$ in $V$; /* In $V$ we store the intersite connectivity of
              each visible node with the node itself */
(24)  }
(25)  Return $V$;
```

Fig. 11.7. Algorithm of **CreateVisibleNodeSet**(W_b, ϵ_v).

The intersite connectivity indicates that 50% of incoming URLs of node type identifier z are not local.   ∎

11.4.3 Luminosity of Web Documents

Reversing the concept of visibility, luminosity of a web document D in a web table W measures the number of outgoing links, i.e., the number of other distinct web documents in W that are linked from D. Similar to the determination of visible nodes, we explicitly specify the node type identifier y based on which luminous nodes are to be discovered and the *luminosity threshold* ϵ_ℓ. The formal definition of luminous nodes is given below.

Definition 11.13. [Luminous Node] *Let y be a node type identifier of web table W with schema $S = \langle X_n, X_\ell, C, P \rangle$, $y \in X_n$. Let y_i be an instance of y. Furthermore, let $N_{out}(i)$ be the number of distinct nodes (instances with distinct URLs) in W containing an outgoing link from y_i and let $N_{max} > 1$ and $N_{min} > 1$ be the maximum and minimum number of outgoing links from the instances of y in W respectively. Then the* **node luminosity** *of y_i, denoted as β_i, is given by the following formula.*

$$
\beta_i = \begin{cases} \left(1 - K_1 \log_e \frac{N_{max}}{N_{out}(i)}\right) & if \ \frac{N_{max}}{N_{out}(i)} < e \ and \ N_{out}(i) > 1 \\ 0 & if \ N_{out}(i) = 1 \\ \left(K_2 - 0.1 \log_e \frac{N_{max}}{N_{out}(i)}\right) & if \ \frac{N_{max}}{N_{out}(i)} \geq e \ and \ N_{out}(i) > 1 \end{cases}
$$

where e is an exponential constant and K_1, K_2, and K are constants such that $K = \frac{N_{max}}{N_{min}} + \delta$, $K_1 = 1.1 - 0.1 \log_e K$, and $K_2 = 1.1 - K_1$, where $0 < \delta < 1$. y_i is a **luminous node** *of y if $\beta_i \geq \epsilon_\ell$, where $0 \leq \epsilon_\ell \leq 1$ is the luminosity threshold for luminous nodes.* ∎

Similar to node visibility, β_i varies between 0 and 1 (i.e., $0 \leq \beta_i \leq 1$). Furthermore, the variability of β_i depends on $N_{out}(i)$ only and its value increases as $N_{out}(i)$ increases. Note that the ratio $(N_{max}/N_{out}(i)) \geq 1$ and in practice the ratios $N_{max}/N_{out}(i)$ and N_{max}/N_{min} will not be too large for a given web table.

The method of discovering luminous nodes of a node type identifier y in a web table W is similar to that of the visible nodes discovery method. We create a web table W_v by removing from each web tuple in W all nodes except instances of y and nodes that are directly linked from y. We eliminate duplicate tuples in W_v to ensure that each instance of y is linked to distinct web documents (nodes). Then, from each tuple in W_v, we remove all the nodes linked from each instance of y. The resultant collection of tuples (with instances of node y) may be a web bag depending on the occurrence of identical instances of y. Similar to visible nodes, the luminous nodes of y are determined from the size of each multiplet in the web bag. For each multiplet in the web bag, we compute the node luminosity β_i using the formula in Definition 11.13. The node luminosity is calculated by replacing $N_{out}(i)$ in the formula in Definition 11.13 with the size of the multiplet containing y_i. The luminous nodes of y with luminosity threshold ϵ_ℓ are determined by comparing each β_i with ϵ_ℓ. The node y_i in a multiplet is considered a luminous node of y if $\beta_i \geq \epsilon_\ell$.

Determination of Luminous Nodes and Intersite Connectivity

Let x be a node type identifier in web table W with web schema $S = \langle X_n, X_\ell, C, P \rangle$, where $x \in X_n$ and x is not a source or sink node type identifier. Then x_{+1} node denotes all nodes in the web table W that have pointers from each instance of node x. The URLs of x_{+1} represent the outgoing URLs of instances of x. A web tuple in a web table may have more than one x_{+1} node depending on the number of links in a Web document of an instance of x reference x_{+1}. The algorithm to determine the luminous nodes for a given node type identifier in a web table is briefly highlighted below. Since the algorithm is similar to that of visible nodes we only discuss steps that are different from the visible nodes algorithm.

Input:

1. A web table W with schema $S = \langle X_n, X_\ell, C, P \rangle$,
2. Node type identifier $x \in X_n$ and x is not a source or sink node type identifier,
3. Luminosity threshold ϵ_ℓ.

Output:

1. A set L of luminous nodes that are instances of x.
2. Intersite connectivity I_j of each luminous node instance of x.

Method

The luminous nodes for the node type identifier x are determined as follows:

1. **Creation of web table W_{lum}.** The procedure to create web table W_{lum} is similar to that of W_v for visible nodes. In the case of luminous nodes, eliminate all nodes except x and x_{+1} from each web tuple in web table W.
2. **Creation of collection of nodes x.** This procedure is identical to that of the visible nodes algorithm. The only difference is that here eliminate the node x_{+1} as opposed to node x_{-1} for visible nodes.
3. **Checking the existence of a web bag and creation of multiplets.** The steps for checking the existence of a web bag and creation of multiplets are identical to those for the determination of visible nodes.
4. **Computation of node luminosity.** The computation is similar to that of visible nodes. Note that in this case use Definition 11.13 to compute β_i. Furthermore, $N_{out}(i) = count(M_{b_i})$.
5. **Determination of luminous nodes.** The procedure to determine luminous nodes is similar to Step (6) of the determination of visible nodes. Note that, in this step, replace the visibility threshold ϵ_v with the luminosity threshold ϵ_ℓ and the set of visible nodes V with the set of luminous nodes L.
6. **Determination of intersite connectivity.** This is similar to Step (7) in the determination of visible nodes. However, here determine the host name of nodes x_{+1} corresponding to each luminous node as opposed to x_{-1} nodes for visible nodes. The computation of intersite connectivity for luminous nodes is based on x_{+1} nodes.

11.4.4 Luminous Paths

In this section, we first provide some basic definitions that we use to illustrate the concept of luminous paths.

Definition 11.14. [Path] *A* **path** $p_{ij} = \langle n_{k_1}(t), n_{k_2}(t), \ldots, n_{k_m}(t) \rangle$ *in web tuple* t *is an ordered sequence of nodes, where* $n_i(t) = n_{k_1}(t)$ *and* $n_j(t) = n_{k_m}(t)$, $n_{k_p}(t) \in N(t), 1 \leq p \leq m$, *and* $\ell_{k_q k_{q+1}}(t) \in L(t), 1 \leq q \leq m - 1$. $n_i(t)$ *and* $n_j(t)$ *are the source and sink nodes of the path, respectively.* ∎

Definition 11.15. [Fragment] **Fragment**$(t) = \{p_{12}, p_{23}, \ldots, p_{ij}\}$ *is a set of all possible distinct paths in web tuple* t. ∎

A web query result in WHOWEDA is a set of interlinked web tuples materialized in the form of a web table. Luminous paths in a web table are sets of interlinked nodes (path) that occur some number of times across tuples in the web table. That is, the occurrence of this set of interlinked nodes is high compared to the total number of web tuples in the web table. An implication is that in order to couple the query result from the WWW, most of the web tuples in the web table have to traverse the luminous paths. The formal definition of a luminous path is given below.

Definition 11.16. [Luminous Path] *Let path p_{ij} occur in n web tuples in web table $W \forall 0 < n \leq |W|$. Then path p_{ij} is called a* **luminous path** *if $n/|W| \geq \epsilon_{\ell p}$ where $\epsilon_{\ell p}$ is the user-defined threshold value for luminous paths and $0 < \epsilon_{\ell p} \leq 1$. The ratio $n/|W|$, denoted as γ, is called the* **path luminosity**. ∎

We now show the procedure to determine the luminous paths between two node type identifiers x and y for the web table W satisfying the luminous path threshold ϵ_{ℓ_p}. We first eliminate all node type identifiers from W except those between x and y and store the resultant collection of web tuples in W_b. Then we check if the collection of web tuples in W_b is a web bag. We compare the set of URLs and connectivities of each web tuple in W_b with that of other web tuples to identify if the set of URLs and connectivities of one web tuple are identical to those of another web tuple. If the sets of URLs of each web tuple are distinct from each other then there do not exist identical web tuples in W_b (no multiplet). The paths between x and y are all distinct and there does not exist any luminous path. However, if there exists a collection of web tuples with identical sets of URLs and connectivities then W_b is a web bag. For each multiplet in W_b, we determine the path luminosity γ using the formula in Definition 11.16. Note that n in Definition 11.16 is equal to the size of a multiplet in W_b. We obtain the set of luminous paths between x and y with threshold ϵ_{ℓ_p} by comparing γ with ϵ_{ℓ_p}.

Note that there may exist a subset of interlinked nodes or paths in a web tuple t_i that may be identical to another web tuple t_j or a path in t_j. The procedure described above only identifies luminous paths from x to y and does not consider paths whose depth is less than the depth of a path from x to y. That is, it does not consider paths with a number of interlinked nodes smaller than the total number of interlinked nodes between the instances of x and y. In order to determine if these paths are luminous paths, for each web tuple t in W_b we create **Fragment**(t) and store them in a collection of fragments F. Then we check for the existence of identical web tuples or paths in F. The determination of luminous paths in F is similar to that of the procedure described above. The algorithm for luminous paths is given in Figures 11.10 and 11.11.

Determination of Luminous Paths

Input:

1. A web table W with schema $S = \langle X_n, X_\ell, C, P \rangle$,
2. Node type identifiers $x \in X_n$ and $y \in X_n$,
3. Threshold $\epsilon_{\ell p}$.

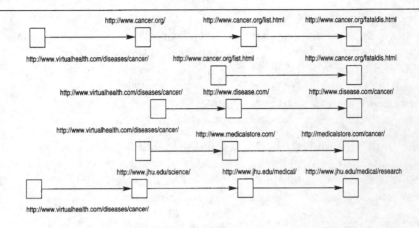

Fig. 11.8. Web table after projecting node instances of x, y, and z.

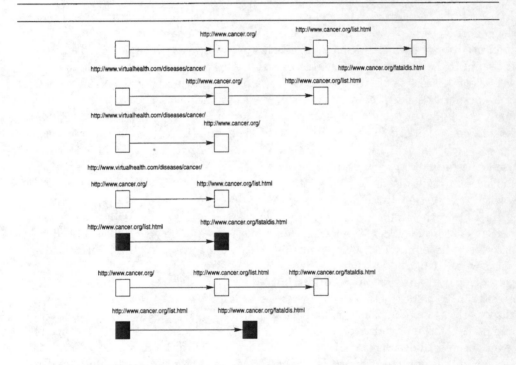

Fig. 11.9. Partial view of collection of web tuples in F.

Output:

1. A set L_p of luminous paths with path lengths (depth).

Method

The luminous paths in the web table W are determined as follows.

Input: Web table W, node type identifiers x and y, ϵ_{ℓ_p}.
Output: Set of luminous paths L_p.

(1)   Initialize web bags W_b;
(2)   Let $P_c = \{start\ x, end\ y\}$;
(3) $W_b = \textbf{WebProject}(W, P_c)$ /* Figure 8.14 */;
(4) $L_p = \textbf{CreateLuminousPath}(W_b, \epsilon_{\ell_p})$; /* Figure 11.11 */
(5)   if $(|L_p| > 0)$ {
(6)   Return L_p; /* Luminous path exists */
(7)   }
(8)   else {
(9)   Open tuple file of W_b;
(10)   for $(j = 1\ to\ |W_b|)$ {
(11)   Create $f_i = \textbf{Fragment}(t_j)$;
(12)   Store f_i in F;
(13)   }
(14) $L_p = \textbf{CreateLuminousPath}(F, \epsilon_{\ell_p})$;
(15)   if $(|L_p| > 0)$ /* Luminous paths exist */
(16)   Return L_p;
(17)   else
(18)   Luminous path doesn't exist;
(19)   }

Fig. 11.10. Algorithm for discovering luminous paths.

1. **Elimination of node type identifiers from W.** Eliminate all node type identifiers from W except those between x and y and store the resultant collection of web tuples in W_b (Step (3) in Figure 11.10).
The next three steps are encapsulated in the construct **CreateLuminousPath**(W_b, ϵ_{ℓ_p}).

2. **Checking the existence of a web bag.** Check if the collection of web tuples in W_b is a web bag. Adopt the following steps to determine this.
   - Compare the set of URLs of each web tuple in W_b with that of other web tuples to identify if the set of URLs of one web tuple is identical to that of another web tuple.
   - If the set of URLs of each web tuple is distinct from the others, then there do not exist identical web tuples in W_b (no multiplet). Proceed to Step (7).
   - If there exists a collection of web tuples with identical sets of URLs then W_b is a web bag.

3. **Creation of multiplets.** Let there be k collections of identical web tuples in W_b. Store each collection of identical web tuples in a multiplet M_{b_i} $\forall\ i = 1, 2, 3, \ldots, k$. Note that each multiplet identifies a collection of identical paths.

4. **Computation of path luminosity.** For each multiplet M_{b_i} in the web bag, compute the path luminosity, denoted as γ, using the formula: $\gamma = count(M_{b_i})/|W|$. Note

that $count(M_{b_i})$ indicates the number of times a web tuple (path) in M_{b_i} occurs in W.

5. **Determination of luminous paths.** The luminous paths between node type identifiers x and y with threshold $\epsilon_{\ell p}$ are determined by the following steps (Steps (3) to (13) in Figure 11.11):
   - If $\gamma < \epsilon_{\ell p}$, the path is not luminous.
   - Otherwise, for each $\gamma \geq \epsilon_{\ell p}$, obtain one of the web tuples (path) from M_{b_i} and store it in luminous path set L along with its path length (depth).

   The following steps determine if some paths in a web tuple in W_b are luminous paths.

6. **Creation of a collection of fragments F.**
   - For each web tuple t in W_b create **Fragment**(t) based on the Definition 11.15 (Steps (10) to (13) in Figure 11.10). For example, the first six tuples in Figure 11.9 are **Fragment**(t) from the first web tuple in Figure 11.8. Recall that each **Fragment**(t) represents the set of all possible distinct paths in web tuple t.
   - Store these fragments in a collection F.

7. **Checking the existence of identical paths.**
   - Compare each path in F with others to determine the existence of identical paths.
   - If all the paths in the collection are distinct from each other then there does not exist any luminous path between x and y. Then ignore the remaining steps.
   - Otherwise, proceed to the next step.

8. **Creation of multiplets.** Let there be q collections of identical paths or web tuples in F. Store each collection of identical paths in a multiplet M_{b_j} $\forall$ $j = 1, 2, 3, \ldots, q$.

9. **Computation of path luminosity.** For each multiplet M_{b_j} compute the path luminosity, denoted as γ, using the formula: $\gamma = count(M_{b_j})/|W|$.

10. **Computation of maximum value of path luminosity.** After determining the path luminosity of each multiplet, compute the maximum value of path luminosity (denoted by γ_{max}).

11. **Determination of luminous paths.** The luminous paths between node type identifiers x and y with threshold $\epsilon_{\ell p}$ are determined by the following steps.
    - If $\gamma_{max} < \epsilon_{\ell p}$ there does not exist any luminous path in F.
    - Otherwise, for each $\gamma \geq \epsilon_{\ell p}$, obtain one of the paths from M_{b_j} and store it in luminous path set L along with the depth of the path (number of nodes in the path).

The following example illustrates the execution of the algorithm for luminous paths.

Example 11.17. Consider the web table Cancer in Figure 6.10. Suppose we wish to find the luminous paths between y and z. In particular, we consider only those paths with threshold values greater than or equal to 0.4. The luminous paths are determined as follows.

1. Instances of node type identifiers x, y, and z are removed from each web tuple of Cancer. The projected collection of web tuples is shown in Figure 11.8.

```
Input: Web table W_b, ε_{ℓ_p}.
Output: Set of luminous paths L_p.

(1)    if (W_b is a web bag) {
(2)        Let |M| = m be the number of multiplets in W_b;
(3)        for (j = 1 to m) {
(4)            Compute path luminosity γ_j for M_{b_j};
(5)            if (γ_j < ε_{ell_p})
(6)                ; /* The path is not luminous */
(7)            else {
(8)                Retrieve a web tuple from M_{b_j};
(9)                Compute the depth d of the tuple;
(10)               Store d and the web tuple in L_p;
(11)           }
(12)       }
(13)   }
(14)   else
(15)       There are no multiplets in W_b;
(16)   Return L_p;
```

Fig. 11.11. Algorithm for **CreateLuminousPath**(W, ϵ_{ℓ_p}).

2. Check the existence of identical web tuples in Figure 11.8. Since all the web tuples are distinct, we proceed to create the collection of fragments F.
3. The partial view of the collection of fragments F is shown in Figure 11.9.
4. Check the existence of multiplets in Figure 11.9.
5. Since the fifth and the seventh tuples in Figure 11.9 are identical to each other, multiplet $M_{b_1} = \langle\{$www.cancer.org/list.html,www.cancer.org/ fataldis.html$\}\rangle$. We assume that these are the only paths in F that are identical to one another.
6. Since the number of tuples in M_{b_1} is 2 and $|W| = 5$, path luminosity $\gamma = 2/5 = 0.4$.
7. $\gamma_{max} = 0.4$.
8. Since $\gamma_{max} = \epsilon_{\ell p} = 0.4$, the path consisting of nodes http://www.cancer. org/list.html and http://www.cancer.org/fataldis.html is a luminous path with depth 1.

Note that a user can impose constraints over the depth of a luminous path in the knowledge discovery query.   ∎

11.4.5 Query Language Design Considerations

We observe the following design considerations in the design of a query language for discovering visible nodes, luminous nodes, and luminous paths.

1. The set of web data relevant to the knowledge discovery task in a web warehouse should be specified in the knowledge discovery query. Since a user may be interested in any portion of data in a web warehouse, a knowledge discovery system should be able to work on any specific subset of web data. This implies that the knowledge discovery process will be triggered by identifying the subtask to retrieve a relevant set of data (nodes in our case) before proceeding to garner useful information from it.

2. The type of knowledge to be discovered should be specified in the query. Ideally, one expects that a knowledge discovery system would perform interesting discovery autonomously without human instruction or interaction. However, since knowledge discovery in a web warehouse can be performed in many different ways on any specific set of data, large amounts and different types of knowledge may be generated by unguided autonomous discovery, whereas much of the discovered knowledge may not be useful to the user. This motivates us to propose *user-driven knowledge discovery*, which specifies both the relevant web data on which the discovery process is to be activated and the types of knowledge to be discovered.

3. Various types of thresholds should be able to be specified to filter out information that is not interesting to the user. A user may wish to interactively specify various types of thresholds that can be used to select interesting knowledge discovered and filter out knowledge that is less interesting, i.e., knowledge that falls below the specified threshold.

11.4.6 Query Language for Knowledge Discovery

Based on the above considerations, a knowledge discovery system in our web warehouse is designed to harness different types of knowledge. The query language consists of the specifications of three major parameters in discovering knowledge in a web warehouse:

- a set of web data relevant to the knowledge discovery,
- the type of knowledge to be discovered, and
- a threshold value of the interesting information to be discovered.

The first parameter, the set of relevant data, is specified by providing the node type identifier(s) in the schema of a web table on which knowledge discovery is to be performed. The second parameter, the kind of knowledge to be discovered, includes visibility, luminosity, or luminous paths. The last parameter, the significance of the knowledge to be discovered, can be specified as a set of different thresholds depending on the type of knowledge to be discovered in a web warehouse.

The syntax for a knowledge discovery query is defined in a simplified BNF grammar ("[ ]" represents zero or one occurrence and words in `typewriter` font represent keywords) as follows.

$\langle WQL \rangle ::=$

    `DISCOVER` $\langle knowledge\_type \rangle$

    `[FOR` $\langle node\_type\_identifier(s) \rangle$`]`

    `[BETWEEN` $\langle node\_type\_identifiers \rangle$`]`

FROM ⟨web_table_name⟩
[WHERE THRESHOLD = ⟨threshold_value⟩]

- "DISCOVER ⟨knowledge_type⟩" specifies that the knowledge to be discovered is of type "⟨knowledge_type⟩". The following kinds of knowledge types are supported in our query language.
    1. Visible nodes.
       ⟨knowledge_type⟩::= visibility
    2. Luminous nodes.
       ⟨knowledge_type⟩::= luminosity
    3. Luminous paths.
       ⟨knowledge_type⟩::= luminous path
- "FROM ⟨web_table_name⟩" specifies that the knowledge is to be discovered from "⟨web_table_name⟩".
- "FOR ⟨node_type_identifier(s)⟩" specifies node type identifier(s) in the web table "⟨web_table_name⟩" on which the specified knowledge is to be discovered. This clause is used for the visibility and luminosity knowledge types.
- "BETWEEN ⟨node_type_identifiers⟩" specifies start and end node type identifiers when the knowledge type is luminous path.
- "WHERE THRESHOLD = ⟨threshold_value⟩" specifies the threshold value for the specified knowledge to be discovered. If the threshold value is not specified by the user then a default value is used.

The following example illustrates the queries for various types of knowledge discovery.

Example 11.18. Consider the scenario depicted in Example 11.12. The query for discovering the visible nodes is as follows.

```
DISCOVER          visibility
FOR               z
FROM              Cancer
WHERE THRESHOLD = 0.8
```

Similarly, the query for discovering luminous paths as illustrated in Example 11.17 is as follows.

```
DISCOVER          luminous path
BETWEEN           y and z
FROM              Cancer
WHERE THRESHOLD = 0.4
```

11.5 Conclusions and Future Work

In this chapter, we have introduced the concept of a web bag in a web warehouse and discussed algorithms to create a web bag and its schema. Our chapter focuses on how web bags may be used to resolve some of the shortcomings of search engines and contemporary web query systems with respect to knowledge discovery from the query results. We have designed algorithms for visible nodes, luminous nodes, and luminous paths that may be discovered using web bags. We have implemented web bag and knowledge discovery algorithms on a UNIX workstation using C++.

The three types of knowledge we discover using web bags may help us in the following ways. Since the results returned from the Web with respect to a query may be enormous, the notion of visible web pages allows a user to see progressively popular web documents in response to her query. Given a threshold, a user can generate a smaller set of visible web pages and browse them for the information of interest. By modifying the threshold, he can progressively change the set of visible web pages. This will reduce the cognitive overheads associated with browsing a set of web pages. From the query processing point of view, a related query can start crawling from one or more visible web pages, which can reduce the number of results returned and the processing cost associated with the query.

Similarly, luminous web pages inform a user about the connectivity with respect to other related web pages. For example, many web sites have popular links under an anchor called "other related sites". Larger numbers of such links represent a web document's awareness of other sources of related references. This information can be used in executing a similar query, so that crawling can start from one or more of those sites. On the same line, the set of luminous paths enables us to identify the common traversal paths in all the results returned. Thus the user needs to browse those web pages only once.

The Road Ahead

This book describes our fundamental work in web warehousing. In particular, we have proposed a data model for representing Web data, and a web algebra for retrieving data from the Web and manipulating them to derive additional information. The algebra provides a formal foundation for data representation and manipulation for the web warehouse. Within the context of a web algebra, we have defined a set of web operators so as to equip the warehouse with the basic capability to manipulate web tables. These operators include global web coupling, web select, web project, web distinct, web join, and web union.

As part of our future work, we intend to achieve the following targets.

- Extending coupling queries and the global web coupling operation.
- Optimizing the number of simple schemas compared to the number of web tuples in a web table.
- Extending the web algebra to incorporate additional web operators.
- Design and implementation of a high-level declarative query language for querying the web warehouse.
- Efficient implementation and performance evaluation of various web operators in the web warehouse.
- Exploring maintenance issues of the web warehouse.
- Currently, we do not consider dynamically generated web pages. In the near future we intend to extend our work to retrieve and manipulate dynamically generated web pages.
- Exploring data mining techniques in the web warehouse and developing the web miner module as described in Section 1.2 in Chapter 1.

We first summarize the work reported here and then highlight the contributions of the book. Next we discuss some of the above goals in detail.

12.1 Summary of the Book

The existence of a huge amount of data in the Web has developed an urgent need for locating the right information at the right time. Simultaneously, the existence of different autonomous Web sites containing related information has given rise to integrating these sources effectively to provide a comprehensive, integrated source of relevant information. The advent of e-commerce and the increasing trend of availability of commercial data on the Web has given rise to the need to analyze and manipulate these data to support corporate decision making. Decision support systems now must be able to harness and analyze Web data to provide organizations with a competitive edge. Yet without any consistent organization, the Web is growing increasingly chaotic. Moreover, it is evolving at an alarming rate. To address these problems, traditional information retrieval techniques have been applied to document collection on the Internet, and a panoply of search engines and tools have been proposed and implemented. Such techniques are sometimes time consuming and laborious and the results obtained may be unsatisfactory. In [165], the author demonstrates some of the inefficiency and inadequacy of the information retrieval technology applied on the Internet. Thus there is a need to develop efficient tools for analyzing and managing Web data. In this book, we address the problem of efficient management of Web information from the database perspective. We build a data warehouse called WHOWEDA (**W**arehouse **O**f **We**b **D**ata) for the managing and manipulating of Web data. This problem is more challenging compared to its relational counterpart due to the irregular unstructured nature of Web data. Managing data in a web warehouse requires (1) design of a suitable data model for representing Web data and (2) development of suitable algebraic operators for manipulating these Web data. To address the first issue, we propose a data model called WHOM (**W**arehouse **O**bject **M**odel) to represent HTML and XML documents in the warehouse. To address the second issue, we define a set of web algebraic operators. These operators enable us to build new web tables by extracting relevant data from the Web, and generating new web tables from existing ones.

The Warehouse Object Model (WHOM) serves as the basic data model for our web warehousing system. It consists primarily of two components: a set of web objects and a set of web operators. It defines the logical structure of a set of objects in a web warehouse and the way these objects are accessed and manipulated. In our web warehouse, sets of web tuples and web schemas are called a web table. A web tuple is a directed graph consisting of a set of nodes and links that satisfies a web schema. Nodes and links are instances of the node type and link type, respectively. Intuitively, nodes and links contain information associated with Web documents and hyperlinks that are embedded in Web pages. Each node and link models the metadata, structure, and content of a Web document and hyperlink, respectively. A node type consists of a name, a set of node metadata attributes, and a set of node structural attributes. Similarly, a link type consists of a name, a set of link metadata attributes, a set of link structural attributes, and a reference identifier. Thus a node consists of a set of metaattribute/value pairs and a node data tree (instance of node structural attributes). Similarly, a link consists of a set of link metaattribute/value pairs, a link data tree (instance of link structural attributes), and a unique identifier. Observe that the metadata attributes of nodes and links represent the metadata associated with nodes and links and the structural attributes represent the structure and content.

The web schema consists of a set of node and link types. It provides two types of information. It specifies some of the common properties shared by the documents and hyperlinks in the web table with respect to not only their structure, but also their metadata and content. In addition, a web schema(s) summarizes the hyperlink structure of these documents in the web table. Web schemas are generated (1) by manipulating the coupling query and (2) by manipulating the schemas of the input web table(s) during local operations to generate a new set of web schemas for a resultant web table. In the former case, a simple or complex web schema is generated first from a valid canonical coupling query. In the next stage, the complex web schema is decomposed into a set of simple web schemas. These two stages are performed without inspecting the web tuples. Finally, in the last stage the set of simple web schemas is pruned by inspecting the hyperlink structure of the web tuples.

To facilitate manipulation of Web data stored in web tables, we have defined a set of web algebraic operators (global web coupling, web join, web select, web project, web union, and web distinct). These web operators enable us to build new web tables by extracting relevant data from the Web and generating new web tables from the existing ones. Each operator accepts one or two web tables as input and produces a web table as output. A set of simple web schemas and web tuples is produced each time a web operator is applied. The global web coupling operator extracts a portion of the WWW when it is applied to the Web. To initiate a global web coupling, a user specifies a coupling query. The result of such a user-driven coupling is a set of related documents in the form of web tuples materialized in a web table. Web union and web join are binary operators on web tables and combine two web tables based on certain conditions. Web select extracts a subset of web tuples from a web table. Web project removes some of the nodes from the web tuples in a web table. The web distinct operator removes duplicate web tuples from a web bag.

A user may wish to view web tuples in a different framework. In Chapter 9, we introduce a set of data visualization operators such as web nest, web unnest, web coalesce, web pack, web unpack, and web sort to add flexibility in viewing query results coupled from the Web. The web nest and web coalesce operators are similar in nature. Both of these operators concatenate a set of web tuples over identical nodes and produce a set of directed graphs as output. The web pack and web sort operations produce a web table as output. The web pack operator enables us to group web tuples based on the domain name or host name of the instances of a specified node type identifier or the keyword set in these nodes. A web sort, on the other hand, sorts web tuples based on the total number of nodes or total number of local, global, or interior links in each tuple. Web unnest, web expand, and web unpack perform the inverse functions of web nest, web coalesce, and web pack, respectively.

Finally, we present some important applications of the web warehouse. First, we show how change management can be performed in WHOWEDA. Our change detection algorithm is based on representing two versions of Web data as web tables and manipulating these web tables using a set of web algebraic operators for detecting changes. We represent the web deltas in the form of delta web tables that can be further manipulated. Second, we show how we can perform knowledge discovery in WHOWEDA. We have designed algorithms for discovering visible nodes, luminous nodes, and luminous paths from query results using the notion of web bags.

12.2 Contributions of the Book

The major contributions of this book are summarized as follows:

- We describe a data model called the Warehouse Object Model (WHOM), which is used to describe data in our web warehouse and to manipulate these data.
- We present a technique to represent Web data in the web warehouse in the form of node and link objects.
- We present a flexible scheme to impose constraints on the metadata, content, and structure of HTML and XML data. An important feature of our scheme is that it allows us to impose constraints on specific portions of Web documents or hyperlinks, on attributes associated with HTML or XML elements, and on the hierarchical structure of Web documents, instead of simple keyword-based constraints similar to the search engines.
- We describe a mechanism to represent constraints imposed on the hyperlinked connection between a set of Web documents. An important feature of our approach is that it can represent interdocument relationships based on partial knowledge of the user about the hyperlinked structure.
- We discuss a novel method for describing and generating schemas of a set of relevant Web data. An important feature of our schema is that it represents a collection of Web documents that are relevant to a user, instead of representing any set of Web documents.
- We present a query mechanism to harness relevant data from the Web. An important feature of the query mechanism is that it can exploit partial knowledge of the user to retrieve relevant data.
- We present a set of web algebraic operators to manipulate Web data in WHOWEDA.
- We present a set of *data visualization operators* for visualizing web data.
- We present the applications of the web warehouse in detecting changes to Web data and in knowledge discovery.

12.3 Extending Coupling Queries and Global Web Coupling Operation

Currently, coupling queries are directed, connected acyclic graphs having a single source vertex. As part of our future work, we wish to generalize the coupling query into cyclic graphs with multiple source vertices. Furthermore, we wish to augment coupling queries by allowing the imposition of conditions based on negation. Note that the inclusion of cycles and negation introduces interesting challenges with respect to the computability of the coupling query [2]. Furthermore, we wish to develop a mechanism to estimate the evaluation cost of a coupling query over the Web. Such a cost may help the user and query processor to optimize the cost of a global web coupling operation.

Finally, in this book we have ignored the processing of forms in the Web. Many Web sites provide information by letting users fill out forms. Search engines do not fill forms autonomously as the number of possibilities is enormous, hence they are forced to miss interesting avenues that humans might follow. We wish to extend our notion of coupling queries to be able to autonomously fill out forms and retrieve results by submission of the forms and further manipulation of these results.

Finally, we intend to optimize the global web coupling operation and adapt it in such a way that it can emulate browsing behavior. One of the issues we wish to investigate is how to guide the search in the most promising direction so that the expected web tuples can be obtained as soon as possible. The queries restricted by time and the number of results will be benefited directly. We wish to use semantic information on hyperlink labels for heuristic search. The semantic similarity between the current set of links and the goal can help the optimizer to decide which is preferred for the next step. Actually, humans employ this to guide their navigation when they browse Web pages manually. For example, when we need to locate the pages containing "Alexander disease", which hyperlink has the highest priority? Obviously, it should be "neurological diseases" since Alexander disease is a type of neurological disease.

12.4 Optimizing Size of Simple Schema Set

We are investigating the problem of reducing the number of simple schemas compared to the number of web tuples in a web table. Recall that if there are n web tuples, then there can be at most n simple schemas. We are developing techniques to reduce the number of schemas in a web table if it exceeds a certain *threshold*. For instance, if two simple schemas S_1 and S_2 share a high *similarity ratio*, then it may be more useful to combine these schemas into a single schema. Moreover, in the nonoverlapping partitioning phase, execution of Case 3 on schemas S_1 and S_2 may not be very useful if the ratios $(T_1 \cap T_2)/T_2$ or $(T_1 \cap T_2)/T_1$ are small. Furthermore, if the similarity ratio of these two schemas is also high, then it may be judicious to ignore the reduction of partitions containing S_1 and S_2 to a set of nonoverlapping partitions.

12.5 Extension of the Web Algebra

Due to the complex nature of the WWW, we believe that additional web operators are necessary to equip the warehouse with the capability to manipulate and restructure Web information efficiently. We highlight these web operators below.

12.5.1 Schema Operators

In this book we have introduced the notion of a web schema with respect to a
web table. We have discussed how schemas are generated in WHOWEDA. As part
of ongoing work, we wish to design and implement a set of operations on these web
schemas [31]. We briefly discuss these operations now.

Schema Goodness

Schema goodness operation quantifies how "good" a simple web schema is with
respect to the web tuples it binds. Recall that each simple schema specifies the
metadata, content, and structural properties shared by some of the nodes and links
in the form of predicates. It also specifies the interlinked structure of the nodes
in the web tuple set. However, it does not indicate the *goodness* of the schema
with respect to the bound set of web tuples. By goodness we mean how much
nontrivial information related to the metadata, content, and structure of the node
and link objects in the tuple set is provided by the web schema. The more nontrivial
information a web schema provides about its data instances, the more useful it is
with respect to query evaluation and query formulation.

Note that the information provided by the predicates on the node and link
type identifiers regarding the metadata, content, and structure of the nodes and
link objects may not be the optimum information the schema can provide about
its data instances. We justify reasons behind this. Recall that the predicates in a
simple web schema are actually defined by a user in a coupling query. There are
two major factors that influence the predicates defined by the user: the information
the user is looking for and his or her perception of the content and structure of
the relevant Web sites. For example, consider the following predicate in a schema:
$p_1(b) \equiv$ CONTENT::b[title] NON_ATTR_CONT "*Genetic Disorder + :END_STR:*".
For simplicity, we assume that there is only one node type identifier b in the schema.
That is, the schema can be expressed as $S = \langle X_n, X_\ell, C, P \rangle$, where $X_n = \{b\}$,
$X_\ell = \emptyset$, $C = \emptyset$, and $P = \{p_1\}$. This predicate specifies that the title of the
instances of b must contain the string "genetic disorder". Of course, the title of
these documents may also contain any other arbitrary string. But the question is
whether this is the optimum information the web schema can provide regarding the
instances of b? We argue that this may not be true always. By inspecting the metadata, content, and structural properties of instances of b we may specify additional
properties satisfied by all the instances of b. For instance, suppose after inspecting
the nodes of type b these common properties are discovered: (1) the title of all the
instances of b is equal to "Genetic Disorder"; (2) the instances of b either belong
to the Web site at www.ninds.nih.gov or at www.genetics.org. These properties
may be expressed by the predicates $p_2(b) \equiv$ CONTENT::b[title]
NON_ATTR_ENCL "*Genetic Disorder*" and $p_3(b) \equiv$ METADATA::b[url.server]
EQUALS "*(www[.]ninds[.] nih[.]gov)| (www[.]genetics[.]org)*".

Intuitively, we may conclude that the amount of information provided by the
above predicates about b is more than that provided by $p_1(b)$. Hence the quality
or *goodness* of the schema with predicates $p_2(b)$ and $p_3(b)$ is better than that of
the schema with $p_1(b)$. Clearly, the predicates $p_2(b)$ and $p_3(b)$ are more helpful in

subsequent query formulation and evaluation compared to $p_1(b)$. This indicates that it is necessary to be able to quantify the goodness of a web schema with respect to the information provided by the predicates. This will enable us to compare whether one web schema is better than another with respect to the set of web tuples it binds. The higher the value of goodness of a schema, the better the schema is in terms of the information it provides regarding its data instances.

Schema Tightness

The *schema tightness* operation is used to improve the goodness of a web schema. A schema tightening operation on a web table may be triggered by the specifying improvement of the goodness of those simple schemas in the web table whose goodness value is less than the *tightness threshold* ϵ. After the tightening operation the simple schemas are modified, if possible, such that their goodness is greater than or equal to the tightness threshold. Formally, let $\mathcal{S}_\epsilon$ be the set of simple schemas in a web table such that $Goodness(S_i) < \epsilon$ where $S_i \in \mathcal{S}_\epsilon$ for all $0 < i \leq |\mathcal{S}_\epsilon|$. Then, $\mathcal{S}_t = Tightness(\mathcal{S}_\epsilon)$ returns a set of modified simple schemas $\mathcal{S}_t$ such that $Goodness(S_j) \geq \epsilon$, where $S_j \in \mathcal{S}_t$ for all $0 < j \leq |\mathcal{S}_t|$. Currently, we are developing techniques to perform a schema tightness operation.

Schema Search

A web warehouse may contain numerous web tables that may not be related to one another. Thus manually searching for relevant web tables to perform web operations on them becomes a significantly difficult and tedious task. The *schema search* operator enables a user to retrieve a set of relevant web tables autonomously whose schema(s) satisfies some *search conditions*. To initiate a schema search operation, the user specifies the condition(s) to be satisfied by the schema(s) of the web table(s). Since the schemas of web tables are more complex than those of relational tables, *search conditions* have to be expressed as node and link type identifiers, connectivities between the node type identifiers, and/or keywords in the predicates. A user may explicitly specify any one of the search conditions or any combination of these conditions to initiate a schema search operation: (1) to retrieve web tables whose schema(s) matches the conditions defined by the user in the form of predicates; (2) to select those web tables whose schema satisfies some user-defined connectivities; and (3) to restrict the number of node type identifiers in the schemas of the set of web tables to be retrieved.

Schema Match

A web warehouse may contain a large number of web schemas. Some of these schemas may be related to each other. Given two schemas, a user may wish to find the *degree of similarity* between these two schemas based on some *conditions*. The degree of similarity is measured as a number varying from 0 to 1. A higher degree of similarity indicates that the two schemas are highly related to each other based on those conditions. The schema match operator is used to compute the degree of similarity between two schemas. The conditions on which the degree of similarity between two schemas can be measured is: (1) Similarity based on the number of node type identifiers in the schemas. (2) similarity based on connectivities of S_i and S_j; and (3) similarity based on predicates as defined in the schemas S_i and S_j. Currently we are exploring techniques for quantifying the degree of similarity between two schemas.

12.5.2 Web Correlate

Recall that different heterogeneous Web sites may provide related information. As a simple example, suppose we are interested in three Web sites. The first contains information about various diseases, the second contains details about drugs and the third contains information about various pharmaceutical manufacturers that have web presence. These three Web sites are operated by three separate organizations, and therefore exhibit a high degree of heterogeneity and autonomy. Suppose we wish to find out details about "drugs that are manufactured by Pfizer for heart diseases and have no side effects". To answer such queries, we may store the data from these three different web tables and then combine them based on the query conditions. Such a combination can be achieved by the *web correlate* operator.

In the *web correlate* operator is used to combine two or more web tables by *integrating* web tuples of one table with the tuples of the other web table whenever there exist *content-related nodes*. It enables us to correlate Web documents containing similar information (but not necessarily identical). A preliminary discussion on the web correlate operator appeared in [29]. We wish to explore the web correlate operator further.

12.5.3 Web Ranking Operator

Presently, in WHOWEDA we have global and local web operators to manipulate information from the WWW globally and locally. The Web information is materialized and displayed in the form of a web table. A crucial problem that a web warehousing system then faces is extracting from the set of web tuples the most relevant web tuples, i.e., *hot tuples*, for a user query. This problem is challenging because these hot tuples might not be displayed in the beginning of the web table. We intend to develop a web ranking operator to rank the web tuples generated by web operation [27].

12.5.4 Operators for Manipulation at Subpage Level

All the web operators discussed until now manipulate Web data at the pagelevel. As future research, we wish to explore and possibly extend the web operators to support manipulation at the subpage level. Note that the growing popularity of XML necessitates the manipulation of a set of documents at the subpage level. For instance, we may wish to select a portion of one document and join it with a portion of another document based on similar contents. Furthermore, we may extract portions of different documents and restructure them in a single Web page. Such manipulation requires us to extend the algebra by adding new operators and modifying the existing set of operators.

12.6 Maintenance of the Web Warehouse

Data in the Web change with time: pages get renamed, pages move, web sites get rearranged, servers get renamed, and users change Internet service providers. Due to this dynamic nature of the Web, we observe the following effects in our web warehouse.

- The Web documents stored in a web table may change with time. Thus the stored Web document in the Web warehouse may not be the current version.
- The topological structure of some web tuples in a web table may change.
- Due to the change in topological structure, the schema binding the set of web tuples of a web table may change.
- The web table may contain information that is not current or it may not contain recent information added to the Web.

As part of our future work, we intend to address the maintenance issues related to the web warehouse in order to solve the above-mentioned problems. We believe that a better understanding of the following issues about the Web is required in order to maintain the web tables in a web warehouse efficiently.

- How often do web pages change?
- How much do they change per time interval?
- How often do pages move? Within a server? Between servers?
- How long do web pages live? How many are created? How many die?

12.7 Retrieving and Manipulating Data from the Hidden Web

Current-day web crawlers retrieve content only from a portion of the Web, called the *publicly indexable Web* (PIW) [108]. This refers to the set of web pages reachable exclusively by following hypertext links, ignoring search forms and pages requiring authorization or registration. However, recent studies [109, 96] observed that a significant fraction of Web content lies outside the PIW. A great portion of the Web is hidden behind search forms (lots of databases are available only through HTML forms). This portion of the Web was called the *hidden Web* in [80] and the *deep Web* in [96]. Pages in the hidden Web are dynamically generated in response to queries submitted via the search forms.

The task of harvesting information from the deep Web can be roughly divided into several parts: (1) formulate a query or search task description; (2) find sources that pertain to the task; and (3) for each potentially useful source, fill in the source's search form and extract and analyze the results. We may assume that the task is formulated clearly. Step (2), source discovery, usually begins with a keyword search on one of the search engines or a query to one of the web directory services. The work in [46, 127, 69] addresses the resource discovery problem and describes the design of topic-specific PIW crawlers. Step (3) (retrieving and analyzing relevant information from the deep Web autonomously) is a challenging problem. At present, users are required to manually provide input values to the forms, and extract data from the returned web pages. However, harnessing data from the hidden Web by manually filling out forms is a cumbersome option. Indeed, this task can be efficiently accomplished by using an automatic form querying system in WHOWEDA supported by a robust data extraction technique. However, the following challenges have to be addressed by such an automated query mechanism in order to warehouse data from the hidden Web.

- `Automatic filling of forms`: The task of automatic filling of forms is a challenging problem in the first place because of the variety of interfaces provided by web forms. In addition, the user may not be aware of the values of all fields necessary to fill up the form.

- `Extraction of results`: Another complex problem is to automatically extract query results from result pages as useful data are embedded into the HTML code. The search and the extraction of the required data from these pages are highly complicated tasks as each web form interface is designed for human consumption and, hence, has its own method of formatting and layout of elements on the page.

- `Navigational complexity`: Dynamically generated web pages may contain links to other web pages containing relevant information and consequently it is necessary to navigate these links for evaluation of their relevances. Also, navigating such web sites requires repeated filling out of forms, many of which themselves are dynamically generated by server-side programs as a result of previous user inputs.

- `Client-side scripts`: Lastly, client-side scripts may interact with forms in arbitrary ways to modify and constrain form behavior. For instance, a text box control containing the total sales price in an order form might be automatically derived from the values in other text boxes by executing client-side script whenever the form changes or is submitted to the server. Scripts written in JavaScript are often used to alter the behavior of forms. Unfortunately, it is computationally hard to automatically analyze and understand such arbitrary scripts.

12.8 Data Mining in the Web Warehouse

Another interesting area of future work involves the development of techniques for mining useful information from the Web [36, 38, 53, 99, 124, 142, 161]. What does it mean to mine data from the Web, as opposed to other sources of information? The Web contains a mix of many different data types, and so in a sense subsumes text data mining, database data mining, image mining, and so on. The Web contains additional data types not available in large scale before, including hyperlinks and massive amounts of (indirect) user usage information. Spanning across all these data types there is the dimension of time, since data on the Web change over time. Finally, there are data that are generated dynamically, in response to user input and programmatic scripts. In our web warehouse, we primarily focus on mining useful information from these different data types.

Any attempt at data mining from the Web requires a discussion of issues of scale. If an operation is performed across all the data on the Web, then it must scale to the size of the Web. If not performed over the entire Web, is it Web data mining? We argue that extracting information from Web pages, even a very small subset of all Web pages, is an instance of Web data mining. In our web warehouse, we focus on mining a subset of Web pages stored in one or more web tables because we believe that due to the complexity and vastness of the Web, mining information from a subset of the Web stored in web tables is a more feasible option. In particular, we believe that the following issues have to be considered in order to perform Web mining in the web warehouse context.

- What is web mining in a web warehouse context?
- How does it differ from conventional data mining?
- How does our WHOM aid in web mining?
- How do we select the type of data in the WWW over which we do web mining?
- What information is readily available in the web warehouse and need not be discovered?
- What knowledge can be discovered in a web warehouse?
- Do we need to transform the selected data to mine effectively? If yes then how do we do it?
- What are the types of information hidden in a web warehouse and useful for decision making?
- How do we justify the significance of the knowledge to be discovered?
- In the case of interactive data mining, what query language is to be considered?
- What are the advantages of performing interactive web mining?
- The types of knowledge to be discovered are: Generalized relation, Characteristic rule, Discriminant rule, Classification rule, Association rule, and Deviation rule. How do these rules fit in our web warehouse?
- What are the algorithms for different types of mining rules?
- Do we need a background knowledge in web warehousing for web mining?
- If so, then how do we create it?
- How do we specify and measure significance of the discovered knowledge in WHOM?
- What are the steps for mining previously unknown knowledge in our web warehouse?
- How do we present the discovered knowledge to users to expedite complex decision making?

A preliminary discussion of web mining in the context of WHOWEDA appeared in [26, 123, 22].

12.9 Conclusions

The work reported in this book has been done in the context of the Web Warehousing Project [140] at the Nanyang Technological University, Singapore. In this project, we are exploring the various aspects of the web warehousing problem.

Building a warehouse that accommodates data from the WWW has required us to rethink nearly every aspect of conventional data warehouses. We believe that web warehousing is an important new application area for databases, combining commercial interest with intriguing research questions.

A Table of Symbols

Symbol	Explanation
Predicates	
$p(x)$	Comparison-free predicate on type identifier x.
$p(x, y)$	Comparison predicate on type identifiers x and y.
$arg(p)$	Argument of a predicate p.
$attr\_path(p)$	Attribute path expression of a comparison-free predicate p.
$attr\_path(p, x)$	Attribute path expression of a comparison predicate p.
$val(p)$	Value of a predicate p.
$op(p)$	Predicate operator of p.
$qual(p)$	Predicate qualifier of p.
P	Set of predicates.
P_a	Set of predicates on type identifier a.
Connectivities	
k	A connectivity.
$lnode(k)$	Source identifier of k.
$rnode(k)$	Target identifier of k.
$link(k)$	Link type identifiers in k.
C_i	Conjunctive connectivity set.
$G(k) = (V_k, E_k)$	Graphical representation of k.
Coupling Query	
$G = \langle X_n, X_\ell, C, P, Q \rangle$	A coupling query.
X_n	A set of node type identifiers.
X_ℓ	A set of link type identifiers.
C	A set of connectivities.
Q	A set of coupling query predicates.
$G(C) = (V, E)$	Graphical representation of C.
G_c	A canonical coupling query.
G_{nc}	A noncanonical coupling query.
G_c^t, G_{nc}^t	A canonical or noncanonical coupling query of Type t.
a_i	An instance of a node or link type identifier a for $i \geq 0$.
u_i	An instance of a free node type identifier # for $i \geq 0$.
$t = (N(t), L(t))$	A web tuple.
$N(t)$	Set of nodes in t.
$L(t)$	Set of links in t.
$n(t), \ell(t)$	A node or link in t.
$n_a(t), \ell_a(t)$	A node or link of type a in tuple t.
Web Schema	
$S = \langle X_n, X_\ell, C, P \rangle$	A web schema.
X_{nc}	Set of node type identifiers in C.
$X_{\ell c}$	Set of link type identifiers in C.

Table A.1. Synopsis of symbols used in this book.

Symbol	Explanation
S	Set of simple web schemas.
$U_i = \langle S_i, T_i \rangle$	A partition.
T_i	Set of web tuples in U_i.
$\mathcal{U}$	Set of partitions.
$W = \langle N, \mathcal{U} \rangle$	A web table with name N.
WHOM Algebra	
$\Phi = \langle M, \Re \rangle$	Selection condition.
M	A set of simple schemas in W.
$\Re = \langle X_{pn}, X_{p\ell}, C_r, P_r \rangle$	A selection schema.
X_{pn}	A set of pairs of node type identifiers.
$X_{p\ell}$	A set of pairs of link type identifiers.
$left(X_{pn})$	Node type identifiers set in the left-hand side of the pairs in X_{pn}.
$right(X_{p\ell})$	Node type identifiers set in the right-hand side of the pairs in X_{pn}.
$\tau = \langle M, P_c \rangle$	Project condition.
P_c	Projection attributes.
$\Psi = \langle M, X_j \rangle$	Join condition.
X_j	Pairs of joinable node type identifiers set.
J	A set of joinable nodes.
I	Pairs of joinable node type identifiers set corresponding to the nodes in J.
$\Omega = \langle \Re_1, \Re_2, P_{comp} \rangle$	σ-join selection conditions.
P_{comp}	A set of comparison predicates.

Table A.2. Synopsis of symbols used in this book (contd.).

B Regular Expressions in Comparison-Free Predicate Values

A regular expression is a pattern that describes a set of strings. Regular expressions are constructed analogously to arithmetic expressions, by using various operators to combine smaller expressions. In this section, we briefly describe various regular expressions that we used in the values of comparison-free predicates and give a few related examples. A synopsis of these regular expressions is given in Tables B.3 and B.4. These regular expressions are influenced by the occurrence of similar expressions in Perl or Python. For detailed exposure the readers are requested to refer to [81].

Standard Regular Expression	Explanation	Examples
.	arbitrary single character	.ating
[]	character group (character matches if it is found inside []) - within the [] the occurrence means the complement of the contained set	Zellw[ea]ger
( )	substring delimiters	(cure)
*	0 or more of the previous character or substring	(treatment)*
+	1 or more of the previous character or substring	(treatment)+
?	0 or 1 of the previous character or substring	tumou?r
|	match the preceding or following substring	(cure)|(treatment)

Table B.3. Synopsis of regular expressions.

Match a Single Character

Based on standard regular expressions, the following are used in predicate values to match a single character.

- "." - Matches any single character. For example .ating will match "eating", "dating", or any other word beginning with some letter followed by the string "ating".
- "[...]" - Matches any one of the characters enclosed in the brackets. If the first character in the set is a circumflex($\wedge$), it matches any one character that is *not* in the set. For example, $\wedge$2 matches any character except "2". A hyphen between two characters in the set indicates a range; for example, [a-d] matches the first four characters after the opening bracket. Note that if the user is not certain of the spelling of a keyword that one is searching for, this construction comes in handy. For example, Zellw[ea]ger (of the neurological disease "Zellweger Syndrome") matches either "Zellweger" or "Zellwager".

Note that the above condition can be expressed as the following predicates in disjunctive form.

Standard Regular Expression	Notation	Examples
\b	:BEGIN_WORD:, :END_WORD:	:BEGIN_WORD: + treatment + :END_WORD:
\B	:NOT_BEGIN_WORD:, :NOT_END_WORD:	:NOT_BEGIN_WORD: + class + :NOT_END_WORD:
\A	:START_STR:	:START_STR: + no class
\Z	:END_STR:	:START_STR: + no cure + :END_STR:
(?= ...)	MATCH( )	MATCH(AE4).*
(?! ...)	UNMATCH( )	.*UNMATCH(class + :END_STR:)

Table B.4. Synopsis of regular expressions.

$$p(x) \equiv \text{CONTENT}::x[\text{html}(.\%)+] \text{ NON-ATTR\_CONT}$$
$$\text{":BEGIN\_WORD: + } Zellweger \text{ + :END\_WORD:"}$$
$$p(x) \equiv \text{CONTENT}::x[\text{html}(.\%)+] \text{ NON-ATTR\_CONT}$$
$$\text{":BEGIN\_WORD: + } Zellwager \text{ + :END\_WORD:"}$$

However, using the regular expression Zellw[ea]ger is a cleaner and more compact way of representing the predicate values.

Alternation

Alternation allows any one of several subexpressions to match at a given point. Each subexpression is called an *alternative*. The alternation operator, "|" is used to match the preceding and following regular expressions. For example, the expression (cure)|(treatment) matches the occurrence of *cure* or *treatment*. Observe the significance of using the alternation operator. Suppose we wish to find documents related to neurological diseases from the Web site of NINDS (www.ninds.nih.gov) which has *no cure*. Note that in some Web pages diseases that are not curable are expressed as *no cure* and in other pages they are expressed as *no treatment*. In order to retrieve these relevant Web documents we may express the alternation operator to express the value of the predicate. Also note that if we disregard the alternation operator then the possible predicate values may be expressed as a set of disjunctive predicates. For instance, the above examples can be expressed as

$$p(x) \equiv \text{CONTENT}::x[\text{html}(.\%)+] \text{ NON-ATTR\_CONT}$$
$$\text{":BEGIN\_STR: + } no \ cure \text{ + :END\_STR:"}$$
$$p(x) \equiv \text{CONTENT}::x[\text{html}(.\%)+] \text{ NON-ATTR\_CONT}$$
$$\text{":BEGIN\_STR: + } no \ treatment \text{ + :END\_STR:"}$$

However, similar to the [...] metacharacter, the alternation operator is a more compact way of expressing these conditions as it can be expressed by a single comparison-free predicate as shown below.

$$p(x) \equiv \text{CONTENT}::x[\text{html}(.\%)+] \text{ NON-ATTR\_CONT}$$
$$\text{:BEGIN\_STR: + "} (no \ cure)|(no \ treatment) \text{ + :END\_STR:"}$$

Greedy Quantifiers

We now introduce the *greedy* quantifiers that we use in our predicate value. The metacharacters ?, *, +, and { m, n} are *greedy*. Furthermore, these metacharacters are called *quantifiers* because they influence the quantity of a match they govern. When one of these governs a subexpression, there is a minimum number of matches that are required before it can be considered successful, and a maximum number that it will ever attempt to match. In other words the metacharacters settle for the minimum number of required matches if they have to, but they always attempt to match as many times as they can up to the maximum allowed. We now discuss the usefulness of these quantifier in predicate values.

- "?" - In the Web a keyword may have dissimilar spellings in different documents. For instance, the keyword *tumour* may appear as *tumor* in some documents. Note that the character *"u"* is optional in this keyword. In order to express values containing these types of keywords we use "?" which matches 0 or one occurrence of the expression immediately preceding it. For example, *tumou?r* will match *tumor* and *tumour*.

- "+" - Sometimes it may not be possible for a user to know the exact spelling of a word occurring in Web documents. In particular, a user may not be sure of how many times a character occurs in a keyword. For example, suppose a user wishes to find documents containing the keyword *Mississippi*. However he may not be aware of the number of times "s" and "p" appear in the keyword. The expression "+" which matches one or more (but not zero) occurrences of the regular expression immediately preceding it can be used to express such constraints. That is, the user may express the value as *Mis+is+ip+i*. This expression matches the following strings: *Misisipi*, *Mississippi*, *Mississippi*, and so on.

- "*" - Matches 0 or more occurrences of the regular expression immediately preceding it. Note that the expression ".*" indicates any collection of characters. We illustrate the importance of "*" with an example. Suppose we wish to match all documents that contain an element which encloses the last names of different customers. These documents may occur in more than one Web site. Thus the hierarchical structure of these documents may not be identical. This indicates that the element containing the last name of the customers may be tagged as any one of these names: *last name*, *surname*, *second name*, or simply as *name* in different Web pages across different Web sites. This condition may be imposed by using the following predicates in disjunctive form.

$$p_1(x) \equiv \text{STRUCTURE::} x\,[\text{customer}] \ \text{SATISFIES } "name"$$
$$p_2(x) \equiv \text{STRUCTURE::} x\,[\text{customer}] \ \text{SATISFIES } "last\ name"$$
$$p_3(x) \equiv \text{STRUCTURE::} x\,[\text{customer}] \ \text{SATISFIES } "second\ name"$$
$$p_4(x) \equiv \text{STRUCTURE::} x\,[\text{customer}] \ \text{SATISFIES } "surname"$$

However, expressing predicates in this way is not only verbose and clumsy, it also requires a user to be aware of all possible names of the element that encloses the last name of a customer. Hence providing all possible values of last name as the value of the predicate is not a feasible option. Consequently, to express these values we may use the metacharacter "*". The above values can be expressed as .*name that matches all words that contain 0 or more characters followed by name. Then the predicate will be expressed as

$$p(x) \equiv \text{STRUCTURE::} x[\text{customer}] \text{ SATISFIES } ".*name"$$

- $\{m, n\}$ - Matches a range of occurrences of the regular expression immediately preceding it. m and n are positive integers. For example, $\{5\}$ matches exactly five occurrences of the preceding expression, $\{5,\}$ matches five or more occurences of the preceding expression, and $\{5, 10\}$ matches between five and ten occurrences. Note that this expression is useful in limiting the number of possible matches for keywords containing the regular expressions "+" or "*". Recall that the expression $Mis+is+ip+i$ will also match keywords such as $Missssisssipppi$. The user may restrict the number of occurrences of the characters by specifying that the occurrences of s or p in each instance in $Mississippi$ does not exceed more than 3. This can be expressed as $Mis\{1, 3\}is\{1, 3\}ip\{1, 3\}i$.

Observe another advantage of using the regular expressions +, *, {m, n}, [ ]. Many documents in the Web may contain typographical errors such as misspelled words in these documents. For instance, $Mississippi$ may appear as $Missisippi$ in one document Similarly, $Zellweger\ Disease$ may appear as $Zellwager\ Disease$. Allowing the usage of these regular expressions enables us to retrieve relevant documents even if they contain misspelled words.

Grouping Metacharacter

The preceding regular expressions are used to match one or more occurrences of a single character. However, when we are considering Web data we are also interested in the ability to express a group of characters together. The metacharacters "(", ")" have much the same meaning as they do in mathematical expressions; they group together the expression contained inside them. For example, one can repeat the content of a group with a repeating qualifier, such as *, +, ?, or $\{m, n\}$. Observe the importance of using "(", ")" for repeating a group of characters. A keyword may occur any number of times in a Web document. In fact ranking functions in some of the current search engines are based on the number of times the specified keywords occur on the Web page. The implication is that if a keyword, say $treatment$, occurs many times in a document then it may indicate that the majority of the document deals with $treatment$. Thus we can impose constraints on the number of times a keyword may occur in a set of documents using "(", ")" and $\{m, n\}$. For example, (treatment)+ will match one or more repetitions of the word $treatment$. (treatment)$\{3, 7\}$ will match minimum occurrences of 3 and a maximum of 7 of the word $treatment$. Note that $treatment$ may appear as a complete word or as a part of another word.

Anchoring

Note that the above regular expressions are used to match a string or substring. Anchoring metacharacters do not match actual strings, but *positions* in the string. We allow the following variations related to anchoring in the predicate values.

Word Boundaries

In Web documents strings may appear as a word or they may be a portion of a word. For example, the regular expression tumou?r may match the words *tumour* or *tumor*. It may also match a word containing the string *tumour*, i.e., *tumourous*. Thus a common problem is that a regular expression that matches the word we want can often also match where the word is embedded within a larger word. In order to support the ability to match the boundary of a word (where a word begins or ends) we introduce the following types of regular expressions.

- ":BEGIN_WORD:", ":END_WORD:" - Matches only at the beginning or end of a word. A word is defined as a sequence of alphanumeric characters and the end of a word is indicated by whitespace or a nonalphanumeric character. For example, the expression :BEGIN_WORD: + *tumour* + :END_WORD: literally means "match if we can find a start-of-word position, followed immediately by *tumour*, followed immediately by an end-of-word position." More naturally, it matches only when *tumour* is a complete word; it will not match when it is contained inside another word. That is, it will not match the words like *tumourous*. Note that the + symbol is used as a separator between the keywords and regular expressions.
- ":NOT_BEGIN_WORD:", ":NOT_END_WORD:" - This is the opposite of the above expression and only matches words when the current position is not at a word boundary. That is, it will patch those strings contained inside another word. For example, :NOT_BEGIN_WORD: + *ache* + :NOT_END_WORD: will match *headache* but not *ache*.

Note that in a standard regular expression, compact symbols are used to express word boundaries. Within this context, there are two distinct approaches. One provides \< and \> to match the beginning and ending location of a word. The other provides \b to match any word boundary (either a word beginning or a word ending) and \B to match any position that's not a word boundary. We follow the former approach; i.e., we separate start-of-word and end-of-word anchors for clarity. Note that this approach is commonly found in tools excluding Perl. Perl follows the second approach; i.e., it has word boundary and nonword boundary anchors. Moreover, notice that we do not use this symbol because although it is a compact form of notation it is not terrribly readable. We envisage that regular expressions in predicate values can become lengthy collections of symbols and using very compact symbols makes them difficult to read and understand.

Start and End of String Anchor

To allow greater flexibility, the following are used to match the beginning and end of the string.

- ":START_STR:" - This expression matches only at the start of the string. For example, :START_STR: + *class* + :START_STR: matches those keywords that begin with *class*, e.g., *classify*.
- ":END_STR:" - This expression matches only at the end of the string. For example, :END_STR: + *class* + :END_STR: matches those keywords that end with *class*, e.g., *subclass*.

Note that the above expressions are influenced by Perl. Perl provides the traditional string anchors, caret and dollar, but the meaning is a bit more complex than simply start- and end-of-string. For a detailed exposition the readers are referred to [81]. Note that in Perl the beginning and end of a string are expressed by \A and \Z, respectively. Furthermore, they are never concerned with embedded newlines. That is the caret can match only at the beginning of the string. The dollar can match at the end of the string, or just before a newline at the end of the string.

Lookahead

Traditionally parentheses are used for grouping in regular expressions. In Perl it is also used for lookahead. It has the special *positive* and *negative* lookahead constructs denoted by (?=...) and (?!...), respectively. The positive lookahead (?=...) checks if the contained regular expression represented here by ... successfully matches at the current location. For example, Data (?= Mining|Archeology) matches *Data*, but only if followed by *Mining* or *Archeology*. In WHOM, we express positive lookahead by the expression MATCH(...). Thus the above example can be expressed as *Data* MATCH(*Mining/Archeology*) as the value of a predicate.

On the other hand, the negative lookahead (?!...) is the opposite of the positive assertion; it checks if the contained expression does not match at the current position in the string. In WHOM, we express negative lookahead by the expression UNMATCH(...). For example, the expression ":BEGIN_WORD: + UNMATCH(*AE4*).* + :END_WORD:" matches those documents that contain a word which does not begin with *AE4* followed by one or more characters.

C Examples of Comparison-Free Predicates

Descriptive power is an obvious requirement of predicates on node and link objects. We now illustrate the expressiveness and flexibility of comparison-free predicates in describing constraints on node and link objects. To realize this, in this section we illustrate different types of comparison-free predicates through examples.

Let x and z be two node type identifiers and let e be a link type identifier. Predicates defined on x, z, and e will be satisfied by the instances of x, z, and e, respectively.

Metadata Comparison-Free Predicates

Some examples of metadata predicates are as follows.

$p(x) \equiv$ METADATA::x[url] EQUALS "$http://www[.]rxdrugs[.]com/$"
$p(x) \equiv$ METADATA::x[url.server.domain name] EQUALS "edu"
$p(x) \equiv$ METADATA::x[date.year] EQUALS "1999"
$p(e) \equiv$ METADATA::e[link_type] EQUALS "$local$"

The first predicate specifies that the URL of the instance of x is http://www.rxdrugs.com/. The second predicate imposes the condition that the domain of the URLs of all instances of x must belong to the edu domain. The next predicate specifies that the year of last modification must be 1999 for all Web documents that are instances of x. The last predicate is used to impose conditions on the metadata of link objects. It specifies that the instances of the link type identifier e must be local links.

We now provide some examples of metadata predicates containing complex predicate values. Consider the predicates given below.

$p(x) \equiv$ METADATA::x[url.filename] EQUALS
        "$.+[.]$MATCH(xml + :END_STR:)"
$p(z) \equiv$ METADATA::z[url.path] EQUALS
        "$.*$MATCH($health/$)$.*$ + :END_STR:"
$p(x) \equiv$ METADATA::x[url.server.geo_location] EQUALS "$sg|au$"
$p(x) \equiv$ METADATA::x[url.path] EQUALS
        "$.*$MATCH(($health$)$|$($disease$)/ + :END_STR:)"

The first predicate specifies that instances of x are XML documents, i.e., documents with URLs containing .xml as the extension to the file name. For instance, a node with the URL http://www.xmlhost.com/intro.xml is an instance of x satisfying this predicate. The next predicate imposes constraints on the path of the URL of instances of z. URLs of those documents that contain the string $health/$ are considered instances of z. For examples, http://www.lycos.com/health/, www.lycos.com/health/AIDS/,   www.yahoo.com/category/health/medicine/ and so on are some of the URLs of the instances of z. The third expression specifies that the host of all the instances of x must be located in Singapore (sg) or in Australia (au). Some examples of URLs of these nodes are http://www.ntu.edu.sg, http://www.sofcom.com.au, and so on. The last metadata predicate is used once more to impose conditions on the path of the URL of instances of x. In this case, the URLs of all instances of x must end with $health/$ or $disease/$. Note that the trailing :END_STR: is required to ensure that the URL matches only those strings that end with $health/$ or $disease/$. Some examples of the URLs of instances of x are http://www.lycos.com/health/, http://www.rxdrugs.com/disease/, and so on.

Content Comparison-Free Predicates

We first illustrate with examples content predicates containing conditions on tagless segments of data. Then we proceed to illustrate with examples predicates on attribute/value pairs associated with elements.

Predicates on Tagless Data

Some of the content predicates containing simple attribute path expressions for imposing constraints on the tagless segments of data are:

$p(x) \equiv$ CONTENT::x[title] NON-ATTR_CONT
    ":BEGIN_WORD: + *customer* + :END_WORD:"
$p(x) \equiv$ CONTENT::x[table.tr.td] NON-ATTR_ENCL "*2*"
$p(e) \equiv$ CONTENT::e[A] NON-ATTR_CONT
    ":BEGIN_WORD: + *customer* + :END_WORD:"
$p(f) \equiv$ CONTENT::f[A] NON-ATTR_ENCL
    ":START_STR: + *brain tumou?r* + :END_STR:"
$p(x) \equiv$ CONTENT::x[form.select.option] NON-ATTR_ENCL "*disease*"

The first predicate specifies that the title of the documents of type x must contain the keyword *customer*. The second predicate indicates that the documents of x must contain a table and the value of a field in the table equals *2*. The next expression is a predicate on a set of link objects represented by the link type identifier e. The anchors of all instances of e must contain the keyword *customer*. The next predicate specifies that the labels of instances of f are either *brain tumour* or *brain tumor*. Finally, the last predicate imposes constraints on an HTML form. Instances of x must contain a form in which one of the options of the select mode is *disease*.

We now examine some content predicates containing regular attribute path expressions containing regular expressions:

$p(x) \equiv$ CONTENT::x[body(.b)?] NON-ATTR_CONT
    ":BEGIN_WORD: + treatment + :END_WORD:"
$p(z) \equiv$ CONTENT::z[name(.last name)?] NON-ATTR_ENCL "Smith"
$p(z) \equiv$ CONTENT::z[orders(.items)|(.products)] NON-ATTR_ENCL
    "cucumber"

The first predicate indicates that the instances of x have a tagged element named body that may include an optional tag b and the textual content contains the keyword *treatment*. Similarly, the second predicate specifies that there may be an optional element last name immediately contained in name. Furthermore, the textual content associated with last name or name is *Smith*. The next predicate states that the instances of z must have an element items or products contained in orders and the textual content between this element is *cucumber*.

We now illustrate with examples content comparison-free predicates containing wild cards.

$p(z) \equiv$ CONTENT::z[name.%name] NON-ATTR_ENCL "Smith"
$p(z) \equiv$ CONTENT::z[disease(.%)+] NON-ATTR_CONT
    :START_STR: + *(no cure)|(no treatment)* + :END_STR:
$p(x) \equiv$ CONTENT::x[html(.%)+] NON-ATTR_CONT
    NEAR(':BEGIN_WORD: + *treatment* + :END_WORD:',
    ':START_STR: + *no cure* + :END_STR:', 1, 5)
$p(x) \equiv$ CONTENT::x[html(.%)+] NON-ATTR_CONT
    "(:BEGIN_WORD: + *treatment* + :END_WORD:){4, }"

The first predicate specifies that the tagged element **name** immediately contains an element whose name ends with "name" and the textual content between this element is *Smith*. The next predicate specifies that there exist zero or more elements inside the element **disease** that lead to a tagged element that contains the string *no cure* or *no treatment*. The third predicate states that all documents in which the keywords *treatment* and *no cure* are separated from each other by at most five words are instances of x. Note that this predicate enables us to impose conditions on those pages in which the string *no cure* occurs in the neighborhood of the string *treatment*. Finally, the last predicate specifies that all instances of x have at least four occurrences of the keyword *treatment*.

Predicates on Tag Attributes

We now illustrate with examples comparison-free predicates imposed on the attributes associated with elements. Consider the following predicates.

$$p(z) \equiv \text{CONTENT}::z[\text{customer}] \text{ ATTR\_ENCL}$$
$$\text{"['}:\text{START\_STR}: + \textit{customer id} + :\text{END\_STR}:',$$
$$\text{'}:\text{START\_STR}: + \textit{10025} + :\text{END\_STR}:']\text{"}$$

$$p(z) \equiv \text{CONTENT}::z[\text{purchase}] \text{ ATTR\_ENCL}$$
$$\text{"[('}:\text{BEGIN\_WORD}: + \textit{clerk} + :\text{END\_WORD}:',$$
$$\text{'}:\text{BEGIN\_WORD}: + \textit{Smith} + :\text{END\_WORD}:'),$$
$$\text{('}:\text{BEGIN\_WORD}: + \textit{type} + :\text{END\_WORD}:',$$
$$\text{'}:\text{BEGIN\_WORD}: + \textit{(phone)}|\textit{(web)} + :\text{END\_WORD}:')]\text{"}$$

$$p(z) \equiv \text{CONTENT}::z[\text{purchase}] \text{ ATTR\_ENCL}$$
$$\text{"[('}:\text{BEGIN\_WORD}: + \textit{id} + :\text{END\_WORD}:',.*),$$
$$\text{('}:\text{BEGIN\_WORD}: + \textit{clerk} + :\text{END\_WORD}:', .*),$$
$$\text{('}:\text{BEGIN\_WORD}: + \textit{type} + :\text{END\_WORD}:',.*)]\text{"}$$

$$p(x) \equiv \text{CONTENT}::x[\text{form.input}] \text{ ATTR\_CONT}$$
$$\text{"['}:\text{BEGIN\_WORD}: + \textit{value} + :\text{END\_WORD}:',$$
$$\text{'}:\text{BEGIN\_WORD}: + \textit{AIDS} + :\text{END\_WORD}:']\text{"}$$

$$p(z) \equiv \text{CONTENT}::z[\text{purchase}] \text{ ATTR\_CONT}$$
$$\text{"[('}:\text{BEGIN\_WORD}: + \textit{id} + :\text{END\_WORD}:', .*)]\text{"}$$

$$p(z) \equiv \text{CONTENT}::z[\text{purchase}] \text{ ATTR\_CONT}$$
$$\text{"[}\textit{id} + :\text{END\_STR}:, \text{MATCH}(E\text{-}).* + :\text{END\_STR}:]\text{"}$$

The first predicate imposes a constraint on the attribute/value list associated with the tag **customer**. The instances of z must contain a tag **customer** whose attribute set consists of the attribute labeled **customer id** having a value equal to *10025*. Note that the operator ATTR_ENCL ensures that there must not be any other attribute/value pairs associated with the specified element apart from those specified in the value of the predicate. Thus the tag **customer** must have only one attribute, i.e., **customer id**. The next expression says that all instances of z must contain an element labeled **purchase** as shown below.

```
⟨ purchase clerk = "Smith" type = "(phone)|(web)" ⟩
   . . .
⟨ /purchase ⟩
```

The third predicate is used to impose conditions on the attribute names associated with an element having any arbitrary value. All instances of z contain an element purchase having the following attributes: id, clerk, and type. The next predicate is used to impose constraints on the documents containing forms. Instances of x must contain a form in which the attribute value of an input element has the value *AIDS*. Note that the operator ATTR_CONT specifies that the predicate is imposed on one of the attributes associated with the specified element. That is, there may exist other attribute/value pairs associated with the element. The last two predicates say that the instances of z must contain the element purchase having an attribute labeled id. The first predicate says that id can have any value and the later one specifies that the value of id must begin with *E-*.

Structural Comparison-Free Predicates

Structural predicates are used to impose constraints on the hierarchical structure of the Web documents and hyperlinks. We classify structural predicates into two types *node* and *link* based on the conditions imposed on the documents and hyperlinks, respectively.

Node Structural Predicates

The following examples of some of the node structural predicates whose values are attribute path expressions are as follows.

$$p(z) \equiv \texttt{STRUCTURE::}z \texttt{ SATISFIES "\{document (name)\}"}$$
$$p(x) \equiv \texttt{STRUCTURE::}x \texttt{ SATISFIES "\{table\}"}$$

The first two predicates specify that the structure of the Web documents represented by z contain element document that immediately contain name and the documents represented by x contain a table. Observe that the node type identifier is not followed by an attribute path expression. Thus the attribute path may not appear in all structural predicates.

The following examples illustrate the structural predicates containing a collection of tag element name or regular expressions over the tag element name.

$$p(z) \equiv \texttt{STRUCTURE::}z\texttt{[customer] SATISFIES "\{(name, date, orders)\}"}$$
$$p(z) \equiv \texttt{STRUCTURE::}z \texttt{ SATISFIES}$$
$$\texttt{"\{customer (name)\}, \{name (first name, last name)\}"}$$
$$p(z) \equiv \texttt{STRUCTURE::}z\texttt{[orders] SATISFIES "\{(items+)\}"}$$

The first predicate specifies that the elements name, date, and orders are contained in the customer element, that is, customer←name, customer←date, and customer← orders. The next predicate specifies that the name element contained in the customer contains the elements first name and last name. The last predicate is used to impose the following condition on the instances of z: the documents represented by z have an element order that must contain one or more items elements. Note that each tag element name is separated by a comma. Observe that structural predicates allow us to fine-tune the amount of constraints imposed on the structure of Web documents via regular expressions. We can say that some elements in the Web documents are optional (e.g. (year)?), some documents allow for multiple occurrence of an element (e.g. (items)+), and so on.

Link Structural Predicates

The structural predicates discussed so far are used to impose constraints on the structure of Web documents. We now discuss predicates used for imposing conditions on the structure of the hyperlinks. One of the key features of hyperlink structures that sets them apart from Web documents is that instances of a link type identifier have a specific location in the corresponding Web pages. For instance, a hyperlink, say a, may occur in a paragraph, in a table, or in a list of a Web page. Thus one should be able to specify predicates on the location of the hyperlinks in the source documents. Our link structural predicates enable us to exploit the location of hyperlinks in the source documents as well as the hierarchical nature of the hyperlinks.

A *link structural predicate* is expressed in the following form.

$$p(e) \equiv [\text{STRUCTURE}::e\{[\text{structural\_attribute\_path\_exp}]\} \text{ op } "V"]$$

where e is a link type identifier, op $\in \{"\text{EXISTS\_IN}", "\text{SATISFIES}"\}$, and V can be either of the following.

1. *Case 1:* If the predicate operator is SATISFIES then the value of V is a collection of tag element names or regular expressions over the tag element name.
2. *Case 2:* V is a structural attribute path expression of the node objects containing instances of e when op $= \{"\text{EXISTS\_IN}"\}$. Note that this is used in order to specify constraints on the location of the hyperlinks in the source documents. That is, $V = o_{x_1}.o_{x_2}.\ldots o_{x_n}$, where o_{x_i} is contained in x and e is contained in x.

We now elaborate on these above cases with examples.

Case 1:

As of today HTML links are *simple* in nature. That is, HTML links are not hierarchical in structure. Consider Case 1. For HTML links $V = A$. Since this is true for all HTML links a predicate of the form

$$P(e) \equiv \text{STRUCTURE}:: e \text{ SATISFIES } "A"$$

does not impose meaningful constraints on instances of e. Thus Case 1 is not applicable for HTML links. However, if we consider XML links then it is possible to have hierarchically structured links (i.e., extended XML links). Thus link structural predicates enable us to impose constraints on the element hierarchy of XML links. For example,

$$p(e) \equiv \text{STRUCTURE}::e \text{ SATISFIES } "\{\text{author (journal, conference)}\}"$$

This predicate specifies that all the instances of e must contain the elements journal and conference that are immediately contained in the link author.

Case 2:

Consider now the predicate based on Case 2. This condition enables us to impose constraints on the location of an HTML or XML link in the source document. Some examples are:

$$p(e) \equiv \text{STRUCTURE::} e \text{ EXISTS\_IN "p.table"}$$
$$p(f) \equiv \text{STRUCTURE::} f \text{ EXISTS\_IN "orders.item"}$$

The first predicate specifies that the instances of e exist in a table contained in a paragraph in the source documents. The next predicate specifies that the instances of f are located in the element `orders.item` in the source documents.

D Examples of Comparison Operators

Given two node or link type identifiers x and y the comparison operator IS_CONTAIN is used to specify constraints on the containment of some properties of instances of x with respect to their metadata, content, and structure in y. For instance, let x represent a set of hyperlinks where the label of these links represents a drug name and y represent a set of Web documents containing information about different drugs. Then a comparison predicate with an IS_CONTAIN operator may be used to specify conditions on those instances of x whose label is contained in the title of the instances of y. That is, if a_1 is the label of x_1 (an instance of x) and t_1 is the title of y_1 (an instance of y) then the operator IS_CONTAIN is used to evaluate whether a_1 is contained in t_1; i.e., $a_1 \subset t_1$. The following comparison predicates depict the usage of the IS_CONTAIN comparison operator:

$$p(x,y) \equiv \texttt{METADATA::}x\texttt{[url.server] IS\_CONTAIN } y\texttt{[url]}$$
$$p(e,y) \equiv \texttt{CONTENT::}e\texttt{[A] IS\_CONTAIN } y\texttt{[html.head.title]}$$
$$p(x,y) \equiv \texttt{STRUCTURE::}x \texttt{ IS\_CONTAIN } y$$

The first predicate is a constraint on the metadata of instances of x and y and specifies that the server name in the URL of an instance of x must be contained in the URL of an instance of y. The predicate $p(e,y)$ specifies that the anchor text of an instance of e must be contained in the title of an instance of y. The IS_CONTAIN operator in the last predicate specifies that the structure of an instance of x must be contained in the structure of an instance of y.

We now discuss the IS_EQUAL operator. Given two node or link type identifiers x and y, the IS_EQUAL operator is used to impose constraints on the equality of the metadata, content, or structural properties of x with the corresponding properties in y. For instance, let x represent a set of hyperlinks where the label of each link represents a particular issue related to diseases (i.e., treatment, side effects, description, and so on). Let y represent a node type identifier where each instance of y contains a detailed description of a particular disease. Then an equality comparison operator, i.e., IS_EQUAL, may be used to identify those pairs of instances of x and y satisfying some equality conditions. For instance, it may be used to identify those instances of x and y where the label of x_1 (an instance of x) is equal to tagless data enclosed in a header tag in y_1 (an instance of y). That is, if a_1 is the label of x_1 and h_1 is a header in y_1 then the IS_EQUAL operator can be used to evaluate if $a_1 = h_1$. Some examples of comparison predicates containing the IS_EQUAL operator are shown below.

$$p(x,y) \equiv \texttt{METADATA::}x\texttt{[url] IS\_EQUAL } y\texttt{[url]}$$
$$p(e,y) \equiv \texttt{CONTENT::}e\texttt{[A] IS\_EQUAL } y\texttt{[html(.\%)+.h\%]}$$
$$p(x,y) \equiv \texttt{STRUCTURE::}x \texttt{ IS\_EQUAL } y$$

The first predicate specifies that the URLs of instances of x must be identical to the URLs of instances of y. In the next example, the equality comparison operator is used to specify that the label of instances of e must be equal to the data enclosed in a header tag in the instances of y. Finally, the last predicate is a comparison predicate on structural properties and the equality comparison operator is used to specify that the structure of an instance of x must be equal to the structure of an instance of y.

Lastly, we elaborate on the IS_CONT_EQUAL operator used to express an equality-containment correlation. From the nomenclature it is clear that this operator is used to express the containment and equality association between the properties of x and y. Note that the containment and equality correlation are in disjunctive form in IS_CONT_EQUAL. That is, a predicate containing this operator is evaluated true if a containment or equality correlation between the node or link type identifiers, say x and y in the predicates, holds. It is not necessary for both of the correlations to be satisfied by instances of x and y. For example, the equality-containment operator can be used to identify those sets of hyperlinks whose label is equal to or is contained in the title of the documents pointed to by these hyperlinks. Similarly, IS_CONT_EQUAL may be used to identify those Web documents whose URL is equal to or contained in the URL of another document. Some examples of comparison predicates containing the IS_CONT_EQUAL operator are shown below.

$$p(x, y) \equiv \texttt{METADATA::} x \texttt{[url]} \ \texttt{IS\_CONT\_EQUAL} \ y \texttt{[url]}$$
$$p(e, y) \equiv \texttt{CONTENT::} e \texttt{[A]} \ \texttt{IS\_CONT\_EQUAL} \ y \texttt{[html.head.title]}$$
$$p(x, y) \equiv \texttt{STRUCTURE::} x \ \texttt{IS\_CONT\_EQUAL} \ y$$

The equality-containment operator in the first predicate specifies that the URL of an instance of x must be either equal to or contained in the URL of an instance of y. The next example says that the label of instances of e must be equal to or contained in the title of the documents represented by y. The last predicate containing an equality-containment operator is used to specify that the structure of an instance of x is either identical to the structure of an instance of y or is contained in the structure of an instance of y.

E Nodes and Links

Tag name	Function	Attributes
Skeletal Tags		
⟨body⟩ ... ⟨/body⟩	Defines the document body	None
⟨frameset⟩ ... ⟨/frameset⟩	Defines a collection of frames	None
⟨frame⟩ ... ⟨/frame⟩	Defines a single frame in a ⟨frameset⟩	name, src
⟨noframes⟩ ... ⟨/noframes⟩	Defines content to be presented by browsers that do not support frames	None
⟨head⟩ ... ⟨/head⟩	Defines the document header	None
⟨html⟩ ... ⟨/html⟩	Defines a complete HTML document	None
Header Tags		
⟨base⟩[*]	Defines the base URL for other anchors in the document	href, target-name
⟨isindex⟩[*]	Indicates that a document can be searched	action, prompt
⟨link⟩[*]	Defines a relationship between this document and another document	href, rel, rev, title, type
⟨meta⟩[*]	Supply additional information about a document	charset, content, http-equiv, name
⟨title⟩ ... ⟨/title⟩	Defines the document title	None
Text Markup Tags		
⟨b⟩ ... ⟨/b⟩	Defines bold content	None
⟨big⟩ ... ⟨/big⟩	Increase font size	None
⟨i⟩ ... ⟨/i⟩	Italic content	None
⟨tt⟩ ... ⟨/tt⟩	Teletypewriter style	None
⟨u⟩ ... ⟨/u⟩	Underlined content	None
Content-Base Tags		
⟨cite⟩ ... ⟨/cite⟩	Indicates enclosed text is a bibliographic citation	None
⟨em⟩ ... ⟨/em⟩	Presents the enclosed text with emphasis	None
⟨strong⟩ ... ⟨/strong⟩	Emphasizes text	None
Formatted Lists		
⟨dir⟩ ... ⟨/dir⟩	Defines a directory list	None
⟨li⟩ ... ⟨/li⟩	List items	None
⟨dl⟩ ... ⟨/dl⟩	Defines a definition list	None
⟨dd⟩ ... ⟨/dd⟩	Defines a definition list item	None
⟨dt⟩ ... ⟨/dt⟩	Defines a definition list item	None
⟨menu⟩ ... ⟨/menu⟩	Defines a menu list	None
⟨ol⟩ ... ⟨/ol⟩	Defines an ordered list	None
⟨ul⟩ ... ⟨/ul⟩	Defines an unordered list	None

Tags with superscript [*] are Type 2 tags.

Table E.5. Set of nonnoisy HTML tags and attributes.)

Tag name	Function	Attributes
Tables		
⟨table⟩ ... ⟨/table⟩	Defines a table	None
⟨tr⟩ ... ⟨/tr⟩	Defines a row within a table	None
⟨td⟩ ... ⟨/td⟩	Defines a table data cell	None
⟨th⟩ ... ⟨/th⟩	Defines a table header cell	None
⟨caption⟩ ... ⟨/caption⟩	Defines a table caption	None
⟨thead⟩ ... ⟨/thead⟩	Defines a table header	None
⟨tbody⟩ ... ⟨/tbody⟩	Defines a section within a table	None
⟨tfoot⟩ ... ⟨/tfoot⟩	Defines a table footer	None
Content Presentation and Flow		
⟨address⟩ ... ⟨/address⟩	Defines an address	None
⟨blockquote⟩ ... ⟨/blockquote⟩	Defines a block quotation	None
⟨p⟩ ... ⟨/p⟩	Defines a paragraph of text	None
⟨iframe⟩ ... ⟨/iframe⟩	Defines an inline frame within a text flow	*src, name*
⟨hn⟩ ... ⟨/hn⟩	Defines one of 6 levels of headers	None
Forms		
⟨form⟩ ... ⟨/form⟩	Defines a form	*action, class, method, name, target*
⟨input⟩*	Defines a form	*class, type, name value, src*
⟨select⟩ ... ⟨/select⟩	Create single and multiple choice menu	*class, name*
⟨option⟩ ... ⟨/option⟩	Defines available options within a ⟨select⟩ menu	*class, value*
⟨textarea⟩ ... ⟨/textarea⟩	Create a multiline text input	*name, class*
Images		
⟨img⟩*	Insert an image into a document	*alt, class, name, src*
⟨map⟩ ... ⟨/map⟩	Encloses client-side image map specification	*name*
⟨area⟩*	Defines coordinates and link for a region in client-side image map	*alt, href, target, title*

Table E.6. Set of non-noisy HTML tags and attributes (contd.).

Tag name	Function
Skeletal Tags	
⟨comment⟩...⟨/comment⟩	Describes comments document body
Header tags	
⟨basefont⟩	Defines the basic size for the font that browser will use to render normal document text
⟨nextid⟩	Define the next valid document entity identifier
⟨style⟩...⟨/style⟩	Defines a document-level stylesheet
Text Markup Tags	
Physical tags	
⟨blink⟩...⟨/blink⟩	Text contained between these tags blinks on and off
⟨s⟩...⟨/s⟩	Abbreviation form of the strike tag
⟨strike⟩...⟨/strike⟩	Put a line though text that appears inside these tags
⟨sub⟩...⟨/sub⟩	Subscript the enclosed text
⟨sup⟩...⟨/sup⟩	Superscript the enclosed text
Content-Based Tags	
⟨code⟩...⟨/code⟩	To present source programs
⟨dfn⟩...⟨/dfn⟩	To define instances of special terms or phrases
⟨kbd⟩...⟨/kbd⟩	To indicate text that is typed on a keyboard
⟨samp⟩...⟨/samp⟩	Indicates sequence of literal characters
⟨var⟩...⟨/var⟩	Indicates a variable name or user-supplied value
Multimedia	
⟨bgsound⟩...⟨/bgsound⟩	Plays a soundtrack in the document background
⟨marquee⟩...⟨/marquee⟩	Create a scrolling text marquee
Tables	
⟨col⟩...⟨/col⟩	Defines a column within a column group
⟨colgroup⟩...⟨/colgroup⟩	Define a column group within a table
Executable Content	
⟨applet⟩...⟨/applet⟩	Insert an application into the current text flow
⟨param⟩	Supply a parameter to an ⟨applet⟩
⟨embed⟩	Embed an object in a document
⟨noembed⟩	Supply content to embed-incompatible browsers
⟨object⟩...⟨/object⟩	Embed an object or applet in a document
⟨script⟩...⟨/script⟩	Define an executable script within a document
⟨noscript⟩...⟨/noscript⟩	Supply content to script-challenged browsers
⟨server⟩...⟨/server⟩	Define server-side Java script
Content Presentation and Flow	
⟨br⟩	Insert a line break into a text flow
⟨center⟩...⟨/center⟩	Center a section of text
⟨nobr⟩...⟨/nobr⟩	Create a region of nonbreaking text
⟨wbr⟩	Define a potential line break if needed
⟨pre⟩...⟨/pre⟩	Render a block of text without any formatting
⟨listing⟩...⟨/listing⟩	Render a block of text without any formatting
⟨xmp⟩...⟨/xmp⟩	Render a block of text without any formatting
⟨plaintext⟩	Render a block of text without any formatting
⟨font⟩...⟨/font⟩	Set the font size for text
⟨div⟩...⟨/div⟩	Define a block of text
⟨multicol⟩...⟨/multicol⟩	Format text with multiple column
⟨layer⟩...⟨/layer⟩	Defines a layer of content within a document
⟨ilayer⟩...⟨/ilayer⟩	Define an inline layer of content with a text flow
⟨space⟩	Define a blank area in a document
Hyperlink	
⟨A⟩...⟨/A⟩	Defines a hyperlink

Table E.7. Set of noisy HTML tags.

Noisy tag attributes
alink, background, bgcolor, bgproperties, leftmargin, rightmargin, link, onblur, onfocus, onload, onunload, style , topmargin, vlink, border, bordercolor, cols, frameborder, framespacing, rows, margin height, marginwidth, noresize, scrolling, version, color, size, onmouseout, onmouseover, enctype, onreset, onsubmit, taborder, face, align, text, onclick, class, compact, type, taborder, notab, checked, align, maxlength, onchange, onselect, loop, dynsrc, height, hspace, ismap, onabort, onerror, vspace, width, coords, shape, behavior, direction, scrollamount, scrolldelay, bordercolordark, bordercolorlight, cellpadding, cellspacing, frame, rules, hspace, span, colspan, rowspan, archive, codemayscript, valuetype, codebase, palette, pluginspage, units, hidden, classid, data, declare, id, notab, standby, tabindex, lang, face, noshade, clip, below, above, top, visibility, z-index, gutter

Table E.8. Some noisy tag attributes.

References

1. S. Abiteboul, D. Quass, J. McHugh, J. Widom, and J. Weiner. The Lorel query language for semistructured data. *Journal of Digital Libraries*, 1(1):68–88, 1997.
2. S. Abiteboul, D. Quass, J. McHugh, J. Widom, and J. L. Wiener. The Lorel query language for semistructured data. *International Journal on Digital Libraries*, 1(1):68–88, 1997.
3. J. L. Ambite and C. A. Knoblock. Flexible and scalable query planning in distributed and heterogeneous environments. In *Artificial Intelligence Planning Systems*, pages 3–10. Science & Technology Books, 1998.
4. J. L. Ambite and C. L. Knoblock. Planning by rewriting: Efficiently generating high quality plans. In *Proceedings of 14th International Conference of Artificial Intelligence*, pages 706–713. AAAI Press, 1997.
5. Y. Arens, C. A. Knoblock, and W. M. Shen. Query reformulation for dynamic information integration. *Journal of Intelligent Information Systems Special Issue on Intelligent Information Integration*, 6(2/3):99–130. 1996.
6. G. O. Arocena and A. O. Mendelzon. Weboql: Restructuring documents, databases, and webs. In *Proceedings of IEEE International Conference on Data Engineering*, pages 24–33, 1998.
7. P. Atzeni, G. Mecca, and P. Merialdo. To weave the Web. In *International Conference Very Large Data Bases VLDB '97*, pages 206–215, 1997.
8. P. Atzeni, G. Mecca, and P. Merialdo. Design and maintenance of data-intensive Web sites. *Lecture Notes in Computer Science*, 1377:436–450, Springer–Verlag, 1998.
9. C. Beeri and Y. Kornatzky. A logical query language for hypertext systems. In *Proceedings of the European Conference on Hypertext*, pages 67–80. Cambridge University Press, 1990.
10. C. Beeri and T. Milo. Schemas for integration and translation of structured and semi-structured data. In *Proceedings of the International Conference on Database Theory*, pages 296–313, 1999.
11. C. Berge. *Graphs*. North Holland Mathematical Library, 1985.
12. P. Bernstein, M. Brodie, S. Ceri, D. DeWitt, M. Franklin, H. Garcia-Molina, J. Gray, J. Held, J. Hellerstein, H. V. Jagadish, M. Lesk, D. Maier, J. Naughton, H. Pirahesh, M. Stonebraker, and J. Ullman. The Asilomar report on database research. *ACM SIGMOD Record*, 27(4):74–80, 1998.
13. S. S. Bhowmick. *WHOM: A Data Model and Algebra for a Web Warehouse*. PhD dissertation, School of Computer Engineering, Nanyang Technological University, Singapore, 2001.

14. S. S. Bhowmick, A. K. Khiong, and S. Madria. Formulating disjunctive coupling queries in WHOWEDA. *Data and Knowledge Engineering Journal (DKE), Elsevier Science*, 46(1), 2003.

15. S. S. Bhowmick and S. Madria. Controlling Web query execution in a Web warehouse. In *Proceedings of 1st International Workshop On Very Large Data Warehouses (VLDWH 2002) (in conjunction with DEXA 2002)*, 2002.

16. S. S. Bhowmick, S. Madria, and W. K. Ng. Anatomy of a coupling query in a Web warehouse. *International Journal of Information and Software Technology (IJIST), Elsevier Science*, 44(9), 2002.

17. S. S. Bhowmick, S. Madria, and W. K. Ng. What can a Web bag discover for you? *Data and Knowledge Engineering Journal (DKE), Elsevier Science*, 43(1), April 2002.

18. S. S. Bhowmick, S. Madria, and W. K. Ng. Constraint-driven join processing in a Web warehouse. *Data and Knowledge Engineering Journal (DKE), Elsevier Science*, 45(1), April 2003.

19. S. S. Bhowmick, S. Madria, and W. K. Ng. Detecting and representing relevant Web deltas in WHOWEDA. *IEEE Transactions on Knowledge and Data Engineering (TKDE)*, 15(2), March 2003.

20. S. S. Bhowmick, S. Madria, and W. K. Ng. Representation of Web data in a Web warehouse. *Computer Journal, Oxford Press*, 46(3), 2003.

21. S. S. Bhowmick, S. Madria, W. K. Ng, and E. P. Lim. Web bags: Are they useful in a Web warehouse? In *Proceedings of 5th International Conference of Foundation of Data Organization (FODO'98)*, 1998.

22. S. S. Bhowmick, S. Madria, W. K. Ng, and E. P. Lim. Web mining in WHOWEDA: Some issues. In *Proceedings of the International Workshop on Knowledge Discovery and Data Mining (in conjunction with PRICAI' 98)*, 1998.

23. S. S Bhowmick, S. Madria, W. K. Ng, and E. P. Lim. Cost-benefit analysis of bags in a Web warehouse. In *Proceedings of the 3rd International Database Engineering and Applications Symposium (IDEAS' 99)*, pages 02–04, August 1999.

24. S. S. Bhowmick, S. Madria, W. K. Ng, and E. P. Lim. Cost-benefit analysis of Web bag in a Web warehouse: An analytical approach. *World Wide Web*, 3(3):165–184, 2000.

25. S. S. Bhowmick, S. Madria, W. K. Ng, and E. P. Lim. Detecting and representing relevant Web deltas using Web join. In *Proceedings of the 20th International Conference on Distributed Computing Systems(ICDCS'00)*, 2000.

26. S. S. Bhowmick, S. Madria, W. K. Ng, and E.P. Lim. *Web Bags: Are They Useful in A Web Warehouse?*, chapter In Book *Information Systems and Databases*. Kluwer, 2000.

27. S. S. Bhowmick, S. Madria, and K. Passi. Ranking of Web data in a Web warehouse. In *International Workshop on Data Semantics in Web Information Systems (in conjunction with WISE 2002)*, 2002.

28. S. S. Bhowmick, S. K. Madria, W. K. Ng, and E. P. Lim. Web warehousing: Design and issues. In *ER '98 Workshops on Data Warehousing and Data Mining, Lecture Notes in Computer Science*, volume 1552, pages 93–104. Springer-Verlag, 1998.

29. S. S. Bhowmick, W. K. Ng, and E. P. Lim. Information coupling in Web databases. In *Conceptual Modeling ER '98, 17th International Conference on Conceptual Modeling, Singapore, November, Lecture Notes in Computer Science*, volume 1507, pages 92–106. Springer-Verlag, 1998.

30. S. S. Bhowmick, W. K. Ng, and E. P. Lim. Join processing in Web databases. In *Proceedings of the 9th International Conference on Database and Expert Systems Application (DEXA)*, pages 647–657, 1998.

31. S. S. Bhowmick, W. K. Ng, and S. Madria. Web schemas in WHOWEDA. In *Proceedings of the 3rd ACM International Workshop on Data Warehousing and OLAP*, pages 17–24. ACM Press, 2000.

32. S. S. Bhowmick, W. K. Ng, and S. Madria. Imposing disjunctive constraints on inter-document structure. In *Proceedings of 12th International Conference on Database and Expert Systems Applications (DEXA)*, 2001.

33. S. S. Bhowmick, W. K. Ng, and S. Madria. On formulation of disjunctive Web queries in WHOWEDA. In *Proceedings of 12th International Conference on Database and Expert Systems Applications (DEXA)*, 2001.

34. S. S. Bhowmick, W. K. Ng, and S. Madria. Constraint-free join processing in a Web warehouse. In *Proceedings of 4th International Conference on Data Warehousing and Knowledge Discovery (DAWAK)*, 2002.

35. A. Borodin, G. Roberts, J. S. Rosenthal, and P. Tsaparas. Finding authorities and hubs from link structures on the World Wide Web. In *Proceedings of the 10th International World Wide Web Conference*, Hong Kong, 2001.

36. T. Bray. Measuring the web. In *Proceedings of the 5th International World Wide Web Conference on Computer Networks and ISDN Systems*, pages 993–1005. Elsevier Science Publishers B. V, 1996.

37. T. Bray, J. Paoli, and C. Sperberg-McQueen. Extensible markup language (XML) 1.0. Online, February 1998.

38. S. Brin and L. Page. The anatomy of a large-scale hypertextual Web search engine. *Computer Networks and ISDN Systems*, 30(1–7):107–117, 1998.

39. S. Brin and L. Page. The anatomy of a large-scale hypertextual Web search engine. In *Proceedings of the 7th World Wide Web Conference*, 1998.

40. P. Buneman. Semistructured data. In *Proceedings of the 16th ACM SIGACT-SIGMOD-SIGART Symposium on Principles of Database Systems*, pages 117–121. ACM Press, 1997.

41. P. Buneman, S. Davidson, G. Hillebrand, and D. Suciu. A query language and optimization techniques for unstructured data. In *Proceeding of ACM SIGMOD Intenational Conference on Management of Data*, pages 505–516. ACM Press, 1996.

42. P. Buneman, S. B. Davidson, M. F. Fernandez, and D. Suciu. Adding structure to unstructured data. In F. N. Afrati and P. Kolaitis, editors, *Database Theory—ICDT'97, 6th International Conference*, volume 1186, pages 336–350, Delphi, Greece, 8–10, Springer-Verlag 1997.

43. L. Carr, W. Hall, H. Davis, D. De Roure, and R. Hollom. The microcosm link service and its application to the World Wide Web. *1st International WWW Conference*, pages 25–34, 1994.

44. L. Carr, D. De Roure, W. Hall, and G. Hill. The distributed link service: A tool for publishers, authors and readers, World Wide Web journal. In *Proceedings of the 4th International WWW Conference*, pages 647–656, December 1995.

45. R. G. Cattell. *The Object Database Standard: ODMG-93*. Morgan Kaufmann, 1994.

46. S. Chakrabarti, M. Van den Berg, and B. Dom. Focused crawling: A new approach to topic-specific Web resource discovery. In *8th World Wide Web Conference*, May 1999.

47. S. Chakrabarti, B. Dom, D. Gibson, R. Kumar, P. Raghavan, S. Rajagopalan, and A. Tomkins. Experiments in topic distillation. In *SIGIR Workshop on Hypertext IR*, 1998.

48. S. Chakrabarti, B. Dom, P. Raghavan, S. Rajagopalan, D. Gibson, and J. Kleinberg. Automatic resource compilation by analyzing hyperlink structure and associated text. In *Proceedings of the 7th World Wide Web Conference*, 1998.

49. S. Chaudhuri and U. Dayal. An overview of data warehousing and OLAP technology. *ACM SIGMOD Record*, 26(1):65–74, 1997.

50. S. S. Chawathe, S. Abiteboul, and J. Widom. Representing and querying changes in semistructured data. In *Proceedings of IEEE International Conference on Data Engineering*, pages 4–13, 1998.

51. S. S. Chawathe and H. G. Molina. Meaningful Change Detection in Structured Data. In *Proceedings of the ACM SIGMOD International Conference on Management of Data*, pages 26–37. ACM Press, 1997.

52. S. S. Chawathe, A. Rajaraman, H. G. Molina, and J. Widom. Change detection in hierarchically structured information. In *Proceedings of the ACM SIGMOD International Conference on Management of Data*, pages 493–504. ACM Press, 1996.

53. M. S. Chen, J. Han, and P. S. Yu. Data mining: An overview from a database perspective. *IEEE Transaction On Knowledge and Data Engineering*, 8:866–883, 1996.

54. W. Chen, M. Kifer, and D. S. Warren. HILOG: A foundation for higher-order logic programming. *Journal of Logic Programming*, 15(3):187–230, 1993.

55. Y. F. Chen, F. Douglis, H. Huang, and K. Vo. Topblend: An efficient implementation of HtmlDiff in Java. Research technical report, AT & T Labs, January 2000.

56. Y. F. R. Chen, G. S. Fowler, E. Koutsofios, and R. S. Wallach. Ciao: A graphical navigator for software and document repositories. In *Proceeding of the International Conference of Software Maintenance, ICSM*, pages 66–75. IEEE Computer Society, 1995.

57. J. Cho, H. Garcia-Molina, and L. Page. Efficient crawling through URL ordering. In *Proceedings of the 7th World Wide Web Conference*, 1998.

58. S. Cluet, C. Delobel, J. Siméon, and K. Smaga. Your mediators need data conversion! In *Proceedings ACM SIGMOD International Conference on Management of Data, Seattle, Washington, USA*, pages 177–188. ACM Press, 1998.

59. S. Cluet, S. Jacqmin, and J. Simeon. The new YAT$_L$: Design and specifications. Technical report, INRIA, 1999.

60. G. Cobena, S. Abiteboul, and A. Marian. Detecting changes in XML documents. In *Proceedings of the 18th International Conference on Data Engineering (ICDE' 2002)*, San Jose, CA, 2002.

61. W. W. Cohen. Integration of Heterogeneous Databases Without Common Domains Using Queries Based on Textual Similarity. In *Proceedings ACM SIGMOD International Conference on Management of Data*, pages 201–212. ACM Press, 1998.

62. D. Cohn and H. Chang. Learning to probabilistically identify authorative documents. In *Proceedings of the 17th International Conference on Machine Learning*, California, 2000.

63. M. P. Consens and A. O. Mendelzon. Expressing structural hypertext queries in graphlog. In *Proceedings of the 2nd Annual ACM Conference on Hypertext*, pages 269–292. ACM Press, 1989.

64. M. Cutler, Y. Shih, and W. Meng. Using the structure of HTML documents to improve retrieval. In *Proceedings of 1st USENIX Symposium on Internet Technologies and Systems, Monterey, California, USA*, 1997.

65. R. S. Davis. The structured information manager: A database system for SGML documents. In *Proceedings of the 22nd International Conference on Very Large Data Bases*, 1996.

66. J. Dean and M. Henzinger. Finding related pages in the World Wide Web. In *Proceedings of the 8th World Wide Web Conference*, 1999.

67. A. Deutsch, M. Fernandez, D. Florescu, A. Levy, and D. Suciu. A query language for XML. *Computer Networks (Amsterdam, Netherlands: 1999)*, 31(11–16):1155–1169, 1999.

68. D. Dhyani, W. K. Ng, and S. S. Bhowmick. A survey of Web metrics. *ACM Computing Surveys (CSUR)*, 34(4):469–503, 2002.

69. M. Diligenti, F. Coetzee, S. Lawrence, C. L. Giles, and M. Gori. Focused crawling using context graphs. In *26th International Conference on Very Large Databases, VLDB 2000*, September 2000.

70. F. Douglis, T. Ball, Y. F. Chen, and E. Koutsofios. Webguide: Querying and navigating changes in Web repositories. In *Proceedings of the 5th International World Wide Web Conference on Computer Networks and ISDN Systems*, pages 1335–1344. Elsevier Science B. V, 1996.

71. F. Douglis, T. Ball, Y. F. Chen, and E. Koutsofios. The ATT Internet Difference Engine: Tracking and viewing changes on the Web. *World Wide Web*, 1(1):27–44, 1998.

72. D. W. Embley. Nfql: The natural forms query language. *ACM Transactions on Database Systems (TODS)*, 14(2):168–211, 1989.

73. H. B. Enderton. *A Mathematical Introduction to Logic*. Academic Press, 1992.

74. G. A. Miller et al. Introduction to Wordnet: An on-line lexical database. *International Journal of Lexicography*, 1993.

75. M. Fernandez, D. Florescu, A. Levy, and D. Suciu. A query language and processor for a Web-site management system. In *Proceedings of the Workshop on Management of Semistructured Data*, Tucson, AZ, 1997.

76. M. Fernandez, J. Simeon, P. Wadler, S. Cluet, A. Deutsch, D. Florescu, A. Levy, D. Maier, J. McHugh, J. Robie, D. Suciu, and J. Widom. XML query languages: Experiences and exemplars. Technical report, AT&T Labs-Research, 2000.

77. T. Fiebig, J. Weiss, and G. Moerkotte. Raw: A relational algebra for the Web. In *ACM SIGMOD Workshop on Management of Semistructured Data*, Tuscon, 1997.

78. D. Florescu, D. Koller, and A. Y. Levy. Using probabilistic information in data integration. In *The International Conference Very Large Data Bases VLDB Journal*, pages 216–225, 1997.

79. D. Florescu, A. Y. Levy, and A. O. Mendelzon. Database techniques for the world-wide web: A survey. *SIGMOD Record*, 27(3):59–74, 1998.

80. D. Florescu, A. Y. Levy, and A. O. Mendelzon. Database techniques for the world-wide web: A survey. *SIGMOD Record*, 27(3):59–74, 1998.

81. J. Friedl. *Mastering Regular Expressions*. O'Reilly & Associates, Inc, 1997.

82. M. R. Genesereth, A. M. Keller, and O. M. Duschka. Infomaster: An information integration system. In *Proceedings ACM SIGMOD International Conference on Management of Data, Tucson, AZ*, pages 539–542. ACM Press, 1997.

83. D. Gibson, J. Kleinberg, and P. Raghavan. Inferring Web communities from link topology. In *Proceedings of the 9th ACM Conference on Hypertext and Hypermedia*, 1998.

84. R. Goldman, J. McHugh, and J. Widom. From semistructured data to XML: Migrating the Lore data model and query language. In *Workshop on the Web and Databases (WebDB '99)*, pages 25–30, 1999.

85. R. Goldman and J. Widom. Dataguides: Enabling query formulation and optimization in semistructured databases. In M. Jarke, M. J. Carey, K. R. Dittrich, F. H. Lochovsky, P. Loucopoulos, and M. A. Jeusfeld, editors, *Proceedings of 23rd International Conference on Very Large Data Bases*, pages 436–445. Morgan Kaufmann, 1997.

86. R. Goldman and J. Widom. Approximate dataguides. In *Proceedings of the Workshop on Query Processing for Semistructured Data and Non-Standard Data Formats*, January 1999.

87. K. Grnbk, N. O. Bouvin, and L. Sloth. Designing dexter-based hypermedia services for the World Wide Web. In *Proceedings of the 8th ACM Conference on Hypertext*, pages 146–156. ACM Press, 1997.

88. K. Grnbk and R. H. Trigg. Design issues for a Dexter-based hypermedia system. *Communications of the ACM*, 37(2):40–49, 1994.

89. M. Gyssens and L. V. S. Lakshmanan. A foundation for multi-dimensional databases. In *The International Conference Very Large Data Bases VLDB Journal*, pages 106–115, 1997.

90. L. Haas, D. Kossmann, E. Wimmers, and J. Yang. Don't scrap it, wrap it! A wrapper architecture of legacy data sources. In *Proceedings of the 23th International Conference on Very Large Data Bases*, 1997.

91. M. Henzinger, A. Heydon, M. Mitzenmacher, and M. Najork. Measuring index quality using random walks on the web. In *Proceedings of the 8th World Wide Web Conference*, 1999.

92. G. Hill, W. Hall, D. De Roure, and L. Carr. Applying open hypertext principles to the www. *IWHD 1995*, pages 174–181, 1995.

93. R. Himmeroder, G. Lausen, B. Ludascher, and C. Schlepphorst. On a declarative semantics for web queries. In *Deductive and Object-Oriented Databases*, pages 386–398. Springer-Verlag, 1997.

94. W. H. Inmon. *Building the Data Warehouse*. Wiley, 1992.

95. J. Jiang and D. Conrath. Semantic similarity based on corpus statistics and lexical taxonomy. In *Proceedings of the International Conference on Research on Computational Linguistics*, Taiwan, 1997.

96. M. K.Bergman. The Deep Web: Surfacing Hidden Value, September 2001.

97. M. Kifer and G. Lausen. F-logic: A higher-order language for reasoning about objects, inheritance, and scheme. In J. Clifford, B. G. Lindsay, and D. Maier, editors, *Proceedings of ACM SIGMOD International Conference on Management of Data, Portland, OR*, pages 134–146. ACM Press, 1989.

98. J. Kleinberg. Authoritative sources in a hyperlinked environment. In *Proceedings of the ACM-SIAM Symposium on Discrete Algorithms*, 1998.

99. J. M. Kleinberg. Authoritative sources in a hyperlinked environment. *Journal of the ACM*, 46(5):604–632, 1999.

100. C. A. Knoblock, S. Minton, J. L. Ambite, P. J. Modi, N. Ashish, I. Muslea, A. G. Philpot, and S. Tejada. Modeling web sources for information integration. In *Proceeding 15th National Conference on Artificial Intelligence*, 1998.

101. D. Konopnicki and O. Shmueli. W3QS: A query system for the World Wide Web. In Umeshwar Dayal, Peter M. D. Gray, and Shojiro Nishio, editors, *21st Conference on Very Large Databases*, pages 54–65, Zurich, 1995.

102. D. Konopnicki and O. Shmueli. Information gathering in the World-Wide Web: The W3QL query language and the W3QS system. *ACM Transactions on Database Systems*, 23(4):369–410, 1998.

103. H. Kozima and T. Furugori. Similarity between words computed by spreading activation on an English dictionary. In *Proceedings of EACL-93*, pages 232–239, Utrecht, 1993.

104. W. J. Labio, Z. Yue, J. L. Wiener, H. Gupta, H. G. Molina, and J. Widom. The WHIPS prototype for data warehouse creation and maintenance. In *Proceedings ACM SIGMOD International Conference on Management of Data, Tucson, AZ*, pages 557–559. ACM Press, 1997.

105. L. V. S. Lakshmanan, F. Sadri, and I. N. Subramanian. On the logical foundation of schema integration and evolution in heterogeneous database systems. In Stefano Ceri, Katsuni Tanaka, and Shalom Tser, editors, *2nd International Conference on Deductive and Object-Oriented Databases*, pages 81–100, Phoenix, CA, 1993.

106. L. V. S. Lakshmanan, F. Sadri, and I. N. Subramanian. A declarative language for querying and restructuring the web. In *6th IEEE International Workshop on Research Issues in Data Engineering Interoperability of Nontraditional Database Systems (RIDE-NDS), New Orleans, February, 1996. IEEE-CS 1996, ISBN 0-8186-7289-7*, pages 12–21, 1996.

107. L. V. S. Lakshmanan, F. Sadri, and I. N. Subramanian. SchemaSQL: A language for interoperability in relational multidatabase systems. In T. M. Vijayaraman, A. P. Buchmann, C. Mohan, and N. L. Sarda, editors, *22nd International Conference on Very Large Databases (VLDB 1996)*, pages 239–250, Bombay, 1996.

108. S. Lawrence and C. L. Giles. Searching the World Wide Web. *Science*, 280(5360):98–100, April 1998.

109. S. Lawrence and C. L. Giles. Accessibility of information on the Web. *Nature*, 400:107–109, July 1999.

110. D. Lee, H. Chuang, and K. Seamons. Effectiveness of document ranking and relevance feedback techniques. *IEEE Software*, 14(2):67–75, March 1997.

111. R. Lempel and S. Moran. The stochastic approach for link structure analysis (salsa) and the TKC effect. In *Proceedings of the 9th World Wide Web Conference*, 2000.

112. A. Y. Levy. Obtaining complete answers from incomplete databases. In *The International Conference Very Large Data Bases VLDB Journal*, pages 402–412, 1996.

113. A. Y. Levy, A. Rajaraman, and J. J. Ordille. Query-answering algorithms for information agents. In *Proceedings of the 13th National Conference on Artificial Intelligence and the 8th Innovative Applications of Artificial Intelligence Conference*, pages 40–47, Menlo Park, 4–8 1996. AAAI Press / MIT Press.

114. A. Y. Levy, A. Rajaraman, and J. J. Ordille. Querying heterogeneous information sources using source descriptions. In *Proceedings of the 22nd International Conference on Very Large Databases*, pages 251–262, Bombay, 1996. VLDB Endowment.

115. A. Y. Levy and M. C. Rousset. CARIN: A representation language combining Horn rules and description logics. In *European Conference on Artificial Intelligence*, pages 323–327, 1996.

116. E. P. Lim, W. K. Ng, S. S. Bhowmick, F. Q. Qin, and X. Ye. A data warehousing system for web information. In *Proceedings of the 1st Asia Digital Library Workshop*, Hong Kong, August 1998.

117. L. Liu, C. Pu, and W. Tang. Continual queries for Internet scale event-driven information delivery. *Knowledge and Data Engineering*, 11(4):610–628, 1999.

118. L. Liu, C. Pu, and W. Tang. Webcq: Detecting and delivering information changes on the web. In *Proceeding International Conference on Information and Knowledge Management (CIKM)*, pages 512–519, 2000.

119. M. Liu, T. Guan, and L. V. Saxton. Structured-based queries over the World Wide Web. In *Proceedings of the 17th International Conference on Conceptual Modeling (ER'98)*, pages 107–120, Singapore, 1998.

120. M. Liu and T. W. Ling. A conceptual model and rule-based query language for HTML. *World Wide Web Journal*, 4(1):49–77, 2001.

121. A. K. Luah, W. K. Ng, E. P. Lim, W. P. Lee, and Y. Cao. Locating Web information using Web checkpoints. In *DEXA Workshop*, pages 716–720, 1999.

122. B. Ludascher, R. Himmeroder, G. Lausen, W. May, and C. Schlepphorst. Managing semistructured data with FLORID: A deductive object-oriented perspective. *Information Systems*, 23(8):589–613, 1998.

123. S. K. Madria, S. S. Bhowmick, W. K. Ng, and E. P. Lim. Research issues in Web data mining. In *Data Warehousing and Knowledge Discovery*, pages 303–312. Springer-Verlag, 1999.

124. S. K. Madria, M. Mohania, and J. Roddick. Query processing in mobile databases using concept hierarchy and summary database. In *Proceedings of 5th International Conference of Foundation of Data Organization (FODO'98)*, Kobe, November 1998.

125. I. Mani and E. Bloedorn. Multi-document summarization by graph search and matching. In *Proceedings of the Fourteenth National Conference on Artificial Intelligence and Ninth Innovative Applications of Artificial Intelligence Conference*. AAAI/MIT Press, 1995.

126. M. Marchiori. The quest for correct information on the web: Hyper search engines. In *Proceedings of the 6th World Wide Web Conference*, 1997.

127. A. McCallum, K. Nigam, J. Rennie, and K. Seymore. Building domain-specific search engines with machine learning techniques. In *Proceeding of AAAI-99 Spring Symposium on Intelligent Agents in Cyberspace*, 1999.

128. G. Mecca and P. Atzeni. Cut and paste. *Journal of Computer and System Sciences*, 58(3):453–482, 1999.

129. G. Mecca, A. O. Mendelzon, and P. Merialdo. Efficient queries over Web views. *Lecture Notes in Computer Science*, 1377:pages 72–86,Springer–Verlag, 1998.

130. G. Mecca, P. Merialdo, and P. Atzeni. Araneus in the era of XML. *IEEE Data Engineering Bulletin*, 22(3):19–26, 1999.

131. A. O. Mendelzon, G. A. Mihaila, and T. Milo. Querying the World Wide Web. *International Journal on Digital Libraries*, 1(1):54–67, 1997.

132. G. Mihaila. Websql—a SQL-like query language for the World Wide Web, 1996.

133. T. Milo and S. Zohar. Using schema matching to simplify heterogeneous data translation. In *Proceeding of 24th International Conference Very Large Data Bases, VLDB*, pages 122–133, 24–27 1998.

134. T. Minohara and R. Watanabe. Queries on structure in hypertext. In *Foundations of Data Organization and Algorithms (FODO'93)*, pages 394–411. Springer-Verlag, 1993.

135. P. Mishra and M. H. Eich. Join processing in relational databases. *ACM Computing Surveys (CSUR)*, 24(1):63–113, 1992.

136. H. G. Molina, J. Ullman, V. Vassalos, and J. Widom. The tsimmis approach to mediation: Data models and languages. *Journal of Intelligent Information Systems*, 8(2):117–132, 1997.

137. I. Muslea, S. Minton, and C. Knoblock. Stalker: Learning extraction rules for semistructured. In *Proceedings of AAAI-98 Workshop on AI and Information Integration, Technical Report WS-98-01*. AAAI Press, 1998.

138. S. Nestorov, S. Abiteboul, and R. Motwani. Extracting schema from semistructured data. In *Proceedings ACM SIGMOD International Conference on Management of Data*, pages 295–306. ACM Press, 1998.

139. Netmind.com. Individual: Track changes on the web. Online, January 2000.

140. W. K. Ng, E. P. Lim, C. T. Huang, S. S. Bhowmick, and F. Q. Qin. Web warehousing: An algebra for Web information. In *Advances in Digital Libraries*, pages 228–237, 1998.

141. P. J. Nurnberg and H. Ashman. What was the question? Reconciling open hypermedia and World Wide Web research. *Proceedings of the 10th ACM Conference on Hypertext*, pages 83–90, 1999.

142. L. Page, S. Brin, R. Motwani, and T. Winograd. The pagerank citation ranking: Bringing order to the Web. Technical report, Stanford Digital Library Technologies Project, 1998.

143. Y. Papakonstantinou, A. Gupta, H. G. Molina, and J. D. Ullman. A query translation scheme for rapid implementation of wrappers. In *4th International Conference on Deductive and Object-Oriented Databases; LNCS*, volume 1010, pages 319–344, Singapore, Springer-Verlag, 1995.

144. Y. Papakonstantinou, H. G. Molina, and J. Ullman. Medmaker: A mediation system based on declarative specifications. In *Proceedings of the 12th International Conference on Data Engineering*, New Orleans, La., 1996.

145. Y. Papakonstantinou, H. G. Molina, and J. Widom. Object exchange across heterogeneous information sources. In P. S. Yu and A. L. P. Chen, editors, *11th Conference on Data Engineering, Taipei, IEEE Computer Society*, pages 251–260, 1995.

146. D. Rafiei and A. Mendelzon. What is this page known for? Computing Web page reputations. In *Proceedings of the 9th World Wide Web Conference*, 2000.

147. D. Raggett. HTML 3.2 reference specification. Technical report, January 1997.

148. D. Sasha and K. Zhang. Fast algorithms for the unit cost editing distance between trees. *Journal of Algorithms*, 11:581–621, 1990.

149. A. Silberschatz and S. Zdonik. Strategic directions in database systems breaking out of the box. *ACM Computing Surveys (CSUR)*, 28(4):764–778, 1996.

150. A. F. Smeaton and I. Quigley. Experiments on using semantic distances between words in image caption retrieval. In *Research and Development in Information Retrieval*, pages 174–180, 1996.

151. J. D. Ullman and J. Widom. *A First Course in Database Systems*. Prentice-Hall, 1997.

152. J. T. Wang, B. Shapiro, D. Shasha, K. Zhang, and K. Currey. An algorithm for finding the largest approximately common substructures of two trees. *IEEE Transactions on Pattern Analysis and Machine Intelligence*, 20(8):889–895, August 1998.

153. J. T. Wang, K. Zhang, and G. Chirn. Algorithms for approximate graph matching. *Information Sciences*, 82(102):45–74, 1995.

154. J. Wei. Entwurf and implementierung einer algebra fur das World Wide Web. Technical report, Diplomarbeit, Fakultat fur Informatik, Universitat Mannheim, Lehrstuhl Praktische Informatik III, February 1997.

155. R. Weiss, B. Velez, and M. Sheldon et al. Hypursuit: A hierarchical network search engine that exploits content-link hypertext clustering. *Proceedings of the 7th ACM Conference on Hypertext*, pages 180–193, 1996.

156. J. Widom. Research problems in data warehousing. In *4th International Conference on Information and Knowledge Management*, pages 25–30, Baltimore, 1995.

157. J. Widom and S. Ceri. *Active Database Systems. Triggers and Rules for Advanced Database Processing*. Morgan Kaufmann, 1995.

158. G. Wiederhold. Mediators in the architecture of future information systems. In M. N. Huhns and M. P. Singh, editors, *Readings in Agents*, pages 185–196. Morgan Kaufmann, 1997.

159. I. Winship. Web search service features. Online, February 2001.

160. D. Woelk, B. Bohrer, N. Jacobs, K. Ong, C. Tomlinson, and C. Unnikrishnan. Carnot and InfoSleuth: Database technology and the World Wide Web. In *Proceedings of the 1995 ACM SIGMOD International Conference on Management of Data, San Jose, CA*, pages 443–444. ACM Press, 1995.

161. A. Woodruff, P. M. Aoki, E. Brewer, P. Gauthier, and L. A. Rowe. An investigation of documents from the World Wide Web. *Computer Networks and ISDN Systems*, 28(7–11):963–980, 1996.

162. C. Yinyan. Querying historical Web information. Master's dissertation, School of Computer Engineering, Nanyang Technological University, 2000.

163. C. Yinyan, E. P. Lim, and W. K. Ng. Storage management of a historical Web ware-housing system. In *Proceedings of the 11th International Conference on Database and Expert System Applications (DEXA'00)*, pages 457–466, London, September 2000.

164. B. Yuwono, S. Lam, J. Ying, and D. Lee. A World Wide Web resource discovery system. In *Proceedings of the 4th International World Wide Web Conference*, 1995.

165. O. R. Zaine. *Resource and Knowledge Discovery from the Internet and Multimedia Repositories*. PhD thesis, Simon Fraser University, Canada, 1999.

166. C. Zloof. Query-by-example: A database language. In *IBM System Journal*, volume 16(4): 342-343, 1977.

Index

Printed by Publishers' Graphics LLC